Women for Hire

Women for Hire

*Prostitution and Sexuality
in France after 1850*

Alain Corbin

Translated by Alan Sheridan

Harvard University Press
Cambridge, Massachusetts
London, England
1990

First published as *Les filles de noce: Misère sexuelle et prostitution
aux 19ᵉ et 20ᵉ siècles,* © Aubier Montaigne 1978 Paris

The preparation of this volume was assisted by a grant from the French Ministry
of Culture and Communication.

This book is printed on acid-free paper, and its binding materials have been
chosen for strength and durability.

Library of Congress Cataloging-in-Publication Data
Corbin, Alain.
    [Filles de noce. English]
    Women for hire : prostitution and sexuality in France after 1850 /
Alain Corbin ; translated by Alan Sheridan.
        p. cm.
    Translation of: Les filles de noce.
    Bibliography: p.
    Includes index.
    ISBN 0-674-95543-9 (alk. paper)
    1. Prostitution—France—History—19th century. 2. Prostitution—
France—History—20th century. I. Title.
HQ194.C6513 1990
306.74'2'09034—dc20   89-15320

Contents

Preface to the English-Language Edition   *vii*
Preface to the Original Edition   *xvi*
Translator's Note   *xviii*

Part I. The Regulationist Project and Enclosed Prostitution

1. The Regulationist Argument   *3*
2. The Enclosed World of Regulationism   *30*

Part II. From Confinement to Surveillance

3. The Failure of Regulationism   *115*
4. Sexual Privation and the Demand for Prostitution   *186*
5. The System Challenged   *214*

Part III. The Victory of the New Strategies

6. The Need for Surveillance   *261*
7. The De Facto Triumph of Neoregulationism   *310*
8. The Twentieth Century: The New Economy of Bodies   *331*

Notes   *371*
Bibliography   *445*
Index   *469*

Preface to the English-Language Edition

In 1974, when I came to realize how urgent the need for a book such as this was, prostitution was not regarded by French historians as a subject worthy of study. It was left rather to literature of a more or less pornographic nature. Astonishingly enough, the word *prostitution* did not appear in the index of the *Bibliographie annuelle de l'histoire de France,* although at that time it included close to a quarter of a million titles.

A few eminent historians did here and there venture some timid allusions to venal sex; one or two even went so far as to describe the prostitute's life, but only when illness, extreme poverty, or death could excuse their daring. Anyone wishing to glean some few bits of scattered information about the history of prostitution had to work his way through chapters of theses devoted to public hygiene, hospitals, prisons, and death. The French historian remained haunted by the ancient links between the prostitute, rotting flesh, corpses, and filth (see A. Corbin, "Commercial Sexuality in Nineteenth-Century France: A System of Images and Regulations," *Representations,* 14, Spring 1986).

This collective attitude is in itself a fascinating object of study; it shows how potent were the images produced by Augustinian moral realism, reinterpreted by officials and social researchers in the early nineteenth century, then firmly anchored in the public's mind by Victor Hugo. The sale of Fantine's hair and teeth in *Les misérables* and the gradual seeping away of the character's very substance symbolized the dehumanization, the loss of identity, the undermining by animality that gradually transformed those creatures of the shadows whose well-being and pleasure could not be imagined—or at least spoken of—other than in terms of the tragic web being woven around them by an ineluctable, unhappy end.

The break occurred in the aftermath of May 1968, when the eyes and pens of a few historians were set free, although it was some time before venal sex was affected by the opening up to research of the field of sexuality. The innovators showed more interest at first in the emergence of the new forms of behavior that they discerned in the nineteenth century, in the rise of neo-Malthusianism, and in the history of homosexuality. Once again the prostitute upset the schemata then being worked out; she suggested too crudely the ambiguities of a slavery that, it was feared, resulted at least in part from a reprehensible desire. The feminist historians, reticent and concerned in their own way about respectability, took on more pressing tasks.

Several premonitory works, however, did encourage the study of venal sex; preeminent among them was the book, which had long remained largely ignored, devoted by Louis Chevalier to the "working and dangerous classes" (*Classes laborieuses et classes dangereuses à Paris pendant la première moitié du XIXᵉ siècle,* Paris, 1958). The stress that this pioneer had laid on the social imaginary and the importance that he attached to social investigation were, for me, decisive. A thesis devoted in part to the temporary migrants from the Limousin who found themselves side by side with those creatures buried deep within Leviathan's intestines (see *Les misérables,* bk. 2, pt. 5) convinced me that light should be shed on those social depths. That is why, in parallel with this work, I began to reflect on the figure of Parent-Duchâtelet. An examination of his thirty-four public health memoranda gave me a better understanding of his fascinating investigation into prostitution (see my introduction to Parent-Duchâtelet, *La prostitution à Paris au XIXᵉ siècle,* Paris, 1981).

To this should be added the influence, if less crucial, of the philosopher Michel Foucault. Not that Foucault paid very much attention to the prostitute: in his reflections on the history of sexuality in the nineteenth century, he was, as we know, concerned mainly with the child, the hysteric, and the homosexual (*Histoire de la sexualité,* vol. 1, *La volonté de savoir,* Paris, 1975). It was only later that his thoughts on the functioning of social control affected my analysis of regulationism. Furthermore, the attention then being given to the study of discourses brought out the interest of the enormous literature concerning prostitution. The nineteenth-century prostitute does not speak to us about herself; what reality we can glean is mediated through male eyes: those of the policeman, the doctor, the judge, and the administrator. Such documentation tells us a lot about the speakers; it enables us to grasp more clearly the configuration of the anxieties and forms of male desire that order the history of venal sex.

From the outset (and in a more systematic way in my essay "La mauvaise éducation de la prostituée au XIX^c siècle," *Bulletin de la Société d'histoire moderne,* vol. 86, ser. 16, 34, no. 2-1987) I tried to follow the logic of the portrait created by the observers of these women. It illustrates in negative the dominant values, while continuing to attest to the naturalness of woman in its essential features: her attitude toward children and animals, her sense of modesty when confronted by the doctor's inquisitional gaze, the emotions aroused in her by flowers, her pity for the wretched.

For anyone undertaking a study of venal sex in the home country of regulationism it is logical to allow oneself to be guided by the configuration of male desire, the social fantasy regarding its dark underside, the modalities of social control. Another path is being followed by British and American historiography, one traced by an abolitionism whose vehemence continued that of the struggle, often waged by women, against the "white slave trade" and slavery in general. But it must be recognized that the nature of the sources created by the social system has its effect on the historian's view. In France, the declared logic of regulationism led to the analysis of its rationality, to a study of the efforts made and the tactics adopted to maintain its coherence; one is driven to understand its functioning, to draw up a balance sheet. I have paid little attention to the question of "redeeming" the prostitute, for this notion had little place in the regulationist system that crushed her; furthermore, as Parent-Duchâtelet noted, redemption was based on the model of the convent and itself looked very much like a form of enclosure.

In England, the forms assumed by the redemption of the prostitute are far more in evidence; the variety of the tactics used to "save" her, of the innumerable assistance organizations, of the charitable bodies that strove to improve the fate of the fallen woman, and the relative lack of supervision of her activities make it easier to discern the relations between the prostitute and society in general. The configuration of a less dehumanizing prostitution gave rise to sources that make it possible, far more than in France, to outline the biographies of individual women and the identity maintained by the prostitute. The history of English prostitution may be more easily constructed in the diachronic mode, whereas the documentation emerging from French regulationism favors the synchronic, the table of the *maison de tolérance,* its management, its personnel, and its functioning.

This contrast is apparent in the differences between this book and those of Francis Finnegan (*Poverty and Prostitution: A Study of Victorian*

Prostitutes in York, Cambridge, 1979) and Judith Walkowitz (*Prostitution in Victorian Society: Women, Class, and State,* Cambridge, 1980), although Walkowitz is careful to compare the archives of redemption with the police and administrative documents produced in the great courts by the short-lived application of the Contagious Diseases Acts. Indeed the quality of her book leads one to regret that no historian of equal talent has attempted a synthesis of prostitution as practiced in the nineteenth century in the United Kingdom as a whole.

But let us return to this book. By the end of the 1970s prostitution had made its official entry into academic history, which was beginning, without condescension or embarrassment, to turn its attention to private life. Even the severe, traditional *Revue historique* dared in 1982 to dedicate its lead article to the history of prostitutes in Venice. (Elisabeth Pavan, "Police des moeurs: Société et politique à Venise à la fin du Moyen Age"). And Pierre Goubert, whose role in French historiography is well known, wrote the preface to Erica-Marie Bénabou's superb work *La prostitution et la police des moeurs au XVIIIe siècle* (Paris, 1978), prepared under his direction.

Although the work carried out over the last ten years has not, it seems to me, challenged what I wrote in 1978, some mention should be made here of the research that has emerged since.

The portrait that, after twenty years' effort, Bénabou has painted of prostitution in Paris at the end of the ancien régime highlights the originality of the regulationism that evolved between the Consulate and the end of the July Monarchy. Although it was rooted in the practices of the previous century, this "French system" was quite obviously a clear break with it. The sexual behavior of venal women in the eighteenth century did not yet strictly determine the identity of the person. The venality of the body, ephemeral and episodic, was omnipresent in the Paris of Louis XV; the overlapping of the various networks led to a confusion between work and prostitution, between shop and brothel. The venal woman was immersed in the life of her district. The police saw their authority come up against the structures of the society of order; they had to show respect for the authority of parents, husbands, and magistrates. The police seemed less interested in the woman than in her client, whether he was a young depraved aristocrat, an unmitigated libertine, or a tipsy ecclesiastic. In addition, a keen concern with stemming disorder in families and a lessening of anxiety about sex itself allowed the police to describe debauchery with a liberty of tone and language that the vice squad of the Louis-Philippe period would not have dreamed of using.

Bénabou brings out these structures of prostitutional commerce, describes the complex *hiérarchie galante,* and untangles the web of pimping. From this picture emerges the originality of the "semi-open house," which not only took account of the fluidity of venal practices but also inaugurated the reordering that would threaten the prostitute's very identity. In addition to the groups formed by the kept women and the *femmes galantes,* which were legion, there began to form in those establishments the outlines of a prostitutional milieu fashioned by repression; a subculture was developing based specifically on the originality of the "arts of the body."

In 1985, in the parts of her book *Policing Prostitution in Nineteenth-Century Paris* (Princeton) dealing solely with the case of Paris, Jill Harsin has meticulously described the emergence of the "French system" in the capital. This historian has not chosen to be guided by sexual privation and the configuration of male desire; from a feminist point of view, which she stresses from the outset, she has focused her attention on the disastrous consequences of the inequality of rights for Parisian women in the reign of Louis-Philippe. By the same token she has placed the prostitute at the heart of the laboring, dangerous, and vicious classes then being described by social investigators. Harsin's book, by working backward, has thus made it possible to establish the link between the Parisian "women for hire" of the second half of the century and Erica-Marie Bénabou's fine work.

Several excellent studies published over the last ten years have pointed out the shifting rhythms with which the regulationist system was propagated and the geographic diversity of its application. With great rigor Jacques Termau (*Maisons closes de province: L'amour vénal au temps de réglementarisme à partir d'une étude du Maine-Anjou,* Le Mans, 1986) has followed the progress of the supervision of venal sex in the most conservative and most clerical regions in France. Sophie de Schaepdrijver ("Regulated Prostitution in Brussels, 1844–1877: A Policy and Its Implementation," *Newsletter of the International Association for the History of Crime and Criminal Justice,* 10, November 1986) and Alberto Cairoli (with Giovanni Chiaberto and Sabina Engel, *Le déclin des maisons closes,* Geneva, 1987) have observed the avatars of regulationism in cities as dissimilar as Brussels and Geneva. And Danielle Javet ("La prostitution à Lausanne au XIXe siècle," *Etudes et mémoires de la section d'histoire de l'Université de Lausanne,* February 1984) has cast light on the more acute sense of human rights to be found in the attitude of the Lausanne authorities. (It goes without saying that this is not an exhaustive list, but one that gives some idea of the work being done in this field. I might also mention B. J. Kam, *Meretrix en medicus,* Zwolle, 1983.)

None of these works questions the chronology I have posed; all highlight the difficulty of applying systematic analysis and of sifting the evidence satisfactorily, the strictness of the 1870s and the relaxation that characterized the Belle Epoque. Some, however, have produced a more subtle description of the decline of the brothel. This process is generally confirmed in the larger towns; but the "French system" retreated, in a sense, when under threat to the smaller towns. It made progress not only, as I had detected, in the rural zones, where large numbers of immigrant workers lived, but also in conservative regions where the grip of the church remained strong. Very revealing in this respect are the cases of Maine and Anjou. At Rambervilliers it was by contrast the left-wing politicians who expected the opening of a *maison de tolérance,* intended to stem the venereal peril, to provide them with a ready extension of their electoral clientele. (see Francis Ronsin, "Les prostituées de Rambervilliers," *Revue d'histoire moderne et contemporaine,* 34, January–March 1987).

Since 1978 the history of the offensive carried out by the morality societies has become more refined. Senator Bérenger, the tireless *père la pudeur;* Emile Pourésy, the implacable enemy of obscene writings and objects; the Protestants of Geneva, the ethical capital of Continental Europe; the complex networks of leagues against vice that grew up in France during the Belle Epoque have inspired theses by Annie Lamarre ("L'enfer de la République," Paris, 1986) and Anne-Marie Koeppeli ("La féminisme protestant de Suisse romande à la fin du 19ᵉ siècle," Paris, 1987). The work devoted to the feminists in the United States and in France allows us to follow more closely the struggle waged by militant women of various obediences against regulated prostitution and the ways of vice. All these studies have confirmed the discreet prohibitionist outlook, whether or not it was admitted, that underpinned that angry struggle. (An exhaustive bibliography of these works can be found in the thesis by Laurence Klejman and Florence Rochefort, "L'égalité en marche: Histoire du mouvement féministe en France, 1868–1914," Paris, 1987). More generally speaking, one can hardly stress too much the impetus given to the history of poor and even venal women by the talented British and American women historians who have joined those working under the direction of Michelle Perrot in France. Together they have been able to achieve a shift in viewpoint and impose on the historical field a feminine point of view, one imbued with empathy for the object of their investigations.

The new history of images of health and illness makes it possible to grasp the roots of the anxiety aroused by venal sex in the late nineteenth century. It now seems to me that in this book I have minimized the obsessive presence of the specter of inherited syphilis, which began to emerge clearly in the 1860s. (See my article "L'hérédosyphilis, ou l'impossible rédemption: Contribution à l'histoire de l'hérédité morbide," *Romantisme*, 31, 1981.) The new scientific conviction accentuated and reoriented the nightmares caused by the old "pox." In the logic of that terrifying morbid entity, the prostitute not only threatened her partner's health but endangered the descendants of her casual client. These women of the people who sold themselves were transmitting a disease "into nature" that destroyed "the heredity in seed" of their bourgeois lovers. The biological threat hanging over the proletariat was both sharpened and reoriented by scientific theory. By lying in wait through a whole lifetime, in oneself and around oneself, the obsessive figure of hereditary syphilis imposed the stigmata of degeneracy.

Pasteur et la révolution pastorienne (edited by Claire Salomon-Bayet, Paris, 1986), the brilliant work devoted to the Pasteurian revolution, also throws light on the emergence of that neoregulationism which, from the 1870s on, took over from the system that had been in place since the Consulate. The difficulty remained, however, of perceiving the respective weights of the Pasteurian triumph and of the hereditarist obsession, since these two major phenomena operated side by side.

There remains what is essential in this domain, that is to say, what belongs to cultural history and the social imaginary. Quite obviously this is a busy site, the full extent of which is for the moment difficult to discern. Since this book first appeared, Peter Gay has set out to write a history of the bourgeois sensibility (*The Bourgeois Experience: Victoria to Freud*), but the sheer scope of his ambitious research has allowed him to devote only a few pages to French prostitution; the work in progress as a whole, however, is full of suggestive insights and stimulating ideas (see in particular volume 1, *Education of the Senses*, New York, 1984, and volume 2, *The Tender Passion*, New York, 1986.) In France, Stéphane Michaud's variations on the role of romantic woman as muse, madonna, and prostitute (*Muse et madone: Visages de la femme de la Révolution aux apparitions de Lourdes*, Paris, 1985, and "La prostitution comme interrogation sur l'amour chez les socialistes romantiques, 1830–1840," in *Aimer en France, 1760–1800,* Clermont-Ferrand, 1980), are helping us to understand better the series of images, both antithetical and complementary, whose contrasts dominate the history of venal sex.

Timothy J. Clark has, almost incidentally, opened up to the history of art the subject of regulated prostitution. His analysis of the indignant reception given Manet's *Olympia* (in *The Painting of Modern Life: Paris in the Art of Manet and His Followers*, New York, 1985) leads him to brilliant reflections on the link between the figures of modernity, the image of the courtesan, and the drawing of the desirable body. Clark suggests that what underpins the functioning of the "French system" may also be read in the reception of the painting. Manet exposes the intolerable: not the naked, offered, desirable, even exciting body, for all this is accepted readily enough, but the image of an unsubmissive woman, whom the spectator cannot imagine as available; the body of an androgynous creature, slyly aggressive, who refuses to exhibit her lack of a phallus and whose cut hair and nonchalant hygiene suggest the insidious threat that they conceal.

Ten years after writing *Les filles de noce* I have no retraction to make in this area. I still think, with even greater conviction, that the history of desire, of male fantasies and anxieties, dominates that of the venal woman, registered or unregistered, in the France of regulationism. A broad detour into the study of private life and the home (Philippe Ariès and Georges Duby, eds., *Histoire de la vie privée,* especially volume 4, Michelle Perrot, ed., *De la Révolution à la grand guerre,* Paris, 1987; *From the Fires of the Revolution to the Great War,* Cambridge, Mass., 1990) has, for me, made even more self-evident the break represented by the 1860s. Then the modernity of the city shattered the yoke of Consular regulationism and made many procedures of supervision obsolete. Those years saw the decline of the social imaginary of the first half of the century, once expressed by Parent-Duchâtelet and brought to its ultimate exaltation by Victor Hugo.

The authoritarian Empire (1853–1859) and Haussmannization cast, as the poet had hoped, a harsh light into the lower depths of the city. The threat now represented by the prostitute came not so much from the fact that she sprang from the people of darkness as from her origins in the gutter. Gambetta was behind the times when he exclaimed in 1878 that prostitution was merely a matter for the public thoroughfare. What those who were trying to reorient the tactics of social supervision feared, often quite rightly, was the blurring of the portrait of the prostitute; the link between her and alcohol, the pox, and tuberculosis; the propagation of hysterical and degenerate behavior which, it was believed, was to be found preeminently in the "whore." Modernity brought with it new images, new practices, and new anxieties; it necessitated changes in the system.

Men were still torn between two contradictory forces. Tortured by the fear of seeing female sexuality liberated, with all the earthly forces that men believed it contained, they were nevertheless fascinated by the animality, the popular vitality, the unrestrained spontaneity, the dark side of prostitution. Hence the force of the image of female sexuality, unbridled but submissive, of a woman at once available, clean, sensual, accessible, and passionate, if only in counterfeit.

The counterpoint being woven between fear and male desire ordered in a broader way many other aspects of the history of sexuality in the second half of the nineteenth century; this too has emerged in the research. (See the synthesis by Angus MacLaren, *Sexuality and Social Order: The Debate over the Fertility of Women and Workers in France, 1770–1920,* London, 1983, and my views on it in *European History Quarterly,* 16, 1, January 1986. On a more limited point, also touched on by MacLaren, see my essay "La petite bible des jeunes époux, *L'histoire,* 63, January 1984.) Male fantasies about lesbianism, the intensity of masturbation, and above all the conjugal norms reiterated by doctors who imagined a sexuality appeased even in its limited eroticization attest to the force of the same emotional mechanisms.

Indeed, the history of prostitution cannot be written without reference to conjugality. The brothel and the unregistered prostitute's room were perceived in the nineteenth century as places of waste, as theaters for a triple degradation—of the prostitute, the client, and money. Overcome with remorse, men fled those places that, a few moments before, had exerted such an irresistible pull on them. The adventure ushered in a period of building up resources again, of latency, gentle sexuality, and laborious saving. It was a balance that implied a clear division, the strict management of waste. Debauchery, defined as the abusive use of sex, of money, of oneself, sometimes invaded the home and private life. Yet it could be got rid of at the brothel; such at least, during the Consulate and the Belle Epoque, was the hope and intent of the apostles of regulationism, the true creators of the registered brothel—the *maison de tolérance.*

Preface to the Original Edition

In *Prostitution in Europe* (New York, 1913) the American Abraham Flexner wrote, "In our time, the demand by men . . . is so common, that it may be regarded as general" (p. 31). The fictional as well as the administrative, police, and legal literature of the time confirms this impression; it provides abundant proof that venal sexual practices were in the forefront of people's minds. But the academic history of contemporary France ignores this essential aspect of social psychology. (Historians of the Middle Ages and of modern times have begun to deal with the problem, as can be seen in the work of J. Rossiaud, B. Geremek, J. Solé, J. C. Perrot, and above all Erica-Marie Bénabou. It should be said that in some countries the history of prostitution is well represented; this is the case in the United States, especially the work of V. L. Bullough and his associates.) This elision poses a problem. The theme that I am proposing to my colleagues is that of the historian and the prostitute. Is the silence the result of some taboo? I cannot say. In any case it is based on a conviction of the nonhistoricity of prostitution. "The oldest profession in the world" seems to be the only one to have escaped history. The few French works devoted to prostitution in the past (see in particular Servais and Laurend, *Histoire et dossier de la prostitution*), like the works by the philanthropists of the Restoration monarchies, operate on such an enormous time scale that it may seem aberrant to deal with prostitution here in the medium term (to be more precise, from 1871 to 1914). So this project requires some explanation.

To begin with, I have tried to approach the subject without resorting to rhetorical devices, pathos, or ostentation; what I had to do, it seemed to me, was to study sexual need and venal pleasure independently of venereal disease and without trying to hide shame behind historical demography. (And not as the few authors who have dealt with this subject have done; see P. Pierrard, *La vie ouvrière à Lille sous le Second Empire,* Paris, 1965, and G. Désert, "Prostitution et prostituées à Caen pendant la seconde moitié du XIXe siècle," *Cahiers des Annales de Normandie,* no. 10, 1977. This criticism may also be leveled at the way I proceeded in writing *Archaïsme et modernité en Limousin au XIXe siècle.*) It is time that the historian of contemporary France entered the bedroom without being accompanied by the local registrar. The sexological history of the nineteenth century, hitherto left to psychosociologists, must be a history of desire, of pleasure, and of sexual need, without regard to morals, the birth rate, or eugenics.

In such an unexplored field how can one fail to open up new perspectives? This book is not an exploration of a thesis but an attempt to discern the coherence between sexual need on the one hand and, on the other, the structural, behavioral, discursive, and political aspects of prostitution. In order to do this I have chosen to study the period during which the prison system set up under the Consulate was gradually falling apart. It was during this time that the regulationism theorized by Parent-Duchâtelet began to totter and the supervision of prostitution in the name of public health began to take shape. Between the end of the Second Empire and the First World War a transition took place between procedures whose origins lay at least as far back as the eighteenth-century Enlightenment (the elaboration of which is exhaustively analyzed by Erica Bénabou) and techniques devised by a twentieth century caught up in dreams of a healthy society.

This book also springs from the conviction that the history of prostitution in the nineteenth century provides us with a particularly fruitful means of understanding that period: what was written and said about prostitution was then a focus for collective delusions and a meeting point for all manner of anxieties.

Finally, I hope to provide food for thought to those who are examining the significance of debauchery—a form of alienation, the result of sexual need, of course, but also a protest, a threat of subversion against which society thought it had to defend itself, especially in the case of female debauchery, which was intolerable to male society and was a victim of collective sadomasochism. The sections at the end of the book devoted to contemporary prostitution (1914–1978), while they fill a gap in historiography, are also intended to distinguish those elements of the prostitutes' movement and present-day attitudes that are simply a backward-looking reaction or an implicit acceptance of emerging structures from those that express a revolutionary will, a rejection of the new economy of the body.

Translator's Note

During the period covered by this book prostitution was not legal, let alone approved, in France. All those involved in it were subject to arbitrary action on the part of the police and other authorities: this varied considerably from time to time and from place to place. Prostitution was, however, in certain circumstances, "tolerated." This specific involvement of the authorities in prostitution had the result of creating a number of technical terms that have no equivalent in English. Where necessary, therefore, I have left them in the original French.

There were, broadly speaking, two categories of prostitute: the registered, who had to submit to various regulations, including health checks, and the unregistered, who operated entirely outside the law. Registered prostitutes were known as *filles soumises* (literally "submissive girls," although it should be pointed out that in the French of this period *fille* itself had the sense of "whore," a respectable girl being referred to as a *jeune fille*). They worked either independently, when they were known as *filles en carte* (on account of their registration cards), or in strictly regulated and supervised brothels known as *maisons de tolérance*, in which they also lived. In the second case, they were referred to as *filles de maison*.

The *maison de passe* was a low-class, unregistered establishment to which women took their clients, encountered in street or bar, for a *passe*, or "short time." The *maison de rendez-vous*, by contrast, was frequented by men higher up the social scale. These were outside official toleration and, unlike the *maisons de tolérance*, which strove for exotic effects, they aimed at reproducing the atmosphere of a respectable bourgeois home. The women, usually a "better class" of unregistered prostitute, tried to pass themselves off as ordinary middle-class women. "Meetings" were arranged by a third party, through whom the money passed; no direct payment was made by the client to the prostitute.

Part I

The Regulationist Project
and Enclosed Prostitution

1. The Regulationist Argument

Parent-Duchâtelet and Regulationism

Although his book antedates by several decades the beginning of the period being studied here, to ignore Parent-Duchâtelet's work[1] would be to condemn oneself to total incomprehension of the debate that raged during the last third of the nineteenth century. Indeed, it was at the beginning of the July Monarchy that the regulationist system, which had been sketched out since the Consulate, found in this physician not only its most prestigious theoretician but also its apostle, one might almost say its bard.

Parent-Duchâtelet brought together into a coherent whole the more or less conscious principles that had guided the administrators of the Empire and Restoration, and he founded the entire system on a masterly study in social anthropology. The harmony of the general structure, the scope of his research, and the methodological innovation explain why his book had such an enormous epistemological impact and served as a limiting model on prostitution for close to half a century.[2] The personality of its author has already attracted the attention of contemporary historians.[3] All I intend to do here is to remind the reader of the outlines of his thought, with a view to helping that reader understand the debate that took place under the Third Republic, at a time when the regulationist system was breaking down under the impact of various upheavals in philosophical and social structures.

Prostitution and Prostitutes

Parent-Duchâtelet's work is concerned only with "public prostitution." Venality, or sex for money, does not for him represent a sufficient criterion for membership in that category; the kept woman, the *femme galante,* and the unregistered high-class prostitute do not concern him. Like Béraud,[4] but unlike his followers in the early years of the Third Republic, Parent-Duchâtelet excludes from his area of concern those venal women with a fixed abode of their own, who paid taxes when necessary, enjoyed civil rights, conducted themselves in a decent fashion outside their homes, and who, for all these reasons, eluded the abitrary action of the authorities. Such women, in his view, represented no real danger to the ruling classes, of which they were de facto members.

Although he constantly emphasizes its long-standing, if not eternal, character,[5] Parent-Duchâtelet does not regard prostitution as an immutable phenomenon.[6] He even denies categorically that it can escape the effects of time; the application of the empirical method and the dominant historicism of his day led him to distance himself in this respect from many of the regulationists; and indeed he even differs from many present-day historians, for whom the supposed permanence of the structures and practices of prostitution justify their lack of interest.

Although a scourge of great antiquity, prostitution is also a necessary evil[7]: "Prostitutes are as inevitable, where men live together in large concentrations, as drains and refuse dumps";[8] "they contribute to the maintenance of social order and harmony."[9] Parent-Duchâtelet, the man of the Paris drains and refuse dumps,[10] takes his place in the purest Augustinian tradition,[11] and his preoccupations reflect the then highly developed obsession with refuse and miasma. Indeed, without the prostitute, "the man who has desires will pervert your daughters and servant girls . . . he will sow discord in the home."[12] In accordance with the then-reigning organicism, Parent-Duchâtelet regards prostitution as an indispensable excremental phenomenon that protects the social body from disease.[13]

What really haunts him—and this has rarely been discussed—is not the existence of public prostitution, which, in his view, it is possible to supervise, nor the existence of unregistered prostitution, to which he pays nothing like the attention that Béraud[14] or his epigones during the period of *ordre moral* were to give it, but the temporary character of the prostitute's "career." They "*come back into Society,*" he writes anxiously, "they surround us . . . they gain access to our homes."[15] From this point of view—which is entirely in agreement with the anxiety felt by the notables of the time about the laboring classes, identified by Frégier with the "vicious classes" as well as the "dangerous classes"[16]—it is essential to know who the prostitutes are in order to prevent them, as far as possible, from acquiring vices that they may pass on after they have abandoned their "career." Above all, society must be protected from "tribadism" (lesbianism), which constitutes as direct attack on the morality of female sexual behavior.

It should be noted that Parent-Duchâtelet strongly stresses the threat of biological contagion. He may rightly be regarded as the precursor of those doctors who, at the end of the century, busied themselves spreading syphilophobia and fear of venereal disease generally. Indeed, in his book all these grand themes are present: "Of all the diseases that can affect mankind through contagion, and which have the most serious repercussions on society, there is none more serious, more dangerous, and more to be feared than syphilis,"[17] the worst scourge of all the plagues. His objectivity forces him, however, to stress at the same time the decline of venereal disease in the social body as a whole.[18]

It is in terms of this acceptance of prostitution and of the threat it presents that Parent-Duchâtelet builds up his masterly anthropology of the woman who belongs "to the class of public prostitution." This class is defined by its marginality; it is "a people apart,"[19] made up of women who place themselves outside society, "differing as much in their morals, their tastes, and their habits from the society of their compatriots, as the latter differ from the nations of another hemisphere."[20] It is this marginality, owing, according to Parent-Duchâtelet, solely to the individuals making up the group, that is the basis of the regulationist project; authoritarian marginalization is justified by a de facto marginality that is prior to it.[21] Like crime, prostitution forms a subterranean counter-society, a social base representing a threat that is at the same time moral, social, sanitary, and political.[22] And who better than the specialist in drains to undertake its study?

This social base was not an undifferentiated magma. Unlike those of his contemporaries who had only a vague view of the laboring classes because fear enfeebled their capacity for observation, Parent-Duchâtelet, with the same conscientiousness that made him spend long periods of time in the drains, analyzes, dissects, and compartmentalizes the "class of public prostitution." He embarks on so precise a study of the categories that compose it that his description was to be repeated endlessly right up to the twentieth century,[23] having acquired such authority that it obscured the vision of later researchers and prevented them from grasping the changes that were taking place. To each class above ground, we might say, there corresponds a category within this subterranean society. "Usually, the most distinguished class of prostitutes chooses its lovers among law students, medical students, and young barristers . . . It is among the shop assistants of every kind, and particularly among tailors . . . that the middle class of prostitutes recruits its lovers. To these may be added the wig-maker's apprentices, traveling and café musicians, jewelers and goldsmiths. The rest are left to workers of all kinds."[24] This hierarchization finds expression in a cascade of contempt, based on the diversity of prices.

By a curious social mimicry, Parent-Duchâtelet notes, each category of prostitute comes to define itself by its clientele. "Since each of those places is frequented by a particular class of men, the women acquire habits, manners, a certain tone by frequenting those men, so that the woman intended for the artisan, the manual laborer, and the mason finds herself ill at ease with an army officer . . . The same goes for the woman who has acquired the habit of living with the educated and polite classes of society; she finds it unpleasant to be among crude people."[25] The existence of this compartmentalization helps to exorcise the anxiety aroused by the risk of social contagion. It was the sense of its destruction, as a result of the diffusion of bourgeois forms of behavior, more than the fear of seeing it break through the dikes of regularization, that was to give rise to the anguished cries of the last regulationists at the dawn of the Third Republic.

A veritable Linnaeus of prostitution, Parent-Duchâtelet throws himself into a very precise description of the *filles en numéro*,[26] the *filles en carte*, the *filles à soldats*, the *filles de barrière* as "streetwalkers" who operate only in the shadows and whose shamelessness ought to make them "unworthy to appear on the registers of prostitution."[27]

The analysis of the causes and the description of the itinerary that leads to prostitution clearly show the presuppositions of the regulationist discourse and indicate a profound wish to condemn the freedom of sexual behavior that sustains it. A girl sinks into "public prostitution" only after a period of "debauchery"[28] following a "disorderly life." Finally, by sinking into "public prostitution" a woman runs the risk of ending up in the depths of abjection—that is to say, lesbianism.[29] This itinerary combines the influence of temperament with that of social mechanisms. It is the initial propensity toward libertinage and laziness that leads women into the fatal trap; fundamentally, prostitution concerns "a certain kind of women."[30] The second fundamental postulate is that the predisposition to debauchery, followed by prostitution, is a matter of family origins: to have "an ignoble origin,"[31] to be a witness to "disorder in the home,"[32] leads to vice.[33] But Parent-Duchâtelet also refers to poverty and low wages. On several occasions Villermé had stressed the prevalence of prostitution as a sideline or an occasional activity among working-class women in the manufacturing centers and, like the socialists and all the authors referred to here, deplored the intermingling of the sexes in workshops and factories. So it is easy to understand the importance to all those who study prostitution of unemployment, the low wages of women, and working-class poverty in general.[34]

Parent-Duchâtelet's portrait of the prostitute was repeated so often in the literature on prostitution and inspired so many novelists that, in addition to distorting the vision of later researchers, as I have said, it probably determined to some extent the behavior of the prostitutes themselves. Thus it is worth listing all the stereotypes that Parent-Duchâtelet assembled or invented in order to understand more fully the hold they were to have on the minds of future writers.

His portrait is based on the central idea that the prostitute possesses all the characteristics that run counter to the values of the time. This stems in part from the fact that, because she is still something of a child, she has not yet been able to assimilate those values. The stereotype of the *immaturity* of the prostitute was, as we know, to have a long future;[35] it derives from the deliberate identification of maturity with an acceptance of the values of society as a whole. To begin with, the prostitute is the woman who rejects work in favor of pleasure[36]: everything about her shows this—her laziness, her love of idleness, the pattern of her day. The prostitute is also the woman who avoids the need to settle down and therefore to work;[37] she represents movement, instability, "turbulence," "agitation." For Parent-Duchâtelet this explains the need for "confinement" and the usefulness of prison. This attraction to movement is expressed not only in the frequency with which these women change their addresses but also by their love of dancing, their sudden shifts of mood, and their inability to concentrate. It finds expression, too, although here Parent-Duchâtelet contradicts himself, in social mobility, since, as in the bourgeoisie,[38] moving her place of residence often represents the prostitute's movement from one class to another.

The prostitute also symbolizes disorder, excess, and improvidence—in other words, a rejection of order and economy. This can be seen in the place in which she lives; its very lack of cleanliness is evidence of this. Her excesses take many forms: a readiness to be "carried away" by various enthusiams, an exaggerated fondness for alcohol, excessive eating, incessant chattering, and frequent bursts of anger. With few exceptions, prostitutes have no notion of saving money;[39] they indulge in useless expenditure, especially for flowers; they easily acquire a passion for gambling, with either cards or lotto.

One is tempted to say above all that the prostitute runs the risk of one day becoming a lesbian; she therefore represents a terrible threat to sexual order, of which she is otherwise the best safeguard. For Parent-Duchâtelet the danger is all the greater in that female homosexuality is an incurable malady whose external characteristics are difficult to observe objectively;[40] the size of the clitoris does not seem to him a very reliable indication. He spends a great deal of time and energy analyzing the illness: it is revealing to observe that the studies of the strictly sexual behavior of prostitutes that he examines are confined to homosexuality; the rest are treated rather allusively. In this field the prison seems to be the only place of observation, which is both useful as such and harmful, since it encourages the spread of unnatural practices.[41] Parent-Duchâtelet recommends that the morals of imprisoned prostitutes be very closely supervised, and that those women who have succumbed to the vice be separated from their lovers and isolated from the younger prisoners.

Thus the catalogue of qualities that the regulationists were unanimously to attribute to prostitutes was drawn up in virtually definitive form by Parent-Duchâtelet. For a century or so commentators continued to stress the persistence of religious sense in fallen women, their attachment to young children, their nostalgia for their native countryside.[42] For them, love often takes the form of a fierce devotion to their lover or their mistress. Their modesty is shown in their refusal to undress in police stations or in front of other women. Finally, their marginality in relation to society arouses in them a deep sense of solidarity and charity. In other words, they possess the same qualities found in honest wives and pious mothers but the true fulfilment of those qualities is prevented by the abject way of life led by the prostitute. The listing of these qualities confirms the bourgeois view of women.

By contrast, the vagueness of the physical portrait of the prostitute that emerges in Parent-Duchâtelet's work is striking. Given the fashion for phrenological and physiognomic theories, one might expect a more precise model, a faithful reflection of moral stereotypes. But there is nothing of the kind.[43] This is because the objectivity of the observation and the immense research carried out by the author into height and color of eyes and hair, for example, led him to conclude that extreme physical diversity exists among prostitutes. Ultimately, although they form a society apart, prostitutes appear to be women like any others; for Parent-Duchâtelet this makes them all the more dangerous in that, let us remember, he is convinced of the temporary character of the profession of prostitution.

Contrary to the then-widespread prejudices, he comes to the conclusion that neither the clitoris, the labia minora, the vagina, nor the anus of prostitutes possesses any peculiar characteristics; the ability of prostitutes to conceive, if not their fertility, is in his opinion scarcely below average. Furthermore, he is led to observe the infrequency of hysteria among these women. Better still, the rigorous application of his method of observation leads him to contradict the then-dominant idea that sexual excess diminishes life expectancy. All in all, the practice of prostitution does not seem to him to constitute a particularly unhealthy profession: "Despite so much excess and so many causes of diseases, their health is more resistant than that of most women who have children and do housework."[44]

Only two physical stereotypes are mentioned, and they are to be repeated endlessly: plumpness of figure, which is easily explained by the prostitute's greed and laziness, as well as by the tastes of her clients; and the raucousness of her voice,[45] which probably stems, the author believes, more from social origin, alcohol abuse, and long exposure to cold than to the practice of oral sex, as popular prejudice had it.

The Need for Tolerance and Supervision

Because it is both necessary and dangerous, prostitution must be tolerated, but closely supervised, with a view to preventing any excess.[46] Indeed, Parent-Duchâtelet comes out against prohibition, which, he believes, history has shown to be ineffective. Similarly he criticizes liberal positions: excess of liberty is mere license, and there are many individuals whose immaturity prevents them from really enjoying their liberty. Prostitutes belong to this category.

The need for tolerance and supervision had found expression since the Consulate in the elaboration of the regulationist system, still called the French system, which rested on three essential principles:

1. It is essential to create an *enclosed milieu*, invisible to children, honest women, and even prostitutes outside the system; enclosure makes it possible to carry marginalization to the limit and to contain extramarital activity; it constitutes a dike to prevent any spillover.[47]

2. This enclosed milieu must remain constantly under the *supervision of the authorities*.[48] Invisible to the rest of society, it is perfectly transparent to those who supervise it. The desire for panopticism, discussed by Michel Foucault in the case of the prison,[49] finds expression in a quasi-obsessional way in regulationism.

3. In order to be sufficiently supervised this milieu must be strictly *hierarchized* and *compartmentalized;* by avoiding as far as possible the mixing of age groups and classes, observation is facilitated and, by the same token, the grip of the authorities is tightened.

This system obviously has its roots in the rationalism of the Enlightenment; it is part of the plan to destroy confusions of category, whether in school, the theater, the hospital, or the cemetery. The history of regulationism was to be that of a tireless effort to *discipline* the prostitute, the ideal being the creation of a category of "enclosed" prostitutes, on the analogy of the enclosed orders of nuns, who would be good "workers" aspiring to the condition of automata, and who above all would not enjoy their work.

As an application of these principles a carceral system was constructed within which a woman moved throughout her prostitutional career. This system called for the organization of four enclosed places: the "house," the hospital, the prison, and, if required, the refuge or establishment where a prostitute could repent of her life and find some rehabilitation. She would circulate from one to the other in the new enclosed carriage, to which Parent-Duchâtelet attached great significance, and whose use, it should be noted in passing, preceded that of the police van.[50] Just as the chain gang both drained off and exalted the criminality that had spread through society, the transfer of prostitutes from police station to prison had aroused spontaneous demonstrations that, in a way, tended to celebrate illegitimate sexuality. "In that procession, which attracted all eyes and was followed by a large number of street urchins, the girls affected a scandalous effrontery, laughed out loud with the soldiers, and took every possible liberty with them."[51]

The axis of the system was the *maison de tolérance*. Ideally the *maison* would be allowed to operate only in certain districts, known as *quartiers réservés,* thus reinforcing the sense of enclosure, making it possible to conceal the building itself from the sight of the female public, and encouraging panopticism, since "in a built-up area one may, at a glance, take in the whole area where places of ill repute exist."[52] Unfortunately, according to Parent-Duchâtelet, experience demonstrated the futility of such an attempt; the establishment of a *quartier réservé* in Paris actually encouraged unregulated prostitution, and the author is more concerned at any rate about vice eluding supervision than about preventing the general public from being aware of it.

Since an establishment that would pass unnoticed in a working-class district would cause a scandal in a residential one, the brothel, adapted to the district in which it was set up, was meant to *concentrate* vice, thus purging the neighborhood of it. When a *maison de tolérance* is opened in a district, "it is a matter of observation that disorder ceases instantly or diminishes; the prostitutes keep to it and no longer spread everywhere; surveillance becomes more active, repression easier."[53]

The house was to be enclosed; entry could be gained only through a dual-door system; the windows were to be of frosted glass and barred.[54] As far as possible placement of rooms on the ground level was to be avoided, thus increasing isolation. The girls would be allowed out only on rare occasions, and medical check-ups would take place in the house. The *maison de tolérance* would be permanently accessible to government inspectors; the doors of the rooms in which the women met their clients would have no locks and would be glazed; the madam or her assistant would carry out constant surveillance, and an attempt would be made not to leave any of the women alone for long, in order to encourage supervision at all times.

The brothel was to be a hierarchized milieu, managed by the representative of authority—that is to say, by the *dame de maison*. The qualities that Parent-Duchâtelet requires of this individual provide a good idea of her functions: they are the same as would be required of a bourgeois wife running a business. The madam would have to be the owner of the property in order not to be dependent on any landlord; the establishment should be as prosperous as possible so as to guarantee the madam's independence. She should have a masculine air of authority about her in order to inspire respect in the girls, who would treat her with deference and submit to the power that she exercised, in a sense, by administrative delegation. "Strength, vigor, moral and physical energy, natural authority, something masculine and imposing, are the requisite qualities in a *dame de maison*."[55] She must not have a husband or lover living in the house, for the influence of a man would have the effect of counterbalancing the authority of the police. Since regulated prostitution must exist in a society of women intended to satisfy male sexual needs under the direct supervision of the public administration, the presence of men who were neither clients nor members of the vice squad could only cause a confusion of roles. The brothel-keepers, Parent-Duchâtelet observes, would educate their children in the best boarding schools; on retirement they might become "charity ladies," devoting their time to various good works.

In other words, the keepers of *maisons de tolérance* were to be the very antithesis of procurers and pimps, immoral, harmful men, ill-defined, creators of debauchery, who as a result represented a terrible threat, especially as they eluded the supervision of the authorities and did their best to impede the surveillance that the police exercised over the prostitutional milieu.

It was quite logical, therefore, to encourage the setting up of *maisons de tolérance* and, in particular, to increase the number of them in the less desirable districts.[56] Nevertheless, Parent-Duchâtelet's lucidity leads him to recognize that some prostitutes very much wish to remain independent and cannot be prevented from doing so. In these circumstances it is preferable to allow them to continue their activities, as was done at the time, while requiring them to carry a card.

Unfortunately, the *maison de tolérance* was not an ideal observatory. Although Parent-Duchâtelet was not afraid to visit the brothels, day and night he was always accompanied by a member of the police. This gives us some idea of the role played by the hospital and the prison in the regulationist system. The required health check for prostitutes was instituted in Paris at the same time that the prefecture of police was established. The coincidence is worth noting: as institutions of similar nature, they were to be reexamined simultaneously at the beginning of the Third Republic. The dispensary where the health checks took place was, for Parent-Duchâtelet, the "finest sanitary establishment, which . . . was set up as soon as the services of medicine were called upon by those in government."[57] Indeed, for the author—and let us not forget that he was himself a doctor—the medical function was above all one of supervision, while therapeutic action was to be applied to things moral as well as, indeed even more than, to the physical. Parent-Duchâtelet turns out to be more impressed by the doctors' "treatment" of the prostitutes' morality than of venereal disease. For him the model practitioner was Dr. Jacquemin, who had made it his rule "to prefer the moral good to the physical advantages where patients were concerned."[58]

These principles are to be found in what Parent-Duchâtelet has to say about the hospital. To begin with, he is in agreement on this matter with the initial position of the medical corps rather than with the views of the police. He therefore demands the setting up of a special hospital for prostitutes with venereal disease. He also criticizes the introduction of venereal departments in the general hospitals and the mingling of sick prostitutes and "unregistered girls" within the same establishment. As a place for observation and preparation for repentance, the hospital to which the sick prostitutes are admitted should be reserved for them. From the overall project also stems the need for *enclosure,* and it is on the model of the prison that the description of the ideal hospital is based (this was the period when the prison-hospital of Saint-Lazare was being established). Similarly, care must be taken, as in prisons, to avoid mixing the various categories of women in the institution: the society of sick prostitutes must reflect in its diversity the hierarchy of the women in their professional lives. Adopting as criteria social and geographic background and sexual behavior, the author proposes to distinguish and to isolate lesbians, the lowest category of prostitutes, from "ordinary prostitutes," "newcomers to the profession," and young women from the provinces.

The logic of the regulationist system requires that the doctor dealing with venereal diseases should be placed under the authority of the *service des moeurs.* The *médecin des moeurs,* like the policeman, the *dame de maison,* and the *dame patronesse* (an organizer of various works of charity), is one of the elements of the system. The qualities that Parent-

Duchâtelet requires of him are very similar to those required of a policeman working in this field; they demonstrate the author's primary concern with moral matters. He must be a man of unblemished reputation,[59] great probity, high morality; he must be a man of mature years, or at least must "have marital ties"; his reserve, his silence, "his modesty when paying visits," his gentleness, "though far removed from familiarity," will help to increase his moral influence; above all, he must demonstrate "his gravity and dignity." In short, by his attitude he must stress the *difference* between the authorities whom he represents and the abjectness of his clients; he will thus avoid any intervention that may run counter to the purpose of marginalization.

But—and this appears to conform to the philanthropic sentiment animating the empiricist sociology of this time—Parent-Duchâtelet demands a greater humanization of the treatment of venereal patients. His hostility to any form of punishment of the victims of disease makes him a precursor of neoregulationism.[60] The precision of the system of supervision removes the need for certain procedures previously regarded as barbarous. In this area what we are witnessing is a development parallel to the one operating within the penitentiary system so brilliantly described by Foucault.

Yet prison is presented, in Parent-Duchâtelet's book, as an indispensable element in the system; his essential aim is to inspire in the prostitute a *permanent terror,* which alone is capable of containing excess and preventing an exaggerated development of prostitution. This certainly points out the fundamentally repressive nature of a system that is not merely regulationist. That prostitution was not actually recognized as a crime by the penal code matters little, since public opinion regarded it as such, in this agreeing "with the principles of civilization, the interest of morals and families, the cry of society, and the fears of mothers."[61]

The function of imprisonment where prostitution is concerned is multifold. As a permanent threat hanging over the prostitute, it is a guarantee of order in the brothels, in the dispensary, and in the hospitals. Also, since each prostitute has been brought there as a result of the arbitrary decision of the authorities, prison constitutes a privileged laboratory for the study of prostitution and, by the same token, provides an improved means of supervising it. The knowledge acquired will enable society to limit the extension of prostitution and above all to prevent "unnatural" sexual practices from developing. (Let us not forget that the function of regulated prostitution, an abject but necessary institution, is to canalize extramarital sexuality and above all to guarantee that it remains "natural.") The prostitutes' prison (indeed, the logic of the system implies that this is a special establishment) furthermore shares the functions then assigned to prisons in general. In this area Parent-Duchâtelet's book is only part of an enormous discourse on penitentiaries that it would be useless and impossible to analyze here. According to the author, prison makes it possible to reveal the deep impulses of a personality and thus prepare it for repentance. Removal to the countryside, work, muscular fatigue, and walking aid this process. There are also better methods of diminishing the manifestations of sexual desire among prostitutes, who are lustful creatures par excellence, even if it is true that they remain frigid while exercising their profession. Parent-Duchâtelet is announcing here the campaign that doctors and hygienists were to launch at the end of the century in favor of physical exercise as an indispensable element in the practice of continence.

The very need for prostitution presents a particular problem, however. What must be the ultimate purpose of the process of repentance? Indeed, would it not be absurd to try to make women whose activities are indispensable to the sexual order return to a life of virtue? In this respect prostitution appears to be radically different from crime, and this fact obviously justifies the distinction made between the two. Parent-Duchâtelet is aware of this difficulty and is forced to recognize the primacy of the smooth running of the system over the process of improving the morality of individuals. The penitentiary system must above all ensure that the prostitute respects the by-laws. What is to be condemned is not so much the exercise of prostitution as disorder. Can this be more clearly expressed than when the author refers to "the fruit that detention must yield, that is to say, the improvement of the prisoner, which, in the case of prostitutes, amounts to passive obedience of police regulations"?[62]

From this point of view, the process of moral improvement and the role of the *dame patronesse* remain strangely limited. If the *dames patronesses* do not wish to compromise the overall project, they can save only a small number of prostitutes, thereby justifying the functioning of the system in the eyes of the church. The *dame patronesse* is the last of the elements that are indispensable to the very existence of regulationism; she mitigates its cynicism in the eyes of public opinion. By leaving open the possibility of remission, the process of repentance, like the establishment of refuge houses, which we know sheltered only a small number of women, facilitated the acceptance of the system by minds imbued with the evangelical message. Indeed, we should note that repentance did not really take a young woman out of the enclosed milieu established by the regulationists, since, unlike the prostitute who "disappeared" and returned to the world, the registered prostitute who repented was condemned to end her days with her hair cut short and wearing homespun in a house most likely based on the model of the convent.

The encounter between the *dame patronesse* and the imprisoned prostitute calls for a systematic analysis that cannot be provided here. The model that Parent-Duchâtelet proposes to hold up to the prostitute-prisoner is that of a wife and mother in whom piety and age have stilled the sexual impulse. For the good influence of the *dame patronesse* to have an effect, the prostitute must be prevented from keeping up any relationships with her family and friends. The madam, the policeman and the police doctor, and the *dame patronesse* are the only people with whom the imprisoned prostitute is to be allowed to communicate.[63]

Parent-Duchâtelet finds justification for the system as he defines it in the evidence of its results; his language is often transformed into a veritable hymn to the regulations. Have these not, from the end of the revolutionary period, profoundly transformed for the better the prostitutional milieu? "Scenes of disgusting lewdness . . . are now very rare inside Paris itself."[64] The repression of proletarian excesses in sexual matters (for that is what regulationism was) finds expression, in Parent-Duchâtelet's own words, in a loss of spontaneity in gesture and language. The domestication of sexual behavior seems to me to be of fundamental importance in that it accompanied and even, it would seem, preceded the reduction of unfocused violence within the proletariat, a process that was at work, as we know, throughout the nineteenth century.[65] This undoubted transformation of attitudes within the milieu very probably led to changes in sexual behavior in society as a whole. Just as certain values of the bourgeois family gradually spread and were partly assimilated and taken up by the working class,[66] so the sexual behavior of the proletariat was gradually influenced by the model presented by the petty bourgeoisie and its attitudes toward the home, and therefore toward prostitution in particular.

But in what form do the changes perceived by Parent-Duchâtelet find expression for the time being? The application of the regulations, time spent in the hospital and in prison, and enforced labor have brought about within the "class of public women" a veritable transformation, which has astonished all foreigners arriving in Paris."[67] "One no longer sees the same haughty, irritating looks, the indecent dress, the lewd gestures and postures, the endless brawls; one no longer hears the filthy conversation and the vociferous shouting that are enough to terrify the visitor."[68] Above all, the prostitutes have partly lost the "turbulence" and "agitation" that had once characterized them. At the same time, the practice of good hygiene has spread. All this, of course, has facilitated the development of repentance and the success of the Bon-Pasteur houses.

Nevertheless, there was still the fear of unregistered prostitution among the poorer classes. On this matter Parent-Duchâtelet shows nothing like the extreme anxiety shown by Béraud, Frégier, and Dr. Potton; for him this is, all in all, a limited phenomenon. Faithful to his empirical principles, he advises the authorities to compromise on their policy and admit the *maison de passe* into the system, even though this is a very different establishment from the *maison de tolérance* as he conceived it. This leaves only the threat of the cheap wineshop with its *cabinet noir*, or private room.[69] Parent-Duchâtelet denounces these shops, but his regulationist optimism overcomes his fears.

Epistemological Implications

Although they are not of direct concern to us, it might nonetheless be worth examining the epistemological implications of the regulationist discourse employed by Parent-Duchâtelet and in other studies of prostitution carried out in the nineteenth century. In no other area do we see more clearly how, at their birth, the social sciences were bound up with the authorities' concern with supervision and punishment. Parent-Duchâtelet's ultimate aim in his long quest was to accumulate sufficient knowledge to allow the authorities to exert their power more easily. He declares this quite plainly at the outset: "Where the government of men is concerned, it is good to know their weaknesses and to use them in order to govern them."[70] The primary purpose of setting up the closed houses that he advocates was, it should be repeated, to facilitate observation and experimentation. The author's project begins to emerge clearly: to enclose in order to observe, to observe in order to know, to know in order to supervise and control—and it is this primacy of observation that makes his book the antithesis of a utopia and one of the masterpieces of empirical sociology.

Parent-Duchâtelet's approach reveals a permanent obsession with the quantitative and a concern for series. By his own admission his principal methodological preoccupation is "to arrive at numerical results on every matter with which I set out to deal."[71] "This method, which I shall call the statistical," he writes again, "will become widespread before very long"[72] and he expresses a wish that it will be rapidly adopted by the medical sciences, for, he declares, "medicine, like science, does not yet exist, but it can become the most positive of the natural sciences by the use of the numerical method in everything that concerns it."[73] Furthermore, the techniques of investigation developed by Parent-Duchâtelet are striking in their modernity: the drawing up of the questionnaire that he proposed to present to the prostitutes on registration, the system of cards that he developed, the establishment and improvement of files on individuals that he proposed and above all his constant concern with checking his findings[74] are abundant evidence of this. His desire for innovation is even to be found in the graphic presentation of the results; it is probably to him that we owe the first diagram using bar graphs to be featured in a work of statistics.[75]

The many different angles from which he approaches the issue of prostitution turn out to be even more interesting; nothing escapes his analysis, which is in turn anthropological, ethnological, linguistic, socio-cultural, sociogeographic, and medical. The passage that he devotes to a study of the literacy rate with the help of signatures foreshadows the work of Maggiolo and corresponds exactly to the most recent concerns of historians.[76] The only omission, which is easily explained by the pro-hibitions of the time, is that he makes no study of the strictly sexual practices of the prostitutes and their clients. But would it not be anach-ronistic to criticize him for this?

Given such a model it is easy to understand why later authors who have set out to describe prostitution have been led to write vast tomes whose breadth would leave flabbergasted the contemporary reader unversed in the literature of the time. It is, therefore, only in reference to Parent-Duchâtelet's book that Dr. Commenge's enormous work on unregistered prostitution[77] between 1876 and 1886 can be explained. The model was to prove so constricting that the sociology of prostitu-tion remained faithful to the initial methods and ignored, for example, the ____graphic techniques of the school of Le Play.

The ____lationist project expounded first by Parent-Duchâtelet, then by ____ud, consists of damming up, containing, and canalizing excesses by ____nt administrative means, without the intervention of the legal ____em, supported by the authorities, the police, and the army, with the tacit approval of the church, would be criticized, of course, just as at the outset penitentiary theories were criticized by cer-tain liberals. Nevertheless, it was not questioned in any profound way before the institutions that developed it and the social forces that sus-tained them were themselves shaken—that is to say, before the triumph of the Republic. It was ultimately the changes in sexual behavior brought about within society as a whole that led to a relaxation of rigor in the early years of the twentieth century.

The Exacerbation of the Regulationist System

Just after the defeat of the Commune regulationism underwent both a renewal and a shift in direction. Whereas, for over thirty years, Parent-

Duchâtelet's book had been *the* work of reference (even in 1857 specialists were placing themselves under his posthumous patronage[78] and, not daring to publish anything new on the subject, were content simply to bring his work up to date), the appearance, between 1871 and 1877 of several important works[79] brought about a marked development in theory. In the wake of the pessimism that weighed on both the conservative and liberal bourgeoisie, tormented by the need to expiate the festivities of the Second Empire and the massacres of the Commune, the regulationist project became exacerbated while the failure of the system was becoming obvious. Severe repression of sexual activity, which was presented no longer as a subterranean threat but as a wave about to engulf society, now became the aim. The growth of anxiety over prostitution reflected the deep unease aroused in those who believed in the "moral order" by the social and political transformations then taking place. Although it remained faithful to its fundamental analyses and to the stereotypes worked out during the Empire and the Restoration, the regulationist discourse assumed, by that very fact, quite a different dimension. The literature of prostitution became one of the most revealing symptoms of the anxieties of this period.

Persistence of the Regulationist Discourse

Whereas its most faithful adepts were themselves aware of the partial failure of regulationism, this approach was becoming more precise. With methods of supervision improving, its failures were attributed not to the system itself but to its initial imperfection. Fundamentally, therefore, there was no break. The plan of Parent-Duchâtelet's book was assumed by his epigones as a veritable yoke, and it was not until the work of Yves Guyot[80] that a fundamental change took place in the problematics and framework for thinking. In 1889 Dr. Reuss showed that he was still the prisoner of a fifty-year-old model when he wrote the book that ends the fine series of anthropological studies inaugurated by Parent-Duchâtelet.

In most of the works of the regulationists prostitution is still presented as an inevitable and incurable ill. The historical passages devoted to the ancient Hebrews, to Rome, or to the Middle Ages always portray the past at the service of the nonhistoricity of the phenomenon, characteristic of works published under the July Monarchy. The inevitable references to Saint Augustine and Saint Paul[81] recall the church's tolerance of regulationism. The improvement in the filing systems of hospital, police, and penitentiary administrations made possible ever more precise investigation, and the anthropology of the prostitute was far from exhausted.

The analysis of the causes of prostitution[82] becomes both more refined and more impoverished. The primacy of instinct over poverty, unemployment, and any other explanation deriving from social structures is now clearly affirmed. The "libidinous temperament," the "desire to live it up," the hereditary predisposition to debauchery are regarded as determining factors. Laziness and idleness are the other main sources of vice. When thought is given to social phenomena it is seldom to the damage done by the exploitation of the proletariat or of women; hunger does not appear to be the prime cause of prostitution. The regulationists of the Third Republic differ in this respect from the philanthropists of the Restoration. "Social changes" are blamed. The discourse on prostitution then echoes all the stereotypes to be found in the inexhaustible complaints of mid-nineteenth-century notables: the weakening of paternal authority in the family; the spread of atheism and freethinking; the decline in the influence of the church; the challenge to the political authorities; the progress of liberalism, which makes police repression more difficult; and the new permissiveness of public opinion are mentioned over and over again. Excessive social mobility, which increases the risk of proletarian contagion; growing uniformity in dress, which makes it difficult to distinguish among the classes and stimulates a taste for luxury and coquetry among the poorer classes; political upheavals; the spread of a sense of transitoriness, which leads people to seek "immediate pleasures"—all these are vigorously denounced, thus revealing the authors' profound anxiety over social developments that are eroding the dikes carefully built during the first half of the century.[83] Of course the effects of industrialization are often mentioned, but usually to deplore the mixing of the sexes in the workshops.

The portrait of the prostitute remained for a long time more or less as it had been during the first half of the century. With astonishing consistency authors note the prostitute's instability and loquacity; her taste for alcohol, and in particular for absinthe; her love of food; her passion for gambling; her propensity toward laziness, lying, and anger. They are also careful to stress her few moral qualities: the sense of solidarity, her love of children, her modesty when confronted by the medical profession, and above all her religiosity. To the prostitute's love of flowers is added her affection for animals, especially birds and dogs.

Among the few changes that the last regulationists nevertheless insist on pointing out are the increasing rarity of tattoos and progress in bodily hygiene. The frequency of homosexuality is mentioned, but very often in relation to the writings of Parent-Duchâtelet; the subject does not seem to arouse as much anxiety as in the past.

We find one important innovation, however: the sudden emergence of the theme of the patriotic prostitute, which, as we know, was to enjoy a rich literary future from Maupassant's *Boule de Suif* and beautiful Irma[84] to La Boulotte, Léon Bloy's heroic inmate of the Saint-Calais brothel.[85] The Comte d'Haussonville seems to have been the first to emphasize the strength of this feeling in his investigation of childhood in Paris.[86] This may well stem from a more-or-less conscious desire to glorify the prostitute as the guarantor of stability in morals and an obstacle to the increase in adultery and the development of erotic behavior among bourgeois women. It may also express a wish to demonstrate the depth of patriotism, which, like religous feeling, remains intact even among such women.

The persistence of the regulationist discourse is evident in the way the *maison de tolérance* is praised and its indispensable character is stressed. Praise of the brothel becomes more frequent with its perceptible decline. Dr. Homo deplores "the abandonment of the *maisons de tolérance* by young men";[87] Dr. Garin wishes to see an increase in the authority of the madams and restrictions on the freedom of the inmates to leave the establishments.[88] "The *maisons de tolérance* are the basis of any regulation of prostitution," Lecour declares. "For the police it is an effective way of localizing the evil by being able to supervise it and repress it, and thus attack unregistered prostitution."[89] Dr. Mireur, following the Marseillais model claims that the *fille de maison* should henceforth be the only officially recognized prostitute.[90] According to him this would have the effect of attracting into the licensed brothels those clients who want to be assured that the girls are healthy.[91] Five years later Dr. Reuss would still be asking the authorities to increase the number of *maisons de tolérance*.[92]

One still finds the obsession with the enclosed and the invisible that had guided the first regulationists. At Lyons, as Garin noted with satisfaction, attempts were being made to prevent the prostitutes from attracting attention when they went to the pharmacy: "Precautions are even carried so far as to lay down an unvarying itinerary and to insist that they wear dark clothes."[93]

The idyllic description of the infirmary of Saint-Lazare by Maxime du Camp,[94] like the eulogistic passages devoted to the *maisons de relèvement* (houses of reform), also suggests the persistence of the regulationist discourse. The obsession with expiation that characterized the conservatives of this period explains why repentance should be such an important concern. Regulationism was based increasingly—as is evident in the case of the Comte d'Haussonville—on the need to encourage the reform of fallen women. Indeed, supervision by the authorities allows charity to come into play; without it the *dames patronesses* would have no hold on vice. In the hospital, in the infirmary, and even more in the prison, the prostitute was accessible to these women, who would otherwise have been unable to meet them in the street or the places where they lived. It should be added that the description of the houses of reform, which the women derisively called *couvinières* (conventlike institutions), were more than ever inspired by the model of the convent.

Obsession with the Theme of Prostitution

Even more than its persistence one should note the broadening of regulationist thinking. In order to understand fully the pervasiveness of the theme of prostitution in the concerns of the time and the wish of some theorists to establish a hyperregulationism, we must go back to the Paris rising of 1871.

The actions of the Commune toward prostitution are highly ambiguous, since its antiregulationism was accompanied in principle by an attempted prohibition on the part of the municipal authorities and an increase in libertarianism in reality. Nevertheless, the theme of licence in the street during the rising, the "saturnalia" of Saint-Lazare, and the barricade of the rue Royale; the myth of the prostitute-*pétroleuses,* "ces entremetteuses de l'Incendie" (those go-betweens of the Fire),[95] setting light to the police prefecture; and the descriptions of the camp of Satory accentuate, for the advocates of the system, the benefits of administrative supervision. According to them the experience of the Commune provides a basis for police regulationism. On this matter the haste with which this "as it were instantaneous and unchallenged reorganization"[96] of the *police des moeurs* (vice squad) took place in late May is revealing. Lecour, aware of the advantages to be derived from the experience by the authorities, hastens to add a few chapters to the book that he had written at the end of the Empire. For his part Dr. Mauriac is content to point out, in his lessons on "syphilography," the consequences of the event on the health of the Parisian population.[97]

Generally speaking, prostitution is seen as much more extensive than before. This greater attention to prostitution is perceptible from 1871 on, and comes well before the great campaigns in public opinion at the end of the decade. Maxime du Camp's analysis, which borders on the delusional, provides an exaggeration of the thinking of the regulationists at the time. [98] Prostitution is seen as a gangrene rising from the lower depths of society and invading the entire social body during the Second Empire.[99] Corruption throughout the laboring classes, the old terror of the early nineteenth century, has taken root. The rise of the *femme galante,* especially of the common prostitute, and the spread of vice within the organism have brought about a "social disorientation." In the tradition of pessimism haunting bourgeois minds, Maxime du Camp suggests to his reader that an irresistible flood has broken through the social dikes. This softening of the social body owing to the instability of its institutions and to the excessive spread of liberalism explains and justifies divine retribution; in turn it determines the wish to enjoy life while it lasts, which is an advantage to the prostitute, who thus becomes the embodiment and symbol of the threat of death weighing on the social body. Only the restoration of order, and above all of *moral* order—that is to say, in the field of prostitution, the application of the regulations—will make a cure possible.

We are, therefore, very far from the regulationist optimism of Parent-Duchâtelet. The threat no longer appears to be contained within a "social base," which would simply have to be supervised, more or less successfully; for the later regulationists it is vital to extend police supervision. This anxiety before "the social circulation of vice" is clearly manifested in the proliferation of the theme of the unregistered prostitute in the literature of prostitution. This fear, which was already perceptible during the Second Empire, as is shown by de Carlier's book,[100] follows the mild anxiety of Parent-Duchâtelet. It reveals, let me repeat, an awareness of the failure of regulationism but does not for all that condemn the system in the eyes of its defenders. The impression of an *invasion*[101] by unregulated prostitution obviously expresses the fear inspired within the bourgeoisie by any idea of sexual liberalization. The demarcation is less distinct than ever between adultery, freedom of morals, debauchery, vice, and prostitution,[102] leaving Maxime du Camp to propose the figure of 120,000 prostitutes for the city of Paris alone[103] and Dr. Reuss to estimate that in 1889 there were over 100,000. The study of unregulated prostitution and its dangers, the analyis of this "group refractory to any systematization,"[104] as Dr. Diday puts it, was to remain the privileged theme of regulationist and neoregulationist literature, while abolitionists strove mainly to stress the disadvantages of the *maison de tolérance*.

The kept woman, ignored by the first regulationists, became by that very fact an object of concern. For Dr. Homo, who studied the problem at Château-Gontier, she is particularly dangerous in small towns: usually a "local girl," she maintains her relations with the society of the area. "Her childhood friends are not afraid to speak to her when nobody else is around; she receives the working girls she employs at her home"[105] and represents a model of luxury and idleness. Now, at Château-Gontier, it is usually the unregistered prostitutes who sexually initiate the young men; indeed, these young men no longer frequent the *maison de tolérance* except to witness "lewd scenes."[106] That sexual pleasure and extramarital activity should leave the ghetto of supervised prostitution represents the most terrible threat. Idleness, luxury, and pleasure, the trilogy opposed to the values of work, economy, and happiness, are embodied by the kept woman and the unregistered prostitute, without, it should be repeated, any plainly operating distinction.

The last regulationist authors describe with newfound precision and vigor the various threats that prostitution, a gangrene on the social body, exerts over the organism as a whole. More use is made of the theme of sanitary, or rather hygienic, danger, and medical authority is appealed to more often than before.[107] Lecour's many references to the works of doctors are a good illustration of this tendency, which bears the seeds of neoregulationism. Syphilis replaces cholera, and venereal disease now symbolizes the risk of contagion from the dangerous classes.

As a result, prostitution represents a terrible threat to the future of the race. Here we are witnessing the emergence of the idea of degeneration that was to culminate at the end of the century in the campaign against the venereal danger. For the time being the theme is more that of a threat to marriage and childbirth than a fear of inherited syphilis. What is evoked is the notion of demographic weakening, [108] and therefore the ebbing capacity of the nation to defend itself, not to mention the fact that prostitution and the sickness it brings with it threaten the soundness of armies directly. According to Dr. Mougeot, "The nation that, by culpable neglect of physical and moral corruption, has allowed the number of its children and the physical strength of each of them to diminish will necessarily become prey to nations who have maintained themselves in greater strength and numbers."[109] What we have then is a set of fears, aroused by the German threat, which were to feed the great campaigns of the repopulationists at the close of the century.

Certainly immorality, and prostitution in particular, together with increasing urbanization were root causes of the falling off in the marriage and birth rates, as well as the supposed increase in morbidity. Sex for money makes young men less eager to marry by making it "so easy for them to satisfy their sexual desires and [explains] their reluctance to give up a life of debauchery, which they see as more agreeable and free of the worries inevitable in the position of head of a family."[110] Besides, prostitution enables "young men to acquire pernicious habits that sooner or later will surface in the privacy of the home and will affect the husbands' self-respect."[111] Finally, unregistered prostitution, by allowing young men to turn to debauchery at an early age (a phenomenon that, at Château-Gontier, dated, according to Dr. Homo, from the Second Empire), weakens their later capacity to procreate and even carries a risk of sterility. "In the name of the declining race . . . which seems to have been poisoned at the very wellsprings of life," for "the protection of the educated classes."[112] Maxime du Camp demands that the prefecture of police in Paris be armed with discretionary powers over prostitution.

Threatened in its very health, the bourgeoisie was also threatened in its fortune. The *mangeardes*[113] (women who "eat up" men's money), the "female minotaurs,"[114] the "parasites,"[115] the vamps who have money of their own or who prey on men's capital, the "ogresses" who invest in promoting prostitutes, are no longer content to ruin the young men of the aristocracy; they are now described as the terror of bourgeois mothers, who will look back fondly to the days when their sons were content to frequent the *maisons de tolérance*. The *femmes galantes* and all the unregistered prostitutes are partly responsible for the "extraordinary mobility of money,"[116] which threatens the most apparently stable positions. What is more, "limited companies and partnerships have been extended to love";[117] men pool their resources to keep a woman in common, and "one may see on the same bed, each on his own day and without any feeling of jealousy, a young man of good family, a draper's assistant, and an actor."[118] The *disorderliness* of vice, at once the cause and symbol of social disorder, was, by its very essence, what haunted the regulationists most.

Unregistered prostitution, if people were not careful, would run the risk of spreading erotic behavior throughout the social body as a whole. Fears concerning the sexual integrity of bourgeois women were of utmost concern to the regulationists of "the moral order." This explains the emergence of that hyperregulationism whose avowed aim was to supervise not only registered or unregistered prostitution but all extramarital sexual activities. It was the logical culmination of the regulationist project, an exacerbation that occurred at the very moment when militant abolitionism erupted. It must be said that in the years following the Commune circumstances were favorable to such an enterprise, since it was an aspect of the liquidation of the Second Empire, a period subsequently symbolized by the social ascent of the demimondaine and the *femme galante*.

From Parent-Duchâtelet's triumphalism the regulationist discourse had become, therefore, the reflection and crossroads of all the bourgeois obsessions of the time. It carried within itself anxiety about the new, especially in sexual matters. Sexual liberation, which was consciously identified with freedom from morals, debauchery, and prostitution, constituted a threat to the family, the fidelity of women, the virginity of young girls, the purity of blood and of the race. The abandonment of regulation would mean the end of any supervision over proletarian sexuality and would increase the risk of contagion that it represented for bourgeois families.

The perception of the danger that the ruling classes incurred through contact with the masses, and especially prostitutes, had therefore been profoundly transformed since the Restoration. Of course, people were still afraid of biological contagion, but an awareness of the threat to fortunes and the sexual integrity of women replaced the physical fear aroused by the spread of criminal violence among the working classes. The reduction of popular violence since the middle of the century and the gradual extinction of widespread illegalities help explain this development.

It is hardly surprising that such feelings fueled the regulationist project. Now the application of the by-laws involved administrative and police action, which was exerted in the political domain, in 1874 and after May 16, 1877; by virtue of this fact it was natural for the debate on prostitution to begin on this terrain, with a fierce confrontation between regulationist conservatives and abolitionist radicals.

The Extreme Remedies

A great many remedies were considered for overcoming the fears of a society threatened by subversion. Fiction, which was only beginning to emerge painfully from the straitjacket of censorship, had hardly begun to express this fear.

Still refusing the intervention of the courts in matters concerning prostitution, and considering that legislation was the only guarantee of police action under the law, Garin[119] at Lyons, Jeannel[120] at Bordeaux, and Mireur[121] at Marseilles demanded uniform legislation throughout the country; the last two even wanted the establishment of international sanitary regulations. In this respect they took up the wishes expressed by Drs. Crocq and Rollet in their report to the 1867 international medical congress[122] in Paris and again by the members of the congress meeting in Vienna in 1873, for which occasion Dr. Mireur wrote his voluminous book *La syphilis et la prostitution dans leurs rapports avec l'hygiène, la morale, et la loi.*[123]

In these works, as in the later works of Reuss, we find a wish to strengthen the links between the various branches of the administration concerned with supervising prostitution. The model for this concentration of regulationist institutions was to be found at Lyons: "The sanitary service occupies the first floor of the old police headquarters, in the rue Luizerne . . . The staircase landing divides this floor into two parts: on the one side [are] the inspector's office, the adjoining accounts offices, and the temporary cell for prostitutes who have been arrested, declared sick, or punished; on the other side are the outbuildings, exclusively used for visits. In the top floor, under the roof, is another police cell . . . with a camp bed, where offenders may be kept for up to four days under arrest."[124]

At Marseilles, Mireur demanded the setting up, if possible close to the red-light district, of a "special house-infirmary," in which would be "concentrated all the departments dealing with prostitution, i.e., the dispensary for visits, the cell, and rooms for treatment."[125] Given that the author is an advocate of the *quartier réservé,* or district reserved exclusively for prostitutes, and of the monopoly of the *maisons de tolérance,* what he is proposing is an almost utopian model of enclosure. The inmates of the "special house-infirmary," divided into age groups, would be obliged, whether they were being held on an offense or on medical grounds, to work in the building's workroom.[126]

In 1887 Dr. Delabost proposed that the prison, dispensary, and hospital intended for the use of the prostitutes of the department of Seine-Inférieure should be grouped together; the whole complex would form a "sort of asylum"; "this concentration . . . might well be set up in some old, unrented factory, which could be converted at little expense."[127] Finally, in 1889 Reuss was to demand that registration, supervision, and repression be placed in the same hands. "It is essential to have unity of direction and viewpoint where prostitution is concerned," he wrote.[128]

The extension of the regulationist system was considered by all these specialists. Mireur, inspired by the efficiency of police activity deployed in Provence between 1871 and 1873, requested that the authorities adopt "the most energetically repressive" measures.[129] The application of two municipal orders dating from 1871 and 1873 had indeed practically succeeded in confining prostitution in Marseilles within the *maisons de tolérance.* Since this "enclosure" had been accompanied by an emigration of the prostitutes out of the city, the general councils and prefects of neighboring departments, for example that of Var in August 1893, had been led to take similar measures.

The most passionate debate concerned visits by sailors, soldiers, beggars, travelers, workers, and civil servants, and their possible sequestration in the event of an outbreak of venereal disease. This was an old idea popularized as early as 1846 by Dr. Guépin,[130] advocated by Diday[131] in 1850 in the *Gazette médicale* and many others during the Second Empire,[132] taken up again by Rey at the Paris congress in 1867[133] and, in a more rigorous way, at the Vienna congress in 1873; the sequestration of venereal patients was then demanded by Drs. Homo, Garin, and

Jeannel.[134] Jeannel, it is true, did not consider subjecting either workers or travelers to quarantine; he did, however, propose the setting up of "hospital–lazare houses for the sequestration and treatment of men found to be suffering from venereal disease."[135] Dr. Homo presented a more ambitious project when in 1872 he advocated health checks for all men "belonging to the army, the navy, and various bodies of workers organized in a military fashion," as well as for merchant seamen, "vagabonds, prisoners, and detainees."[136] After giving it due consideration, however, he rejected the idea of subjecting to such examinations "civilian workers employed in the large-scale industries (factories, railways, mines, etc.)."[137] Such projects stemming from social medicine were ostensibly based on a wish to control the transmission of syphilis among the working classes, but in fact they were basically, for the time being, intended to stop the contagion from spreading to the rest of society.

More revealing of the nature of regulationism in the early years of the Republic are the projects that tended to repress, or at least to control, all forms of extramarital sexuality under the pretext of supervising prostitution. In 1872 Dr. Homo demanded the registration of all kept women, on the grounds that their activities constituted a disguised form of prostitution.[138] Of course the idea was not new, but those who had considered this method, such as Dr. Strohl of Strasbourg, had usually rejected it in the end. Dr. Homo declared that society must defend itself against the danger of the kept woman. "How many young men choose not to marry, how many households are riven by discord, how many fortunes swallowed up in our time by this pernicious influence?"[139] Besides, the moral justification of such a measure was, for him, self-evident by virtue of the regulationist principle previously laid down by Dr. Potton, according to which "vice must never be deprived of its shame."[140]

The hyperregulationist scheme that then developed in fact provided for the repression or supervision up to the time of marriage of the individual's entire sexual activity, and in particular that of women; all this was advocated in the name of the struggle against prostitution. Here is Dr. Mireur lavishing his advice on parents wishing to prevent their daughters from falling into prostitution: from the age of four or five, the age "that is truly that of first impressions,"[141] girls should be supervised day and night, with special attention being paid to their gestures and words."[142] "Whatever the social position of the young girl, or rather of her parents," the author writes in his work on prostitution in Marseilles, "it still seems to me to be indispensable that she should be initiated at an early age into manual labor . . . It is rare for a working woman to be amenable to ideas of bad conduct."[143] At school, moral teaching must not been neglected. "Moderate your daughters' taste for luxury,"[144] he advises middle-class mothers. Unfortunately, the real difficulty will arise when the young girl first enters the store or workshop. There she will meet her enemy: man.[145] There is no need to go over the arguments; the ideology is well known. Here the regulationist literature simply echoes the overall enterprise of repressing premarital sexuality then being pursued by medical science, as can be seen in the crusade launched by Dr. Bertillon to denounce the dreadful dangers of using the genital organs before the age of twenty-one.[146]

More original is the regulationism of Professor Diday, who seems to have been the only specialist of the time to hold sensible views on the functions of prostitution and to base his thought on a coherent sociological analysis. An eminent writer on the subject of syphilis, he links the spread of prostitution not to the satisfaction of the baser instincts or to the attractions of vice but to the existence of late monogamous marriages; from this fact he makes the logical deduction that one should cease to vituperate against prostitution and, on the contrary, make it more accessible. His serene lucidity makes him an isolated case, much criticized by the abolitionists and repudiated by the regulationists. He was not afraid to develop his ideas on the role of prostitution as a "social safeguard." "Rightly condemned in the name of morality, prostitution is tolerated as the only means, in a civilized state, of preventing disorder, discord, scandal, offenses, and crimes deriving from the obstacles that our social organization places in the way of the satisfaction of one of the least controllable needs of human nature."[147] What should be done, then, is to organize prostitution, to guarantee its correct functioning so that it may be capable of "keeping in check the sort of people who need to find satisfaction from it, those whom society has an interest in diverting in this way from amorous relationships that would prove fatal to marital peace."[148] Such arguments led nowhere; regulationism was to base its survival on other, apparently less cynical arguments.

With the exception of Diday the regulationist discourse remained faithful to the traditional analysis of the causes of prostitution. More than ever it stressed the primacy of instinct; the portrait of the prostitute still conformed to stereotypes dating from the Restoration and Louis-Philippe periods. By definition the remedies envisaged always involved regulation and surveillance. But whereas Parent-Duchâtelet claimed to be dealing only with a problem of the public thoroughfare, to be remedying only a subterranean threat that above all should be sealed off and canalized, the regulationists of the "moral order" were dealing with a problem that concerned the sexuality of the entire social group. As a result, prostitution became a major preoccupation. The regulationist discourse now exposed its underlying aim, the total repression of sexuality.

It is clear that it was this anxiety, this anguish, perceptible in the writings of the technicians, that was to bring about the sudden emergence of the theme of prostitution in fiction; in many respects *Nana* is the daughter of post-Commune regulationist obsessions.[149]

2. The Enclosed World of Regulationism

Les Filles Ordonnées au Vice

A woman entered the enclosed world of officially tolerated prostitution by registration;[1] by that very fact she became a *fille soumise* whether she decided to join a *maison de tolérance* or to practice her profession on her own. In the first case her name would be included in the brothel-keeper's book and she would thus become a *fille à numéro,* a prostitute with a number; in the second case she would be given an identification card and be regarded by the authorities as a *fille en carte*. Registration indicated the adoption not of a profession, for prostitution could not be regarded as such, but of the state of being, which certain regulationists were not afraid to compare with being in the military. It is an important difference because from it derives in part the arbitrary nature of the penalties handed down by the authorities.

Methods of Registration

Methods of registration varied from one municipality to another. In every case, however, a distinction was made between those women who had registered voluntarily and those who had been registered by the authorities. In Paris voluntary registration was a simple procedure: the applicant, armed with a copy of her birth certificate, turned up at the second bureau of the first division of the prefecture of police and asked to be registered. She was questioned by the assistant head of the bureau, who asked her to declare her matrimonial status and the professions of her parents. She would declare whether she still lived with them, and if not, give the reasons for the separation. The applicant then had to declare how long she had been living in the capital, and if she had any children, whether she had them with her. Finally, she was asked why she had decided to apply to be registered.

The woman then underwent a medical examination at the police dispensary. An investigation carried out in her home commune made it possible, if deemed necessary, to check her statements and to build up a file. If she was married, the vice squad summoned her husband. When these formalities had been complied with, the applicant had the right to go to the house of her choice or to set up on her own; it should be noted, however, that in Paris the brothel-keepers could no longer bring girls to the prefecture of police to be registered, as they had once been allowed to do.

In the case of compulsory registration a more complicated procedure took place, especially after October 15, 1878, the date when the Gigot regulations came into force. Upon arrest the *fille insoumise* caught soliciting was questioned "without delay"[2] by the local police superintendent. If she was arrested in the evening, this meant spending the night in the police station. The superintendent then decided whether to release her or to send her to police headquarters, where she might be isolated in a cell. The assistant head of the vice squad, after questioning her, had her sign the report drawn up by the police and sent her off for a medical examination at the dispensary.

If the prostitute was found to have a venereal disease, she was sent to the infirmary of Saint-Lazare. If she was healthy and it was a first arrest, she was usually released, while a recidivist would be registered, if she agreed, on the spot. If she protested and refused to submit to the administrative obligations incumbent on registration, she was sent back to police headquarters to await a final decision. This rested not with the superintendent who had questioned her, as had formerly been the case, but with a commission made up in theory "of the prefect or his representative, the head of the first division, and of the interrogating superintendent," but in fact of the head of the second bureau, assisted by two police superintendents. If the unregistered prostitute was an adult, these officers were content to follow the opinion of the interrogating superintendent. In the case of a minor, the decision belonged to the commission. The vice squad then carried out an inquiry and built up a file on the woman, which was communicated to her family through the local mayor;[3] it was only at the end of this rather long procedure that the minor was finally regarded as a *fille soumise*.

It goes without saying that if the members of the vice squad made a mistake, there was considerable risk of a scandal: an "honest woman" arrested by mistake some evening in a Paris street had to spend the night in the local police station in the company of criminals and vagabonds.

If the police superintendent confirmed the vice squad officers' report, she was then sent off to the central police station, where she would be forced to submit to a medical examination of her sexual organs. It was errors of this kind that were to give rise to the great abolitionist campaigns.[4] It should be added that any registered prostitute regarded as having "disappeared," and therefore removed by definition from the register, was reregistered compulsorily and punished if caught soliciting.

At Marseilles[5] the procedure laid down by the by-laws of 1878 was rather different. The prostitute who wanted to be registered filled out a form that comprised no fewer than twenty-four questions; she then submitted to a medical examination. Her file was sent to the central police station, then to the mayor. When this file had been approved and returned to the vice office the girl received a card on which were written the dates on which she would have to report for medical examinations.[6] In the case of a minor the applicant was questioned with greater care, but the procedure was identical. The unregistered prostitute caught soliciting was questioned by an inspector of the vice squad; taking the report and the result of the questioning into account, this inspector then decided whether or not the girl was to be registered. If she was married, the decision was made only if her husband refused to take her back.

In the small and medium-sized towns the procedure was even simpler. The investigation carried out by Gigot in 1882[7] leads one to believe that in most of these municipalities any woman caught in the company of a man who did not previously know her and who would not answer for her was compulsorily registered at this time. The results of these investigations suggest the frequency of denunciations: these were made by soldiers, neighbors and other local inhabitants, and, quite simply, registered prostitutes who were jealous of the competition provided by the unregistered *filles*.

According to Hennequin,[8] who analyzed the 445 by-laws in force in 1904, the procedure for voluntary registration was set out in 279 communes and compulsory registration in 403. Although most of the regulations stated that the woman must be in the *habit* of practicing prostitution,[9] few made provision for guarantees against discretionary punishment. In over two hundred localities no mention is made of the authorities possessing the right of compulsory registration. In fact this right belonged to administrators of all ranks, from superintendents down to sergeants. Thirty-four regulations stipulated that the mayor should delegate this power to the superintendent, and sixteen granted it to some unspecified person. In 150 towns "the exercise of this power is reserved to the mayor."[10] Apparently only seventy-three by-laws reveal any attempt to provide guarantees before proceeding to compulsory registration. In forty communes this was imposed only after complaints had been lodged by neighbors or local inhabitants; seventeen by-laws required an investigation into the woman's background, her family, and her prospects for returning to the straight and narrow. At this time only the orders enforced at Marseilles and Narbonne made provision for an appeal procedure in the magistrate's courts. Furthermore, it should be noted that twenty-five municipal by-laws stipulated that before a married woman was registered her husband had to be warned and urged to exercise his authority. At Limoges a woman was registered only "after her absence or her husband's connivance had been confirmed, or if the husband found it impossible to prevent his wife's conduct."[11] At Cherbourg he was also made to sign a certificate to the effect that his wife had abandoned him.

Up to about 1880 the number of voluntary registrations seems to have exceeded the number of compulsory ones. At Bordeaux between 1855 and 1861, "out of a total of 1,216 registrations, 1,005 were voluntary and 211 were compulsory."[12] In the last ten years, Mireur wrote in 1882,[13] in Marseilles 2,510 girls were registered voluntarily and 1,074 were registered compulsorily. As time went on, however, the latter procedure began to be more common, as is shown by the results of the 1902 investigation in the five departments making up the sample in Table 1.[14] Furthermore, it would seem that voluntary registration was more frequent in the Midi than in the regions north of the Loire.[15]

The *fille insoumise* was free to leave the way of life that she had chosen

Table 1. Registrations and removals of prostitutes from the register, 1886–1901, in five departments.

Department	Compulsory registrations		Voluntary registrations		Total registrations	Removals from the register	
	Number	%	Number	%		Number	%
Finistère	1,759	99.7	6	0.3	1,765	1,688	95
Seine-et-Oise	365	93	28	7	393	97	25
Charente-Inférieure	788	74	278	26	1,066	407	38
Hérault	2,781	59	1,890	40	4,671	2,468	52
Meurthe-et-Moselle	1,072	79	279	21	1,351	453	33.5
Total	6,765	73	2,481	26	9,246	5,113	55

or that had been imposed on her; to do this she had, in theory, to follow the procedure of having her name removed from the register, although in fact it was usually enough quite simply to "disappear." The by-laws operating in Paris made provision for several official reasons other than death for removing a name from the register: a prostitute who married could have her name removed on presentation of the marriage contract; the same applied when a lover recognized as serious made the request, after a meticulous investigation into his prospects and the duration of the liaison. Her family could also request that her name be removed; for this the parents had to be reasonably well off and not to have encouraged the prostitution of their daughter in the first place. Finally, a prostitute suffering from some infirmity could be removed from the register immediately; it should be noted, however, that old age was not always regarded as sufficient reason for a woman's name to be dropped from the register. In 1904 the doyenne of the *filles en carte* in Paris was seventy-three; she had been registered in 1848. The next-longest-serving prostitute had been registered in 1866 and was now sixty-five.[16]

In some cases a name was removed only after a probationary period of between three and nine months.[17] Prostitutes who had been taken into refuge-workshops devoted to the reformation of fallen women by *dames patronesses* and those who had decided to work continued to be supervised by the vice squad. Furthermore, those *filles soumises* who had set up a *maison de tolérance* on their own, those who had been condemned for some common-law offense, those who had left for the provinces without passports, and especially those who had "disappeared," were temporarily removed from the register.

At Marseilles[18] it was the inspector of the vice squad who alone decided on removals from the register; apart from this, the procedure was almost identical. Here, however, a prostitute who wanted to live as her lover's wife was not removed. The *fille soumise* who wanted to leave the city stated her destination, underwent a medical check-up, and was automatically removed from the list.

According to Hennequin,[19] by 1904 almost all municipal by-laws provided for removal from the register; the matter was usually decided by the mayor at the written request of the interested party or those standing surety for her. In some twenty towns, however, a probationary period of about three months was required. Four reasons for removal were mentioned in the various by-laws: good behavior and a guarantee that the young woman could work for a living or would be kept by some honorable person (221 by-laws), marriage (55), return to the family (33), old age and illness (19); only 11 by-laws refer to all these reasons together.

In fact it was very rare for a prostitute to have her name removed from the register because she had found some other means of existence, because she had married, or because she had resumed work. In Paris from 1880 to 1886 only 233 *filles soumises* benefited from such a measure. During the same period 262 prostitutes had died, 490 had been temporarily removed because they had served a prison sentence, and 11,510 had disappeared or left for the provinces without passports.[20] The reluctance on the part of the vice squad to remove names from the register was scarcely diminished in later years: between 1888 and 1903, 314 prostitutes died in Paris, 378 were removed on account of marriage, and 545 by administrative decision; during this period 22,397 prostitutes "disappeared."[21] Disappearance, therefore, was certainly the most effective way of escaping police control. It should be remembered, however, that the women who disappeared benefited only from a temporary removal. It should finally be noted, as Table 1 shows, that in 1902 the figures for registrations in the five sample departments remained much higher than those for removals.

All this proves the great mobility of the *filles soumises;* for most of them registered prostitution was only a temporary way of life. Despite the frequency of reregistrations, the high number of disappearances and discrepancies between the strictness of the procedures and actual behavior demonstrate quite clearly the failure of the regulationist project. Furthermore, this mobility made it extremely difficult to calculate the exact number of *filles soumises* who were actually practicing prostitution at any given time. The total of what Lecour calls *filles actives,*[22] Garin *filles en exercice,*[23] and Richard *filles en circulation*[24] includes in effect registered prostitutes plus reregistered prostitutes minus prostitutes removed from the register, prostitutes who had disappeared, those under treatment for illness, and those in prison.

It is the prostitutes of this group—the registered prostitutes—that I shall now try to describe as a whole; I shall then discuss the various enclosed establishments organized for them under the by-laws. In order to do this I have consulted an abundance of archival documents emanating from the vice squads and from the last major works of the regulationist literature, for, it should be remembered, one of the elements of the project was to marginalize the group in order to study it all the more closely and, by the same token, to supervise it the better. It should also be remembered, however, that registered prostitution was not representative of prostitution as a whole; far from it. Although she had usually been unregistered before and was destined to return to that state, the registered prostitute, bound by the by-laws to obey the regulations of an enclosed system, became an object of administrative scrutiny. In her way of life and her attitudes she differed to a marked degree from the unregistered prostitute, whom she saw above all as a competitor.

Geographical Distribution

It is relatively easy to find out the numbers of officially registered prostitutes between 1851 and 1879. Indeed, in the three censuses of 1851, 1856, and 1872 the authorities provided a special category for prostitutes. In 1879 the Ministry of the Interior, at the request of Dr. Desprès[25] and under the direction of Dr. Lunier, carried out a national inquiry into the numbers of registered prostitutes practicing in France at the end of 1878; the results of this operation appeared in Desprès's book.[26]

Three years later, while writing his book, Yves Guyot carried out an investigation among the mayors of the country's major cities. He received replies from thirty-three municipalities; twenty-eight of them provided annual figures for the period 1876–1881, while the others were content to provide numbers for the years 1880 or 1881. Unfortunately, the results of this investigation do not always concur with those published by Desprès. In fact Desprès's seem to correspond more closely with reality; and they have the additional advantage of covering the whole of the country. The 1879 investigation had something of an official character; it was carried out by members of the administration. By contrast, Guyot's very partial report seems to be motivated mainly by a wish to support his own thesis. The questionnaire drawn up by Guyot was interpreted differently from town to town. What is more, the many errors in arithmetic and the enormous numerical variations from year to year lead one to doubt the validity of the results obtained.

After 1879 little is known about the figures for official prostitution: at the time of censuses prostitutes were no longer considered to form part of the active population and, for that reason, prostitution was not listed as an occupation. Fortunately, we have data deriving from the wide investigation approved on January 20, 1902, whose aim was to study the best administrative measures for improving the situation of the prostitutes.[27] We know that the memoranda, centralized in Paris, were kept at the disposal of the extraparliamentary commission of the vice department, formed in 1903. I hope at some point to carry out an exhaustive analysis of this investigation, but it will involve an enormous body of work. For the time being, I shall be content to analyze the results from seven departments distributed across the country.

There are also a few additional fragmentary data: those provided in 1881 to the Senate commission chaired by T. Roussel concerning the prostitution of minors[28] and those of the investigation ordered in 1904 by the Société générale des prisons.[29] In the case of Paris and Marseilles, the police archives provide a continuous series of figures.

Between 1851 and 1878, if we take into account territory acquired or lost,[30] the number of registered prostitutes remained relatively stable throughout the country (see Table 2). It is true that one can note a slight decrease from 1851 to 1872, which is almost compensated for by a rise between 1872 and 1878; this phenomenon, however, should be treated with caution on account of discrepancies in the sources. The vice squads, which were asked to make the investigation in 1879, tended to overestimate the numbers involved; as Henri Hayem remarked in 1904, it was the practice in certain towns "to keep on the police registers the names of prostitutes of whom any trace has long since been lost."[31]

So, as we shall see, this relative stability actually conceals a decline in the number of *filles de maison* (prostitutes attached to a particular brothel), which is compensated for by an increase in *filles isolées* (prostitutes working on their own). On this matter it will be noted that the total number of prostitutes in the *maisons de tolérance* (see Table 3) was even higher in 1878 than that of the *filles en carte* (registered prostitutes outside the *maisons*).

Everything seems to suggest that, despite the abolitionist campaign and the challenges made to the regulationist system, the figures for official prostitution increased after the middle of the 1880s. This increase is very marked in the capital (see Figure 1) after remaining steady during the government of *ordre moral* and then decreases sharply between 1876 and 1883, with the triumph of the republicans and the first great campaign of the abolitionists; the figures then increase markedly between 1884 and 1902, despite the decline in the number of *filles de maison*.

The trend is less marked in the other centers of prostitution, as is apparent in Table 3.[32] One may note, however a slight increase in numbers in Hérault, Meurthe-et-Moselle, and Charente-Inférieure. At Marseilles the increase remained modest, and at Brest, Toulon, and

Table 2. Changes in number of prostitutes in France between 1851 and 1878.

Year	Number of prostitutes	Prostitutes per 10,000 women aged 15–49
1851	16,239	17.35
1856	14,413	15.21
1872	11,875	12.83
1878	15,047	16.01

Table 3. Changes in number of prostitutes between 1878 and 1902 in five departments and in Paris, Marseilles, Toulon, and Paris.

Region	Filles de maison		Independents		Total		% increase	% decrease
	1878	1902	1878	1902	1878	1902		
Finistère (Brest)	152	76	112	164	264	240		− 9
Seine-et-Oise	165	125	32	38	197	163		−17
Charente-Inférieure	136	125	43	148	179	273	+52.5	
Hérault	234	85	14	371	248	456	+84	
Meurthe-et-Moselle	92	161	183	255	275	416	+51	
Total	779	572	384	976	1,163	1,548	+33	
Marseilles	448	87	216	700	664	787	+18.5	
Toulon	246	236	29	16	275	252		− 8
Paris	1,343	382	2,648	6,257	3,991	6,639	+66	

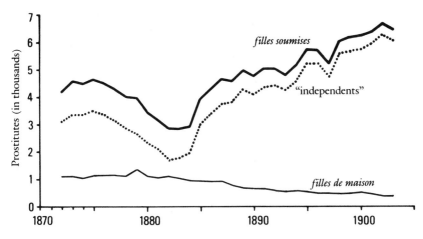

Figure 1. Changes in the number of *filles soumises* in Paris, 1872–1903. (Archives of the Paris prefecture of police.)

Seine-et-Oise there was a slight decrease, although not enough to challenge the overall impression of a rise in numbers. In almost every case[33] in 1902 the number of *filles en carte* was greater than that of *filles de maison*. We must now look at this phenomenon, which is crucial for the destiny of the regulationist system.

The geographic distribution of registered prostitution (see Figure 2) brings out the influence of factors whose relevance has long been noted.[34] It is apparent that official prostitution is an urban phenomenon and increases with the volume of the urban population. This is easily explained: the society of the large urban centers is differentiated; the variety of categories that make it up itself gives rise to a multiform prostitution. Furthermore, the anonymity of the city is a factor favorable to an increase in the number of prostitutes. It will be noted that, for the same reason, the proportion of *filles en carte* increases with the volume of the population (see Table 4); whereas in the subprefectures as a whole, those registered in *maisons de tolérance* are almost twice as numerous as those working on their own, in Paris the proportions are reversed.[35]

Three other factors proved to be a determinant in the detailed results of the investigation of 1878 (see Figure 3). First, the situation of a town in relation to the great axes of circulation: the rate of official prostitution was higher in the ports and major road and rail centers (Dunkirk, Le Havre, Cherbourg, Brest, Nantes, Rochefort, Bordeaux, Marseilles, and Toulon). Second, the existence of certain urban functions: garrison towns, places of pilgrimage, spas, and tourist centers generally had the

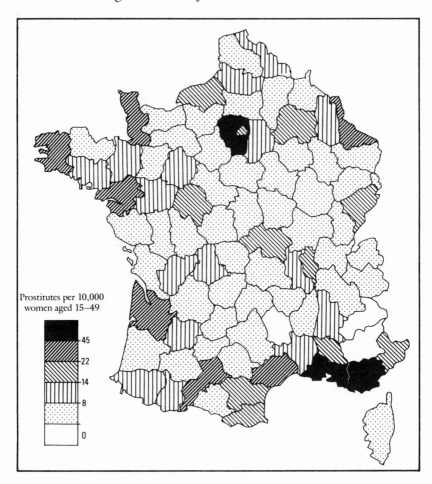

Figure 2. Number of prostitutes in France, 1872. (Based on the census.)

highest chance of seeing the growth of tolerated prostitution. Exactly
how much is in evidence at Belfort, Nancy, Verdun, Toul, Versailles,
Saumur, Vichy, Issoudun, and Cauterets, and even near the army camps
of Mourmelon, Saint-Maixent, and Farge-en-Septaine. Large-scale
industry, which determined the presence of a proletariat made up of
newly arrived immigrants, encouraged both registered and unregistered
prostitution, as in the towns of the Nord. This was sometimes also the
case in university towns, although this factor tended to increase above
all the figures for unregistered prostitution. Third, certain regional traditions, bound up with particular sexual practices, helped increase the
numbers. Thus it is clear that prostitution in *maisons de tolérance* was
particularly well developed in the towns of the Languedoc and in those

Table 4. Number of registered prostitutes, 1878.

Region	Maisons	Filles de maison		Filles en carte		Total filles soumises
		Number	%	Number	%	
Paris	128	1,340	33	2,648	66	3,988
Other prefectures	698	3,764	54	3,153	45	6,917
Subprefectures	414	2,313	65	1,228	34	3,541
Chief towns of cantons	79	396	75	129	25	525
Other communes	9	46	60	30	39	76
Total	1,328	7,859	52	7,188	47	15,047

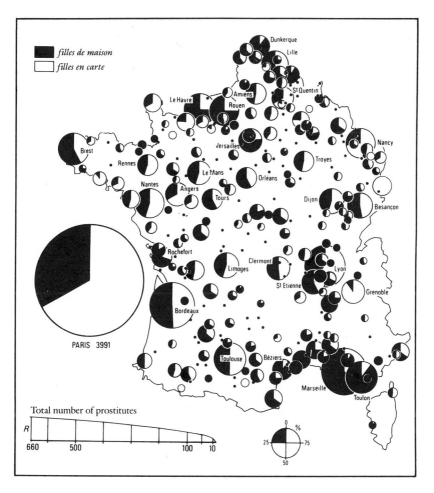

Figure 3. Number of registered prostitutes (*filles de maison* and *filles en carte*), 1878.

close to the Mediterranean coast (Toulouse, Béziers, Montpellier)[36] and that the number of independent registered prostitutes was high in Lower Normandy.

In certain other regions official prostitution was practically unknown. These were usually characterized by weak urbanization, by backwardness in communications, and by an absence of large-scale industry. Thus the heart of the Massif Central (Creuze, Corrèze, Haute-Loire, Cantal, Aveyron, Lozère, Ardèche), the Pyrenees (Ariège), the Alps, and the mountainous regions in general were rather unfavorable to the development of prostitution.

In short, a study of the geographic distribution of prostitution in itself gives some inkling of the nature of the clientele and the functions that the prostitutes served in the sexual life of various social groups.[37]

A Sketch in Social Anthropology

Most *filles soumises* were registered between the ages of twenty-one and twenty-five. Among the 5,440 prostitutes registered in Paris between 1880 and 1886, 73.91 percent were over twenty-one at the time of their registration, 23.73 percent were between eighteen and twenty-one, and only 2.35 percent were between sixteen and eighteen.[38] Out of 3,584 women registered at Marseilles between 1872 and 1882, 3 percent were under eighteen, 8 percent were between eighteen and twenty-one, and 89 percent claimed to have reached their majority.[39] As Figure 4 shows, the age distribution of the 9,689 women registered between 1886 and 1901 in the five sample departments confirms these observations on the whole; it should be noted, however, that the number of prostitutes who were underage on registration formed a not inconsiderable group.

Data on the age at which prostitutes had lost their virginity suggest that the overwhelming majority of *filles soumises* had already been having venal sexual relations for several months, if not years, before applying for registration. There are, it is true, a few examples of girls who were virgins on the day of their registration, but there can be little doubt that these were very rare exceptions. The work carried out between 1891 and 1899 by Professor Barthélemy at the infirmary of Saint-Lazare[40] confirms this hypothesis: he came to the conclusion that, on the average, prostitutes lost their virginity at the age of sixteen. Seventy of the 195 *filles soumises* whose past he studied were registered during their first year of prostitution, 47 during the second year, 53 between the third and sixth year, and 19 more than five years after they had first accepted money for sex. It may therefore be assumed, the author adds, that the registered prostitute had abandoned herself to prostitution, on the average,

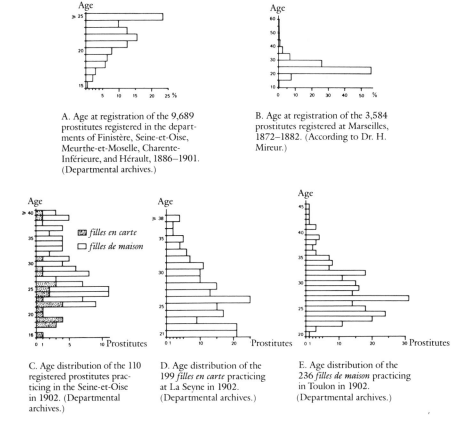

A. Age at registration of the 9,689 prostitutes registered in the departments of Finistère, Seine-et-Oise, Meurthe-et-Moselle, Charente-Inférieure, and Hérault, 1886–1901. (Departmental archives.)

B. Age at registration of the 3,584 prostitutes registered at Marseilles, 1872–1882. (According to Dr. H. Mireur.)

C. Age distribution of the 110 registered prostitutes practicing in the Seine-et-Oise in 1902. (Departmental archives.)

D. Age distribution of the 199 filles en carte practicing at La Seyne in 1902. (Departmental archives.)

E. Age distribution of the 236 filles de maison practicing in Toulon in 1902. (Departmental archives.)

Figure 4. Age distribution of *filles soumises* (registered prostitutes).

three years and nine months before registering.[41] On this matter it is worth pointing out that one of the stereotypes endlessly repeated at the end of the century at trade union conferences[42] does not appear to be borne out by the facts: this is the image of the working-class virgin seduced by a young bourgeois or by her employer. In the overwhelming majority of cases the prostitute had lost her virginity with a man of her own background. The investigation carried out by Dr. Le Pileur[43] among 582 prostitutes interned at Saint-Lazare confirms Dr. Martineau's conclusions concerning unregistered prostitutes.[44] Thirty-eight percent of them had lost their virginity to laborers, 17 percent to tradesmen, 11 percent to individuals practicing the "more or less liberal professions," 5 percent to their husbands, 3 percent to their employer or his son, and 1.3 percent to members of their own families. The rest were unaware of their seducer's occupation. Only nineteen (3 percent) claimed to have been raped.

The distribution by age of the prostitutes of La Seyne, Toulon, and the department of Seine-et-Oise in 1902[45] is evidence of the youth of the *filles soumises*. This is explained by the temporary character of official prostitution, although it should be added that at this time the police were reluctant to register minors. It also appears that the average age was lower among the *filles en carte* than among the *filles de maison* (see Figure 4). Contrary to widely held belief, prostitutes over thirty were proportionately more numerous in the brothels than in the streets.

The prejudice that prostitutes are almost always illegitimate[46] does not stand up to analysis: of the 3,584 prostitutes of known parentage registered at Marseilles,[47] 90.3 percent were born in wedlock and only 9.7 percent were illegitimate; it should, be pointed out, however, that 6.5 percent were born of unknown parents. Ten years earlier Dr. Homo had reached similar conclusions about the prostitutes of Château-Gontier, scarcely 10 percent of whom were illegitimate.[48] Of 234 registered prostitutes in the Marne in 1882, 23 (9 percent) were illegitimate; 204 had been brought up by their families (197 by their father and mother or by one of them and 7 by some other relative). Of the remaining 30, 14 had spent their childhood at the Bon-Pasteur institution, 9 were raised in an orphanage, and 7 had been in care.[49] The rates broadly correspond to the national average. It would be difficult to establish a correlation between illegitimacy and a propensity to registered prostitution.[50] The *filles soumises* were, it goes without saying, almost all unmarried at the time of their registration; the married woman and even the widow were rare exceptions. Only 7 of 151 prostitutes at Château-Gontier were married.[51] Of the 3,584 registered prostitutes at Marseilles, only 239 (6 percent) had been married, and 67 of these were widows.[52] In Paris the proportion was 5.88 percent of the prostitutes registered between 1880 and 1886.[53] Of the 87 inmates of the "enclosed houses" of Marseilles in 1902, 84 were unmarried and only 3 married.[54] In the same year 96 percent of the *filles de maison* and 89 percent of the independents in Versailles were unmarried. At Brest the proportions were then respectively 92 percent and 84 percent.[55] Once again, it should be noted that the rates are more or less identical for the various urban milieus.

The town of origin of the *fille soumise* was more or less distant according to the size of the city in which she practiced. Of the 5,440 prostitutes registered in the capital between 1880 and 1886, 4.74 percent had been born abroad, 65.39 percent were from the provinces, and 2.92 percent came from the suburbs; only 26.95 percent had been born in Paris.[56] The proportion of foreign-born prostitutes was higher at Marseilles:[57] of the 3,584 women registered in the city, 878 (24 percent) were foreigners;[58] the largest numbers were provided by Italy (342), Spain (219), Switzerland (128), and Germany (93).

It will be noted that the area of recruitment for prostitution in Marseilles (see Figure 5) was very large indeed at this time, extending to every department. The Bouches-du-Rhône provided only 270 prostitutes (9 percent of the total), hardly more than the Rhône (212) or the Alpine region, which, although it had few practicing prostitutes itself, nevertheless contributed generously to the brothels of Marseilles. The other large contingents were provided by the Mediterranean coastal departments, by those of the Rhône valley, and by those in which the

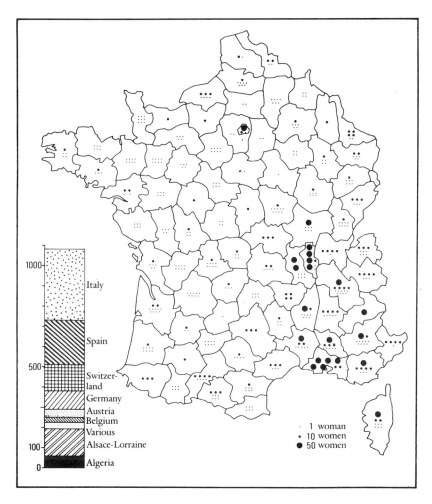

Figure 5. Area of recruitment of prostitution in Marseilles (places of birth of 3,584 prostitutes registered with the vice squad: 2,513 Frenchwomen and 1,071 foreign and Algerian women). (According to Dr. H. Mireur.)

country's main ports were to be found; this would suggest a movement of prostitutes between the ports. One still must explain why so many girls came from Alsace-Lorraine. Many of them probably left that region when it was ceded to Germany. This area of recruitment was to prove relatively stable, as is shown by a comparison of earlier figures concerning *filles soumises* with those for 1902.[59]

By contrast with Marseilles, the recruitment of registered prostitutes at Château-Gontier between 1862 and 1869 had been carried out largely in the neighboring departments, with the exception of those situated immediately to the north (Manche, Orne). Very few prostitutes in that small town had been born near the place where they practiced; only 16.5 percent had been born in Mayenne and 2.6 percent in the arrondissement of Château-Gontier.[60]

So what Parent-Duchâtelet once noted about the Parisian prostitute was not specific to the capital, or even to the big city; although her birthplace tended to be less distant if she practiced her activities in a small town, the registered prostitute was almost always uprooted. This phenomenon is sufficiently explained by the way in which the personnel of the *maisons de tolérance*[61] were recruited, as well as their own wish for anonymity.

The social background of the prostitutes poses a delicate problem. There are two opposed myths in this area: that of the women's aristocratic or bourgeois origin, skillfully kept up by the brothel-keepers and pimps with a view to making them more desirable and tempting to their prospective clients, and that of the obligatory link between poverty and prostitution, created by the philanthropists and populist writers during the first part of the century and later reinforced by socialist analysis. In fact Mireur's work[62] concerning 3,102 prostitutes registered in Marseilles, the results of which, furthermore, do not differ markedly from those that Parent-Duchâtelet had obtained in Paris half a century earlier, refutes both these myths (see Table 5). Although his investigation is not absolutely valid, since he used the answers provided by prostitutes to questions asked at the time of their registration, it seems quite clear that registered prostitutes came, albeit in unequal proportions, from every social background.

The comparison with the socio-occupational distribution of the population as a whole does show, however, that the majority of them had urban origins; families of agricultural workers are markedly underrepresented.[63] It also seems clear that industry was not the great provider of brothel inmates. The majority of the prostitutes came from a proletariat of artisans, day workers, small shopkeepers, and various marginals. It is not surprising to see well represented in the list in Table 5 café proprietors and innkeepers, itinerant merchants, commercial travelers, hotel waiters, singers, and actors.

Members of the liberal professions and people of independent means are better represented than in society as a whole, although it is true that these are essentially urban categories. Nevertheless, it is quite surprising to find among the ranks of the registered prostitutes of Marseilles daughters of thirteen teachers, six court ushers or bailiffs, four lawyers, four magistrates, and one inspector in the vice squad. One feels the same sense of surprise at finding among the parents a larger number of retired soldiers (fifty-nine, including seventeen officers) and policemen.

There would seem to be little point in investigating the occupations of prostitutes before their registration (see Table 6) since we know that most of them were already practicing unregistered prostitution. In this case the occupations they declared served merely to hide their real activity; also, there often exists confusion between the vague status of apprenticeship and the actual practice of a trade. It cannot be denied, however, that some did practice an occupation, sometimes in addition to prostitution, so the list of occupations in Table 6 is not entirely without interest. Nonetheless, there is nothing to prove that in arresting unregistered prostitutes the police did not exercise choice; that is, it may be that the police decided, more or less consciously, to register only members of certain occupations, in which case the list of occupations formerly practiced by registered prostitutes might not correspond precisely to those practiced by unregistered prostitutes.[64]

When one considers the results of the investigation at Marseilles in 1882[65] concerning registrations during the previous ten years, one notes that, in the majority of cases, prostitution was, by the women's own admission, their only previous activity. Furthermore, as Table 6 shows, it was the maid's room, the drinking den, the laundry, and the garment workshop, not the factory, that served as the antechambers to the brothel. The large number of domestic servants and cooks requesting registration aggravated ruling-class anxieties about the morality of their servants.[66] We shall return later to the cases of theatrical artists and governesses who decided to register;[67] it was their situation that aroused the vehement campaigns against "the trade in singers and governesses"—the white slave trade.

A reading of the results of the investigation of 1902 (see Table 7) confirms these conclusions, except that the proportion of those who list no prior occupation (41 percent) is very high among the registered prostitutes of La Seyne and Toulon. A comparison with the status of the parents of registered prostitutes from the first of these towns leads one to conclude that the brothel was now mainly a recourse for the prosti-

Table 5. Occupations of fathers of prostitutes registered at Marseilles between 1872 and 1882, according to police questioning.

Occupational category	Number	Category as % of total
Men of independent means	207	
Members of the liberal professions, lawyers, teachers	43	
Artists	47	
Army officers	17	
Manufacturers, merchants	38	
Subtotal	352	11.3
Wholesale merchants	34	
Shopkeepers	125	
Owners of cafés, inns, restaurants, tobacconists	97	
Traveling merchants	97	
Subtotal	353	11.3
Employers and workers in crafts		
Building	126	
Metals	127	
Wood	113	
Leather	107	
Textiles	119	
Books	23	
Food	88	
Transportation	65	
Other	87	
Subtotal	855	27.5
Public employees		
Middle-ranking	3	
Lower-ranking (clerks, postmen, policemen, customs officers)	55	
Subtotal	58	1.8
Railway employees	60	1.9
Retired soldiers	42	1.3
Foremen in industry	14	0.4
Agents and commercial travelers	28	0.9
Clerks and public writers	67	2.1
Hotel and café waiters	38	1.2
Factory workers	22	0.7
Day workers, navvies, sweepers, porters	562	
Domestic servants and concierges	60	
Beggars, blind men, wrestlers, traveling musicians	19	
Prisoners	2	
Subtotal	643	20.7
Fishermen	44	1.4

Table 5.   (continued)

Occupational category	Number	Category as % of total
Agricultural workers, farmers, vineyard workers	467	15.0
Gardeners, nurserymen	37	1.1
Shepherds	4	0.1
Woodmen, coalworkeres	18	0.5
Total	3,102	

Table 6.   Previous occupations of prostitutes registered at Marseilles, 1871–1881.

Occupation	Number
Prostitutes	1,822
No occupation	213
Housewives	61
Apprentices	203
Total	2,299
Other occupations declared:	
Of independent means	13
Schoolteachers, governesses	7
Theatrical artists	40
Café employees and barmaids	58
Florists and traveling saleswomen	34
Other commercial employees	23
Subtotal	115
Dressmakers, linen maids, embroiderers, laundresses, ironers	265
Tailors	91
Milliners	28
Glove makers	16
Boot stitchers	26
Hairdressers	38
Various other trades	80
Subtotal	544
Workers in large-scale industry	11
Domestic servants and cooks	305
Chambermaids	202
Charwomen	14
Subtotal	521
Total	1.251

Table 7. Previous occupations of prostitutes registered in the Var and Seine-et-Oise, 1902.

Occupation	La Seyne Filles en carte		La Seyne et Toulon Filles de maison		Total		Seine-et Oise All registered prostitutes
	Number	%	Number	%	Number	%	
None	19	9.5	112	41.3	131	27.8	5
Housewives	15	7.5	3	1	18	3.8	1
Schoolteachers, nurses	—	—	1	0.4	1	0.2	1
Singers, dancers	4	2	4	1.5	8	1.7	
Shop assistants, commercial employees, cashiers	—	—	6	2.2	6	1.3	2
Merchants, saleswomen, fruiterers, florists	3	1.5	6	2.2	9	1.9	3
Laundresses, ironers, linen maids	33	16.5	28	10.3	61	12.9	16

Needleworkers (dressmakers, milliners, embroiderers, corsetmakers, tailors, passementerie-makers, stitchers)	61	30.5	28	10.3	89	18.9	16
Workers and other tradeswomen: hairdressers, silk-folders, rice-huskers, printers, clockmakers	7	3.5	5	1.8	12	2.5	3
Factory workers	—	—	8	3	8	1.7	2
Farmers	1	0.5	—	—	1	0.2	
Domestic servants, chambermaids, cooks	54	27	64	23.6	118	25.1	53
Day workers	3	1.5	6	2.2	9	1.9	6
Total	200		271		471		108

tute without any other occupation, whereas a woman who had already practiced a trade preferred to remain an independent operator.

There is no evidence that the educational level of the prostitutes was very much lower than average. Among the 5,440 prostitutes registered in Paris between 1880 and 1887, only 19.65 percent were illiterate.[68] At Marseilles, it is true, the situation seems to have been worse, since among the 3,584 prostitutes registered between 1871 and 1881 the literacy rate was only 55 percent.[69] But this situation was only temporary; in 1902, 72 percent of the inmates of enclosed houses could read and write, and two of them even had final school-leaving certificates.[70] At this same date only 9 percent of the registered prostitutes in Versailles were illiterate, while 7 percent had lower-school certificates.[71] Some brothel-keepers were careful to recruit only girls with some education; in 1902 all the inmates of the *maisons de tolérance* at La Seyne could read and write, and "one of them . . . had even been to secondary school, was an excellent musician, and since the age of nine had been with the same mistress."[72] All the women working in the brothel at Château-d'Oléron in 1902 could also read and write.[73] These examples represent a literacy rate higher than that of the total female population in certain departments of the Centre and of Brittany.

Although the fertility rate of the registered prostitutes was very low, a number of them did give birth to the children they had conceived. Usually they had to be separated from them after birth. Seventy-three prostitutes gave birth in this way at Marseilles during 1901;[74] thirteen of the children were stillborn, seventeen died shortly after birth, nineteen were entrusted to public assistance, and only twenty-four were kept by their mothers. Of the children born to registered prostitutes at Versailles between 1899 and 1901, eleven were handed over to public assistance. At Toulon in 1902 forty-eight inmates of the enclosed houses, out of a total of 236, had children; six of them had two and two others had three. Twenty-one of these mothers placed their children with their own parents, twelve entrusted them to nurses or guardians, and eight to hospitals.[75]

Although the roads leading to official prostitution were fairly well marked, it seems that the women of the voluntarily marginalized world of the *filles soumises* were recruited from highly varied social categories. If we consider the illegitimacy rate, the occupation of the parents, and educational level, it seems that the registered prostitutes did not appreciably differ from the averages calculated for the society as a whole. This shows very clearly that we should beware of any simplistic explanation or correlation.

Yet we must also be mistrustful of averages. Regulated prostitution was an extremely heterogeneous microcosm. We shall find this diversity throughout the description of the enclosed houses to which regulationism confined the *filles soumises*. It is ultimately only a reflection of the variety of demand, itself a consequence of the widespread nature of sexual frustration, which, as we shall see, affected every category and every social class, albeit in different ways. Thus it was those frustrations, more than poverty or lubricity of temperament, that accounted for the breadth and social diversity of prostitution. There is no need to bemoan the lot of the virgin deflowered by the bourgeois or the unmarried mother reduced to selling herself, thus proving the primacy of poverty; nor is there any need to vituperate with the regulationists against the salaciousness of women doomed to prostitution, thus demonstrating the primacy of temperament. Women of almost every background turned to prostitution because the social structures of the time created an enormous demand and, by the same token, a profitable industry.

Indeed, it is not the least of the paradoxes of the regulationist discourse that its proponents claim to be concerned with a category of women apart, while the sociological and statistical methods used to study that category tend to show that the registered prostitute was in many respects, apart from her sexual behavior and her refusal to work, very much like most other women. But was it not precisely the fundamental aim of this discourse to create a difference and thus to marginalize so that the *fille soumise* would constitute a counterideal, enabling the honest woman all the more easily to define herself?[76]

"The Seminal Drain"

The study of the *maison de tolérance*—or, as Dr. Fiaux called it, "the seminal drain"[77]—comes up against special difficulties. The regulationist project, based on both the enclosure and constant surveillance of venal sexuality, was in fact unrealizable. The discrepancy, abundantly noted by the abolitionists, between everyday reality and the by-laws, which the brothel-keepers, doctors, and sometimes even the police of the vice squad scarcely respected, makes description difficult. Furthermore, evidence concerning the *maisons de tolérance* often merely reflects the fantasies of those providing it.

On this subject one may distinguish among four types of description. First, there is the description that appears in fiction. Second, there is the description emanating from specialists who, in their professional capacities, had contacts with the personnel of the *maisons de tolérance*; these doctors, policemen, and magistrates drew up a precise but rather static picture of the *maisons*. Usually regulationists, and therefore advocates of enclosed prostitution, they allowed themselves to be largely influenced, it should be repeated, by the stereotypes deriving from Parent-Duchâtelet. Besides, their concern for anthropological observation and their fear of sexuality as such produced a picture that was fairly cold, external in a sense, one that scarcely grasped the living reality of the system in its functions or explained its behavior.[78] Third is the evidence provided by clients or individuals who admitted to carrying out investigations of their own; this immense picturesque literature often has all the flavor of personal experience, along with a taste for scandal or quite simply for the erotic that leads one to treat its findings with caution.[79] Fourth, there are the books or pamphlets written by journalists, polemicists, and publicists of various kinds or by politicians whose aim was to convert the reader to their opinion. These authors were usually abolitionists and had the best of intentions, of course, but they often had very little experience of the brothels; as a result they were frequently susceptible to the most fantastic rumors, providing these were attractive and melodramatic enough to serve their purposes. In particular, they show no understanding of the prostitute herself.[80] Furthermore, hostility in principle to the church, the army, and the police often distorts their evidence.[81]

Despite the immense scope of the bibliography, one cannot but deplore the absence of any accounts or memoirs written by the prostitutes themselves. Indeed, it was not until our own time that such women dared to recount their lives; we do have, however, a few letters written by inmates of brothels to their friends or lovers and complaints sent by the registered prostitutes to officials. Furthermore, I have been able to consult the registers of three *maisons* in Lyons,[82] and the archives of the vice squad in Marseilles contain a series of files on brothel-keepers[83] and "places of debauchery."[84] Unfortunately, most of these documents concern only the period between 1900 and 1914. In spite of these difficulties, I shall try to sketch a picture of the *maison de tolérance* as it functioned during the last quarter of the nineteenth century.[85]

The Topography and Typology of Enclosed Prostitution

Few towns in France had *quartiers réservés* at this time, although several towns in the Midi and certain ports did. As late as 1882, eighty-eight of the registered brothels in Marseilles (that is, nearly all of them) were situated in the district bordered by the rue de la Reynarde to the east, the rue Radeau to the west, the rues de la Loge and Lancerie to the south, and the rue Caisserie to the north.[86] Thus the rue Bouterie had fifteen *maisons,* the rue Lanternerie thirteen, and the rue de l'Amandier twelve. It should be added that at Marseilles, enclosed prostitution was highly developed at this time; indeed, there were proportionately far fewer independent prostitutes than in the other large cities in the country. It should be noted that, for a long time, inmates of a *maison* who, after leaving the establishment, practiced independent prostitution were punished with imprisonment.

During the same period, the registered prostitutes at Montpellier all lived in a district called Cité Pasquier,[87] whether they worked out of rooms, enclosed houses, or mixed houses, which sheltered the activities of women who had contracted debts and who were practicing prostitution temporarily under police surveillance. At Toulon the *quartier réservé* known as Chapeau Rouge enjoyed, according to the mayor,[88] a "felicitous geographical situation" in the least busy part of the city, at the foot of the city walls; it was reached, however, by very busy streets. In 1902 it contained fifty-five brothels. In 1878[89] and again in 1902 the administration was forced, by intense police activity, to make sure that the enclosure was respected, for *filles soumises* tended to live in the city itself. These were somewhat belated counteroffensives typical of the attitude of vice squads in the country's ports. For example, the by-law of September 9, 1896, stipulated that registered prostitutes in the town of Cette must be housed within the district of Souras-Haut.[90] But the most backward-looking initiative was that of the mayor of Aix-en-Provence, who decided in October 1907 to set up a *quartier réservé,* bordered by the rue Fonderie, the rue des Bretons, and the rue des Jardins.[91]

At Brest enclosure was less strict than at Marseilles, although in about 1874 the authorities tried to concentrate the brothels close to the port, in the rue des Sept-Saints, the rue Haute-des-Sept-Saints, the rue Neuve-des-Sept-Saints, and the impasse Kléber,[92] and permission was refused for the opening of brothels on the rue Kléber and the rue Guyot. This new voluntarist geography of vice was made necessary, the subprefect declared in 1875, by alterations in town planning; in his opinion the rue Kléber, which joined the rue de Siam, the town's principal artery, had become too busy to allow *maisons de tolérance* to multiply there.[93]

The location of the *maisons de tolérance* in towns that had no *quartier réservé* had to comply with certain prohibitions. These were most numerous in Paris; the Gigot regulations of 1878 forbade the opening of a brothel near a school or place of worship or close to any large public building. Furthermore, the brothels had to be situated at a minimum distance from one another, thus making it impossible to set up two establishments in the same building. In short, in the fight against unregistered prostitution the prefecture of police had opted for the dissemination rather than for the concentration of vice. In the provinces, regulations forbade the opening of brothels near municipal monuments and buildings, places of worship, schools, and public walkways. In 1904 eighty-two orders were issued containing prohibitions of this kind.[94]

From the beginning of the century transformations brought about by town planning and the decline in the number of *maisons de tolérance* had profoundly changed the geographic distribution of the *maisons*. Of course the old permitted locations survived; a large number of brothels, often the most sordid ones, were still situated in town centers, in old buildings packed together in dark, narrow back streets close to cathedrals and other medieval buildings. Certain districts in Paris, such as the area around the Hôtel de Ville and especially around the Palais-Royal, were good examples of this relative permanence of the places of prostitution.

Still, the enormous changes brought about in the center of the capital had already caused the disappearance of certain of the ancient red-light districts: thus the Cité and Ile Saint-Louis, which had been the center of prostitution in Paris since the Middle Ages, were thus cleaned up by Haussmann's urban development. The extension of the rue de Rivoli, followed by the construction of the Hôtel and Magasins du Louvre, had brought with it the destruction of the main brothel districts, made up of the rue Froidmanteau, the rue Pierre Lescot, and the rue de la Bibliothèque.

So there were now, in addition to the traditional inner-city nuclei, several new types of site. This may be illustrated by the case of Paris. Since the Restoration, the major *maisons de tolérance* had been opened in busy side streets, close to the broad main roads that now formed the commercial center of the town. The *maisons* set up near the Madeleine, the Opéra, and above all the Bourse are a good illustration of how the development of prostitution was bound up with the expansion of upper-class commerce and high-density use; the establishments in the rue Chabanais, for example, were already internationally renowned.

The extension of the towns, and sometimes the construction of lines of fortification, had, since well before the beginning of the Third Republic, brought an increase in the number of brothels as urban development progressed. In Paris the building of fortresses had been accompanied by the formation of a new prostitutional "folklore"[95] side by side with inner-city traditions. Establishments had been opened between the outer boulevards and the fortifications; to be more precise, after 1840 the prefecture of police had given official tolerance to the wine shops that had become centers of illegal prostitution. Indeed, it was on this occasion that the administration recognized the right of the brothel-keepers to open a wine shop, a privilege that the madams in the center of the city, jealous of their colleagues, later had withdrawn. It should be said, however, that in those districts the number of unregistered brothels far exceeded that of the *maisons de tolérance.*

The development of communications and changes in commercial activities created a great many more places where people could meet and separate. Brothels were therefore set up close to railway stations, markets, and new harbors. Sometimes these new factors merely reinforced the traditional location, as in Paris, with the building of Les Halles, or the covered markets. Finally, the constitution of a national army and, accordingly, the construction of a large number of barracks further changed the location of the *maisons de tolérance.* The number of these establishments increased in garrison towns and places close to army camps. An example was the brothels set up near the Ecole militaire, which, as we know,[96] inspired Edmond de Goncourt to write some of the finest passages in *La Fille Elisa.*

Furthermore, the geographic distribution of the *maisons de tolérance* did not necessarily correspond to the places of activity used by the unregistered prostitutes or by registered prostitutes working independently, both of whom found their clients in the street. Before trying to define the space of prostitution in its entirety, one must describe these subtle, shifting circuits.

The typology of the establishments generally corresponds to the prostitutional topography. From this point of view the case of Paris is the most revealing. At the top of the hierarchy were the first- and second-class *maisons,* intended for an aristocratic or bourgeois clientele men concerned above all with luxury and discretion. Preeminent among these were the great *tolérances* of the Opéra district, the description of which provides the authors of works devoted to enclosed prostitution with their bravura passages. Without describing, for the moment, the fantastic furnishing and decoration intended to satisfy the clients' exotic tastes or perversions,[97] I shall simply list the broad features of the interior of these establishments. The rooms contained a bed, open on three sides, surrounded by columns and draperies, covered with a simple bottom sheet, and surmounted by a canopy or large mirror.[98] A washstand with a marble top, on which were arranged splendid scent-bottles, stood in a corner of the room. On the mantelpiece some bronze statuary suggested fauns or bacchants; near the bed or in a small adjoining boudoir a chaise-longue and a sofa were intended to satisfy the client's erotic whims. The light was filtered by the stained glass of the windows or cleverly diffused by the gas lamps over the mantelpiece.

In the corridors, stairs, and sitting rooms, throughout the premises in fact, were thick carpets, mirrors, and a profusion of bronze statuary; the ceilings and walls were decorated with mythological scenes.[99] An abundance of exotic flowering plants reinforced the impression of sensuality lent by the decor. Sofas and armchairs were arranged along the walls. "The air was dominated by a sickening, perfumed smell, reminiscent of face powder and musty cellars: an indefinable smell in a heavy, oppressive atmosphere like that of steam rooms where human bodies are pummeled."[100]

In the salon of the great *maison de tolérance*, the mecca of aristocratic and bourgeois pleasure, silence and discretion reigned. Whereas in the cheaper establishments noise, activity, singing and dancing, alcohol, the suggestive negligee, and, even more, manual arousal helped to excite the senses, desire was aroused in the *maison de luxe* by a combination of almost total nudity, suggestive but aesthetic poses, solicitation from a distance by looks and gestures, and the general quiet air of luxury. Degas expressed all this in his admirable series of monotypes devoted to one of the grand *maisons de tolérance*. The same atmosphere of silence and discretion, though without the nudity, is to be found in Toulouse-Lautrec's *Salon*.

Although intended for a much larger clientele, the second-class *maison de tolérance* was also arranged in such a way as to guarantee absolute discretion.[101] An ingenious system eliminated any possibility of clients meeting one another; the new arrival was shown into a small waiting room, where he would make his choice; a maid was posted on guard at every landing, and a system of bells made it possible to effect entrances and exits without risk of being seen. This kind of establishment was noted for its large number of salons. The bedrooms contained a flat, many-sided bed surrounded by mirrors; on the floor a thick carpet assisted discretion.

The so-called *maisons de quartier* were intended for a lower-middle-class clientele; the "regulars" were assured of being left in peace in a mirror-lined salon with red velvet sofas along the walls.[102] A bed with a single opening, hung with curtains and covered with an eiderdown, was the only furniture in the bedrooms. The *maisons de quartier* was reminiscent of a bourgeois *pension;* in addition to the communal reception room and the bedrooms, there was a dining room where clients could get something to eat.[103]

Very different, though also very varied among themselves, were the brothels intended for a popular clientele. Usually these were *maisons à estaminet,* or brothels with a bar attached. The arrangement of the bar was hardly different from that of an ordinary wine shop, except that it featured more mirrors and better lighting.[104] Amid all the noise, smoke, and smell of alcohol, the women, outrageously made up, wearing tiny costumes consisting of tights and a small, short skirt that stopped at the thighs or just a dressing gown designed to reveal shoulders, arms, and breasts, and satin stockings, drank with the clients before going up to the rooms with them. Here discretion was not called for, and brawls were frequent; the *garçon de tolérance,* or brothel waiter, served as a bouncer. The client would get drunk on beer before selecting the girl of his choice. The bedrooms were furnished like those of a cheap hotel.

Some of these establishments, situated near barracks or ports, were reserved for soldiers or sailors. Indeed, it was rare for soldiers in uniform to be accepted in houses where they did not make up the majority of the clientele. The descriptions by Edmond de Goncourt and Maupaussant of these brothels for soldiers or sailors are unforgettable.[105]

At the very bottom of the scale were the brothels set up near the city fortifications, at Montrouge and Charonne and in certain districts within the city, like the ones at the place Maubert, for example. There the bar was next to a common reception room furnished with a table and wooden seats; the women, most of them old,[106] their faces heavily made up to conceal their wrinkles, drank beer or absinthe and gave themselves to the clients in rooms furnished with an iron bed or just a mattress. Similar were the *maisons d'abattage,* or "quickies," where the woman would be lucky to get even a glass of beer. In some soldiers' establishments in the Grenelle district the client paid fifty centimes and was given a number and told to wait in line; this was also the custom in the brothels of North Africa.[107] This practice was found in some provincial establishments at times when large numbers of soldiers were expected.[108]

This summary description—a long picturesque portrayal is not my purpose here—suffices to show the extreme diversity of the Parisian *maisons de tolérance.* As we can see, this diversity merely reflects the social pyramid itself. In the provincial towns the hierarchy of the *maisons* was less subtle. Thus at Toulon in 1902 the authorities distinguished between only two kinds of tolerated establishments: the enclosed houses, frequented by a better-off clientele and by army and navy officers, and the "ordinary houses frequented by workers, sailors, and soldiers."[109] At Brest, according to the mayor, there was "little difference in the way the houses are run and in the comfort they offer. The clientele is the same and so is the price."[110] At Rambervilliers[111] commercial travelers, shop assistants, clerks, and a few laborers would frequent the brothel on weekday evenings and Sunday afternoons. Sometimes, it is true, as at Fécamp in Maupassant's *Maison Tellier,*[112] the popular clientele was received in the bar while the bourgeoisie waited in the salon; this distinction was based on the fact that in the smaller towns, bourgeois customers would be served drinks in an upper room over a café frequented by working people. This literary example, like the typology pertaining in the capital, is a good illustration of the influence of the dominant modes of social life, since the bourgeois salon and the popular café were the models on which these establishments had been based.

The Diversity of the Clientele

What defines a brothel is first of all the clientele that frequents it. The extreme variety of the clientele is explained by the multiplicity of functions fulfilled by the *maisons de tolérance*. The brothel was at once a source of initiation for youths, of sexual consumption for all those who were deprived in this area, of compensation for husbands dreaming of extramarital sexual activity. It was also a meeting place for the male bourgeoisie of small towns lacking in other entertainments and a mecca of eroticism for the maimed, the perverse, or simply those curious about strange or refined practices forbidden to bourgeois wives. Finally, it could also be quite simply a place of passing entertainment for tourists or pilgrims who wanted to "get away from it all" and experience something new in their sexual life.

Now, quite obviously, the importance of these various functions varied throughout the second half of the nineteenth century. Thus, as we shall see, although the brothel remained a source of initiation and sexual consumption for those on the fringes of society, it gradually lost interest for bourgeois husbands and bachelors, who were now attracted to other forms of venal sex. In this milieu the *maison de tolérance* came to be identified over the years as a "temple of the perversions,"[113] except in smaller towns, where it was to develop a role that might be termed sociocultural, if one were not afraid of being accused of provocation.[114]

We have to recognize that the client of the great *maisons de tolérance* is still unknown to us. It is revealing in this respect to note that he hardly appears in the accounts of novelists and painters,[115] except in a few of Degas's works, in the form of a shadow or barely sketched outline. In Toulouse-Lautrec's *Salon* it is the very absence of men that creates the obsessive expectation of the women, who seem to exist only to satisfy the invisible male. Of course it must be admitted that it would be difficult to capture this fluctuating clientele of individuals who passed through briefly and discreetly in the course of their respectable lives. The grand bourgeois scarcely appears in the literary or artistic brothel at the time quite simply because, in reality, he was never seen. This probably explains his enormous attraction to voyeurism: the concern for discretion provided the basis for the erotic power of violating someone else's privacy.[116] By contrast, we are fairly well informed about the clientele of the *maisons de quartier,* of the small-town brothels, and popular establishments. Here the promiscuity was such that it would not have been possible to describe the girls without depicting the male clientele at the same time.

Regulations forbade the brothel-keepers to receive male minors in their establishments; of 294 by-laws in force in 1904, 181 specifically forbade admission of minors or schoolboys to the *maisons de tolérance.*[117] In fact such boys were frequently admitted, and it was in a prostitute's bed that most of the sons of the lower and, to an even greater extent, middle class had their first sexual experiences.[118] There is abundant evidence of this. "It is in the convents of pleasure, under the protective eye of the police," Paul Bourget notes, "that almost all the young virginities are culled."[119] Describing the yard of his provincial school on a Thursday (Thursday being a half day in French schools), he adds: "There was always one of our comrades whom we would regard as one might the Alps. He was the one who had been there! . . . Where? Out there, on the edge of the town! We would point out the little alleyway as we walked in line through the streets." When he went to complete his studies in a Paris lycée, he saw that things were the same in the capital, but— and the remark is a significant one—"while the poor provincials continued their pilgrimage to the one place in their town where they could find a good woman who wasn't too expensive, the Parisians were beginning to set out on adventures of their own."[120] The author rightly insists on the incalculable consequences that this initiation into sin, shame, and often disease could have on the sexual behavior of adults. "The young man will continue to carry from his strange adolescence," he writes, "an inevitably blemished idea of woman."[121]

The essential function of the *maisons de tolérance* was nevertheless to satisfy all those excluded from, or on the fringes of, sexual life. In the circles in which the practice of late marriage was widespread, visiting the brothel represented, together with masturbation, a form of provisional sexuality for young, still-unmarried men. This was particularly true in the case of shop assistants, waiters,[122] and office clerks, who were too poor to keep a mistress or even think of marrying.

To this clientele should be added all "marginals," those who traveled in the course of their work, were recent immigrants to the place in which they lived, or were not sufficiently integrated into the town to satisfy their sexuality in any other way, either because they were too poor, because they did not have the time, or because women rejected them.

This explains why commercial travelers[123] formed the basic clientele of the brothels of small provincial towns. Similarly, students in the provincial universities often went to the brothel in groups, if only to "play an ace of hearts,"[124] that is, to gamble at cards for the privilege of going to a room with one of the women. Nevertheless, it must be recognized that this student clientele, tempted by other forms of venal sex, was to frequent the *maisons de tolérance* less and less. The sons of the wealthier families in the small towns, who were often too well known locally to consort with prostitutes, would go to the *maisons de tolérance* of the nearest city.[125] On the day of their "medical," prior to their military service, or simply on the occasion of some local festival, it was traditional for the young men of the area to indulge in a *partie montée*.[126]

In the popular establishments the clientele of marginals was made up of day laborers, unskilled workers, navvies, road sweepers, ragmen,[127] and migrant or foreign laborers[128] who were not integrated into working-class society and usually lived in lodgings while their wives and fiancées stayed at home. The case of sailors and soldiers is an even more obvious example, since both tradition and the wishes of the military authorities drove them to satisfy their desires in a registered establishment.[129] It should be noted, however, that this behavior was to change rapidly with the disappearance of the professional army.[130]

To this economic proletariat one should add the clientele of all those excluded from love,[131] members of a proletariat of ugliness and infirmity, who were rejected by prostitutes working for themselves but whom the inmate of a *maison de tolérance* was obliged to accept. Finally, men with venereal diseases who wanted to relieve their desires had no other outlet but to go to a *maison de tolérance,* whose personnel were not so particular.

To satisfy all the marginals in a permanent state of sexual privation was to remain throughout the period under study the essential function of the registered brothels. Indeed, it was the purpose assigned to it by society, according to the Augustinian viewpoint shared by Parent-Duchâtelet and the regulationists before him. For them, let me repeat, this was the very function to which the establishments should be confined.

In fact, the *maisons de tolérance* also played the role of satisfying the needs of married men whose everyday sexual activities had for some reason been interrupted. Husbands wishing to pursue continuous extramarital relations, however, now preferred the prostitute working for herself, whether or not she was registered, or a mistress. For foreigners staying in Paris or for provincials who came to the capital for a few days, the pilgrimage to the brothel had become a rite.[132] Prostitution associated with travel and leisure was a full-scale industry. This explains the enormous activity of the large *maisons de tolérance* during the universal expositions of 1878, 1889, and 1900. The circumstances of prostitution were essentially determined by events of this type. Pleasure trains carried to the nearest city the men of small towns wanting to have a good time in a *maison de tolérance*. As Dr. Bergeret wrote, on festival days and holidays the "debauched men" of Arbois would organize "pleasure trips" to Besançon, Dijon, and Lyons.[133] The same function was fulfilled by the *maisons* in the medium-sized towns, which on fair days and market days, would suddenly be filled with a clientele of peasants.[134]

The Establishment and Its Managers

The *maison de tolérance* was a commercial enterprise, and its functioning was determined by the profit motive. At its head was the keeper, usually a woman, though sometimes, in certain provincial towns where the regulations allowed it, a man.[135] The mistress of such an establishment was usually a former prostitute herself who had managed to save enough money to set up on her own; otherwise she might be her mistress's former assistant. Sometimes she was quite simply a *fille soumise* who had made good; in a few rare instances the keeper was the daughter or niece of the previous mistress. Finally, it sometimes happened that the keeper was an honorable bourgeois shopkeeper who had decided to set up a *maison de tolérance* purely as a commercial investment or the proprietor of a hotel that was failing to attract customers and who hoped to increase the profitability of the establishment by turning it into a brothel.

An analysis of the files on seventeen women who had been given permission to open *maisons de tolérance* in Marseilles between 1908 and 1913 enables us to construct a fairly detailed picture, albeit at a fairly late period, of the *dame de maison*.[136] We know the ages of sixteen of them: they ranged from twenty-six to fifty-two. Three of the keepers were between twenty-six and thirty-six, six between thirty and forty, another six between forty and fifty, and the remaining one was fifty-two. The files contain the places of birth of eleven of them. Only two were born in Marseilles; two were from the Loire, two more from Brittany, one from Paris, one from the Jura, one from the Landes, and one from Puy-de-Dôme. One more had been born in Italy.

Nine of these women were married, three were unmarried (two of whom were employees of *maisons de tolérance*), and four, including a widow, were living with men outside marriage. We should note the stability of three of these relationships, which had lasted for six, twelve, and seventeen years. The occupations of the husbands and lovers were very varied: among them we find a bagger, a former docker now retired from work, a sailor, a mechanic, a traveling jeweler, the owner of several lemonade carts, a former wine merchant, and a billiards instructor. One of them, who claimed to be a restaurant waiter, was in fact a supplier to brothels. It would not appear that the fortunes of their husbands and lovers had enabled the women to establish themselves as brothel-keepers; on the contrary, the men seem rather to have been pimps whose women were inured to the profession.

Indeed most—and this is their only characteristic feature—of the registered brothel-keepers at Marseilles had begun in the profession: four of them had been registered as *filles soumises* in the city, and two had been struck off the register. Furthermore, three of the applicants had worked as assistants to keepers. Eight of the registered keepers had already managed a *maison de tolérance* (five at Marseilles, two at Toulon, one at Riom), six had managed lodging houses, and four had run a bar. A study of the files also reveals that seven of them had begun by running unregistered brothels. Only one appears to have been new to the profession, since she had previously managed a clothing workshop, but of course this could have been a front.[137] Finally, four of the seventeen had already been found guilty of theft, assault and battery, or corruption of minors, although this did not prevent their being given a license.

In all, an already marginalized personnel included several former offenders and a number of unregistered brothel-keepers for whom the new license represented both a promotion and a constraint, since they would now have to conform to regulations and assist the authorities in their work of surveillance.

In theory, the brothel-keeper was not supposed to be dependent on a business partner: "In no circumstances must the running of a *maison de tolérance* be carried out in the interests of a third party," Lecour wrote in 1874.[138] But in fact, despite the exceptional difficulties presented by a study of these enterprises, since neither the commercial courts, nor the registration authorities, nor even the notaries could recognize them as such, it seems clear that, in the provinces at least,[139] some brothel-keepers owned several houses and entrusted their running to managers. The mother of Jeanne Salabert, a keeper at Cahors, herself ran a house in the town and another at Condom.[140] Furthermore, upholsterers, decorators, and even rich private individuals invested in this sort of business. They bought the buildings in which brothels were situated; sometimes they advanced the keeper the capital required to enable her to buy the premises and furnish them.[141] Carlier even provides a list of the proprietors of the main Paris *maisons de tolérance* in 1870.[142]

It will be noted (see Table 8) that the owners of the buildings in which the *tolérances* were situated were rarely brothel-keepers but, more usually, men of independent means, members of the liberal professions, or businessmen. In Paris the written permission of the proprietor and of the principal tenant was indispensable for a licensed brothel to be opened; these individuals required the keeper to pay a hefty bribe and a much higher than average rent. It was these often exorbitant demands that forced the *dames de maisons* to put pressure on the women they employed. The gratuitousness of the registration of a *maison de tolérance* by the prefecture of police contributed in the end to making the proprietors of the buildings in which they were situated the main beneficiaries of this industry. In time the registration came to be attached to the building and not personally to the keeper; the new mistress would be given permission to run the *maison* by the prefecture of police without payment, but she would have to buy back the furnishings of the establishment and, above all, satisfy the demands of the proprietor before obtaining a new lease.

From the early years of the Republic the value of some *maisons de tolérance* rose to an exorbitant level because of these practices. In theory,[143] it was always the authorities who set the purchase price of such a *maison* or, to be more precise, of the "furnishings of the premises," since these were what was really being sold. In fact, vendor and buyer usually agreed on the payment of a sum as "key money." According to Carlier,[144] the average price of such a lease during the 1860s in Paris was 10,000 francs. The three highest prices reached 150,000, 260,000, and 300,000 francs, while the cheapest *maisons de tolérance* went for 1,500 francs. In 1901 Champon, the mayor of Salins, estimated that the pro-

Table 8. Occupations of owners of the principal *maisons de tolérance*, Paris, 1870.

Occupation	Number
Of independent means	97
Members of the legal profession (barristers, solicitors, notaries, magistrates)	6
Stockbrokers, businessmen	4
Merchants	4
Managers of *tolérances*	22
Factory owners, shopkeepers	6
Various (contractor, haulage contractor, spinning-mill owner, lodging house owner)	4
Total	143

vincial *maisons de tolérance* were worth, on the average, between 25,000 and 30,000 francs.[145] This was certainly the case in Seine-et-Oise in 1902.[146] The price of the "ordinary house" in the Var around the same time, however, was no more than 6,000 francs.[147] At Brest, the subprefect wrote, the establishments "usually do not reach a very high price; the most important one was acquired for 30,000 francs."[148] But once again this was the cost of buying the "furnishings of the premises." The keeper would still have to pay an additional high rent. At Toulon in 1902 a *"maison fermé"* (that is, a first-class establishment) rented for about 4,000 francs a year and a *maison ordinaire* for between 1,500 and 2,000 francs.[149] At La Seyne the rent of such an establishment rose to 2,700 francs;[150] at Brest the average was 2,500 francs.[151] It goes without saying that the negotiation of this sort of business gave rise to substantial profits for certain legal practices that specialized in such private agreements.[152]

Despite the size of the initial capital required, the profits were often considerable. This obviously depended on the nature of the establishment and on the prices charged. In areas around certain army barracks the charge could fall as low as fifty centimes, but that was exceptional. The lowest category of establishment usually charged between two and three francs.[153] In the first- and second-class houses the entrance fee was five, ten, or twenty francs, to which should be added the payment given the prostitute herself and the tip for the submistress, which in fact doubled the price.[154] According to the mayor of Brest, a prostitute earned "on average ten francs a day in the house," but "the daily expenses of each inmate, for food, upkeep, and lodging are estimated at three francs."[155]

It should not be forgotten, moreover, that in the popular brothels the profits derived mainly from drinks consumed in the bar or in the rooms.[156] Women were usually forbidden to go with a client before drinking with him, and once in the room they would suggest that the client order another round of drinks. Some keepers gave bonus tokens at the end of the month to the women who had persuaded their clients to spend the most on drink; these tokens served as currency inside the establishment. At Marseilles, Lyons, and Clermont-Ferrand, the woman who accumulated three hundred francs' worth of bonus tokens was entitled to a silk chemise.[157] As the abolitionists insisted, not without exaggeration, some of the *maisons de tolérance* had regular clients who were veritable gold mines for the keepers. There was, for example, one bachelor who, in the course of a few years, spent his entire fortune of forty thousand francs in the *tolérance* of the small town of Salins.[158] So it is easy to understand the solicitude shown by the keeper of this establishment toward certain members of her clientele: "When a young man of means was short of money," the mayor wrote, "the keeper accepted a cheese or a demijohn of brandy by way of payment."[159]

Figure 6 shows the profits made, according to Carlier[160] and Dr. Fiaux,[161] by the main *maisons de tolérance* in Paris in the decades 1860–1870 and 1878–1888. It should be pointed out that the first set of data are mere estimates, whereas the second derive from more rigorous calculations.

The estimates are obviously open to criticism, but in the absence of sufficient private archives they are the only overall indications at our disposal. The results show very clearly the evolution taking place: the disappearance of a mass of small *maisons de tolérance*, some of which had been turned either into *maisons de rendez-vous* or unregistered establishments, was accompanied by a marked increase in profits made in the larger *maisons*. Between these two periods enclosed prostitution changed markedly; this process was to continue and even to accelerate at the end of the century.

But let us return to the regulationist procedures. When, with the agreement of her husband if she was married, a woman decided to run

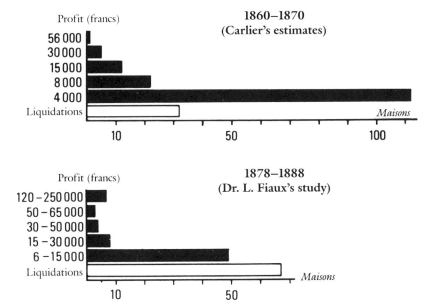

Figure 6. Paris *maisons de tolérance:* average net annual profit and number of liquidations.

a *maison de tolérance* in the capital, she first had to obtain the consent of the owner of the building; she would then send a written request to the prefect of police. The officers of the second bureau of the first division then carried out an investigation into the applicant's background; if the results were favorable, and if in particular it was proved that she was no longer practicing prostitution, the woman was given a book in which she would have to record the names of all the women who would be working for her, and in addition the results of health checks. The authorities reserved the right to close down an establishment temporarily at any time or to withdraw the book and thereby ruin the keeper. In this way, they had total control over the brothel-keeper. Indeed, it should be understood that the establishments were not authorized but merely tolerated.

The prefect of police was the only recourse left to the keepers when they were robbed or swindled. Of course, the law did not recognize commerce in human flesh. All transactions concerning the *maisons de tolérance* were, in fact, unlawful; Article 1133 of the civil code declared that "any obligation the cause of which is contrary to good morals is null and void." A brothel-keeper could not, therefore, prosecute an inmate who stole from her or a client who behaved badly. For the same reasons she could not claim bankruptcy or even mortgage her capital, since she did not pay a patent and her business was not registered with the commercial court. We must not forget that, in theory, she owned no more than the fittings and furniture. The police, however (and this was a matter of some controversy), often took it upon themselves to support a keeper against a client who failed to pay up; in the regulationist scheme, it should be remembered, the keeper represented the authority of the administration inside her establishment.

In the provinces the procedure varied from town to town; usually the authorities proved less rigorous; the municipal administration, however, always had the upper hand in both the opening and the running of the *maisons de tolérance* and reserved the right to close them down. Of the 445 by-laws in force in 1904,[162] only 294 dealt with the *maisons de tolérance*. Of the latter, 290 required previous permission and 4 a mere declaration; 249 required that the mistress keep a register of her inmates, 200 that she inform the police of any change in personnel; 93 by-laws forbade keepers to admit foreign women into the house and 146 prohibited the admission of minors.

The Paris by-laws forbade the *dame de maison* to live with her husband or lover inside the brothel; the reasons for this prohibition are obvious. Furthermore, she was to employ only male servants, although the large *tolérances,* in which the women's salon clothes changed every month, employed a large female staff of linen maids, dressmakers, chamber-maids, and cooks.[163]

The keeper's husband, when he did not prefer to do nothing, some-times ran a café or a lodging house in the neighborhood; this allowed him to operate unregistered prostitution. More usually he became a pro-curer for his wife's establishment. It should not be forgotten, moreover, that many brothel-keepers were lesbians, which sometimes created bitter jealousies inside the house.

In the first-class *tolérance* Madame would leave the everyday running of the establishment to a submistress and go off to take the waters in some fashionable resort. The profits from such a business were enough for the keeper to retire to an honorable position in the provinces. On July 25, 1890, Aimé Pruvot, a brothel-keeper at Melun, bequeathed a million francs to the city of Paris for the foundation of an asylum that would bear his name.[164]

The role of the submistress now becomes clearer. A former registered prostitute in her thirties or, much more rarely, some relation of the keep-er, the submistress received the clients, for whom she would open the door after looking through the peephole, summoned the girls to the salon, and assisted the visitor in making his choice. It was she who took the entrance fee. Usually she knew how to examine men and would intervene if the girl chosen, anxious about her partner's sexual health, consulted her. The girls had to obey the submistress as if she were Madame herself. Usually her pay was modest: between twenty-five and forty francs a month, according to Dr. Fiaux,[165] in the middle-ranking establishments; between twenty and thirty francs plus lodging, food, and clothes, according to Dr. Reuss.[166] In the best *tolérances* this pay could reach between 2,400 and 6,000 francs. The sale to the client of various small items—cigars, candy, or condoms—allowed the submis-tress to make some extra money. Finally, she received tips from visitors and presents from inmates eager to win favor.

The Functioning of the Establishment

Despite the virulent campaign waged against the "trade in virgins,"[167] there is little doubt that the *fille soumise* who entered a *maison de tolérance* was rarely a beginner; usually she had done her apprenticeship as an unregistered or independent prostitute.[168] This facilitated the recruit-ment of personnel. In Paris this procedure was easy enough;[169] most keepers simply had to choose among the women who offered themselves for work. Yet the need to make frequent changes, the extreme mobility of prostitutes who wanted to work independently as soon as they had paid off their debts, and the frequency of illness sometimes presented the keepers with a personnel problem. This was especially so in the provincial establishments, but it could also occur in certain Parisian *tolérances* when the keeper made life impossible for the women in her employ. Furthermore, the reputation of a *tolérance* depended on the quality of the personnel. The clever keeper was able to offer her clientele a majority of blondes, but there also had to be brunettes and at least one redhead on hand. She also had to be sensitive to the diversity of temperaments and types of behavior, maintaining a certain "ethnological variety,"[170] juxtaposing "big-breasted girls" and "skinny girls with the figure of a vicious schoolboy . . . the Jewess of Portuguese origin beside the Flemish girl, the girl from Bordeaux or Marseilles pretending to be from the Middle East, side by side with a kid from the Paris suburbs,"[171] not forgetting the black woman. This ethnic variety also had to be reflected in a range of psychological types: "The gay ones, always laughing out loud, with their teeth showing, look good when mixed with the dreamy ones; the affected or pretentious ones are as useful to the keeper as the crude, terribly cynical ones."[172] In short, there was an art of diversity that required continual recruitment, a systematic analysis of which might enable us to understand the sexual fantasies of the time. It was necessary, especially when the clientele was stable, as in the provincial towns, to renew the personnel frequently if the regulars were to be constantly stimulated. All this explains the existence of a vast network of recruiting agents.

Procuresses wanting to take on girls in their unregistered establishments haunted the employment agencies,[173] hospitals, and dispensaries, waited for prostitutes when they came out of prison or lay in wait for provincial girls arriving in the railway stations. More usually the keeper used less roundabout methods of recruitment. Sometimes she would hire an independent agent. At Bordeaux[174] the brothel-keepers even recruited directly at the dispensary. Jeanne Salabert, a keeper at Toulouse, recruited at the labor exchange.[175] Some of her colleagues also used as agents hotel or restaurant waiters, club managers, even coachmen.[176] The inmates of the establishments at Versailles were sent by wine merchants with businesses on the outer boulevards of Paris.[177] Occasionally recruitment[178] was carried out directly by the police; on June 5, 1908, the authorities decided to shut down one of the *maisons de tolérance* at Draguignan; the police superintendent, fearful that the inmates might disperse and turn to prostitution on their own account, "directed them to Antibes, where a brothel-keeper agreed to take them in and to pay their travel expenses."[179]

Usually, however, as I have said, the keeper's husband or lover acted as recruiting agent; this was the case at La Seyne and at Toulon in 1902.[180] With this purpose in mind, he would travel the country, visiting various establishments, trying to persuade the young women of his choice to come and work in his wife's establishment or offering brothel-keepers an exchange of personnel; sometimes the recruiting agent would pass himself off as a commercial traveler.[181] Keepers could also turn to agencies offering their merchandise through small advertisements in newspapers. The sale of these "parcels," whose qualities were described in detail in the press, stimulated a profitable commerce long before the development of the "white slave trade," a subject to which we shall return at length. The brothel-keepers of Brest used female agents to whom they paid a commission of five or six francs according to whether or not the recruit came from the town in which the agent worked.[182] Finally, the keeper might wish to eliminate any intermediary and deal directly with a colleague; in that case the price of the "parcel" corresponded approximately to the debts accumulated by the young woman, who thereby became as dependent on her new mistress as she had been on her previous one.

These transactions gave rise to an abundant correspondence, widely used by the abolitionists,[183] in which we find notices, recommendations, and various details about the technical quality or state of health of the merchandise. Sometimes these were not permanent transactions but merely temporary transfers required by changes in demand. Dumas, a former examining magistrate, told members of the commission set up by the municipal council of Paris[184] that the arrival of reservists brought about an influx of girls from the *tolérances* of Melun into those of Fontainebleau or vice versa.

The area of supply or of exchange varied according to the locality: whereas the Parisian *tolérances* recruited throughout the whole of France and even abroad, the keepers at Brest,[185] for example, drew on Nantes, Rennes, Lorient, Quimper, Morlaix, Rouen, and Le Havre; at La Seyne[186] the keeper obtained her personnel from the houses at Marseilles, Aix-en-Provence, Nîmes, and Montpellier. An analysis of the registers of three brothels in Lyons whose archives have been preserved[187] allows us to follow the movement of their personnel in detail.[188] We should note the considerable Parisian contingent as well as the contribution of local recruitment. As to the rest, most of the inmates came from towns of average size situated fairly close to Lyons itself: Geneva (46), Saint-Etienne (41), Grenoble (26), Mâcon (19), Villefranche (13), and to a lesser extent Roanne, Vienne, Saint-Chamond, and Chambéry. Few came from very far; fifteen were from Marseilles, which is not very many in view of the extent of prostitution in that city. The three establishments at Lyons recruited mainly in the Rhône valley and in the Massif Central. Apart from the capital, the northern regions of the Loire provided very few individuals.[189] This demonstrates a relational model quite different from that of the Marseilles establishments, which recruited from both the region and other ports.

It is difficult to compare the provenance of the women who entered the establishments with their destination after their departure: sixty-one of them disappeared without a trace.[190] Nevertheless, it would seem that the balance of exchange with Paris was negative, whereas it was clearly positive with the towns of the region; this allows us to draw up an itinerary, which partly corresponds to the definitive migrations in that period of rural exodus. The Lyons brothels attracted young women from the neighboring towns. Although it is true that one day most of them went home—and it is this that makes the migrations of prostitutes unique—some merged into unregistered prostitution, while others submitted to the attractions of Paris. From this point of view Lyons seems to have been a staging area, just as the larger cities of the region were a staging area for girls born in the surrounding countryside. For the rest, the geographical distribution of the points of destination corresponds closely with the area of recruitment.

It is tempting to analyze the monthly distribution of movements of the personnel in order to find out whether renewal was continuous or seasonal (see Figure 7). It should be noted at the outset that we are not dealing with establishments in decline: during this period they preserved their total numbers intact. The impression of continuity is strong, except that the movement was more intense in late spring and early summer: the inmates took fewer risks in leaving the establishment in a period of fine weather, and it may be that the clientele preferred to see a renewed personnel after the summer break. Winter seems to have been a period of relative stability; and indeed it is easy to understand why a woman wanting to leave would postpone her decision during the colder months. One thing emerges quite clearly: recruitment was at its lowest in February, which is probably due to the effect of Lent.

The duration of the inmates' stay in the same establishment varied considerably; on the whole, however, most of them moved around a good deal. This can be seen in Figure 8, which shows the average stay of women working in the *maisons de tolérance* at Versailles and Toulon in 1902.[191] At Brest, according to the mayor, they stayed on average of fifteen months in the same establishment.[192]

Figure 8 also shows that of the 573 prostitutes registered between 1885 and 1914 in the three Lyons establishments whose archives have

Registrations

Departures

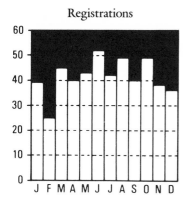 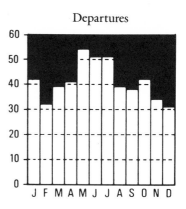

Figure 7. Monthly distribution of registrations and departures in two *maisons* in Lyons, 1902–1914.

been preserved,[193] 471 (82.2 percent) made only one stay, 76 (13.2 percent) stayed twice, 11 (1.9 percent) three times, 6 (1.2 percent) four times, five (0.8 percent) five times, and 4 (0.7 percent) more than five times. If we consider only the duration of the single stays and that of the first stay of the 102 girls who stayed more than once, [194] we observe three patterns:

• Fifty-six prostitutes (9.7 percent) stayed less than a week, either because they did not adapt to the profession or to the practices of the house, or because they did not suit the tastes of the clientele, or because they were there simply as short-term replacements.

• Another 169 (29.4 percent) stayed for a period of between seven and thirty days; 111 (19.7 percent) worked for a period of between thirty and sixty days. Half the numbers were made up, therefore, of a mobile personnel, the renewal of which corresponded to the wishes of the clientele. And 190 (33.1 percent) proved to be more stable, even though their stay did not exceed 12 months.

• Finally, each *maison de tolérance* included a small number of permanent inmates, or "seniors," whose role was probably to perpetuate the style of the establishment, to give the regular customers a sense of continuity, and to help the mistress exercise her authority over the more mobile personnel. Between 1900 and 1914, forty inmates stayed for a period of between one and five years; five worked for a period exceeding five years, and one stayed in the establishment for over ten years. Furthermore, of the women who returned several times, some were in fact pillars of the establishment; they were content to take a few days' holiday at irregular intervals. Célestine B——, "Esther" to her clients, entered the Chevillat *maison de tolérance* on May 8, 1901; she did not

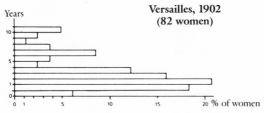

A. Average duration of stay in the same establishment by prostitutes practicing in the *maisons* of Versailles in 1902. (Departmental archives: estimates made during the inquiry of 1902.)

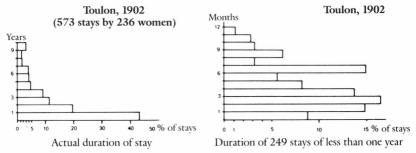

B. Duration of stay in each of the establishments frequented in the course of their careers by the women working in the *maisons* of Toulon in 1902. (Departmental archives.)

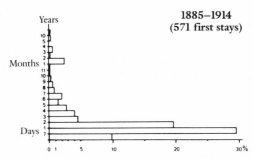

C. Duration of stay of the inmates of three Lyons *maisons*, 1885–1914, according to the registers of the establishments. (For women who had worked in the establishment on several occasions, the duration of only the first stay was recorded.) The differences between Figures A and B, on the one hand, and C, on the other, stem essentially from differences in the methods used. In A and B the investigation concerned inmates at a particular date, whereas in C all the first stays in the *maisons* were recorded. This second method leads us to take into account many short-term stays; in an investigation carried out on a particular date, by contrast, what I shall call the "meteors" are, for the most part, overlooked.

Figure 8. Duration of stay of inmates in *maisons de tolérance*.

finally leave it until March 4, 1919. During those seventeen years and ten months she was absent only eleven times, six of these to spend a few days at Montargis, probably her hometown; it was there that she finally retired in 1919. On four occasions she spent a short time in Paris. Two of her stays away were fairly extended: she left the house on April 25, 1911, for Orléans, moved on to Paris, and did not return until June 25, 1912. In 1915, first at Montargis, then in Paris, she spent seven months outside the establishment. Marie ——— joined the same *tolérance* on March 25, 1909, and did not finally leave it until March 8, 1920, after thirteen absences. It should be noted, however, that different brothels followed different practices; it is evident that the personnel of the *maison* Chevillat was more stable than that of the other two establishments.

Although the average stay in a *maison de tolérance* was often short, many inmates did have long careers as *filles soumises* behind them. Figure 9, which shows the seniority in the profession of Versailles prostitutes in 1902 and the number of establishments already frequented by the inmates of the brothels of Marseilles and Toulon at the same date, indicates this clearly.[195] It should be added that the inmates of the Brest *tolérances* had, at that time, spent on the average six years in the house.[196] L———, an inmate of a brothel in Toulon in 1902, had been in the house for fifteen years; she had worked in twelve such establishments after joining, at the age of fourteen, a *tolérance* in Versailles through an agent who had fabricated false papers for her.

Figure 9 allows us to appreciate another aspect of the mobility of the inmates of *maisons de tolérance,* since it shows both the number of establishments and the number of towns in which the inmates of the Marseilles *tolérances* had worked previously. Sometimes the itinerary followed by the inmates had led them into regions very distant from one another. P———, who was thirty-three in 1902, born in the Charente-Inférieure,[197] and a seamstress by training, had been working since the age of twenty; she had joined the *tolérance* at Toulon six years before; previously she had been an inmate at Bordeaux, Pau, Toulon, Paris, Versailles, Le Havre, and Marseilles. By contrast, some of the Toulon prostitutes had never left the Mediterranean. Rachel M——— was thirty; born at Castres, she had previously worked as an ironer in a laundry. She had been in the profession for ten years and had worked in establishments at Bastia, Ajaccio, Montpellier, Nîmes, Tarascon, Marseilles, Cette, and Toulon. Finally, some inmates remained faithful to their establishment. In 1902 Marie B———, a former milliner and a widow, had been in the same house for seventeen years; Phil——— G——— had been in the same establishment for thirteen years, and it was the only one she had ever been in.

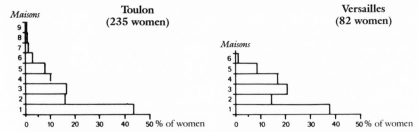

A. Number of establishments in Toulon and Versailles in which the *filles de maison* then working had worked previously. (Departmental archives.)

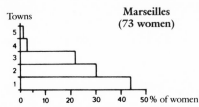

B. Number of towns in which the inmates of the Marseilles *maisons* had worked as *filles soumises*. (Departmental archives.)

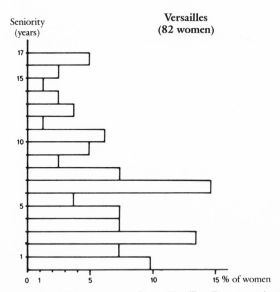

C. Seniority in the occupation of *filles de maison* working at Versailles. (Departmental archives.)

Figure 9. Filles de maison, 1902.

When a prostitute entered a *maison de tolérance*, she lost her name[198] and went by a pseudonym, which she usually kept throughout her career, even when she moved to a different establishment.[199] In this area onomastics can teach us a lot. If one compares the first names of the inmates of the three Lyons *tolérances* with the pseudonyms that were given to them,[200] one notices at once that the most common baptismal names—Marie, Jeanne, Louise, Joséphine, and Anna—do not appear on the list of pseudonyms. Conversely, the most common pseudonyms—Carmen, Mignon, Suzanne, Renée, Andrée, Marcelle, Simone, Olga, Violette, Yvette, Paulette—hardly appear at all on the list of given names. With the exception of Berthe and Blanche, baptismal names and pseudonyms form two different onomastic series.

The pseudonyms given to the inmates of the Lyons *tolérances* in the Belle Epoque make up a fairly short list; the most common were to be found in every establishment. One can detect in their choice the influence of literature and, even more, the musical theater: Carmen and Mignon are the most frequent, and the presence of Manon, Camélia, and Fantine betray the same influence. One also notes the large number of diminutives ending in "-ette" (Violette, Yvette, Paulette, Brunette, Blondinette, Odette, Arlette, Georgette, Lucette, Marinette, Ninette). In all these account for 65 percent of the pseudonyms. Their purpose was probably to emphasize youth; they express the taste for juvenile prostitution, which was often denounced in the early years of the century. By contrast, with the exception of Sapho,[201] none of the pseudonyms has a specifically erotic character of its own, and none suggests sexual specialties or perversions. This should probably be seen as evidence of the modesty commonly attributed to prostitutes and to the wish of the clientele to find in the brothel a transposition of the bourgeois home as well as sexual stimulation. It is also quite surprising to note how few of the pseudonyms (apart from Carmen) bear an exotic charge or suggest biblical eroticism, although the presence of Suzanne maybe linked to the pictorial theme imbued with senile voyeurism and the erotic charge provided by denuded, offered chastity.

Inside the house the prostitutes were subjected to a set of rules that reflected the logic of the system. These rules, peculiar to each establishment, allowed the keeper to exert a strong hold over the inmates. From the first day a double-entry account was opened between the mistress and the new prostitute. In theory the keeper owed her employee lodging, food, indoor clothes, heat, light, and laundry; in return, in Paris at least, she received all entrance fees and "session fees." A *fille d'amour* had to be content with *gants* (gloves), the name given to presents from clients. A prostitute who was a mere *pensionnaire,* however, pocketed half the amount of the entrance fees but had to pay the keeper a monthly rent amounting to between ninety and two hundred francs, depending on the house.[202] The accounts were kept by means of a system of tokens; this allowed the keeper to cheat by means of what the prostitutes called *sauter la passe,* or "missing the entrance fee." In the provinces, whether or not they were *pensionnaires,* the prostitutes usually received half the money paid by the clients. In 1902 in the Var[203] the residents of the *maisons ordinaires,* which had a popular clientele, managed to earn five or six francs a day, and the inmates of the *maisons fermées,* with their bourgeois clientele, earned on the average fifteen francs.[204]

If the keeper was shrewd, she tried to get her employee to amass debts. In fact, nothing was easier: the commission paid to the recruiting agent, the traveling expenses, the hiring of the "change," or clothes worn during the journey, and of the dressing gown were charged to her. Later, tips to the servants; the regular appointments with the hairdresser, the chiropodist, and the manicurist; the cost of medical examinations and medicines; extra laundry fees; the hiring of jewelry in the high-class *tolérances;* the purchases of all sorts of commodities at the shop run by the keeper—all these expenses helped keep her in debt. Since the inmate of a *maison* was seldom given permission to go out, she had to buy from the keeper her cigarettes, her perfumes, her soap, her candles, and all the fashionable articles that tempted her, and she had to do so at exorbitant prices. At the table and in the salon, all the extras that she ordered in the course of the day, including the champagne and the liqueurs, were charged to her; and the keeper was very skillful at getting her employees to drink more by making fun of any lack of generosity. On this matter we should remember the temperament of the prostitutes and, in particular, their sense of solidarity. These communities of women were subjected to very precise forms of sociability: each one paid for her round of burgundy or champagne; a woman who lost at cards had to buy a round for her companions; the same went for the inmate who was celebrating her birthday or who had decided to set up a liaison with one of her companions. At certain times in the year, and above all on Madame's birthday, the personnel were expected to lavish presents on the keeper. And any infringement of the rules incurred payment of a fine, whether it was a matter of being late to meals, some mark of disrespect to the keeper, or, more frequently, a failure to behave properly to the clients.

If a prostitute, laden with debts, tried to escape, the police would make sure that the keeper recovered what was owed her. As late as 1907 the legal officers of the government[205] recognized that the widow Talazac, a brothel-keeper at Bagnères-de-Bigorre, was in the right when she refused to hand over papers and clothes to one of her employees who wanted to leave the establishment while still in debt to her for the sum of forty-five francs. Yet it should not be imagined that the prostitute was kept in the brothel mainly by force; this somewhat melodramatic view should be left to the abolitionist literature. The guarantee of living in some comfort and having no fears of the morrow, the relative abundance of food and liquor, the idle existence that allowed her to get up late, the long afternoons spent gambling and chatting—these bound a prostitute to the system by much more subtle ties. If necessary, debts were there to guarantee the permanence of the way of life despite changes of establishment.

Outings with Madame survived only in a few provincial towns; in Paris and Marseilles they had gone out of fashion. There, not more than once every fortnight, each woman was allowed to go into town and do whatever she liked. She could meet her lover and, if necessary, hand over to him her meager savings (it was on the occasion of one of these outings that Goncourt's *fille* Elisa murdered her soldier-lover). In the evening the women would come back with flowers for Madame or cigars for Monsieur.

Generally speaking—and this was the case in Paris—the compulsory health checks would take place in the house.[206] In some provincial towns, however, as at Lyons, as we have seen, the inmates of the *tolérances* would set off together in small groups for the vice-squad dispensary. Yves Guyot attributes his decision to devote himself to freeing the enclosed prostitutes to the sight of those processions of *filles* in the Rennes of his childhood.[207]

The Quest for Clientele

The clientele of a first-class Parisian *maison de tolérance* was recruited by recommendation; there were few external signs, except for the closed shutters, to suggest to the passer-by the character of the establishment. By contrast, the *maisons de quartier* and working-class brothels were easily distinguishable: in both Paris and in the provinces the presence of a lantern and the large house number, which, in some of the outlying districts, could be as much as two feet high, clearly indicated the nature of the enterprise. In 1904[208] twenty-two municipal by-laws still required the presence of the lantern and the large number, and sixty-nine required that the entrance to the building and the staircase leading to the establishment itself should be illuminated after nightfall.[209] In the suburbs the walls were often decorated with brightly colored stripes.

At Marseilles the women exhibited themselves in turn at the entrance or in the corridor of the establishment, while a maid was installed at the door. Until 1878 in Paris a former prostitute was employed to stand in front of the *maison* to attract clients by touting the pleasures that awaited them inside. Although abolished by Gigot, this practice[210] was gradually reestablished, apparently with the tacit approval of Prefect Cames-casse.[211] Sometimes, although this practice tended to disappear in the early years of the Third Republic, inmates would be sent out in turn to solicit in the street in front of the house.[212]

The traveling client could, if he so desired, obtain the addresses of the various *tolérances* in the town in which he found himself by consulting the *Annuaire reirum: Indicateur des adresses des maisons de société (dites de tolérance) de France, Algérie, et Tunisie et des principales villes de Suisse, Belgique, Hollande, Italie, et Espagne.* Apart from the addresses of the brothels and the names of the keepers, this work contained, in its advertising sections, a great deal of information about the suppliers and various businesses that revolved around the prostitutional industry.

The brothel-keeper also distributed in the street, in hotels, or in railway stations cards, attractively decorated with a cupid or a female nude, indicating the nature and address of her establishment. Café or restaurant waiters, hotel porters, coachmen, and sometimes individuals who were especially paid for the purpose were delighted to inform potential clients, and, if need be, to accompany them to the door of the brothel. Sometimes although this was particularly true of the *maisons de rendez-vous*,[213] advertisements were placed in newspapers clearly indicating the address and specialties of the better houses.

It is difficult, of course, to assess the professional activity of the women in the *maisons.* Everything seems to suggest, however, that it was much more intense than that of prostitutes working on their own or of unregistered prostitutes. The keeper, for whom nothing mattered but profit, would force her inmates to receive any client who turned up and to satisfy all his needs. A few questions asked of the visitor before his departure allowed the keeper to assess her employee's degree of compliance. It was the usual practice for inmates to work even during their menstrual periods; the keeper used skillful makeup to conceal from the client the condition of his partner. Similarly, when demand was heavy even a sick girl had to continue working; some subkeepers specialized in makeup that consisted in applying small pieces of colored gold leaf to lesions and carmine on the sexual organs of inmates suffering from gonorrhea or syphilis.[214] Even when a prostitute became pregnant, this did not mean that she stopped working; such a woman might even be specially requested by a client.

Dr. Level, a member of the Paris Municipal Commission, worked out that the average inmate of a *maison de tolérance* saw seven or eight clients a day.[215] In 1902 the inmates of the *maison de tolérance* at La Seyne had, on average, five visits a day.[216] In fact these averages mean very little, for many prostitutes, after doing very little on weekday evenings, had to receive a large number of clients on Saturdays, Mondays, carnival days, fair days, and days when army medicals were being given or when a big exposition was being held in the city. The documents examined by Dr. Fiaux suggest that in the better *tolérances* it was rare for a woman to receive fewer than four men a night[217] more usually she received seven, eight, ten, or twelve clients. The author cites the case of Rolande, an inmate of one of these houses, who received sixteen men in the course of a night.[218] In the *maisons de quartier* and the popular establishments, the average was often lower because the influx of clients was less regular; clerks, shop assistants, and laborers tended to come at the beginning of the month, especially on Saturdays and Mondays, when they received their wages. Yves Guyot estimates that the number of clients received by one inmate could at such times mount to fifteen, twenty, or even twenty-five a day,[219] while "from the fifteenth of the month, many nights have the figure 0 against them."[220] The monthly distribution of activity in these establishments seems to have followed that of sexual delinquency; that is to say, the maximum occurred in May, June, July, and August and the minimum in February, around Lent.

In fact, the records of *passes* (entrance fees) and *couchers* represent only one of the aspects of the inmate's work: sadomasochistic practices, lesbian scenes, and tableaux vivants gradually came to make up the main activities of the better class of *tolérance*. This was already the case in the early years of the twentieth century.[221]

The Everyday Life of the Inmate

In Paris and in 124 provincial towns in 1904[222] the by-laws forbade brothel-keepers to allow two inmates to sleep in the same room and required them to provide women with decent accommodation; but in fact, these regulations were seldom complied with. All observers agree, even as late as 1914, in describing in the blackest terms those sordid "kennels," "henhouses," or "boxes" in the attics in which the prostitutes were crammed two by two.

An iron bed with a flea-infested mattress, a wooden table, and a straw-stuffed chair were usually the only furniture in the rooms available to the inmates. All the windows of the establishment had to remain shut;

as late as 1904, 199 municipal by-laws stipulated that they were to be barred.[223] Furthermore, seventy-nine by-laws forbade the girls to appear at the doors or windows. In this respect the inmates of the first-class establishments were hardly better off the. , their colleagues in the working-class brothels.[224]

The inmates would get up late, between ten and eleven usually. The first part of the day was devoted to bathing, grooming, and hairdressing, whose complications required the extended attentions of the establishment's wig-maker. Then came the makeup, when their faces would be painted in an exaggerated white or pink, with tiny blue veins drawn on to simulate a transparent skin. In the lower-class houses the older prostitutes were content to smear their wrinkles with a preparation made of fish glue[225] after sticking on wigs of poor quality.

After lunch, the long afternoon was spent playing cards or lotto, accompanied by an endless stream of chatter in an atmosphere heavy with cigarette smoke. The women who knew music would practice the piano; others might read novels. There was little variety in the conversation; according to Dr. Fiaux it centered mainly on professional matters.[226] The provincial *maisons de tolérance* usually had a garden[227] where the inmates were able to get a little exercise.

Meals were frequent and copious. They were eaten in the presence of the mistress of the house in an atmosphere of bourgeois respectability: the women stood up when she entered and usually remained silent. An unseemly word, any lack of respect, or even excessively noisy conversation would, in the better houses, be reprimanded. It is true, however, that the timetable for these meals hardly corresponded to that of a *pension de famille*. In Paris[228] the inmates of the bourgeois *tolérances* had four meals a day: the first, at 11 A.M. or noon, consisted of three dishes, a dessert, and half a bottle of wine. A second meal, the dinner, served at 5 or 6 P.M., was the most copious of the day, being as large as lunch but with the addition of soup and coffee. At midnight and again at 5 A.M., according to Macé, but only at 2 A.M., according to Dr. Reuss, light suppers were served, consisting of cold meat, salad, and wine.

After dinner, before receiving their clients, the women would go to their rooms to wash and change into their working clothes: "white, pink, or black fish-net silk stockings, very open, high-heeled shoes, and a very transparent dressing gown or chemise made of lace or black or white gauze."[229] The inmates of houses intended for a bourgeois clientele also wore bracelets, rings, and necklaces. In the working-class establishments the timetable was more or less the same, although the food was not as good and the appointments of the place were less luxurious.

In the provinces opening times varied from town to town.[230] Some by-laws, like those of Amiens, for example, called for the houses to close at midnight; others (Bordeaux, Brest, Montpellier) insisted on 11 P.M., and still others (Nantes) on 10 P.M. In the best Paris *tolérances,* by contrast, the high point of activity was between 11 P.M. and 2 A.M. This period was then followed by long waits in the salon. On arrival, the *michet* ("sucker," "dude," in other words the client) was shown into the main salon; there he found the inmates assembled in two lines in a previously arranged order. None of them was to solicit his choice by a verbal invitation, but they all tried to tempt the visitor with winks, smiles, movements of the tongue, or exciting postures. After offering his hand to the woman of his choice, the visitor then left the salon, accompanied by the subkeeper, went upstairs with the prostitute, and waited for her to wash before she rejoined him. In the lower-class brothels the choice was made in the adjoining bar, where each woman would solicit the clients in turn. If a client accepted one of them she would drink with him and try to persuade him, by gestures as well as words, to continue their conversation in one of the rooms of the establishment.

This, then, was the simple, regular life of the inmates of the *maisons de tolérance.* There were few opportunities to break with the everyday monotony, especially since outings with the keeper had lapsed; the most one could expect was a "marriage" between two of the girls, Madame's birthday, and, later, participation in the Quatorze Juillet.[231] The closing in *La Maison Tellier* to allow the inmates to attend the First Communion ceremonies in the local church and the organization of an escape were clearly no more than brilliant literary ideas.

Now, although it is certainly a fact that inmates sometimes "disappeared,"[232] they did not use violence to break out of their confinement; protest remained verbal. The only example of a violent revolt known to me dates from 1867. In that year the inmates of a house at Parthenay set fire to the establishment in order to regain their freedom.[233] The theater of the prostitutes' rebellion was above all the hospital,[234] and later the prison,[235] but never their place of work. What aroused the prostitutes' violent protest was their being prevented from working.

The tolerated brothel was, in a way, the very opposite of a hovel or dump—the opposite, that is, of the unregistered brothel. Of course, it provided an outlet for that sexual excess that Molinari regarded as indispensable to the survival of the human species,[236] but at the same time it was an expression of the prohibition of group sex and a condemnation of promiscuity. It reflected in its own way bourgeois home life[237] in that, in accordance with the by-laws, each couple was assigned a bedroom of their own. In this it is revealing to observe that, throughout the century, it was not the brothel bedrooms that aroused the ire of observers and administrators but the places where out-of-work prostitutes would congregate. It was there that the anarchic promiscuity of bodies, and worse, that of bodies of the same sex, occurred.

The *Filles en Carte:* A Transitional Stage

According to Dr. Mireur,[238] the *filles en carte* constituted the aristocracy of registered prostitution. Indeed, their existence was officially tolerated by the authorities, who thus hoped to control itinerant, usually unregistered prostitution. It should be noted from the outset, however, that certain municipal by-laws did not recognize the *filles en carte*. At Draguignan, for example, the by-laws, which dated from 1874, forbade prostitutes to reside outside the *maisons de tolérance*.[239]

The prostitutes who worked independently were compelled to undergo health checks.[240] In Paris they were forbidden, in theory, to rent furnished rooms; instead they had to rent a room or apartment and furnish it themselves, thus coming under the control of the landlord and decorator.[241] The rise in rents gradually drove them from the center of the city to the outskirts. The prefecture of police, however, allowed certain independent prostitutes to work in the *maisons de tolérance,* which thus served them as *maisons de passe,*[242] or places where they could take their clients from the street. In 1878, 36 of the 127 *maisons* in the capital had been given this permission.

At Bordeaux the by-laws were more complex; the authorities required the second-class independent prostitutes to reside in the furnished rooms of an established *tolérance* in the district assigned to low-class prostitution. There they rented rooms on the ground floor, opening directly onto the street; sitting on their doorsteps, they would solicit throughout the day and part of the night. The higher-class Bordeaux *filles en carte* were, by contrast, tacitly allowed to frequent the *maisons de passe* and even the more respectable *maisons de rendez-vous*.[243]

In theory the independent prostitutes of Marseilles were supposed to live in the *quartier réservé;* in fact they tended more and more, with the passing of the years, to leave this enclosure. In 1872[244] the mayor, and then in 1876[245] the commissioner of police, noted the spontaneous creation of a sort of *quartier réservé,* the theater of operations of the *filles en carte,* unrecognized by the local authorities.[246] Sixty buildings in this district were known to be *maisons de passe;* furthermore, fifty-five furnished lodging houses in the city were occupied by independent registered prostitutes, often mixed with unregistered ones. By 1902[247] the process had developed to the point where 448 of the 700 *filles en carte* lived "unofficially" in 170 furnished lodgings and hotels in Marseilles or in rooms that were rented to them by private persons.

The municipal by-laws laid down precise requirements for the behavior of the independents. In Paris they were forbidden to solicit or even to appear in the street or in public places before 7 p.m. and after 10 or 11 p.m. They had to avoid provocative dress and behavior and could not circulate wearing a hat. The obsessional fear felt by the regulationists toward soliciting explains why prostitutes were forbidden to touch passers-by in any way, to provoke them by gestures or by obscene words, and above all to attract attention from their windows.

The analysis carried out in 1904 by Hennequin of all the prohibitions affecting the *filles en carte* demonstrates the rigidity of the way of life that the authorities intended to impose on them and shows clearly that it was only with regret that the authorities allowed them to carry out their activities outside an enclosed house. Even at this date 351 by-laws forbade them to enter a café, 329 to loiter in a public place, especially in the vicinity of schools and barracks, 247 to appear at their windows, 51 to use obscene language that could be overheard, and 62 to keep children in their living quarters; 334 by-laws laid down the times at which they could walk the streets; 17 forbade them to go out in open carriages or to travel in carriages with men, 13 to attend the theater without permission. At La Rochelle[248] an order of 1886 provided that they should keep to certain parts of the auditorium assigned to them by the commissioner of police. The by-laws in force at Nancy since 1874 established that "the windows of apartments where independent prostitutes live must be glazed with frosted glass and remain permanently shut, unless they have lockable shutters . . . Inside their homes, prostitutes will abstain from all noise, brawling, and generally whatever might attract the attention of neighbors and passers-by."[249]

It goes without saying that these were theoretical prohibitions, impossible to enforce; they allowed the police to arrest any *fille en carte* at will, on the grounds of contravening some by-law. In fact the vice squad was faced with a real dilemma: the independent prostitute who practiced soliciting had to refrain from any scandalous behavior that might reveal the nature of her activity to honest women, and especially to young females and children; at the same time she had to adopt behavior that clearly indicated to prospective customers that she was a prostitute.

In practice the registered independent prostitute merged into the huge mass of women who worked illegally, and her behavior differed little from that of the unregistered prostitute, which has so often been described. She constituted in a way a transition between the enclosed milieu, the ideal of regulationism, and the diffuse sexual illegality that reigned in the big cities and often spilled over into venality. Sometimes the independent prostitute was a former inmate of a *tolérance* who had decided to regain a partial freedom.[250] It should be remembered, moreover, that the registered prostitute was generally a former unregistered one, and that most of the *filles en carte* "disappeared" and rejoined the ranks of the unregistered; between the two categories, therefore, there was a contant interchange. Sometimes, too, *filles en carte* pretended to be unregistered in order to attract the bourgeois clientele who refused to frequent the registered prostitutes; this was the case of a great many *filles à parties,* who recruited in the fashionable Bois de Boulogne and Champs-Elysées.

More often than the unregistered prostitute, because the permission of the authorities allowed her to do it more easily, the *fille en carte* set up what might be called a clients' partnership; that is, she reserved her favors for a group of gentlemen who knew her, decided to buy her services en bloc, and divided up among them the days on which she could be visited. This type of partnership among honest men had the advantage of reducing considerably the risk of venereal contagion.[251]

Jealousy aroused a lot of tension between the *filles en carte* and the unregistered prostitutes; the latter were often the victims of their colleagues' denunciations. This is understandable: in districts where the surveillance of the vice squad was inadequate, the *filles soumises* saw their clientele melt away, to the profit of the unregistered prostitutes.

Of course it would be wrong to imagine that the independent registered prostitute was entirely in the grip of the authorities simply because her name appeared on their records. Like the unregistered prostitute, she was generally under the thumb of a pimp, and what I shall have to say later about the unregistered prostitute often applied to the *fille en carte*. Although the latter practiced her profession outside the bounds desired by the regulationists, she escaped neither the constant surveillance of the police nor confinement to the hospital or prison.

The Hospital

A twofold evolution was taking place in accordance with regulationist theory. On the one hand, health checks for registered prostitutes had been considerably improved and much more widely enforced since the beginning of the July Monarchy. The establishment of special departments in certain general hospitals or infirmaries in prisons intended for prostitutes; closer cooperation in the cities between the health services and the vice squad; frequent, more thorough compulsory health checks; better conditions for the medical examination of women; and, above all, the setting up of what was sometimes an extremely detailed filing system—these were all manifestations of progress in health supervision, quite apart from improvements in therapeutic techniques. By the same token, improved medical controls allowed the officials of the vice squad to supervise the prostitutes and to tighten their grip on them. In short, the regulationist project was becoming more and more a reality.

On the other hand, one may observe the decline of the old practices that tended to turn the treatment of venereal disease into a punishment. We need not be reminded that the victims of the "pox" had, since the Renaissance, been subjected to violent treatment and often even to public corporal punishment intended to castigate them for their misconduct and to make them repent for the pleasures of the flesh. The disappearance of the whip, the marked decrease in the practice of solitary confinement in these cases, the abandonment of such brutal practices as deprivation of food at certain times or the denial of the most basic comforts came fairly rapidly in the cities; this merely expressed the overall evolution of penitentiary theory and methods.

This twofold evolution shows how eager the authorities were to move away from the primacy of avowedly moral concerns to issues associated with health; it quickly took the form of the emergence of neoregulationism and a shift from phallic to venereal anxiety. Yet the rapidity of the transformation in outlook and practice varied from region to region and depended on the size of the urban areas; indeed, one is struck by the considerable variations in this process. In some of the larger towns, in Paris especially, but also at Lyons, a distinction was drawn between prostitutes suffering from venereal disease and members of the general public suffering from it. This in itself tended to marginalize the prostitutes still further. Prostitutes were often treated in hospitals or in special departments; although they too benefited from more humane forms of treatment, this did not prevent the authorities from keeping them as tightly controlled as ever.

In a large number of towns of average size, however, the general hospitals still refused to accept patients suffering from venereal diseases.[252] Similarly, the statutes of most mutual aid societies stipulated that victims of shameful diseases be deprived of the services usually provided by these associations.[253] In these provincial towns, patients with venereal diseases were primarily prostitutes, and although other patients were sometimes admitted to the premises reserved for them, the inmates were usually treated with old-fashioned severity. Padlocked gates, bars, and solitary confinement remained common in some regions right up to the First World War.

The Development of the Health Check

The *contrôle sanitaire,* or compulsory health check, was both a part of the official supervision[254] exercised over all the activities and living conditions of the registered prostitutes and the particular means by which this supervision was carried out. In fact, it should be remembered, it was the dispensary and not the prison hospital that was the true locus, or, to use Dr. Reuss's term, "the cornerstone,"[255] of the regulationist system in practice.

The health check figured prominently among the prostitutes' concerns and in their conversation.[256] In order to understand this, we have to take into account the prejudices of the time, which helped to make the medical examination of women's sexual organs an assault on their modesty, if not actually rape. We find this concern in most of the writings of the abolitionists.[257] On this matter there is a very evident embarrassment on the part of even the most fervent regulationists: Dr. Mireur, who regarded the health check as necessary, nevertheless called it a "stigma," "a degrading act," "an affront to human dignity."[258] In 1859 Procurator General Dupin of the Cour de Cassation considered the locking up of prostitutes a less serious matter than the health check.

Unfortunately it is very difficult, given the extreme diversity among localities, to give even a moderately accurate account of the development of the health check for prostitutes. In the late 1880s in Paris and Nantes the independent prostitutes were examined every two weeks; in most of the cities the by-laws insisted on a weekly check. This was the case at Marseilles, Bordeaux, Lyons, Lille, Amiens, Besançon, Reims,[259] Brest, Rennes, Toulouse, and Montpellier.[260] The independent prostitutes at Dieppe, Dijon, Angoulême, Chalon, Dunkirk, and Laval underwent three checks a month. In 1904, 208 by-laws out of 322 requiring a health check for registered prostitutes stipulated that it should take place every week, 55 that it should take place three times a month, and 46 twice a month,[261] although it is true that at this date the development of neoregulationism had already strengthened the supervision of prostitutes' health.

In Paris and its surburbs the medical examination of the inmates of the *maisons de tolérance* took place in the establishment itself, each of which had to be provided with an examination chair, a speculum, forceps, and other necessary instruments. One of the fifteen physicians attached to the vice squad came every week. The result of his examination was recorded in the keeper's book; every inmate recognized as suffering from venereal disease was sent to the infirmary of Saint-Lazare. When, between visits, the keeper saw that one of her employees was ill, she was to have her examined at the dispensary; the same applied to new inmates. In fact, as we have seen, the keepers took great care to conceal lesions; moreover, they preferred to have the women treated by a doctor in the city so as not to be deprived of their services for too long. It should be added that certain independent prostitutes who could not travel were given permission to be treated at home by the physicians of the vice squad. At Marseilles[262] and Lille the inmates of the *tolérances* were also examined at home.

In the capital the dispensary was open for health checks every day, except Sunday, between 11 A.M. and 5 P.M. It was here that the registered independent prostitutes, and the unregistered ones caught soliciting, were examined. Furthermore, the prostitutes treated at Saint-Lazare and regarded as cured by the doctors of that establishment had to come to the dispensary for a further health check.

The tax imposed on the Paris prostitutes for these check-ups had long since been abolished. This sort of imposition, which had enabled the municipality to cover the expenses of the health department, had been strongly criticized as immoral. Nonetheless, many municipalities were still keeping up this practice at the beginning of the Third Republic and even beyond. In 1873 at Brest the taxes received for health checks on *filles de maison* "amounted to 14,400 francs,"[263] which was the cause of innumerable complaints by brothel-keepers. At Marseilles the tax was commensurate with "the style, standards, and category of the *maisons de tolérance*"[264] or "to the more or less luxurious appearance of the independent prostitutes."[265] These independent prostitutes could change their category on presentation of their reasons for doing so. The price of the health checks was one, two, or three francs, according to category. As late as 1904,[266] 86 municipal by-laws out of the 168 that mentioned the subject specified the levying of a tax. In eighty-two other towns the health checks were free of charge either completely or to prostitutes in financial difficulties. It should be said that these taxes did not appear in the municipal budgets after 1879, when the Conseil d'Etat declared them to be illegal. According to Hennequin, the health check was very often a source of financial benefit to the municipality.

In the early years of the Third Republic, at Bordeaux, Rouen,[267] and Lyons, a more subtle system made it possible to draw up categories of registered prostitutes quite spontaneously: certain times were reserved for those who wanted to be examined free of charge; others, the better-off ones, had to pay a tax if they wanted to be given more individualized treatment. The Paris dispensary, which had initially been situated in the rue Croix-des-Petits-Champs, had been set up in 1843 on the quai de l'Horloge, in the courtyard of the prefecture of police, adjacent to the cells and offices of the vice squad. A similar organization operated in Lyons,[268] and we know that this concentration was highly approved of by the regulationists. The city of Marseilles had had a dispensary since 1821.[269] It was situated in the rue de la Prison in the same premises as the jail. At Laval, too, there was a "special establishment next to the prison.[270]

In accordance with the regulationist scheme—and this lasted until 1888—the physicians who performed health checks on prostitutes in Paris were chosen by the prefecture of police. They worked under the orders of a physician in chief who specialized in questions relating to the unregistered prostitutes in general and to medical examinations on them in particular. Similarly, in Marseilles it was the prefect who selected from a list presented to him by the mayor the inspector-physicians of the health department.

The functioning of the Paris dispensary soon came under violent attack; as the pivot of the system, it would always be the most strongly challenged institution.[271] It should be said, however, that the criticism was well founded. The health checks were carried out at an extremely rapid rate: according to Dr. Clerc,[272] who boasted that he could examine a woman every thirty seconds,[273] a single practitioner saw four hundred women in twenty-four hours. As early as the Second Empire, Carlier observed that the average number of patients examined in an hour was fifty-two.[274]

Until 1887 one patient out of every two had only a *petite visite;* that is to say, contrary to the practice at Lyons or Marseilles, she was examined without a speculum. The most elemental hygiene was neglected, and uncleaned speculums were accused of being agents of contagion.[275] In order to carry out rapid examinations a special apparatus was developed; for example, the ingenious chair used by Dr. Jeannel at the Bordeaux dispensary made it possible to examine women of different heights without adjustment while allowing them to keep on their clothes and, above all, their hats.[276] In Paris, after a fire at the prefecture of police in 1871, Dr. Denis's chair-bed was abandoned in favor of the table with speculum, which the prostitutes of Lille were to nickname "the rocker."[277] This innovation is evidence of a shift in attitudes and the beginning of a less shameful attitude toward sex.

In the short time allowed him, in Paris and Marseilles the physician examined the vulva, the vagina, the neck of the womb, the lips, and the inside of the mouth. In order to palliate the effects of the ablutions and makeup used by sick women before undergoing a health check, the patients were forced to wait for a long period of time before the examination. It goes without saying that, despite this precaution, and given the difficulty of diagnosing disguised venereal sores, many illnesses escaped the practitioner's attention.

The compiling of the file and the various documents arising from the health checks was gradually improved. In the early years of the Third Republic, the large number of these documents (eight per patient) indicates that more than medical care went into this operation. Under the name of each registered prostitute the dispensary had an "individual card," on which appeared the dates of her examinations; this made it possible to alert the vice squad when a woman disappeared. Furthermore, an individual "statistical sheet" remained in the office of the physician in chief, who was thus able to draw up a periodic bill of health for the personnel.

When a prostitute was found to be sick, she was sent to Saint-Lazare, together with a "notice," which would be tied to the foot of her bed; the dispensary would then keep under her name an "observation card," on which would be recorded the various stages of the disease. By means of this document syphilitics could be placed under special observation. When an independent prostitute wanted to join a *maison de tolérance,* or when the inmate of a house wanted to change establishments, she had to undergo an additional medical examination; the results were recorded and sent by the dispensary to the administrative department. There was also a "special postponement register," which contained the names of all the prostitutes for whom the diagnosis had been considered uncertain and whose move had, therefore, been postponed.

Furthermore, we should not forget that the independent prostitute was provided with a card that she had to present on demand and which recorded all her sanitary and administrative obligations. Finally, the results of the health checks carried out in the *maisons* were recorded not only on the keepers' registers but also on special forms.

Although different,[278] the organization, at least before 1878, was almost as meticulous and complex in the health department of Lyons. The participation of members of the vice squad at health checks and the implementation of a complex system of symbols (tokens, letters) enabled the physician to know the exact status and previous health record of each woman he examined.

In short, all this goes to show the scope of the statistical efforts made in controlling venereal disease. These efforts were rendered quite pointless, it is true, by the very failure of regulationism—that is to say, by the endless interchange between registered and unregistered prostitutes.[279] The health check was too broad-meshed a net, despite the untiring labors of the personnel, but it did enable the administrative department to observe the movements of registered women, at least until they disappeared.

The statistics concerning ratios of illness among registered prostitutes and unregistered ones caught by the police are not devoid of interest. They allow us to discern the seasonal evolution of disease and its annual variations; furthermore, they enable us to know the approximate age at which the syphilization[280] of prostitutes took place. Unfortunately, the investigations carried out by the physicians of the health department and by those of Saint-Lazare did not produce identical results, although all indicate the high rate of illness among the young. The police commissioner of Marseilles, E. Dietze,[281] noted that out of 214 young registered prostitutes in 1875 and 1876, 112 were sick; some, aged fifteen or sixteen, had already been treated for venereal disease several times. The observation carried out by Dr. Maireau on 135 prostitutes led him to conclude in 1884 that "every prostitute is syphilized by her second year in prostitution,"[282] although in the detail of his study a few exceptions emerge. An investigation carried out at a later date by Dr. Jullien was more rigorous.[283] His study (see Figure 10) concerns one thousand prostitutes, first-time inmates in his department at Saint-Lazare, consisting of 177 registered prostitutes and 823 unregistered ones, almost all of whom were forced, as a result of their arrest, to become registered after their cure.

It will be noted that the venereal diseases (consisting here of 651 cases of gonorrhea, 421 cases of syphilis, and 36 soft chancres) affected above all the prostitutes under twenty; as Dr. Jullien remarks, nineteen was the peak age, closely followed by eighteen and twenty.

These results differ quite appreciably from those obtained in the same period by Professor Barthélemy,[284] who, it is true, confined his study to syphilis alone; moreover, his methods of investigation seem less than rigorous. The study of a group of 153 prostitutes led him to observe that 28.7 percent of them developed syphilis in their first year in prostitution, 41.1 percent between one and three years later, 20.2 percent between three and five years later, 7.8 percent between five and ten years later, and only 1.9 percent after more than ten years of prostitution. This led the author to draw up this stereotype of the prostitute: she lost her virginity at sixteen and a half, became a prostitute at nineteen and a half, caught syphilis at twenty-three, and ceased, according to him, to transmit the disease at twenty-seven or twenty-eight. The publication in

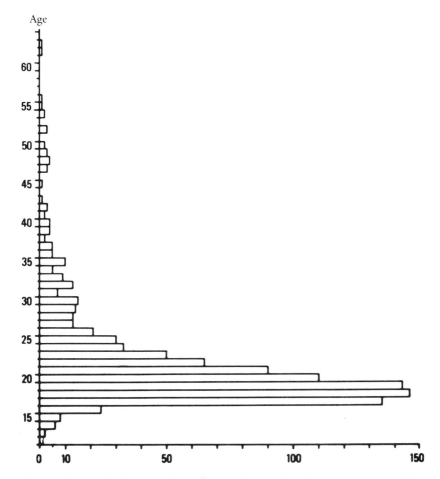

Figure 10. Age distribution of one thousand venereal patients entering the infirmary of Saint-Lazare for the first time, 1890–1900. (According to Dr. Jullien.)

1909 of the results of Dr. Le Pileur's observations tended to confirm Dr. Jullien's work;[285] out of five thousand venereal patients treated by him at Saint-Lazare, 28.7 percent were under eighteen and 63 percent under twenty-one.

The Prison Treatment

The infirmary at which prostitutes were treated for venereal diseases in Paris was only part of the penitentiary establishment at Saint-Lazare, and it is somewhat artificial to deal with this infirmary in isolation from its environment. This symbiosis between prison and hospital—"the prison treatment"[286]—advocated by Parent-Duchâtelet came into force under the July Monarchy, when regulationism was at its height. In 1834 the municipal council had voted funds for the construction of an infirmary inside the prison; the building was opened in February 1836. The by-laws, in force up to the reform of 1888, were passed on July 11, 1843; those of August 29, 1875, concerning the establishment as a whole still made provision for its continued application.

The infirmary of Saint-Lazare was situated in the faubourg Saint-Denis in the premises of a former monastery; women other than prostitutes suffering from venereal disease could be treated at the Hôpital de Lourcine and male venereal cases at the Hôpital du Midi. The description of Saint-Lazare and its infirmary is an inexhaustible theme in the prostitutional literature of the Third Republic. The institution lay at the heart of the debate between abolitionists (and even neoregulationists) and traditional regulationists. As a result, it is very difficult to draw up an objective account of the place: the idyllic portrayal of a Maxime du Camp and the sinister description of Yves Guyot,[287] who visited the premises in 1877, are merely the work of polemicists. It cannot be disputed, however, that the infirmary of Saint-Lazare was then inferior in therapeutics to the major hospitals of the capital.

The patients were divided up into dormitories, which in all comprised four hundred beds; these dormitories were broken down into cells of about twenty beds, each cell being separated from the next by partitions with holes in them. This allowed the Sisters of Marie-Joseph to carry out an effective surveillance and, in theory, to prevent any nocturnal debauchery. The registered prostitutes occupied the second floor, the unregistered ones the third and fourth. Minors were treated separately. On arrival the patients were dressed in the infirmary uniform and a white cap, which made them easy to recognize. Here the prostitutes were not forced to work. There has been a great deal of criticism of the poor quality of the food, although it does not seem to have been worse than ordinary hospital food at the time,[288] but the hours at which meals were served resemble those of a prison more than those of a hospital. Indeed, the by-laws of November 29, 1875, still provided that "meals would be distributed in the second section [the prostitutes' section] of the infirmary at 6:30 A.M. and at 1:15 P.M., with additional soup at 4 P.M." It was this schedule above all that unleashed the criticism of the abolitionists.

Of course, the prostitutes treated in the infirmary were prisoners, just like the other inmates of Saint-Lazare. They could not leave until the departmental head was satisfied that a cure had been effected and gave his permission accordingly, an opinion that had to be confirmed by a second medical examination carried out by the dispensary physicians. Furthermore, the patients were almost totally cut off from the outside world; visits took place as if through a convent grille, under the supervision of the nuns, on Tuesdays and Fridays between midday and 2 P.M. Communication by letter was strictly supervised. These decisions were intended to prevent the pimps from continuing to associate with their *marmites* during the treatment or to come in and recruit. The infirmary inmates were allowed two hours' exercise during the day; in order to prevent any contact between the categories, the registered prostitutes had their walk at different times (between 10 A.M. and 11 A.M., and between 3 P.M. and 4 P.M.) from that of the unregistered ones (between 11 A.M. and midday, and between 4 P.M. and 5 P.M.).

The syphilitic patients of Saint-Lazare were treated with mercury and potassium iodide.[289] In fact, the length of treatment was limited and its efficacy dubious, especially since hygiene was in a lamentable state at that time in the infirmary, as Professor Bourneville remarks in his report to the municipal council in 1880. It was only during the next decade that washbasins and bidets were installed. Meanwhile, patients were unable to wash their private parts. "Neither baths, nor washbasins. A shared nozzle, an excellent vehicle for contagious diseases; no towels, no handkerchiefs," observed Yves Guyot after his visit.[290]

According to Dr. Reuss,[291] the average length of treatment was six weeks for registered prostitutes and three months for unregistered ones. First Guyot[292] and later Corlieu[293] referred to a note from the prefecture of police which provides the following information on the stay of syphilitic patients in 1879: 27 women had stayed over three months; 88 stayed between two and three months; 127 stayed between one and two months; 77 stayed between twenty and twenty-nine days; and 123 stayed between ten and nineteen days.

The average length of treatment did not exceed thirty days, therefore, whereas at the Hôpital de Lourcine[294] it lasted, depending on the year, between fifty-eight and sixty-five days. In fact, as the abolitionists repeated tirelessly, the patients, on leaving, had simply had their symptoms covered up.

On the whole, the situation appears to have been the same in the other cities that had set up special departments for the treatment of diseased prostitutes. At Lyons, where a hundred beds had been reserved for them in a special quarter of the Antiquaille[295] before a prefectural order in 1878 condemned the functioning of the health department, the average length of treatment was twenty-one or twenty-two days.[296] At Marseilles the regimen was theoretically extremely harsh, since in the

Sainte-Magdeleine department of the Hôpital de la Conception the sick prostitutes, all dressed in a uniform of gray sackcloth, were forced to carry out manual labor in compliance with the by-laws. It should be noted, however, that in 1882, when Dr. Mireur published his work,[297] this by-law was no longer applied. The special building in which the prostitutes were treated consisted, apart from the wards of twenty-nine beds,[298] of a refectory and a yard, which made it possible to isolate the prostitutes completely from other patients. As at Saint-Lazare all mail was opened, and two hours were allowed for exercise; a number of punishments were laid down for those prostitutes who disturbed order: deprivation of wine, a diet of bread and water, confinement to a cell. In the case of rebellion, the authorities could call on the authorities to restore order. Between 1871 and 1881, the annual average stay of the venereal patients ranged from twenty-three days (in 1881) to thirty-five days (in 1878).[299] It should be added that there was no other department in the city for the treatment of venereal patients who were not prostitutes.

At Bordeaux in the early years of the Third Republic, according to Dr. Lande,[300] "those suffering from diseases of a sexual order [and] uterine diseases," even when nonvenereal, were relegated to "near the scullery and water-closets" of the Hôpital Saint-André. When, in about 1887, a project was afoot to build a special establishment for the city's venereal patients, the order was still given to the architect to include a series of subterranean cells.

In most medium-sized towns the treatment of venereal patients was still very backward[301]: prostitutes and debauched women were mixed with merely sick women, and the regimen was conceived implicitly as a punishment. In this respect the case of Nancy is particularly significant. Until 1914, when prostitutes were transferred to the Hôpital Hippolyte-Maringer in the former Sacré-Coeur monastery, venereal patients were treated at the Maison de Bon Secours in appalling conditions.[302] The gray façade and the almost windowless walls of the building rose from the street like those of a prison. This impression was reinforced still further by the gates that one encountered at the entrance. The quarters had no outside windows and were lit from the cloister, which served as an inner courtyard for the women's department; it was bordered on one side by a series of cells, each of which had a reinforced door. Inside, the only furniture was a small wooden bed fixed to the wall; a small, barred skylight allowed in a little sun.

At the Maison de Bon Secours the venereal patients were assembled in a "day hall" or workroom, which was badly lit and ventilated, where they were forced to work at sewing and embroidery. The tiny, sinister-looking recreation yard, surrounded by high walls, got hardly any sunlight at all. In the chapel the venereal patients were segregated in a gallery. Inside dormitories planned for 60 patients, 100 or even 120 women were packed.[303]

Until 1880, when the medical faculty opened a clinical department of dermatology and syphilography there, the institution was the sole responsibility of the prefect, who appointed the department head. Later, sanitary conditions remained poor, as can be seen from descriptions of the bandaging room,[304] which was also where the weekly medicals of the registered prostitutes took place.

It is understandable, therefore, that the prostitutes should have rebelled against their confinement in the "Brique," as they called the Maison de Secours. In 1904 the inner yard was completely laid waste; the police were obliged to intervene, and several venereal patients were jailed. "Here and there," Professor Spillmann wrote in 1914 on the last years of the institution "a few particularly restless and violent women organized small revolts. The administration then called in the vice squad, which took the culprits off to solitary confinement and the discipline hall."[305] In 1913 two women who had been locked up in the discipline room destroyed it in one night, "breaking the windows, ripping mattresses and sheets, using a fork handle to smash the woodwork, detach the plaster from the walls, and prise off the windows."[306] It is hardly surprising, then, that, in 1914 the authorities assigned a large contingent of police when the venereal patients were transferred to their new hospital.

The conditions in Nancy were in no way exceptional: on the contrary, they seem to be quite representative of the manner in which venereal patients were treated. The investigation carried out by Professor Bourneville in 1887 and the polemics that it gave rise to in *Le progrès médical* throws a harsh light on that situation.[307]

At the Hôtel-Dieu in Saint-Etienne the venereal department was too small. "The latest arrivals slept on pallets in a first-floor room, with a tiled floor, open to a prison yard from which the snow had not yet been swept";[308] the door did not fit and it was colder inside than out; the tables and benches were rickety. That year the angry patients broke down a door and smashed a window with "the iron bar they used to unblock the pipe from the latrines."[309] They then escaped into the town. This kind of escape was quite frequent here, especially at times like Shrove Tuesday and Easter. That same year at Lyons the venereal patients in the Antiquaille also rebelled against being deprived collectively of wine and part of their meals;[310] instead of escaping, however, they barricaded themselves into a room, where they did damage estimated at four hundred francs.

These rebellions were traditional; in 1830 and 1848[311] the Paris prostitutes confined in Saint-Lazare mutinied with the support of the populace. The fact that such hospital revolts could continue right up to the First World War without the municipalities taking the most elementary humanitarian steps as a result is very revealing of the attitude of the public toward sexuality.

Let us return to the report that Bourneville made after his investigation of the hospitals in eastern France. At Château-Thierry the women patients suffering from venereal disease—and there were very few of them—were treated in rooms occupied by senile women; originally it had been the intention (significantly) to put them in a cell next to the insane, far removed from the other patients, above the autopsy room.[312] At the Hôtel-Dieu in Epernay the venereal patients were isolated from the others. At Bar-le-Duc they were treated in an attic room; the windows were obscured "by a fine-meshed grill," and the door had locks and bolts. "Next door was the indispensable 'solitary' cell."[313] We again find the isolation of the venereal patients, bars, and locks at the civil and military hospital at Saint-Dié. At the Hôpital Saint-Maurice at Epinal there was an even greater desire to segregate the venereal patients; the wall of the hospital yard was itself surmounted by a palisade. In this establishment the venereal patients had no beds but only simple pallets. The solitary cell, next to the lavatory, was in frequent use. At the civil hospital at Belfort twelve beds were reserved for venereal patients. Bourneville notes the "defective furniture, lack of washbasins and injection apparatus, inadequate cubic space, bars, railings, etc."[314] At Gray the rooms reserved for the venereal patients were clean, but the windows were padlocked. The other hospitals in the region refused to treat this type of patient; the venereal patients in Chaumont were sent to Besançon, those of Bar-sur-Aube to the hospital at Troyes, and those from Lunéville were taken by the police to the Bon Secours at Nancy.

This situation was not peculiar to eastern France: in 1881 at Brest sick prostitutes were often locked up and were unable to communicate with the outside world.[315] At Dinan venereal patients and prostitutes suffering from other vaginal infections were treated as prisoners and not as patients. During the Second Empire the nuns of the hospital at Château-Gontier refused to accept venereal patients, who were sent off to be treated in the prison infirmary at Laval, where they were sequestered.[316] At Boulogne things were a little more complicated: venereal patients who were not prostitutes and the unregistered prostitutes were treated more humanely, while registered prostitutes were received in a different department and locked up in a room with barred windows.[317]

A former intern in the hospital at Orléans describes in even more sinister fashion the room set aside for the town's venereal patients.[318] It was an attic room whose only furniture consisted of the beds, a bench along the wall, and a few rickety chairs; the doors, which were usually kept locked, were opened only once a day for an hour's exercise in the gardens. Solitary confinement was still in use, and a few years earlier the venereal patients in the department had also been deprived of wine. This establishment took in some hundred patients a year and was not confined to prostitutes. Since 1886 at the Hôpital Saint-Sauveur at Lille, the "municipal department for syphilitic prostitutes" had occupied a special building which, as Dr. Patoir wrote in 1902, was "like a prison, or rather a prison infirmary."[319] The women could not leave the establishment before they were cured; they were subjected to an extremely harsh regimen and tight surveillance.[320] In 1882 the venereal patients at Montpellier were still being deprived of wine.[321] At Reims until 1902— that is to say, before Dr. Langlet, the departmental head, set about implementing neoregulationist reforms—the registered prostitutes were treated in the Salle Helvétius, which was reserved for their use. Even at that late date there were bars on the windows and secure locks on double doors; "no visits, no work, no books"[322] but "solitary" cells, declared Dr. Langlet in his open letter to Dr. Wiet, the administrator of hospitals, who had criticized him for allowing venereal patients into his departmental common room. At Clermont-Ferrand in 1887 the department for female venereal patients was placed under the supervision of "a well-built guard." "Here there is no yard or anywhere for the inmates to exercise . . . The sheets, stained with mercurial ointment, etc., are changed only every month . . . Next to this room is a *punishment chamber*."[323] The municipal by-laws in force in 1904 at Castelnaudary, Saint-Quentin, and Langres still stipulated that sick prostitutes be treated at the prison infirmary.[324]

There is little point in citing further examples: well after the beginning of the abolitionists' campaign and after the neoregulationists had demanded more humane conditions, the treatment of venereal patients, laid down by the authorities with the tacit support of a majority of public opinion and part of the medical profession, was still based on a desire to lock up and punish the patients. Indeed, the rise of the theme of the venereal peril helped, in a way, to reinforce this attitude.

The discrepancy between the improved supervision of the health of registered prostitutes' and the persistence in many places of archaic attitudes toward venereal disease appears to have been evident to the majority of the members of the medical profession from the 1880s on, and it was this awareness that gave rise to the development and ultimate victory of neoregulationism, which advocated the humanization of treatment in order to get the public to accept more readily the need for health checks and the confinement of sick prostitutes.

The archaic treatment of venereal patients in the small towns should not make us lose sight of the coherence of the regulationists enterprise in Paris and the country's main cities. Since the time when Parent-Duchâtelet wrote his famous work, the links between the vice squad and the health departments everywhere had grown closer. Hospitals and special departments had multiplied, largely inspired by the penitentiary model; within these enclosed institutions the compartmentalization advocated by the regulationists of the July Monarchy was sometimes strict, as at Saint-Lazare. When we read the works of the medical advocates of the system, whether they were in charge of dispensary departments (Jeannel, Homo, Garin, Martineau, Commenge) or of the treatment of venereal patients (Jullien, Barthélemy, Butte, Le Pileur, Corlieu), we see clearly the importance that "prison treatment" had in their preoccupations; yet the role of these same practitioners turns out to be practically nonexistent in the development of syphilography. Indeed, progress in this area resulted mainly from the efforts of physicians (Ricord, Mauriac, Fournier) working in hospitals intended for (mainly male) venereal patients who were not prostitutes.

The therapeutic mediocrity of the "compulsory hospitals" resulted from the system that had given rise to their creation: the close ties between the vice squad and sanitary supervision led to the appointment by the prefect of none-too-competent doctors only too inclined to regard their patients as offenders; confinement and the Draconian by-laws still in force affected the quality of care and impeded cure; furthermore, the progress of medical science made it ever more clear that it would be impossible, using "prison treatment" as practiced, to provide the prostitutes suffering from syphilis with definitive cure. It should be added that the severity of the treatment led the venereal patients to try to conceal their disease in order to escape what was in fact a form of detention. It was this failure of the health departments that was to provide the abolitionists with their best argument.

The Prison

Unlike vagabondage and begging, prostitution was not in itself an offense. Article 334 of the penal code refers only to "l'outrage et l'attentat aux bonnes moeurs";[325] prostitutes could not, therefore, be tried, as such, in the magistrates' court. When they contravened municipal by-laws in the provinces or even those affecting the prefectures of police at Paris and Lyons, however, the administrative authorities subjected them to fines or periods of punitive detention. The illegality of such measures did not pass unnoticed.[326] The abolitionists made it one of their main arguments, and even the neoregulationists came to recognize that their criticisms were well founded; both demanded the intervention of the legislature to bring the prostitutes back under common law. The regulationists did not evade the debate, and, especially between 1872 and 1882, when the prefecture of police was exposed to mounting attacks, they replied to their adversaries with a series of legal arguments that should be briefly examined here.

The Theoretical Justification

Like Lecour, who was in charge of the first division of the prefecture of police during the period of *ordre moral* and who confronted the critics most energetically, the regulationists derived their best argument from legislative silence. Indeed, since the ancien régime, the legislature had refrained from intervening in the matter in order not to be forced to recognize prostitution. On 17 Nivôse, Year IV (January 7, 1796), the Directory had sent a message from Rewbell to the Council of the Five Hundred asking it to legislate on this point; it advocated that prostitution should be declared an offense, that a special legal procedure should be set up for prostitutes, and that they should be punished by periods of imprisonment exceeding five days. The commission formed for this purpose by the council, which included, among others, Dubois-Crancé and Tournier, failed to define the prostitute and balked at envisaging a procedure incompatible with the forms of justice. On 7 Germinal, Year V (March 27, 1797), Bancal asked the Council of the Five Hundred to set up a new commission on brothels, gambling places, and theaters. This proposition caused an outcry in the hall. Deputy Dumolard declared that it was unworthy of the assembly to deal with such subjects; he reminded his fellow members of the existence of police by-laws and demanded that the motion be set aside; this was adopted by a large majority.[327] Since then no assembly has ever passed legislation on the matter.[328] On May 8, 1877, the Senate in a motion stated that it was wise to touch on what it regarded, quite wrongly, as "legislation on this matter" with the greatest prudence.

Article 484 of the penal code establishes that in all matters not dealt with by the code, the courts should continue to observe the local by-laws. The regulationists interpreted this article as providing the basis of the power enjoyed by local authorities in the matter of prostitution.[329] In Paris they referred to the ordinances of the ancien régime, and in particular to the one issued by Police Lieutenant Lenoir in 1778 and to Article 14 of the ordinance of November 8, 1780, to justify the practices then in force. Throughout the century the central government left it to the mayors to issue regulations on the matter;[330] the municipal law of 1884, together with Article 471 of the penal code, reinforced this position.

According to the advocates of regulation, prostitution was a matter that affected the public thoroughfare and was related to the maintenance of order and decency in the street and in public places; the authorities were therefore directed to supervise the prostitutes. In any case, for them[331] recourse to normal legal procedure was utopian: the courts would be congested with matters arising out of prostitution; it would take too long for sentences to be handed down; and health procedures in particular would be impeded. Thus the authorities took the place of the magistrates, not in finding offenders guilty and passing sentence, but in inflicting punishment.

In the course of the century certain lawyers had tried to justify the intervention of the authorities in another way. Dupin,[332] the procurator general at the Cour de Cassation, wrote in 1859: "Prostitution is a *state* that subjects the creatures who practice it to the discretionary powers delegated by the law to the police."[333] It was not, therefore, any more an infringement of individual liberty to apply the by-laws to prostitutes than to inflict punishment on soldiers or to search travelers at the frontiers. "Such measures are legal because they are the necessary consequences of things";[334] they "constitute merely means of policing" and "may result legally from the exercise of discretionary powers left to the administration, a power that the police exercise freely under constitutional guarantees."[335]

The theory by which legislation constitutes, between the prostitute and the administrative authority, a veritable contract implying recognition of the legality of punishments was also advanced.[336] It must be remembered, however, that the civil code does not recognize contracts whose cause is contrary to good morals.

Put more simply (and we shall see this type of argument develop with neoregulationism), the advocates of the power of the authorities invoked the need for the sanitary supervision of prostitution; they refer to the sequestration of travelers put into quarantine on arrival at ports to justify the confinement of venereal patients and, by the same token, the punishments inflicted on prostitutes who fail to turn up for their health checks. Venal sex was for them merely one insalubrious industry among others; it should, therefore, be subjected to health regulations. It is true that this theory logically implies that men should also have health checks and that male venereal patients should be confined; and indeed some regulationists, as we have seen, were not afraid to envisage such a thing.

It should be added that the advocates of administrative authority also derived arguments to justify this system from judgments passed by the Cour de Cassation; but it is not my purpose here to enter into a detailed study of these texts.[337] In fact, the main point is certainly that of the legislative silence on prostitution, a silence that, in spite of many campaigns to change public opinion, lasted into the twentieth century. It resulted from the fact that legislators found themselves in a dilemma: to recognize by law the existence of the prostitute and of prostitution in order to supervise them or, against all sense of realism, to decide that venal sex was illegal although the structures of sexuality ordained its existence. This legislative silence abandoned the field to the authorities and, however weak the legal arguments of the regulationists might have been, in fact provided a basis for administrative confinement.

The "Woman Hunt"

In Paris, as I have mentioned, the vice squad at this time consisted of the second bureau of the first division of the prefecture of police; until 1881 the sixty-five policemen entrusted with these problems formed, under the title *inspecteurs des moeurs,* a specialized *brigade des moeurs,* or vice squad. In 1881, following a campaign against the prefecture of police,[338] Prefect Andrieux abolished this brigade[339] and transferred the men to the *service de sûreté,* or detective division. This reform had little effect, as the abolitionists were to remark, except that, contrary to its avowed aim, it allowed the members of the detective squad to intervene in the matter of morals; this in fact led to a reinforcement of surveillance.

The police in the capital tried to implement the by-laws of November 16, 1843, and then those of October 15, 1878, which did not in fact represent any great alteration of the preceding ones.[340] To begin with, they had to exercise daily surveillance of the *maisons de tolérance* in order to make sure that they were properly run; that the keepers refused entry to schoolboys, minors under the age of eighteen, and soldiers in uniform; that the inmates, on their days out, wore decent clothes and respected the hours imposed on them. During health checks, they accompanied the physician who was to carry out the examinations. The abolitionists quite rightly criticized both inspectors and police for not enforcing the by-laws in the first-class *maisons de tolérance* and for closing their eyes to irregularities in establishments where the keepers were good informers or the inmates too complaisant.

In fact, the police concentrated their surveillance on the activities of the registered independents and the way they respected the by-laws of September 1, 1842. They made sure that the women did not miss health checks, walk the streets hatless, offer provocation in a public thorough-fare, solicit in groups, or get drunk; that they respected the prohibitions pertaining to times and places where they were allowed to solicit and were not accompanied or followed by their pimps. During their checks on lodging houses, the police also made sure that the women were not living several to a room. The prostitutes were not to offer any resistance to the police when being investigated or arrested.

The prohibitions imposed on the registered independents were so numerous; the difference between the solitary, the lawful practice of soliciting, and provocation on a public highway was so minimal; and the areas where the independents could not operate were so large that the unfortunate women found themselves constantly subjected to the arbitrary action of the police. The large number of arrests proves this conclusively, and it was this arbitrary action that drove the registered independents to "disappear."

With the specific purpose of arresting unregistered prostitutes and formerly registered ones who had disappeared, the inspectors of the vice squad and, later, the officers of the detective force organized raids, espe-cially on the *grands boulevards* (Saint-Denis, Poissonnière), on the outer boulevards,[341] and outside the dance halls commonly frequented by the prostitutes; sometimes the Paris police even raided hotels and lodging houses. Readers of Zola's *Nana* will remember the passages devoted to such raids, which terrorized the women and shocked the public. These "purging operations," to use Camescasse's term, which the prefecture of police made little attempt to deny and which took place in broad day-light, led to serious blunders and aroused the indignation of the aboli-tionists.[342] It should be said, however, that they were usually organized at the request of the local inhabitants, especially the tradesmen of the district.

The police surveillance exercised over prostitutes in the provinces was almost identical, although it differed in severity from district to district. The vice squad of Lyons and its suburban communes[343] remained, like that in Paris, under the direction of the secretary-general of the prefec-ture, even after the central *mairie* (town hall) had been restored in 1878.

In the other large cities its direction lay with the police commissioner; this was the case at Brest,[344] Bordeaux, and Marseilles, where the vice squad was a special department of the municipal police.[345] The work of the police was more or less the same in every case: their main task was to follow up failures to attend health checks.

In Paris each *fille soumise* was, on the average, arrested and detained several times a year. The prison of Saint-Lazare, which the prostitutes nicknamed their *campagne,*[346] was part of the everyday life of the registered prostitutes. Guyot[347] calculated that in 1880, each of them had, on the average, been arrested twice. In fact, some prostitutes benefited from the protection of the authorities and were never bothered, while others were constantly harassed and had only one obsession—to evade the police. It goes without saying that the *filles en carte* (independents) were much more frequently charged than the *filles de maison.*

Figure 11 illustrates very clearly how repressive periods were closely bound up with political circumstances. Between 1856 and 1871, during

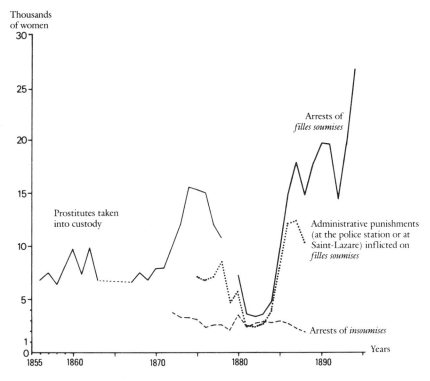

Figure 11. Police repression of prostitution in Paris. (Archives of the prefecture of police; Richard, op. cit.; Reuss, op. cit.)

the Empire and the government of national defense, the number of arrests remained relatively stable, at an average level of between six and seven thousand a year. Between 1872 and 1877 repression was intense. Under Lecour, the first division of the prefecture of police practiced strict surveillance in accordance with the policies of Thiers and his successors against the workers' movement[348] and all forms of delinquency. The intensification of repression appeared in the first weeks following the defeat of the Commune; between June 3, 1871, and January 1, 1872, the police made 6,007 arrests (3,072 registered and 2,935 unregistered prostitutes), twice the average for the period 1860–1870. This resumption of repression was accompanied by a very lax attitude toward the *maisons de tolérance,* a policy that succeeded in halting for some years the decline in the number of such establishments in the capital.[349]

The triumph of the Republic, the progress of abolitionism, a greater awareness of individual liberties, the campaign against the prefecture of police, Lecour's resignation, followed by those of Gigot and Minister of the Interior de Marcère, and finally the appointment of Andrieux were also marked by a very sharp decrease in the number of arrests and sentences.[350] This relative moderation continued from 1881 to 1884. Then, after 1885, under the direction first of Camescasse then of Gragnon, repression intensified once more, especially, as Macé recognizes,[351] against the poor prostitutes of the outlying districts; the slowing down of the abolitionist campaign, the emergence of neoregulationism, and widespread anxiety about the dangers of venereal disease are enough in themselves to explain the phenomenon. In fact, this evolution was paralleled by that of overall repression throughout the legal system. All this goes to show that the prostitutes were subjected to the much tighter surveillance practiced over all forms of deviance.

Repression was no less severe in some of the provincial towns: at Reims, for example, between January 1, and August 1, 1881, 753 police reports were filed against *filles soumises* who had failed to turn up for their health checks, gone out after 10 P.M., frequented certain streets and places that were out of bounds to them, or gone out with their pimps.[352] Between November 1, 1883, and November 1, 1884, 2,744 sentences were handed down as a result of charges made by members of the vice squad against prostitutes in the magistrates' court at Lille; these sentences involved at least 13,000 francs in fines, 4,830 days in prison, and 3,000 days of civil imprisonment.[353]

The recapitulative investigation carried out in 1902, just prior to a profound theoretical transformation concerning the repression of prostitution, came up with some striking figures. In Marseilles, since 1876, 143 sentences had been passed against registered prostitutes, 100 for *vol au canapé* (literally, "theft on the sofa," that is, stealing from a client),

30 for insulting behavior to policemen, and 30 for pickpocketing. Above all, 22,256 reports were made for various offenses: 19,541 (88 percent) for failure to attend health checks, 1,741 (7 percent) for soliciting and scandalous behavior in the public thoroughfare, 494 (2.2 percent) for being in a café, 420 (1.8 percent) for soliciting in their doorways or at their windows, 66 (0.3 percent) for performing acts of prostitution in public places, and 21 (0.1 percent) for breaking regulations inside a *maison de tolérance*.[354] These offenses were liable to prosecution in the magistrates' court and could be punished by fines of between one and five francs and a day in prison if the offense was repeated, not, of course, including administrative detention, which lasted between forty-eight and seventy-two hours. As many as 21,943 registered prostitutes were detained in this way at the municipal jail over the five years preceding the investigation.[355]

At Toulon the repression was no less severe. Between 1897 and 1901, 14,322 charges were made against registered prostitutes, 820 against inmates of *maisons de tolérance,* and 13,502 against independents. These charges led to 5,266 prison sentences. To these should be added 163 cases of prosecution for theft, assault and battery, indecent behavior, use of forged papers, drunkenness, and being out of bounds. Furthermore, it should be noted that, at the same time, 556 charges were made against brothel-keepers; these led to 241 prison sentences. Finally, charges were brought against 51 *dames de maison*.[356]

It is difficult to say whether repression in the provincial towns was modeled on that existing in the capital.[357] It is clear, however, that an increase in police action in the period following the Commune can be noted in certain regions. Many of the by-laws date from 1872.[358] In that year Guinot, mayor of Marseilles, intensified the struggle; he set out to bring the prostitutes back into the *maisons de tolérance,* which many had abandoned, and to increase the number of these establishments, thus halting their decline. Furthermore, he asked that there be set up at Marseilles "a special house that would be used for the prostitutes as prison, workshop, and hospital."[359] This project was to be taken up again and developed in 1875 by Police Commissioner Dietze, who proposed setting up for the prostitutes a "moralizing penitentiary system."[360] These efforts were to be crowned with some success, at least temporarily.[361]

Prostitutes in the Penitentiaries

All the unregistered prostitutes caught committing offenses and the *filles soumises* arrested at night in Paris spent the night in the local police station before being taken the next day to the prison of the prefecture of police. If the arrest took place during the day, they were taken directly to the quai de l'Horloge. At the central police station,[362] while waiting to be questioned by the deputy head of the vice squad, they were put with the prostitutes undergoing prison terms of under four days. Unlike the unregistered prostitutes, who were locked up in cells, the registered ones, numbering between 150 and 200 a day, were crowded into a large common room under the supervision of a nun.[363] They were not able to wash; messengers, however, were sometimes allowed to go to their places of residence to deposit the clothes that they had worn so that they would not become crumpled [364] and to bring back fresh linen, camisoles, and nightdresses. At night mattresses were brought in and the women "crowded into the corners to sleep packed one against another."[365]

At Marseilles the lockup was a damp hall fifty meters square, with a reinforced door and two barred windows; even the system of ventilation provided by the windows was recent, since it dated only from 1876.[366] In one corner was a "latrine cabin"; opposite was a washbasin, where the women could have a quick wash before going for their health checks; close by was a long line of hooks where they could hang their clothes. Between fifteen and twenty women could be piled into this room, their only sustenance consisting of bread and water; here too, however, a messenger could be sent to their place of residence to fetch clothes, blankets, or food.

In the police cells at Marseilles and Paris, amid all the shouting and laughter, the women lived without any rules whatsoever, playing cards,[367] sharing their food, writing obscene graffiti on the walls, and practicing homosexuality.[368] This anarchy, this promiscuity, which accorded so little with the development of penitentiary theory and practice, shocked both the Comte d'Haussonville and Dr. Mireur. The latter, as a good regulationist, demanded not the abolition of administrative detention but the establishment of obligatory work and silence—in other words, the belated application of the Auburn system.

Until 1902 the police cells at Toulon were very like those at Marseilles. The inmates, however, were totally cut off from the outside world. "They were given soup at midday, a portion of vegetables in the evening, and bread and water as required."[369] The premises were aired every twenty-four hours. Wine, tobacco, and alcohol were forbidden.

In both Paris and Marseilles it was the interrogating superintendent who, until 1878, decided on the penalties to be passed against a registered prostitute who had committed an offense.[370] Later, as a result of the Gigot by-laws, the prostitute, could appeal the decision before the commission set up for this purpose. In every case penalties were, in the last resort, passed by the prefect of police on the recommendation of the interrogating superintendent, with the approval of the head of the first division. In fact, the appeal procedure remained theoretical; experience soon showed the women that the commission usually confirmed or even increased the sentence initially proposed by the superintendent. Thus, between 1880 and 1886, the commission upheld 180 penalties, made 4 heavier, and reduced only 48.[371] Grécourt, head of the second bureau in 1903, wrote on this matter, "The women never appeal because they know that, not only is their punishment justified, but that they are not punished every time they deserve to be."[372]

In theory, the sentences passed on the prostitutes in the capital were not to exceed two weeks' imprisonment. The most common were sentences of between six and eight days. The registered prostitute who caused trouble, however, or who resisted arrest could be punished with one to three months' imprisonment. It should be noted on this matter— and the fact is revealing—that if the prisoner was sick, the time spent in the infirmary was counted as part of her sentence.

In the provinces it was generally the mayor who, on the recommendation of the police commissioner, decided on the terms of imprisonment to be imposed; it sometimes happened, however, as we have seen in the case of Lille and Marseilles in 1902, that, contrary to all legality, the arrested prostitute was brought before the magistrates' court and sentenced by the judicial authorities.

In Paris a prostitute sentenced to more than four days' imprisonment was sent to the second section of Saint-Lazare prison, which was reserved for prostitutes. These women were subjected to the same obligations as common-law offenders, from whom, however, they were strictly segregated, just as were the minors, who formed the third section and who benefited from a special regimen. The women undergoing punishment slept in dormitories that were never heated;[373] their food, which was served at 8:45 A.M. and 3 P.M., consisted, in addition to seven hundred grams of bread twice daily, of boiled vegetables accompanied once a week[374] by a slice of beef; water or a sort of coconut milk made on the premises was the only drink.[375] Unlike the sentenced offenders, they were not allowed to buy things for themselves.

The registered prostitutes undergoing short sentences wore a black cap; if their sentence did not exceed one month, however, they were not forced to wear the black-and-white woolen penitentiary dress. The prisoners were given only one chemise a week, even during their menstrual periods. They had to do eleven hours' work and keep silent in damp workshops, where they wore their fingers to the bone sewing mailbags under the supervision of a nun, who read them pious novels and other books. As with the sick prostitutes, their correspondence was opened, and they were allowed to communicate with visitors only through the parlor grille.

The Sisters of Marie-Joseph were harsher toward the prostitutes than they were toward other prisoners;[376] the women were not allowed visitors,[377] nor could they get clothes or food from outside. The old custom whereby the brothel-keepers would bring them fresh linen and a basket of food disappeared when the by-laws of 1875 were implemented.[378] The imprisoned prostitutes were not allowed to work for themselves during their few hours of recreation. In cases of insubordination, insolence to the nuns, or refusal to work, they were given disciplinary punishments ranging from withdrawal of food or visitor privileges to "solitary confinement, with dry bread and straitjacket."[379] Under the circumstances, it is understandable that prostitutes facing charges should have accused themselves of minor larcenies in order to be put in with the thieves.[380]

Since the visit made by Josephine Butler in 1874 and that of the municipal councillors of the Seine in 1878, the running of Saint-Lazare had been at the center of the prison debate. The intense campaign against the establishment waged by the abolitionists and the accusations launched by the public against the Sisters of Marie-Joseph explain the timid reforms finally initiated between 1887 and 1890[381] and the placing of the prison in 1887 under the authority of the Ministry of the Interior.

As we have seen, administrative detention was also current practice in the provincial towns. In 1887 the number of prostitutes under detention at Rouen was such that the prison premises could not cope with them. During the three-year period 1884 to 1886, at a time when there were between 185 and 290 registered prostitutes in the city, the prison authorities recorded 4,037 admissions of prostitutes to the Bonne-Nouvelle prison; the total number of days of detention rose to 36,853, not counting the 8,572 days spent in custody for nonpayment of legal expenses and fines. During the same period, the registered prostitutes of Rouen were fined 73,775 francs in fines but paid only 819 francs, preferring to be locked up rather than pay their debts.[382]

At Lyons, sentences of three to twenty-one days were served in the *maison de correction* of Saint-Paul.[383] At Marseilles, because of the by-laws of 1878, prostitutes served their sentences in the police cells or in the prison of Les Présentines. In 1904,[384] after neoregulationism had become widespread, ninety-six municipal by-laws still required the sequestration of prostitutes who failed to turn up for their health checks, and twenty-seven of them specified no maximum sentence. Sentences were served in the police cells in forty-three of these towns, in the local prison in eight, in the high-security cell in eleven, and in the *maison d'arrêt* (short-term prison) in seven. As a result, in sixty-nine localities there was a confusion between administrative detention and the detention of those accused or found guilty of offenses. Only fifteen municipalities removed any penal character from this kind of detention by sending the punished prostitutes to a hospital, a dispensary, or some other kind of care facility.

Regulationism was only one element in the overall scheme of the exclusion, marginalization, and confinement of all deviants and of the surveillance of widespread illegalities. If the prostitute was treated differently from the beggar or vagabond, it was because prostitution was recognized as having a social function that necessitated tolerance. It is clear that the system was a result of the anxiety inspired among the ruling classes by the biological and moral threat exerted by the laboring classes; despite the theoretical universality of the by-laws, only prostitution for the lower classes was severely supervised.

The extent of regulationism very soon became international. The practices set up in Paris during the first part of the century came to be known abroad as the "French system," and were widely imitated. When the abolitionist campaign erupted in France in 1876, the system had not yet been very seriously questioned. Since the defeat of the Commune, it had become worse in Paris and in Marseilles. Its advocates were in the upper reaches of the army and police and included a large number of the senior members of the medical profession; the church, at a time when the cult of Mary Magdalen was growing, gave its tacit approval. Since the Directory, the silence of the legislature on the matter also helped.

The failure of regulationism had long since been plain, however. The notes that Carlier had made during the Second Empire makes this abundantly clear, and the plentiful literature of the 1870s is thoroughly imbued with anxiety about the diffusion of illegal practices throughout the entire social body. It was because its failure was so patent, even in the eyes of its most faithful defenders, that the regulationist project lost impetus, while, in the abundant literature on syphilis, one can see the emergence of the arguments that were to form the basis of the success of neoregulationism, then the supreme attempt to justify repression.

We have seen the coherence of the system that confined the registered prostitutes in enclosed milieus. Let us now move on to a study of the simultaneous failure of and challenge to this system.

Part II

From Confinement
to Surveillance

3. The Failure of Regulationism

The Decline of Enclosed Prostitution

The number of establishments in the capital reached its maximum in the early years of the July Monarchy. Thereafter the decline was continuous; after 1856 it also affected the total number of inmates. Already very marked during the second decade of the Empire, the decline, which slowed down for a time, accelerated after 1881. The change touched even more widely the *maisons de tolérance* of the rest of the department of the Seine. In most of the larger cities the pattern became clear from 1856 on and increased between 1877–78 and 1885: the drop in the number of *maisons* was marked at Marseilles, Lyons, Bordeaux, and Nantes (see Figure 12).[1] Lille, which had had twenty-three tolerated establishments in 1876, had no more than six in 1888.[2] At Le Havre the number declined from thirty-four in 1870 to twelve in 1890. In 1874 the subprefect of Brest noted the decline of enclosed prostitution.[3] Yet during the same period, all these urban areas saw an increase in population. It should be noted that the crisis in the *maisons de tolérance*, which appeared so clearly and so early in the larger cities, was a European and even a worldwide phenomenon.[4]

If one analyzes the results concerning nine of the main urban centers,[5] one is led to observe that the decline in the number of tolerated establishments and of their inmates was not general; it affected the medium-sized towns as a whole only later. In these towns the decrease was scarcely perceptible between 1876 and 1886, when the number of establishments fell only from 731 to 717. Between 1886 and 1901, the decline continued to be gradual: at the beginning of the century 632 tolerated establishments were still functioning in these medium-sized towns. Table 9,[6] which shows the rise and fall in the number of establishments

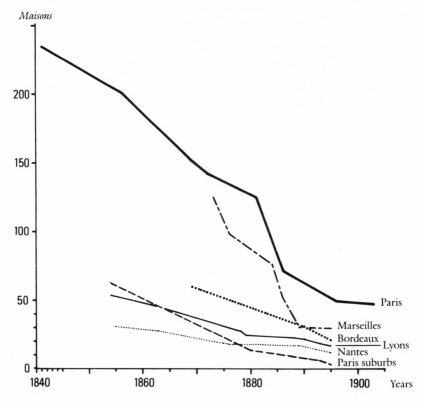

Figure 12. The decline in the number of *maisons de tolérance*. (Unpublished documents of the extraparliamentary commission of the vice squad, reprinted in Fiaux, 1988, I, 355.)

in the five departments forming our sample, confirms both the overall decline and the diversity of the regional situations.

Ever since the Second Empire,[7] specialists have pondered the causes of this decline, without always perceiving the main reason. Haussmannization resulted in the destruction of a number of long-standing *maisons* situated in sleazy districts of the larger cities. The brothels destroyed in the Ile de la Cité and in the area around the Louvre were not replaced. The sudden expansion of the cities meant that the traditional location of the brothels no longer corresponded to that of the clientele, who had moved out to the periphery. This dispersal of demand gave rise to a certain neglect of the specialized quarters. When establishments were set up in accord with the new geographic distribution of the clientele, they were usually lodging houses for independents or unregistered brothels.

Several economic factors also militated against the *maisons de tolérance*.

Table 9.   Changes in the number of *maisons de tolérance* in five departments between 1856 and 1901.

Department	Number of *maisons*					
	1856	1866	1876	1886	1896	1901
Finistère	14	17	15	20	21	12
Seine-et-Oise	18	21	21	19	17	13
Charente-Inférieure	12	15	17	18	20	19
Hérault	27	33	39	43	20	9
Meurthe-et-Moselle	18	14	16	18	20	19
Total	89	100	108	118	98	72

Even during the Second Empire, the exorbitant rise in price of the *tolérances* and increasing rents made the acquisition of a *maison* a hazardous undertaking. This period saw more closings of small and medium-sized establishments. Opening an unregistered brothel or turning a *tolérance* into a lodging house for independents involved fewer risks and smaller investment. It should be added that running a lodging house open to independent prostitutes did not require bookkeeping as meticulous as did operating a *maison de tolérance.*

Above all, the running of a *maison de passe,* a *maison de rendez-vous,* or a bar with a back room did not present problems of recruitment, whereas, after 1880, the keepers of the *tolérances* had some difficulty in finding employees.[8] They were increasingly forced to resort to agents, who constantly raised the price of their "parcels"; the emergence of the theme of the white slave trade was, to some extent, merely a reflection of the new difficulties faced by the brothel-keepers. This situation enabled the women to demand better pay, and it became difficult for their mistresses to exercise over them the total control they had once enjoyed.

Since the introduction of the regulationist system, the *maisons* had benefited from the protection of the authorities and, in Paris, from the vigilant attention of the prefecture of police. From 1876 on, the latter was violently criticized by the radicals on the municipal council, and it became difficult for the police to act as openly in favor of the *maisons de tolérance* as they had previously. Fearing scandal and press campaigns that would stir up public opinion, the prefecture granted licenses to open *maisons de tolérance* with some reluctance. Some provincial municipalities, albeit not many, were now also hesitant to grant new licenses; those of Salins, Pontarlier, Courbevoie, and Amiens even went so far as to forbid, either temporarily or permanently, enclosed prostitution in the areas under their jurisdiction. In short, the struggle against arbitrary police action in the capital, the greater susceptibility of public opinion to human rights, and the development of what I shall call a concern for municipal respectability, not to mention the spread of anti-Malthusian ideas, represented so many factors whose influence combined to the detriment of the *maison close*.

In fact, they merely expressed indirectly the influence of the real cause of the decline: a change in sexual demand.[9] The *maison de tolérance* declined because it had lost most of its clientele. In the larger towns, and especially in Paris, the masses of immigrants had now been to some extent integrated; the spread of the values and behavior patterns of the petty bourgeoisie had altered attitudes. The brothel, the "seminal sewer" to which men came to satisfy a physiological need, had lost much of its attraction. Meanwhile, the urge to seduce had considerably increased. In the working classes and in the lower middle class, the unregistered prostitute gained ground daily, while the nudity and paraphernalia of the brothels were rejected with disgust by more and more men. The competition offered by the independents and new forms of prostitution[10] put certain categories of *maison* out of business. Even in the provinces, "the *maison de tolérance* died of itself: the commercial traveler, who was its most faithful client, turned away from it; instead he had relations with barmaids and servant girls," declared Iriart d'Etchepare,[11] with some exaggeration it is true, to the extraparliamentary commission.

Public opinion found it increasingly difficult to accept the enclosure and confinement of women; it goes without saying that the spread of feminism was not unconnected with this development. In a society that exalted work,[12] prostitution was less and less easily tolerated. To appreciate this, one has only to consider the number of complaints that flooded in to the vice squads.[13] There was an increase in petitions and in court cases brought by landlords against brothels for lowering property values. Carlier had already stressed in the notes he had made in the closing years of the Empire that the *maison de tolérance* was being isolated, whereas, under the Restoration, it had been valued by a larger number of small tradesmen whose fortune it had helped to make.[14] The shift in attitude of the local people and shopkeepers to the *maison close* merely reflected the new distaste in public opinion for this form of prostitution.

This process was considerably accelerated with the passing of the law of July 17, 1880, which deregulated the sale of alcoholic drinks. This gave rise to an immediate increase in procuring in wine shops; many wine merchants set up back rooms where unregistered prostitutes, whether or not they also worked in the shop, could sell themselves.[15] Sometimes the prostitutes, acting alone or in association with others, opened a drinking place with the intention of selling themselves to their clients.

By the end of the century, in Paris at least, the *maison de tolérance* intended for a popular or petty-bourgeois public no longer had a place: if it were to escape ruin, it had to specialize or be turned into something else. Léon-Joseph Malbraque, the keeper of a *maison* at 106 boulevard de La Chapelle, expressed the problems of establishments along the periphery of the capital in a letter addressed to the prefect of police in 1893:

> I am invaded on every side by unregistered prostitution, and it would not be untrue to say that here everything is prostitution except me; the street women are constantly soliciting in front of my building and are not moved on from morning to night . . . Nobody, whether from the provinces or abroad, can come to the *maison* without being harassed, pulled to one side, and solicited a hundred times; these women tell clients not to go there, that it will be too expensive, that they'll be robbed, beaten, etc.[16]

According to him, the hotel at number 104 housed between fifteen and twenty prostitutes, not to mention those who worked in the back room of the wine merchant on the ground floor, where the pimps gathered. The hotels at 114 and 116 were also brothels.[17] To conclude, the keeper requested an audience with the prefect in order to explain to him the difficulties of those like himself, among whom, he writes, taking up in simple language the lineaments of regulationism,

> there are many good family men, honest tradesmen, serious taxpayers, who, if they were given some support, could be of real service to the police, to morality, and to good morals. For close on ten years I have had the misfortune to invest my meager savings in this business, which I have defended selflessly and steadfastly; I have made a study of real morals, and many of my colleagues working in the same line of business honestly and morally could, I believe, be of service if summoned and listened to by the departmental chiefs when small changes are made in the by-laws.[18]

Such complaints, one may be sure, were not isolated; on April 26, 1876, the keepers of the *maisons de tolérance* in Marseilles signed, in the name of public morality, a petition against the soliciting practiced by independent and unregistered prostitutes.[19] In 1903 the situation of the keeper of the brothel of Saint-Nicolas-du-Port proved particularly difficult: his *maison* was in crisis; he could not reconvert it because the building, especially designed to comply with the authorities' requirements, "is good only to be used for the thing required of it";[20] it had no opening onto the street, and the internal arrangement of the premises corresponded to its use. Furthermore, it had been agreed in 1881, when the *maison* had been opened, that the tenant should pay two hundred francs a year to the office of charities; this he had regularly done. If, on top of that, he had to pay for a license,[21] it is understandable that he should claim that he could not "earn [his] living."[22] He also complained that the inmates were leaving his establishment to become café maids or unregistered prostitutes. He called for "serious" police repression and demanded that those inmates who wanted to leave his establishment should be expelled from the city. The keepers also criticized the severity of the health check. The keepers of Nancy sent a petition to the prefect complaining about Dr. Vigneron, whom they accused of ruining them.[23]

Despite the crisis, new establishments were set up, especially in the Midi; most of them did little more than get by, which confirms the longer-term malaise. The most typical example of these failures is perhaps that of the *maison de tolérance* opened at La Seyne in 1901. Situated outside the town itself "in an airy district,"[24] the establishment was specially built to conform to the most modern rules of hygiene; the personnel consisted entirely of educated young women; the house rules guaranteed the inmates' "well-being."[25] No disease had been detected during health checks. Despite all its advantages, the establishment failed to prosper. This example, however, is testimony to the permanence of a utopian project of the ideal brothel.[26]

From the Maison Close to the Maison Ouverte

Certain keepers were able to adapt and managed to turn their establishments partly into *maisons de passe* or *maisons de rendez-vous*. The relative openness of the officially tolerated establishments is remarked by almost all witnesses; it demonstrates the final failure of the regulationist project. The practice of clients giving presents to their partners began to spread,[27] and in some of the *tolérances* the inmates enjoyed greater financial independence from the keeper. It was becoming increasingly easy for them to come and go as they pleased. The obligation to padlock the windows had gradually ceased to be complied with, at least in the capital.

The keepers of the *maisons* intended for a petty-bourgeois clientele tended more and more to take in *pensionnaires*—prostitutes who were free to lead their lives as they wished, who were paid by the client and simply owed rent to the keeper. These establishments became, therefore, more *maisons de passe* than *maisons closes*. To attract a reluctant clientele, some brothel-keepers in Paris had even taken to sending the inmates out to solicit on the boulevards or outside dance halls.[28] The practice also developed of hiring *filles de maison* for parties that took place outside the establishment. At Salins, the keeper obtained girls for petty-bourgeois clients who wanted to give "naturist balls"[29] and sometimes even to schoolboys wanting to spend an agreeable afternoon. In order to stay in business the keeper at Saint-Nicolas-du-Port had to send his girls out to find clients in the town.[30]

Sometimes the keeper used various subterfuges to attract a clientele whose new tastes she was familiar with. Thus certain officially tolerated establishments deliberately gave themselves the appearance of unregistered brothels and required unnecessary precautions on the part of the client.[31] Dr. Fiaux even mentions certain *maisons closes* disguised as fashion workshops, in which the keepers would offer clients what were supposedly underage apprentices but who were in fact registered prostitutes on the list of the prefecture of police.

Gradually the *maison close* was also turned into a sort of tolerated *maison de rendez-vous;* the keepers, in addition to performing their traditional activities, arranged meetings between their clients and local working-class women. The spread of bourgeois adultery provided new opportunities; indeed, many unfaithful wives had realized that the *maison close* offered greater security than bachelor apartments or hotel rooms. As a result, some tenants partly reconverted their establishments; others received couples in a separate apartment.[32]

The changes undergone by the *maisons* situated inside the *quartier réservé* at Marsailles are clear evidence of this openness and certainly prove that the process was irreversible. Here, however, one cannot attribute the change to the competition offered by unregistered prostitutes working in nearby brasseries or wine shops, for there were none in the district. The clientele, made up for the most part of sailors, remained faithful to the *maisons* and to the registered prostitutes and seemed less attracted than others to the unregistered ones. Within the red-light district itself, there was scarcely any competition from unregistered establishments. In Marseilles the administration continued to favor the *tolérances,* and the position of the police remained firm; their authority had not yet been undermined by press campaigns. In short, tradition was entirely on the side of the *maison close*. And yet, even inside the *quartier réservé* the *maison close* was undergoing extensive changes as a result of a common accord reached between keepers, prostitutes, and their clients. More and more the women tended to live outside rather than in the *maisons,* which gradually became tolerated *maisons de passe.*

Thanks to the work of Dr. Regnault we are able to follow this process in detail. The *maisons closes* as such, which numbered 125 in 1873, numbered no more than 31 in 1889 and 12 in 1897. Most of the keepers applied for their establishments to be turned into *maisons ouvertes* or *maisons libres,* which were a sort of lodging house set up in the *quartier réservé* and officially tolerated. The women did well out of them: they came and went as they pleased and had only to pay the keeper the price of their room (between 2.50 and 5 francs a day around 1890). They were paid for their services directly by the client. According to Dr. Regnault, the prostitute could thus make between 15 and 20 francs a day, and 30 or 35 francs on Sundays.[33] It is true, however, that she had to pay for her own clothes and medical examinations and ran the risk of being thrown out by the keeper if she could not pay her rent.

The keeper of a *maison ouverte* no longer had to concern herself with recruiting inmates or getting them from agents; she did not have to worry about clothes or health checks; her accounts were greatly simplified; she could set up her establishment without a large amount of capital; waiting rooms and salons were no longer necessary; and her profits were often higher than before. In the *maisons ouvertes* the prostitutes had to attract their clients themselves; they stood in front of the building or on the lodging-house stairs. This enabled the keeper to do without the services of the duenna, who, at Marseilles, had accompanied the prostitute, for the authorities now allowed the prostitute herself to stand in front of the *maison close.*[34] As for the client, he was pleased to be able to make his choice even before going into the establishment.

The early transformation of prostitutional structures at Béziers is an even better illustration of the openness of the *maisons de tolérance,* but it has to be admitted that the situation there was unique, as was the extent of prostitution in the town. By the beginning of the twentieth century, the *maisons closes* had long since disappeared from the town and the by-laws of 1861 governing them had become obsolete. Certain furnished houses at Béziers were regarded by the authorities as "not unregistered *maisons de débauche*"[35] and "not subject to regulation . . . The women who live there in exchange for the payment of a fixed sum are free to come and go as they please and *to receive whom they like.*"[36] They were neither *maisons de tolérance* nor *maisons de passe* in the strict sense. "The landladies or keepers were registered only as licensees and payers of indirect taxes. There is no by-law concerned with the closing of such establishments."[37]

From the Maison de Tolérance to the Maison de Débauche

As we have seen, the *maisons closes* survived, especially in town centers. Indeed, the crisis did not affect the better class of *tolérance*. As a result, the institution continued, but it no longer corresponded to the regulationist prescriptions which called for plainly furnished brothels where sexually excited men could, quite simply, satisfy their desires. The turn-of-the-century *maison close* survived because it became a veritable *maison de débauche,* if not a temple to the perversions, intended to satisfy an aristocratic or bourgeois clientele largely consisting of strangers in search of refined eroticism.

In short, the only *tolérances* to survive and even to expand were those that were not in competition with the hotels and lodging houses because their functioning involved both considerable investment and a specialized personnel. Of the forty-seven *tolérances* surviving in Paris in 1903, eighteen were first-class *maisons* worth between 200,000 and 300,000 francs.[38]

The elaborate decoration and extensive equipment of these establishments explain the high prices levied on the clients. The interior decoration of the great fin-de-siècle *tolérances* was extravagant. Many keepers were determined to renovate their establishments on the occasion of the universal exhibitions of 1878, 1889, and above all 1900. Again, although picturesque description is not my purpose here, I shall quote from the accounts of some of these establishments to be found in the Meunier report:

> A Swiss rock, with a marvelous grotto and a rustic staircase, is one of the curiosities and one of the mysteries of the establishment [situated in the rue Chabanais]. The grand staircase is monumental. There are mirrors everywhere, on all the walls and all the ceilings; there are soft, very thick carpets everywhere and in every room; there are hangings everywhere; dazzling electric lights everywhere; and everywhere perfumes in this temple of Love, the priestesses of which are naked.[39]

The ground floor of the establishment in the rue M—— was occupied "by a very rich Greek temple."[40] Here were opera settings, there scenes of an Oriental paradise, Louis XV salons, Calypso's caves. Everywhere was an "electric fairyland," a novelty for most of the clients and one that Dr. Fiaux accused of abetting "sexual hypnotism" and "derangement of the brain."[41]

One finds the same refinement in the paraphernalia intended to satisfy what were now being defined as the perversions. These practices had, of course, long been current in the brothels, but industrialization and the spread of an aristocratic eroticism to the bourgeoisie led to a proliferation of new equipment. Thus machinery for voyeurism was much improved. Forty years before, wrote Dr. Fiaux in 1892, these were simply oblique holes drilled into walls or cupboards; "nowadays, by a skillful arrangement of draperies hung over doors, wall hangings on which engravings and pictures have been clumsily applied, or thanks to tubes fixed into walls and fitted with binoculars, or acoustic horns, the spectator can see and hear from a small adjoining room: an installation with adjustable seat, night-light, etc., is conveniently provided."[42] Here "one pays for one's seat as one might for a stall at the theater."[43]

The first-class *tolérances* thus increased the number of spectacles and tableaux vivants, in which the inmates, entirely naked, abandoned themselves to homosexual practices on a large black velvet carpet or in rooms hung with black satin to bring out the whiteness of their bodies. In other establishments the inmates were content to assume plastic poses on turntables operated by an electrical mechanism.[44] Sometimes sexual monstrosities such as hermaphrodites or scenes of bestiality were displayed. According to Dr. Fiaux,[45] certain *tolérances* had made a specialty of the spectacle of women having sexual intercourse with Great Danes, which had become fashionable in society, or with Newfoundland mongrels, which were very common in the capital.[46]

The keepers of the deluxe *tolérances* possessed "a complete arsenal of sexual tortures,"[47] in particular for flagellation,[48] and a whole series of gadgets now to be found in sex shops but then produced in a much more refined manner. In this area, too, there was a marked shift; "straps with thongs of perfumed leather, silk cords for binding, small bunches of nettles" were now out of fashion.[49] Now Belgian or German factories provided the keepers with new equipment, such as Dr. Mondat's suction pump,[50] machinery for giving localized electric shocks, condoms of all kinds, not forgetting dildoes from England[51] and the harness that allowed a woman to strap on an artificial penis to satisfy "shameful sodomites"[52] or high-society lesbians. The keeper also had at the disposal of the clientele a series of supposedly aphrodisiac drugs such as tincture of phosphorus and Spanish fly.

Collections of licentious albums, some from Japan (*The Island of Women, The Island of Men*), were presented to clients at the most expensive *tolérances*. In the art of obscene photography isolated nudes gave way, more and more, to tableaus of group sex or scenes that often depicted couples disguised as monks or nuns having sex.

Obviously the use of all this equipment involved a qualified personnel, who sometimes had to undergo a veritable apprenticeship. As Dr.

Fiaux remarks, the inmates of the *tolérances* often acquired a certain sense of professional duty and took a pride, for instance, in outdoing their colleagues in the way they stroked their client's bodies.[53] The practice of oral sex, then regarded, like sodomy, as the most abject of all, and which Professor Ricord once defined as "insanity of the genito-labial nerve,"[54] was widespread in the first-class *tolérances*. According to Léo Taxil—and this is evidence from a client—some brothel-keepers kept *essayeurs* whose role was to teach the inmates such practices.[55] The women of a deluxe *tolérance* also had to learn kissing of the anus (anilingus) and anal sex, and how to satisfy lesbian clients. All the evidence goes to show that there was a marked increase in upper-class lesbian demand during the first decades of the Third Republic. In 1881 Dr. Paul Dubois declared that the Maison du Chabanais had specialized in satisfying that demand. In some of the deluxe *tolérances* the keepers made it quite plain to new inmates that they "would also be for women."[56]

It goes without saying that group sex, supper orgies, and in particular the *partie carrée* (partner-swapping) were common practices in these establishments. Rooms furnished with two beds, two sofas, and two washstands and decorated with huge mirrors were especially designed for this purpose. The women also had to wear all kinds of costumes to satisfy clients who, through substitution, were trying to possess a beloved who had jilted them. In some establishments this was a regular feature: to satisfy male fantasies the inmates dressed up as brides, nuns, or bluestockings of the Directory period.[57] Often the clothes matched the decor.

Despite the regulations, certain deluxe establishments also accepted homosexual men, who could dismiss the women who had accompanied them upstairs and be left alone in the rooms designed for *parties carrées*. When a gentleman requested it, the keeper might send for a young man of her acquaintance who would be willing to sodomize the client.

It is not my intention to embark on a detailed description of all the various practices that the inmates were expected to perform for their clients[58] but simply to mention these activities insofar as they went beyond venal sex. It is quite clear that during the final decades of the century, venal practices had become much more elaborate. Of course sadism, masochism, bestiality, and other refinements had existed in the brothels long before they became objects of study for the sexologist.[59] It cannot be denied, however, that, just as the 1970s saw the proliferation throughout society of erotic images, records, magazines, and gadgets, so the final decades of the nineteenth century, despite all the efforts of legislation and of the innumerable societies for the improvement of morals, saw the spread, at least through the lower-middle and middle classes, of tastes, fantasies, and techniques that had formerly been the preserve of aristocratic eroticism.

It is also clear that this development was bound up with artistic and literary movements that had brought eroticism to the forefront. Prostitution and its world had become essential themes in fiction and painting;[60] symbolist and decadent literature and art testified to a collective neurosis that found expression through a vertiginous attraction for, as well as a morbid fear of, female sexuality. It was also at about this time that serious efforts were made at classifying what were now being termed the perversions: while Sacher-Masoch gave his name to practices that may be regarded as traditional,[61] Krafft-Ebing proposed an exhaustive table of sexual behavior.[62] Throughout Europe homosexuality was the subject of trials that aroused a great deal of attention; Ricord, Charcot, Magnan, Ball, and Westphal turned their efforts to what they regarded as a pathological phenomenon. The study of hysteria was making great strides; in short, the *scientia sexualis* was being founded in the West.[63] Is it surprising, then, that refined erotic practices, which bourgeois husbands may have wanted to ask of their wives but could not, should be the object of an industry and commerce whose prosperity contrasted with the crisis then afflicting many of the smaller *maisons de tolérance?*

These considerations also explain the relative stability of the number of *maisons* in the smaller and medium-sized towns. In those places too, practices were changing; as early as the beginning of the Third Republic, Dr. Homo was stressing the alterations that had come about in the sexual behavior of clients, as perceived by the older prostitutes in the *tolérances* of Château-Gontier. In the past the *filles de maison* did not usually practice oral sex, and when one of them did, her fellow inmates would make her "eat by herself."[64] Recently, however, the young men who frequented the brothels only wanted to have their pleasure "by unnatural means, usually *ab ore*,"[65] and were avid spectators of female homosexual acts. This type of establishment, which was often the only one in a small town, also became the focus in the last decades of the century for the kind of circle that Maupassant had described in *La Maison Tellier.* Here men came to be initiated into the latest Parisian eroticism. They would listen to fashionable music-hall singers on the earliest gramophones, surrounded by women wearing negligees inspired by the couture of the capital, while leafing through, under elaborate electric lighting, magazines or albums of licentious photographs. The brothel became a place of escape, a place to get away from one's ordinary life, a place where one could make up for the austerity of life at home. There, new forms of sociability were developed between the petty-bourgeois men of the area and a society of women who, in a way, helped to refine their sensibility as well as their sensuality.

The evolution that I have described seems to have had contradictory consequences. Whereas the inmates of the second-class establishments saw their situation improve, the living conditions of the inmates of the deluxe *tolérances* deteriorated. "The greater the elegance of a *maison de tolérance*, the more odious the situation of the inmate becomes," Turot wrote in 1904.[66] The capital now needed to open a deluxe *tolérance* capable of satisfying the tastes of a blasé clientele, together with the expense of running it, drove the keepers to make their employees work harder than before. This is what emerges from the inquiries carried out by the Paris municipal council,[67] by the extraparliamentary commission, and by Dr. Fiaux.

In 1904 the inmates of the great Parisian *tolérances* had to respond to the first summons at any time between midday and 3 A.M. and go down to the salon ready for work; it is evident that the daily number of clients accepted by each of these women had increased. Their living quarters were as unhealthy as ever. In the same year, in forty-five cases out of forty-seven, the employees were forced to live in.

One cannot, therefore, speak without qualification of the decline of the *maison de tolérance* in the second half of the nineteenth century. Nonetheless, the evolution that I have described is evidence of the failure of the regulationist plan to confine extramarital sex to certain enclosed places, under strict administrative supervision, thereby, it was hoped, arresting the development of excessive, unnatural, or quite simply illegal sex. The failure of enclosure was evident in the case of a large number of *tolérances;* affected by competition from the lodging houses and by the shift in sensibility, they were gradually forced to open up in order to survive and to some extent transform themselves, the humbler ones into *maisons de passe,* the others into *maisons de rendez-vous.*

The failure of surveillance was no less evident, and the end of the century was certainly the high point of the deluxe brothel. If only the larger deluxe *tolérances* continued to prosper, this was not merely because of a process of concentration but rather because of a greater demand for elaborate eroticism. Far from being the sexual outlet envisaged by Parent-Duchâtelet and the regulationists, the brothel became a laboratory in which new sexual requirements were worked out. This was certainly what des Esseintes realized when he imagined initiating, free of charge, a young worker into the eroticism of the great *tolérances* and thus leaving him, for the rest of his life, frustrated in his everyday sexuality.[68]

The dual evolution that I have discerned corresponds to a dual transformation in demand: the new taste throughout society for seduction and for more exotic practices among a minority of privileged people. It was not until the 1870s, a time when the decline of the *maison de tolérance* was well under way and was perceived as such, that we see the beginnings of the abolitionist campaign against the *tolérance*. The anti-*tolérance* discourse was, it seems, simply the belated reflection of changes in behavior; it merely expressed, after some delay, the evolution in sensibility and in the nature of demand in venal sexuality. The latter phenomenon, to which I shall return at length, seems to have been one of the major elements in the social evolution. Before approaching it, however, I shall analyze the other aspects of the failure of the regulationist project.

Changes in the Traditional Forms of Unregistered Prostitution

Since the establishment of the regulationist system, the authorities had distinguished between tolerated (registered) and clandestine (unregistered) prostitution. They claimed to be involved in a tireless campaign to root out the latter, with a view of its ultimate disappearance. But in fact, the term *clandestine* had lost almost any meaning by the middle years of the Second Empire.[69] In Paris and in the larger provincial towns, the "clandestine" prostitutes solicited quite openly or were openly available in lodging houses and drinking places. The terms *filles soumises* and *filles insoumises* would be more appropriate, although it should not be forgotten that the latter ran a constant risk of being arrested and having their names recorded in the registers of official prostitution.

It is obviously very difficult to draw up a table of the various forms of unregistered prostitution and of the procuring that went with it. To begin with, one must define what was then understood by prostitution, because it has to be admitted that those who have examined this problem are far from being in agreement. Littré's dictionary regarded as a prostitute any woman who indulges in indecent behavior ("any woman of bad morals"). Many authors failed to distinguish clearly, in the case of women, between sexual freedom, debauchery, and prostitution, which, it will be remembered, were for Parent-Duchâtelet the successive stages of female decline. In 1888 Dr. Reuss still made no distinction between debauchery and prostitution, and saw the latter only as the popular form of the former.[70] Indeed, the imprecision and semantic evolution of the terms *demimonde* and *demimondaine* are significant in this regard; originally[71] they referred to women who had become free (widows, separated women, foreign women) but who lived on the fringes of society and whose matrimonial status was unclear. In short, these women, as a result of some public scandal, constituted a sphere separate from the *monde* (high society) and from honest wives, yet separate too from the world of courtesans, who accepted money for their favors; they gave themselves to whomever they pleased but did not sell themselves.[72] Very soon, certainly after the fall of the Empire,[73] and probably before,[74] the *demimonde* came to refer to those women who frequented the first *maisons de rendez-vous;* the term *demimondaine* now referred to a high-class prostitute.

For some, *venality,* the selling of sex, was the criterion of prostitution. For them, therefore, the kept woman was a category of prostitute; by the same token, they were led to regard as such a woman who gives herself to a particularly generous lover or the woman who gives herself to her husband's boss in order to improve his career prospects.

Most specialists, however, agreed on four criteria: (1) habit and notoriety;[75] (2) venality, to the extent that for the woman who practices it prostitution is an actual job, the main source of her income; (3) the absence of choice (that is, the prostitute gives herself to whoever asks her); and (4) the absence of pleasure or any sensual satisfaction as a result of the extent of her clientele. This definition, which was offered by way of example in 1890 by E. Richard,[76] chairman of the commission set up by the Paris municipal council, and by Dr. L. Butte, dispensary physician,[77] leads to excluding from the category of prostitutes courtesans, kept women (especially those who work), and occasional prostitutes, working women who try to increase their earnings with a little prostitution on Sundays or petty bourgeoises who sell themselves in order to pay some urgent bill.[78]

This last definition was agreeable to both liberals and neoregulationists; indeed, the latter tended to regard as prostitutes only women who presented a real risk of contagion—that is, those who gave themselves, without exercising any real choice, to a very large clientele. It goes without saying that such a definition—and it is the one most commonly accepted in quantitative inquiries—tends to minimize if not to exclude bourgeois prostitution and to underestimate the relative importance of working-class prostitution, a fact that must be taken into account.

Whereas the notion of the *fille soumise* is an uncontroversial one, since it refers to the prostitute who is included in official registers, that of the *fille insoumise,* or "unregistered prostitute," varies considerably, depending on the meaning given these terms. To the very extent to which they eluded the regulationist scheme, the "clandestines" represented a category of women that was not strictly marginalized. The image of the *fille insoumise* is therefore excessively vague. In attempting to describe her one might use stereotypes as clearly marked as those that define her counterpart. The unregistered prostitute merged into the community of "honest women," from which she emerged only intermittently. To a greater extent than the *fille soumise,* she was recruited from and operated in various milieus; it is therefore much more difficult to locate her in the social pyramid, especially as the constant circulation of the *insoumises* among the various categories of prostitution makes analysis difficult and any attempt at categorization unworkable. This mobility, which was strongly marked by Carlier at the end of the Second Empire, and even more so later, merely reflects the increasing mobility within urban society. Was it not one of Zola's more obvious intentions to make the reader of *Nana* sense the perpetual movement upward and downward to which the woman who had entered the cycle of venality was subjected? In short, if the unregistered prostitute inspired such terror in the specialists,[79] it was because she only *appeared* to be like other women, while moving throughout society and thus presenting an increased risk of moral and physical contagion. All this explains the relative failure of the attempts carried out by doctors who, like Martineau and Commenge, had been inspired by the methods of Parent-Duchâtelet to study unregistered prostitution.

One can also understand the uncertainty of authors who have tried to assess the numbers of women practicing unregistered prostitution. Sometimes the numbers proposed tell us about nothing but the fantasies or quasineurotic fears of those who advanced them. Whereas Carlier[80] estimated the number of unregistered prostitutes in the capital at between 14,000 and 17,000, Maxime du Camp,[81] in the years after the Commune, cheerfully proposed the figure of 20,000. After him, Lecour[82] arrived at a total of 30,000, the number most widely accepted during the 1870s, and which his adversaries Guyot and Fiaux[83] made their own. In 1881 Coué, the head of the second bureau, declared before the municipal commission that the number of unregistered prostitutes in the capital was 40,000,[84] while Dr. Desprès, who, as we know, had benefit of the help of the departments of the Ministry of the Interior, reached the figure of 23,000.[85] A few years later the detective force proposed a total of 50,000,[86] while Lassar estimated the number of prostitutes practicing in Paris in 1892 at 100,000.[87] In his report Richard reached different conclusions; refusing to take account of kept women, and therefore of the large numbers of linen maids and seamstresses who received subsidies from their bourgeois lovers, he came to the conclusion that only 10,000 or 11,000 unregistered women made prostitution a genuine profession.[88]

A reading of later estimates would suggest a fairly marked increase in numbers between 1890 and 1900. Indeed, Lépine, the prefect of police, proposed a total of between 60,000 and 80,000 for the early years of the twentieth century.[89] The most modest estimate comes from Turot, who, in his report to the municipal council, used the figure of 20,000 unregistered prostitutes in the capital. Again, it is true that the result varies according to the definition of the term. Thus Lépine, returning to the question in 1905, declared to the Society for Sanitary and Moral Prophylaxis that of the total number of unregistered prostitutes in Paris, only 6,000 or 7,000 walked the streets and were comparable in their behavior to the *filles soumises;* the others were "part-timers" (seamstresses with little work, unemployed maids and working girls), married women who frequented the *maisons de rendez-vous,* or kept women who were unfaithful to their lovers.[90] Similarly, in 1908 Dr. Le Pileur estimated that Paris had only between 12,000 and 15,000 unregistered prostitutes, but he did not include kept women.[91]

We have at our disposal, it should be said, the annual numbers for arrests of unregistered prostitutes carried out in Paris by the vice squad (see Figure 11); but once again fluctuations, if fairly small, are more a reflection of the intensity of repression than of the extent of unregistered prostitution. Nevertheless, if one is to accept the most moderate estimates, it would seem clear that in Paris unregistered prostitutes were far more numerous than registered ones, a fact that the large number of disappearances[92] has already suggested. Could there be more obvious proof of the failure of the regulationist system?

Inquiries carried out in the rest of France led to the same uncertainties. Desprès[93] arrived at a total of 18,061 unregistered prostitutes for the country as a whole, excluding the capital. It should be noted that he did not regard kept women as prostitutes and did not include them in his calculations. The breakdown according to the administrative function, and therefore the approximate size, of the towns is as follows: 12,585 unregistered prostitutes in the prefectures (5,000 at Lyons, 2,000 at Bordeaux, and 420 at Marseilles); 3,096 in the subprefectures; 1,697 in the main towns of cantons; and 585 in other communes.

Unfortunately, it is clear that the authorities who responded to the inquiry did not adopt identical criteria. How otherwise is one to explain the results: 105 unregistered prostitutes at Foix, 400 at Troyes, 150 at Bourges, Perpignan, and Orléans, 485 at Nîmes, 200 at Elbeuf, 90 at Caudebec, and only 100 at Lille, whereas there were 40 at Haumont, 50 at Rennes, 25 at Amiens, 10 at Versailles, 6 at Quimper, and above all 420 at Marseilles, where Dr. Mireur had estimated the number to be between 4,000 and 5,000, which is quite probable?[94]

We have to take into account, of course, regional habits and attitudes, which differed widely on this subject. Thus the answers to the inquiry tend to stress the prevalence of unregistered prostitution in the manufacturing towns (Lyons, Limoges, Troyes, the textile towns of Normandy), in the principal towns of the Midi (Nîmes, Montpellier, Béziers, Perpignan), and in Paris and Bordeaux, while the phenomenon seems to have been less developed in the ports (Brest, Marseilles, Toulon), where registered prostitutes were very numerous. The addition of the numbers proposed by Després concerning registered and unregistered prostitutes points out the overall prevalence of prostitution in the largest cities and in the main towns of Aquitaine, Provence, and above all Languedoc.

But once again, all these results must be regarded in a modal way; at most they allow us to produce an overall estimate of the scope of a phenomenon that in reality is beyond our grasp and to detect the places where it reached its maximum intensity.

There is unanimous agreement that unregistered prostitution expanded in the provinces between the beginning of the Second Empire and the end of the century; a comparison of the results obtained in 1879 with those of the investigation of 1902 for our sample also supports this view. Despite the absence of valid numerical data, it would be unscientific to deny the reality of this increase, which, in both Paris and the provinces, closely corresponds to the decline of enclosed prostitution and the emergence of new forms of prostitution, which I shall try to describe later. It is quite possible, however, that the violent campaign that attracted the attention of public opinion to prostitution led many observers to take account of phenomena that they had previously ignored and therefore to overestimate the growth of venality.[95]

Whatever the quantitative imprecision, one must still describe the structures of unregistered venal sex. "Unregistered prostitution is an institution that, while having no formal rules, functions nevertheless according to an established order," Dr. Martineau wrote.[96] Let us now try to discern, at every social level and through the most varied prostitutional practices, the nature of that order and the forms of procuring that determined it.

Demimondaines, Femmes Galantes, and Women of the Theaters and Restaurants

I shall rapidly describe the high-class prostitution associated with the pleasure-seeking society of the Second Empire. There exists an enormous, picturesque literature devoted to this milieu; I would simply direct the interested reader to it.[97] My purpose here is merely to situate these forms of prostitutional behavior in the social spectrum of venal sex. To do so I shall first try to discern what the *femmes galantes* had in common.

They were almost all unregistered, although, as we have seen, certain registered prostitutes sometimes managed to maintain fine careers.[98] The courtesan, whatever her origins and past, was seldom investigated by the police; were they to do so, her male protectors would soon have put an end to their tiresome inquiries.

All these women operated in isolation, at home, at whatever times suited them, whether they lived in an apartment, which was generally the case, or in a townhouse, as the wealthiest of them did. Their clientele was exclusively composed of rich men,[99] foreign aristocrats, *grands bourgeois* of finance or industry, members of the Parisian *bonne bourgeoisie*,[100] or rich provincials who specialized in immoral women on the decline. As good courtesans the *femmes galantes* exercised choice and were able, therefore, to maintain the illusion with which they surrounded themselves. Sometimes, if with decreasing frequency, they reserved their favors for a single lover. Generally, like certain independent registered prostitutes, they formed partnerships with a number of lovers, being careful to allow each his own day and night. The *femme galante* never practiced soliciting; she sold herself to whomever she pleased after some semblance of courtship or resorted to a "pick-up,"[101] as was done by the women who frequented cafés and late-night restaurants and even by the *grandes horizontales* on their rides through the Bois de Boulogne.

Of course, these *femmes galantes* were encountered only in the large cities, specifically in Paris, Lyons,[102] and certain watering places and seaside resorts; in the capital they frequented only the smart quarters in the center of the city, where they sometimes displayed, at their lovers' expense, a degree of luxury indispensable to the maintenance of their rank.

Usually the high-class prostitute was "launched"; she was the creature of some important procuress, an "ogress," sometimes simply her own mother. In fact, the structures of this form of procuring had evolved in the course of the century, as may be seen if we compare the activity of Asie in *Splendeurs et misères des courtisanes* with that of Zola's Tricon. Originally, launching was mainly the work of the local dressmakers or even laundresses. These women would lend magnificent clothes, sometimes belonging to their clients, to young women whose beauty or savoir-faire had caught their attention in the street. In return, they demanded substantial hiring fees. These dressmakers also acted as pawn-brokers, usurers, and intermediaries for the women they had helped to launch.

Although they did not completely disappear—far from it—these pro-curess-dressmakers seem to have declined in influence during the last decades of the century, probably because they were by then incapable of providing the considerable sums required to launch a *femme galante*. Meanwhile, the role of various tradesmen, especially upholsterers, had greatly increased. These upholsterers would set up the courtesans of their choice in apartments that they either owned or rented, and which they decorated and furnished in luxurious fashion. Furthermore, they would force the women to pay an exorbitant rent and to buy the decor and furniture on an installment plan. It often happened that such a woman, becoming insolvent before having paid off her debts, did a "moonlight flit"; this enabled the upholsterer to set up a new courtesan in an apartment whose contents he had already partly been paid for. Certain tradesmen did the same, and when the women had dragged themselves down with debts, had them completely under their control.

The procuresses extended their activities; like Tricon, who reigned over the elegant demimondaines of Longchamps, some of them had at their disposal a wide network of clients that enabled them to recruit and launch, with the help of agents who were sometimes dressmakers, not one or two young women but a whole group of *femmes galantes* in whose careers they invested large sums of money and from whom they earned substantial profits. By the end of the century this type of pro-curess had become hardly distinguishable from the mistresses of *maisons de rendez-vous*.[103] In short, high-class procuring, which was a genuine commercial enterprise, became structured throughout the century and probably concentrated among a smaller number of establishments, while the profits to be derived from it increased as this type of conduct spread throughout the bourgeoisie and enclosed prostitution declined.

By means of this process the *femmes galantes* became mere tools whose temporary fortune—and ruin—produced profits for "industrialists"[104] or tradesmen, who, like the landlords of the *tolérances,* were the principal beneficiaries of the constant changes at work in the world of commercial sex. Far from being parasites, the courtesans enriched these procuresses and upholsterers, not to mention the lovers (of either sex) who, very often, lived off them. The wretched end of the *femme galante* was not just a literary theme; the last moments of Lucie Pellegrin,[105] described by Alexis, seem to have been like those of most of the women of that class, although, in the absence of any quantitative study, the notion should be regarded with caution.

The world of *galanterie* was in fact more differentiated than I may have suggested so far. It represented a veritable melting pot at the center of which were the *déclassées*, aristocrats or bourgeois women and girls from the lower orders who had made good. Pierre de Lano stresses this variety in recruitment and the attraction, not to say obsession, that this social anomaly exerted over bourgeois males: "A bored lady of the manor, a misunderstood *bourgeoise*, a failed would-be actress, a peasant girl who had lost her innocence—she is all these things . . . She is the eternally unsolved riddle that intrigues and terrifies man."[106]

At the top of the pyramid was the *demimonde*, in the new sense of the term, comprising the *déclassées* or simply those women without class, victims of a scandal, divorcees,[107] those separated from or abandoned by their husband or lover, merry widows, rich foreign women whom the authorities could, when they pleased, send back out of the country.[108] It included the "poor lionesses," described by Emile Augier, who depended on *galanterie* to be able to buy the clothes that tempted them. Finally, it included young women from the lower classes who had been launched. Most of this last category do not seem to have come from the working classes as such[109] (Zola is in error here), but from the ranks of the *bourgeoisie populaire*,[110] young women who had reached a certain educational level without being able to take up an honorable profession. Very often this category included unsuccessful theatrical artists who had been forced to turn to *galanterie* as their main means of subsistence.

These demimondaines, who were variously called *lorettes*,[111] *lionnes*, and *cocottes* under the Second Empire, then *belles petites* and finally *grandes horizontales* under the Third Republic, soon invaded the world of fiction. The legendary escapades and glamorous lives of La Païva, Blanche d'Antigny, and Anna Deslions are still remembered.[112] It was this milieu that Zola researched before writing *Nana*, which claims in part to be a portrait of it; it was also this milieu that Flaubert, who knew it well, describes at length in his correspondence and which many artists depicted.[113]

The *grande horizontale* lived in a townhouse in the avenue de Villiers or near the Etoile or the Trocadéro, or, more modestly, in an apartment near the Madeleine or the place Saint-Georges, surrounded by a large household of servants, often supervised by her parents. There, in the midst of the most ostentatious luxury, she led an idle existence, mainly devoted to her toilette. She would not go out until 4 P.M., when she would be driven to the Bois, accompanied by her splendid equipage, to attend the races or to be seen at some private event, which would enable her to improve her conversation; the rest of her time would be taken up by evenings spent at the theater, especially at important first nights, followed by supper in a restaurant or at the home of friends. She would regularly receive her very mixed acquaintance at home.[114] This applied, however, mainly to the *cocottes* of the Second Empire and to the *grandes horizontales* of the first decades of the Republic; later, a relative democratization may be observed.

More representative of the new times, and also more numerous, were the women who frequented late-night restaurants and cafés, who usually sprang from the world of shop assistants and prostitutes working in "shops" that were in reality brothels. The women who frequented these restaurants lived in comfortable apartments let to them by upholsterers; they went out only in the evening; after receiving "old friends" and dining, they would go off to the vaudeville theaters, dressed rather outrageously, and, with the complicity of the maître d'hôtel, waiters, and even the manager,[115] end the evening in the *cabinet particulier,* or private room, of a late-night restaurant in the company of some rich foreigner or young man "living it up."[116]

The *femme de café*—and one is reminded of Zola's first descriptions of his Satin—represented the lowest type of *galanterie,* on the frontiers of unregistered prostitution. Unlike the street prostitute, what she was really looking for, with the help of the café waiter, was a *coucher,* "an individual she could spend the night with"[117] in a furnished room that she would rent, often by the night, in the district circumscribed by the rue de Rochechouart, the rue de Châteaudun, the rue Blanche, and the outer boulevard. In this quadrilateral, apartments, even whole buildings, were divided into furnished rooms and sublet to these *femmes de café* by the tenants, who also provided whatever refreshments the couple might want during the night. At dawn the *femme de café* would go off to join her pimp in Montmartre, before coming down again the next day at the aperitif hour, when she would sip absinthe. Among the *femmes galantes* who set out to pick up a lover who might subsidize their expenses, one ought to mention all the courtesans who concealed their identity,[118] those who claimed to be the wives of sailors at sea, soldiers on active duty, commercial travelers on their rounds, or unconsolable widows, who haunted the cemeteries like Les Tombales, described by Maupassant, and whom Macé calls *pierreuses de la mort*[119] ("streetwalkers of death"); they were not simply the product of the literary imagination.

Femmes d'Attente and Kept Women

These women lived on the frontiers of venal sex, since the union in which they lived with their lovers was often based on the bourgeois matrimonial model. These pseudowives were usually *femmes d'attente,* who enabled young bourgeois, artists, students, and clerks to enjoy sexual activity before contracting a late marriage or allowed impecunious petty-bourgeois bachelors, who could not afford to start a family, the illusion of living *en ménage.*

These *femmes d'attente* were, then, "substitute wives" for men who could not afford to marry, but sometimes, like Huysmans' Marthe, they were the mistresses of elderly gentlemen who were tired of the faded charms of an ill-tempered, frigid, or simply boring wife and who could not, like the eternal bachelor-students of the bourgeoisie of the Southeast, be content with affairs with servants.[120]

In Paris the kept women[121] were usually laundry maids, seamstresses, milliners, or sometimes florists employed in workshops in the center of the city. Being inadequately paid,[122] they sometimes had to use their charms to earn extra money. Conversations in the workshop,[123] the example of older women, and rivalries and jealousies soon persuaded the young apprentice to find herself a bourgeois lover, sometimes with the secret hope of eventually marrying him.

Usually the kept woman was installed in a furnished room or small apartment,[124] or the bourgeois man was content to buy her clothes and to take her out. Sometimes the lover would keep not only a married woman but also her husband. "A lot of old bachelors in Paris live in this way with honest couples,"[125] supporting these ménages à trois, notes Louis Puibaraud, former principal private secretary to the prefect of police.

In cities where there was a large amount of industry, the men of the local bourgeoisie recruited their mistresses from among the young factory workers. This was the case, during the Restoration, among the needle-makers of Rugles,[126] in the silk factories of Lyons,[127] and in the textile factories of Lille[128] and Valenciennes.[129] Sometimes the owners, but more often the foremen and other superiors, would extort compliance from the prettier working girls by offering the prospect of a job. The abolition of this *droit de cuissage* was tirelessly demanded at workers' and trade union congresses.[130] Such practices were common, for example, among the seamstresses of Roubaix,[131] who repaired faulty pieces of material at home, and among the porcelain-makers of Limoges,[132] who were forced to give themselves to the boss when they were held responsible for breakages, or even to the foremen when they wanted to be hired. It was the hostility of the workers to two of the foremen accused of these practices that triggered off in the porcelain capital the attempted uprising of 1905 and led to the "satyr hunts" which then spread through the streets of the town.[133]

The importance of these unions, or quasiménages, cannot be over-emphasized. These interclass sexual relations did indeed cause a double frustration and, to use Maurice Barrès's term, "irremediable misunder-standings."[134] They gave the young bourgeois an intimate knowledge of the proletariat, but only through its daughters and wives. It was with a pretty, young, but uncultivated working girl, whom he would soon tire of,[135] that he made his first sexual experiments. The difficulty of finding satisfaction in a relationship based on money is obvious, and by their very nature these unions reinforced the young man's tendency to see poor women as merely an instrument of pleasure. This image of sexual-ity was later to prove constrictive: it was to impede real fulfillment for couples in a genuine relationship and was to be the model, when disen-chantment with marriage set in, for some new, tempting relationship. It was these considerations that accounted, albeit only in part, for the unjust hostility of bourgeois parents to their sons' young mistresses and led Alphonse Daudet, for example, to dedicate his book *Sapho,* which he saw as a lesson for youth, "to my sons, when they are twenty."

It was inevitable that, for the kept women, such contacts beyond social barriers should result in confused feelings. Of course, the young mistress often continued to keep an *amant de coeur* from her own class; sometimes it would be the man who had taken her virginity. Neverthe-less there was a risk that she would feel sexually and emotionally torn between the two milieus.[136] The distant attitude of her bourgeois lover could not fail to increase her hostility toward the bourgeois male, a hos-tility sometimes tinged with nostalgia that could later be prejudicial to complete satisfaction when she tried to maintain a relationship with a young worker.

Increase in demand, bound up, as we shall see, with the numerical expansion of certain categories of bachelors, explains the development of these venal practices. From the last years of the Empire the young men of Château-Gontier were in the habit of keeping mistresses;[137] the young bourgeois of Roubaix and Tourcoing had mistresses at Lille,[138] while the sons of the local landowners chose theirs at Béziers. In Paris the demand was such[139] that kept women and *femmes galantes* often took on several lovers at once; at Marseilles some of them organized what were veritable gentlemen's clubs.[140]

While prostitution of various forms spread into new circles and tend-ed to be diluted, while, at the same time, the stereotype of the prostitute became blurred, the barriers separating various categories of venal wom-en were collapsing. "The *grisette* has disappeared; she has merged into the *insoumise,*" Carlier protested.[141] He added that the kept woman, as formerly understood, was also disappearing. The widespread demand by men for sexual pleasure and the vagueness of the boundaries between venal sex and the new habits of kept women now made it much easier for a young woman to slide into prostitution; a series of subtle transitions was in place to help her. It would be illogical, therefore, to approach unregistered prostitution in the strict sense without at least touching on fundamental forms of sexual behavior that are indispensable to any understanding of sexual practices in the last century but which only studies particularly devoted to them would have elucidated fully.

The Unregistered Prostitute

I shall now try to describe the oldest and most widespread forms of unregistered prostitution: those in which women living in lodging houses solicited in the streets or bars. It was from these categories that the *filles soumises* were directly recruited and within which most of the registered prostitutes who disappeared took refuge. This permanent osmosis explains the social proximity of the unregistered prostitutes and the *filles en carte;* the structures of procuring, however, were different in each case, and it is this that is the most important factor.

Itinerant prostitution. The essential task of the street prostitute was to solicit or to "pick up" clients. "Streetwalking" was no longer the same under the Third Republic as it had been at the beginning of the century;[142] the prostitutes were more itinerant than before.[143] When the *maisons de tolérance* were dispersed at the heart of an expanding urban space, the streetwalkers correspondingly enlarged their field of activity. They had begun in the shadowy districts of the center, moved to the outlying boulevards, then gradually took possession of the whole city. Their endless quest took the form, in Paris at least, of complex itineraries. The journey of the women from the periphery, where they lived, to the center, where they met their clients, was the broadest movement. This occurred in veritable waves; one may remember the tumultuous descent from the Bréda quarter to the area around the Opéra described by Zola[144] or the meticulous descriptions of Blanche's itineraries in Charles-Louis Philippe's *Bubu de Montparnasse.*[145] This movement was in stark contrast to the motionless string of prostitute-sentinels, who, positioned on a winter's night under the lampposts of the outer boulevards awaiting a client, seemed to Gervaise to be guarding Paris against some imaginary enemy.[146] Contemporary accounts provide a wealth of detail about these districts of the capital and the work of the prostitutes.

This geography was a shifting one; it varied according to the time of day and night, which makes description difficult. Prostitution began around 2 A.M. around Les Halles[147] and the rue de Venise. This quarter was then the area worked by the dregs of the prostitutes in the center of the capital. They roamed around the vegetable sellers' carts, sold themselves for fifty centimes or one franc,[148] and "accepted anything, even payments in kind, cabbages, carrots, whatever vegetables the tradesmen were selling in the nearby streets."[149] Between dawn and midday the streetwalkers were not very active, except, again, around Les Halles, which was frequented by a clientele of restaurant-owners, bursars, and servants come to buy provisions.

"It was only from one o'clock in the afternoon that the market in women began in Paris."[150] From then until nightfall the women would come down from La Villette, Ménilmontant, Belleville, Saint-Ouen, Clichy, and the eastern suburbs. Usually the prostitute, who worked in the afternoons, had a husband or lover; this explained why she never worked in her own district. The location of daytime prostitution, unlike nighttime prostitution, remained fairly precise. The main centers of activity were (1) the streets and alleys linking the Bourse with the Palais-Royal, via the rue Vivienne and the rue de Richelieu; (2) the boulevard Sébastopol and the streets that led down to the Louvre and the Palais-Royal, particularly the arcades of the rue de Rivoli, where the prostitutes solicited provincials,[151] foreigners, or Parisians who had left their wives in the department stores; (3) the district of the Bastille and the boulevards that link it to the place de la République (boulevard Voltaire, boulevard Richard-Lenoir); and (4) the *grands boulevards,* which, from the Château d'Eau to the Madeleine, linked the other three sites as well as three of the railway stations (the gares de l'Est, du Nord, and Saint-Lazare), the skating rinks, the Hôtel des Ventes, and the racetrack.[152]

By evening the prostitutes were everywhere. The thousands of women who tirelessly circulated on the sidewalks make localization imprecise, but certain itineraries and certain places were notable for a high density of prostitution. These may be listed, moving inward. First, on the very edge of the urban center was the ring of fortifications, where the *pierreuses* and *filles à soldats* prostituted themselves in the open air, at least when the weather was fine, for twenty sous and a half-liter of wine;[153] the same applied to the Bois de Boulogne and the Bois de Vincennes, especially around the camp of Saint-Maur. The Champs-Elysées had also, since the Second Empire, become a popular place for nocturnal soliciting. A third site was the line of the inner boulevards from the rue Poissonnière to the Madeleine. Next, the larger arcades, especially those around the Opéra, were the preserve of the more expensive prostitutes, especially in cold weather. The passage des Panoramas was the special preserve of such prostitution. In fact it was not without reason that Zola made it the center of prostitutional activity for the heroine of *Nana;* this was because the arbitrary arrest of Mme. Eyben was to trigger off the most serious of the campaigns undertaken against the prefecture of police. Mention should also be made of the passage Jouffroy, the passage Verdeau, and the passage de l'Opéra. Nearer the center, the districts traditionally given over to nocturnal prostitution such as the Palais-Royal, which has always attracted foreigners, the area around the place du Châtelet (rue de la Reynie, rue Quincampoix), the Bonne-Nouvelle district, the area around the portes Saint-Denis and Saint-Martin, the place des Vosges, the place de la Bastille and the surrounding area, as well as the streets bordering on the north of the Latin Quarter, close to the Seine (rue de la Harpe, rue Saint-Jacques, rue Saint-Séverin, rue Galande) also became the preserve of the lowest type of nocturnal prostitution. Finally, there were the large public gardens: the Luxembourg, the Jardin des Plantes, and, since 1871, the Tuileries. The distribution by district of the unregistered prostitutes arrested by the police[154] confirms this prostitutional geography.

Inside these sectors there were certain points of particular activity: the railway and bus stations and certain vaudeville theaters (the Moulin de la Galette, the Casino de Paris, the Jardin de Paris, Bullier, the Elysée-Montmartre, and above all the Folies-Bergère, whose "lower promenade, in other words the Marché aux Veaux, is a permanent whores' fair").[155] Mention should also be made of the dance halls, where very young men came "slumming" from the center, and which, to the great scandal of right-thinking people,[156] were veritable seedbeds for young prostitutes.

The situation in Paris[157] leads one to observe that there was no coincidence between the prostitutional space and the popular space, any more than between the criminal space and the popular space. Furthermore, this lack of coincidence tended to increase as the century went on, for both prostitution and crime. And only the kernels of prostitution survived within the popular space, since they also existed within bourgeois space.[158]

The links between prostitutional and festive space, though not very close, are sometimes clearer; thus it is obvious that the shift from the second district to the bourgeois districts of the center (from the Tuileries to the Champ-de-Mars) corresponds to a conquest of those same quarters by the prostitutes.

The descent of the women from the heights of the periphery to the center of the capital was seen all the more strongly as a threat in that it was identified, in 1871, with the descent of waves of common people in a revolutionary form. The Bastille, "a focal point . . . from which the revolutionary space was undoubtedly structured,"[159] as was proved by the resistance to the Versaillais, was also a center of venal sex. We should not be overhasty, however, and conclude that the prostitutional space and the revolutionary space were identical. The influx of women into the center expressed the subjection of the proletariat and not some plan for subversion;[160] it merely followed the movement of the labor force.

In the end, "the prostitutional space" of Paris, like the "alimentary space" defined by J.-P. Aron, is original.[161] Even more than "the popular space," whose resistance to Haussmannization has been demonstrated by J. Gaillard[162] and J. Rougerie, it was characterized by a certain rigidity.[163] But it also tended to expand with the opening up of the city and the increased mobility of the women at the very time when prostitutional practices were spreading through society as a whole.

The unregistered prostitutes were less dispersed, it goes without saying, in the large provincial cities. At Lyons they met in the parc de la Tête d'Or and in the neighboring streets; in Marsailles in the cours Belsunce, outside the *quartier réservé,* and along the allées de Meilhan; at Rouen their preserves were the Boulingrin and the cours Cauchois.[164] In 1902 Roubaix and Tourcoing had not yet regulated prostitution. The women preferred, therefore, to live there and come to work in Lille in the Saint-Sauveur district, around the rue des Etaques, where "a train brought them each evening and another took them back around two in the morning."[165]

The technique of soliciting varied according to the category of prostitute and the appearance of the client. "Are you going to make me rich?" was the usual formula for approaching a client. Some prostitutes were not afraid to grab a man by his sleeve and cling to him, even yelling insults at him if he refused their attentions. This is what happened when, according to Léon Bloy, the poet Barbey d'Aurevilly was nearly stoned by the crowd during the siege of the capital.[166] With the complicity of coachmen who specialized in this activity, the practice of soliciting from a carriage also began to spread.[167] By contrast, soliciting through an open window became less common,[168] which is explained by the increase in mobility. Certain particularly well-situated windows, however, were veritable gold mines; according to Macé, several apartments in the rue de Provence or the rue de la Chausée d'Antin were rented for up to a thousand francs a month on account of their particularly convenient windows; in that district "any window brought in between thirty and a hundred francs a day."[169] Distinctive signs were placed at the window: ribbons, flowers, a birdcage, or lamps indicated to the client whether "the prostitute was at home."[170]

It was in the rooms of lodging houses, which were also, it will be remembered, frequented by the *filles en carte,* that the unregistered streetwalkers prostituted themselves. Commenge estimated in 1896[171] that ten thousand lodging houses and restaurants in the capital were given over to this activity. They were mainly to be found in the central districts or, at the other extreme, in the most outlying areas.[172] It was rare for a prostitute to live in the same room to which she took her clients; generally speaking, she was content to use it for her work and to go back in the early hours of the morning to the hotel room she occupied on the edge of the city. Some prostitutes, it is true, built up a clientele among the owner and the usual tenants of the same lodging house. The price per room was generally between two and three francs in this type of hotel; it could vary, however, between twenty-five centimes and twenty francs, depending on the client's appearance.[173] A certain complicity grew up between the women and the landlord, who would warn them when the police arrived.[174] Of course, the erotic techniques used in such places were hardly refined;[175] what mattered was the number of visitors.

This form of prostitution was very widespread in the provinces. At Lyons[176] it was by far the most common; in that city it was directed at a relatively select male clientele. At Marseilles, according to the police commissioner in 1876,[177] go-betweens lodged the unregistered prostitutes in rooming houses, in groups of between four and nine. Each one paid three francs a month for her room; in addition, she spent nearly ten francs a day on her clothes and food and had to pay about ten francs to her pimp. In the evening, she had to earn an average of twenty-three francs to survive.

"Pretext shops." Even at the beginning of the century the clothes shops around the Palais-Royale had been converted by the women who ran them into centers of prostitution. This practice subsequently became more widespread: glove shops, collar and tie shops, and tobacconists in particular specialized in this activity in the 1870s.[178] By the end of the century many more kinds of shops had gone the same way. The glove shops, which were under strict police surveillance, were now "out of fashion," according to Virmaître,[179] a connoisseur on the subject. The practice had now spread in the center of the capital to shops selling engravings and photographs, to wine merchants,[180] perfume shops, bookshops, and above all "novelty" shops, which had either a back room or a room on the entresol or in the basement where the salesgirls prostituted themselves. According to Virmaître, there were over three hundred such shops in the capital, and the chairman of the extraparliamentary commission noted in 1904 that there had been a considerable

increase in this kind of procuring. At this time a large number of massage parlors or bathhouses[181] had also been converted to this kind of activity; some of them functioned as veritable *maisons de rendez-vous*.[182] The phenomenon also existed in the provinces, but its development was very unequal: pretext shops were rare in Lyons but very common in Bordeaux.[183]

Since I am dealing with the links that grew up between retail trading and prostitution, I should also mention—and this was a favorite theme of popular melodramatic, postromantic fiction at the end of the century—the women who owned small mobile stalls, especially the many flower-sellers, who were often lesbians and haunted the streets of the center of Paris and the Champs-Elysées.[184] Georges Berry, who devoted himself especially to the defense of young beggars, brought the problem before the deputies in 1892. That same year at Toulouse[185] the authorities shut down four of the eight florists' kiosks in the avenue La Fayette. These establishments, which had been veritable employment agencies for prostitutes, were kept by procuresses who sent little girls of twelve and thirteen "to deliver flowers" to customers' homes.

But to return to the pretext shops: each of these shops had two or three prostitutes, who were fed by the *patronne* but who received no pay. Indeed, the women had to share the money paid by their clients with the mistress of the establishment. According to Martineau,[186] the second-class shops were usually kept by two women who shared the profits. Originally the clientele of these clothes shops consisted mainly of rich old gentlemen who were regular customers of the firm and who were compliantly received by the young women, during working hours, in the workshops behind the store, and who were allowed certain familiarities in exchange for presents. Later the clientele consisted of very correct gentlemen, sent by pimps operating in the large cafés or late-night restaurants, as well as porters, waiters, and even interpreters in the case of foreign clients.[187]

When the client went to the counter to settle his purchases, he was unequivocally made to understand that he could, for an additional sum, purchase another sort of merchandise. In view of the small number of prostitutes working in each of these shops, there were frequent changes of staff, effected with the help of specialized procuresses. These were often, at the same time, go-betweens working at home; posing as agents claiming to sell liquor or objects d'art,[188] or even as charity organizers,[189] they gained access to people's apartments, ever on the lookout to corrupt the young women they met or lying in wait for them outside their places of work. As we have seen, it was from among these shop girls, who soon got used to the ways of bourgeois men, that the women who haunted late-night restaurants and cafés were recruited.

Mention should be made here of the most degrading form of prostitution to have emerged in the course of my research: that practiced in many of the public lavatories in Marseilles. Each of these establishments was run by a manageress who employed one or two women who, apart from cleaning the premises, had to satisfy the sexual requirements of the clientele. On April 1911 the police kept one of these public lavatories, in the Quai du Port, under surveillance; it was run by a seventy-year-old widow, a native of Corsica. The police observed the two female attendants go into the cubicles with the men and leave ten minutes or a quarter of an hour later. The first of these prostitutes was a forty-one-year-old married woman, a former seamstress from the Aude; she had been working for the manageress for two years. The second was a forty-six-year-old widow from Lyons who lived in a nearby lodging house. "For the past ten years," she confessed, "I have been employed as an unpaid servant in the public lavatory . . . I give myself to men's pleasure, doing whatever they want of me. I charge one franc a time and share it with the keeper."[190]

After forbidding the manageresses to employ women under forty,[191] the mayor decided in 1902 to shut down several of these establishments. The offensive failed because the Court of Appeals considered the municipal ordinance to be illegal.[192] In 1911, as part of the struggle against unregistered prostitution then being waged in Marseilles, several of these public lavatories were closed temporarily after being officially declared "places of debauchery."

Wine-shop procuring. The law of July 17, 1880, which made the ordinance of December 29, 1851, and the abrogation, in 1882, of the measures taken in 1852 obsolete, had the effect of liberalizing the sale of alcohol, increasing considerably the number of places where alcohol could be sold and, at the same time, introduced fierce competition. Many wine-shop owners then decided to employ unregistered prostitutes in order to tempt their clientele and to sell their products more easily. This brought a considerable increase, in various districts of the capital and in particular around Les Halles,[193] of wine shops that had not only a back room[194] but also a bedroom attached, unless they were situated on the ground floor or next door to a hotel. These wine shops haunted by the unregistered prostitute should not be confused with the *maisons de tolérance* with bar attached, which were also to be found in the working-class quarters.

In each of these wine shops two usually quite young prostitutes worked;[195] often they also helped the owner to serve drinks. So that the clientele would not grow tired of them they stayed, on the average, only three months in the same establishment. They were fed by the wine merchant but were given no wages and had to pay for their room, which varied between three francs and five francs a day. It should be noted that in Toulon until 1902, from which time they were subject to severe repression, the waitress-prostitutes, who sometimes numbered as many as ten per establishment, were fed free of charge and paid only one franc for their room.[196] Marie R——, a waitress in a café at Pauillac in 1901, paid her boss one or two francs whenever she had a client; nevertheless, in a week she had set aside about sixty francs.[197]

In Paris the prostitute's pimp set up his headquarters in the wine shop; he lived there, played cards there, and therefore became one of the owner's best customers. When, at night, he went up to his room with the prostitute, after she had taken leave of her last client, she paid a "night rent" to the owner. Sometimes the unregistered prostitute who operated out of a wine shop did not live there but was content, with her boss's approval, to frequent the establishment, thereby bringing with her the pimp's clientele and helping to keep the shop going.

The clientele of these wine shops essentially consisted of workers and soldiers, who now preferred women whom they regarded as barmaids and for whom they could imagine that they exerted a certain charm, to the more overt form of prostitution found in a brothel. And of course the "barmaids" were a great deal cheaper: they could usually be had for one or two francs.

The extension of this form of prostitution was even more marked in certain regions other than in the capital; this is understandable enough, since it was directed at a huge popular clientele during their leisure time, and in the very establishments that they had long been in the habit of frequenting. The case of the Nord is revealing in this respect: the popular beer halls were of particular importance in the social life of northern France.[198] From the 1880s on there was a large increase in the number of beer halls; there too the owners were forced, by competition, to bring in prostitutes, who often came from the surrounding countryside.[199] Before long, the main breweries, which owned whole chains of beer halls, realized the advantages of the system and routinely encouraged the development of unregistered prostitution, thus becoming, in turn, great beneficiaries of venal sex.

At Lille some registered prostitutes, in order to be removed from the register, even managed to buy certain beer halls and, with their accomplices, continued their previous activities.[200] Even by 1881 the police of Roubaix noted that, to their knowledge, seventy-four beer halls in the town were serving, "more or less openly, as *maisons de passe*."[201] Furthermore, three kilometers away the Belgian hamlet of Mont-à-Leu "has about forty beer halls served by two, three, or four women who publicly work as prostitutes."[202] The police commissioner requested the mayor to sign an order forbidding owners of beer halls to employ servant girls. In 1886 *Le matin* launched a campaign against the spread of this form of prostitution in the town of Valenciennes.[203]

The inquiry carried out in 1904 by Henry Hayem, under the aegis of the Société générale des prisons, gives some idea of the scope of the practice: at Grenoble between fifty and sixty "low dives" employed between 150 and 200 unregistered prostitutes. Such establishments were equally common in the ports—at Cherbourg and Marseilles, for example. The municipality of Cherbourg was well aware of the problem and was even resigned to regulating the alcohol-prostitution connection by giving each wine shop owner the right to have a registered prostitute on the premises.[204] This woman paid the owner a daily fee that varied from four to twelve francs but which was generally between eight and ten francs. At Brest there were about fifty such dives; at Lyons they could hardly be counted.[205] According to Dr. Etienne, about a hundred barmaids working in Nancy were also prostitutes.[206] At Saint-Malo sixteen owners of such establishments were found guilty, in 1912, of employing underage barmaids whom they encouraged to practice prostitution.[207] The phenomenon was also to be found in the smaller localities; Dr. Bergeret pointed out the disastrous consequences for health of the establishment that functioned in the small town of Arbois.[208]

Nonetheless, it was at Béziers, a veritable prostitutional nebula, that the links between drinking places and venal sex were most obvious. New structures were being set up, the complexity of which was to be noted by the police commissioner in a report to the prefect on July 2, 1900. In that year the town had, in addition to lodging houses recognized as being houses of ill repute,[209] "twenty-five cafés each run by three women, the owner and two others, who are in fact prostitutes and regularly undergo health checks; thirty cafés run by an owner and one other woman, who also undergo health checks; and twenty other cafés run by one or two women who also prostitute themselves, but who refuse the health check, which the authorities cannot force them to take."[210]

After 1880 the vice squad was all the more powerless in that the wine-shop owners were now covered by law and had become extremely powerful electoral forces. Unquestionably, expansion of wine-shop prostitution was the form of unregistered prostitution best adapted to the new sensibility of the working public, who were in the habit of frequenting women for money.

Faced with an avalanche of complaints,[211] however, many mayors, following the example of the mayor of Le Havre, forbade café owners to employ women, other than members of their own families, on public view. There can be little doubt that this regulation was applied unevenly.

At La Rochelle, for example,[212] certain café owners got around the problem by forming fictitious partnerships with their barmaids; others put the women in a room at the back. Despite this, a study of the towns taken as a whole suggests that, in the early years of the century, a brake was placed on the extension of this practice.

Prostitution in the countryside. To complete the account of the traditional forms of unregistered prostitution all that remains is to draw up a picture of itinerant prostitution, the lowest form of all. Unlike the other forms that I have described, this does not seem to have undergone much expansion in the second half of the century. Nevertheless, itinerant prostitution also saw profound changes bound up with the evolution of the nature of demand.

The stereotype of the *fille à soldats* has often been drawn:[213] thin, ugly, "dirty, badly dressed, and badly combed," she was, it was said, usually over thirty-five or forty. She would often arrive in the wake of a regiment; abandoned by her lover, she was forced to live in a hovel, sometimes in a hut. She would sell herself to her clients for the derisory sum of two, four, or six sous,[214] sometimes even for a hunk of bread, taking her client to a piece of waste ground, a thicket, a wood, a building site, or ruined ramparts. Most of these *pierreuses,* as they were called, were said to be only *manuelles;* in other words, they merely masturbated their client, who was often too disgusted to have sexual intercourse with them.

One cannot but think of the *pierreuse* in "La Boue" by Léon Bloy, a poor creature suffering from tuberculosis, whom the soldiers in the camp of Conlie had nicknamed "Epitaph" and who would console "anything up to a dozen men for the sum of fifty centimes,"[215] before she was killed, suffocated by "a big fellow from Pont-l'Abbé or Concarneau," who "worked her too hard."[216]

It must be admitted that this portrait, as drawn in picturesque fiction, is largely the work of imagination; contemporary sociologists of the facts found it quite impossible to assess those prostitutional activities that eluded the knowledge of the authorities. Fortunately for the historian—and indeed this case is quite exceptional—the police tried, from 1896 onward, to carry out surveillance in the rural communes around Toul.[217] A systematic study of the files provides us with a more accurate picture of the *fille à soldats*.[218] We shall see in due course how little this resembles the fictional portrait made at the time.

In 1896 the military and prefectural authorities, disturbed by the development of venereal disease in the garrison at Toul, decided as a first stage to carry out an investigation into rural prostitution as it affected the soldiers garrisoned at Dommartin-lès-Toul, Le Bois-le-comte in the commune of Domgermain, La Justice, La Madeleine, and Les Baraquements in the commune of Ecrouves. It emerged from this inquiry that, in addition to the eighty full-time prostitutes at Toul, twelve "barmaid-prostitutes" and eight girls living with their parents had had sexual relations with soldiers from the garrison. The mayors, under pressure from the prefect, with the help of the police of Toul and subsidies from the War Ministry, then drew up a set of regulations. From that date barmaids would cease to prostitute themselves: in particular, it was decreed that "any girl or woman found dancing with clients, whether soldiers or civilians, or sitting on soldiers' knees would be immediately registered as a prostitute." A certificate of "good morals and behavior" would be required of new barmaids. Owners who did not comply with the regulations would have their establishments placed out of bounds to army personnel.[219] Notorious prostitutes, now subjected to the health check, chose to leave these communes; of the "eight girls living with their families," two went to Nancy and six, when admonished, claimed to have given up their wicked ways. The coast had now been cleared for the *filles à soldats* in the strict sense.

From the files of the 153 prostitutes arrested once or several times in those three communes between the second quarter of 1903 and June 30, 1909,[220] the *fille à soldats* emerges as a *young* woman and a native of the neighboring countryside. Half the women investigated turned out to be under twenty-one and over three-quarters (77 percent) under twenty-five at the time of their first arrest. Out of this total only twelve (7.8 percent) were married, one was a widow, and two were divorced. The woman who decided to continue working as a prostitute after her arrest was registered, which required her to abandon her clandestine activities. This explains why of the 153 prostitutes arrested, only 11 (7.2 percent) tried to practice again in the area around the barracks. Thus, the *fille à soldats* of the garrison at Toul was a young woman just beginning her career; the unregistered prostitution that she practiced around the barracks was temporary, in that she later returned to ordinary life or else decided to become a registered prostitute and settle in the town.

Most of the women arrested were, it should be repeated, natives of the rural communes, and, unlike the inmates of the *tolérances,* who often came from far off, most of them had been born in the Meurthe-et-Moselle or in neighboring departments. It is obvious that the presence of a large garrison represented what contemporary witnesses regarded as a ferment of moral dissolution for the youth of the area. In 1900 a scandal broke out at Dommartin: it appears that a large number of local girls were having sexual relations, without their parents suspecting the fact; the police commissioner estimated that this represented "a veritable misfortune for the small village."[221]

Some of the women were natives of Troyes, Nancy, Paris, or departments farther afield; they had usually come to join lovers who had been conscripted and, as chance would have it, had been sent to the garrison at Toul; in order to survive, they prostituted themselves to other soldiers. Some of them were the companions of workers employed in the construction of the railways or the fortifications.

Unlike the unregistered prostitutes of the larger towns, few of the *filles à soldats* of these rural regions admitted that they had practiced any profession before selling themselves. Among their number one may note eight former barmaids, one domestic servant, one day worker, and five former factory workers, not to mention, it is true, a few prostitutes from Toul, who were attracted, during the fine weather, by the clientele of soldiers from the garrison, and four singers from *cafés-concerts* who had come to live for a time with officers.

The *filles à soldats* of the region of Toul lived in small rooms rented from neighboring peasants, in sheds built in the middle of vineyards, in wooden huts, even in stables or derelict outbuildings; some lived with a worker in a canteen or in a caravan parked in a field.[222] Sometimes two women would get together to find accommodation in the village; in this case they drew their clientele from both the soldiers and the young men of the neighborhood. After 1896 the wine shops were under too close surveillance to be able to harbor prostitutes.

Soliciting was not carried out very often at the gates of the barracks. The files show that some of the women preferred to try to seduce the guards at isolated posts: four on the rifle range, two in the fodder store, three in the ammunition depot, three in the balloon depot, one at the engineering school, four in the washhouse, two at the abattoir, and one in the soldiers' baths; eight awaited the return of the soldiers in the evening on the banks of the canal linking the Marne and the Rhine and one on the Barine road. Each woman appears to have had her own habits.

Clandestine prostitution in the wine shops, which had flourished before regulation, thus gave place after 1896 to a more diffuse prostitution; the women sold themselves in the open air, in the fields, on the banks of the canal,[223] in sheds or huts, a few at home.

The prevalence of venereal disease among the unregistered prostitutes arrested in the garrison communes was dreadful: depending on the time of year, a third to a half of the women checked on the orders of the authorities were suffering from venereal diseases. Finally, it should be noted that the level of prostitutional activity varied with the time of year: fine weather and the arrival of the reservists brought a sudden increase and even attracted the registered prostitutes of neighboring towns. Police surveillance was impeded when territorials did not hesitate to claim that the women that they were with were their own wives.

In the countryside there were thousands of *rôdeuses,* itinerants who haunted the fairs and markets; some were the daughters of circus people, who sold themselves to the peasants in a field or in the woods. In 1903, in the Charente-Inférieure, a troupe of circus artists parked their caravans and set up shop; "while the women received their temporary lovers," the managers of the troupe set about, like real pimps, "publicizing their traveling *maison fermée.*"[224] According to Dr. Vigneron, this form of prostitution was also practiced in eastern France, especially at fair time; at the shooting stand or at a conjuror's stand "there was usually a young woman soliciting more or less discreetly and making appointments for that evening."[225]

In 1900 the members of the Health Council of the Hérault complained that the villages were now as undermined by prostitution as the towns; they particularly criticized the owners of wine shops who took on barmaids during patronal festivals.[226] At Castillon-sur-Dordogne in 1903, three restaurants and a café were thus turned on occasion into brothels; in preparation for the coming fair "the procurers were always recruiting the required women."[227]

During their husbands' absence sailors' wives in Finistère sometimes went into the surrounding countryside at haymaking or harvest time to prostitute themselves.[228] "Not a year passes," wrote Dr. Bergeret, "but I see, at Arbois, women giving themselves covertly or quite openly to prostitution."[229] According to the subprefect, this was how the oyster-sellers of the arrondissement of Marennes supplemented their earnings.[230] Isolated inns situated at crossroads attracted agents, carters, and above all the itinerant workforce employed on the construction of canals and railways; such inns were often hotbeds of unregistered prostitution. At Frontignan a wine shop, situated on the canal side in the hamlet of La Peyrade, became a rendezvous for the prostitutes of the neighborhood.[231] This was also the case in 1903 with an inn frequented by the Italian workforce, five or six kilometers from Bormes.[232]

Certain parts of the countryside were noted for intense prostitutional activity. In 1903 the prefect carried out a meticulous inquiry in the countryside of the Var and found fifty-five cafés "that could be regarded as brothels in twenty-eight communes having a population of under five thousand inhabitants."[233] Twenty-six of these establishments were kept by café owners, who prostituted their barmaids in rooms adjoining the public room; twenty-two were run by women of ill repute, who used either their barmaids or local women who would come at certain days and certain hours to be at the disposal of lovers that the *patronne* would procure for them; eight of these cafés had been opened by partnerships of prostitutes. The prefect was disturbed by his findings and remarked that "prostitution is tending to become nomadic."[234] It follows "the needs of the clientèle . . . , moving from commune to commune according to festivals, fairs, and the workers' paydays."[235] The failure of the stabilization desired by the regulationists had thus led to a resurgence of earlier prostitutional habits.

Nevertheless, it must be recognized that, in the end, venal sex was not particularly widespread in the countryside, except perhaps near the Mediterranean coast, in Aquitaine, and near barracks and mines. There is every reason to believe that the examples I have cited were not representative of the country as a whole, that the spontaneous development of a network of prostitution in a small village or hamlet remained exceptional.[236] Dr. Lardier, who made a special study of prostitution in the countryside, tried to explain its relatively low frequency: the peasant, he writes, will not pay for one of his peers.[237] In that milieu servant women had little opportunity to sell themselves; the woman who wished to do so had to move to the town. Also, the peasant could frequent prostitutes only on certain fair days or after a wedding feast; otherwise he would not have anonymity. And Dr. Lardier adds, "I have to note that the need for sexual intercourse is not, in general, very widespread among our country people."[238] He continues, "The girl of the fields, inured to hard work, does not have a highly developed carnal appetite."[239] This type of remark, which springs from a bourgeois vision of the peasantry, not to mention a desire to exalt the morality of the rural population, has little scientific value; one must admit that, ultimately, it is impossible to assess the number of countrymen who had recourse to prostitutes in the towns.[240]

One final area of prostitution in the countryside was the mining towns. The deployment of the employers' strategy with a view to creating in the mining areas a workforce selected or raised in the area, housed, and supervised not only during their work time but also during their leisure time, has been brilliantly described.[241] This strategy, however, came up against the requirements of constant recruitment and the repression of any threat to the employers' intentions. As a result, side by side with the garden cities built by the companies there developed in a sort of symmetrical process urban centers of immorality, disease, and violence. The hygienic, moralizing urbanism of the employers was undone by the disorder of temporary dwellings, hotbeds of alcoholism and prostitution, whose nature in turn justified the policy of the companies.

The mining area of Briey was an extreme example of this duality. Here the disorder was increased by proximity to Germany and Luxembourg, which fact brought with it a "frontier" prostitution that finally attracted the attention of the authorities.

In 1908[242] unregistered prostitution there took three forms. In the first place, 325 barmaids and 200 (out of 400) café owners' concubines were in fact unregistered prostitutes: they came from Luxembourg, Belgium, Germany, and Italy and had been sent by foreign employment agencies; very few had come from Nancy. Second, of the 800 married women who took in workers as lodgers, many sold themselves to those lodgers. And third, a number of parents prostituted their daughters.

These hundreds of women practicing venal sex had as their clients unmarried Italians who had come to work in the mines. Indeed, out of the 10,881 workers in the mining area in 1911, only 3,500 had brought their families with them to live in the garden cities. About 4,000 were lodgers in workers' houses; the others, who were often reluctant to live in the bachelors' quarters built by the companies, crowded into privately owned sheds, of which there were then about 220 in the mining area as a whole. These very crude constructions were built "out of old planks, covered with tarred cardboard, in turn covered with the bottoms of sardine tins."[243] Usually the keeper was himself an Italian.

Near the frontier, in the territory of Joeuf and Homécourt, along the Montois road, about forty of these hovels had been erected. On Saturday nights, according to the police, scenes of uninhibited debauchery took place quite openly. There were plenty of dance halls,[244] which contrasted with the austere morality of the garden cities; professional "dancers" came to liven things up and to supplement the numbers of the local prostitutes.

Groups of about ten Italians would often get together and rent a shed where they could eat together, the meals "being prepared by a woman who, in addition to acting as cook and housekeeper, also provided other services that one can easily imagine."[245] The mining engineer who related these facts states that, contrary to all expectations,

> this regime of private communities was relatively stable and did not give rise to any more quarrels than that of the free market; . . . the partners made sure that they excluded participating members whose particular tastes might give them an unfair share of the woman's favors, and it was quite common, on Sundays, to meet the colony walking

arm-in-arm, with the mistress-servant at the center of the group, pre-ceeded by a comrade playing the accordion.[246]

According to the police and the engineers, there was a terribly high level of venereal disease in the mines. The agent estimated that 38 per-cent of the unmarried workers were suffering from gonorrhea or syph-ilis. Whole families had been contaminated, and the patients usually did not seek treatment. Professor Spillmann cites the case of a young servant girl, who was not yet registered, whom the *patronne* forced to prostitute herself with "more than fifty individuals"[247] in five or six weeks, and who, on her arrival at the venereal clinic, displayed repulsive lesions of the vulvar region.

Neither public opinion, the employers, nor the local authorities could remain indifferent to the spread of these urban centers of debauchery, alcoholism, and violence, whose way of life eluded any regular surveil-lance. At first, attempts were made to replace this uncontrolled venality with enclosed, supervised prostitution. In 1908 Spillmann demanded the opening of one or two *maisons de tolérance* in the mining area.[248] This was a failure. The brothel opened at Homécourt did not thrive, owing, according to the mining engineer, "to the passionate and some-what naive character of the Italian worker, who disdains easy pleasures and prefers intrigue and adventure."[249]

That same year, in an article entitled "On Debauchery, Blood, and Alcohol," the newspaper *L'Est républicain* launched a campaign, heavily tinged with xenophobia, and denounced what it saw as a scandal. The association formed for the abolition of the white slave trade, under its president, Laboulaye, alerted the government. In 1910 the government ordered an investigation into "the health situation of the mining region," and in August 1912 the prefect, at the request of the minister of the interior, formed a commission to study "the health conditions of the population of the mining area of Briey." It was then decided to organize, with the help of the employers' association of heavy industries, a venereal service to cover the region as a whole. The administration made excellent progress. "In three months," the subprefect of Briey was to write in 1913, "we have been able to carry out a most effective sur-veillance of the prostitutes in the area."[250] With the exception of four communes, the vice squad now worked normally everywhere. Further-more, there was close supervision of the dance halls, and so-called dan-cers were now forbidden. The policy carried out in the Briey area is a good example of the increased repression that, in the name of health, was turned upon the world of prostitution in the years leading up to the First World War.[251]

The Many Faces of the Pimp

The popular image of the pimp very often makes him seem the main, if not the only, beneficiary of prostitution; but, as we have seen, prostitution profited, and probably to a wide extent, a variety of beneficiaries, and these did not come from the working class alone. Of course the "Alphonse" who robs his *marmite* of most of her earnings is not merely a figure of melodrama; but we may well ask whether all the fuss made about him did not, in a way, blind bourgeois opinion to the existence within its own ranks of the true profiteers of venal sex. The pimp, therefore, could all the more easily play the role of scapegoat in that he represented the link between prostitution and crime. He was perhaps, in the figure of the "tough guy," the last embodiment of the physical threat exerted by the laboring classes over the bourgeoisie at the end of a century that was marked by a decline in proletarian violence. The hostility of Marxists to the lumpenproletariat and that of socialists to idleness and immorality probably helped to sustain this myth of the pimp, or at least to exaggerate his real importance and, by the same token, to mask the real structure of procuring. It is revealing in this regard that the refusal to legislate against prostitution did not extend to the pimps; they alone, together with the owners of the lodging houses, were affected by a law that, in fact, spared the real profiteering middlemen. Thus, during the three years from 1904 to 1906 (that is, in the period immediately following the passage of the law of April 3, 1903, which strengthened the provisions of the law of May 27, 1885), 1,154 pimps were brought before the courts in the department of the Seine alone, and 573 of them were found guilty.[252]

Before trying to draw my own rapid portrait of the pimp, let me distinguish between the *amant de coeur,* the "lover" who was "kept" by the prostitute, and the true pimp. The first merely satisfied her need for tenderness and affection; she might, of course, lavish presents on him, but she never became completely dependent on him or expected any protection from him. During the first half of the century, the *fille de maison* thus had an *amant de coeur*[253] whom she preferred to all others; as we have seen, this practice tended to disappear later. The *amant de coeur* of the barmaid-prostitute was often a student, artist, or young bourgeois; but, it should be repeated, a kept woman often reserved her affections for a young man from her own background,[254] without his being, strictly speaking, a pimp.

Closer to the true pimp, or *souteneur,* though not fulfilling all the same functions, was what Reuss calls the *soutenu,*[255] that is to say, a man (or woman)[256] who lived off a *femme galante* or a woman who haunted the late-night restaurants and cafés, without her having any real need of his services to carry out her activities and without his having any domination over her. Again, according to Dr. Reuss,[257] some young journalists, lawyers, doctors, and writers earned up to six or eight hundred francs a month from their mistresses.

The *souteneur,* or pimp, was an individual who lived off the prostitute or prostitutes over whom he kept permanent watch, ready to intervene against an overly rough client. It was he who would warn his *marmite* of the arrival of the vice squad; in the event of a police raid, he would take her arm[258] or try to facilitate her retreat by keeping the police talking. The *souteneur* would tell her what hotels or drinking places to frequent; if necessary, he would help her rob or blackmail her clients.

In short, he was her guide, and he was obeyed, because, very often, it was he who had trained her, and sometimes it was he who had deflowered her. Finally, and probably above all, the *souteneur* was the prostitute's real lover, with whom she lived. The prostitute, frigid in her work, found compensation in the pleasure she took with her man.[259] Of course, he took most of her earnings from her, demanded her daily "loan," beat her when she proved to be refractory or simply did not earn enough, and, if necessary, prevented her from leaving him. The report of Deputy Paul Meunier to the extraparliamentary commission contains a picturesque text in which are listed, in the name of a supposed "sidewalk syndicate," the prostitute's obligations toward her *poisson.*[260] The sadomasochistic nature of the prostitute's relations with her *souteneur* have been described too often to require repetition here. We should be on guard, however, against some degree of exaggeration and must take into account the nature of marital behavior in a milieu in which feelings were expressed in a manner quite different from that current among the bourgeoisie.

The only available written testimony consists of statements made by prostitutes, reported in the *Gazette des tribunaux,* and a few letters from prostitutes in prison or simply being detained in an infirmary or hospital,[261] or accounts of contemporaries who had seen extracts from letters and so on. These demonstrate the deep affection most of the prostitutes felt for their men. Conversely, the solicitude shown by some *souteneurs* to their *marmites* when they were in prison went beyond the mere wish to benefit once again from their services. Charles Louis Philippe describes very well the ambiguous, brutal love of Bubu of Montparnasse for his Berthe, though, of course, we must remember that they are literary creations.

Tattooing, an incomparable source, allows us to assess the intensity of feeling of the prostitute for her *souteneur.* Of course, a number of these tattoos were the work of professionals; they were chosen from an album of examples by the women, who gave in to envy or a wish to compete with some rival. Nonetheless, most of the tattoos on prostitutes were naive works, clumsily executed by the lover, who was himself tattooed. The girls were very attached to these symbols, and there were very few who, after breaking with a *souteneur*, contemplated having them removed.

The semiology of amateur tattooing in the case of the prostitute is simple. To begin with, it should be noted that the false beauty spot on the face usually indicated the presence of larger tattoos. The designation of the name or initials of the lover on the forearm or upper arm, followed by the words *P.L.V.* or *pour la vie* ("for life") and often preceded by *J'aime*, was the commonest tattoo. This mark of attachment was sometimes accompanied by a pansy (*pensée*), also meaning "thought," of which it is the symbol, a heart, or, more rarely, a portrait of the lover. Two crossed hands over a dagger indicated the wish to be faithful unto death. The more elaborate professional tattoos often involved doves, a winged Cupid, or a vase of flowers. Other symbols sometimes indicated the lover's occupation or the site of his military campaigns; a star represented service in the colonies. Sometimes the tattoo expressed a wish for fidelity to a lover who was doing his military service in distant parts; a single bird also indicated the prolonged absence of the loved one.

A break-up is clearly indicated on the woman's body by an arrow through a broken heart. When the prostitute took a new lover, apart from the arrow that signified a break with the previous one, a second tattoo, placed beneath the first or on the other arm, designated his successor. If the break was accompanied by great distress, the heart pierced by the arrow was accompanied by symbols that indicated a desire to be revenged or to drown one's sorrows: sometimes the abandoned mistress had a grave or a bottle of wine tattooed on her body. The death of a lover who could not be forgotten was expressed in a superimposed cross or, more simply, by a pansy with its petals turned back over the tattooed heart.

Tattoos traced by Dr. Leblond and Dr. Lucas[262] are certainly the most moving documents available. They are indisputable evidence of the depth of feeling and love that the women felt for their *souteneurs* or for their *amants de coeur;* the fact that such practices may be regarded as the sign of sadomasochistic relations is of little consequence. There were very few obscene inscriptions; the simplicity and intensity of the love felt by these women bound to the men on whom they depended was expressed in a naive and childish but indelible symbolism. This evidence of fidelity and abandonment, taking the form of a concern to redeem the sold body, is the best possible definition of the condition of the prostitute at the end of the last century.

The *souteneur* was a complex individual. Almost all the evidence points to an evolution in his character; over the years he is depicted less and less as a suburban Hercules[263] and more and more as a lower-class would-be dandy,[264] a skillful young rogue.[265] Like the unregistered prostitute off whom he lived, the Parisian *souteneur* of the last years of the century had given up flashy clothes, the black silk "three-decker" cap, the light checked bell-bottom trousers. He now dressed like anyone else; at most he might go on wearing light ties, the rings given him by his mistress, and yellow gloves, if he frequented the cafés in central Paris.[266] The pseudonym, though, survived, and we hear of the Lady-Killer, the Bull, the Pasha of Montrouge, and the Terror of Grenelle.

The propensity of the sociologists of the time to draw up categories and to embark on a veritable entomology leads them to distinguish the following:

• The *souteneur* of the *maison de tolérance,* who had become an *amant de coeur* and who, it should be repeated, was rapidly disappearing, although as late as 1902 he still survived among the prostitutes of Versailles. Even at this date *souteneurs* sometimes placed their mistresses in the town brothels.[267]

• The shameful *souteneur,* sometimes a hard-working laborer, who devoted his spare time to supporting a mistress, whom he would often marry when she was old.[268]

• The *souteneur* who had married his *marmite* in order to avoid the threat of banishment since the passing of the law of July 9, 1852, or who was simply a systematically complaisant husband.

• The *souteneur* who roamed the suburbs and who, as well as keeping watch over his women, did not hesitate to rob passers-by. This type was widespread at Grenelle, La Villette, Belleville, and Ménilmontant, as well as in the center of Paris around Les Halles and the place Maubert. In the same category may be included the *nervi,* who, according to the police, numbered over a thousand at Marseilles in 1875.[269] The police commissioner for Lille wrote to the prefect in 1903 that not a night passed that individuals were not robbed in the rue des Etaques; the victims, concerned about their reputation, usually refused to press charges. In the end, the police found out only about those "who were attacked and remained on the ground, because they defended themselves."[270]

• The *souteneur* of the cafés in the center of the capital and the "launcher" of demimondaines. The former might pass himself off as a ladies' hairdresser, a circus athlete,[271] a *café-concert* singer,[272] or a bookmaker.

The "launcher," like Prado and Pranzini, who murdered their mistresses,[273] was depicted by Dr. Commenge as a "swarthy, foreign-looking individual with greasy hair and dazzling rings."[274]

• Finally, there was the *souteneur* of young men who practiced homosexual prostitution, but he is not part of this inquiry.

Whatever is said to the contrary,[275] there is no trace of any real syndicates of *souteneurs* before the First World War.[276] The most one can discern is a great solidarity based on long familiarity. This grew up during the long, idle afternoons around a billiard table or card table, or simply during endless promenades in the street.[277] The older ones trained the younger ones, who thus did their apprenticeship on the job and began, from the age of fifteen, to play the role of lookout.[278] At Marseilles, however, when several prostitutes worked the same street, their *souteneurs* acted together and "dispersed on scout duty to the periphery of the territory exploited."[279] When the police arrested one of the women, the *souteneurs* came together and tried to facilitate the escape of the others. In Marseilles, too, two *souteneurs* would sometimes form a partnership to work the same prostitute.[280]

Apart from the inquiry carried out in the Seine-Inférieure in 1899, there exists no quantitative analysis that would enable one to describe the features of any group of *souteneurs* that might be representative of the category as a whole. Carlier tried, at the end of the Second Empire, to carry out a systematic study of individuals accused of procuring.[281] Out of 695 *souteneurs*, or those supposed to be such, arrested in the capital over six years, 371 (53 percent) were natives of Paris, and 324 (47 percent) were from the provinces or abroad; it is clear, then, that the proportion of Parisians was higher than among either the registered or unregistered prostitutes. At this time the *souteneurs* very often had criminal records: indeed 330 of them (47.4 percent) had already been prosecuted 575 times, including 275 cases (involving 95 individuals) of assault and battery and resisting the police, 262 cases (91 individuals) of larceny and breach of trust, and 38 cases (31 individuals) of carrying weapons, attacks at night, and robbery with violence. The Parisian *souteneurs* certainly belonged, at this date, to the criminal world, which explains why it was often advocated that they be sent to the colonies. In 1896 Commenge remarked that over a hundred *souteneurs* had been condemned to death or to hard labor for life during the preceding twenty years.[282]

At Rouen in 1889, forty-seven individuals "lived exclusively off the prostitution"[283] of their wife or mistress, although they all claimed to have an occupation: seventeen described themselves as artisans or workmen, eight as day laborers, seven as commercial travelers or hawkers, six as singers or traveling musicians, two as tradesmen, two as café waiters, two as shop assistants, and two as sailors. Nine of these pimps had already been convicted of larceny or assault and battery.

Usually the *souteneur* was young. According to Carlier, some were as young as eighteen, but none was older than fifty. The distribution by age of the *souteneurs* of Rouen confirms this evidence (see Figure 13). The archives of the prefecture of police contain several accounts of actions by groups of individuals described as *souteneurs*. Unfortunately, it seems quite obvious that the police, like the press and public opinion, systematically confused certain forms of illegality on the part of groups of young men with the activities of *souteneurs*. Thus in 1902 the police regarded as *souteneurs* members of a gang made up of fifty boys and girls who, every Monday evening, on leaving a dance hall, would indulge in scenes of violence and "lewdness" on the passenger boats that operated

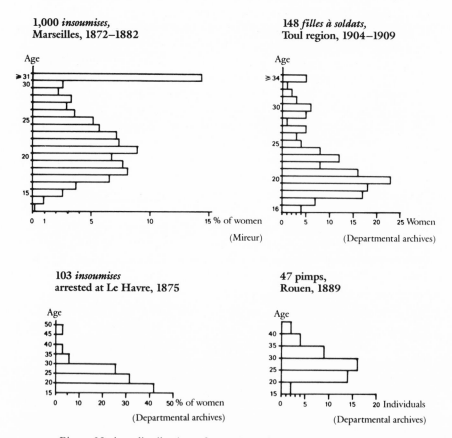

Figure 13. Age distribution of unregistered prostitutes and pimps.

between the Tuileries and Suresnes. Indeed, each week they would board the boat at Puteaux about 5 P.M. "The boats," according to the report, "were taken over. The pimps made women and children give up their seats, damaged the equipment, sang obscene songs, and threatened with death any travelers who protested. They then smashed the electric lamps, and the scenes of lewdness began."[284] In an ambush and raid organized by the police, "the pimps, numbering about thirty-five, most of whom were youths between fifteen and nineteen,"[285] were apprehended. It was against these alleged *souteneurs,* who were in fact young hooligans, that the press demanded the intervention of the police.[286]

More revealing was the affair that took place on the evening of October 28, 1902.[287] On that day at 9:30 P.M., some twenty *souteneurs,* who were already named as such in police files, were involved in a brawl involving revolvers and knives at the corner of the rue Boyer and the rue de la Bidassoa. Two of the participants were wounded: a nineteen-year-old tiler and a washhouse boy of twenty-three. The police arrested on the spot a twenty-year-old cutter and an eighteen-year-old day laborer. In a haul carried out at 1 A.M., the police also seized members of a gang at 4 rue de Ménilmontant and arrested six of the men who had been involved in the brawl the night before: an eighteen-year-old tiler, a nineteen-year-old laborer, a seventeen-year-old glazier, a twenty-year-old leather cutter, a seventeen-year-old joiner, and a twenty-four-year-old pattern cutter. Apart from the last, all were very young and all claimed to have a trade in response to policy inquiry, a practice that dated from the application of the law on recidivists.

This leaves unanswered the most important question: the actual number included in the category of *souteneurs.* Research in this field is very hazardous. I shall simply provide, as far as Paris is concerned, two extreme estimates. In 1891 *Le temps,* in an investigation into the *souteneurs,* estimated their number at fifty thousand, while the experts in the prefecture of police believed that there were then over ten thousand of them.[288] The second estimate is certainly closer to reality. It must be admitted, however, that any attempt to carry out a study of the evolution in their numbers is, for the moment, out of the question.

A Demographic Portrait of the Insoumise

It is much more difficult, on the basis of quantitative data, to sketch the portrait of the *insoumise* than of the *soumise.* The unregistered prostitute usually eludes the investigation of sociologists, as she does that of the police, for the specific reason that there is little to distinguish her from other women. There is no file in the vice squad archives, no brothel-keeper's book, no periods in prison to help us study her. Our only raw materials are the case histories recorded in the hospitals that were open to venereal patients and the documents concerning the arrests and health checks of the *insoumises,* who, as a result of being arrested and examined, were thus no longer unregistered, and, in the majority of cases, moved on to swell the ranks of the registered prostitutes. It should be added that these documents do not allow us to include the courtesans, and that the quantitative investigations carried out hardly affect the unregistered streetwalker at all.

It might seem useless to take account of the results of these investigations, insofar as the *insoumises* either had already been registered or were destined one day to be so before disappearing. Indeed, we know very well that clandestine activity was merely the apprentice stage or the "obligatory preface"[289] to official prostitution. In immediately joining a *maison de tolérance,* Goncourt's Elisa was an exception; the very different destiny of Huysmans' Marthe corresponds more closely to reality. It is important, however, to examine the similarities and try to discern the features that distinguish the *insoumise* from the *soumise,* or registered prostitute.

From the considerable medical literature dealing with the question,[290] it emerges that the family background of the unregistered prostitutes was, at first glance, just as typical as that of the registered ones. Out of a group of a thousand *insoumises* released by the Marseilles police between 1872 and 1882,[291] only 112 were illegitimate; Commenge finds that only 184 were illegitimate out of a total of 2,368 sick unregistered prostitutes whose family background he studied.[292] The number of orphans and of young women who had lost one parent, however, turned out to be higher than average. As of their arrest, 27.1 percent of the released *insoumises* in Marseilles had lost both parents; in addition, 16.6 percent had lost their father, 15.3 percent their mother, and 7.3 percent were born of unknown parents.[293] Of the Parisian *insoumises* studied by Commenge, 692 (29 percent) were orphans; 811 (34 percent) had lost their father and 456 (19 percent) their mother.

The geographic origins of the unregistered prostitutes seem less distant than those of the *filles soumises.* In Paris, according to Commenge, 34 percent were natives of the Seine and 6 percent of the Seine-et-Marne or the Seine-et-Oise. As for the remainder, the area of recruitment was the same; that is, the contribution of the southern regions of the country was insignificant, while that of Brittany and the Nord was fairly large. The biggest contingents came from the outlying districts of the capital and from the eastern arrondissements: these arrondissements were, in decreasing order of representation, the eleventh (boulevards Voltaire and Richard-Lenoir), the eighteenth (Montmartre, Clignancourt, and La Goutte d'Or), the twentieth (Belleville, Ménilmontant, and Charonne), the nineteenth (La Villette), and the tenth (faubourg du Temple and portes Saint-Denis and Saint-Martin).

Most of the *insoumises* of Brest were natives of the city; the commune of Marseilles provided proportionately more (26.2 percent) unregistered than registered prostitutes. Most of the *insoumises* in the city, however, came from the other communes of the Bouches-du-Rhône and neighboring departments. Furthermore, there was a good number of foreigners (22 percent). During 1875 the police of Le Havre arrested 103 *insoumises;* 22 of them had been born in the city and 26 in another commune of the Seine-Inférieure; 16 were natives of Calvados, an adjoining department.[294]

The distribution by age of the *insoumises* arrested and then released by the Marseilles vice squad reveals, in comparison with that of the registered prostitutes, a larger proportion of young girls and of fairly old women. This is easy enough to understand. One finds that certain unregistered prostitutes were still practicing their profession in their sixties. An analysis of the ages of the 103 unregistered prostitutes arrested at Le Havre in 1875 leads to the same conclusions (see Figure 13).

The stated occupations of the *insoumises* (see Figure 14) differ very little from those claimed by the *filles soumises* at the time of their registration. One finds a majority of workshop employees, domestic servants, cooks, chambermaids, shop assistants, and barmaids. One also finds on the list of one thousand *insoumises* drawn up by Dr. Mireur fifty-six singers and actresses, twelve teachers of languages or the piano, and five primary school teachers. Two hundred twenty-five venereal patients passed through Professor Février's department at the Maison de Secours at Nancy,[295] and the 403 women treated in the same establishment during the period 1895–1900[296] belonged to the same categories as the Marseilles *insoumises.* Although the region was industrialized, factory workers provided only a fairly small contingent, whereas at Nancy, café employees, whose contribution had markedly increased, formed almost half of the total number at the end of the century. The occupational distribution of 6,342 sick *insoumises* arrested in the capital between 1878 and 1887 brings out particularly strikingly the preeminence of dressmakers, linen maids, laundresses, and above all domestic servants.

The studies carried out by Dr. Martineau[297] on the venereal patients treated at Lourcine provide details about the age at which future unregistered prostitutes generally lost their virginity (see Figure 15). Indeed, the data provided by this practitioner go well beyond the limits of this

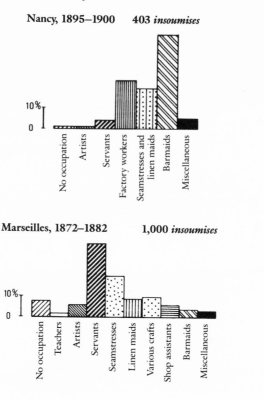

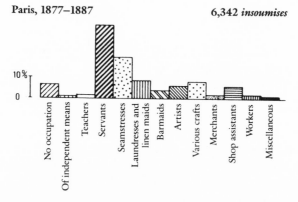

Figure 14. Occupations claimed by unregistered prostitutes. (According to Dr. Vigneron, Dr. Mireur, and Dr. Commenge.)

study; they do, however, throw considerable light on the sexual activity of working-class adolescent girls and make it possible to carry out a sociological study of the networks of seduction (see Figure 16). Such a study complements the scholarly researches of demographers on marriages and illegitimate births. Of course, it may be objected that Dr. Martineau's work is less rigorous and that the sample chosen is not representative of women as a whole. Moreover, although the patients questioned probably had not forgotten the age at which they lost their virginity, some must, in good faith, have provided erroneous information concerning the occupation and above all the age of their first sexual partner. Finally, others may have been tempted to lie, either to justify their behavior or to paint a rosier picture of the past and to conceal a sordid adventure. This almost unique attempt to quantify a completely obscure phenomenon is nevertheless extremely interesting.

We see that most of the prostitutes treated at Lourcine had lost their virginity at an early age, which confirms the result of the studies carried out at Saint-Lazare. A large majority of the patients (78 percent) lost their virginity between the ages of fifteen and twenty-one; one will also note the high proportion of those who lost it before the age of sixteen

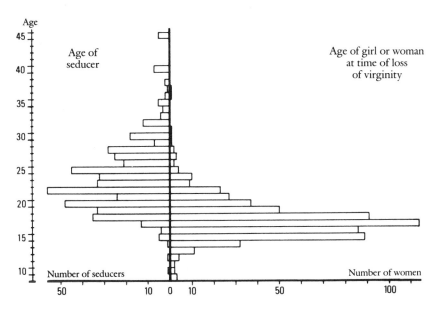

Figure 15. Age at loss of virginity of future unregistered prostitutes treated at Lourcine by Dr. Martineau, according to their own evidence. (Several of the women were unable to give the age of their seducer.)

WOMEN SEDUCED \ SEDUCERS (•1 woman)	Servants	Day workers	Farmers	Craft workers and employers	Soldiers	Industrial workers	Waiters	Clerks and traveling salesmen	Artists and designers	Employers in commerce and industry	Liberal professions and students	Landowners, of independent means	Middle managers in industry and administration	Clerks
Servants	••••• •••••		•	••••••• ••••••• •••••••	••	•••	••••	•••• •••	•••	•••• •••	•••••	••••	•	•	••••
Day workers	•	••		•••	•								•		•
Agricultural workers														
Linen maids, laundresses, ironers	••	•		••••••• •••••••		•		•	•	•••	•••	•		•••
Seamstresses		•		••••••• ••••••• ••••••	••	•••	••	•••	•••	••••	••••• ••••	•••	•	••••
Other crafts			•	••••••• •••••••	•	••••		•	•	•	••	•		••
Factory workers			•	••••• ••••	•	•••	•	•				•		••
Barmaids	•			••						•				•
Shop assistants				••			•			•		•		••
Traveling saleswomen				••		•				•		•	•	•
Artists, models				•				•			•		
Teachers											•		

Figure 16. The seduction of future unregistered prostitutes in Paris by profession. (According to Dr. Martineau.)

(21 percent). The age of highest incidence is between seventeen and eighteen; after twenty-two, virginity is exceptional.

The men involved were older, which should go without saying; very few (5.2 percent) were under eighteen. The loss of virginity did not take place, therefore, between adolescents of the same age. The great majority of the seducers (73.5 percent) were between eighteen and twenty-eight, with the age of highest incidence being twenty-two. Mature men, still less older men, are poorly represented in this group; those over thirty make up only 10.4 percent of the total and those over forty 2.7 percent.

If one concentrates on the occupations of the women concerned (see Figure 16), three models emerge from the investigation. First, domestic servants lost their virginity with men of the widest variety of occupations. The household servant, the cook, and the chambermaid had a considerable range of contacts, including their employers, men also in service, artisans, suppliers, and shop assistants, and this explains the range of occupations among their seducers. Second, the laundresses and drapers were, for the most part, seduced by men of their own artisan category (66 percent); the same was true, to a lesser degree, of the other prostitutes who worked in factories or workshops, with the exception of seamstresses. And third, the results concerning seamstresses, and particularly dressmakers, reveal an unusual fact: not one of them had been seduced by a domestic servant, while all the other male occupational categories feature among their seducers, and members of the liberal professions and students (17 percent) represent a fairly large proportion of the total.

An analysis of the results concerning these seducers provides information on the ways in which men of different milieus tried to satisfy their sexual desires outside marriage. It will be noted from the outset that soldiers are almost totally absent from the list; the fact that the investigation concerns Parisian women is not enough to explain this absence. Artisans and workers seem to have been the primary seducers of the future venereal patients at Lourcine; they can boast of conquests among every category of woman represented. The multifarious attraction that they exerted contrasts with the relatively narrow contacts of the women in their own circle.

The discrepancy between the behavior of the men and that of the women is even more marked among those in domestic service, but here the situation is reversed: the seduction practiced by the male domestics is narrowly located within their own society. Seventeen of the twenty-one women seduced by male servants were servants themselves. Members of the liberal professions and students who indulged in such "flings" did so overwhelmingly with seamstresses and servants. They very rarely seduced women working in workshops or factories. Shop assistants and commercial travelers adopted an identical form of behavior; this similarity is expressive of a wish to imitate, which is itself revealing of social ambitions. Employers in commerce and industry practiced much of their seduction on the same two categories, although ancillary seduction is apparent here.

This brief sketch is enough to show the diversity of the networks of premarital and extramarital sexual relations. The everyday proximity of bodies was often the determining factor; it explains the relations between men and women who found themselves working side by side in the kitchen, in the workshop, or in the privacy of a bourgeois home. Yet it scarcely accounts for all the complexities of desire and seduction.[298]

We have to admit, with Commenge, that "one may be too disposed nowadays to exaggerate the moral influence of the school." Of the ten thousand sick *insoumises* that he questioned between 1878 and 1887, only 16 percent were illiterate, which was very close to the average, although it is true that at Marseilles the proportion in 1882 was 42.3 percent of the women arrested and then released, a percentage higher than the regional average.

All in all, the unregistered prostitutes arrested by the vice squad or those treated in hospitals for venereal disease largely resemble, even in their diversity, the *filles soumises* at the time of their registration. This is hardly surprising. At the very most they seem a little better integrated in the urban milieu in which they operated. They were more often local women than were the registered prostitutes; they almost always claimed to have an occupation; and their educational level was a little higher than that of their colleagues.

New Forms of Prostitutional Activity

Let us now approach the principal phenomenon of prostitution in France in the last third of the nineteenth century: namely, the development of venal practices which can no longer be called clandestine on the part of women and girls who, without being courtesans of the highest rank, almost totally eluded the regulationist system. These women were not prosecuted by the police;[299] when suffering from venereal disease, they were not regarded as prostitutes and denounced as such by members of the medical profession. Unlike the *insoumises,* they no longer lived in fear of the police. They were very seldom dependent on a *souteneur,* although some kept an *amant de coeur.* Yet they were victims of a new kind of procuring. Under cover of genuine commercial enterprises this new form of procuring held groups of women in its grip and formed networks whose sheer size helps to explain the currency of the theme of the white slave trade during the early years of the twentieth century. Finally, and perhaps above all, because it is this that defines them, all these new forms of prostitutional activity necessitated that the woman give her client the impression that she was allowing herself to be seduced and was no longer a mere animal deprived of the freedom to refuse.

The Femmes de Brasserie

Almost every year since the problems of prostitution had moved to the forefront of public concern—in other words, since 1876—a public opinion campaign, based on the fact that a large number of barmaids were suffering from venereal diseases, demanded the closing of the *brasseries à femmes* (cafés specializing in the serving of beer and frequented by quasiprostitutes).[300] These establishments saw the light of day under the Second Empire, on the occasion of the Universal Exposition of 1867; it was then that barmaids began to replace barmen.[301] The law of July 17, 1880, gave rise to a fairly marked increase in the number of these establishments and of their female staff until a by-law issued by the prefect of police, Léon Bourgeois, on February 24, 1888, checked the process.

The *brasseries à femmes* (see Table 10[302]) were set up in the central districts of the capital; most of them, and the most thriving of them, were on the Left Bank, in the Latin Quarter. Usually these establishments were managed on behalf of rich bedmates. Unlike the *maisons closes,* the *brasseries à femmes* involved an essentially male form of procuring.

Their signs were picturesque or suggestive; the most celebrated of them were called the brasseries du Caïd, des Nounous, des Dernières Cartouches, de Cupidon, des Odalisques, or de l'Enfer.[303] At carnival time the managers would organize brilliant cavalcades advertising the specialties of their establishments.

The patrons were served by *verseuses* (pourers), pretty young women wearing short skirts and a costume that often looked theatrical. Thus the waitresses would appear as Andalusian, Italian or Scottish peasants.[304] The *verseuse* would sit at the table of the customer she had just served, drink with him, and encourage him to drink more. If he so wished, she would go with him to a room in a nearby *hôtel de passe,* the manager of which had an agreement with the manager of the brasserie. Less often, she would give herself to him in one of the rooms or in a back room of the establishment itself, which was sometimes richly decorated and converted into a "cave of Venus."[305]

The girls were fed by the *patron,* except in certain of the brasseries on

Table 10. Growth in the number of *brasseries à femmes* in the capital from 1872 to 1893.

Year	Number of brasseries	Number of barmaids
1872	40	125
1879	130	582
1882	181	881
1888	203	1,100
1893	202	1,170

the Right Bank; they paid a "right to serve" fee, although this was fairly modest, amounting to no more than fifty centimes or one franc a day in the Left Bank brasseries, in addition to a payment that varied according to the situation of the table assigned to them. Furthermore, the *patron* received a tax proportional to the quality of the waitress and the number of sexual contacts made; he could also levy various fines, in particular for breakages. Finally, the *verseuse* had to pay for her own costume and for the matches that she lit for her client;[306] in some establishments she was even, according to Dr. Martineau, supposed to tip the waiters.[307] In spite of this, Macé estimates that a *fille à brasserie* earned between five and twenty francs a day.[308]

The periodic change of costumes and settings obviated a frequent change of personnel.[309] Unlike other categories of prostitute, the *femmes de brasserie* seldom moved from one establishment to another; they were thus able to build up a clientele of regulars. Indeed, the best *verseuses* were set up by the *patron* in an apartment nearby; this enabled them to carry out their activities more easily. The timetable of these girls was less restrictive than that of the inmates of a *tolérance:* the *verseuses* worked between 3 P.M. and midnight; the rest of the time the establishment was run by only a few women especially recruited for the mornings.

The clientele of the *brasseries à femmes* consisted mainly of young men: *lycée* and university students, artists, and young clerks or shop assistants could meet in a warm atmosphere; in the brasseries of the Latin Quarter the young intellectuals were at home. It was now in these establishments, rather than in the theaters, as had been the case during the Louis-Philippe period, that young students found a sense of community. The *brasseries à femmes* unquestionably facilitated group identification and the integration of young provincials into Parisian society. The attachment of students to the *verseuses* even found expression in their practical jokes. For example, at a meeting organized in April 1883 by members of a morality society that aimed at having the brasseries shut down, five hundred participants shouted in unison that these establishments were a public utility.[310] Of course, the beauty and youth of the *verseuses,* as well as their permanence in the establishment, made it possible to have relations with them that were not devoid of sentiment. Each of the young men harbored the hope of becoming the *amant de coeur* of one of the *verseuses* without running the risk of competing with a true *souteneur.*

Huysmans directed his sarcasm against this disguised prostitution and against the naiveté of the young men who allowed themselves to be taken in by it.[311] Yet an elderly Barrès looked back nostalgically at the *brasseries à femmes* of his youth, which allowed a "student proletariat"[312] to have love affairs involving sex, which had become more difficult with the decline of the *grisette*. It was one such brasserie that Barrès' Racadot placed his mistress Léontine in order to benefit from her "useful pity."[313] Even the serious Roehmerspacher, another Barrès hero, who had spent his first night in the capital in the company of one of these girls, offered to initiate Sturel into this milieu.[314] "At this time," Barrès writes, "the two dominant factors in the life of the quarter were the races and the *brasserie à femmes*,"[315] and he evokes "the compact mass of girls and students packed together in that smoking-den . . . So many varied youths shouting and gesticulating together gave the impression that there was no more than one of them. They formed one and the same federative animal, all its hands outstretched, all its mouths open to alcohol and prostitution."[316] "Every shade of free love had merged in those innumerable brasseries that, in 1883, filled the rue des Ecoles, the rue Monsieur-le-Prince, and near the Odéon, the rue de Vaugirard."[317]

The fashion for the *brasserie à femmes,* like that of the *cafés-concerts,* had also spread to the larger provincial towns; they had existed at Lyons, Marseilles, and Toulouse since 1882. Henri Hayem's investigation also shows how common they were at Caen, Dijon, Grenoble, Lille, Orléans, and Roubaix-Tourcoing.[318] Meanwhile, aware of the hostility of public opinion, the mayor of Antibes had closed them.[319] Of course, the spread of these establishments aroused the hostility of the lemonade sellers and café waiters; in 1885 those of the rue Bayard sent a petition to the mayor of Toulouse.[320] The year before, the waiters and lemonade sellers of Marseilles had attacked the brasserie waitresses.[321]

In the ports, and particularly at Brest, Toulon, and Marseilles, certain *femmes de brasserie* set up opium dens in their apartments.[322] In 1913 an anxious Garde des Sceaux (the senior law officer in the government) decided to carry out an inquiry into the link between prostitution and drugs. At Brest, Lorient, and Rennes the smoking dens were frequented almost exclusively by naval officers or by officers of the colonial army, and by a few young men who frequented the *brasseries à femmes*.[323] At Marseilles, opium could be smoked in the back rooms of certain of these establishments. At Toulon, where the consumption of drugs was more widespread, suitably decorated, even luxurious, smoking dens had been set up.[324]

The Fille de Beuglant and the Artiste-Prostitute

We are now dealing with a phenomenon that was more specifically provincial. The fashion of the *cafés-concerts* had become widespread in the provinces in the 1870s; after that there was hardly a town, however small, that did not have its *beuglants,* or *cafés-concerts.*[325] There were eight at Périgeux, seven at Oyonnax, six at Draguignan and Evreux, five at Mende: 388 in all. This does not include the establishments of the same kind, but of inferior class, such as the six *cafés-concerts* that, in 1895, were in operation between Longwy and Gouraincourt.[326] In the summer some villages in the Languedoc and Provence would embellish their patronal festivals or bullfights with concerts. In all, *beuglants* and *bouibouis* employed several thousand women; indeed, each of them recruited, depending on its size, between five and twenty singing artistes. The fashion for the French *café-concert* had meanwhile spread abroad, especially to Holland and the Russian empire.

Under cover of music, the *beuglants* were in fact places of prostitution. In 1906 André Ibels demonstrated this conclusively in the tumultuous campaign he launched in *Le matin* against the "trade in singing artistes." Indeed, the client who so wished could drink with one of the artistes during the show and, afterward, "have supper" with her in a private room. This form of prostitution was enormously successful with men of the bourgeoisie, and even with provincial shopkeepers. In addition, there were a great many that recruited a more working-class clientele.[327] Of course, the atmosphere created by the music and the gaiety that reigned in the *beuglants* certainly had its attractions. Moreover, male vanity was satisfied in these liaisons with artistes, whom one could sometimes pride oneself on having taken from some other habitué.

Unlike the brasserie owner, the *patron* of a *café-concert* did not profit directly from the prostitution of the women in his employ.[328] For him it was essentially a matter of increasing the quantity of drinks consumed in his establishment and of encouraging his customers to spend recklessly. To do so he had to embellish his café with a variety of pretty young women. It is worth repeating, however, that the *patron* was himself only a manager and that the *beuglants* usually belonged to rich absentee owners. Ibels cites the case of a wealthy distiller in the Nord who owned over thirty such establishments.[329]

The network that made it possible to recruit prostitutes was relatively simple: the *patron* turned to a Parisian *agent lyrique,* who was usually to be found in the République quarter, near the boulevard Sébastopol or the portes Saint-Denis and Saint-Martin. This agent was not supposed to respect the by-laws regulating employment agencies. All he had to do was to attract, by means of tempting advertisements, young women who wanted to become "artistes" and, after going through the motions of an audition, send them off to one of the centers of this activity, such as Avignon or Toulouse. Indeed, a number of such *agents lyriques* recruited more *soupeuses* (supper girls) than real *chanteuses*.

Having arrived at her destination, the woman was presented with a standard contract, the clauses of which were all too clear: it allowed a *patron* to keep a strong grip on the personnel he recruited. Usually the artiste was under the obligation to sing, to accommodate, and above all to "give supper" to a client who requested it up to 2 A.M., and sometimes even 5 A.M. The contract very seldom made provision for a salary; it was usually specified that the women would have to be satisfied with the takings from the house lottery and the collections made among the audience.[330] In addition, most of the contracts stipulated that they had to pay for their board as well as their clothes and even pay a borrowing fee for using scores, not to mention the fines that might be imposed on them for failing in their duties. Sometimes they were expected to gamble in the company of the clients. Finally, the *patron* almost always reserved the right to dismiss a young woman whenever he liked and thus to condemn her very often to rejoining the ranks of the *insoumises*.

Between 1890 and 1893 the ephemeral Union syndicale des artistes lyriques waged a vigorous campaign against the "trade in artistes." In 1903 a reconstituted union, which now had over two thousand members and was affiliated with the trade union confederation (CGT), took up the struggle again with the support of the labor exchanges. In 1905 alone, the union put up five thousand posters denouncing the scandal.[331] On several occasions it wrote open letters to mayors. In 1906, above all, André Ibels handed the results of his investigation to Clemenceau and Albert Sarraut, then undersecretary of state at the Ministry of the Interior; he also obtained the support of Senator Bérenger, the indefatigable enemy of the pimps. On December 6, 1906, a ministerial circular forbade collections during shows, the "posing of artists on the stage," and "any communication between spectators and artists during the shows."[332] It also forbade managers to feed the artists, house them, or make them eat in their establishments. Meanwhile, 150 mayors signed ordinances with a view to ending the abuses.

In fact, the results of this campaign were disappointing. The measures taken by the municipalities and the ministerial circular were fairly inadequately applied and often fell into disuse after a few months. The Société des auteurs, compositeurs et éditeurs de musique refused for a long time to commit its support. In addition, the *patrons* of the *cafés-concerts* were vitally important electoral forces, and the municipalities that subsidized these establishments found it difficult to deal severely with them and officially recognize that they were in fact centers of prostitution. Above all, the demand for prostitution was so pressing that it was difficult to prevent the licensees of *beuglants* from satisfying it.

The Maisons de Rendez-Vous

The *maison de rendez-vous*, which naturally must not be confused with the *maison de tolérance* or the *hôtel de passe*, is certainly the institution whose development, improvement, and, between 1900 and 1910, official recognition provides the most revealing evidence of the evolution of prostitutional behavior and, more generally, of the sexual behavior of the bourgeoisie.

Of course it was not, strictly speaking, a novelty: for a long time the *lionnes pauvres* (poor lionesses) and gentlemen too shy to seduce women themselves[333] had called on the services of pimps, who would arrange meetings. The *maison de rendez-vous* was also, in a way, the heir to the *maison à parties* of the first half of the century and of the genuine *maison de passe* that succeeded it, the main examples of which in Paris were, in about 1885, grouped around the rue Duphot, the rue Lavoisier, and the rue du Château-d'Eau.[334] Between this date and the end of the century, a parallel decline occurred in the number of *maisons de tolérance* and a rapid increase in *maisons de rendez-vous* in the strict sense. I shall now try to describe them as they flourished in the capital, before the prefecture of police set up a special set of regulations governing them. I shall then analyze, using the example of Marseilles, the way in which they functioned in the large provincial cities during the first decades of the twentieth century.[335]

In principle, the Parisian *maison de rendez-vous* had no residents. As its name clearly indicates, it provided a means of arranging meetings between rich clients and women who, although they were willing to sell themselves, claimed to be honest bourgeoises; they might be actresses, married women, widows, or divorcees. In fact, if the evidence of the prefecture of police is to be believed, the women who used the *maisons de rendez-vous* were often genuine prostitutes who passed themselves off as good bourgeois women, or even as foreign princesses. In the second-class *maisons* the mistresses even took on women who used the establishment regularly and imposed on them a fairly strict timetable,[336] perhaps even going so far as to force them to have lunch or dinner in the establishment. The licensee of the *maison de rendez-vous* always reserved the right to refuse a client whose looks she did not like.

The meeting between the partners involved a simulated seduction, apparently without money being discussed: it was to the mistress of the establishment that the gentleman paid the agreed-upon sum with a view to obtaining the favors of the woman of his choice, whom he sometimes selected from a photograph album. The better *maisons de rendez-vous* were in no sense temples of eroticism: what one hoped to find there was another man's wife. In short, the *maison de rendez-vous* was the shrine of venal adultery. At the level of sexual desire, it represented a veritable mutation that in turn determined a shift in female sexual behavior within a large section of the urban bourgeoisie; without the widespread development of adulterous practices[337] such an institution would not have been able to proliferate so far or so fast. As to changes in male sexuality, the increased taste for adultery, even if venal, was perhaps related to the quest for virginity that also seemed to characterize the sexual behavior of that period.[338] In either case, desire was stimulated by breaking taboos.

The *maison de rendez-vous,* unlike the *maison de tolérance,* usually consisted of only one or two apartments in the building it occupied, and no particular sign pointed it out to the curiosity of the passer-by or visitor. These apartments were set up in the fashionable quarters of the center, often close to the department stores, which allowed women to frequent them in the afternoon without arousing too much attention.

In 1888 there were still very few *maisons de rendez-vous:* only about 15. By the early years of the century there were probably 200 of them.[339] In 1904 the police officially listed 114: 83 second-class ones and 31 first-class ones.[340] For the same date Turot lists 72.[341] According to him, these were frequented by 313 *pensionnaires,* but he was obviously counting only the second-class establishments—that is, those that were regarded as lodging houses and were therefore under surveillance by the appropriate section of the vice squad.[342]

The decoration and furnishing of the apartment were luxurious, of course, but not flashy. The aim here was to suggest the hygiene and comfort of a bourgeois home. Often the drawing room and adjoining bedrooms contained expensive furniture; on the walls or mantelpiece a few works of art completed the illusion of a respectable home intended to satisfy gentlemen who were tired of or repelled by the outrageous luxury of the *tolérances.* Of course, there was no question of a bar in such establishments, and the drawing room in which the meetings took place was very different from that of the first-class brothels. The women usually wore afternoon clothes of a sober, decent kind. The atmosphere was that of afternoon tea in the apartment of a demimondaine. "There was no trace of vulgarity. The atmosphere was that of the best society."[343] Sometimes a lady might go to the piano to accompany one of her friends who sang. Certain establishments, it is true, specialized in female nudity,[344] others in the practice of certain perversions such as flagellation,[345] but they were rare and unrepresentative. By a process of contamination, one might say, the *maisons de rendez-vous* had usurped the role that had been fulfilled by the first-class *maisons closes*.

The rendezvous would take place in the afternoon; activity usually ceased by 7 P.M.,[346] although some, it is true, closed fairly late, at 11 P.M. or midnight. But "the ladies admitted never spent the night."[347]

It goes without saying that the prices were much higher than in the *maisons closes,* although they varied according to the category of the establishment. When, in 1900, Prefect Lépine was preparing a by-law for the Paris *maisons de rendez-vous,* he divided them into two categories: those charging under forty francs and those charging more. In the more expensive, those around the district of the Etoile, for example, such as the former residence of Arsène Houssaye in 1903,[348] and those of the rue de Provence or the rue Boudreau frequented by the stockbrokers of the Bourse, the charges reached astronomic proportions. In 1903 the minimum fee for a meeting in the better establishments was between sixty and a hundred francs.[349] The most common charge was five hundred francs, half of which went to the manager. Certain society ladies, however, "allowed themselves to be *contacted*," according to Dr. Fiaux, "only at a charge of several thousand francs."[350] By contrast, in some second-class establishments, known after 1900 as *maisons à registre,*[351] the women sometimes sold themselves for five francs; they would await the clients lying on a sofa, playing cards, or reading serial fiction. Here the atmosphere was somewhat like that of a *maison de quartier,* except for the absence of vulgarity.

We must now try to understand how the system functioned and who profited from it. At the head of the establishment was the mistress of the house, the successor to the procuresses of the past. She usually had the air of a respectable woman and received visitors formally dressed. The mistress of a *maison de rendez-vous* employed a network of recruiters, advertisers, and intermediaries to assist her in organizing meetings. The women whom she attracted to her establishment were, it should be repeated, sometimes, perhaps often, registered prostitutes. Most of them, however, were what Carlier termed "inadequately kept women,"[352] whether by a lover or a husband. The evidence suggests that they were often the wives of clerks or small tradesmen.[353] Sometimes it was truly a marital form of procuring, the husband being perfectly aware of what was happening and consenting to it. Zola had presented a couple of this type in *Nana.* We know that Flaubert, just prior to his death, was planning several novels devoted to this marital procuring as it flourished in bourgeois society.[354] By the end of the century this practice seems to have spread into the ranks of the petty bourgeoisie.

The *maisons de rendez-vous* were also the recourse of widows in financial straits or dowerless daughters who hoped to obtain the necessary capital to make a marriage to which their rank in society would permit them; for the latter, the mistress would procure serious lovers, by the month or the year.[355] Finally, one should not forget the trade in the false virgin, a specialty of the *maisons de rendez-vous,* and a subject to which I shall return. In all the personnel was varied, made up of very different types of women who might, using Virmaître's terms, be grouped, depending on the degree of their activity, into two categories: the *plat du jour* and the *intermittentes.*[356]

The way in which the women, who were often perfectly respectable at the outset, were drawn into the system was very subtle. Recruitment was by recommendation: the confidences of a friend or of a woman met in a park while walking with the children, the indiscreet suggestions of a tradesman as to how his bill might be paid, accounts overheard by chance in a shop, the idle chatter of a hairdresser or simply of a chambermaid, the suggestions of an herbalist who sold abortion-inducing drugs,[357] the direct advances of an *entremetteuse* sent by the mistress of a *maison de rendez-vous* and who, using the pretext of a delivery, would hold out the tempting qualities of some potential lover. Often the spectacle of prostitutional activity or its presence in certain places was enough to disturb a woman's peace of mind sufficiently to bring about her fall. Literature is full of examples of this permanent soliciting. There are the feelings of moral vertigo felt by Renée Saccard at the end of an evening spent with a prostitute friend or with her lover in the private room of a late-night restaurant, from which she could observe from the window the activities of the streetwalkers in the boulevard; it was there that she committed incest for the first time. Similarly, it was her presence in Sidonie Rougon's *maison de rendez-vous* that had previously led her to give herself to a young clerk and to let herself go for the first time. Such behavior illustrates the importance of these places in the attraction exerted by the atmosphere of prostitution on bourgeois women. It was to a similar sense of vertigo that the young Baronne de Grangerie gave in; after observing at length the behavior of a prostitute soliciting from the window opposite and noticing that the duration of the contacts was between twelve and twenty minutes, she was seized by an irresistible desire to compete with the prostitute. This game finally forced her to sell herself for two louis to a handsome fair-haired young man whom she invited up and whom she could not reject without causing a scandal.[358]

In the first-class *maisons de rendez-vous* the woman fixed her own price; if it was too high, she would not get her client and would be forced to lower it. Of course, the literature and reports of the time are full of amusing anecdotes,[359] unexpected meetings, and comical adventures set in the *maisons de rendez-vous*. They probably involve a great deal of exaggeration, but above all, they are a clear sign of a wish to cast scorn on the bourgeois *ménage*; this also seems true of the theater of the time.[360]

It was mainly through contacts that those gentlemen who wanted to were led to frequent the *maisons de rendez-vous*. Sometimes, too, they came as the result of an invitation. Rich men or men who were suspected of being in search of companionship would receive at their place of residence cards inviting them to visit the salon of Madame X and inspect her collection of fashions, pictures, or jewelry, learn a language, or visit her Oriental pied-à-terre.[361] Then, there were the classified advertisements in the newspapers, which, though less explicit than those for the *maisons de tolérance,* were no less readily understood.

According to Goron, a former head of the *Sûreté,* or detective force, the clients were often married men looking for an affair, who refused to visit the brothels but who "had no desire to waste their time in preliminaries, in flirtatious behavior in doorways, and who organized liaisons by the month, the fortnight, the week, the hour, one might also say on the run."[362] Sometimes these hour-long meetings were extended; they became "real affairs," some of them even sanctioned by marriage, in a slide from the venal to the legal, which in itself says a lot about the evolution of sexual behavior. In addition, there were the rich foreigners or men passing through Paris, a clientele in which certain *maisons* specialized, even going so far as to organize receptions at which the necessary introductions might be made.

It is not my purpose here to describe these establishments in all their picturesque detail; I refer the reader to the plentiful bibliography concerning the Paris *maisons de rendez-vous*. I shall take only one example, a fairly early one it is true, since it dates from 1888. It concerns the running of a *maison* managed by a Mme. Frétille, a widow, according to Macé,[363] head of the first division of the prefecture of police. Fortunately for us, this woman kept a record of all her activities, and when the police raided her establishment, thousands of documents were seized. Macé, who was able to consult them, left a succinct but extremely valuable summary of them.

Mme. Frétille, a sociologist unbeknownst to herself, classified her clients according to their rank in society and according to the price that could be demanded of them. She also wrote down in registers the names of the partners who had met in her establishments. Her male clientele consisted of the following categories: "Jockey Club, army, navy, judiciary, Stock Exchange, industry."

The list of the procurers of both sexes who had helped the establishment to prosper is a very long one.[364] It might be useful, however, to list them more or less exhaustively in order to show the scope of the network involved, with all its far-reaching ramifications: dressmakers, milliners, laundresses, manageresses of fashion houses; music, singing, and dancing teachers; piano tuners; managers of employment agencies and marriage bureaus; theater agents, photographers, fortunetellers, dentists, hairdressers, chiropodists, manicurists, depilators, midwives, club coachmen; café, restaurant and hotel waiters. In short, in the center of the capital the bourgeois wife was positively besieged, solicited on every side, by a mass of intermediaries who were not afraid to earn extra money by taking commissions from the profits of venal love. If one reads the correspondence of Mme. Frétille it becomes obvious that the recruiters were everywhere, "at the watering-places, at the seaside, in the forests of Bohemia."[365] The profits, although little is known about this, were sometimes astonishing. Meunier cites the case of a second-class *maison de rendez-vous* that charged less than ten francs, but which nonetheless brought the mistress an annual income of seventy thousand francs.[366]

It has to be admitted that, in the forms that I have just described, the *maison de rendez-vous* seems at first glance to be an essentially Parisian phenomenon: indeed, its prosperity and extent required the anonymity of a very large city. Furthermore, apart from a few data of a statistical order, the nature of the documentation I have used presents its own problems. Was not the expansion of the *maison de rendez-vous,* as attested to by contemporaries, whether police, administrators, doctors, or mere eyewitnesses, exaggerated at a time when it was a favorite theme of both novelists and dramatists? To what extent and in what forms was the process able to develop in the larger provincial cities? Was the female personnel that frequented the *maisons de rendez-vous* composed mainly of prostitutes or, on the contrary, the married women whose misbehavior obsessed so many? These questions ought to be examined with the help of firsthand documents.

As luck would have it, there is a very fine series of documents in the archives of the Bouches-du-Rhône concerning the apartments and buildings in Marseilles declared by the prefectural authorities to be "places of debauchery" between 1909 and 1913.[367] This collection comprises forty-eight extremely well filled files; they contain various reports by policemen who, sometimes for several weeks, kept a close watch on a particular establishment before raiding it with a view to finding proof that is was indeed a house of prostitution. A meticulous analysis of these files shows that thirty-six of them were *maisons de rendez-vous,* as I have just defined them.[368] Of course, the picture that these documents allow us to draw cannot take the place of my earlier description. Furthermore, there is nothing to prove that what was the case in Marseilles was representative of the country as a whole; we know very well how unique were the structures of prostitution in France's second city. The files do show, however, that, contrary to my expectations, the *maison de rendez-vous* was not, at the beginning of the century, a specifically Parisian phenomenon. They also allow one to analyze precisely the form these institutions took in the largest of the provincial cities.

The thirty-six *maisons de rendez-vous,* kept by thirty-two women,[369] were dispersed throughout the city and were to be found in twenty-five different streets.[370] So the location of these establishments differed profoundly from that of the *maisons de tolérance,* which were confined to two *quartiers réservés* or red-light districts. The keeper was always a tenant;[371] this fact is specifically mentioned by the police in the case of seventeen of them, and it is easy enough to check in the case of the others, since notification of the decision of the prefecture was given to the owner.

By definition, the *maison de rendez-vous* did not occupy the whole of the building in which it was situated but only a single apartment. Sometimes, however, the rooms that formed this apartment were distributed over several floors; this is specified in the case of eleven of the thirty-six establishments. Usually the building was a respectable one; thus the other tenants who lived at 9 rue de l'Arbre, in which the *maison de rendez-vous* run by Marcelle V—— was situated, were a newspaper owner, a woman living on a private income, a dancing teacher, and a dressmaker. It is worth noting, moreover, that it was usually denunciations emanating from these respectable tenants that triggered a police investigation. Some of these letters of denunciation were astonishingly detailed and expressed above all the then-widespread fear that family life would be disturbed by the visual and, worse, auditory evidence of sexual freedom. Take, for example, the cutler, aged twenty-eight, who denounced Mme S——, whose apartment was situated above his, because he frequently heard "the bed move." He added: "The bed is being made and unmade all the time so that I can tell more or less how many clients are being received."

The Marseilles *maison de rendez-vous* was never situated on the ground floor or entresol of the building; it was usually on the second floor, fairly frequently on the first, sometimes on the third, rarely on the fourth. At a distance from both the concierge's lodge and the maids' rooms, it was therefore on the most elegant, most expensive floor in the building. The apartment usually consisted of between three and six rooms.[372] In almost half the cases it was a five-room apartment consisting of three bedrooms, a drawing-room, and an entrance hall or kitchen. Everything about the apartment—situation, size, arrangement, distribution—was like that of an average bourgeois home and quite different from the model of the *maison de tolérance*.

Only six of the keepers were to my knowledge unmarried; two of these lived with a lover, and the other four were former *filles soumises* recently removed from the register. Usually the woman who managed a *maison de rendez-vous* was a widow (at least six out of these were widows) or a married woman separated from her husband and living alone. At the outset of an investigation there was seldom any question of a husband; with one exception it was the woman who was the tenant of the apartment. In order to elude police investigations more easily thirteen of the thirty-two keepers used a pseudonym: eight of them had chosen first names often adopted by *filles de maison,* while five of them had adopted false surnames.

The keepers of the *maisons de rendez-vous* were, on the average, somewhat older than those of the *maisons de tolérance*.[373] Only seven of the twenty-two whose dates of birth are known to us were under thirty-five, and eleven were over forty; the oldest was seventy-one. The distribution of places of birth seems to be comparable: of the seventeen whose place of origin is known to us, only three were born in Marseilles, two were born in Paris, two came from abroad (Spain and Italy) and one from Algeria; the others were born in various departments.[374]

The *maisons de rendez-vous* were, with a few exceptions, kept by a single woman; one of the keepers was assisted by her mother, another worked with her sister-in-law. Ten out of the thirty-two declared that they had an occupation, which in some sense allowed them to pass in society: four of these women claimed to keep a massage parlor, two a hairdressing establishment; one called herself a milliner, another a seamstress; yet another said she ran a fashion house; and the last claimed to hold meetings of lace-workers and cigarette-makers in her apartment. The *maisons de rendez-vous* of the early years of the century belong, therefore, to the tradition of the pretext shop, except that the police, when they raided these establishments, found practically nothing to justify claims to such activities.[375]

The makeup of the personnel remains the essential issue. The meticulous descriptions made by the police stress its great complexity. One may, very roughly, divide the women into four types:

• To begin with, there were the underage girls. Several of these establishments specialized in juvenile prostitution. Thus Marie B——, who called herself Elvire, prostituted Pauline T——, an eleven-year-old girl who had been solicited by a woman friend while selling the newspaper

Le radical on the cours Saint-Louis. "From that day on," the girl declared to the police, "I go every day from 11 A.M. to 12:30 A.M. and from 5 P.M. to 7 P.M. to the lady's apartment and she gives me between two francs fifty and five francs." Her sexual activity was confined to her hands and mouth: "Only one man possessed me completely," she added, "and it hurt a lot." Mathilde S——, known as Titine l'Apache, prostituted girls of fourteen and fifteen. For three months one of them had gone each day to the keeper's house; she was given half the ten, twenty, or thirty francs paid by the clients, although Louisette, who had introduced her to the *maison,* insisted on taking half of that. Louisette herself was only fifteen; she was Titine's mistress. She solicited for another keeper as well, Louise M——, who also prostituted young girls to her clients. Some of these girls were brought to her by their mothers; thus a thirty-five-year-old woman came regularly to sell her thirteen-year-old daughter. Most of them, however, were shop assistants.

• It often happened—and this seems to be confirmed in most cases—that the personnel was partly or totally made up of *filles soumises,* or "notorious unregistered prostitutes," who had come either from the world of lower-class prostitution or from the *galanterie* higher up the social scale. This tends to confirm the police thesis that those women in the *maisons de rendez-vous* who claimed to be married were in fact prostitutes who knew how to adapt to the new tastes of the clientele. This was the case at Anna O——'s, Anna N——'s, the C——'s, Madame I———'s, and at the establishment run by Rose G——, who had already run *maisons de tolérance* at Privas (1896–1901), Ajaccio (1907–1909), and Marseilles (1909–1912).

• Some tenants[376] used unemployed women or working women who were already on the threshold of prostitution and who, if they had not met a procurer, would probably have entered a *maison de tolérance* or resigned themselves to soliciting in the streets.

• It seems fairly certain that the prostitution of married women was not a myth, even if all those who claimed to be so could not do so legally. Certain keepers of third-class *maisons* arranged rendezvous with women of the petty and middle bourgeoisie. Furthermore, one also found in some of these establishments shop assistants and young women claiming to be musical or theatrical artists.[377]

The keepers of the Marseilles *maisons de rendez-vous* also arranged a few hours of privacy for illicit couples who had met elsewhere; some of the establishments confined themselves to this activity. Unfortunately for us, the police, usually so prolix, remained very discreet on this point.

In many cases—and it is this that makes any description so complicated—the keeper kept under the same roof and set to work different types of personnel, which I have somewhat artificially divided up into categories: the *filles soumises* and the "married women," whether real or false, would merge in an establishment that also received couples. At Halima B——'s, underage girls worked in the morning, adult women in the afternoon. At Madame C——'s, the "married women" received their clients in the salon, the others in the kitchen. But all the women—and this, it should be remembered, was what characterized the *maison de rendez-vous*—wore formal town clothes; they wore hats when they entered or left the building. The introduction of the client, whether in the salon or in the kitchen, was followed by conversation, sometimes assisted by liqueurs or champagne. Again we are very far, here, from the padded silence and animality of the high-class *tolérance,* although occasionally, in exceptional cases,[378] the women wore dressing gowns inside the establishment; the hold of the model provided by the *tolérance* was too strong for all the keepers to shake it off.

With two exceptions the thirty-six *maisons de rendez-vous* operated only during the day; one of them remained open in the evening as well as the daytime. Only two were open in the morning. We know why. The tireless surveillance of the police[379] provides us with the hours during which twelve establishments were frequented. Taken as a whole, the maximum activity of the Marseilles *maisons de rendez-vous* occurred between 4 P.M. and 6 P.M., and not between "five and seven," as the popular prejudice had it. Between 3 P.M. and 4 P.M., and again between 6 P.M. and 7 P.M., activity was fairly intense. The establishment that opened before 3 P.M. or received clients after 7 P.M. was exceptional.

As always, the client appears very little in the documents, although he is not completely absent. The police are kind enough to describe him as a *monsieur,* but a *monsieur* who may belong to any of various social milieus, which means that members of the upper and middle bourgeoisie, and even certain aristocrats passing through Marseilles,[380] frequented the *maisons de rendez-vous;* but there were also petty bourgeois, artisans, and shopkeepers. There were, however, no workers, sailors, or soldiers—or almost none. Certain *maisons* seem to have specialized in a particular type of clientele; others prided themselves on serving men of different social positions. Madame B——, Josephine L——, and Marguerite G—— received men from "good Marseilles society"; three *conseillers généraux,* one local councillor, three mayors, and one deputy mayor intervened with the authorities on behalf of Henriette D—— and a senator in favor of Elise C——. During one afternoon when he was on duty in front of the building in which Jeanne G——'s apartment was situated, a policeman saw seven *messieurs,* including one *décoré* (the honor not being specified) and a naval officer; Céline G——, for her part, received "the commercial high life" of the city.

The client stayed a little longer in the *maison de rendez-vous* than in the *maison de passe;* this is understandable because part of the time was taken up with introductions, conversation, or the consumption of drinks. Guided by the same concern for detail, the police on duty set about calculating, for nine of the thirty-six establishments, the average duration of the client's stay; it lasted between twenty-five minutes and an hour and a half.[381] In one of the *maisons* certain habitués spent the whole afternoon with the *belles de jour.*

The analysis of the prices at ten establishments enables us to distinguish between two types of *maison de rendez-vous:* in six of them the price varied between three and five francs; in the other four it varied between ten and thirty francs, depending on the status of the client and that of the keeper. In every case the keeper received half the sum. From the little evidence available it would seem that the number of contacts made by the women was lower than in the *maisons de tolérance*—on the average between two and four a day. As a result, the number of clients that these establishments could receive in the afternoon was limited; according to police calculations, it varied between four and twenty a day.[382]

The hairdressing salon run by Halima B—— in the rue Venture was a typical example of the first-class Marseilles *maison de rendez-vous.* The establishment consisted of five rooms; the bedrooms were luxuriously furnished. The keeper "put the underage girls to work in the morning." When the police raided the *maison* one afternoon in 1913, the salon was filled with young women; one of them was playing the piano. Of the others, one was seventeen and married; she earned between nine and fifteen francs per client. Two women, aged twenty-five and twenty-eight, were musical artists; they earned ten francs. The fourth, aged thirty-one, had been frequenting the establishment four times a week for six months. Furthermore, the police discovered a woman of thirty-three, another of twenty-four who claimed she was there by mistake and was expecting to have her hair done, and a married woman of twenty-two who declared she was looking for a job in the salon. Two clients were present: a fifty-three-year-old insurance underwriter and a fifty-one-year-old doctor, whom the keeper had charged forty francs.

It would seem, then, on the basis of what emerges from the police archives of Marseilles, that prostitution in the *maisons de rendez-vous* was, at the beginning of the century, a widespread form of venal sex. It was because he was both aware of and disturbed by the increase in the number of such establishments that the prefect had decided to do everything possible to halt the expansion. These establishments seemed all the more dangerous for the protection of public morals in that they sheltered, sometimes at the same time, *filles soumises,* unregistered prostitutes, married women, and adulterous couples. The efforts made by the keepers to deal separately with these various elements of their personnel could not entirely offset the risk of moral contagion. A comparison between Paris and Marseilles leads one to conclude, however, that the proportion of real prostitutes was higher in the provincial *maisons* and that of married women larger in the establishments in the capital; the anonymity enjoyed by Parisian women helps to explain this.

Even if one considers only working-class society, it is clear that, from the earliest decades of the Third Republic, the regulationist strategy elaborated at the beginning of the century had failed completely. Its archaic character was so obvious that after 1880 it found hardly any defenders. But the failure of regulationism did not stem only from the expansion of traditional unregistered prostitution; it is also clear that, at every level, venal sexuality was now imbued with various suggestions of seduction.

I shall now move on from description to an attempt to link together, in order to explain, if only in a summary way, these radical changes in sexual behavior with what historians have taught us of contemporary economic, social, and intellectual developments. A study of the language used to discuss prostitution may enable us to grasp how that language affected, and at the same time tried to stem, developments in behavior.

4. Sexual Privation and the Demand for Prostitution

The failure of the attempt to enclose the prostitute in an establishment; the sight of prostitutes swarming the streets; the spread of unregistered prostitution in drinking places and luxury shops; first the invention, then the spread of the *brasseries à femmes, cafés-concerts,* and *maisons de rendezvous* are all evidence of a shift in the demand for prostitution. During the reign of Louis-Philippe, when immigrants piled into a traditional urban setting that was ill equipped to receive them, this demand emanated above all from individuals who were not yet integrated into urban society and were forced to satisfy their most elementary sexual needs at the lowest cost. Over the decades, this demand, which was declining and had itself been affected by the dislocation caused by urbanization, was succeeded by a demand that was developing in an expanding bourgeoisie that, with increased prosperity, was gradually adopting social practices borrowed from the aristocracy. In these circles men were finding it more and more difficult to bear the constraints of a sexual model that was becoming widespread—indeed almost universal—with the *embourgeoisement* of the new social strata and the moral integration of the working classes. Thus there grew up a new clientele that sought eroticism within the appearances of a bourgeois home: such desires could not be satisfied simply by moments of genital release.

The Slow Destruction of the Earlier Model

An Errant Sexuality

Again, it is not my purpose here to study prostitutional demand during the first half of the century, but some sketch must be made of this model if we are to appreciate its decline. The example of Paris will serve. Louis

Chevalier has shown how difficult it proved to integrate completely the influx of immigrants into urban society.[1] Up to the 1860s, immigration involved a great imbalance between the sexes, resulting in a considerable shortage of girls and women, and in particular young women.[2] The extent of working-class concubinage[3] and the large number of temporary unions, and therefore of illegitimate births and unmarried mothers abandoned by their lovers, demonstrate how difficult it was for the traditional extended peasant family to adapt to the model of the urban nuclear family lacking a broader family base.[4]

The formation of a huge male proletariat in a state of sexual privation was then aggravated by the massive influx of temporary migrants from the countryside, who, like the masons from the Creuse, whose sexual frustrations I have described elsewhere,[5] were crowded into the lodging houses of the Left Bank and of the poorer districts of central Paris, Lyons, and Saint-Etienne. Living constantly in groups, obsessed by the wish to save money and to go home for the winter or summer, they found it impossible to forge lasting relationships with their workmates who were already established in the city, and who, in any case, despised them. This marginalization, which is reminiscent of that suffered by migrant workers in the twentieth century, deprived them of any opportunity to meet women in the urban environment.

All these factors stimulated the development of popular prostitution, so much so that in certain circles, sexual activity and the demand for prostitution tended to be indistinguishable, just as the boundaries between the sexuality of the couple and the sexuality of the group tended sometimes to disappear. Some of the memoranda of the inquiry carried out by the Chamber of Commerce into the lodging houses of Paris in 1847 are highly significant in this regard.

The bourgeoisie had not yet taken possession of the city, however. It feared the laboring classes; it had an exaggerated sense of the connection that then existed between crime and prostitution, and which was based on the common marginalization taking place. In that "introverted" city,[6] in which town planners increased the number of enclosed or semienclosed spaces (squares or walks planted with trees), the bourgeoisie avoided mingling with the working people in the streets, a fear of contact that still finds expression in the fragmentation of space in theaters and the very delicate hierarchization of other public places.

For the bourgeois, the prostitute remained essentially a creature of darkness, enclosed in the brothels of the proletarian districts of Paris or haunting the dimly lit alleyways of the poorer quarters. Like other figures emerging from the masses, she was often, for him, little more than a mask, sometimes harshly lit by a gas lamp.[7] The regulationist project, which culminated in 1830 with the decision of Prefect Mangin to forbid the streets of the capital to all prostitutes, was well adapted to this image of the city and to the nature of the social relations at work in it.

The need for venal sex of a bourgeoisie that invested more than it consumed could not, for the time being, be brought out into the open. Moreover, the bourgeois found it difficult to size up a prostitution that was, for him, still essentially a mass phenomenon, the cesspool that Parent-Duchâtelet made himself to explore, as if he were going off to study refuse and the drainage system.

The Birth of the Working-Class Home

The structures that had given rise to the spread of popular prostitution were gradually to come apart. The decisive period in this process is unquestionably the second decade of the Second Empire.[8] It was during those years that the integration of the immigrant proletariat began to take place. This adaptation took many forms: it found its passion at first in the return to demographic "normality." After 1860 the influx of immigrants slowed down. The balance between the sexes gradually tended to improve, although there was still a shortage of young women and, in certain districts and streets, the distribution of the sexes was still extremely uneven; for a long time, certain of the back streets, with their lodging houses, remained almost entirely male.[9] Unquestionably, the behavior of the temporary migrants was changing, although the speed of the process has been exaggerated. Their trips home became less frequent; the better integrated among them sent for their wives; temporary migration was gradually transformed into more or less permanent settlement.[10]

Above all the models of the nuclear family and of the bourgeois home were slowly assimilated by the urban proletariat. The period of disarray and of sexual illegality that was bound up with the abandonment of the rural family was followed by a period of adaptation. Integration in the city was first of all a familial integration. As Jeanne Gaillard has remarked, "The workers longed for a home, married life, a normal existence."[11] This process, which accelerated considerably during the 1860s, was reflected and perhaps accentuated by a populist literature of positivist inspiration, of which Jules Simon's *Ouvrière* is perhaps the best example. Pierre Peirrard has also noted a spontaneous movement to regularize working-class unions in Lille, and the success of the work of the Society of Saint-François-Régis speeded up this normalization.[12] Working-class discourse at the end of the century recorded and amplified this familialization. Analyzing its content, Michelle Perrot was led to note the formation of a new working-class household, in which the bourgeois marriage constructed around the child was grafted onto the peasant household of an older France: "The worker was primarily the head of a household with a wife and children, and his wage claims and other demands, his thoughts on education, work, apprenticeship, and security, were constantly based on this reality."[13]

Integration was encouraged by a decline in abject poverty and, in particular, of that "chronic poverty," which, as Gaillard has shown, diminished with the spread of Haussmannization.[14] The collection of highly detailed and very convincing essays edited by A. Daumard[15] and P. Léon, [16] Yves Lequin's thesis, [17] and, in greater detail, the researches of F. Codaccioni[18] prove that the workers in the country's main cities (Paris, Lyons, Toulouse, and to a lesser degree Lille and Bordeaux) shared in the overall economic upturn of the latter half of the nineteenth century. Furthermore, certain marginalized and therefore "dangerous" nuclei, which lay at the centers of the big cities, were tending to disappear, as were, for example, the ragmen[19] and water-carriers of Paris.

Better education also facilitated integration; we now know that, even in the most backward regions, illiteracy had become almost nonexistent in the cities by the end of the Second Empire.[20]

While violence and widespread illegal activity were diminishing among the urban proletariat, the links between crime and prostitution tended to become looser. This phenomenon is connected to the same process as the assimilation of the conjugal model and the model of the home. Charles, Louise, and Richard Tilly have demonstrated convincingly that there was an overall decline in proletarian violence during the second half of the nineteenth century,[21] and Michelle Perrot has shown how "urban violence tended to decrease, to become less widespread, and more specific"[22] as a result of the regulation brought about by industrial civilization, which is "capable of subjecting to its ends" all man's instincts, including those of pleasure.[23] Delinquency itself was transformed: cunning tended to replace brutal violence and swindling the theft of food.[24] In this new context the independent or unregistered prostitute would no longer inspire the same fear in the bourgeois.

One can hardly overstate the importance for the present investigation of this popular moralization, of the decline of widespread illegality, including in sexual matters. In the eyes of the bourgeoisie itself, the laboring classes gradually ceased to be identified as the dangerous classes. Crime and delinquency were now regarded as the exclusive domain of a subproletariat, which, Michel Foucault believed, was cleverly marginalized.[25] Like familialization, this moralization was apparent in working-class discourse.[26] Indeed, the traditional view had been turned inside out: it was now the bourgeois who embodied vice. The boss was reproached for thinking about nothing but eating, drinking, sleeping, and surrounding himself with luxuries; he was now represented as a pleasure-loving decadent, much given to orgies.[27] Work and pleasure were again perceived as being antinomic, but this time in working-class discourse, which thereby assumed the values on which industrial civilization was based. At the same time, the factory worker or miner was gradually adapting to the demands of mass production.[28]

Since the appearance of Michelle Perrot's work, Lion Murard and Patrick Zylberman have carried out a more systematic analysis of the process of working-class moralization and of the strategy implemented by the companies to accelerate it in the mining communities. They discern a "vast revolution operating between 1860 and 1880 simultaneously in the home, at work, and in morals."[29] The major purpose of this revolution was the formation of the working-class home. This event appears to have been only a new stage in the "somatic *dressage*" of the worker; indeed, during the first half of the century, what mattered above all was getting the producer to work, and this then involved, on the part of the bourgeoisie, an acceptance of heterogeneity and congestion. Meanwhile, from about 1860 to 1880 a vast attempt was initiated to separate one social element from another, "to eliminate confusions." This led to the building of public housing from which the brothel was excluded and to a systematic effort to normalize morals.

This somatic *dressage* and this moralization, which were two inseparable aspects of the same scheme, since production required the high moral quality of the worker, were to be expressed in slum clearance and the birth of the working-class home. With this in view, "an attempt was made to isolate, to distribute the members of the same family inside the home, in such a way as to avoid body-to-body contact."[30] Thus, a "sexually peaceful"[31] space was constituted; a "painless subjugation of sexuality"[32] took place, accompanied by an exaltation of familial feeling. It became the aim "to assign precise, enclosed, and obligatory places for lovemaking,"[33] to compress "the volume of erotic behavior,"[34] to arrange things in such a way that the bedroom became the exclusive place of lovemaking. *"It was a victory over the wine shop, the bar, and other evil places."*[35] Thus triumphed the principle of each individual in his own bedroom and in his own bed, and the bourgeois fear of the promiscuity, the hovel, and the common bed of the proletarians was exorcised.

The creation of this type of home life implies the elimination of celibacy and concubinage. This explains the policy of "apartheid of bachelors,"[36] systematically carried out by the mining companies (and society as a whole),[37] and the diatribes against paying guests taken in by working-class families. This strategy is of fundamental importance to this study because it impeded the sexuality of bachelors and therefore condemned them to resort to the prostitute. Not only was concubinage condemned by the clergy, but it was actually prohibited by the by-laws of the mining communities.

At the same time, attempts were made to isolate families from one another within buildings in such a way as to reduce to a minimum opportunities for meeting and thus eliminate "the eroticism of corridors and staircases."[38] These various schemes succeeded as well in undermining the old horizontal relationships, destroying, for example, the men's clubs that encouraged popular prostitution. Employers also tried to fill the hours between the worker's labor and rest. He was encouraged to take up raising vegetables during his leisure time: the aim was nothing less than to turn the dancer, the pillar of the wine shop and brothel, into a gardener.[39] Thus, the process of moralization advanced, and the model of a home life for a new race of workers forged by production was created.

It is an attractive schema, a demonstration that is often convincing in that it is based on a thorough analysis of the by-laws of qualitative evidence, of the structure of the urban landscapes and of the new working-class communities. It is an argument that has confirmed, from a particular example, what my study of prostitutional behavior was beginning to suggest. Nevertheless, these hypotheses must be supported. Unfortunately, there is very little work in quantitative history that would enable me at present to confirm or deny them. The differential demography of the second half of the nineteenth century is only just under way.[40] A distinction can be made now, however: we must be careful not to confuse a strategy proposed by the employers with what actually happened. Thus, M. Gilet and his pupils note a decline in concubinage in the department of the Nord, but only at the very end of the nineteenth century. In that region the period 1850-1890 was even marked by a spread of this practice and by an increase in illegitimate births. G. Jacquemet's conclusions on the population of Belleville also urge prudence. Indeed, this researcher fails to discern any marked decline in working-class concubinage between 1860 and 1910. In fact, only a subtle analysis based on a typology of behavior related to concubinage could throw light on this delicate problem. In particular, we must distinguish between the fate, on the one hand, of *concubinage de fréquentation* (the equivalent of an engagement), a form of temporary sexuality, as well as permanent concubinage of a kind to be found in the Nord, which differed little from marriage except that the relationships were not legalized, and, on the other hand, that of an erratic ephemeral concubinage closely bound up with prostitution, and which constituted the only barometer of "morality."

In any case, it seems to me that, overall, the state of research suggests that a familialization and moralization of the working class did take place during this period.[41] No doubt this process accelerated during what Michelle Perrot felicitously calls "the workers' century" (1880-1936),[42] a period during which there emerged a strengthened sense of identity that found expression in the use of special slang, in specific forms of sociability, in a new pride at being a manual worker and living off one's wits, and, most important, in a lively sense of independence from authority. The moralization process, even if it stemmed from the employers' strategy, expressed and therefore helped reinforce this working-class pride.

All this explains why the old structures of prostitution were declining. Broadly speaking, prostitution was ceasing to be *above all* an indispensable outlet allowing a suddenly marginalized male proletariat to satisfy its sexual needs as best it could. The prostitutes gradually tended to form a voluntarily marginalized group at the service of a proliferating bourgeoisie that was still the prisoner of its sexual model. Prostitution was changing its function and style; this mutation reflected a new stage in the development of capitalist structures in urban society.

It goes without saying that this was a very slow process. There were still groups of unmarried proletarians in a state of sexual privation in the large towns and, sometimes, where one might least expect to find them, for example in the heart of Haussmannized Paris.[43] Later a new type of subproletariat was to form, made up largely of foreign workers who found assimilation difficult and who were separated from the French national group by a barrier of incomprehension. The influx of Italian and Belgian workers, of Jews from central Europe, and of colonials was to bring about an expansion in new forms of lower-class prostitution, often of an unregistered kind, as we have seen in relation to the mining area of Briey. A sizable popular prostitution did survive, therefore. But after 1860 it was no longer this from of prostitution that spread; it no longer satisfied an expanding demand, and it was no longer a subject of national concern because it was no longer seen or feared by the bourgeoisie. Furthermore, the tastes, needs, and prostitutional habits of the proletariat had themselves evolved, at a time that was seeing, as I have shown, a diminution in violence and the assimilation of bourgeois values and morals. In imitating the petty bourgeois, the proletarian inherited some of the latter's frustrations and fantasies. He too now demanded that he be allowed some semblance of seduction in his dealings with prostitutes.

The New Demand for Prostitution

"Monsieur's Expenses"

The new demand resulted initially from the numerical growth and above all the increased wealth of social groups within the bourgeoisie. A. Daumard[44] observes that, during the second half of the nineteenth century, the members of the business bourgeoisie (merchants, industrialists, bankers) benefited from an extremely rapid increase in wealth, one that was more marked, in particular, than that of the bourgeoisie of property owners and senior civil servants that had dominated urban society under the reign of Louis-Philippe. This shift in wealth within the governing classes is of fundamental importance to this study. Most researchers who have investigated this problem have concerned themselves with the expansion of the intermediary stratum formed by what was then called the urban middle classes,[45] which also, but in an uneven way, shared in this increased wealth.[46] On the subject of Paris, Daumard believes that it was at the level of the middle and upper bourgeoisie that the largest increase in fortunes occurred[47] and lays considerable emphasis on this *"movement upward of average conditions."*[48] The increase in wealth of the small enterprise, the shop, and the workshop seems to have been less rapid and that of the clerks and lower-ranking civil servants much below the average. Nevertheless, these groups benefited from the general movement, as did members of the liberal professions, middle management, and, at the end of the century, engineers, whose rise during the decades before the First World War has been demonstrated by Maurice Lévy-Leboyer.[49] In these circles the changes in habits of consumption and venal sex should be regarded like those in any other type of consumption. Daumard and P. Léon are well aware of how this increase in wealth was accompanied by a shift in the composition of fortunes: it was above all personal fortunes that increased—that is to say, wealth that was easily transferable. Moreover, income gradually gained primacy over acquired wealth.

The increased mobility of bourgeois men and, accordingly, time spent away from their places of work offered ample opportunities for sexual adventure. The development of international tourism,[50] the presence of large numbers of foreigners in Paris and in the watering places, train travel,[51] voyages at sea, holidays by the sea,[52] the new fashion for long pilgrimages, the massive influx of provincials into the capital during the universal expositions,[53] theatrical tours, the density of the network of commercial representation—all these were factors contributing to an increase in the demand for prostitution on the part of bourgeois males.

The analysis of account books carried out by Marguerite Perrot[54] has demonstrated the significance of such headings as "Monsieur's Expenses," "Alms," and "Traveling Expenses." Of course, a wife who kept her husband's account books would never dream of adding up his entertainment expenses. Nevertheless, the increase in such expenditure probably points to an expansion in this type of consumption. Was it not a tradition among the provincial bourgeoisie that the income from government stock should be devoted, at least in part, to Monsieur's entertainment? And did not Victor Hugo jot down in his notebooks under the heading "Charity" sums of money paid to prostitutes?

The Intensity of Sexual Frustration

The blossoming of male sexuality in those bourgeois milieus that tended both to expand and to grow richer was impeded by a number of factors, not all of which (far from it) were related to the obligation to make marriages dictated solely by considerations of fortune.[55] Theodore Zeldin has rightly remarked, in his study of the emotional relations of the bourgeois couple, that the romantic idealization of the wife made prostitution even more necessary: the cult of the purity of the young women of that class made them inaccessible.[56] Freud long ago discerned that the two erotic poles of Victorian man—idealization and degradation[57]— were in fact complementary. This is what Jean Borie describes as "the cardiac rhythm" of the male sexuality of the time—that is to say, the alternation of "exploits in brothels" and "angelic, passionate petitions." This bipolarity tended finally to be resolved, after the experience of a double failure, in an anesthetizing married life.

The rise of the religion of the wife-mother, preached, after Michelet, by the prophets of progress (in the first rank of which are to be placed first Hugo then the Zola of the period after *Le docteur Pascal*), and reinforced by medical discourse,[58] had long since impeded the blossoming of marital sexuality. "Pleasure in sexual intercourse," Zeldin writes,[59] "could not in such circumstances be sought with [wives], who were dedicated to motherhood." For her part, Noami Schor, through the behavior of Hélène Grandjean and her daughter, rightly concludes that the idea of a mother enjoying sexual pleasure was then the supreme scandal, or rather the unthinkable.[60] Borie, in agreement with both

Sartre and Foucault, observes that a reversal had taken place in this regard since the eighteenth century. Desire and pleasure, which were no longer exalted as ends in themselves but were associated with generation, were relegated to the new status of genetic instinct. Sexual intercourse in marriage was now closely bound up with the notion of duty.[61] The influence of positivism and the progress of materialism and free-thinking did not fundamentally put into question this marital model.[62] The work of Jules Simon on this subject is very revealing; progressives, like radicals, were as eager as Catholics to promote the notion of duty rather than pleasure.

More generally, the intensification of familial feelings and the painless subjugation of sexuality that characterized bourgeois marriage and home had the effect in the end, as it spread through the whole of society, of making eroticism a specialty. It was the very nature of Mme. Arnoux's attractions, the warm welcome received in her home, that formed the basis of Rosanette's success. The sentimental education of the young bourgeois was inconceivable without this duality, even if he refused, unlike Frédéric Moreau, the old-fashioned temptation of aristocratic eroticism.

Throughout the century the physiologists tried to provide a scientific basis for this conception of woman as wife and mother.[63] It remained dominant until about 1900, although the evolution of male taste and of the forms of desire leads one to believe that a profound transformation was then taking place. Dr. Louis Fiaux, describing, in the footsteps of the famous Dr. Garnier, the sexual behavior of the women of his time and of his world, considered in 1880 as axioms of "positive sociology" the following propositions: "The generative crisis (or the need for intercourse) is manifested in most women every twenty or twenty-five days. In the case of adult, healthy men, it is much more frequent; it no doubt varies according to the strength and habits of the subjects, but with Haller, Trousseau, and most of the physiologists, I believe that it occurs every three or four days at the latest." He goes on to express satisfaction that "their [women's] more passive role in generation, the less frequent character of their crises and of their sexual desires generally preserve us from their tyranny." "I even believe," he goes on, "that women are more demanding out of coquetry than out of debauchery, out of self-interest rather than out of sensuality. Knowing our needs, they demand much in order to bind us to them and thus to protect themselves from our infidelities."[64]

This passage is a good enough summary of what was then the received wisdom concerning womens' sexual behavior. A reading of the gynecological literature,[65] and, in particular, of the articles devoted to the struggle against sterility, reinforces the impression that the act was extremely short and very monotonous.[66] This is all the more understandable in that, before the spread of Neisser's discoveries, gonorrhea and urethritis were attributed to "overpassionate"[67] sexual intercourse. The most eminent scientists, such as Professor Alfred Fournier, believed that "special excitements" and sexual intercourse too frequently repeated had pathological consequences. The female reserve that resulted from this theoretical environment is sometimes described in an aggressive way. Dr. Fiaux notes the large number of individuals bitten by their wives who refused to practice oral sex.[68]

It is understandable enough that wives' behavior should have led husbands to seek satisfaction outside marriage and, if necessary, with prostitutes. The unequal frequency of sexual desire in men and women, regarded as a scientific fact, justified the existence of prostitution and led to male adultery being regarded as "a safety valve."[69] Furthermore, as Theodore Zeldin notes,[70] the conditions of monogamous marriage did not at this time allow the husband to have regular sexual intercourse with his wife. It was, of course, quite common for women to refuse to fulfil their marital duties. In addition, menstruation, pregnancy, and strictures that sexual intercourse should be moderate, indeed infrequent (nonexistent if possible), during the nursing period, and above all the prevalence of genital diseases in women[71] had the effect of aggravating the supposed difference in frequency of sexual desire between the sexes and led to male frustration. Finally, it goes without saying that for all husbands anxious that their wives avoid an unwanted pregnancy, the prostitute was a partner with whom it was not necessary to practice coitus interruptus.

Since Michelet, the influence exerted by priests on the behavior of wives has often been faulted. Insofar as he was a director of conscience, the confessor was the only man to receive women's sexual confidences. By increasing the number of prohibitions, he prevented couples from enjoying sexual fulfillment, whatever erotic value transgression might have had. Indeed, we know that many confessors at this time urged women to refuse their favors to husbands who practiced coitus interruptus. Some even praised the virtues of continence by mutual consent after procreation, advising them to avoid anything that might inflame desire in the husband and proposed as models the chaste couple, Mary and Joseph. The clergy spoke of man's needs and not of the couple's pleasure; it presented sexual relations as an act of submission.[72] There was a total coherence between this conception and Augustinian ideas on prostitution. It should be added that, on the advice of their confessors, women frequently felt that they had a duty to convert their freethinking husbands; of course, this did not advance good relations between husbands and wives. By turning to prostitution, however, the husband could experience that "comradeship between men and prostitutes" described by Zola.[73] The bourgeois male's frequenting of prostitutes and his behavior toward them represented, from this point of view, a protest against the sexual ideas of his class.[74]

The Proliferation of Ghettos

The growth in the number of petty-bourgeois bachelors is one of the major aspects of the shift in prostitutional structures. Many categories of individuals who were not well off but who belonged to the petty or middle bourgeoisie by virtue of their culture, their tastes, their way of life, and their ambitions replaced the unmarried proletarians of the first part of the nineteenth century and played a crucial role in the demand for prostitution. Ostensibly well integrated into urban life, these bachelors in fact led a marginal existence, especially in the sexual domain.

Those who might be grouped generically as public and private employees formed the first of these categories, which included clerks and shop assistants. This category had grown extremely rapidly in number. Men made up the personnel of the wholesale businesses in the rue du Sentier as well as of the retail clothing shops and hardware stores in the city center; in the department stores too it was men who ran the fashion departments. Furthermore, we should not forget the large increase in the numbers of shop assistants, since we know that, at least up to 1880, the upheavals in the structure of commerce did nothing to prevent the expansion of many branches of the retail trade.[75] In fact, the effect was quite the reverse.

Daumard, writing about Paris, and Léon, discussing Lyons, demonstrate clearly that the distribution of wealth within this group took the form of an inverted spinning top. The bulk of these employees, as far as money was concerned, were deeply rooted in the working class; only a very small elite managed to free themselves and enter the middle bourgeoisie. Furthermore, if these clerks and shop assistants shared in the general increase in wealth during the second half of the nineteenth century, it was to a degree well below average.[76]

In the offices, the dependence of the clerk was striking: when he entered a business it was very often for life.[77] Let us not forget the works of Maupassant or even those of Courteline, not to mention the tragic fate of Ferdinand's father in Céline's *Mort à crédit (Death on the installment plan)*. Such clerks were confronted by a severe sexual problem:

many did not have enough money to start a home when they were young or even to live with a woman; in any case, they did not have enough money to keep a family in a respectable manner. Celibacy and late marriage were for many of them the only possibilities. By the Second Empire, Paris led the country in the number of unmarried adult males and late marriages.[78] The evolution of these two indicators at Bordeaux[79] and in the capital is revealing.

Sexual privation among the clerks and its palliatives were an inexhaustible fictional theme in the second half of the nineteenth century. Too poor to marry or to keep a woman, the young clerk nevertheless did earn enough to pay for a prostitute. From Flaubert to Maupassant and Charles-Louis Philippe, the novelists described a whole range of venal sex to which the clerk, shop assistant, and artist could have recourse when they escaped, through bachelorhood, marital misery. Yet it was Huysmans, the purest representative of this "bachelor literature," the emergence of which after 1850 has been pointed out by Jean Borie, who, in all his novels, best describes the sexual frustrations of the petty-bourgeois male and of the relief he sought. The problem of the *ménage* lies at the center of his work; along with the venereal danger, it constitutes one of the fundamental obsessions of his heroes. André, in *En ménage,* returns to his unfaithful, frigid wife after exhausting various forms of venal sex; Cyprien *(Les soeurs Vatard, En ménage)* decides to live with an elderly prostitute after ruining himself keeping a young working-class woman; Léon attempts to live with Marthe, who is on the edge of prostitution, but this ends in failure; Folantin, the clerk of *A vau-l'eau,* old before his time, has given up sex but indulges in a final, unhappy experience with a none-too-young unregistered prostitute. Marriage itself is essentially conceived by Huysmans' characters, as is apparent in *En rade,* as a palliative, as a means of guaranteeing comfort and sex, a profoundly pessimistic vision, a reflection of the terrible sexual privation endured by a large portion of urban society. Furthermore, such works of literature reveal the extent to which fear of "trouble to follow"[80] led the bachelor to the prostitute, thus avoiding any of the problems that might attend seducing an honest young woman.

The fate of another sexual proletariat seems closely related: that of the students, both in the provinces and in Paris—in other words, all those "young men without roots" partly destined to swell the number of "proletarians with degrees" whose troubles Jules Vallès has described, unless, as they sometimes did, they resigned themselves to becoming tutors, whose sorry condition has been evoked by Paul Gerbod.[81]

This category saw a marked increase in size, while the absence of higher education for women deprived these young men of partners who could have shared their aesthetic tastes and intellectual interests. Today it is difficult for us to imagine what the sexual lives of those groups of male students lacking the company of women students must have been like.

Of course, we do know that recourse to venal sex was traditional among these young men. In 1799 the comrades of the young Henri Beyle (the future Stendhal), uprooted young men from Grenoble, had recourse to the services of low-class Parisian prostitutes.[82] It was by living with Sapho that Jean, Alphonse Duadet's hero, solved his problem. Literature offers innumerable examples of young men who, during their student days, keep a prostitute or are kept by her.[83] Sexual illegality was the rule in that milieu: student sexuality and venal sex were then inextricably linked. But what sexual privation these literary descriptions must conceal! None is more revealing in this regard than Paul Alexis' novella *Les femmes du père Lefèvre*. There the sexual frustration of the students at a provincial university (Aix-en-Provence) are laid bare; they explain the sudden collective release that follows the arrival in the city of a truckload of *pierreuses* recruited in the port of Marseilles by old Lefèvre, a former soldier and the young men's drinking companion.

More generally, the "sexual ghetto"[84] in which the bourgeois adolescent was trapped grew ever larger with the growth in numbers of the petty, middle, and upper bourgeoisie. Indeed, although the young working-class man, from adolescence on, was able to have sexual relations with girls from his own milieu, the young bourgeois was almost condemned to initiation by a prostitute, followed by the practice of venal or ancillary sex.[85] The importance attached by this class to the virginity of its young women, delivered intact, complete with dowry, on their wedding day, and the refusal until the very end of the century[86] to use techniques of provisional sexuality, once the rule in rural society, provided prostitutes, despite the work of the vice squad, with a large clientele of adolescent schoolboys.

The establishment of conscription, on July 27, 1872, certainly had complex effects on prostitution.[87] It led to an immediate massive increase in the demand for prostitutes in the garrison towns and military ports. These young men, at the height of their sexual desire, released from the pressures exerted by family and village, where prostitution was relatively infrequent, enjoying a new anonymity in the big cities, could not but be tempted during their free hours by the delights vaunted by the older soldiers, and often even by officers. In this regard Dr. Vigneron[88] discusses the role of the "rounds" that the new recruits were forced to offer their comrades. Furthermore, many reservists took advantage of their thirteen- or twenty-eight-day periods of service to throw off the conjugal yoke.[89]

Finally, it is possible that after 1880, probably in a fairly small section of the working class, a new phenomenon began to impede the process of moralization then under way. Indeed, we know that the development of technology and of the forms of industrial management resulted in depriving the worker of much of his technical skill.[90] This development seems to have resulted in an increased desire for pleasure: the frustrated producer wanted to consume. This mental process seems to have involved mainly the more highly skilled categories of workers. If this hypothesis is true, it would help to explain the development of new forms of prostitutional behavior within the working class itself.

A bourgeoisie that was expanding and getting richer but whose sexual frustrations were intense, an increase in sexual ghettos in which a growing number of young men found themselves trapped, a rapid increase in the number of urban bachelors—all these things helped create a new demand that, it should be repeated, reinforced the demand already emanating from a proletariat of workers living on the boundaries of the city. It goes without saying that this new demand was different in kind; it no longer involved only lodging-house prostitution, the result of a mere demographic anomaly. The transfer of clientele was accompanied by a mutation in sensibility and, consequently, in behavior where prostitution was concerned.

Changes in the Forms of Desire

Of course, this mutation was modulated according to social category. It found expression, however, in overall phenomena that should first be described. In order to understand those phenomena, we must take into account the nature of the bourgeois home and of bourgeois sexual behavior, precisely to the degree that they tended to spread throughout the whole social pyramid.

The prostitute's client now demanded some semblance of seduction, of feeling, even of attachment; this involved a certain continuity in the relationship. In any case, the mass consumption practiced in the popular brothel was now found repugnant, unless it was accompanied by a technical specialty. If the act were not given a particular value by a genuinely erotic environment,[91] the client felt ill at ease and frustrated; disappointed and humiliated, he would beat a hasty retreat.[92]

These feelings explain the repugnance for anything smacking too much of professionalism and a preference on the part of men for the clandestine. Even the *fille en carte,* the independent registered prostitute, had to try to pass herself off as unregistered, or actually present herself

as such. As we have seen, the numbers of pseudo-unregistered prostitutes increased as the *maison de tolérance* declined, giving rise to pseudo–
maisons de rendez-vous and, later, to the fashion for the pseudo-minor.
All these practices strengthened the impression for bourgeois observers
of an extremely rapid increase in unregistered prostitution.

The client, especially if he was a comfort-loving bourgeois, often
wanted his relations with a prostitute to be based on the conjugal model,
with, of course, the addition of eroticism. He wanted those relations to
form a parallel union if he was married or a substitute for marriage if he
was not. This explains the increase in the number of kept women, or at
least of prostitutes who were "seen again," and also the attraction at the
end of the century of the *maison de rendez-vous,* where the client could
believe that he was practicing venal adultery or, better still, imagine that
he was possesing a woman who belonged to a higher social class than
his own, to which he could aspire but could make no claim.[93] It was no
longer a matter of giving vent to sudden sexual urges. What a male
satisfied when he bought a woman whom, in other circumstances, he
could not possibly seduce was fantasy.

In the upper and middle bourgeoisie and at certain levels of the petty
bourgeoisie, a trickling down of aristocratic tastes was taking place. We
understand many of the aspects of the process: J. P. Aron has analyzed
the way in which gastronomy gradually penetrated middle-class circles,[94]
while Gaillard has shown how the department stores brought within
reach of these social groups a standard of quality in clothing hitherto
reserved for the aristocracy.[95] The same went for "illicit" sex—a little
later it would seem, than for gastronomy. The link between these forms
of imitative social behavior is obvious. I have examined the development
of prostitution in the fashionable cafés, the late-night restaurants, and
the deluxe shops. The new forms of behavior where sexuality and pleasure are concerned were only one element in a totality of new needs.

These needs and the forms of behavior that they determined were
transmitted by osmosis to the base of the social pyramid. The attraction
felt by the shop assistant for the *fille de brasserie* and the feeling that led
the worker to desert the prostitute of the proletarian brothel for the
barmaid are also expressions of this process.

The case of the soldier is more complex and sufficiently meaningful
to be examined separately. As long as the army consisted of men who
enlisted for seven years, became real professionals, were kept in enforced
celibacy, and condemned to frequent changes of garrison, the brothel
seemed to be the indispensable complement to the barracks. Even the
officers, who had often risen from the ranks and were largely petty bourgeois in origin,[96] were not averse to frequenting the *maisons de tolér-*

ance.[97] The difficulty experienced by members of the armed forces in integrating into society as a whole justified, therefore, the role of prostitution. Furthermore, the solicitude with which, throughout the century, the military hierarchy regarded the brothel is explained by a wish to safeguard the health of the troops, to canalize the sexual needs of officers and men, and, by the same token, to provide a safety valve for the sexual tensions that the presence of a large garrison could not fail to arouse in a town.

The relations between civil and military society, which were imbued with a reciprocal sexual anxiety, made the *maison de tolérance* virtually necessary if conflict, which might well degenerate into civil disorder, was to be avoided. In short, the army brothel, or rather the brothel frequented by soldiers, was the mode best suited to carry out the function assigned to it by regulationism, for it was here that sexual frustration was most intense. It was hardly surprising, therefore, that the military hierarchy was the most faithful and long-lasting advocate of the system.

The fact that the brothel was one of the points of contact between the two societies[98] explains both the attraction and the hostility it aroused among soldiers. This ambivalence is well conveyed by Léon Hennique's novella *L'affaire de grand 7,* from which the author describes the sacking of a *maison de tolérance* and the massacre of the inmates by an enraged garrison after the murder of one of its members by the *patron*. The author puts the conclusion in the mouth of the garrison's commanding officer: "All those young braggarts are more stupid than children! . . . They have smashed their toy." It goes without saying that the Franco-Prussian war emphasized the role of the brothel in military society. Its description now became a leitmotif of the naturalist novel.

National conscription and, until 1905, the gradual shortening of the length of military service, together with a return to the conception of the citizen-soldier, gradually altered these forms of behavior. Of course, it should be repeated, the enlistment of massive contingents could not fail to give rise to an overall increase in prostitution, but here too this was accompanied by a mutation in sensibility. The reduction in the length of military service assisted the integration of the soldier into civilian society, or at least went some way toward bridging the gap that had opened up between the two worlds. The sexual marginalization of the soldier was somewhat mitigated. He now kept "*the memory* of his old civilian life";[99] he kept in close touch with his family and with the girls back home, even if he did not actually have a fiancée. The adoption of the principle of regional enlistment and an increase in the amount of leave reinfo ced this process. The citizen-soldier had a much better idea than the Second Empire trouper of what real erotic relations were; he had often experienced a wealth of sexual relations that transcended mere genital release. The brothel seemed less necessary and the reality of it more disappointing. The frequenting of prostitutes gradually ceased to be a military dogma, and this has to be seen as one of the major causes of the crisis in the lower- and middle-level *maisons*.

Furthermore, especially during the early years of the twentieth century, changes in barracks life loosened still further the ties with the brothel: there was a growth in education and an attempt to inform the soldier about the dangers of sex;[100] in addition, the barracks became a pleasanter place to be, with more soldiers' clubs and libraries. As these and other factors made continence easier, the officers, more of whom now came from military academies and were often aristocratic in background, refused to lead or to accompany their men to the brothel, even when the keeper reserved for their use, as was often the practice, her best rooms and her most luxurious salon.

To sum up: the circumstances had gradually changed; customs and practices had altered; and, in the years prior to the First World War, this process was reinforced by a campaign of sexual moralization carried out by the military authorities. The period from approximately 1860 to 1914 saw the development, therefore, of a new kind of demand for prostitution. The change was more qualitative than quantitative. It was the demand of a different social and mental nature that was to give rise to more conspicuous forms of consumption, forms that were much more open. It was a demand that now resulted mainly from the frustrations that stemmed from the sexual repression inherent in maintaining and diffusing the bourgeois conjugal model. Naturally enough this demand, and the change in socioeconomic structures that gave rise to it, were to determine in turn and development of a corresponding supply; and this was made easier by the fact that the new needs, which cost more to satisfy, now brought considerably higher profits to those involved. Can it be said, however, that prostitutional activity as a whole had increased, as contemporary observers suggested? Despite the obvious progress of unregistered prostitution, and taking into account the decline of the *maison de tolérance*, it would be difficult to prove that this was the case. In sexual matters, the measure of phenomena depends more on the degree of perception and on the fantasies of the observer than on the reality of the facts.

Adapting Supply to Demand

As the way in which the prostitute presented herself to the client altered, then, so did the recruitment of prostitutes adapt to the new sensibility.

It must be recognized from the outset that this would not have been possible without a profound mutation in the urban context. As a result of that mutation, the bourgeois and the prostitute simultaneously took possession of the city; the new urbanism carried within it the failure of the plan for an enclosed regulationism.

Woman as Spectacle

This mutation was one of the results, and probably the most evident one, of what we call, somewhat inaccurately, Haussmannization. A series of studies—of Paris by C. M. Léonard and J. Gaillard, who coined the term "extroverted city,"[101] of Lille by P. Pierrard, of Lyons,[102] of Bordeaux by P. Guillaume, of Marseilles and Toulouse—has demonstrated very clearly, barring a few small differences,[103] that the expanding bourgeoisie took simultaneous possession of the center of the city in which they lived. The enclosed spaces typical of the town planning of the Restoration were supplanted by wide arterial roads bordered by huge sidewalks. The creation at the center of the larger cities of a business quarter, in which banks, company headquarters, and department stores sprang up, gave rise to an increase in fashionable cafés and restaurants. The building of the railway stations and the increasing number of places where people could pass the time helped change the face of the city and the behavior of its population. The atmosphere of the street changed as the sidewalks were "cleaned up"[104] and made less crowded; gas lighting and, at least in the capital, the establishment of a proper police force made the city safer. In his novel *Au bonheur des dames,* Zola magnificently describes the impression of invasion brought about at this time by the seizure of the city by its inhabitants and, above all, by its bourgeoisie. In clever counterpoint the author describes at the same time the spread of roadworks, the shift in commercial structures, and the invasion of the crowd. It is no longer possible to say whether Haussmannization created the influx or merely stemmed an irresistible tide.

It was then that the prostitute emerged from the shadows. She now sought the lighting that would emphasize her makeup; she dared to show herself; she circulated tirelessly. Animated by the same movement that drove the bourgeoisie, battalions unfurled from the neighboring heights. At Lille[105] the prostitutes flooded in toward the Haussmannized center, attracted by the high prices they could extract from the bourgeois clientele. This transfer of prostitutes toward the center appears to have been a general phenomenon in the larger cities.

Never had so much been on show in the cities as in the second half of the century. There were exhibitions everywhere, and we know the role they played in relation to prostitution. The windows of the large department stores were themselves exhibitions. Paris had become "the city of food on offer."[106] The prostitute in turn came to show and offer herself. All this explains the impression noted by all observers of an invasion of the street by prostitution, without anyone being too sure whether it was the result of an actual increase in numbers or of greater mobility and display. Indeed, mobility and display were accompanied by a blurring, a social confusion, that made inoperable earlier attempts at redistribution. This was to involve, on the part of the vice squad, the development of new strategies.

For the moralists the danger appeared all the greater in that this flood was accompanied by the triumph of luxury. The prostitute intended for the bourgeois male had also become woman as spectacle. She paraded or exhibited herself on the terraces of the high-class cafés, in the brasseries, in the *cafés-concerts,* and on the sidewalk. Toulouse-Lautrec, the painter of the salons of the bourgeois *maisons de tolérance,* was also the painter of those women on offer, if not in broad daylight, at least under the bright artificial light of Paris by night, whose ostentation now stimulated the fantasies that sprang from all the frustrations of that milieu. It was then and in this way that the primacy of the visual in sexual solicitation originated.[107] Such exhibition, more than anything else, expressed the failure of regulationism and at the same time gave rise to the fearful hyperregulationism already described. The fact that this mutation should have been attributed to the decadent, pleasure-seeking Second Empire and condemned unanimously after the fall of that regime did not halt the process.

From now on the vice squad was to focus its attentions on the surveillance of the street. Their prime aim was to keep the streets clear and keep people moving; they became obsessed with soliciting. The harassing presence of the prostitute in the streets made it impossible to allow home life to spill over into the world outside. Almost all the complaints lodged against prostitutes at this time came from respectable gentlemen who were outraged that they could not walk the streets with their daughters or young children. The fiction of the period provides rich testimony to what was a veritable phobia and a repressed desire for contact.[108] Until the First World War, the moralization of the street was to remain a major theme in bourgeois discourse, as proletarian violence and criminality had once been. The increase in the number of moral societies whose essential aim was to combat the licentiousness of the streets provides further evidence. The moralizers certainly perceived the serious threat to traditional ethics of a supply that was addressed also—

indeed, perhaps above all—to a bourgeoisie that was more and more preoccupied with venal sex.

The Temptation of Venality

But let us return to the changes brought about in supply. Of course, if we do not go beyond the official terminology,[109] the categories of prostitution appear to differ very little from those analyzed by Parent-Duchâtelet, or by Richard Cobb for the period of the French Revolution,[110] or even those described by Restif de la Bretonne[111] or Mercier,[112] but we should not be taken in by this apparent permanence. The new supply, which corresponded to the expansion in bourgeois or *embourgeoisé* demand, came from social categories that had also seen their living conditions change.

Domestic service was more than ever a breeding ground for prostitution, and the number of female domestic servants had increased considerably in urban society. In a city the female domestic servant was no longer part of the family, indeed was hardly part of the household; the creation of the close-knit bourgeois home brought with it a relegation of the household staff to the sixth floor. We know from the literature of the period what fears this removal from paternalistic supervision gave rise to. After the publication of Jules Simon's *Ouvrière*[113] the diatribes against the "sixth floor" and its maids' rooms, in which were brought together not crime and immorality as before but theft and immorality, constitute a leitmotif of bourgeois complaint. In 1896 Dr. Commenge devoted long and learned passages to it.[114] Madame Avril de Sainte-Croix, under the pseuydonym "Savioz," dealt with this problem.[115] Even in 1912 Dr. Morin lavished his prophylactic advice with a view to "trying to prevent the contamination of the apartment by what the maid will bring from the sixth floor: obscene literature or venereal microbes."[116]

Furthermore, it should be noted that the domestic staff was very hierarchized. Ladies' companions and chambermaids, who were often chosen for their beauty,[117] constantly in contact with Madame, whose secrets were sometimes known to them through the husband's confidences, tried to imitate their mistresses; as a result, they acquired new needs and harbored new ambitions. Thus was formed a class within which proximity to the bourgeoisie[118] gave rise to a desire for escape: marrying a male servant was now seen as a relegation. The relative isolation of the maid on the sixth floor enabled her at last to elude the surveillance of her mistress and facilitated a possible liaison with Monsieur.[119]

We know that the attraction of the maid was a permanent element in the sexual behavior of the bourgeois male of this time. It is frequently mentioned in fiction: one thinks of "the bitter, mysterious seduction" of the Goncourts' heroine in *Germinie Lacerteux,*[120] of the character of Trublot in *Pot-Bouille* or of Monsieur Lanlaire in Octave Mirbeau's *Journal d'une femme de chambre.* Maupassant makes it the subject of his novella *Sauvée;* abroad, de Ryckère[121] discusses it at length, while both Ibsen *(Ghosts)* and Tolstoy *(Resurrection)* describe the temptation offered by a maid in the house. The sexologists of the time, and Krafft-Ebing in particular,[122] even offer an explanation: at a time when dress was setting up a veritable barrier between the sexes, the apron was reminiscent of a female undergarment and suggested easy intimacy. Indeed, this fetishism of the apron made certain prostitutes adopt the attitude of young domestic servants when they solicited in the streets.

So it is understandable if the maid, used to free sexual behavior, intoxicated by Monsieur's caresses and compliments, and very often by the approaches of his friends, gave in, when finally sacked and confronted by the prospect of poverty, to the temptation of venal sex.

The number of female shop assistants, or *demoiselles de magasin,* and of barmaids had also increased considerably. At the same time, many more shops provided hostel accommodation[123] for their staff, in which the apparent rigor of the regulations was accompanied, in fact, by great permissiveness. The *demoiselle de magasin,* like her male counterpart, was no longer under her employer's moral guardianship. Moreover, in the large commercial enterprises the middle managers and other supervisors adopted toward her the same techniques of seduction by blackmail that were traditional among the foremen in certain industries. We know that these practices were the subject of Zola's *Au bonheur des dames.* "Retained in the working class, not only by her social origins, but also by the living conditions imposed upon her by her wage, the *demoiselle de magasin* was part of the fringe that was in daily contact with the other world: the rich and all their attributes."[124] Even more than the chambermaid, she was "in a situation of escape,"[125] especially as she felt threatened by lack of security in work, which was particularly great in this milieu.

For many a salesgirl who tried to make herself as attractive as her female clients, marriage was a dramatic step. It amounted to a return to her real social class; it meant abandoning forever any hope of becoming a lady. So it is understandable that very few marriages took place between employees. Indeed, management was hostile to such unions; it was not until 1900[126] that the department stores encouraged marriage between their employees.[127] Yet becoming a kept woman might well seem a way of satisfying a salesgirl's ambitions. The temptation was all the greater in that most of her friends had a lover; otherwise it would be impossible for these *dames à peu près*[128] (near-ladies) to dress as they wished, or in other words to appear in public.[129] The presence of certain young women in a shop was even negotiated by bourgeois gentlemen; thus the position of milliner often gave a kept women a social front. This penetration of the milieu by venal sex added an element of excitement to it.

The example of Paris allows one to observe a large increase in *ouvrières de l'aiguille* (seamstresses), *couturières en chambre* (dressmakers working at home), and women who made various luxury articles; moreover, and this is the important point, this occurred in the center of the city. Contrary to what a simplistic analysis might suggest, Haussmannization was not accompanied by a general exodus of the humble away from the business center; for the categories described here it was even responsible for the opposite movement. The activity of dressmakers was stimulated by the growth in department stores. Indeed, it should not be forgotten that these establishments appealed to a female clientele's taste for luxury and, at the same time, its sense of economy. This ambivalence is well described by Zola when he contrasts Madame Marty (and her daughter), who ruins her teacher-husband by her unconsidered purchases, with Madame Bourdelais, who is happy to get some good bargains. The novelties department, which initially was responsible for the success of these establishments, was no more than a department selling raw materials; the customer bought the fabrics that took her fancy and brought them to her dressmaker. Similarly, the upholstery department stimulated the activity of upholsterers, whose role as procurers in bourgeois society I have already examined.

Furthermore, far from disappearing, the small workshop, whose proprietor was particularly anxious not to move too far away from his suppliers and his clientele, proliferated in the center of the capital. This expansion was based on the "very flexible renovation of the traditional trades" that was then taking place.[130] As Jeanne Gaillard shows very well, this phenomenon, far from being a survival from the past, represented "a preoccupation with modernity."[131]

This "persistent polarization exerted by old Paris," which testifies to "a rejection by the inhabitants of radical change in the city,"[132] found expression in the large numbers of dressmakers, women working at home, and shop assistants living in lodgings in the center of the city, now deserted by certain categories of workers or marginals who had been expelled to the outskirts. The coexistence in the center of the cities of students, male shop assistants, and clerks on the one hand and *demoiselles de magasin* and seamstresses on the other, as well as the creation of intense commercial and festive activity, which attracted the gentlemen of the bourgeoisie, explains the widespread character of the prostitutional relations formed there, outside the system set up by the authorities.

Indeed, in those sectors of activity the wages were inadequate to maintain the young working woman who did not have access to extra money provided by a man. The fact is well known: it has been remarked in every social inquiry since the reign of Louis-Philippe. It was noted by Jules Simon,[133] by Benoist,[134] and by Bonnevay.[135] It was tirelessly repeated at workers' congresses, in works on prostitution, and in fiction. More generally, without a man it was difficult for a woman to become integrated into the urban society of the day.[136] It was almost impossible to find lodgings: "the well-kept rooming-houses," writes Picot, in *La réforme sociale,* "were closed to her, and independent, unfurnished rooms were expensive. Outside her work, few distractions were available to the virtuous young woman: the unmarried working girl could not, like a man, go to drinking places alone—even the street was dangerous for her."[137] Furthermore, in these industries there were long periods of idleness that could last as long as four or even six and a half months. Finally, these activities were extremely sensitive to economic ups and downs; the great vulnerability of industries in which a growing proportion of production was intended for export explains the closed link in these sectors between economic fluctuations and fluctuations in the volume of prostitution. The activity of the shop, too, was subject to the same fluctuations. Jean Le Yaouanq has demonstrated that retail trade in the fourth arrondissement, after undergoing a period of expansion between 1870 and 1880, was severely affected by the crisis between 1880 and 1890.

Furthermore, the special conditions of apprenticeship in the cities encouraged the prostitution of young girls. The young female apprentice was cut off from her family; she was used to make deliveries, which necessitated long walks through the streets;[138] she was ill equipped to resist a man's persuasions.

For the seamstress, whose ambitions had often developed through her relations with a rich clientele,[139] marriage was difficult. When the male shop assistant or clerk married, he preferred, if he could, to choose his fiancée "from a family,"[140] or marry the boss's daughter. The case of Le Vieil Elbeuf, the management of which was placed successively in the hands of former owners' sons-in-law, is revealing if not exemplary. Since marriage was hardly a possibility for young women of this class, they had to find a lover who would help keep them or else turn, either temporarily or permanently, to venal sex. So it is understandable if prostitutes were recruited in greater numbers in the workshops than in the factories. In the workshop in which Marthe serves her apprenticeship or in which the Vatard sisters work,[141] the lovers of these young women are the main subject of conversation and pride. "In some industries," Bonnevay writes on the subject of the Lyons work force, "the girl who, after the age of twenty, has not yet found a lover, is regarded as a monster."[142] Jules Simon notes, "There are mothers who advise [their daughters] to find a lover."[143] Thus there developed venal relations that satisfied the new requirements of demand.

But the new prostitution was not nourished by this influx alone. A supply of a different kind was developing on the part of women tempted by the consumption of luxury goods. Indeed, the new commercial structures took the form of a stimulation and exploitation of women's desires. Octave Mouret, in many ways symmetrical with Nana, put in charge of one of those "commercial *maisons de tolérance*,"[144] is an instrument of just such an exploitation. It is significant in this regard that the lingerie department appears to Zola as a vast dressing room in which a multitude of women, in the grip of desire, abandon their underclothes.[145] In the extroverted city, within which she now moved in broad daylight, the bourgeois wife could indulge in adultery more easily than in the past. Shopping provided her with an alibi that could not be checked and facilitated assignations that ran little risk of compromising her. Busy public places were turned into anonymous meeting places. The temptations were all the stronger in that, as we have seen, the demand for this type of woman was considerable, and many gentlemen were prepared to satisfy the expensive tastes of a respectable partner. Just as the expansion of the department stores gave rise to the appearance and proliferation of kleptomania in high places,[146] it facilitated the spread of bourgeois prostitution, especially on the part of petty-bourgeois women, who were always on the margins of their class, perpetually threatened by relegation and tempted to sell themselves in order to keep their rank.

Progress in women's education, including the establishment of secondary education for girls, helped increase the number of what d'Haussonville regarded as the "unclassified"—that is to say, "women, or rather girls, who, born in a popular milieu, have made efforts to rise to a higher station, without yet succeeding in doing so, and who oscillate, uncertain of their future, between the condition that they have left and the one that they have not yet been able to attain."[147] For many of these governesses, piano teachers, and schoolmistresses the loneliness and moral distress were intense. The products of the new secondary education for girls constituted, from the end of the century, a group symmetrical with the one formed by the proletariat of university graduates, but its living conditions were even harsher. Like the working girl, the woman who aspired to the bourgeoisie but was not integrated into a family had to have the support of a man. But it was difficult for an "unclassified" woman to find a husband who would satisfy her aspirations. Is it surprising, then, that some of those girls ended up in the *maisons de rendez-vous*, if not as inmates in the first-class brothels?

The growth of the new prostitutional demand and supply was probably not linear; it merely expressed the evolution of the structures of urban society.[148] The processes that I have described were perceptible and measurable during the Second Empire: the increasing wealth of citizens, changes in the urban context, and cosmopolitanism characterized the period, as we know. But, contrary to the often-expressed view,[149] despite the pessimism and desire for moral expiation manifested during the first decade of the regime, the Third Republic, from 1871 to 1914, was far from being marked by a decline in the new prostitutional activities. Beyond the difficulties of the 1880s, which in any case stimulated supply if not demand,[150] the expansion of urban consumption between 1896 and 1913 spurred the growth of these activities. It was, as we know,[151] a period of rapid economic growth based on the expansion of urban demand, which was expressed in turn by an increased rate in the creation of wealth.[152] It is easy to understand that bourgeois prostitution should have found its golden age during this period.

Toward the Abandonment of the Corset

The proliferation of new prostitutional practices would have been less marked if these socioeconomic changes had not been accompanied by an increased permissiveness. The exacerbation of frustration widened the cracks in the bourgeois union. The male quest for sexual fulfillment was carried out more and more openly during the last years of the century. At a time when large sections of the proletariat were adopting some of the values on which the greatness of the bourgeoisie had been based, one observes a relative freedom of female sexual behavior within that class, a contradictory development that makes it particularly difficult to assess the phenomenon as a whole.

The causes of these cracks are evident: the growth in numbers of the petty and middle bourgeoisie broke open the dominant model. Several factors in sexual repression saw their influence decline; the drop in religious practice after the failure of the Catholic counteroffensive of the 1870s also affected the ranks of the bourgeoisie, and the episcopate of Monsignor Dupanloup ended sadly.[153] A reverse process from the one to which the social fear of 1848 had given rise gradually restored skepticism in these circles. The advance of freethinking, the development of the secular ideal, the close connection between clergy and political conservatism led to a decline in the influence of the church—and we know how large a part the church had played in repressing sexuality since the post-Tridentine offensive.[154] The establishment of secular secondary education for girls and, furthermore, the changes to which, out of fear of competition, this innovation gave rise in the religious schools speeded up the evolution in women's attitudes.

Generally speaking, the decline of political conservatism and the principle of authority in the wake of the failure of the government of *ordre moral*, the growth of a liberalism springing from the principles of 1789, and the new sensitivity to individual liberties created a favorable climate for such moral changes. The influence of radicalism on feminism and the establishment of divorce following the triumph of the Republic are clear indications of this connection. Moreover, the abandonment of censorship, followed by the liberalization of the press laws in 1881, allowed the spread of the *scientia sexualis* and of notions of sexual liberation.

Indeed, a very revealing development took place between 1876 and 1879—that is to say, at the time of the decisive battles that were to lead to the triumph of the Republic. At this time there emerged an explicit sexuality in literature and art, through, as it happens, the representation of prostitution. It is no accident that *Marthe, La fille Elisa, Nana, La fin de Lucie Pellegrin, Boule de Suif,* and the Comte d'Haussonville's articles devoted to debauchery and vice in the *Revue des deux-mondes* appeared around the same time. By imposing on the reading public descriptions of the brothel or the *maison de passe,* Huysmans, Edmond de Goncourt, Zola and Maupassant, whether they were aware of it or not, had won a political victory: to appreciate this, one has only to think of the trouble that censorship caused Flaubert and Barbey d'Aurevilly.

This breach in the moral order brought about by the stark description of venal sex[155] was accompanied, as we know, by many other such breaks that cannot be studied here. I would simply suggest that, in my opinion, the progress of feminism, the spread of adultery, and the establishment and proliferation of divorce, as well as demands for the right to free union, the neo-Malthusian campaign,[156] propaganda in favor of women's sexual emancipation,[157] and progress in disseminating sexual information to adults[158] belonged to the same process. The medical discourse on the double nature and therefore on the specificity of the nature of women tended to give way to the discourses on depopulation. Motherhood ceased to be a destiny and became a duty.[159] While "male sensibility was changing and taste moving away from a full, round, motionless model of beauty to that of a slimmer, more vivacious, more similar companion,"[160] women's bodies themselves changed form and significance. In 1906 the great couturier Poiret persuaded women to abandon the corset.

Although we await progress in the study of historical sexology, it is already possible to discern the main aspects of the evolution of urban society and of the urban attitudes that encouraged, if they do no explain totally, the changes that the mere description by eyewitnesses reveals in prostitutional structures and practices. It goes without saying that this evolution, which found expression in the failure of the regulationist project and in the decline of the institutions that it had inspired, gave rise to new prostitutional discourses.

5. The System Challenged

Vigor and Diversity of Abolitionism, 1876–1884

Never had the debate around the subject of prostitution reached such intensity as in this period. Indeed, the enormous international effort put into investigation and reflection during the early years of the twentieth century was to proceed in a much calmer atmosphere. If the existence of official prostitution was a burning question between 1876 and 1884, it was because it was implicated in the great political and social debates of the time. It was then that, in the course of virulent campaigns that often seemed like veritable crusades, not one but several abolitionist discourses were built up, which is why anyone who tries systematically to unravel the threads is struck by an apparent complexity and even confusion. The task of the historian is complicated by the simultaneity, especially as he must at one and the same time write a history of the battle fought around abolitionism and relate the emergence and gradual construction of coherent antiregulationist theories.

In the interest of clarity, I shall not follow chronology strictly. What matters is to integrate the ups and downs of the abolitionist campaign within the long-term debate on the subject of prostitution and to discern in which spheres and with what arguments a challenge was made to this regulationist system, whose failure had by now become evident.

Josephine Butler and the Beginning of the Abolitionist Federation

It was in English and Swiss Protestant circles that the challenge to the "French system" began. Indeed, between 1866 and 1876 an evangelical tendency, imbued with aggressive feminism, had developed in Great

Britain and the Swiss cantons of Geneva and Neuchâtel, with views on this matter that were repressive and prohibitionist.

The Contagious Diseases Act of 1866, 1867, and 1869 had introduced an embryonic regulationism into England by creating in certain cities a prostitution that was officially tolerated and supervised. In 1869 this initiative was opposed by a group of doctors in Nottingham. Then, on January 1, 1870, Josepine Butler, the wife of the principal of a college in Liverpool, published in the *Daily News* a manifesto of the Ladies' National Association in which the new legislation was strongly condemned. Victor Hugo, who, in *Les misérables,* had popularized the principal themes of the future campaign,[1] associated himself officially with this protest. From this point on, throughout the country,[2] the Quakers took up the struggle for the repeal of the acts. Over three hundred associations were set up with this end in view. In March the magazine *The Shield* was founded to propagate the new cause and to coordinate the action of the British Federation, which had been formed with the purpose of having regulated prostitution abolished.

For four years the English women's campaign was confined to Great Britain and focused on the repeal of the acts. But on June 25, 1874, at a conference held at York, Josephine Butler and her friends, in association with Aimé Humbert of Neuchâtel, launched an abolitionist crusade on an international scale. In December the new crusader crossed the channel. At first she confined her attention to Paris, requesting an interview with Lecour, who received her somewhat curtly. She nevertheless obtained permission to visit Saint-Lazare, which scandalized her. She made contact with certain Protestants, who then gave her their support: she was given a warm welcome by the economist Frédéric Passy, Théodore Monod and Dr. Gustave Monod, his uncle, and by the pastors of the Baptist church. Victor Schoelcher, Jules Simon, and Louis Blanc offered further encouragement. Jules Favre agreed to see her, with the result that he turned violently against regulation,[3] and gave her letters of introduction to several leading Catholics. Finally, Mme. Jules Simon invited her to attend a feminist meeting held by Mme. Lemonnier.

Mrs. Butler visited Lyons and Marseilles, where she won some support, then Genoa, where she met disciples of Mazzini. Her crusade then took her to Switzerland, where she resumed contact with the Humberts and the Genevan abolitionists, who had launched their own campaign, in particular with the publication of the Comtesse de Gasparin's *Lèpre sociale.* On her return to Paris, Mrs. Butler met Emilie de Morsier, who, with her husband, was to be a particularly active militant of the new cause. Dr. Armand Després, a specialist in the study of prostitution, also showed great regard for the English feminist. This first crusade was still a strictly private affair. Aside from a small circle of Protestants and well-intentioned individuals, Mrs. Butler did not have a group capable of orchestrating a large-scale movement. The situation began to change two years later, after Yves Guyot's violent attacks on the vice squad.

Early in 1877 Josephine Butler, accompanied by the principal representatives of the organization, crossed the Channel once more with a view to launching a public campaign.[4] She came to support the extreme left in Paris against the vice squad and addressed three fairly small middle-class audiences. In addition, she took part in a large public meeting, consisting of over two thousand people, organized in the hall in the rue d'Arras by Yves Guyot and his friends. Finally, on January 30, at the request of a "ladies' committee of the workers' congress," Mrs. Butler gave a lecture at the Salle Pétrelle to the local seamstresses. Apart from the considerable radical public, attracted to the meeting in the rue d'Arras by the extreme leftist municipal councillors, the audience was not very large, which shows that the crusade had made little impact. It should be said, however, that the working-class public of the capital would have been put off by the political complexion of the movement and by Josephine Butler's own verbal excesses. Furthermore, the hostility of the police, who had forcibly evacuated one of the meetings and condemned its chairman for breaking the law of 1868, may well have dissuaded the well intentioned from lending their support. Yet, the fact that participants from such varied backgrounds—radicals and socialists on the municipal council and in parliament, leaders of the bourgeoning feminist movement, members of the workers' movement, Protestant pastors and rich Protestant bankers—should have rallied to Josephine Butler and her British federation testifies to the creation of a not inconsiderable pressure group that was to be the embryo of the future French committee of the federation. It should be added that "the Paris lectures" paved the way for the Geneva congress and the setting up of an international federation.

At this date the leaders of the association intended to give it a religious character. For Josephine Butler, the "French system," and the Contagious Diseases Act that had been inspired by it, were doubly evil: they caused the enslavement of women and encouraged immorality in men. They were, therefore, an attack on both liberty and morality. The struggle against this system was to be carried out in the name of Scripture and of the "political Bible,"[5] that is to say, the "great constitutional principles"[6] contained in Magna Carta, the Petition of Rights, and the Bill of Rights. This struggle was to be part of the larger struggle against the modern democratic and socialist tendencies that were leading to the "fetishism of socialistic State worship"[7] and to "medical domination and legislative tyranny."[8]

Josephine Butler was calling for a defense, on the one hand, of the "freedom and purity of our English Commonwealth,"[9] and particularly of the liberty of women, and, on the other hand, of morality and the family. The second aim of the crusade was directed not simply at "legalized prostitution" but at debauchery in general, that is to say, all extramarital sexual relations. "We must pursue vice to its source," Edouard de Pressensé declared in 1876. "We must pursue it in all its forms, to all its lairs; we must attack the infamous literature, the impure art, and the degraded drama that are closely related to it. Above all, it is our duty to combat that disastrous illusion, lodged in so many minds, that vice is inevitable."[10] Josephine Butler, for whom true hygiene necessarily tended to moralization, was not afraid to use coercion to bring about the reign of virtue. In 1882 she declared: "The best of the restrictions imposed by law is that which encourages and, if necessary, forces citizens of both sexes to practice self-respect."[11]

Mrs. Butler, it should be repeated, based her crusade on the model of the abolitionist campaign, which had developed in the same milieus and had led to the abolition first of the sale and then of the enslavement of blacks. A veritable "Deborah of modern times,"[12] she directed her attack mainly against Paris, "the great Babylon."[13]

The pastors and the friends who joined her struggle had also declared war on vice. They all rejected the basic postulate of regulationism— namely, to recognize the normality, even the necessity, of extramarital relations for young unmarried men.[14] They all launched into vibrant eulogies for continence, whose benefits they vaunted—a view they shared with many doctors of the time.[15] The leaders of the federation did, however, stress the dangers of celibacy, "the most shameful of things," Louis Sautter declared to the young men of the Christian Union, since "it leads us inevitably to depravity."[16] Debauchery and the celibacy that leads to it bring about, furthermore, a drop in the birth rate as a whole and an increase in illegitimate births. Here the abolitionists' discourse finds an echo in the fears of the Catholic repopulationists.

All these anathemas had been brought together in the speech made by de Pressensé at the London conference in May 1876, six months before Yves Guyot launched his campaign. Attacking the regulationist ministers, he had declared, "You have forgotten that this profligacy which you facilitate contributes to the corruption of the youth of the nation, and sends them back to the domestic hearth blighted, corrupted, prematurely aged, when they are not separated forever from the domestic hearth, as is the case now in certain countries where complaint is made of the diminution of marriages, and (as in the decline of the Roman Empire) rewards are held out to those who will marry and bring up children."[17] Rather than systematically facilitating the corruption of youth, as the Second Empire had tried to do, the government ought to eliminate tolerated debauchery.[18]

This prohibitionist abolitionism, which attacked both the enslavement of the *fille soumise* and the official tolerance of extramarital relations, inspired the congress held at Geneva between September 17 and September 22, 1877. This congress, which brought together some six or seven hundred people, including, as a representative of the French extreme left, Louis Codet,[19] set up the British and Continental Federation for the Abolition of Prostitution. The double struggle of the prohibitionists is clearly expressed in the final declarations that constituted the real charter of this abolitionism and which clearly reveal its profound motives. I have extracted the following articles, which seem to me to be particularly revealing.[20]

"Self-control in sexual relations is one of the indispensable bases for the health of individuals and peoples" (Resolution 1 of the hygiene section, to which Dr. Armand Desprès and Dr. Gustave Monod brought the authority of the medical faculty). "The state sanctions the immoral prejudice that debauchery is a necessity for man" (Resolution 8, moral section, on which Edouard de Pressensé sat). "The practice of impurity is as reprehensible in man as in woman" (Resolution 1, moral section). *"The true function of public hygiene is to develop all the conditions favorable to health, which finds its highest expression in public morality"* (Resolution 2, hygiene section). "Compulsory registration is an affront to liberty and to common law" (Resolution 5, moral section). "The police must ensure that decency in the street is respected" (Resolution 6, hygiene section).

During the proceedings of the hygiene section Dr. Philippe de La Harpe, referring to Dr. Neuwmann's book *On Continence Considered as Necessary to Health,* demanded that the federation should strive to make it understood that "continence is not only a virtue, but a source of health, of physical as well as moral strength." To conclude, he declared: "Let the *maisons de tolérance* be closed, therefore, the vice squad abolished, and prostitution combated to the death. *Delenda Carthago*—I have spoken."[21]

The ambiguity inherent in the new abolitionism is understandable: the defense of common law and of individual liberty coincided exactly with the aims of the French extreme left. Yet, the prohibitionism advocated by the membership of the new federation, the struggle for decency in the streets and for early marriage, which were to be the aims of the morality societies that they would give rise to, and above all the desire for sexual repression and the prohibition of all extramarital relations alarmed the liberals.

The resolutions of the second congress of the federation, held at Genoa between September 27 and October 4, 1880, and in which Yves Guyot and Emilie and Auguste de Morsier took part, reflected to a greater degree the influence of this second liberal and radical faction. To them the most important thing was to limit the functions of the state and to guarantee clearly the rights of the human being. Only guarantees of individual liberty, the application of common law, and the abolition of registration and administrative detention were demanded; the repression of extramarital sexuality had officially disappeared from the aims.

By this time the federation was more securely rooted in France.[22] In September 1877, at the occasion of the Geneva congress, the great Rabbi Zadock Kahn gave his support; but despite the words of encouragement given by Monsignor Dupanloup to Emilie de Morsier,[23] the Catholic hierarchy continued to be reticent, only a Father Hyacinte[24] giving his complete support. The first annual conference of the federation took place in Paris on September 24 and 25, 1878. It was a time of great hope for the members of the association.[25] The general secretary, James Stansfeld, had been received by Minister of the Interior de Marcère.

After his predecessor, Gigot, had refused to recognize the committee, which had been in existence since November 1878,[26] Prefect of Police Andrieux officially authorized, in an ordinance issued on June 16, 1879, the setting up of a French section of the British and Continental Federation, to be called the Association pour l'abolition de la prostitution réglementée. Presided over by Victor Schoelcher, the new body brought together radicals, leading feminists, and the membership of the Protestant abolitionist groups. The committee, chaired jointly by Yves Guyot and Mrs. H. Chapman, included, notably, Maria Deraismes[27] and Emilie de Morsier. That same year[28] the morality section of the Société pour l'amélioration du sort des femmes, presided over by Maria Deraismes, sent a petition to the Chamber of Deputies demanding the abolition of the registration of underage girls; the petition was presented by Couturier, the deputy for the Isère and a member of the federation.

In April 1880 another visit to Paris by Josephine Butler marked the climax of the federation's effect on public opinion. On April 10 a meeting, held in the rue Lévis, attracted about two thousand people, including "a fairly large number" of women;[29] according to a police officer's report, "The petty-bourgeois and working-class element predominated."[30] It has to be admitted that public opinion had been aroused by Yves Guyot's new campaign in *La lanterne*.[31] The leaders of Paris's extreme left were present, together with members of the federation. The tenor of the speeches revealed the influence now exercised by the feminist movement in this context.

Later on, the evangelical abolitionist movement, which had presided

over the creation of the federation in France, was to merge increasingly
with the morality societies. The Comité parisien pour le relèvement de
la moralité, founded in 1875 during one of Josephine Butler's visits to
Paris, which was affiliated with the federation and which included
Edouard de Pressensé, Dr. Gustave Monod, and pastors of the Wesleyan
church, was now to broaden its activity; in May 1883 it was transformed into the Ligue française pour le relèvement de la moralité
publique.[32]

The new league came to be much more widely established in the
country than the association had been. By the end of 1883 it already
had eight provincial committees; in addition, it organized a large number of lectures, especially in regions with a sizable Protestant population.
The concern for public decency, however, became increasingly dominant in this movement over that for the abolition of regulated prostitution. This shift became clearer after the death of de Pressensé in 1891.
The activities of the association, after an initial upsurge, declined.[33]
Then, in 1898, with the problem of prostitution again in the forefront,
a French branch of the international abolitionist committee was founded;[34] it was grafted onto the league, which had kept the message alive
over the intervening years. This suggests that it was largely thanks to
the active support of radical abolitionists that this movement was able
to develop its activities between 1876 and 1883.

The Extreme Left versus the Vice Squad

The struggle carried out by the Parisian radicals against the prefecture
of police belonged to a wider battle for individual liberties and the rights
of man, which were threatened by arbitrary police action, first under
conservative and then under opportunist (centrist) governments. This
abolitionism, which was liberal but not libertarian, differed quite markedly from Josephine Butler's prohibitionism. Furthermore, the campaign had deep roots in the rancor felt by the people of Paris toward
the Versailles government and was an expression of the autonomist aspirations of the inhabitants of the capital. In its struggle against the prefecture of police, the extreme left attacked the vice squad first because it
was now evident that it was the most easily criticized and therefore the
most vulnerable branch of the police.

Like all police and penitentiary institutions in the first half of the nineteenth century, the vice squad was originally the object of violent criticism.[35] It was not until the early years of the Third Republic, however,
that these extremists began to attack the arbitrary action of members of
official bodies. In 1872, in a report that became famous,[36] the councillor

Ranc condemned the vice squad on behalf of a commission formed within the municipal council with a view to studying the administration of the prefecture of police. After criticizing Prefect Léon Renault for the scandalous raids carried out by the vice squad in the streets of the capital and denouncing the exorbitant powers of the prefecture, the councillor demanded guarantees of individual liberty, the reform of Saint-Lazare, and above all the passing of legislation that would bring prostitutes back under common law. In short, the Ranc report broached the main themes that were to be developed during the campaigns of the extreme left against the prefecture of police. But the majority of the municipal council was made up at that time of moderates (the center right), and Ranc's protest was not taken up.

It was in November 1876, six months after the lifting of the state of siege, that Yves Guyot gave the signal for the campaign directed against Lecour, the chief of the first division, against Prefect Félix Voisin, and, above them, against the minister Dufaure and Marshal de Mac-Mahon himself.[37] According to Guyot, it was reading, in two Lyons newspapers (*Le progrès* and *Le petit lyonnais*), the account of the dramatic arrest, followed by the suicide of two *filles soumises,* that had moved him to take up his pen. The first of the women, Mélanie M——, after having her legs crushed by an omnibus while resisting the vice squad, finally managed to throw herself out of the carriage that was taking her to the police station, and drowned herself in the Rhône. The second, Marie D——, in order to escape the police, who were raiding the lodging house in which she lived, threw herself from a third-floor window; seriously wounded, she died a few hours later in the hospital. Shortly afterward, the actress Rousseil was brutally assaulted by members of the vice squad while out walking on the boulevards.

On November 2, in the columns of *Droits de l'homme,* Guyot attacked the vice squad in indignant terms. This article was the first episode in an endless campaign that was to see many successors. For two months the newspaper, now supported by the English abolitionists, relentlessly attacked the vice squad; it opened its columns to Josephine Butler. At the same time, the left-wing and extreme left-wing press took up the cause, and the revolt against the prefecture of police spread.[38]

Yves Guyot then carried the struggle to the municipal council. On November 4, during the debate on the budget for the prefecture of police, he demanded that the section on the vice squad be treated separately. On November 30, before Voisin and Lecour, who had come to attend the session, he delivered a violent attack on the vice squad. On December 2 the council appointed a commission to study the running of the prefecture of police. At the request of the government, the president of the Republic, Mac-Mahon, annulled this decision by a decree dated December 6. Ignoring this, the council elected a new commission; war was thus declared between the government and the Paris municipal council.

On December 7 Yves Guyot was found guilty by the eleventh court of summary jurisdiction, fined, and given a six-month prison sentence. During the trial, required to confine himself to answering the charge of insulting behavior toward the police, he thus found it impossible to pose the problem of the legality of the action taken by the vice squad. During the first two months of the following year, the radicals supported the Paris campaign of Josephine Butler and her friends. In April 1877, Guyot went to prison. Despite the financial help of the British federation, his imprisonment brought with it the disappearance of *Droits de l'homme*[39] and put an end to the first act of the campaign.

During the period of repression that followed May 16, the problem disappeared from the forefront of people's minds. Yet from November onward, after the electoral victory of the republicans, *La lanterne,* successor to *Le radical,* which had itself succeeded *Droits de l'homme,* initiated a new polemic, which ended, on December 17, with the departure of Voisin and the appointment as prefect of Albert Gigot. A new and much more violent campaign was to excite public opinion between October 1878 and July 1879.[40] The Republic was now triumphant. In the context of the purging then taking place in Paris, the extreme left hoped to dismantle the powers of the prefecture of police and bring it under the control of the municipal council. In this it was not particularly successful, but it did get the dismissal of the minister of the interior, de Marcère, and of Gigot, who had received little support from Waddington's opportunist government.

Yves Guyot took up his pen again on October 10, 1878, to attack the vice squad in the columns of *La lanterne.*[41] For two years he had been building up a file; furthermore, he had obtained the cooperation of a number of officials in the prefecture. In a series of anonymous articles entitled "The Revelation of a Former Member of the Vice Squad," "Letters of a Physician," and above all "Letters from an Old Clerk," he denounced in great detail the activities of the staff of the prefecture of police. After the initial attacks, Lecour resigned and set about writing articles to defend his honor.[42] Then the newspapers entered the fray again, giving their support to Guyot. Already the affair of Augustine B——, a working-class woman arrested by the vice squad after a day's hard work, had triggered off the almost unanimous protest of the Paris press.[43]

The prefect Gigot, indignant at the violence of the attack, had *La lanterne* prosecuted and its business manager condemned to three months in prison and a fine of a thousand francs. In January 1879, however, de Marcère, shaken by the precision of the criticism, appointed a commission of inquiry into the running of the prefecture of police. This commission was made up, in particular, of senators Schoelcher and Tolain, deputies Tirard and Brisson, Prefect Gigot, and a Dr. Thulié. On February 16, 1879, this commission, which was not favorable to the vice squad, resigned, arguing that it had found it impossible to carry out its task. The affair now reached the Chamber, where the extreme left of the municipal council won the support of radical leaders, who, it is true, were more interested in seeing a purging of personnel than in ending regulated prostitution. Thus Clemenceau reproached de Marcère for the poor quality of the staff at the prefecture of police and for his insistence that the inquiry be carried out in secret. He demanded that the institution be reorganized to the advantage of the republicans. Meanwhile, Gambetta and his friends had long since distanced themselves from the struggle; on April 14, 1879, in the columns of *La République française,* Ranc criticized in strong terms the campaign then being waged by *La lanterne* against the vice squad. Finally, after the Chamber refused to pass a vote of confidence in the minister, who was being accused furthermore of being too closely bound up with financial circles, de Marcère resigned, dragging Gigot down with him. Waddington, the president of the Council of Ministers, and Lepère, the new minister of the interior, replaced Gigot with Andrieux. Thus this second stage ended in a dual defeat for both *La lanterne* and the prefect.

Between June 1879 and the spring of 1881, the struggle continued, this time against Andrieux. Once again the debate went beyond the context of the municipal council and divided the Chamber. The successive arrests of M. Bonnefous and his niece, on June 22, 1879, followed, on June 24, by that of Mlle. Bernage, a *pensionnaire* of the Comédie-française, who was eighteen years of age, brought new protests from Yves Guyot in the columns of *La lanterne.* Andrieux, who relates these events with amused detachment in his memoirs, refused to give in to what he regarded as the newspaper's blackmail. On June 28 he ordered the seizure of *La lanterne.* He had this action approved by the Chamber on July 1, 1879, thanks to the protection of Gambetta, who declared in a lordly manner that he saw the regulation of prostitution as a matter of concern only to the public thoroughfare. The next month the manager of the newspaper was convicted again.

Relations became more tense between the municipal council, which Guyot had joined once again after a by-election in 1879, and Andrieux. Unlike his predecessor, Andrieux refused to attend the meetings of the commission of inquiry set up by the council. After being reformed, this commission began its work at last on January 27, 1879.[44] Furthermore, on December 28, 1880, the municipal council adopted the proposition presented by Guyot and Lanessan, which called for the abolition of the vice squad. On March 29, 1881, the arrest of Mme. Eyben, who was stopped and questioned by the police while standing in the passage des Panoramas waiting to meet her children, blew up the whole affair once again. On April 10 Pascal Duprat challenged the government in this matter. Andrieux, thanks to his wit, some kindly words from Gambetta, and the support of the opportunist leaders, managed to amuse the assembled deputies and win their support. By 324 votes to 91, and despite the opinion of an ad hoc commission, the deputies rejected on July 18 a request presented by Mme. Eyben to permit prosecutions against the prefect of police, who was a member of parliament. It should be noted that, according to the abolitionist press,[45] Andrieux won the day because he was able to flatter the centralizing sentiments of the majority. The hostility of the Chamber to abolitionism was nourished at this time by that of the provincial deputies to the capital.

The government now regarded Andrieux as a liability, however, especially as his relations with the municipal council had become strained once more, and the left-wing press was suggesting that the prefect was compromised in some sex scandal.[46] So Jules Ferry and Minister of the Interior Constans readily accepted the resignation of Andrieux, who regarded the government's plans to bring the prefecture of police partially under the authority of the Ministry of the Interior as inadequate. Once again Yves Guyot's campaign had failed, but the prefecture of police emerged from it diminished.

The final phase of the struggle was really no more than an endless but strictly localized guerrilla war between the extreme left on the council and Andrieux's successors. The victory of the radicals in the municipal elections of 1884 thus led the council to refuse to pass the budget for the prefecture of police. Furthermore, on December 26, 1882, the general council of the department of the Seine passed a resolution proposed by Mesureur in favor of abolitionism.[47] It was probably the strength of this opposition that, for the second time, in October 1883, brought about the failure of plans, prepared by Waldeck-Rousseau, to bring the prefecture of police under the authority of the Ministry of the Interior.[48] It should be noted, however, that the abolitionist campaign hardly impeded the activities of the vice squad at this time; never had arrests of prostitutes been so numerous. Quite obviously, despite the support of abolitionist precepts by a number of newspapers that had hitherto been reticent,[49] the opposition had lost its enthusiasm for this endlessly debated subject.

Two significant events had marked the history of abolitionism during these years: the publication in 1882 of Yves Guyot's book *La prostitution,* and the adoption by the commission of the municipal council on March 29 and April 16, 1883, of Dr. Louis Fiaux's report, which concluded that the vice squad should be abolished. This report was handed over to a new "health commission," set up by the council to study in a more general way the problem of hygiene in the capital. Seven years later this commission was to arrive at slightly different conclusions, as is apparent in the book published by its chairman, E. Richard,[50] which is of markedly neoregulationist inspiration.

Throughout these ups and downs, which form a kind of counterpoint to the activities of the members of the British and Continental Federation, an abolitionist discourse finally emerged that was somewhat different from that which had sustained the activities of the prohibitionists.

Unlike regulationism, liberal abolitionism was not the result of inquiries carried out by doctors belonging to official health bodies and inspired by the methods of an empiricist sociology; it owes nothing to the experience of police administrators. What is revealing in this respect is the tenor of Yves Guyot's important book, which is a veritable antithesis to that of Parent-Duchâtelet. It becomes quite clear, despite the statistical apparatus that he presents, that the author did not possess a thorough knowledge of prostitution and had not carried out investigations of his own; he does nothing to alter the stereotype of the prostitute. The theoreticians of liberal abolitionism tended to be publicists more or less involved in political action, lawyers (sometimes eminent ones), philosophers, and moralists. They were struggling against a system that, to them, was merely one element of conservatism; and they did so in the name of a political and moral ideal that went well beyond the context of regulated prostitution.[51]

The fundamental aim of this project was not the abolition of prostitution but the freeing of the prostitutes from registration, the destruction of the whole system that tended to create a marginal milieu outside common law. This discourse, therefore, was above all a critical analysis of regulationism and, more particularly, of the institution that dominated it, the *maison de tolérance.*

The principles invoked to justify this aim are clear. It was in the name of respect for individual liberty, equality before the law, common law—in short, it was by referring to the great principles of 1789 and the Declaration of the Rights of Man—that the abolitionists demanded the disbanding of the vice squad. Yves Guyot was the first to analyze, in terms that are astonishingly modern, the way in which society has enforced the exclusion and marginalization of prostitution—not only the prostitutes themselves but also their allies, the procurers and brothel-keepers.

But this was not a libertarian abolitionism, as some of its adversaries claimed. None of its adherents advocated extramarital sexual relations or, still less, exalted pleasure. After asserting that sexual desire precedes or at least accompanies puberty, Yves Guyot[52] refused to conclude that the adolescent has a right to pleasure. This was quite simply because the condemnation of sexual relations outside marriage was for him, as for Dr. Fiaux, an unquestionable presupposition.[53] Homosexuality and perversion were subjected to attacks from the liberal abolitionists, whose virulence went well beyond that of the most ardent regulationists. Guyot waged his struggle with a view to creating sexual order and defending marriage and the family. If he was in favor of emancipating women, it was to free them to become wives; it was to encourage in them a rebirth of "honesty." For Dr. Fiaux, the *maison de tolérance* was to be condemned because, among other misdeeds, it diverted working-class women from marriage.[54] The hostility of these liberal abolitionists to neo-Malthusianism was almost as marked as that of the neoregulationists spreading the gospel of an increase in the national population. Where they differed was in their choice of means; in order to limit sexual disorder—that is to say, debauchery—the liberal abolitionists rejected the path of regulation.

They refused to allow the state to intervene in individuals' sexual relations[55] and therefore, unlike the prohibitionists, demanded the freeing of private prostitution when it was not an offense to the eyes of the public. While condemning debauchery, as well as asceticism, Yves Guyot believed that women must be able to dispose of their bodies and their beauty freely, just as men have the free use of their brains and hands.[56] The development of a sense of responsibility in the individual, of self-control,[57] and progress in education were to usher in the triumph of sexual order; the application of liberalism and the programs of individual morality were enough to guarantee social morality. Above all, therefore, we should not confuse law and morality; the function of law is not to moralize.

Liberal abolitionism expressed here an optimism of positivist inspiration placed at the service of sexual repression. Whereas, for the regulationists, recourse to prostitution was an indispensable technique of temporary sexuality, Yves Guyot, like Dr. Fiaux, declared himself to be deeply convinced that the development of civilization, the progress of culture and hygiene, in short, the sense of history, lead to greater reserve in sexual relations.[58] This moral reflection, allied to a concern with defending common law, finds its theoretical fulfillment in the work of

Renouvier and his disciple F. Pillon, who, in the name of natural morality, then set out to justify the abolitionist precepts in *La critique philosophique, politique, scientifique et littéraire.*[59]

The abolitionist reasoning implied several corollaries that were to emerge only later in the debate: the equality of men's and women's responsibility was thus to lead Dr. Fiaux to propose first the legal search for paternity,[60] then recognition of the damage caused by intersexual contamination. Furthermore, when criminal anthropology later constructed the theory of the innateness of prostitution, the liberal abolitionists were to proclaim loudly their belief in the possibility of redemption, though without carrying very far the analysis of the social causes of the phenomenon.

The wish to defend individual liberty led the abolitionists to point to the existence of new threats; and it was there that their discourse becomes most modern. It is true that, like the English prohibitionists, they wanted to defend the individual against the "new spirit of inquisition"[61] practiced by the police and even more so by doctors, whose interconnection they stressed, being the first in France to denounce the abuses of medical power. The long passages devoted to condemning compulsory health checks on prostitutes, which they regarded as "medical rape,"[62] also demonstrate the reticence that medicine had to overcome in conquering sexual inhibitions and taboos, which together went under the term *modesty*. From 1882 onward, Yves Guyot exposed one by one the excuses offered by the police and doctors (at first respect for religion and morality and protection of public peace, then a guarantee of public health) for maintaining a system of which the essential aims were profit, police intelligence, and the pleasure of exercising arbitrary power.[63] The lucidity with which this abundant abolitionist literature unmasked the presuppositions and the pseudoscientific character of medical discourse on the subject of sexual regulation represents one of its major achievements.

The critical analysis of the system represented in Paris by the vice squad constituted, it should be repeated, the principal element of this abolitionist discourse. One has only to study the way in which that criticism was carried out. The fundamental criticism made of the institution was that it represented a threat to individuals. In view of the small number of removals from the register, the vice squad was in fact the machine for turning temporary prostitutes into permanent ones. The system set out an itinerary that encouraged the kept woman first to register, then to enter a *maison de tolérance,* and finally to find herself outside society. This marginalization allowed another category, itself marginalized, to exercise a tyrannical, arbitrary power over the first, to which it was constantly linked: this second category consisted of members of the vice squad.[64] These men shared the womens' ignominy; usually drunkards motivated by sheer brutality and a desire for vengeance, they were frequent clients of the *maisons* and were convinced that they were allowed to do anything to these women. In connivance with the keepers, they commonly practiced blackmail; worse, their very existence presumed that of the *souteneurs,* themselves products of the system, who had been denounced by Yves Guyot as indispensable mediators between prostitutes and the police.

The registered woman had become, arbitrarily, the perpetual prisoner of the police. Denunciations of "women hunts,"[65] or raids and inspections of the lodging houses, which were daily occurrences in the larger cities, are a leitmotif of the abolitionist literature. As we have seen, it was scandals of this type that marked the various stages of the campaign. The keeper, too, was denounced as an essential part of the system, as an indispensable agent in the sequestration of the women desired by the police. It was certainly the *dame de maison* who took it upon herself to apply the by-laws; it was she who, encouraging her inmates to contract debts, prevented their liberation.

This system, which led to the suppression of individual liberty, was *illegal:* the existence of "administrative detention" placed the prostitute outside common law. The abolitionists, unlike the regulationists, were keen to put the debate on legal terrain: hence the interminable refutation of the arguments of their adversaries, larded with the opinions of eminent lawyers[66] and innumerable judgments from the Appeals Court stressing the illegality of arrests as punishment and condemning the usurpation by the regulating authority of strictly judicial functions. Indeed, according to the penal code itself, prostitution was not an offense; and if it had been, one would have to consider that it involved two guilty parties. Furthermore, the registration of minors,[67] which was common practice in Paris and in the larger cities, was a serious offense against the articles of the penal code dealing with the protection of children. The same was true of the attitude of many keepers, who, with the tacit complicity of the police, allowed male minors to enter their establishments.

Arbitrary and illegal, this sequestration of women, who became "the things" of the police, was also immoral and inefficient. This ought to have condemned it in the eyes of the regulationists themselves, for it represented unassailable proof of the failure of their plan. It was immoral because the *maison,* far from being the regulated drain that allowed the practice of a normal, tolerable, temporary sexuality, had in fact become "first a centripetal, then a centrifugal focus of every ultravenereal vice."[68]

The inmate of the brothel was now the woman who satisfied the pleasures that one did not ask of one's wife.[69] The system was immoral, too, because it created an almost insurmountable obstacle to the redemption of the prostitutes. The day they wake up in a *maison,* "they feel above them the entire social organization, from the keeper, who represents capital, to the policeman, who represents the whole of social authority, to the doctor, whom she meets as a sort of tormentor and jailer."[70] According to Mireur himself, the prostitute is a slave "who has sacrificed her own personality."[71] Guyot shows how important it was to the regulationists to link in the public's mind the ideas of prostitution, the hospital, imminent death, and hell—in short, crime and its punishment— and how scandalous it would seem in their eyes to do anything that might allow the prostitutes to get rich easily and, subsequently, become respectable. Far from working, as they declared, for the redemption of fallen women, then, the regulationists were supporting a system that was by nature hostile to such a redemption.[72]

These reflections led liberal abolitionists, Louis Fiaux in particular, to make a few minor alterations to the portrait of the prostitute, which had hitherto been almost immutable, and to challenge the stereotypes concerning her sense of modesty, her religious outlook, and her maternal instincts, and to stress her "irremediable hopelessness,"[73] her inertia, her moral destruction, and ultimately her acquiescence, even her sense of professional duty.

Precisely to the extent that they perceived the rise of the hygienic argument within the regulationist discourse, the abolitionists insisted on the failure of the system in this domain. Health checks were too cursory;[74] they did not allow an accurate detection of gonorrhea or syphilis. Worse still, the dispensary was a place of contamination. Finally, the brevity of the treatment prevented any real cure. The prison infirmary was in fact the synthesis of the vices of regulationism, since sequestration, rape, and inefficiency were combined. The medical staff, appointed by the prefect of police, were poor practitioners; the treatment given was outdated; the harshness of the nuns toward the patients they called "our women," as did the members of the vice squad, was proverbial; they could not give up the idea that the treatment of venereal patients had to represent an expiation of the pleasures of the flesh. In order to prove the system's failure from the point of view of health, Yves Guyot set off the interminable debates concerning the effectiveness of the Contagious Diseases Act and the comparative disease rates of registered and unregistered prostitutes.[75] Although he did not himself apply a rigorously scientific method (far from it), he did produce a judicious critique of the statistics drawn up by the regulationist doctors.

This analysis of a system gave rise to proposals for reform; these are to be found summarized in the report adopted by the commission of the municipal council in 1883. The commission demanded, for all the reasons I have mentioned, the abolition of the vice squad and of official prostitution; at the same time, it demanded a general liberation of prostitutes. "All prostitutes would then be free"; they would come back under the common law; if they then broke the law or police regulations, they would be brought before the magistrates' court.

In the opinion of the commission, laws relating to prostitution were necessary, but only with a view to enforcing "respect for public decency." This time it was a question of giving a legal basis to repression. This new legislation would increase the penalties incurred by those prostituting children, extend the protection of minors up to the age of eighteen, be particularly harsh to punishable vice[76] (that is to say, homosexuality and perversion), and above all make it an offense to solicit noisily, insistently, or by obstinately standing in the public way. For their part, the police would disperse any gatherings of prostitutes in the street.

In the area of hygiene, the commission demanded the abolition of the prison hospitals as special establishments for venereal patients; such patients would be treated in the general hospitals if they so desired. Venereal disease itself would no longer be regarded as "a mysterious monstrosity that should be studied separately, treated separately, and designated by a separate language."[77] Syphilis in particular would be recognized as one disease among others, and even as less serious than many others. The administration would try to increase the number of out-patient medical consultations and provide free treatment and medicines to patients wanting to be treated. Finally, the majority of the members of the commission considered that progress in the education of girls and the adoption of a few vague measures concerning women's work would be enough to reduce prostitution, if not to make it disappear entirely.

The abolitionist analysis laid bare in a masterly way the presuppositions and motives of the regulationists. It proved the illegality of the system and, perhaps less successfully, its inefficiency. This explains the optimism with which these publicists believed they could counter the spread of prostitution. Despite the elaboration of a critique of regulationism based on an analysis of the social and sexual structures of industrial civilization, abolitionism was to remain, for the overwhelming majority of public opinion, at least until the beginning of the First World War, just as I have described it, the movement demanding that the great principles of the Revolution be applied to the one remaining sector of the population that had still not benefited from it.

Abolitionism among Feminists and in the Workers' Movement

A few references here and there have no doubt made the reader aware of the part played in the abolitionist campaign by the apostles of feminism and the members of the workers' movement. In fact, their positions were not, at the time, original ones. Solicited and sometimes even subsidized by the abolitionist federation, the feminist and workers' organizations rallied to the campaign, directing their extreme left-wing arguments against the prefecture of police. Indeed, we know that, generally speaking, these groups originally belonged to the radical orbit. Their own preoccupations, however, led their members to stress the weight of social phenomena and to try to influence the thinking of the abolitionists in this direction.

Many of the feminist leaders belonged to the French Association for the Abolition of Official Prostitution; Maria Deraismes, Emilie de Morsier, and Caroline de Barrau were its most active organizers. Albert Caise, one of the founders of the *Journal des femmes,* on November 15, 1876, at the beginning of the abolitionist campaign, launched one of the first petitions against toleration, demanding the closure of the *maisons,* the abolition of the vice squad, the passing of a law concerning provocation in the public thoroughfare, an increased number of dispensaries, and the return of the prostitutes to the rule of common law, as well as free, obligatory education and new legislation covering women's work. This petition came up against the refusal of senators to intervene in the matter.[78]

The positions adopted by the Democratic League for the Improvement of the Lot of Women, founded after the workers' congress of 1876 with the encouragement of Josephine Butler, and soon to be chaired by Maria Deraismes, were, obviously, the same as those of the federation. In September 1878 in Paris, during the first conference of the international federation, Léon Richer, the editor of *Droit des femmes,* developed the principles of a feminism of radical inspiration. When, in 1882, with the support of Victor Hugo, he founded the French League for the Rights of Women, he included in that association's program the abolition of regulated prostitution.

This demand was now a leitmotif of feminism, although what was actually a new argument passed unperceived.[79] Suffice it to say for the moment that when the abolitionist movement revived in France, between 1898 and 1901, it immediately received the support of all the feminist organizations.[80] In 1900 the two international feminist congresses that met in Paris voted unanimously for the abolition of any exceptional measures affecting morals. In 1901 all the members of the committee of the National Council of French Women, with the exception of Mme. Jules Siegfried, were also members of the abolitionist federation. Not a single feminist society was set up that did not include in its program the abolition of regulation and acceptance of a single standard of morality for both sexes.[81] The feminist magazines and newspapers—*La fronde, Le féminisme chrétien,* and *Le journal des femmes*—had all come out against the vice squad. "From one pole of feminism to the other the opinion is the same."[82]

The first abolitionist demonstrations had also benefited from the active presence of delegates from the workers' movement. Early in 1877 Mlle. Raoult had described the dramatic condition of the Parisian working-class woman to the bourgeois audience of the Paris conferences;[83] she returned to the subject at the Geneva congress, with the foundation of a new federation. The first workers' congresses also gave a prominent place to demands for the abolition of regulated prostitution. It was at the outset, when it was partly under the influence of positivist and radical ideologies, that the workers' movement gave the greatest importance to this problem.[84]

Already condemned at the Paris congress in 1876, even before the campaign opened, prostitution was discussed at length at the workers' congress at Lyons (January 28 to February 8, 1878), in the context of an overall discussion of the condition of the workers. In these debates one finds the same anxiety toward sexuality that then characterized the workers' movement. The danger to the honor of workers' families represented by the behavior of supervisors and foremen was denounced. Salomon demanded, in the name of public morals, the abolition of the employment agencies and their replacement by organizations run by the trade unions. Mme. Carraz, a delegate representing the women of Lyons, analyzed at length the causes of working womens' demoralization in the industrial centers. She blamed both ignorance and poverty, and stigmatized regulated prostitution. She concluded by declaring: "We must bend all our strength to this aim: the disinfection of our cities by the abolition of the *maisons de tolérance* and of every kind of legalized prostitution."[85] A delegate from Reims criticized the presence of men and women side by side in the workplace and the immoral behavior that resulted from it. In the end, the congress supported the conclusions presented by Malinvaud, the chairman of the commission devoted to vagabondage and morals in the industrial centers: the vice squad was declared to be immoral, illegal, useless, and ineffective, and its abolition was demanded. During the "immortal congress" at Marseilles (1879), Louise Tardif blamed male prejudice and behavior for driving women to prostitution.[86] A year later the question of the vice squad was debated at the Le Havre congress. Auguste Desmoulins, a member of the abolitionist federation, spoke on the subject, and at the proposal of the women's commission the institution was condemned once more, in particularly vehement terms. After 1879, however, this opposition took the form of socialist abolitionism rather than the earlier form.

Let us now assess the importance of the results obtained during this ardent, many-sided campaign. Unquestionably, the movement had aroused public opinion: between 1876 and 1884 the press, literature, and the visual arts had made prostitution a major theme. The abolitionist discourse was now structured and the arsenal of legal, hygienic, and moral arguments established. Yves Guyot's book was the reference to throw at Parent-Duchâtelet's epigones.

Several official bodies were led to take part in the debate, and the politicians responsible for these matters were forced to adopt a position. The abolitionists, in 1883 and 1884, won an unquestionable victory when the municipal council commission approved the Fiaux report and the council itself refused to pass the vice squad budget. Nonetheless, in 1878 and 1881 the opportunist majority in the Chamber had rejected the campaign being carried out by the Parisian extreme left; even among the radicals, such leaders as Clemenceau refused to commit themselves too strongly.

In practical terms the gains were few. As Dr. Fiaux was to recognize twenty years later, the problem had hardly aroused the passions of the provincial municipalities. Although the campaign had led Gigot in 1878 to soften the regulation of prostitution in the capital and moved Andrieux to abolish the vice squad as such, very few municipal administrations allowed themselves to be seduced by the arguments of the abolitionists. The list of initiatives is a short one. In 1878 the mayor of Bourges forbade the sequestration of prostitutes in the *maisons de tolérance* and insisted that the text of the prohibition be hung up in all the brothels. That same year the abolitionists met to prevent the opening of a *maison* at Belley. On July 15, 1880, a women's demonstration took place at Chambéry with the same purpose; the abolitionists won the day. No municipality at the time, however, dared to prohibit tolerated prostitution. Indeed, even between 1884 and 1900 only four such measures were taken. In 1891 the mayor of Amiens, Senator Frédéric Petit, had the *maisons* shut down, but they were reopened in 1895 after the election of a new mayor.[87] In 1893 the municipality of Courbevoie was the first to abolish regulated prostitution permanently. On April 28, 1897, Champon, the mayor of Salins, by an ordinance that was thereafter regarded as a model by the abolitionists, closed the *maison* that had been in the town since 1861, after detailing the scandals that had taken place there over the previous thirty-six years. Finally, in June 1900 the municipality of Pontarlier refused to give permission for the opening of a *maison* within the commune. This list is not a long one. Public opinion may have been stirred up, but it was not persuaded. The relative failure of the petitions is revealing in this regard.[88] The abolitionist campaigns had been sufficiently vehement, however, to stimulate the reflection of those in positions of responsibility, and, in return, gave rise to a very coherent form of neoregulationism that was to prove convincing.

It is clear that the abolitionist movement had been weakened by the coexistence within it of, on the one hand, an evangelical, moralizing prohibitionism dominated by an obsession with sexual repression and, on the other, an atheistic liberalism. Nevertheless, the two tendencies were not so far apart as they might seem at first sight: did not Yves Guyot dedicate his book to Josephine Butler? They were in agreement not only on the need to criticize the enslavement of women, to defend the individual, and to abolish official prostitution, but also to expect the moral development of the individual to result in the disappearance of the scourge. Although they both recognized, as regulationists, that poverty, bad pay, in short factors of a social order played a role in the genesis of prostitution, they scarcely pursued this aspect in their analysis. Here their discourse stops short: the same may be said, a fortiori, of their thoughts on the functions of prostitution.

Furthermore, the liberal abolitionists, deeply committed to individual liberty in sexual relations, also aspired to the triumph of reserve, to a domination of the sexual drives, to an internalization of repression. It was this that made for the ambiguity of these abolitionist tendencies, carrying a message of liberation for enslaved woman and yet of repression, insofar as the individual is invited to exercise a self-censorship in order to submit to the sexual order. This subtle mixture of evangelicism, positivism, and Kantian morality, so characteristic of the time, paved the way in bourgeois society for the "moralization" of youth, which coincided, in the years prior to the First World War, with the rise of nationalism.[89]

Regulation, Abolition, and the Rise of Socialism

The Socialist Discourse on Prostitution

This is not the place to retrace, however briefly, the history of socialist thought with regard to sexuality and the family, prostitutes[90] and prostitution;[91] to do so would require another book. I intend simply to study the attitude toward prostitution of the socialists of the Third Republic and to analyze their positions in terms of the quarrel between regulationists and abolitionists. This amounts to pointing out the relative similarities of the critical analyses carried out by socialists of various tendencies and the abstention of the leaders during the campaign.

Despite the differences that existed, where sexuality was concerned, between the various apostles of utopian socialism, and despite the relative vagueness of the Marxists on this matter,[92] the analysis of the causes and consequences of prostitution later carried out by the French socialists of the Third Republic is simple, clear and unanimous. The work that received most attention was *La femme dans le passé, le présent, et l'avenir,* a French translation, published in 1891, of *Die Frau und der Sozialismus* by the German socialist leader Ferdinand August Bebel. In France itself, several theoreticians, who were more or less directly engaged in the socialist struggle, had studied this problem. Some of them, such as Benoît Malon,[93] Charles Bonnier,[94] Charles Andler,[95] and above all Edouard Dolléans,[96] had made it a veritable specialty. At another level, that of the discourse emerging from the mass membership at congresses, the analyses were more simple: anything that threatened the morality of the working-class woman was tirelessly denounced.

Prostitution was regarded by the socialists as a scourge that was spreading. In this their analysis confirmed the obsessions of the hyperregulationists; it was a growing evil, for, like vice, it progressed in parallel with the development of capitalist structures. "Class organization means that prostitution is an essential cog in the system of production and distribution of wealth," wrote Dolléans.[97] Much earlier Bebel had remarked that "prostitution becomes a necessary social institution, like the police, a standing army, the church, the bosses"[98] because the capitalist regime creates "a state of contradiction between man, qua natural sexual being, and man considered as a social being."[99]

"Without the bourgeois family, there would be no prostitution."[100] Indeed, the capitalist system had created a veritable "matrimonial mercantilism"[101] within the bourgeoisie. On account of its purpose, its modalities, and its structure, the bourgeois conjugal family was in itself an unofficial form of prostitution, which found its material expression in such notions as the dowry, joint estate, patrimony, and inheritance. The mother who married off her daughter according to bourgeois criteria was little more than a procuress,[102] and the very notion of "marital duty" was, for Bebel, "worse than prostitution."[103]

Now, the very structure of the bourgeois family, derived from the economic structures of capitalism, involved the destruction of the proletarian family.[104] Indeed, the late marriages imposed on bourgeois males, the habits of debauchery that this postponement tended to create, "class morality," and in particular the value placed on the virginity of girls and on the fidelity of women, determined, within the bourgeoisie, an abnormally developed sexual demand that could not be satisfied solely by the women of that class. Furthermore, the marriages contracted for financial reasons, typical of the bourgeoisie, led within marriage itself to a lack of sexual satisfaction and recourse to the prostitute, as well as causing an increase in adultery and unnatural vice.[105] "The wish to preserve the financial power of the family intact requires the supply by the proletariat of a number of its girls ready to serve the pleasure of the wealthier classes."[106]

A veritable minotaur of modern times, the bourgeoisie sought in factory, workshop, and store the contingents of girls necessary to satisfy this demand; the factory was thus turned into the "capitalist's harem," and the boss came to symbolize the vice that threatened proletarian virtue.

It was by a triple process that the bourgeoisie set about creating the necessary prostitutional demand.

1. For the reasons that Proudhon, Pecqueur, and Engels had pointed out,[107] the workshop, by the very promiscuity that it engendered, was a place of demoralization; this theme recurs endlessly in nineteenth-century literature.[108] The idea that excessive hours, night work, the very conditions of labor (temperature, the physical gestures required) brought about the demoralization of women and girls was nourished among working-class militants by the fear of competition from women's labor, as this complaint, constantly expressed at trade union congresses, clearly shows.[109] The *droit de cuissage (jus primae noctis)* demanded by the bosses and, even more so, by the foremen demonstrated, for the socialists, the demoralizing effect of the factory, the workshop, and the store.

2. The low pay given to women was deliberate. It was intended not only to increase profit and reduce production costs but also to impose prostitution on large numbers of working women. In this manner "capital has found the means of regulating prostitution."[110] By regulating wages and the volume of employment, it has provided the reserve of prostitutes necessary to maintaining the bourgeois family and the virtue of bourgeois girls. Industrial capitalism needs the daughters of the proletariat to fill the brothels, just as it needs their sons as cannon fodder. Moreover, the economic rationality that determines the volume of employment is in inverse correlation to the prosperity of business, thus allowing the bourgeoisie to enjoy the women of the proletariat at a better price when profits decline. Karl Marx had already drawn a connection between the crisis in the cotton industry and the increasing numbers of young English prostitutes.

3. Thus capitalism gave rise to proletarian prostitution by making it impossible for working-class couples to enjoy the full harmony of marriage. By preventing the sexual fulfillment of the proletariat, it facilitated recruitment for debauchery. The length of the working day, the distance between home and the workplace, the excessively high rents demanded for tiny accommodations, and habits of drunkenness and wife-beating caused by this way of life were all obstacles to the harmony of the working-class couple. "For the proletarian," Benoît Malon complains, "there is no leisure time in the evening after a respectable, moderate, fruitful day's work, no rearing of the children in common—that sweetest of bonds—nothing of what constitutes the normal family."[111] To this should be added the disturbing effect of late marriages, the practice of birth control,[112] the application of rules of continence and "unnatural practices," which also paved the way for prostitution. Moreover, poverty has brought about the physiological undermining of the proletarian: diseases of the organs and menstrual problems, which were common among working women, also led to the development of "unnatural practices" and of "artificial sexual pleasure."[113] Finally, the sedentary nature of the work, in particular the use of the sewing machine, according to Bebel, "encourages the accumulation of blood in the belly and, by the compression of the sitting organs, produces sexual excitement,"[114] thus leading to debauchery.

In order to stem the rising tide of prostitution imposed by capitalist structures and systematically regulated by the bourgeoisie, immediate remedies would have to be implemented: to begin with, a reduction in women's work, itself, it should be remembered, being "one of the great problems facing the trade union movement at the first federal sittings";[115] then the raising of women's wages and the "moralization" of the workshop, with a view to abolishing night work, the mixing of the sexes, and the abusive solicitations of owners and foremen. Revealing in this regard is the campaign waged by the socialist press—and the tenor of the speeches made in the Chamber by extreme left-wing speakers—after the revolutionary strike that took place at Limoges in 1905, which was caused by the immorality of a foreman. At the level of ordinary trade union discourse the struggle against prostitution then turned into a defense of the morality of a working-class family whose values were in many respects very similar to those of a bourgeois family: premarital chastity, fidelity, exaltation of motherhood. There was no longer any reference here to the need to reform the bourgeois marital model or to remedy the repression of the sexual instinct made necessary by the capitalist system.

As far as the status of prostitutes was concerned, the socialist theoreticians were in agreement in demanding the abolition of the vice squad, mainly because its attentions were directed exclusively at working-class women and, as a result, "police regulation sanctions class exploitation."[116] This is certainly what the socialist councillor Henri Turot intended when he entitled his book on prostitution *Le prolétariat de l'amour*.

Curiously enough, at least at first sight, the coherence and self-confidence of the theoretical discourse were accompanied, in the case of the French socialists, by a marked reluctance to engage resolutely in the struggle against regulated prostitution, and an unquestionable reluctance to participate in the great debates that excited public opinion on this subject during the first years of the twentieth century. Not only was socialism not a dominant voice in the struggle for the abolition of the vice squad, but it sometimes seemed as if the socialists were in fact in favor of legislative silence on the matter. My main purpose here is to understand the reasons for this attitude.[117]

Those reasons emerging from ideology are clear enough. In this area the socialists did not expect a profound revolution from the application of common law and respect for individual liberty, any more than they foresaw the development of an individual moral conscience where male sexuality was concerned. The abolition of regulation and of the vice squad would not, therefore, in their opinion, represent decisive remedies in themselves. The true solution lay in the destruction of capitalist structures and, accordingly, in the disappearance of the bourgeois family and all its accompanying evils. Only this profound change would allow sexual relations to blossom in the proletariat—in other words, in the creation and development of a true proletarian family. To regard as a unique and indispensable remedy a fundamental social revolution amounts to seeing prostitution as a secondary problem. This hardly led socialists to participate in the campaign of the liberal abolitionists.[118]

Furthermore, the vagueness and even divergences to be found among the socialist theoreticians, beginning with Marx and Engels themselves, on the subject of a socialist sexual order, which alone would be capable of putting an end to prostitution, was an obvious impediment to any such commitment to the struggle.[119] The socialists had certainly connected the volume of prostitution with that of unsatisfied sexual demand, and thus with the widespread nature of celibacy, but they did not explain in detail how the disappearance of any prostitutional demand in a socialist society would occur in practice. Here the discourse on prostitution turns to a utopia whose optimism resulted in a lack of interest in the struggle then being waged by those who were working toward an immediate improvement of the prostitute's lot.

A certain political opportunism thus explains the socialists' reticence.

Since 1876 the terrain had been occupied by the abolitionist movement, a heteroclite coalition containing, side by side, strict Protestants, progressives, and radicals, who, with a few rare exceptions, were of aristocratic or bourgeois origins. First the British and Continental Federation, then the morality societies that took up the struggle, claimed to be outside any philosophical tendency and to bring together members of every political complexion, an assertion that aroused the suspicion of the socialists, who had long been regarded with mistrust in these movements. The primacy of the moral over the social was clear enough in the case of the abolitionist leaders, with their overriding concern for moral redemption. The "good works" organized by the "charity ladies" of the federation were deeply imbued with paternalism: was not redemption mainly a matter of providing servants for the bourgeoisie? There was no question in this context of incriminating the bourgeois family, as the socialists did, at least at the theoretical level.

The abolition of regulation had also become the battle cry of feminism, then dominated by radical ideology. It was *La fronde* that adopted the most determined attitude on this subject, and we know how difficult the spread of feminism in the socialist movement turned out to be and how its scope and influence were limited in that movement right up to the First World War.[120] When, at the beginning of the century, the struggle against the white slave trade was organized, it took the form of a league led by aristocrats and members of the upper bourgeoisie. In short, abolitionism in its initial form, as the campaign against white slavery, looked too much like the bourgeois morality societies for socialists to feel impelled to join in any large numbers.

At a deeper level, the socialist leaders, who were almost all of petty-bourgeois origin, were imbued with the morality of that class: like all the parliamentarians at the time, they felt an obvious repugnance for discussing sex and prostitution. They did not believe it to be a good electoral issue, that, on the contrary, defending the prostitute and demanding her liberty would run the risk of alienating a large segment of the public. The attitude of Marcel Cachin in the fifteenth arrondissement is revealing in this regard.[121] Indeed, in view of the ambiguity of the problem, the socialists found themselves caught in a serious dilemma. To declare themselves advocates of the status quo would be to present themselves as the defenders of the arbitrary action of the vice squad, and there could be no question of that. To demand legislation on prostitution amounted, in view of the dominance of hygienic neoregulationism, to granting the full sanction of the law to a form of repression of the prostitutes, who were largely of working-class origin, and this the socialists could not bring themselves to do. But to make themselves apostles of total liberty in prostitution did not correspond to the deepest convictions of the movement's leaders, who saw venal sex as a capitalist canker and who wanted to see the further development of social hygiene. Nevertheless, this was to be the position defended by certain socialist leaders who dealt with the problem, but in an unquestionably discreet manner. Not one of them made an effort to bring the problem of prostitution to the attention of the deputies and senators.

Reticence did not mean total abstention, however. During the congresses of the various groups and socialist parties, men would sometimes stand and, in simple but strong terms, attack the prostitution of working-class women, which was seen as an evil brought about by the capitalist system, the sad consequence of the unsatisfied sexual urges of a vicious, demoralizing proprietor class. After 1898 and the reform in France of a branch of the International Abolitionist Federation, expressions of sympathy and actual membership increased from the socialist side; this was because, under the influence of Auguste de Morsier, the abolitionists now refused to link their campaign with the defense of morality and bourgeois marriage.[122] Jaurès, when officially asked for his support in 1902, declared at last that he favored the abolition of regulation; in the municipal council the socialist Turot led the struggle against the vice squad. Above all, F. de Pressensé, the socialist deputy from the Rhône, led a tireless battle against the regulation of prostitution within the federation and in the League of the Rights of Man, of which he was president. Of course, it may be thought that, in his case, religious convictions and family tradition weighed more heavily than political loyalties; at least his criticisms of the lukewarm attitude of his socialist friends helped to bring the problem to the forefront of the party's concerns. The "people's universities" and the trade union centers, which, it is true, were dominated by the anarcho-syndicalist ideology, now welcomed lecturers from the federation.[123] When Paul Meunier tried to persuade the Chamber to legislate on prostitution, he was given the support of the extreme left.[124]

Nevertheless, it all amounts to very little. The socialist analysis, now guided by Marxist ideology, did not accord a very large place to sex. The prevailing view was that the disappearance of prostitution would not outlive capitalist exploitation and the spread of early marriage.[125] Neither monogamy nor premarital chastity was in question; no reference was made to the demand created by ugliness, shyness, infirmity, and old age. Such preoccupations did, however, emerge, not within the socialist groups but in the minds of certain individuals, often themselves marginal, who belonged, broadly speaking, to either the libertarian tendency or to the neo-Malthusians.

Prostitution and the Anarchist Discourse

The anarchist press and the writings of anarchists gave a much larger place to sexual morality than did the socialists; the former, quite clearly, did not have the same reluctance to confront the subject as the latter. Unfortunately, it is not possible, when faced with such a proliferation of individual expressions (typically, Charles-Albert's remark that prostitution was "a powerful aid for adapting to the capitalist system")[126] to produce a very clear picture of the libertarian stand. I shall therefore do no more than present what, as a result of wide reading,[127] seems to me to be the dominant intuitions of anarchist thinking on prostitution.

The anarchists, like the other socialists, believed that capitalism produced prostitutes ("the typical beloveds of the capitalist system"),[128] but they strove to show above all else that prostitution was a means of adapting to the system. In order to explain this, the libertarian discourse, which differed profoundly in tone from the socialist discourse, frequently denounced the evils of the "industrial prisons." In particular, it set out to show how capitalism gave rise within the proletariat to the development of specific extramarital sexual practices that made it possible not only to satisfy bourgeois sexual demand but also to give the worker an elementary form of satisfaction, which was indispensable to maintaining the use of his labor.

Three themes constantly recur in the writings of the anarchists on the subject of prostitution.

1. The denunciation of the employers' *droit de cuissage* was a veritable leitmotif.[129] I shall not return to this practice, which I have already discussed several times. The anarchist press regarded this scourge as inherent in the "industrial prison" and indissociable from the existence of a population of female wage earners. Often, as in the case of the housemaid, sexual favors were a tacit clause in the contract binding the working girl to her employer.[130]

2. Unlike the socialists, who were fierce defenders of the working woman's morality, the anarchists, in the purest Proudhonian tradition, seized upon the thin line between female wage-earning and prostitution. Following a reasoning diametrically opposed to bourgeois discourse, which presented prostitution as antinomic to labor, the anarchist showed that prostitution was itself a form of labor. Like working women, prostitutes wore themselves out working; among themselves the prostitutes spoke of "their work." Moreover, working-class women were also, by force of circumstance, prostitutes. The seamstress who, in the evenings, augmented her wages by giving herself to a client was acting no differently from the clerk who, on his return home, wore out his

sight doing accounts to earn a little extra money. "Flesh for work, flesh for pleasure"[131] was simply the dual aspect of the same enslavement of women, made necessary by the capitalist system. As Proudhon suggested, the factory and the brothel were two similar, interlinked institutions. Work for wages could not be opposed to prostitution, because the two phenomena were ultimately identical. "All wage-earning is a form of prostitution, because, by hiring out one's labor, it is always one's body— muscles or brain—that one hires out."[132] Libertad scandalized his audience when, on October 25, 1906, at a meeting organized by the abolitionist branch, he declared, before being expelled: "In present-day society, there is not only the prostitution of sexual organs; there is a prostitution of arms, bodies, brains . . . The working woman who works for the profit of her employer is just as much a prostitute as the woman who sells her flesh. What I deplore and what will be abolished only when the rotten society we are living in is crushed is prostitution in general."[133]

3. In capitalist society, prostitution fulfills a triple function. First, it is made necessary by the structure of the bourgeois family, by bourgeois morality. Here the anarchist discourse is at one with socialist discourse, so there is no need to belabor the matter: prostitutes are necessary because bourgeois girls and women are not allowed to initiate young males and "because they are not free to respond as they wish to the desires that they arouse."[134] But this is not the essential point. Second, regulated prostitution, an institution of capitalist society, has for that society the advantage of removing from the threatening army of the unemployed a contingent of girls and women whom it then places under surveillance.[135] Finally, and above all, capitalism gives rise to the development of a utilitarian prostitution, "an outlet for poor virilities." Whereas the socialists place the greatest emphasis on the extent of bourgeois sexual demand, which determines in turn, and in a sense automatically, proletarian supply, the anarchists stress the existence of a project inherent in the capitalist system. This consists of arousing in the worker a form of sexual behavior that will not weaken his zeal for work and of creating a prostitution adapted to this behavior—that is to say, adapted to the mode of production.[136]

Capitalism so arranged things that the worker did not experience, or experienced very little, the love that transcends mere satisfaction of physical need, and this was one of the fundamental aspects of the alienation of the workers. Indeed, in that system what mattered was "to keep a watch . . . over anything that might divert the masses from steady work, such as love, and to have ready to hand the means of doing without it."[137] Here, it is true love that becomes antinomic to work. Capitalism seemed to be aware of this: for "the slaves of the machine and capital . . . love . . . is the exaltation of an organ and the satisfaction of that organ."[138]

From this point of view, the development of a utilitarian prostitution bound up with the existence of a wage-earning class became a "powerful aid in adapting to the capitalist system." Thus, things were organized in such a way that prostitution fulfilled its function: this was the origin of regulationism. This organized prostitution made it possible, therefore, both to defend the bourgeois family against the unmarried male and to prevent true love from diverting the worker from his labor. Is it surprising, then, if the volume of prostitution increased with the development of industrial society? In order to carry out their functions, the "saleswomen of love" were no longer recluses. With the assent of the police, they swarmed over the sidewalks: "They are everywhere." Here the libertarian discourse links up with the fears of the hyperregulationists. "At any time and at any place, for a few sous if necessary, the rut of the impatient male, of the poor male, of the male exasperated by a poor life must be satisfied."[139]

Retailers of low-cost sex that leaves no traces, "prostitutes are the typical beloveds of the capitalist system." They were also, by this fact, the very symbol of the rottenness of the world[140] and "the sore from which the social pus flows."[141] In such circumstances the campaign for the abolition of the vice squad became even more urgent.[142]

Unlike the socialists, who were all too ready to excuse the fallen woman because she was a victim of the social organization but not to regard her activity with sympathy, the anarchists looked favorably on the prostitute in the practice of what they regarded as her job. Quite logically, they considered that the prostitute should be no more despised than the working woman. A more precise analysis of sexual privation in society and of the function performed by venal sex led them to an awareness of the normality of the prostitute. Needless to say, the libertarian press vigorously opposed the theory of the born prostitute, the ultimate attempt to marginalize her. Recognizing her function, the anarchists were the only ones to reintegrate the prostitute into society.

Hence the profoundly original view that they had of her. It is not my intention here to provide a large number of examples or to analyze the content of the image of the prostitute in the libertarian press or in anarchist-inspired songs.[143] Innumerable portraits of prostitutes in the depths of degradation nonetheless arouse sympathy, for example, that of Margot,[144] alcoholic, consumptive, suffering from the most extreme loneliness, whose wretched existence symbolizes that of the prostitutes of the Latin Quarter. Indeed, the prostitute often appears in the anarchist press as a woman worthy of love, in a way that suggests that anarchist sentiment was the heir to romanticism and was close to the redemptorism that, under the influence of Dostoyevski[145] and Tolstoy,[146] animated a Catulle Mendès[147] and, above all, a Léon Bloy.[148]

> Et les yeux humbles des putains
> Aux cils voilés, experts aux feintes . . .
> Et les yeux humbles des putains
> Nous consolent mieux que les saintes.

wrote Jacques Damour in *Le libertaire*[149] in 1899, before Apollinaire wrote of the "regrets des yeux de la putain."[150]

The measures advocated by the anarchists to remedy the evils of prostitution are profoundly different from those offered by the socialists. They proposed that the prostitutes should form a trade union, as other working women had. On November 12, 1899, Alla observed in *Le libertaire* that prostitutes, robbed, robbed, and robbed again, "terrorized, plundered, beaten by wretched pimps, tracked down, charged, and brought before the courts by the law," form a "real and officially recognized professional body."[151] He advocated the formation of a trade union that, in view of the large number of prostitutes, would be the most influential of all. "It would also be the most powerful trade union through the individual action of each of its members on every class of society; it could publicize in the most splendid way the profession of love, and demand the consideration that has so far been refused."[152] It could also exercise a beneficial influence on hygiene. It should be said that the idea of a prostitutes' trade union had long since aroused a sarcastic response in the satirical press: *Le grelot* had brilliantly described the possibility of a strike by the prostitutes.

Like the socialists, the anarchists declared that only a complete transformation of society would bring about the disappearance of prostitution, but their analysis gave more emphasis to the necessary disappearance of all authority in sexual matters; the overthrow of bourgeois sexual morality was an indispensable precondition. There now developed a critique of the monogamous family. Léopold Lecour, the apostle of free union, thundered against the housewife, who was just as much a product of capitalist society as the lady and the whore, the three symbols of the enslavement of women.[153]

The right to pleasure was invoked; there was no question here of blaming, as the liberal abolitionists and the feminists did, the depravity of male youth; the present behavior of young males was necessitated by the sexual structures. The true juvenile depravity was, in fact, the practice of continence. "The chaste," Henri Duchmann wrote,[154] "are usually shy people, whose overheated imaginations, combined with the vice of Onan, delights in unhealthy parodies. This is just as terrible a depravity, the result, precisely, of the difficulties that prevent the sexes from satisfying themselves freely." The anarchist press demanded—although theirs was an isolated voice—the right of the unmarried male to sexuality and, furthermore, "the right of virgins to pleasure." In 1904[155] the same Henri Duchmann urged unmarried women to have sexual relations, for "virginity is renunciation, abstention, death."

In the society of the future, when women will have emancipated themselves from the morality that enslaves them,[156] and when sexual freedom will be able to blossom, prostitution will lose its raison d'être and disappear in all its forms; only then will women, bourgeois and proletarian alike, cease to be prostitutes, whom capitalist authority needs for the time being, and true love will triumph.[157]

The notion of prostitution seems to be of fundamental importance here; as we can see, it takes on dimensions well beyond the subject of this book. What is usually regarded as venal sex was merely one aspect of a phenomenon that concerned almost all women. So it was illusory to hope for the disappearance of prostitution in the strict sense without a radical revolution taking place in the economic, social, and above all moral structures. "As long as men remain subjected to the influences of an environment governed by the laws of property, incapable of acquiring economic freedom and moral freedom, they will neither be able nor, for the most part, wish to rise to the higher form of the sexual instinct, love, and will instead encourage women to sell their bodies."[158]

Paul Robin, that unclassifiable but fascinating character, turned his attentions to, among other things, the fate of the prostitute.[159] None of his contemporaries regarded the problem with so much openness of mind. In the first place, we owe to him the most precise of the plans to unionize prostitutes that were drawn up during this period. He proposed that the offices of Gabrielle Petit's *Femme affranchie* should serve as the headquarters of the organization, but I have been unable to discover whether it actually functioned. In line with the neo-Malthusian campaign that he undertook, he demanded better sexual information for prostitutes in order to protect them from "two risks,"[160] the risk of venereal disease and the risk of becoming pregnant. He demanded that the use of condoms[161] become general among prostitutes and that the physical conditions in which they practiced their profession be reformed so that the principles of sexual hygiene could be applied.

But the real solution of the future, which he saw more clearly even than the anarchists, lay in "pure, simple, unqualified freedom,"[162] respect for the right of each individual to pleasure, and "joy" for all. Recounting "the lamentable sexual history of mankind," and considering that "marriage and divorce are abominable survivors of those universal tortures,"[163] he regarded with optimism that "there is a possibility of sexual satisfaction for all, without lack or excess for anyone."[164] In the kind of society he advocated there would no longer be any prostitutes; love would be "a joy . . . forever truly free, spontaneous, never enforced, never enslaved, never mercenary."[165]

Carrying out a veritable Copernican revolution, he was no longer content to demand the right of unmarried women to pleasure; he actually pitied virgins as much as prostitutes, seeing the former as the main victims of the sexual order. In his *Propos d'une fille* he puts into the mouth of the prostitute with whom he claims to be speaking the following exhortation: "And you, you who are probably the most unhappy of all, you women who grow old neglected, vainly desiring a little of those pleasures whose excess burdens us, and the sharing of which would make both you and us happy! When will we want, when will we be able to unite together and fight the good fight?"[166] By stressing above all else sexual privation and the inequality of satisfaction among individuals, this theoretician of pedagogy[167] was the first to discuss the problem in adequate terms, long before Wilhelm Reich.

A New Calculus of Transparencies

Amplification of the Venereological Discourse

The elaboration of a neoregulationist system was the response of members of the medical profession to the campaigns of the liberal abolitionists. It also resulted from the theme of venereal danger, which had been gaining prominence since the end of the Second Empire. It was above all a manifestation of the efforts of the medical profession to develop its power and exert its authority, first through social hygiene, then through the prevention of disease.[168]

As we have seen, the denunciation of the venereal peril led doctors, in their international congresses, to advocate a stricter regulationism. The vigor of the abolitionist campaigns then brought them to an awareness of the archaic and defective nature of the "French system" and to try to reform it in order to save it.

The rise of the venereal theme in the medical literature is explained, first, by the scientific progress achieved. Clinical study had made it possible to assess the development of syphilis and to define the manifestations of its three successive stages. The discovery of the tertiary stage, of its seriousness and of all its effects, stimulated the fear of degeneracy, which was very widespread in the 1870s, and which marked in Europe the height of the influence of Darwinism. Biological anxiety, which had hitherto been generalized, now began to focus on a few scourges of the first order, which now included the danger of venereal disease. Among the prominent clinicians responsible for progress were, along with Neisser, those of the medical schools of Paris and Lyons, in particular Ricord and his pupils and followers: Toussaint Barthélemy, Lancereaux, Mauriac, and above all Alfred Fournier. The rise of this new pope of syphilography corresponds to the emergence of neoregulationism, of which he was, in many ways, the creator and most active apostle.

Since what conditioned neoregulationism was the extreme seriousness of the venereal threat,[169] the way in which it was then exposed should be analyzed in detail. In my opinion it was Dr. Mauriac who, in his lectures of syphilography between 1875 and 1881, best described the progress of the scourge in modern times. Referring to the number of consultants at the Hôpital du Midi, which was far from being a rigorously scientific sample, he established circumstances of morbidity and proved that they were based on "circumstances of pleasure," that is to say, on prostitutional activity, itself determined by fluctuations in personal wealth. Indeed, "sexual commerce" evolved, according to him, parallel to other forms of commerce.[170] Thus pleasure, immorality, and wealth were presented, in the discourse of the venereologists, as antinomic to health.

In the final analysis it was the factors that act on wealth, and therefore on prostitutional activity, that determined for Mauriac, the oscillations of morbidity. Economic downturn, by diminishing sexual consumption,[171] impedes the course of the disease. This observation leads quite naturally to an emphasis on the beneficent effect of economic crisis; his argument here echoes the desire for penitence and abstinence to be found in the thinking of conservatives in the years following the pleasure-loving days of the Second Empire. The other factors he saw acting on prostitutional activity were the proportion of bachelors in the population, and therefore the marriage rate (marriage was now presented as the best remedy to the venereal danger), and above all else the way in which the by-laws were applied. According to Mauriac, morbidity is inversely proportional to the number of arrests and registrations and directly proportional to that of "disappearances."

The action of these three factors found expression in a decline of venereal morbidity in 1870 and 1871, during the war and siege, then between 1873 and 1876, thanks to intensive activity by the vice squad. Between those two periods a slight revival could be noted that should be attributed to a thirst for pleasure, "the temporary drunkenness of the senses,"[172] a simple compensation for previous privations. But, as Professor Mauriac and his Lyonnais colleague Dr. Horand had been anxiously stressing since 1876, the disease was spreading rapidly; its growth had accelerated in 1878 on the occasion of the Universal Exposition, which attracted crowds of foreigners and provincials to Paris. In 1879 and 1880—that is to say, at the height of the abolitionist campaign—venereal diseases reached "a development that they had perhaps never attained before at any time."[173] Mauriac attributes the revival to, among other causes, the relaxation of the activity of the vice squad, which followed the violent attacks made on it by the abolitionists. According to him, 5,000 new cases of syphilis developed each year in Paris; ten years later Richard estimated the number of venereal cases in the capital at 85,000.[174]

Now this scourge, whose progress was assuming the shape of a veritable invasion, was rising up from the depths; like the prostitute, disease circulated throughout the social body at precisely the points at which, through venal sex, the various classes are in contact. Syphilization from below rebounds on syphilis from above, declared Professor Fournier. "Experience proves," wrote Professor Barthélemy, "that venereal disease, wherever it appears, always comes from the street"; he added, "Clean up below (streets, sidewalks, bars, dance halls, wine shops, etc.) and you will clean up the rest . . . Clean up the cities and you will clean up the whole country. Clean up every capital, and you will clean up the whole world."[175] The biological threat was identified once again with the social threat. Unlike cholera, however, which had disappeared since 1859, this was a continuous, endemic threat from a disease that was smoldering, growing, it seemed, in an unavoidable way with the increase in wealth and the attraction of the pleasures of which it was merely the reflection.

The works of Professor Mauriac[176] showed, it was thought, that venereal geography was based fairly reliably on social geography, and even on that of political riots: the center of the capital and the suburbs of the north, the east, and the south were infected, whereas the west and outlying suburbs remained relatively healthy. The 5,008 women who had contaminated the patients at the Hôpital du Midi included a large number of registered prostitutes (35 percent), but even more unregistered ones (40 percent) and "miscellaneous" others: servants, working girls, barmaids, and artists. Unpaid mistresses, however, turned out to pose very little danger (6 percent). These results led Mauriac to insist on the need to counter unregistered prostitution in a determined way and to limit extramarital sexual relations. This ought to be all the easier in that the occupational distribution of the diseased working women (16 percent) was precise: they consisted almost entirely of laundresses, seamstresses, milliners, florists, mattress-makers, polishers, and feather dressers.[177]

As for the male victims of the contagion as a whole, or at least Professor Mauriac's hospital patients (these excluded members of the bourgeoisie, who consulted doctors privately), this group certainly reflects the working-class clientele of prostitution as we have encountered it so far. We meet again the unmarried proletarian males of the capital, who had made up most of the clientele during Louis-Philippe's reign (workers in the building trades, navvies, day workers, domestic servants), as well as a good number of office clerks and shop assistants.

The venereal danger was all the more serious, the specialists urged, in that, coming as it did from the social depths, it attacked not only the guilty but also the innocent bourgeois. The "syphilis of the innocents," which had long since been recognized[178] but had been given new immediacy by Fournier, increased the public's horror of the disease. Syphilitic newborn babies, the midwives who had delivered them, wet nurses diseased by the babies they were suckling, glassblowers contaminated in the course of their work, patients infected by badly cleaned medical instruments[179] or by tattooing[180]—these victims of chance represented, according to Fournier, 5 percent of all syphilitics. And this figure did not include "the syphilis of honest women"[181]—fiancées made victims by the kisses they accorded their betrothed, young brides contaminated by their grooms, faithful wives who paid for their husbands' behavior. On the basis of 842 cases treated in his private practice (in other words, men and women from a bourgeois milieu), Fournier concluded that these honest women constituted at least 20 percent of the total number of female syphilitics. This "contagion by rebound"[182] led him, with the neoregulationists, to demand the humanization of the treatment of venereal patients.

This seemed especially important as the psychosocial context added to the gravity of the venereal danger; the consequences of the disease on the psychology of the patient and on his or her environment were particularly devastating. Alfred Fournier's writings swarm with anecdotes on this subject that are almost too painful to read: virgins, their bodies covered with lesions, dying in appalling pain because their sense of modesty did not allow them to benefit from early treatment; young men who commit suicide rather than contract a marriage that would risk contaminating a beloved wife, fathers who murder sons-in-law who had infected a dear daughter; and, after 1884, wives, revolted by their husband's disease, demanding a divorce. What we have here is a whole dramatic repertoire on which authors of later decades were to draw.

Professor Diday devoted voluminous works to the psychology of the venereal patient and to his behavior within the family. He details all that was done and said to conceal the disease from one's spouse. The practitioner even goes so far as to explain how to undress and "keep one's partner amused"[183] in bed without risking contagion, but he still came up against the most difficult problem: how was one to refuse sexual intercourse? For his part, Dr. Lardier describes the torments of the peasant who dared not have recourse to the village quacks, was prevented by the possibility of gossip from confiding his disease to anyone in his community, and who was forced to go, alone, to the nearest city to consult a doctor.[184]

Shame; despair, sometimes leading to suicide, at learning of the chronic nature of the disease; the cruelty that drove the venereal patient to infect a prostitute intentionally with syphilis or even to deflower a virgin, because, according to popular belief, to transmit the disease to an innocent party[185] brought a cure; or simply the confusion of the young man who dared not tell the family doctor about his disease but placed his trust in drugs touted by advertisements in public lavatories[186]—such were the various psychological attitudes brought about by the ravages of the dominant prejudices. It should be noted, incidentally, that nineteenth-century doctors, otherwise so scrupulous of medical secrecy, showed little such scrupulousness where sexuality was involved.[187]

In the end, as the medical literature on the subject emphasizes, the venereal danger led to a decline in marriages, the breakup of households, an increase in divorce, and therefore to a decrease in population. If the degeneracy of the race has not yet become a constant topic of observation,[188] the risk of depopulation through venereal disease was, in 1885, denounced in fearful terms by Professor Fournier before his colleagues at the Academy of Medicine. It was apparently this information that caused the psychological shock that was indispensable to the later success of neoregulationism.

Although it was not yet the object of systematic propaganda in the battle of public opinion, the venereal danger already bore within it, like the prostitution with which it was confused in many people's minds, the major anxieties of the time concerning health, sex, population, and the proletarian threat; this confluence explains the dithyrambic tone adopted by the specialists calling for a veritable sanitary crusade.[189] It goes without saying that this denunciation of venereal disease in frightful terms was in itself a call for continence and a restraint on extramarital relations;[190] these preoccupations were to become self-evident with the deployment of the great campaign in the first years of the century.

The rise of venereal anxiety was the main element in the hygienic terror that was beginning to gain ground. It was already clearly perceptible in literature. The work of Huysmans is thoroughly imbued with it. This anxiety, which contrasts with the mocking, relaxed attitude displayed by Flaubert on this subject,[191] partly forms the basis of his physiological pessimism. It is found again in counterpoint, like prostitution, in almost all the novels written before his conversion. It is sometimes clearly described, whether in the anxiety of an eighteen-year-old schoolboy losing his innocence to a streetwalker after a student supervisor has shown him "portraits of men chimerically ravished by syphilis,"[192] or the torments of the infected bachelor reading the medical advice displayed in public lavatories.[193] It is while preparing an album illustrating all that is most horrible about syphilis, the chancres of the patients at the Hôpital Saint-Louis that Cyprien finally devotes himself to his art after renouncing both love and worldly success.[194]

Venereal anxiety is openly invoked in the recounting of the many nightmares and fantasies that mark Huysmans' novels: one remembers the character of des Esseintes terrorized in a dream by the invasion of the "great pox" or fascinated by plants of a chancrous appearance.[195] This feeling is perceptible at each step, even when it is not explicit; it determines the author's view of sexuality. Woman, with her gaping sex, is often identified with death-carrying pox; all those female bodies whose beauty dissolves, whose eyes burst,[196] are evidence of this same anxiety, as is the attraction for the works of Félicien Rops,[197] which also reflect the grip that the venereal danger held over men's minds.

With Huysmans this obsession is expressed in the very structure of the narrative: the evolution of the feeling of love, or rather of desire for woman, is described in his novel *En ménage* according to the model of syphilis, in three successive, increasingly serious stages.[198] One can already sense in his works the ambiguity concerning neurosis and tertiary syphilis characteristic of certain Scandinavian works, in particular Ibsen's *Ghosts*. Yet it is worth noting that Huysmans, imitated in this by Zola, did not take the easy way out by having Marthe die of a venereal disease. The work ends with the description of the alcoholic pimp's autopsy, although it is true that, by stressing the link between prostitution and alcohol, the author was again echoing medical literature.

The venereal peril is a central theme in Huysmans' earlier books, and one finds it again, like a second voice, in the work of several other novelists of the time, fiction that was sometimes no more than a reflection of the phallic anxiety and fear inspired by castrating woman. It was not only the condition of being a prostitute but the most ignominious death, that rottenness, that leprosy by which the body dissolves alive, which, for Barbey d'Aurevilly, represented the vengeance of the Duchesse de Sierra Leone.[199] By making prostitution and syphilis, which had become symbolic, the means of self-destruction through sex, the author inaugurated, in 1872, an inexhaustible theme. One has only to think of the more discreet but moving description of the illness, which was to strike down Maupassant in dramatic fashion. His misogyny, which has so often been denounced, turns out, on this matter, to be less profound that Huysmans', but it reveals the same tenderness for the venereal patient that the author felt for prostitutes; he is not afraid to denounce male cowardice and the scandalous way in which the victims of the disease were then treated.[200]

Even when it was one of the major themes of a work, even when it generated the profound anxiety that structured the work, the venereal peril was not yet the *subject* of literary works. It was not until fifteen years later that novelists and playwrights, often with some intention of social prophylaxis, were to devote their writing to systematically describing venereal disease, its torments and ravages.[201]

Scientific Prophylaxis and the Sanitary Police

The elaboration of the neoregulationist discourse and the propagation of its major themes were mainly the work, it should be repeated, of one man, Professor Alfred Fournier. Indeed, the new chief of French syphilography believed himself to have a double mission: to denounce the venereal peril and to propose reforms capable of eliminating it. To do so he set out to give a new direction to the abolitionist campaign, some of whose aims he supported, by popularizing certain of the recent achievements of medical science.

It was in 1880 that, for the first time, he proposed his reform plan to the commission set up by the Paris municipal council.[202] In 1885 Fournier denounced before the Academy of Medicine the dangers that venereal disease presented to the population. Declaring himself to have been deeply impressed, but also aware of the advantage that he might derive from the operation in establishing his authority, the prefect of police appointed a commission of scientists and administrators to work out a program of reforms.[203] This was presented in 1887 by Dr. Le Pileur;[204] it closely followed the ideas of Alfred Fournier.

In the same year Fournier demonstrated to the Academy of Medicine the widespread nature of "syphilis of the innocents" and thus prepared his colleagues for a possible humanization of the treatment of venereal patients. Finally, in 1888, some months after the Academy of Belgium had taken up its position, Fournier presented to the Academy of Medicine a coherent plan. This project was to become the reference text of the neoregulationists.[205] It should be noted, however, that it was not adopted in its initial form on account of the isolated opposition of Brouardel, a defender of traditional regulationism, who supported maintaining the prerogatives of the prefecture of police.

It was the neoregulationist scheme worked out in 1887 and 1888 by Dr. Le Pileur, Professor Fournier, and Professor Léon Le Fort, with the assent of the majority of their colleagues in the academy, that I shall now analyze, before going on to show how it was later altered by each one of them.

This new discourse was based on simple but very firmly expressed principles: the progress of medical science, especially that of syphilography, had entrusted the doctor with a new mission, that of organizing sanitary and social prophylaxis. "Above sanitary policing," Professor Mauriac was to write, "float the medicine and hygiene that have inspired, directed, and illuminated it."[206] "I declare myself to be a convinced advocate of regulation," Dr. Corlieu wrote in 1887, but of a regulation worked out "not according to the ideas of the Administration, but according to a plan emerging from the physicians of the Dispensary and a few syphilographers, gathered together in a special commission, a plan that would be submitted for the approval of the Conseil d'hygiène et de salubrité de la Seine, while awaiting the creation of a general directorate of public health."[207]

This new mission was no longer based, as some of the regulationists at the beginning of the century believed, on arguments stemming from a confessional ethics. Moral and political preoccupations were officially relegated to the background: "Why mix politics or religion with measures that should only emerge from the field of prophylaxis?" Dr. Commenge was to ask.[208] One can hardly find an allusion to these considerations in the accounts of academy debates.[209] Professor Mauriac, ten years earlier, had already warned his listeners that he had banished all moral considerations from his analysis of the venereal situation.[210] Yet the extreme seriousness of the venereal danger required the adoption of measures of social prophylaxis. Thus it was no longer the provocation to debauchery that justified and even required repression, but the fact that it was at the same time a provocation to syphilitic contagion.[211]

From these principles derived a critical analysis of the existing system, which was, indeed, in the eyes of the neoregulationists, archaic, intolerable, and inefficient. The position of the traditional regulationists and of certain prohibitionists of the abolitionist federation, which amounted to regarding venereal disease as a divine punishment and demanding treatment that was also punishment, was totally incompatible with the new scientific spirit. Alfred Fournier criticized sharply the functioning of the prison infirmary of Saint-Lazare. The poor organization of the care dispensed to the venereal patients, the inadequate number of beds reserved for them,[212] the exclusion practiced by the mutual aid societies, the attitude of certain nuns who refused to treat this category of patient were denounced in turn.

The system was intolerable. Furthermore, the neoregulationists, taking up certain arguments of the abolitionists, criticized in turn the exorbitant powers of the prefecture of police and the scandals to which they had given rise. The registration of minors was denounced as contrary to respect for paternal authority.

Finally, traditional regulationism had proved to be inefficient; the prefecture of police found itself weaponless before the campaigns of its adversaries. Even Lecour, with whom Le Fort had debated, recognized the powerlessness of the vice squad and the inaction to which it had been reduced. Did not the decline of the *maison de tolérance* itself point to the failure of the system? Moreover, the stays in the prison hospitals and general hospitals imposed on venereal subjects were too short to be effective; these establishments had simply become places of asylum,[213] and as a result the system did not really guarantee prophylaxis.

These considerations necessitated a series of urgent reforms: a scientific prophylaxis had to be established, carried out by an effective sanitary police, whose action would be to legalize and control through the courts; these reforms would ensure the return of the prostitutes to common law.

Modern prophylaxis and the scientific recognition of the syphilis of the innocents implied abolishing the punishments still being inflicted on venereal patients and abandoning the collective medical examinations practiced by army doctors. Yet they also required the continuing registration of prostitutes and a more determined campaign against unregistered prostitution, which presented a grave health risk. Indeed, in the debate over the comparative rates of illness among registered and unregistered prostitutes, the neoregulationist physicians (Mauriac, Le Pileur, Butte, Corlieu, Martineau, Commenge, and Barthélemy) found themselves on the same side as the regulationists (Garin, Mireur, and Jeannel), who also believed that the risk of contagion was greater among the unregistered than among the registered.

Registration was not to involve retaining all the obligations deriving from an earlier age that the municipal by-laws still imposed on the *filles soumises*.[214] Sequestration in an establishment was not directly specified in the early pronouncements of neoregulationism. The discretion shown toward the brothel certainly indicates that no hostility was felt in principle to the institution. Molé-Tocqueville's lecture, which, in 1879, became one of the first texts of neoregulationism, had even come out strongly in favor of sequestration. In particular, one reads in the final report: "Do not all these occasions of contact [with the prostitutes], of cohabitation, of inevitable relations blunt contempt? . . . Would it not be better to sacrifice some areas of land on the outskirts of the town, constitute an *asylum* for vice in which the police and the physician could, successfully, ensure good order and health?"[215]

The registered prostitutes, then, would now be compelled to submit to thorough medical examinations once a week. Moreover, the system of allowances should encourage the unregistered prostitutes to report to the dispensaries, which would be increased in number. The hospitals annexed to prisons would be abolished; the venereal patients would be treated in special hospitals open to all who sought treatment. An establishment of this type would be set up in each town of a certain size. Fournier, however, came out against the opening, urged by the abolitionists, of special services in general hospitals. Out-patient consultations were increased; Professor Bourneville had been demanding this for years, and the success of Fournier's work at the Hôpital Saint-Louis proved their efficiency. These consultations were without charge, as were the medicines prescribed for the patients. In these special hospitals the venereal patients would be sequestered until their complete cure was certified by the doctor in charge.

This new organization presupposed an improvement in the quality of the medical profession. To begin with, it required a reform in teaching. Only 13 percent of new doctors had seen a syphilitic in the course of their studies.[216] All the departments treating venereal patients should therefore be open to students, and training in venereology should be made compulsory in their fourth year. As for the doctors at the dispensaries and special hospitals, they would no longer be appointed by the prefecture of police but recruited through competition. Finally, an attempt would be made to disseminate medical knowledge of venereal disease throughout the population at large.

This prophylaxis would be imposed by an efficient sanitary police; the repression of provocation in the public thoroughfare would be increased; the unregistered prostitutes and those who frequent cafés, shops, and bars would be more closely supervised; special steps would be taken by the police around army camps to track down the *pierreuses;* the reporting of infected women would be systematically organized.

The action of the sanitary police would be based on law; the neoregulationists agreed with the abolitionists on the need to legislate on prostitution. Of course, the application of this law would cover the whole of the national territory. The new legislation would establish not the offense of prostitution but, as the abolitionists proposed, the offense of soliciting. Furthermore, certain neoregulationists proposed even before their adversaries did—and this accords with the logic of their system—making an offense of contamination.[217]

This neoregulationism involved recourse to the courts and, more precisely, to the courts of summary jurisdiction or magistrates' courts. These would have to judge women who failed to undergo health checks, and would be able to impose temporary and renewable registration on unregistered prostitutes caught soliciting members of the public. The new police would now confine their attention to enforcing the sanitary regulations, to noting offenses of solicitation, to handing the delinquents over to the legal authorities, and to enforcing the decisions of the court. This would put an end, therefore, to the arbitrary action of the vice squad.

Thus structured, the neoregulationist project, under the pretext of abolishing abuses and arbitrary action, was expressing in essence the wish to legalize repression. It was at one and the same time an updating and reinforcement of traditional regulationism, and it benefited the medical authorities. This intention was not lost on the abolitionists; it was even publicly admitted by some of those who were designing the new system. Professor Le Fort declared in the course of a discussion at the Academy of Medicine that, far from seeking to weaken it, he was trying "to strengthen the action of the administration by removing, by law, the obstacles opposing its effective intervention."[218] This declaration was repeated several times during the discussions.

The new plan was even perceived, and quite rightly, as the ultimate attempt to save regulationism. As Le Fort declared once more: "Salvation will come only through the intervention of the courts."[219] It was partly to maintain the principle of authority at a time when public opinion was shifting more and more toward liberalism that the highest medical authorities in the country erected this neoregulationism, which tended toward the legal recognition of the marginalization, if not the sequestration, of prostitutes in the interests of preventing disease.

The ideas of Professor Fournier did meet with hostility from several advocates of the traditional system, of whom Professor Brouardel was the spokesman, as well as from such admitted abolitionists as Dr. Fiaux. Furthermore, from 1888 on, the members of the Society of Practical Medicine were to condemn, through the pen of Dr. Malécot,[220] the positions of the academy, in particular the sequestration of venereal patients.

Finally it should be noted that, in the same year, *La semaine médicale* also adopted a position against the Fournier report.

Nevertheless, most of the doctors who tackled the question took up once again the professor's main propositions, each adapting them in his own way. From 1885 on, Dr. Martineau[221] expounded a set of neoregulationist health measures, which he refused to bring under legal authority. Dr. Corlieu,[222] for eleven years attached to the health dispensary, also demanded the application of a reform inspired by the medical profession, and one that went well beyond the framework of regulated prostitution. Dr. Verchère[223] also approved, in large measure, the neoregulationist project. In 1889 Professor Barthélemy,[224] whose role was later to be the determining one when a question arose of organizing at an international level a policy for the prevention of venereal disease, declared that he agreed with Fournier. Furthermore, he formulated a few practical propositions that were highly indicative of the nature of the neoregulationism that he advocated. He demanded that the members of the vice squad be made health inspectors and called for the establishment of a health certificate for prostitutes and barmaids, a measure that had already been advocated by Professor Diday. He proposed that in the "preservative houses," as he called the brothels, the "matron" should examine the genital organs of each client. Finally, he demanded that offenses against the health regulations should be punished by detention in workhouses, a proposal that, it is true, is typical of traditional regulationism.

The progress achieved by neoregulationism in shaping opinion between 1885 and 1890 was to find expression in the final report of the health commission set up by the Paris municipal council. Whereas Dr. Fiaux's text of 1883 constitutes a catalogue of the reforms proposed by the abolitionists, the 1890 report,[225] which was to have considerable impact on public opinion, and on which Georges Berry would closely base his parliamentary bill in 1894, reflects the work of both commissions; in the end, it formulates an attenuated neoregulationism placed at the service of the municipal council. Indeed its author, Councillor Richard, demands that the supervision, which, contrary to the abolitionist views expressed by Dr. Fiaux in 1883, was to be maintained, be removed from the prefecture of police and placed under the authority of the municipal council. The report retains the principle of compulsory hospitalization of venereal patients, but expresses the view that this should take place in special services set up within general hospitals. Finally, Richard also condemns administrative detention and proposes to hand over the registration of *filles soumises* to the magistrates' courts.

Generally speaking, the primacy accorded in this work to the venereal danger is in itself revealing.

In 1888 one stage came to an end in the debate that divided public opinion as to how the prostitute should be treated. The abolitionist campaign had lost much of its strength, and the socialists had very little interest in the problem. A precise plan of reform was drawn up, however; its authors tried to adapt regulationism to the progress of science and changes in public awareness. This discourse reveals very clearly the claims of the medical profession; it follows in direct succession the progress achieved by the notions of social hygiene and disease prevention. The exaggerated place it gives to the venereal danger, now depicted as the most terrible of the threats to health, also reveals the phallic anxiety that sustained it. In proposing to maintain, and even in a way to increase, the marginalization of prostitutes by demanding increased repression of unregistered prostitution and the sequestration of venereal patients, it also reveals the grip of the ancient fear that the laboring classes inspired in the bourgeoisie.

For the time being the neoregulationist project was scarcely implemented at all.[226] Between 1888 and 1898, the medical literature kept turning over the ideas of Fournier and Richard. For ten years, within the medical profession polemics proceeded and statistical series were drawn up; there were endless disputes concerning comparative morbidity, without it occurring to anyone that this was not at the heart of the problem and that they were confronting a question that was impossible to solve in a scientific manner with the data at their disposal. The major fact of that decade, from our point of view, is unquestionably the entry onto the stage of the indomitable Senator Bérenger. This strong personality was to some extent to bring about a shift in the various positions. Taking up the principal elements of neoregulationism, he was, in effect, trying to give it back some moral content. Although a liberal Catholic, Bérenger was linked to de Pressensé and the founders of the Society for the Revival of Public Morality. He was to become the life and soul of this movement, the destroyer of pornographers of all kinds, the scourge of the white slave trade, the defender of underage prostitutes. By officially linking neoregulationism to the desire for moralization that sustained it, Bérenger was to give it the coloring that it was to acquire at its triumph, just prior to the First World War, after the period between 1898 and 1906 when the problems of prostitution would once again grip public opinion.

Part III

The Victory of the New Strategies

6. The Need for Surveillance

In the 1902 elections the Bloc des Gauches (an alliance of parties stretching from the extreme left to the radicals) triumphed; the radicals, who had always been friendly to the ideas of the abolitionists, came to power. Ever-wider divisions were opening up in bourgeois morality: divorce was increasing rapidly, women were demanding emancipation, the behavior of the young was being transformed by greater permissiveness, "free union" found passionate advocates, and the Dreyfus affair had sensitized public opinion to every aspect of individual liberty. In short, the climate seemed favorable to the liberation of the prostitute, and the abolition of regulation appeared to be imminent. But let us not forget that the advocates of surveillance were already planning for battle. A system had been worked out that involved the implementation of new strategies, but whose fundamental aim remained the marginalization of the prostitute.

Before retracing the history of this second abolitionist campaign and analyzing the new policy toward prostitution, we ought to consider the way in which the advocates of regulation had denounced the venereal peril, the white slave trade, and the innate nature of prostitution. These campaigns, cleverly orchestrated, had had a profound effect on public opinion; they had managed to persuade a large segment of the public, against the logic of political history, to accept the continued surveillance of prostitution.

The Venereal Peril at the Turn of the Century

Although prostitution had been described in detail in fiction since 1876 and had been widely discussed in the press between 1876 and 1883, at the time of the abolitionist campaign against the vice squad, it was only during the first years of the twentieth century that it became a subject in the forefront of public concern. The mass-circulation newspapers, encouraged by the morality societies, found, in denouncing in their own way the white slave trade, a theme capable of arousing the interest of most of their readers; at the same time, the venereal peril had become the subject of a multifold obsessive literature. It was in a situation dominated by fear of these two scourges, and by a concern for protecting oneself against them, that there arose at this time a movement to promote sex education, which was initially conceived as sexual dissuasion.

Unfortunately, the framework of this study is too narrow to deal with these ideas in depth. One can say, though, that the rise of these two themes, together with the often favorable reception given by French scientists to the theory of the born prostitute, expressed the anxiety of a large segment of the bourgeoisie, which was all too aware of the threats of subversion in the sexual order, and formed part of a much broader plan for safeguarding morality. Indeed, the combined efforts of the moralists, educators, and doctors succeeded, to all appearances, in stemming the movement toward sexual liberation that had taken root in the bourgeoisie. The decade prior to the First World War, which, as we know, was marked by a violent upsurge of nationalism, was also a period that saw a moralizing counteroffensive, offering proof, if any were needed, that, like de-Christianization, the collapse of the sexual order was not a continuous, linear movement. It followed the lines of a set of circumstances in which one's attitude toward prostitution was a primary indicator.

Between 1899 and 1910, the white slave trade and the venereal peril became international issues, beyond the scope of this book. Since 1902 sex had also been an object of concern to diplomats. From then on, French history very often does no more than reflect decisions made at international meetings; and national associations were merely the antennae of world organizations. Thus, the subject took on new dimensions as a result of changes in the means of mass communication and the worldwide organization of space.

A Terrifying Danger

The last years of the nineteenth century and the first decade of the twentieth were the golden age of the venereal peril.[1] Two international conferences especially devoted to it were held in Brussels in 1899 and 1902. It was then that an organization was set up that, while demanding the humanization of the treatment of venereal patients, proposed to disseminate throughout public opinion, by means of an obsessive propaganda, the idea of a terrifying danger.

Around 1900, syphilis appeared to be a more serious disease, more contagious and more durable, than had previously been thought. The emergence of the notion of parasyphilis tended to make the old "pox" regarded as the disease that conditioned a large number of other morbid phenomena. This theory attributed to venereal disease "new, overwhelming responsibilities,"[2] especially when mercury and iodine were found to be ineffective against parasyphilitic complaints. In 1902, in his report to the international conference at Brussels, Professor Burlureaux declared that, for this reason, doctors "ought to be so familiar with the study of syphilis that the idea of syphilis would occur to them when confronted with any patient."[3]

An increasing number of publications implicated syphilis in the incidence of stillbirths. Even in 1889, Dr. Le Pileur[4] declared that "out of a hundred children conceived in Paris, thirteen would die on account of their mothers' syphilis." In 1901 Dr. Paul Bar[5] estimated that the proportion was between 7 percent and 8 percent. That same year Professor Pinard, citing work carried out at the Baudelocque clinic by one of his pupils, declared that "on a statistical basis of 20,000 cases of pregnancy, the author has found, as the cause of infant mortality, the syphilis of the parents to be in the proportion of 42%."[6] Infantile polymortality in the same family was regarded from this point on as evidence of syphilis.[7] The lack of scientific rigor in this work did not prevent it from arousing people's anxiety.

Above all, the currency throughout the medical profession of the notion of inherited syphilis had a profound effect on a public haunted by the fear of degeneracy. Following the work of Edmond Fournier, the son of Professor A. Fournier, the existence of syphilitic degeneration[8] was recognized by many as an incontrovertible truth. Almost every kind of malformation and abnormality was attributed to it; this became the golden age of syphilitic teratology.[9] Supporting the ideas of Parrot, Professor Pinard declared to Professor Fournier: "In all my practice, I have never observed a single case of rickets unconnected with syphilitic parents."[10]

So this terrible and highly contagious disease was, in the opinion of the specialists, very widespread; indeed, the number of its victims was thought to be increasing at a rapid rate concurrent with the progress of civilization.[11] Essentially an urban phenomenon in the past, syphilis was now spreading throughout the countryside, as Dr. Léon Issaly noted in a thesis whose conclusions, often cited, seem to have left their mark on many.[12] Following Dr. Le Noir, [13] Alfred Fournier conjectured that, in Paris alone, from 13 to 15 percent of the male population (about 125,000 individuals) were infected. Professor Barthélemy even suggested that the proportion was as high as 20 percent.[14] In 1902 Emile Duclaux, director of the Institut Pasteur, reached the conclusion that there were as many as a million *contagious* syphilitics in the French population.[15] In 1906, in Lyons, at a congress for the advancement of science, Dr. Manquat repeated again the terrifying estimates of Dr. Le Noir and Professor Fournier.[16] Furthermore, Emile Duclaux believed that more than 2 million individuals in the country were suffering from gonorrhea. So cautious an authority as Dr. Morhardt was not afraid to adopt the then-widespread opinion that most men fall victim to the gonococcus once in their lives.[17]

Thus it becomes easier to understand the inflammatory language used by those syphilographers, in particular by Barthélemy, Dieulafoy, and Fournier,[18] when they denounced the venereal peril. The discourse of the venereologists, even more so than in the past, accorded with the anxieties of all those who perceived and deplored the decline in the French birth rate. From this point of view syphilis was all the more serious in that it struck very early. The investigation carried out by Edmond Fournier into 17,406 cases[19] indeed shows that contamination occurred at an early age. The peak period for contracting syphilis through sex (that is, not including the "syphilis of the innocents") occurred between eighteen and twenty-one for women and between twenty and twenty-six for men. Those infected, therefore, were at the height of their procreative ability.

At the same time, syphilis threatened the future of the country. It acted as a scourge on the army and navy, and the Société de prophylaxie set up a commission to study "the venereal peril in the French colonies." Even more grave, by reducing fertility the disease deprived the nation of future soldiers. "Would not a half or a third of the children that will be killed by syphilis this year, I wonder, have made up as many conscripts in twenty years?"[20] Alfred Fournier asked members of the Extra-parliamentary Commission for the Regulation of Morals.

In short, the venereal danger represented a death sentence for mankind as a whole; thus Dr. Patoir[21] declared that he was convinced that the syphilization of mankind as a whole was unavoidable. Following Tarnowsky's declarations, he added, "In certain districts of Russia, this syphilization seems to be an accomplished fact."[22] In all, public opinion was confronted by a terrifying discourse whose dissuasive effects on sexuality proved lasting.[23]

The Organization of the Campaign

It was in an international context that the struggle against the venereal danger was organized. The much-demanded conference took place in Brussels in 1889, at the initiative of Dr. Dubois-Havenith and members of the Belgian Academy of Medicine, who, with their French counterparts, had pointed out the extreme danger of the epidemic. Most European countries were represented at Brussels, whether they were regulationists like the French, hyperregulationists like the Belgians, or abolitionists like the British since the abandonment of the Contagious Diseases Acts and the Norwegians since 1888. The French delegation consisted of determined regulationists, such as Professor Barthélemy, who had tirelessly called for such a conference, as well as abolitionists who were either longtime converts (Dr. Fiaux) or recent ones (Professor Augagneur).

Of course, these abolitionists carried off a great succès d'estime, of which they were inordinately proud. At the end of long debates concerning above all the comparative intensity of the disease among *filles soumises* and unregistered prostitutes, the conference, in its final resolution, in fact adopted the point of view of the neoregulationists. The most evident result of its work was the formation of an International Society for Sanitary and Moral Prophylaxis, the aim of which was to coordinate the efforts of all those who were determined to combat the venereal peril.

The second conference, which took place in Brussels in 1902, did little more than confirm the positions adopted in 1899. At the suggestion of Professor Landouzy, however, the system of surveillance of prostitution then in force was this time strongly condemned by the participants at the meeting.

The war carried out in France against the venereal peril took various forms; nevertheless it was centered on the Société française de prophylaxie sanitaire et morale, founded in 1901 as part of an international society.[24] A veritable league against syphilis—and this was how Alfred Fournier, who was largely responsible for founding it, defined it—it was, from the outset, in contact with the morality societies, the medical societies of neoregulationist tendency, and the senior officials of the prefecture of police; later, its members came into contact with the military hierarchy. The Société française de prophylaxie became, therefore, the center of a pressure group whose role was considerable not only in maintaining the regulation of prostitution, but also in the new thinking on sexuality being carried out in France by educators, doctors, soldiers, and the families of the liberal upper and middle bourgeoisie. It was there that, thanks to the venereal peril, was born and became popularized the notion of sex education. The action of that society and of everything connected with it, under the pretext of struggling against the venereal peril, obviously consisted above all of a campaign, partially successful, to dissuade youth from indulging in sexual activity.

In 1901 the Société de prophylaxie had 406 members, 11 of whom were women; of the 395 male members, 358 (90 percent) were Parisians; only 34 lived in the provinces, and 3 abroad. The society brought together the leading lights of the medical profession; fully 75 percent of its members were doctors, dentists, and pharmacists. The other members belonged, for the most part, to the upper bourgeoisie of fortune and talent, whose salons were frequented by the doctors. They consisted of Parisian barristers and notaries (5 percent of the members practiced law); senior civil servants, deputies, senators, even government ministers (4 percent in all); stockbrokers, industrialists, and merchants (7 percent); professors at the Sorbonne and men of letters (4 percent); artists (2 percent); and army officers (2 percent). The list also includes a few aristocrats, two students, and one porter from Les Halles! It seems quite obvious that family and social connections determined recruitment.

The aims of the Société de prophylaxie were clearly defined at the outset. Officially, its concern for health took precedence over moralizing intentions; its object was to assess the venereal peril precisely and to combat it in cooperation with the international society that had been formed for this purpose. This implies a reflection on the prophylactic means likely to check the spread of the disease and on the attitude to be adopted toward prostitution; it also implies the organization of a propaganda campaign intended to stress the dangers that freedom in sexual relations, particularly among the young, brought with it.

Precisely to the extent that the members of the society, believing that the measures of preventing social disease already being taken were inadequate, assumed the aim of promoting individual protection,[25] a concern for moral preservation was implied in the health campaign. Indeed, as Alfred Fournier observed, the best way to fight the venereal peril would be to eliminate all extramarital sexual relations: "If mankind could return to a golden age of innocence, the days of syphilis would be numbered."[26] This explains how the ultimate aim of the association came to be the extinction of syphilis through "moral uplift, the purification of morals, an awareness of duty, respect for virgins, and early marriage."[27] In 1902, before the members of the Brussels conference, Professor Burlureaux, who had been entrusted with a report on individual prophylaxis, declared: "Marriage is quite obviously the safest shelter against the venereal peril. It is clear, then, the extent to which the struggle against the venereal peril and the precepts of religion are inseparable." He added, "Ministers of all denominations have a major interest in seeing the continuation of our campaign against the venereal peril, because they know very well, in the final analysis, it is moral education that will be the essential factor in preventing venereal diseases."[28]

As Dr. Debove was to write in 1904, "You see, gentlemen, that by approaching this very serious question of the prophylaxis of venereal diseases exclusively on the medical terrain, we are led to advise chastity on all."[29] In his *Conseils aux avariés,*[30] Dr. L. E. Monnet declared: "Heading the treatment of genital herpes, we must write as an absolute rule marital fidelity. Having only one woman is a strict, indispensable rule, so true is it that morality and medicine, here as always, show their indissoluble union."[31]

It would, therefore, be pointless to try to separate the moralizing intentions from the sanitary ones: they form a whole. Nowhere does the close relationship between the medical discourse and its moral presuppositions appear more clearly than in the literature and publications of the Société française de prophylaxie sanitaire et morale. Indeed, the society's very name reveals the connection.

The society now set about organizing debates and undertaking inquiries into public opinion on such crucial subjects, for anyone concerned with the sexual behavior of the bourgeoisie, as the use of contraceptive methods, the freedom of marriage and eugenism, the criminalization of intersexual contamination, the advantages and disadvantages of continence, and the influence of sport on juvenile sexuality. In this society, which might at first glance seem marginal and insignificant, there developed a new strategy concerning sexuality and, more particularly, juvenile sexuality. For the first time, people dared to approach such subjects in open, public debate, other than in terms of prostitution. The discourse on prostitution, and therefore the policy advocated concerning it, were suddenly integrated into a wider discourse on sexuality. The abundant literature of the Société de prophylaxie is evidence of this widening interest; it seems to me to represent a turning point in the history of attitudes toward sexuality.

An Obsessive Propaganda

"There is nothing wrong in provoking the obsession of one's fellow-citizens when such a praiseworthy aim is to be attained,"[32] Professor Burlureaux declared at Brussels in 1902. These words from a leading doctor, who had dared to confront publicly the issue of sex education for young girls, gives some indication of the way in which members of the Société de prophylaxie built up a sexual curriculum that essentially took its bearings from the idea of venereal peril.

In fact, it should be repeated, this education was above all a form of dissuasion: it was right to inform a young man in order to put him on his guard against pre- or extramarital sexual relations. "In reality, what must be achieved is that young people would marry as virgins," Dr. Queyrat declared in a report read to the Société de prophylaxie in 1902.[33] He added, "It is important that each of us, moralists and doctors, should carry out an energetic campaign . . . against that harmful stupidity"[34] that consists of believing that a young man must be allowed to amuse himself before marriage. Believing that premarital experiences are simply "a few hours of carnal epilepsy,"[35] he summed up his thinking thus: "As far as young men are concerned, let us keep them pure, let them marry young, and, I would add, let them be faithful husbands."[36]

The same intentions appear in pamphlets published by the society. Most of the ones written by Burlureaux[37] and that by Alfred Fournier[38] are devoted to a description of the symptoms of venereal diseases. In 1906 Dr. Manquat declared that, for him, the purpose of sex education for girls was to stress "the dangers that they run, now and in the future, whenever they agree to sexual relations outside marriage."[39] Professor Delorme, summing up, in April 1907, the results of the information campaign in the army, declared that this education had created in the soldier "slowly, but surely," a "salutary fear," a "reasoned and in a way instinctive repulsion."[40]

This form of sex education was only one aspect in the denunciation of the venereal peril; many other means were then implemented to sensitize public opinion. The Société de prophylaxie had posters put up, even in public lavatories, in order to fight the deceitful advertising of charlatans. In 1902 at the Brussels conference Burlureaux advocated the use of light projections, colored plates, and models to inspire a "salutary terror" and advised setting up museums of syphilis in the larger cities;[41] we know that his advice was followed, at least to some extent.

There were more and more lectures: Professor Pinard spoke on the venereal peril at the Sorbonne, and Father Sertillanges broached the subject in two Lenten lectures at Notre-Dame. In 1903 the deputy Georges Berry introduced a bill on prostitution in the Chamber; the text of the bill is a learned exposé of the venereal peril. Far from demonstrating the decline of the scourge, the author claims that it had been on the increase since 1900. The previous year Waldeck-Rousseau had decided to set up an extraparliamentary commission to study ways of fighting the peril.[42]

The success of Ibsen's plays in Europe had raised the fear of degeneracy among the educated public. In a preface to the French edition of *Ghosts,* Edouard Rod recalls "the sense of gnawing fear"[43] that he saw spread through the audience during performances of the play. The "spectacle of the fatal scourge on the stage,"[44] the evocation of a world peopled by men doomed at birth by the sins of their ancestors, nourished a deep anxiety that scientific discoveries had aroused. The fact that "general paralysis,"[45] a form of inherited syphilis, is not mentioned in the play, any more than is "neurosis," makes the final scene all the more moving; by its very ambiguity it aroused the secret terror that the spectator of the day felt for syphilis.

With Brieux's *Les avariés* the venereal peril was overtly named on the stage. This work, inspired by Dr. Cazalis' *Science et le mariage,* and of which Yves Guyot was to say that it was not a play but a dramatized interview with Dr. Fournier, was a propaganda piece, probably instigated by the Société de prophylaxie. The play shows the disastrous consequences wrought by syphilis on individuals and families. The author denounces the conspiracy of silence, and the ignorance and calamities that it is producing; he advocates the dissemination of medical information and demands that the "damage" be treated, without shame, as in the case of other diseases. His hero, Georges Dupont, a twenty-six-year-old future notary engaged to a deputy's daughter, contracts syphilis in a final fling before marriage. The father-in-law, convinced by the family doctor, recognizes in the end that his son-in-law is not solely guilty and decides to reconcile the couple during divorce proceedings following the birth of a syphilitic child. The deputy even goes so far as to present a bill of social protection against syphilis in the Chamber.

At first prohibited in France, then performed before a wide audience and eventually published in 1902, Brieux's play brought the venereal peril into the headlines. It provided the bourgeoisie, which it depicted, with the terms *avarie* (damage) and *avariés* (damaged), which offended the ears of the audience less than *syphilis* and *vérole* (pox). This allowed polite society to discuss the scourge as overtly as alcoholism or tuberculosis. From this point on, there was a large increase in the number of medical books intended for a general public; it was to Brieux that Dr. Fernand Raoult dedicated his *Etude sur la prophylaxie de la syphilis* in 1902. Dr. L. Monnet published his *Conseils aux avariés,* and Dr. H. Mireau published in *Le petit provençal* a series of popularizing articles that he collected in 1906 under the title *L'avarie: Etude d'hygiène sociale.* He too dedicated the book to Brieux, "who has done more on his own, through the three acts of his play, than all the hygienists put together have done for fifty years."[46] He observes that "there is not a single newspaper that has not devoted a few columns to the study of the disease."[47]

Les avariés represents, therefore, an essential stage in the spread of venereal fear among the public.

In 1900 André Couvreur published a terrifying novel, *Les mancenilles,*
which he himself regarded as a "clinical study"[48] of syphilis intended for
male readers alone. In the novel Paris is compared to the manchineel, a
poisonous tree that is deadly to anyone who sleeps in its shade, and the
women of the capital are regarded as *mancenilles,* responsible for the
moral and physical collapse of the men who come in contact with them.
In this book one finds references to the "popular dung heap"[49] from
which syphilis rises, as well as a hostility to the city and an exaltation of
country life typical of the traditionalist current, and deeply rooted xenophobia and racism.[50]

In essence, the novel is a documentary work on the evolution of syphilis; a number of visits to the Hôpital Saint-Louis enable the reader to
follow the various stages of the disease. This course in venereology is
completed by a description of the development of the disease in Maxime
Duprat, the hero of the novel, who, having become a government minister at thirty-six, is struck down by tertiary syphilis contracted twelve
years before. The individual, familial, and social consequences of venereal disease are meticulously analyzed: a late marriage with a virginal
country girl, a brilliant political career in ruins, the contamination of the
innocent wife, the birth of a monstrous child, who is mercilessly
described by Couvreur, with its "greenish belly, apelike hands, feet
twisted into gnomelike attitudes."[51] Maxime is himself a victim of inherited syphilis, and the final madness that brings him down reinforces in
the minds of readers the link that venerealogists were making between
venereal disease and mental illness.

In all such novels, the author speaks through the mouth of a doctor,
a friend of the hero. This scientist dreams of a "moral antiseptic"[52] and
tries to spread a fear both of the disease and of moral disintegration.[53]

In 1903 Paul Bru similarly devoted his novel *L'insexuée* to the consequences of gonorrhea. The plot is simple: Raymond Morel, only son
of a successful furniture manufacturer, marries Simone Laugier; they
adore each other, but the young man has contracted the "clap." During
their honeymoon Simone falls ill; she is suffering from salpingitis and
has to undergo an operation on her ovaries and fallopian tubes. She will
no longer be able to be a mother; "she will no longer have a sex." Learning of her fate by chance and realizing that her life is in ruins, she loses
consciousness. Later, she turns to mysticism before finally going insane
on hearing of her husband's infidelity.

Many other books helped to spread the venereal fear, not all of them
emanating from sympathizers of the Société de prophylaxie. An element
of neo-Malthusian propaganda pervaded these works. In his novel

Vénus, ou les deux risques, Michel Corday showed how the fear of pregnancy and disease prevented couples from fully enjoying their sexual lives together. His character, the poet Léon Mirat, sees his experience of marriage ruined by his concern with avoiding making his wife pregnant. Having become a widower, he comes up against the same obstacle when sleeping with his mistresses, although each of them uses different methods of birth control. Having finally contracted syphilis during an escapade with a former lover, a shop assistant turned courtesan and well-known actress, he is driven to kill himself. His friend Dr. Reiset, who, since the suicide of his own syphilitic brother, has been involved in desperate research at the Institut Pasteur to discover a serum against the disease,[54] has convinced him of its inexorable character.

This terrifying novel, with its very modern language and tone, represents a desperate appeal in favor of a right to pleasure without risk and progress against "the shame vaguely attached to anything associated with sex: love, pain, motherhood, contagion."[55] Again, we see in the novel a description of "that fear, followed by the anxious waiting of a man who, for weeks, examines himself, scrutinizes himself, asks himself if he is not poisoned . . .[56] and suddenly, the *that's it* comes like an electric shock, like a syncope in the mind."[57] The novelist describes, without benefit of any metaphor, the horrors of venereal disease: "It eats away the bones: the patient spits out his teeth like Pangloss, loses his nose, assumes that hideous death's-head one sometimes encounters in the streets, or crumbles away, melts, dissolved by necrosis."[58] At the end of the book Dr. Reiset delivers a concluding speech that might have come from the pen of Alfred Fournier. Profoundly pessimistic, the book had a terrible influence on readers; according to Dr. Monnet, many venereal patients, after reading the book, rushed to their doctor to ask if, in all frankness, he regarded the disease as incurable and suicide as the only possible way out.[59] Thus the book helped to spread syphilophobia.

It was in the army, it should be repeated, that the most widespread educational effort was made. Since 1902[60] the young recruit had been lectured in the matter upon enlisting; army hygiene manuals dealt at length with venereal disease.[61] "Demonstrative tableaux," projections, and advice printed on leave passes spread this information. On September 23, 1907, in a memorandum that caused a scandal, Undersecretary of State for War Chéron demanded that sex education be extended, officially advised on the use of methods of birth control, and called for the setting up of disease-prevention rooms where soldiers would be able to go after having had sexual relations. On April 7, 1912, the minister of war, at the request of members of the Société française de prophylaxie, strengthened measures intended to give information to soldiers.

Since 1902 all punishments directed at soldiers suffering from venereal diseases had been abolished, and health checks had become personal. In order to avoid temptation, attempts had been made to keep soldiers inside the barracks by increasing the number of clubs, recreation rooms, and libraries.[62] Longer leaves, allowing soldiers to visit their families, were encouraged in place of one-night leaves; *maisons du soldat* and *jardins militaires* were opened in the main garrison towns.

The moralization of the soldier, as the American Abraham Flexner observed in 1913, was general throughout the European armies. Indeed, for him it was part of preparing soldiers for war: "The nation that first manages to reduce [venereal disease] will gain a considerable superiority over its enemies."[63] Everywhere "the enlisted man is being taught that continence is possible and healthy . . . Almost simultaneously, the military authorities in Europe have set about struggling against the tavern and lust."[64]

The effect of this systematic, obsessive propaganda is perceptible in literary works far removed from any concern with the military. One has only to read Charles-Louis Philippe's *Bubu de Montparnasse*[65] to get some idea of the extent to which the risk of venereal infection surrounded juvenile sex with anxiety; one might almost think that the book had been published by the Société prophylaxie, whereas we know that this was not at all the case. Venereal anxiety was one of the obsessions that structured Huysmans' work, but here it became the main subject of a book devoted to prostitution that might have had as its subtitle "A Sociological Study of the Psychological effects of Venereal Disease." Bubu, the young pimp, after suffering the torments of waiting for the disease to attack, is eventually reassured by his colleague "le Grand Jules," who has had syphilis and who has proved himself to be "stronger than the pox."[66] With some pride Jules manages to convince his young friend that venereal disease is part of their lot in life. Perhaps this should be seen as the emergence of a counterdiscourse that gives some indication of the sociological limits on propaganda concerning venereal disease.

Victor Margueritte's novel *Prostituée,*[67] a veritable summa on venal sex, is also steeped in the fear inspired by syphilis. This work is essential for our purposes in that it helped to spread the idea of the irresistible progress of the disease, and above all the certainty that this spread was inevitable precisely insofar as it was bound up with the development of civilization.[68] Referring to the thoughts of one of the heroes of his book, an eminent syphilis specialist, the author writes:

He, Montal, would have made a considerable contribution to demonstrating the growing invasion, the hereditary devastation, and how, propagated on every side as the horizons of peoples broaden, as the routes of commercial exchange increase and intersect, *it had grown at the same time as civilization,* corrupted, constantly corrupted, each day more rapidly, each day more. Syphilis, once restricted to a few individuals, circumscribed in small centers, was now spreading, with parasyphilitic accidents, over every race, infiltrating its poison from vein to vein, from family to family. For it was not only prostitution that conveyed it; the immense vicious circle was growing larger, getting closer and closer.[69]

That final, crucial thought suggests that any regulationism, whose ineffectiveness had been demonstrated, was now inadequate, and that, in order to limit the progress of the venereal peril, it would be necessary not only to renew it, but, above all, to exert closer surveillance over sexual behavior through education, hygiene, and morality.

The Venereal Peril and the Vice Squad

The new emphasis given by doctors to the venereal peril had, as far as prostitution was concerned, both strengthened and exacerbated neoregulationism, had even given rise to a sanitary hyperregulationism, and, as a result, impeded the progress of abolitionism. Indeed, the outraged feelings with which the scourge was denounced are evidence, it should be repeated, of the desire of the medical profession to justify the regulation of prostitution. We know that, since Pasteur's discoveries and, as far as venereal diseases are concerned, those of Neisser, the notion of "social hygiene," to borrow the title of a book by Dr. Emile Duclaux, was gradually becoming more ordered and complex. In the synthesis that he published in 1902, the director of the Institut Pasteur and the Institut des hautes études sociales devoted a chapter to the vice squad,[70] concluding that it needed to be transformed into a sanitary police. As a good pupil of Fournier he did no more than reaffirm the principles of neoregulationism, while showing how they were to be integrated into a coherent, overall project of social hygiene, and of the "socialization of doctors"[71] (that is to say, the assumption by the medical profession of the administration of health) and of various other social groups.

Only too aware of the support that the denunciation of the venereal peril gave to the neoregulationists, the abolitionists set about, albeit in vain, to expose the exaggerations of the campaign. The reasoning of their adversaries was simple. The venereal diseases were spreading. Meanwhile, the sanitary regulation of prostitution reduces morbidity, as was proved to their satisfaction by the low number of diseased prostitutes in the *maisons de tolérance* and by the "law of balance" according

to which male venereal morbidity was, in a given locality, inversely proportional to the activity and severity of the vice squad. It was therefore
necessary, they argued, to maintain and improve the surveillance of prostitutes. Within the army, whose influence at a time of growing nationalism is well known, the authorities were aware of the function performed by the regulated prostitute, and attempts were made, in
particular, to halt the decline of the *maison de tolérance*.

As I have mentioned, the venereal peril even gave rise in medical circles to a hyperregulationism, different from that of the 1870s in that it
no longer appealed openly to moral or religious principles. Thus Dr. G.
Fischer[72] suggested that prefectural ordinances should require all venereal patients to indicate the name and address of the individual who had
contaminated them. The local police superintendent would then send
this individual an "antivenereal booklet" and an invitation to receive
treatment; at the third such complaint, the guilty party would be fined,
or even imprisoned, and would be hospitalized by force.

In a booklet that appeared in 1900, Dassy de Lignières saw the venereal peril as "the most atrocious, the most fearsome scourge"[73] of all and
described the *maison de tolérance* as "a pillar of social order."[74] He
demanded that clients be subjected to a medical check and, before going
with a prostitute, be given a "health ticket" stating the exact time of the
check. "The healthy woman and the healthy visitor in a medically supervised and hygienically transformed brothel must be the formula of the
expedient to be attempted."[75] Such ideas, which indeed were to triumph
in time of war, had already been expressed by Scandinavian and German
doctors. In 1906 Dr. Manquat demanded, more moderately, that a
health certificate should be issued, which the client could demand to
see.[76] Dr. Carle supported this proposal; he believed that this certificate
ought to be given to any woman who had contracted syphilis three years
or more before.[77]

The fear-inspiring, obsessional advertising of the venereal peril
unquestionably helped to spread, through public opinion, the idea that
it was necessary to regulate prostitution. This was the view expressed by
Dr. P. Lévêque in one of the few doctoral theses to defend the point of
view of the abolitionists. "Professor Fournier, with the authority of science," he writes, "has spread before us the museum of horrors. . . One
shudders and falls at the knees of the prefect of police."[78]

Unlike the strictly sexological discourse on perversion or on mental
illness, which by its very diversity solidifies the multiplicity of ways of
achieving pleasure,[79] the discourse on the venereal peril seems to be
unifying; around it and in terms of it the reflection on sexuality is *ordered*
in a way, at least insofar as this reflection is intended for public opinion.

It is an imperialist discourse, therefore, that, thanks to the decline of the religious and the ascent of the medical, tends to conceal the moral discourse, the pedagogical discourse, even the discourse that deals with the etiology of mental illness. It is a confluence around a central theme, around a unifying obsession.

And so we come finally to what Michel Foucault calls the "repressive hypothesis,"[80] for that which unifies around the venereal peril all reflection on sexuality also carries a dissuasive strategy directed principally at the young. While a *scientia sexualis* was being worked out, while doctors and sociologists were classifying behavior or treating the role of sex in the genesis of mental illness, the information that reached public opinion about sexuality came to it only through the lens of the terrifying, obsessive propaganda surrounding the venereal peril. Banal as it may seem in the end, the excessive fear of "pox," a formidable obstacle erected in the face of pleasure, took up where sin left off; and it was this that syphilophobia nourished.

The White Slave Trade

If there is one subject in which it is difficult to disentangle myth from reality, it is certainly the white slave trade. Indeed, this is a theme made more significant by the fear-ridden literature that conveyed it than by the reality that it concealed. It was the crossroads of all the obsessions of the period, a subject on which the most balanced minds of the era lost their bearings.[81]

In fact, the term expresses a certain ambiguity. We might, with Lenoble,[82] draw a distinction between a "small trade" and a "large-scale international trade." Indeed, in the mind of the public, and even for certain lawyers such as advocate-general Feuilloley,[83] the white slave trade was synonymous with selling women; it was to be condemned because any trading in human flesh was forbidden. It was the meaning given to the term by the first writers to popularize the idea: Guyot in his work on prostitution and Tacussel in the first book devoted to the scourge.[84] Similarly, the campaigns carried out by Ibels in the columns of *La lanterne* and *Le matin* against the trade in *chanteuses* (nightclub singers) were aimed at a commerce that scarcely went beyond national frontiers. In short, what was usually meant by the white slave trade was the trading that the brothel-keepers, agents, and suppliers were obliged to carry out if they wanted to recruit and renew the staff of the officially tolerated establishments. The existence of this trade was therefore based on that of the regulationist system. Furthermore, the abolitionists made

their denunciation of the white slave trade one of their own main arguments. It should be noted, however, that they preferred to choose examples from England or Belgium—that is to say, countries where inquiries
had already exposed the existence of this trade.

For specialists in international law, for diplomats, and for neoregulationists anxious not to question the rationale for tolerated prostitution,
the white slave trade referred solely to the commerce that took place
across frontiers. "It is a hiring in one country for another country,"
Louis Renault wrote. "It is a fact of export or import."[85] After the Paris
conference of 1902 there was even a tendency, in those circles, to apply
the term only to criminal acts—that is to say, not to the international
trade in women as such but the sale of minors and that of women when
it was accompanied by violence, fraud, or abuse of trust.

From 1880 to 1914 one may observe a semantic slide; the latter con-
notation of the term gradually gained ground over the former. This phenomenon is in itself revealing of the progress made by neoregulationism
at the expense of abolitionism through the struggle against the white
slave trade; an ambiguous campaign if ever there was one, it managed
to combine good feelings with a wish to preserve whatever could be
salvaged of the traditional system.

The Genesis of the Myth

A simple argument in the hands of the first abolitionists, who included
in their condemnation any form of white slave trade, the denunciation
of the scourge was first directed at practices exposed by British parliamentarians and Belgian judges.[86] In the report that he had published on
July 26, 1881, on behalf of a commission set up by the House of Lords
for the protection of young women, Lord Snagge had uncovered the
existence and procedures of a traffic between the United Kingdom and
the Continent. The publication of extracts from the correspondence
between British suppliers and Belgian agents and keepers had created an
enormous scandal. In the correspondence seized, the age, the physical
description, and the professional qualities of the "parcels" were vaunted
shamelessly. During the preceding three years (1878–1880), thirty-four
young Englishwomen including three who had been virgins, had been
sent from London to Brussels; the current price was three hundred
francs, payable on receipt and verification of the good condition of the
merchandise.

Following these discoveries the Belgian courts, in a trial that opened
in December 1881, tried to throw light on this affair and concluded that

such a traffic did in fact exist. The progress of the trial in Brussels was copiously related in France by the abolitionist press. A novel in French, dedicated to Josephine Butler, was published in Belgium; it described at length the traffic in women between England and the Continent.[87] Guyot deals with these facts at great length, providing details about the way in which, according to him, the recruitment, the enlistment, and the transportation of prostitutes was carried out in France. On July 3, 1885, the *Pall Mall Gazette* began a series of revelations that tended to prove the existence in London of markets dealing with very young girls taken by force into houses of ill fame in order to be raped.[88] A French translation of this inquiry appeared the same year in Paris under the title *Les scandales de Londres;* the somewhat scabrous text contained the detailed confessions of a tout.

Under the pseudonym of "Dr. Minime," Dr. Lutaud, a recent convert to abolitionism, strove to popularize these revelations. In his book *La prostitution et la traite des blanches à Londres et à Paris,* which appeared in 1886, one can detect all the themes that were to make the campaign of the large-circulation newspapers successful in 1902. Of the original notion of the white slave trade all that remained was the idea of the martyrdom of virginity; it was not the fact of a woman being sold, but the idea of the virgin ravished that aroused its rather salacious disapproval. "Rape of Virgins," "Trade in Virgins," "Virgins are Delivered," "An Order for Five Virgins," "Why Does No One Hear the Cries of the Victims?" "Little Girls Are Tied with Straps"—these are some of the chapter headings in his book. Lutaud smugly details, district by district, the wholesale price of "fresh girls." He tells what it would cost a customer in search of virginity: £5 ($25) at Mrs. M——'s and Mrs. Z——'s, £10 ($50) in the east End, £20 ($100) in the West End.[89] Of course, these prices involved the presentation to the customer of a certificate of virginity properly drawn up by a qualified practitioner. According to the author, ten thousand girls were prostituted in this way in the British capital; he cites the case of a customer who had the habit of consuming three virgins a fortnight. These revelations did not cause much widespread concern in France; the time of the large-circulation newspaper had not yet come.

Abroad, however, the white slave trade had already been the object of official denunciations. Thus, as early as 1864 a decree from the government of Hungary[90] had drawn the attention of those responsible to the shipping away of girls destined for America. In March 1867 some Hungarians living in Egypt sent a petition to the deputies of their country begging them to take steps against this trafficking. Above all, in 1874, this time in Austria, the Chamber of Deputies called for an international conference that would deal with this problem; it demanded that a clause be inserted into the new penal code then being drawn up. At its fifth conference, which met at Geneva in 1889, the British, Continental, and General Federation for the Abolition of Regulated Prostitution solemnly denounced the existence of an international white slave trade.

In 1895 the French Senate approved a bill presented by Bérenger[91] that included arrangements against "the hiring by violence or fraud for purposes of prostitution, [or] the use of the same means to force a woman, even a major, to give herself to prostitution." This bill, it is true, was never debated by the deputies. In the same year the international penitentiary conference in Paris passed, at Paul Robiquet's request,[92] two propositions aiming to eliminate any form of constraint where prostitution was concerned and demanded the convening of an international conference on the white slave trade.

Only the German Reich was to take concrete steps.[93] In 1897, after Reiniger, Bebel, and Forster had brought up the question several times in the Reichsrat, steps were taken against the traffickers. A clause introduced into the emigration law punished with from two to five years' imprisonment and a fine of between 150 and 6,000 marks anyone who, by concealing his intentions, persuaded a woman to emigrate with the purpose of delivering her into prostitution. Several extradition treaties were then signed with neighboring countries.

It was mainly private initiative, however, that was to bring about the international campaign against the white slave trade. Once again, most of the impetus came from Protestant circles in Great Britain and Switzerland. The National Vigilance Association, founded with this aim in mind in London in 1885, tried to set up an international organization that would be able to oppose the international network of traffickers. Coote, its secretary, made several trips to the Continent with the aim of setting up national committees. Senator Bérenger became the organizer of the French committee; he now made the struggle against the white slave trade his main political aim. He succeeded in gathering around him well-known individuals from different backgrounds. As a "work of concentration,"[94] the committee brought together neoregulationists and abolitionists, Protestants, Jews, and Catholics, opponents and supporters of feminism; in short, from the outset it was presented as a unanimist movement capable of making the most exalted abolitionists forget about the priority of the struggle against regulation.

It was the National Vigilance Association that, in June 1899, organized a meeting, at the Palace Hotel in London, of the first international conference on the white slave trade. Members from twelve countries were present; as far as western Europe was concerned, only the Spanish and Italians were missing. Of course, the somewhat mistrustful British government was not officially represented, and this led to the abstention of foreign governments.[95] These governments, however, had sent individuals authorized to speak unofficially. Each national committee appointed two spokesmen to describe the situation of the white slave trade in its own country and the steps that had been taken to defeat the scourge.[96] Thus this conference gave a scientific basis to the existence of something that, for many, had hitherto been no more than a myth.

After noting the astonishing silence of the penal codes about the problem, the members of the conference passed a unanimous resolution to set up a permanent international organ to combat the white slave trade; the national committees were invited to put pressure on the authorities in their own countries to make this trade a legal offense. Above all, the conference proclaimed the need for an international conference to organize the struggle on a worldwide scale.

During the debates a sometimes intense confrontation had exposed the contradictions in the attitude of certain of the national committees, and in particular of the French committee. The British and Swiss representatives were indignant, as were the feminists present, to observe that one could, as Bérenger did, set out to battle the white slave trade while, at the same time defending regulated prostitution. They thus asserted the existence of a fundamental contradiction that, for them, rendered the efforts being made almost pointless.[97]

At the end of the conference, moved by a concern for effectiveness, Pastor Comte, despite the strong feelings of the British representatives, agreed, in the name of the French abolitionists, not to link together the regulation of prostitution and the white slave trade. His position, which in the end was accepted by all the representatives, made possible the adoption of unanimous resolutions. This concession was to be fraught with consequences and, in France at least, was to transform the crusade against the white slave trade into a tool in the hands of the neoregulationists around Bérenger.[98]

Parallel to this organizational effort and internationalization undertaken by the National Vigilance Association, a number of charitable associations now devoted themselves to the protection of girls, with the official aim of keeping them out of the hands of the traffickers. Founded in Geneva in 1877 as a result of the abolitionist conference, the Union internationale des amies de la jeune fille was, to my knowledge, the first element in the international campaign to protect the sexual morality of youth. In 1902, just after the Paris conference, it owned 240 homes for the "protection" or the "raising up" of girls; it kept agents in the railway stations of 27 towns and ran 84 employment agencies that charged no fees. Furthermore, it published such periodicals as *L'amie de la jeune fille*.[99] On the same model there then sprang up the Oeuvre catholique internationale de la protection de la jeune fille. In addition, the Jewish Association for the Protection of Girls and Women and the Alliance israélite also took part in the struggle against the white slave trade.[100]

In France, at least 1,300 associations were now devoted, totally or in part, to the protection or "raising up" of girls. The passage of the law of April 19, 1898, on "the suppression of assault or acts of violence on children" had given rise to an increase in this type of institution. There would be little point in repeating here the catalogue of all these societies listed by H. Joly in London.[101] The important thing is to observe both their increase in the last years of the century and the efforts then being made to list them and to coordinate their actions.

After the London conference the white slave trade became one of the most talked about subjects of the day.[102] In 1901 a conference in Amsterdam brought together representatives of the national committees, and the following year, at the initiative of the Radical government, the long-awaited international conference took place in Paris; it ushered in a new stage in the crusade. All that remains is to determine what reality lay behind the myth of the white slave trade, then at its height.

The Reality behind the Myth

The development of the white slave trade was, quite obviously, one of the consequences of European economic expansion. It resulted not so much from the extension of colonization as from the vast movement of emigration that took millions of Europeans to every other part of the globe. This is not the place to review what has been so well analyzed elsewhere. The last, and by far the largest, of the great migratory waves largely involved emigrants from the northern end of the Mediterranean basin (Greeks and Italians), from the Austro-Hungarian empire, and from the Russian empire. It coincided first with the emergence, then with the rise, of the myth of the white slave trade. This is easy enough to explain: this massive, largely male emigration involved predominantly poor and underqualified young men. It gave rise to a demand for prostitution, as the imbalance between the sexes that then characterized the populations of the new countries (Australia, Latin America) and the pioneer fronts testified. This demand was again stimulated by the "breakup" of China and then, between 1899 and 1902, by the Boer War. The revolution in transportation now made it possible to satisfy these needs more easily.[103] More generally, the increased mobility of individuals, facilitating uprooting and the anonymity that resulted from it, made virtue more fragile and made it easier for the traffickers to tout their wares. It should be added that certain internal political events also encouraged the development of the white slave trade. Thus, as Prince Sergei Wolkowski remarked,[104] the persecution of which they were victims drove many young Jewish girls in the Russian empire to give in to the advances of traders.

Nevertheless, the white slave trade was not only the result of a new and growing demand on the part of a transplanted European population unable, on account of the disequilibrium of the sexes, to resolve its frustrations through means other than prostitution.[105] How otherwise is it to be explained that France, which took so little part in the movement of European emigration, should have been so haunted by the white slave trade? It also reflected the decline of the brothel throughout western Europe. Aware of the irremediable character of a crisis bound up with a profound mutation in male sexual sensibility and a lessening tolerance on the part of public opinion, the traffickers, touts, agents, and suppliers very soon perceived the extent of the substitute markets that were opening up to them, providing they were able to adapt to the new situation and establish international networks. Thus the white slave trade was merely the reconversion and extension of the activity of agents who at the time ensured a constant supply of women to many brothels in western Europe. Far from being a new scourge, it was a direct descendant of the regulationist system; and it goes without saying that effective suppression could not be carried out as long as the official commerce associated with tolerated brothels survived.

Was this transformation in and this new expansion of the market for prostitutes accompanied by a concentration, like that at the center of the milieu in the first decades of the twentieth century? The large-circulation newspapers had competed with one another in voicing this notion.[106] In 1912 Pierre Goujon, referring in the Chamber to "the truly prodigious expansion" of the evil over the previous fifteen years, declared: "It is so to speak methodically organized. The white slave trade is practiced by an international association that has its own regular agents in every country of the world, which has its own bankers, which even has its own emergency fund for those of its affiliates who find they have to settle their accounts with the law."[107] The reports presented at the conferences, the results of official inquiries, the documents preserved in legal and police archives[108] urge prudence in judgment. Indeed, what seems striking—and I shall come back to this—is the discrepancy between the current of public opinion (I shall not call it rumor) and the verifiable facts. The police archives in particular lead one to formulate the provisional hypothesis that the white slave trade was not yet radically different in structure from the trading of women then being practiced and tolerated in regulationist states. There was adaptation, perhaps an increase in the volume of activity, but there were no profound innovations in the methods, techniques, or financing.

If the specialists of the Société générale des prisons are to be believed, the white slave trade, in the widest sense, was traditionally practiced by two kinds of personnel: modest touts and the richer suppliers for whom they worked. "The supplier," declared Feuilloley, an advocate-general at the Cour de Cassation, who, by his own admission, had made a specialty of studying this type of business, "has the appearance and manners of an honest bourgeois; he pays his rent regularly; he has a good reputation in the building in which he lives. He's a businessman, his neighbors say."[109] Puibaraud noted the large number of jewelers involved in this activity.[110] The suppliers "had a subordinate staff of recruiters usually made up of hairdressers' assistants, young men working in hotels, cafés, and public dance halls, who procured the women for them." The introduction of the girls never took place at the home of the supplier, or even at the home of the recruiter. "It usually took place in the street, in a public garden, sometimes in a café, but never twice in succession in the same place . . . The recruited woman was then given some money . . . When he had managed in this way to recruit a number of women, the supplier formed what was called a *convoy,* which he then set about sending in the direction of the provinces or a port for embarkation abroad."[111] This description also tends to accredit the idea of a hierarchization in the world of trafficking and of a relative concentration in the trafficking in women. A consultation of the archives will enable us to see more detail.

In 1902, just prior to the Paris conference, the prefecture of police made a list of all the individuals convicted of involvement in the white slave trade;[112] eighty-one "supplier-agents" are listed in the file that I have had the opportunity of analyzing. Of course, it is possible, if not probable, that the Paris police knew more about the activities of the touts than about those of the suppliers; but is the distinction as clear as Feuilloley implies? It would not seem so. Indeed, it appears that the traffickers were individuals engaged in a system of official tolerance; most were brothel-owners, madams or their husbands, touts working for a particular brothel, lodging-house keepers, and wine merchants. It has to be recognized, however, that later on, the link became less clear; thus, four years later Ferdinand Dreyfus, using the analysis carried out by civil servants in the Ministry of the Interior of four hundred files on the white slave trade compiled between 1902 and 1906, observed that the traffickers were usually referred to as agents or sales representatives, wine merchants, hotel owners, proprietors of employment agencies, managers of *cafés-concerts,* or managers of theatrical companies,[113] although it is true that all these professions had from time immemorial served to conceal the true activities of the suppliers of women to brothels.

The second fact that emerges, when we know for whom these traffickers were working and what the destination of their "parcels" was, is that the trade usually involved either the provinces or the provinces and foreign countries at the same time. The tout, agent, or supplier who specialized in large-scale international trade remained exceptional. We should add that those who sent "subjects" abroad were usually the agents of a particular *maison de tolérance;* in the sample studied, these were mainly brothels in Holland. The white slave trade and recruitment for the *maisons de tolérance* were two inextricably linked activities; this is, of course, quite logical, but it also proves, if proof were required, how vain were the efforts of a Bérenger and the French committee.

When the mass-circulation newspapers described the traffickers, based on a few unrepresentative cases, they were usually foreigners, often non-Europeans. Savioz, in *La grande revue,*[114] spoke in August 1902 of Levantines, Galician Jews, and South Americans, yet, according to the police, the overwhelming majority of individuals dealing in such trafficking were French, often from the provinces. There were a few Jews, a few Belgians, and a few Russians, which confirms the links that the French traffickers forged with the dealers' countries of origin. It should be added that the foreign trafficker usually hid behind a pseudonym.

The "supplier-agents," those individuals who practiced trading in women, were generally older men and women (see Figure 17). In this they differed considerably from the *souteneurs,* with whom they should not be confused, and had more in common with the staff running the *maisons.* Finally, and this will come as no surprise, only 66 percent had no police record.

The Parisian geography of the trade in women is fairly precise, although it did shift with the movements of police repression. In 1902 the thirty-four establishments frequented by the agents of this traffic were concentrated in the ninth arrondissement (16), mainly in the rue du Faubourg-Montmartre; in the second (7), in the rue Montmartre, boulevard Saint-Denis, rue Saint-Martin, rue Blondel, and boulevard Sébastopol; and in the tenth (5), in the eighteenth (4), and in the third (2). They consisted of ten *débits de vins,* six "cafés," four "taverns," two "brasseries," two "bars," two "restaurants," and eight establishments of

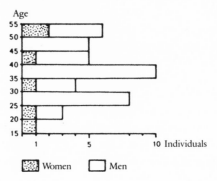

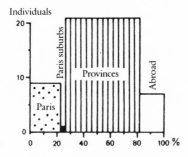

Figure 17. Parisian "supplier-agents," 1902. (Archives, prefecture of police.)

various other designations. The geographic distribution noted by the police is not unlike that described by Mme. Avril de Sainte-Croix,[115] who claims that the touts had been meeting on the heights of Montmartre and in the cafés around the intersection of Châteaudun, the rue des Martyrs, and Notre-Dame de Lorette ever since the police had forced them to abandon the area around the Palais-Royal.

The majority of "subjects" at this time came from a few clearly specified suburbs, often those in which the suppliers lived; in 1902 these were Conflans, Fin d'Oise, and above all Andrésy,[116] then the national center of trafficking in women. The techniques of touting were obviously quite similar to those that kept the *maisons de tolérance* supplied. Also involved were shady employment agencies, lodging-house owners in league with the traffickers, newspaper advertisements, touts (male and female) operating in the hospitals or public parks, and, in Paris in particular, in the square de la Tour Saint-Jacques and the place des Vosges. In one innovation, however, the railway stations seem to have become the special field of action of the touts. There they awaited the lonely, disoriented young women arriving in the big city from the provinces. All that had changed were the methods of transportation and transit. The manufacture of forged papers for minors, the medical check, the "apprenticeship" before departure for those who might still be novices, the concentration in one area in the suburbs—all these preceded the formation of the convoy to the railway station and thence to the port of embarkation.[117] For the few recruits who really did not know what they were letting themselves in for, receiving sexual advances during the crossing and then finding themselves, on arrival, with no money, abandoned by all friends, and faced with mounting debts did the rest. In the Russian empire, the activities of the traffickers were often hidden behind an official search for brides for bachelors in the new colonies; thousands of honest young girls were thus recruited cheaply by profiteering brothel-keepers overseas.

The young Frenchwomen who were the objects, for one cannot always say victims, of the international white slave trade were mainly, like most prostitutes, domestic servants or shop assistants.[118] There were also many, if contemporary witnesses are to be believed, who were "unclassified," such as qualified schoolmistresses or piano teachers without pupils, who, in the Russian empire, and particularly in Poland, were attracted by the offer of jobs as governesses or tutors.[119] When, on arrival, they realized that they had been deceived, they had very little alternative but to accept the propositions of agents acting for brothel-keepers. Their situation was rather that of the singers in *cafés-concerts,* who, once they reached their destination, had to agree to prostitute themselves in order to find work.

One should point out, however, as did Feuilloley[120] and the magistrates and officers of the court questioned by Paul Appleton[121] in the course of his researches, that the virgin abducted against her will or the woman raped and transported either by force or by deception to a far-off brothel was a rare exception. Of course, the commission of inquiry and the abolitionist societies proved the existence of such incidents, but the trafficking in women, whether on a large or small scale, concerned almost exclusively girls and women who were well aware of what was expected of them and who, without compulsion, were willing to be sent abroad. Generally speaking, by agreement with the agents who accompanied them,[122] they concealed their true activity during the crossing and pretended to be fiancées, salesgirls, or governesses in order not to attract the attention of the authorities. Once again, the white slave trade, insofar as it concerned fairly large numbers of women, followed the same modalities as the national trade in women; it simply involved crossing frontiers. In Georges Picot's felicitous words, the difference was that there was no longer unity of place.[123] And it was precisely this everyday trafficking, whose legality was in question up to this point, that the diplomats of the world were to legalize by codifying it, or rather by defining its legal limits at the Paris conference.

Like that of any other product, the international trade in women had its own routes, its own warehouses, and its own markets; and this commercial geography evolved rapidly with the transformations in demand, fashion, and obstacles.[124] The reports read at the London conference in 1899 enable us to sketch an initial picture of the international trade.[125] At this time there existed simultaneously a discontinuous intra-European traffic and an extra-European trade that operated in terms of regular currents. Indeed, Europe, it goes without saying, exported more than it imported; hence the term *white* slave trade.

Vienna and Budapest were the main Continental markets; European women, particularly Jews, from Bohemia, Hungary, and Galicia, were taken to Trieste or Genoa, then sent to ports throughout the world. It seems that 180 prostitution agencies operated in the Austrian capital, with 1,500 women permanently at their disposal, ready to set sail to satisfy any demand.[126] The Russian empire [127] was the other great market of supply; it was mainly through Odessa that the Jewish prostitutes, Circassian women in particular, but also girls from Warsaw, Kiev, and the provinces of Petrow and Kalisch, set out in groups of fifteen or twenty. According to Dr. Alfred Garofolo,[128] each year 1,200 young women destined for prostitution sailed from Genoa; they came from Hungary, Russia, Switzerland, and France. Naples and Messina were other centers of embarkation, especially used by emigrating Italian women. In southern Italy[129] the trafficking was controlled by the Camorra and the Mafia. France, like England, was essentially a country of transit; through Le Havre, Bordeaux, Marseilles,[130] and Southampton passed Italians, Germans, Belgians, and even Russians, in addition to a few Frenchwomen.

All the European nations, except Sweden, then depicted as the country of good morals and family tradition, added a contingent to the international trade. Despite police activity, it was also practiced at Antwerp and Hamburg. France supplied above all the European markets, and more particularly the brothels of Belgium, Holland, and the Russian empire. According to the report made by Balkenstein,[131] a police officer put in charge of an investigation by the government of the Netherlands, there then existed at Amsterdam, Rotterdam, and The Hague eleven

Fransche Huizen, or French brothels; four of these establishments imported their inmates directly from France, then sold them again after a few weeks to other, second-class brothels. In fifteen months seventy-nine French girls were imported in this way, and their movements from one establishment to another gave rise to 221 transactions. The case is cited of a Breton girl sold, without her consent, three times in the space of eight weeks. A fairly large number of Frenchwomen were also sent to South America, especially to Argentina.

In fact, the principal importing countries were those of South America; the demand from the United States seems to have declined somewhat with the settling of the West and tighter immigration controls.[132] In any case, it was now the regions of the Pacific coast that attracted most of the trade, and not New York, which nevertheless remained the principal "warehouse."[133] Similarly, the role of Rio de Janeiro declined on account of the reaction caused in the country by the excessive spread of venal sex.[134]

Until 1914 the largest markets in women remained Buenos Aires and Montevideo. According to a statistical study carried out by the vice squad in the Argentinian capital and cited in the Chamber by Pierre Goujon,[135] 6,413 prostitutes had been registered in the city between January 1, 1889, and December 31, 1901; 4,338 (68 percent) of them had come from Europe, including 1,211 (19 percent) from the Russian empire, 857 (13 percent) from Italy, 688 (11 percent) from the Austro-Hungarian empire, 606 (9 percent) from France, 350 (5 percent) from Germany, 326 (5 percent) from Spain, 96 (1.5 percent) from Switzerland, 76 (1 percent) from Rumania, 65 (1 percent) from Great Britain, and 42 (0.7 percent) from Belgium. According to a report from the Swiss consul at Buenos Aires in 1897,[136] the traffickers were largely Polish Jews; 2,200 girls appeared to have been crowded into the brothels of the Calle Lavalle alone, which had been nicknamed "the street of blood and tears." According to the same report, 40 percent of the prostitutes had originated in Poland, 15 percent in Russia itself, 11 percent in Italy, 10 percent in Austria-Hungary, 8 percent in Germany, 5 percent in France, 4 percent in England, 4 percent in Spain, and only 3 percent in Argentina. These estimates differ considerably from those of Goujon, suggesting that imports from the Russian empire increased considerably in the last years of the century. It may be noted that in both cases most of the women came from the countries that were then providing the largest proportion of international emigration, although the small number of British subjects and the larger number of French shows that the conformance was not perfect; tastes, traditions, fashions, as well as social structures and sexual attitudes also played a role.

The other great axis of this trade was in the east. This involved large numbers of Italian, Russian, Maltese, Rumanian,[137] Greek,[138] Jewish, and above all Austrian women, for, according to Appleton,[139] 75 percent of the girls imported into Egypt came from the Austro-Hungarian empire and landed in Alexandria, a major center for the trading of women in the eastern Mediterranean. A report presented by the Egyptian national committee to the Paris conference[140] states that it was often on the banks of the Nile that "women underwent their apprenticeship into the debauched life," although Vittorio Levi was to write six years later that almost all the prostitutes from Russia, Rumania, and Hungary had already undergone an apprenticeship of two or three years on the Bosporus before settling in Egypt.[141] These contradictions suggest that there was considerable movement of women between Constantinople and Alexandria. Indeed, we know that a number of the prostitutes brought together on the banks of the Nile went off to fill the houses and harems of the Ottoman Empire, particularly those of Smyrna, Beirut, and the towns of Anatolia and the coast of the Bosporus. In Turkey the trade was carried out to the benefit of the aristocracy and the sultan himself.[142] It should be pointed out that prostitutes of eastern origin were extremely rare in France, even at Marseilles; this seems to prove that the Mediterranean trafficking in women was then very unbalanced.

At Alexandria the Far Eastern agents came to buy women for the brothels of Bombay and the Chinese ports. According to the report of the Egyptian committee, their usual itinerary was "Europe, Alexandria or Cairo, Port-Said, Bombay, Colombo, Singapore, Saigon, Hong Kong, and Shanghai, and vice versa on the return trip, but, need we add, that once those women reached China, they rarely returned?"[143] Egypt had no law forbidding this trafficking; so it was at Alexandria and Cairo that the conveyors who had come from Europe with the merchandise, the wholesale merchants of Egyptian nationality, and the eastern buyers met. Egypt was then the real stock exchange of the market in women.

The white slave trade was also practiced in Australia and South Africa. Furthermore, trafficking in women of the "yellow races"[144] flourished in eastern Siberia and in those regions of Manchuria that were under Russian domination and in territories in which there was a particularly large imbalance between the sexes; thus, many Japanese women stocked the brothels of Vladivostok and Harbin.

Between the London conference of 1899 and the conference held in Paris in 1906, several modifications affected the geography of the trade in women. The role of the North American market continued to decline, although Frenchwomen were still highly valued and fetched two or three times the price of other women.[145] During the Boer War the Transvaal became the main region of consumption; thousands of European women, including a large number of French, set out for the Cape in order to satisfy the demands of the British soldiers.[146] Johannesburg was then the main center of this trade.

Since 1899, too, a fairly profound change in prostitutional structures had taken place in South America. It took the form of an increased dispersal of the brothels. The special district in Montevideo[147] had been abolished, and since January 1, 1904, the administration of the city of Buenos Aires had closed the large establishments there; prostitution was now practiced in "three-girl houses." This shows that there too a mutation in attitude took place rather like the changes that, for half a century, had been affecting the brothels of western Europe.[148]

The International White Slave Trade and Public Opinion, 1902–1910

A new minotaur. When in 1895 Robiquet suggested to the international penitentiary conference in Paris that it should deal with the problem of white slavery, his words aroused, we are told, the angry disapproval of those present. Several speakers referred to the presence in the hall of nuns and called on the speaker to behave in more seemly fashion.[149] Until quite recently, Moncharville declared to the London conference in 1899, the white slave trade, a phenomenon little known to the public at large, had aroused astonishment and skepticism, when it was not met, as Savioz wrote,[150] with smiles of disbelief. A journalist for *Le matin* announced, in the issue of April 20, 1902, his intention of mobilizing public opinion, "which has always remained uninterested in the question." In short, up until the first years of the century, the public tended to see the white slave trade as fiction.

A few years later, when the Paris conference opened in 1906, the same Robiquet wrote: "The question of the white slave trade now figures on the list of good works to which right-thinking people and the ladies of the most aristocratic world devote themselves."[151] The president of the Republic received the members of the conference at the Elysée Palace; finally, six years later, in the Chamber of Deputies, Pierre Goujon showed in fiery terms the extent to which fear had taken over the population as a whole.[152]

The sudden eruption of public concern over the theme of the white slave trade took place in 1902. On July 27 a journalist for *La République* was already denouncing white slavery as "one of the worst scourges of our time and one that is raging with increasing intensity in every civilized country." It may be compared, he added, to "a considerable moral cancer, which is gnawing away and pitilessly destroying a section of European youth." According to him, it was amassing more victims than tuberculosis. It was a formidable force directed "against *universal moral-ity* by creatures who are more dangerous than sharks."[153] What caused this sudden awareness of a very ancient practice that had already been denounced at length by the abolitionists for a quarter of a century?

The first reason is clear: the large-circulation newspapers, and *Le matin, Le journal,* and *Le petit parisien* in particular, had been "solicited" and financed by the French committee,[154] now called the Association pour la répression de la traite des blanches, to prepare public opinion for the international conference that was to take place in Paris in July 1902; it was in April that the campaign was started. These newspapers had just proved their power in the Dreyfus affair, which they had imposed on public opinion. The radicals now in power had, when in opposition, indignantly defended individual liberties. Of course, neither Waldeck-Rousseau nor Emil Combes had been personally involved in the abolitionist campaign, but many of their supporters had fought for the cause and expected reforms.[155] Clemenceau himself might well have felt committed by his earlier statements; now a new crusade, much less embarrassing then the one demanding the abolition of regulation, could bring together all right-thinking individuals.

For the large-circulation newspapers the white slave trade provided a splendid theme which made it possible, depending on the case in question, to arouse, in turn or simultaneously, the readers' xenophobia, anti-Semitism, hostility toward England or Germany, anticlericalism, even the vague anxiety about population growth and the undermining of the race. Were not the dealers in women, like the neo-Malthusians, partly responsible for this loss of national substance then being denounced by Dr. Bertillon's alliance? It goes without saying that the subject also, through the salacious or at least suggestive stories recounted, made it possible to call for every form of repression. More than the theme of prostitution itself, that of the white slave trade, by relating the fall rather than the life of the fallen woman, was charged with immense emotional power. This is a key point. The denunciation of the white slave trade came just in time. The myth—for the way in which white slavery was described corresponded only in small part to the reality—fed to some extent on the anxiety aroused by a general awareness of sexual liberation on the part of women and an increase in "debauched" behavior. When the white slave trade was being discussed, the unfortunate woman her-self was no longer the issue. Public opinion regarded her as necessary, indeed often considering her, in the purest regulationist tradition, as indispensable to safeguarding female virtue; this explains why the success of the abolitionist campaign remained limited. What was being described was instead the "social mutation,"[156] the moral decline, the journey; no attempt was made to illustrate the fragility of feminine virtue, but rather to describe the risks to virgins and honest women and to relate their metamorphosis into inmates of foreign brothels as a result of being uprooted and subjected to violence. This account of a double loss of caste, both social and sexual, accompanying a long trip abroad, which, by the anonymity that it provided, undermined a sense of modesty and made the woman more vulnerable to male desires, was unbearable to the group.

This psychological context explains why the white slave trade should have so excited and disturbed public opinion. Whereas the brothel-keeper who employed the woman was tolerated as an inevitable social factor, the tout was odious because he was responsible for women losing caste. Finally, it goes without saying that it was easier for journalists to justify what they wrote with moralizing intentions than by simply describing the depravity of the brothels. What a service they were performing for innocent girls when they described the torments that awaited them if they gave in to seduction!

It now becomes clear why the large daily newspapers rivaled one another in zealously denouncing and fighting the new scourge.[157] In 1902 *Le matin* had a regular section entitled "White Slave Trade," while *Le journal* prided itself on being the cause of the arrest of the supplier Loutchnik. *Le petit parisien* financed—or at least claimed it did—the organization of the Paris conference.[158] Most of the newspapers devoted articles to the scourge; for 1902 alone[159] I found items in twenty-two newspapers dealing with the problem.

This research allows one to discern the structure of the accounts devoted to the victims of the white slave trade: they form a sort of serialized biography that borrows all the stereotypes of melodrama. Unlike the members of the prostitutional milieu—the client, the brothel-keeper, and the professional prostitute, who all merged together in the reader's disapproval—the characters in stories involving the white slave trade are in a perfectly antithetical opposition. The victim is always young—even very young, hardly past childhood—considered a virgin even when her innocence is not self-evident; she has been sold by touts who were able to win her confidence and dazzle her with the prospect of an artistic career. Indeed, what occurs is not a real seduction that might put into question the victim's virtue. Like the young Greek girls delivered to the Minotaur, a comparison that constantly recurs in these articles, the virgin is sacrificed to devouring vice. The dealers, "gentlemen of between thirty and forty, bloated and ugly, whose fingers are covered with thick rings, whose appearance is reminiscent of the well-known figures of respectable bookmakers, members of the vice squad, and brothel-owners,"[160] are powerful sharks. Their names usually sound foreign or are too typically French to be true: in 1902 they included M. de Beaucourt, Hayem (known as Hayum), Loutchnik. The first two were arrested as they were setting sail for the Cape with five underage girls, while Delaunay, known as Loutchnik, assisted by his mistress, Louise Tourneux, a singer, had persuaded Germaine Nicoud, a fifteen-year-old girl, to go to London as a prostitute.

The newspaper describes first the railway journey that followed contact with the girl, then the crossing by boat. The use of exoticism remains limited; stress is placed, rather, on the homesickness of the girl, and attempts are made to arouse the reader's xenophobia. The articles then describe the fall from grace, the social mutation. There is no shortage of scenes of violence and perversion, for the girl, still innocent, refuses to give her consent. Of course, the anti-Semitic press had no difficulty in identifying the guilty parties: "The white slave trade, is, I repeat, with Jewish finance, one of Israel's biggest commercial organizations . . . Through this trade, the international Jewish association provides colossal dividends to its shareholders," wrote Raphael Viau in an article in *La libre parole*[161] entitled "Hayum, Israel and Co." He goes on to cite all the affairs involving the white slave trade in which Jews appear to have been compromised. He describes the arrest in Lemberg, in 1892, of "some forty Hebrews" from whom were seized a correspondence in "Hebreo-German patois" concerning "parcels," and again the misdeeds, in 1896, of the "Jewish" recruiters Isidore Bicktaden and one Rosenkranz. For him, the white slave trade was, in France, solely confined to Parisian Jews. This was how the Orléans rumour took hold. *La tribune française,*[162] criticizing the inefficiency of the leagues that were formed to combat the white slave trade, assured its readers that "indeed, before a week is out, they will be stuffed with Jews who will put in an appearance there . . . so that nobody will speak of the Jews, whereas they monopolize the trade." Meanwhile, the anticlerical press challenged the clergy. On September 2, 1902, in an article devoted to the white slave trade, *La lanterne* denounced actions supposedly taken by the "procuring clergy" in South America. On December 3 *Le rappel* attacked the "clerical marriage agencies."

That year Anglophobia was still more widely exploited than anti-Semitism, and much mention was made, especially during the Beauchamp-Hayem affair, on the amount of trade destined for the Transvaal. On May 12 *L'aurore* referred to a memorandum from General Roberts, dated 1866, "ordering the setting up of harems in all the camps of the British army in India," and the author wondered whether the general "was not secretly encouraging the odious trade" that was being operated and which had South Africa as its outlet. After the Loutchnik affair it was London that was presented by *Le journal*[163] as the "headquarters of the white slave traders." After the signing of the Entente Cordiale and the Moroccan incidents, Franco-German tensions became perceptible in the literature devoted to the white slave trade. At the Paris conference in 1906 the delegate from the French police, Hennequin, responded indignantly to Wagener, [164] who had been sent by the German committee to investigate the white slave trade being carried out by his compatriots in South America and had questioned the role played in this affair by the port of Le Havre.

The press also gave considerable coverage to the pain felt by parents, and in particular mothers, whom the journalists tried hard to meet; the reader was very sensitive to this approach, which made it possible to emphasize the unpredictable, everyday character of the white slave trade, presented here as the result of an abduction. The outcome, which was usually a happy one, crowned the melodramatic character of the story: the charity worker sometimes appeared like a good angel and vanquished vice. On January 21, 1904, *Le journal* devoted an article to the Gabrielle Deixheimer affair, of which the various sequences were subtitled: "Sold," "The Disappearance of a Young Sixteen-Year-Old Girl from Belleville," "The Slave Market," "A Black Band in the Place de la République," "A Mother's Calvary."

While satisfying the reader's fantasies, these stories gave an incomplete picture of the traffic that was taking place and tended to exaggerate the danger incurred by a girl who allowed herself to be seduced. By making the trading in women a monstrous, rare act committed by creatures of exceptional perversity, the mass-circulation newspapers distracted attention from, or at least failed to implicate, the regulationist system then in force, all the frustrations that underpinned it, and the everyday trafficking that it involved. The press waxed eloquent about the violence done to a few virgins, but only occassionally made any mention of the massive trade that was taking place in girls and women, more or less consenting, it is true, but whom it is difficult not to see as the real victims of the existing sexual structures and regulations.[165]

The Difficulties of Organizing International Action. In December 1901, two years after the London conference, the French national committee formed the Association pour la répression de la traite des blanches et la préservation de la jeune fille. The new society proposed to wage a propaganda campaign against the scourge, to persuade the authorities to implement a reform of laws that gave impunity to "traffickers in human flesh," to coordinate the action of every attempt to protect virginity, to raise up the fallen, and to create new institutions of rescue. The "crusade" that it initiated belonged to an overall campaign aimed at arresting the progress of immorality, fighting pornography, and removing licentiousness from the streets. As early as 1902 the new association had five local committees, in Le Havre, Cherbourg, Brest, Bordeaux, and Marseilles.[166] Furthermore, it boasted that it had already succeeded in bringing the trafficking between Paris and Bordeaux to an end.

Thanks to the influence of Senator Bérenger and of the men around him—Georges Picot, Henri Joly, and Ferdinand Dreyfus—the international commission, formed at the London conference in 1899 to determine which state would organize the international conference, chose France, whose government had already been given prior notice by the senator. It is not one of the least paradoxical aspects of the affair that the country that had given birth to the "French system" of prostitution was chosen to lead the official crusade against the international traffic in women.

The conference opened on July 16, 1902, with sixteen nations officially participating.[167] The program had been prepared by the French committee. The preliminary notes cited the inadequacy of legislation dealing with the trafficking in women.[168] The task of the conference was to urge the various states to adopt legislative measures, to decide on the procedures and authorities in the various countries concerned by such international trafficking, and to urge governments to adopt administrative measures for supervising the traffic and repatriating the victims. From the outset, by the limited definition that he gave to the white slave trade,[169] Louis Renault so arranged matters that regulationism was not put into question.

Quite logically, the conference ended with the publication of two very different documents. One, a plan of "administrative arrangement," involved a number of measures that tended to guarantee the defense and repatriation of the victims. This arrangement would come into force as soon as the various governments had ratified it. This presented no difficulty; ratification was officially made on May 18, 1904, by thirteen countries,[170] and the proposal was promulgated in France on February 7, 1905. For applying this arrangement, an Office national pour la répression de la traite des blanches was set up at the Ministry of the Interior. The other measure, a plan for a convention, would have to be ratified by the parliaments or corresponding bodies in the various countries. This measure specified a series of minimal penal arrangements and provided for establishing a new international offense. Owing to the fury of some of the French press,[171] however, the conference had to make a distinction between actions involving female minors and those involving adult women; in doing so, it implicitly advised the legalization of the trade in the latter.[172]

This is certainly how we have to assess the effect of the Paris conference. If, as Ferdinand Dreyfus noted, it was the first demonstration of any concern on the part of diplomats with the problems of prostitution and the trade in women, it nevertheless ended up by recognizing the legality of most of that trafficking. Of course, the reader might well conclude that such an affirmation stemmed from a love of paradox; let us simply say that this was also the conclusion drawn by the prefecture of police. A document, emanating from the office of the prefect and dated November 22, 1902,[173] provides a summary of the meeting and concludes: "It may be said, therefore, that the international conference has in no way suppressed the abject, immoral trafficking known as the white slave trade, but has laid down the conditions that the traders must fulfill if they are to continue their activities without fear of interference." What this plan proposed to suppress was solely that which evoked the disapproval and fears of public opinion, that is to say, acts of violence perpetrated on innocent virgins. As for stopping the trade in adult women sold through fraud, violence, or threats, it was, in the opinion of the prefecture of police, practically inapplicable. "In the world to which these women belong, a complaint to the courts or even simply to the police is a rare occurrence because it is so dangerous. Furthermore, it would have to be proved before the courts that fraud, violence, etc. had taken place—proof is always very difficult to supply and it would be a bold woman indeed who would depend on evidence that would be withheld out of fear."

In order to set an example, the French parliament passed the law of April 3, 1903, which condemned the trafficking in minors and in adults sold through violence, fraud, or threat, losing no time in applying the resolution of the convention. Those found guilty now ran the risk of prison sentences of from six months to three years and fines of between fifty and five thousand francs. Furthermore, Article 4 provided for the same penalties to be applied to anyone who, "by the same means, held against her will, even on account of debts contracted, any woman, even a major, in a house of debauchery," or who "forced her to practice prostitution."

Not every country showed the same dispatch, despite the efforts of the French government, which had been given the task by the conference of urging the necessary steps. Germany, Great Britain, Norway, and Sweden refused to join in. It then became necessary to determine what alterations could be made to the 1902 plan in order to achieve ratification. In 1910 the German government agreed to ratify at a conference in Paris on the suppression of obscene publications. The French government was quick to agree. Thus the white slave trade was at the forefront of a second international conference held in the French capital in April and May 1910. The new convention of May 4, 1910, submitted for approval by the states, repeated the terms of the French law of 1903; it therefore involved no change in the French legislation.[174]

Official efforts to organize international suppression certainly did not bring an end to private initiative. At Frankfurt in 1902, Paris in 1906, and Madrid in 1910,[175] three international conferences assessed the work that had been done. The publication of the proceedings of the second of these conferences gives us some idea of the effects of the application of the law of 1903. In the country as a whole, "between April 3, 1903 and August 1906, 144 individuals had been prosecuted for hiring female minors; 17 had been acquitted, 6 fined, 121 sent to prison; 35 individuals had been prosecuted for hiring adult women, 3 of whom had been acquitted, 2 fined, 30 sent to prison."[176] Furthermore, as a result of the new legislation, "754 individuals known to be pimps have been prosecuted for special vagabondage, 56 have been acquitted, 6 fined, 692 sent to prison."[177] These figures are considerable if one takes into account that the pimps, who hitherto had come under the law of May 27, 1885, on vagabondage, found it easy enough to avoid police prosecution. So one cannot deny the development of a wave of repression against all those who tended to deprive prostitutes of their freedom, a wave of internal repression that went hand in hand with the "opening up" of prostitution and with the movement of reform demanded by certain social critics and imposed on Prefect Lépine by public opinion.[178]

Yet the statistics undermine the myth of an international white slave trade involving violence against innocent virgins. Of course, at the same time, four hundred files had been lodged in the Ministry of the Interior, and the prefecture of police had dealt with ninety-three cases of white slavery in the strict sense; but out of this second total, sixty-three of the charges were found to be without basis. This demonstrates the prevalence of fantasy in this matter. Thirty cases were reported, but only ten were brought before the courts, and eight defendants were found guilty. In the country as a whole, 754 *souteneurs* were sent to prison, but only eight individuals were found guilty of practicing the white slave trade in Paris. The comparison is most telling. In four years, throughout the country as a whole,[179] forty-one women and girls, real or supposed victims of the white slave trade, were repatriated at the expense of the state: twelve had come from the Transvaal and from the Cape Colony, twelve from the United States, seven from Egypt, seven from Russia, and three from Germany and Austria. Finally, in 1908, the international arrangement made it possible to try 93 cases of "cosmopolitan procuring" throughout the world; 146 individuals were charged, and 125 were found guilty.[180]

Everything goes to show that the white slave trade, in the narrow sense given it by lawyers and diplomats—that is to say, the export of underage girls and nonconsulting adult women—far from being the terrible scourge denounced by Bérenger and his associates, by the mass-circulation press, and by Goujon in the Chamber, was a minor phenomenon. It was a mere corollary of the trafficking officially tolerated by a regulationism that neither international conferences nor the gatherings organized to oppose the white slave trade were then willing to expose. What is more—and it did not escape the attention of the prefecture of police—the Paris conference of 1902, by narrowly defining the criminal act, struck down the moral barriers that might have been erected against the traffic in consenting adult women. The prestige that a Bérenger was able to derive from chairing so many dazzling meetings was put at the service of neoregulationism; the advocates of this system showed great skill in turning into an asset a campaign directed against the scandal that ought to have weighed against them, so closely linked was it to the existence of official prostitution and the *maison de tolérance*. By achieving greater suppression of the corruption of minors, which had always been condemned by the advocates of regulation, without questioning the "French system," they had merely allowed the police to supervise the prostitutional milieu more readily; they had succeeded in convincing even more of the public of the need for surveillance. In any event, they diverted and aborted a campaign, originally begun by the abolitionists, which soon became recognized as highly dangerous to the survival of regulated prostitution.

It is evident that throughout this business the abolitionists were out-maneuvered. As a result of misunderstood pragmatism they agreed to take part in this crusade, side by side with conservatives and regulationists of every kind, and the latter were only too delighted to deflect the hostility of their adversaries and above all to engage them in the moralizing campaign that had become their primary objective. Let there be no mistake: the leaders of the struggle against the white slave trade saw that struggle as, above all, a means of widening the campaign to moralize youth, a campaign that found expression in those circles in the wish to forbid obscene publications or to ban licentiousness from the streets.

The discrepancy between the real extent of the evil and the picture that was painted of it is in itself revealing. It provides evidence of a wider plan: to persuade young girls that they were daily threatened by seduction and violence, that, for them, youth was a veritable trial, a time of danger, during which they would have to know how to "preserve" themselves in order to reach the safe haven of marriage.[181]

Prostitution, Madness, and Degeneracy

The links between prostitution, madness, and hysteria were a fundamental theme in contemporary writing on prostitution. Then, as the century came to an end, a complete change of perspective on the subject took place. The emphasis was not so much on the frequency of mental illness and hysteria among prostitutes, the hardships of their existence, the evil effects of alcohol, and the influence of certain diseases, but rather on regarding the practice of venal sex as in itself a disease, a form of madness of which the various kinds of behavior practiced by prostitutes were the symptoms and of which degeneracy was the cause. With this end in view, there was a sudden increase in studies of the prostitute and the "honest woman" that may be said to belong to comparative anthropology and psychophysiology. This new discourse, bound up with the evolution of criminal anthropology, claimed to provide a scientific basis for the genesis of the stereotypes that the empiricist sociology of the Louis Philippe period had catalogued.

The Traditional Issues

The frequency of mental illness among prostitutes. This was a cliché tirelessly repeated by almost all psychiatrists, neurologists, and sexologists in the nineteenth century, without its being based on any real clinical studies; it was a hypothesis that was not felt to be in need of verification, so self-evident did its validity appear. From this point of view it is revealing that nobody at the time suggested that mental illness might be less widespread among prostitutes than among the rest of the female population.

It was Esquirol[182] who was the first, in 1832, to refer to the practice of prostitution in the etiology of mental illness. For a long time he was the only specialist to carry out a clinical study of the problem; based on this study he observed that 5 percent of the female mental patients admitted to Salpêtrière had practiced prostitution as a profession. After Cullerier,[183] Parent-Duchâtelet,[184] carrying on from Esquirol's work, devoted several pages of his book to the occurrence of mental illness among prostitutes. The relation was now recognized as a scientific truth; it was taken up by Rossignol,[185] Griesinger,[186] Guislain,[187] Renaudin,[188]

Chatelain,[189] and, at the end of the century, by Reuss.[190] Krafft-Ebing, in *On Insanity, Based on Clinical Observation,*[191] repeats that prostitutes easily develop mental illness.

Poverty and privation, unhappy love affairs, the practice of free sex, and, even more, the damage caused by alcohol and syphilis seemed to be sufficient explanation of mental disturbance. Prostitution was regarded as a station on the way to madness. The inadequacies of social organization and the moral disturbance of the individual are used to explain each other, without any real reference in these works[192] to the influence of hereditary characteristics.

The only clinical study that can make any claim, however small, to being scientific, the one that Dr. François Gras carried out in the asylums of the Rhône in 1899,[193] fails to confirm the frequency of mental illness among prostitutes. Out of 5,137 women who had entered the asylums of the department between 1879 and 1899, the author records the presence of only forty prostitutes; that is, only 0.8 percent of the inmates. It is true that these figures included only registered prostitutes: to be more precise, seven *filles de maison,* sixteen *filles en carte,* and seventeen *insoumises* who had been placed under official surveillance before being registered. In 1900, 3,338 registered prostitutes and unregistered prostitutes under surveillance were practicing in town. In seven cases out of forty the author attributes mental illness to alcoholism. The somewhat varied forms of madness that had necessitated the internment of the women are given, in order of decreasing frequency, as "excesses of maniacal excitation," "general paralysis," "attacks of melancholia with suicidal tendencies," and "mental confusion accompanied by hallucinations." By contrast, dementia was uncommon among the prostitutes of the Rhône.

This modest work, the conclusions of which, it is quite clear, embarrassed the author, had little impact; it does, however, suffice to show the importance of presuppositions in the medical discourse of the time and how little scientific rigor was employed by the most eminent psychiatrists in theorizing about the links between madness and prostitution.

The frequency of hysteria. In the enormous literature devoted to hysteria,[194] references to prostitution are no more than elements in the debate between advocates of different theses on the genesis of the illness. It explains why authors, as Pierre Briquet had observed in 1859, should "have oddly varied on the subject of the influence that prostitution might have on the production of hysteria."[195] For those who, like Dr. Landouzy, supported utero-ovarian views and regarded continence as the cause of this illness, it goes without saying that the activities of prostitutes preserved them from hysteria. Thus Parent-Duchâtelet discusses at length how rarely this illness is found among prostitutes.[196] Yet for the adversaries of this theory, and particularly for those who, beginning with Briquet, saw it as a disease of the nervous system and not of the genital organs, continence was a secondary factor;[197] these doctors were happy to note the frequency of hysteria among prostitutes.

In 1859 Briquet published the results of the study that he had been carrying out, with the help of la Morlière and Bois de Loury, of 197 registered prostitutes, aged between sixteen and thirty, being treated in the infirmary of Saint-Lazare.[198] Out of this total, 106 were hysterics[199] and 28 "impressionable" women; only 65 seemed to him to be lacking in any symptom of the illness. These results allowed him, he believed, to establish as a principle that "over half the total number of prostitutes are affected by hysteria of every degree."[200] This affirmation was accepted without question by Despines, Legrand de Saulle, and Gilles de la Tourette,[201] who were only too happy to prove that if continence did not predispose one to neurosis, venereal excess encouraged it.

For these doctors the genesis of the illness was obvious. For Briquet,[202] "poverty, sleepless nights, the abuse of alcoholic drinks, continual anxiety about police activity, or ill-treatment from the men with whom they live, enforced sequestrations brought about by the diseases that they contract, the uncontrolled jealousy and violent passions that they experience" explained the development of the illness. Gilles de la Tourette considered that it resulted "not so much from organic lesions as from continual fears, psychic disorders, the moral abjection in which their shameful profession throws them."[203] Legrand de Saulle considered heredity a determining factor.

In 1890 one of Charcot's pupils, Dr. H. Colin, questioned Briquet's statements. He carried out his own meticulous examination of 196 women suffering from venereal disease at Saint-Lazare.[204] He detected among them only nineteen hysterics and observed that "in general hysterics are intelligent or at least of a higher intellectual level than prostitutes."[205] This work did not stop certain practitioners from reaffirming the frequency of hysteria among prostitutes.[206] In fact, after 1890 the debate was somewhat superseded; the problem of the links between mental pathology and prostitution were now being presented in different terms.

The "Born Prostitute" and Genetic Instinct

We know that the primacy of individual temperament in the genesis of prostitution was explicitly recognized by the regulationists and by a large number of the neo-regulationists, even those who accorded a major role to the environment; and for a long time certain specialists such as Ball[207] and Dr. Moreau of Tours[208] referred to heredity in explaining prostitutional behavior. But these were merely incidental reflections, unrelated to the coherent undertaking being carried out in the last years of the century by a school of criminal anthropology with the aim of establishing scientifically the innateness of the disposition to prostitution.

The born prostitute was seen as an incomplete creature who had undergone an arrested development, who was a victim of morbid hered-ity, and who presented signs of physical and psychological degeneration relating to her imperfect development. Prostitution was to women what crime was to men: the result of degeneracy, even of regression. In the psychological domain the born prostitute, and her counterpart in soci-ety, the wife who indulged in repeated adulteries, was the victim of a "moral insanity." All in all, the stigmata of degeneracy made her a crea-ture far more removed from the honest woman than was, for example, the thief. Of course, not all prostitutes were born prostitutes; some were merely "occasional prostitutes," but these were without much interest to specialists. Such was the tenor of the theory that was developing in these schools of criminal anthropology, the leading lights of which were Pauline Tarnowsky in Russia and Ferrigani, Lombroso, and Ferrero in Italy. Their works, although severely criticized, were quickly translated into French,[209] and they strongly influenced the discourse on prostitu-tion between 1890 and 1914. Since their appearance of extreme scien-tific rigor could not but impress, it is essential to analyze their results with more precision.

Anthropometry revealed the abundance of signs of degeneracy in the prostitute. In many ways the prostitute gave the appearance of a prim-itive woman; this amounted to saying that she remained closer to the male than did the "honest woman." Thus, in these last years of the nine-teenth century, a new portrait of the prostitute emerged out of these endless anthropometric studies that was more precise than ever and which was now based on an overall theory.

From a comparison of groups of criminal women, prostitutes, peasant women, and honest women, it was observed that the prostitutes were characterized by their weak cranial[210] and orbital capacities. Yet the weight of the mandible was found to be much higher among prostitutes than among honest women.[211] Above all, they presented frequent anom-alies: hypertrophied parietal bumps, a large irregularity of the occipital hollow, receding or narrow forehead, abnormal nasal bones, prognath-ism, a masculine type of face, huge jaws, asymmetry in the face and

eyebrows, badly distributed and defective teeth. Their pelvises were
shorter than the average for "normal women" and had an atavistic character: the opening of the sacred canal. The upper limbs were also shorter
than in the case of honest women; the feet were smaller and prehensile.
Their eyes were most frequently dark.

Three essential characteristics linked the prostitute to the savage,
primitive woman, who was closer to the male: (1) a plumpness, the
result of shorter stature and heavier weight than for honest women (on
the average, prostitutes had thicker thighs than honest women); (2) a
greater appearance of virility, which found expression in the exaggerated
development of body hair, in particular around the sexual organs, by an
abundant head of hair, and by the large number of *noevi piloris* (41 percent among prostitutes, 14 percent among honest women), and in addition the prevalence of "masculine" voices, resulting from the excessive
size of the vocal chords; and (3) the abundance of tattoos.

These characteristics taken as a whole, which made it possible to
define the anthropological type of the born prostitute, did not prevent
the women in question from being beautiful in their youth. Indeed, the
fatty layer, as well as makeup and other adaptations to the need to attract
men, made it possible to conceal for a time the anomalies that, unfortunately, became accentuated with age; in time the face became quite
virile and even "uglier than that of a man."[212] All these observations
made it possible to declare that the prostitute, far more than the female
criminal, recalled the primitive type of woman; indeed, Lombroso
observes, "the primitive woman . . . was always a prostitute."[213] Virility
was much more a characteristic of the savage woman; to see that atavism
was the cause of excessive plumpness one had only to refer, the same
author suggests, to the appearance of Hottentot women.

Physiobiology confirmed the results of anthropometry. To begin with,
the born prostitute was characterized, in this field, by *precocity,* another
sign of degeneracy. Her menstruation was premature and irregular, as
was confirmed by the observations of Dr. Rossignol;[214] loss of virginity
came early, another characteristic of primitive women.

Again, the born prostitute was characterized by greater *insensitivity.*[215]
Thus the algometer showed that her tongue and clitoris were less sensitive to pain than those of normal women. Insensitivity to taste and
olfactory blindness were common among prostitutes, and their visual
field was limited. This did not prevent the born prostitute from display-
ing a more precocious lasciviousness than the "honest woman," a characteristic that again made her closer to the male. On this matter, however, scientific discourse comes to an end; the time for physiological
measurements of sexual activity had not yet come. Basing their argu-

ments on much earlier work, and even on Parent-Duchâtelet's book, Lombroso and Ferrero pointed out the frequency of lesbianism among prostitutes; the born prostitute was tempted by masculinity, another sign of the degeneracy of that "tendency to atavistic return to the period of hermaphrodism."[216]

The psychic degeneracy of the born prostitute determined her *moral insanity*.[217] This affliction, which was essentially characterized by a lack of modesty, was the fundamental cause of the genesis and development of prostitutional behavior. According to Pauline Tarnowsky, who set out to define this type, the characteristics of this "moral insanity" are many: lack of affection, violent jealousy, and a wish for revenge; the weakness of the sense of property and of the feeling of friendship; atrophy of the maternal instinct, which made the born prostitute a persecutor of children and, in time, the procuress of her own daughter; an attraction for delinquency, in particular for theft and blackmail; a tendency to physical violence and to greed.

Furthermore, the experts said, the intelligence of the born prostitute was below average; the decline of this function, along with the atrophy of the instinct for reproduction, meant that the primacy of nutrition was given free rein; this found expression in a liking for alcohol, in greed, even in voraciousness. A fondness for play, an attraction for laziness, a low susceptibility to boredom, a readiness to do nothing, to think nothing, contrasting with the enthusiasm with which they threw themselves into a love of dancing, were characteristics of degeneracy. These features were reminiscent of the juxtaposition of laziness and orgiastic practices observed among savages. Furthermore, the born prostitute was a liar. Like all the "morally insane," she was very much attached to animals and devoted herself to her pimp as a dog would to its master; the religious sense found in many prostitutes was in itself, for Lombroso, a sign of degeneracy.[218]

The main characteristic, it is worth repeating, was the lack of modesty. This feature represented, par excellence, the psychological symptom of moral degeneracy. It was this phenomenon that resolved the contradiction that had always been detected between sexual precocity, prostitutional activity, and frigidity; the born prostitute practiced her profession driven by a disorder that was more moral than sexual. Furthermore, frigidity was for her an advantage, "a Darwinian adaptation."[219] It is because the sexual act appeared to her to be insignificant, morally as well as physically, that the born prostitute performed it so easily.

Genealogy was said to prove that the theory of the born prostitute was well founded. We know—and the work of Zola is the best example of this—the importance attached to the reconstitution of families by nineteenth-century authors who wanted to prove the hereditary origin of crime, debauchery, and all other moral weaknesses. The recourse to heredity was aimed above all at tracking down and explaining the morbid, the unhealthy; it sprang from a wish to naturalize moral weaknesses and misdeeds. The scientific discourse on the born prostitute is a particularly convincing example of this approach. Tarnowsky demonstrates the frequency of alcoholism, consumption, syphilis, and nervous and mental diseases among the parents of Russian prostitutes. She notes that the signs of degeneracy are particularly marked when it is the mother who has taken to drink.

Of course, there were also occasional prostitutes whose characteristics were acquired. Usually these were unregistered prostitutes; in society these *insouciantes,* to use Tarnowsky's term, were adulterous women who reserved their favors for a single lover. "The absence of any taste for evil in itself"[220] distinguished these women from the born prostitutes. In order to take up venal sex, they had to be driven by poverty, bad family example, or abandonment by a seducer, or be victims of trafficking in women. Once having fallen, they displayed a greater sense of modesty than the born prostitutes; they remained accessible to shame and remorse, and showed much more affection for children.

The theory of the born prostitute, which was widely criticized, nevertheless had a considerable effect on the French medical profession and imbued a large number of works, even when the authors showed some reluctance to give full approval to the theories of Tarnowsky or the Italian criminologists. As early as 1888 Dr. Féré, a physician at Bicêtre and a well-known sexologist, equated prostitution and criminality; according to him, prostitutes and criminals were both unproductive "invalids of civilization," [221] "the rejects of adaptation,"[222] "impotent and sick out of congenital infirmity."[223] The refusal to work, like the seeking after pleasure and the "disposition to irritability . . . the biological condition most favorable to art,"[224] were, for him, signs of degeneracy; they characterized the members of neuropathic families. Dr. Corre [225] theorized that prostitution offered an advantage that nobody had ever thought of before: it provided a distraction for the female criminal. In an article whose content was merely a popularization of the theory of the born prostitute, and in particular of the works of Lombroso and Ferrero, Dr. Emile Laurent described the considerable role of alcoholic parents in the genesis of prostitution; he observed that there were many families in which every member was either insane, a criminal, or a prostitute.[226] Although his clinical observations tended to prove it wrong, Dr. Gras rallied in the conclusion of his thesis to the theory of the born prostitute.[227]

But in France it was Dr. Octave Simonot who led the way in providing evidence for and extending the theory of the born prostitute. After examining two thousand venal women, to use his term, this physician attached to the vice squad set out to describe the psychophysiological features that defined what he called inherited insanity, a form of mental alienation peculiar, according to him, to prostitutes. His work, which dates from 1911, marked the culmination of this long anthropological discourse on the French prostitutes inaugurated by Parent-Duchâtelet in 1836. Simonot first set out to refute the causes offered by the sociologists; for him, *"prostitution is a pathological organic affliction."*[228] Taking over the anthropological observations of Tarnowsky, he based his theory mainly on neurology and, more particularly, on disturbances in cerebral activity. For him, "prostitution is an automatic reflex action" and the life of the prostitute "a pure reflex."[229] This "inherited insanity"[230] results from "a chemical, biological modification of her inherited plasma."[231]

According to Simonot, 80 percent of the women treated at Saint-Lazare were suffering from cerebral asthenia, which involved loss of memory and the inability to concentrate. Among prostitutes, as among savages, all that survives is "spontaneous attention." Both are incapable of the "voluntary attention" that is required by work, and which marks an advanced degree of human evolution. To this feature may be linked a constant tendency to be distracted and a susceptibility to idées fixes, two symptoms of degeneracy.

The woman suffering from "inherited insanity" is incapable of volition; this was the case with 70 percent of the prostitutes treated at Saint-Lazare. Their desire to work did not go beyond the stage of "inner dreaming." Moreover, the prostitute is sensitive to illusion because her brain is unable to carry out the work of synthesis required by perceptions; as a result, she is the victim of great "confusion of cerebral sensorial images."[232] Sometimes the brain remains "completely without life or existence"; the prostitute, the victim of such a "physiological decapitation,"[233] is now subject only to impulsive actions.

Of the prostitutes treated at Saint-Lazare, 90 percent devote their entire energy to the search for pleasure; this is yet another symptom of "inherited insanity." They remain under the grip of "the lower senses, whose constituents are the peripheric nerves";[234] hence their attraction for lively colors, music, and sexual relations. This continual search for pleasure links the prostitute with the child and the savage. For the prostitute, love is identified with the reproductive act; from this point of view, she is "arrested in her development at the batrachian or bird stage."[235] "The reproductive act" gives rise in her to veritable passions, whereas the emotions it arouses in "the normal, well-developed man are temporary and passing." "The passion that springs from the generative act," Simonot concludes, "is prostitution."[236]

The vulnerability of the prostitute to suggestion, the instability that characterizes her, the "mental vagabondage" for which she is criticized and which is to be condemned like any other form of vagabondage stem from the fact that she produces within herself, in the "cerebral mechanism," "a solution of continuity, preventing the coordination of ideas, movements, and actions."[237] Finally, Simonot attaches enormous importance, in the genesis of prostitution, to spinal irritation owing to heredity; according to him, this affliction is accompanied by a "reflex excitability" caused by "a more or less complete interruption of the continuity of the spinal chord with the brain."[238]

The "insane" character of the author's arguments do reveal the extreme tension to be found in medical discourse when it had to confront the fact of prostitution. But Simonot's work is not as negligible as might be thought—not because it appeared in an important, widely circulated review, but on account of the constant concern shown by this former vice squad doctor to justify, in a way that he claims to be scientific, the stereotypes of early regulationist literature. To conclude, Dr. Simonot, like all earlier anthropologists, proclaims the marginalization of the prostitute, but he bases this exclusion on a pseudoscientific arsenal borrowed from psychophysiology. "Strong, well-adapted, collective mankind continually evolves; the weak, individual prostitute does not adapt."[239] It is the intense dislike of work, the flight from pain, the refusal to settle down, and the perpetual search for pleasure that together, according to this practitioner, make up "inherited insanity," which is the result of a process of degeneracy.

The theory of the born prostitute, whatever its influence may have been, was greeted with considerable mistrust; even Lombroso was later led to retract it. Apart from the predictable hostility expressed by the socialists,[240] by libertarians, and by all those who refused to admit the primacy of temperament in the genesis of prostitutional behavior, a good deal of doubt was voiced within the medical profession itself.[241] The reservations, which found prudent expression through the pen of Dr. Gras, soon swelled into open hostility. In 1897 Dr. G. Daniel of Brussels published a severe criticism of Pauline Tarnowsky's book. By what criteria, he asked, are we to recognize the honest woman? "Innocently enough," he went on, "I did not believe that there was any more reason to carry out a special psychiatric study of the prostitute than of a dressmaker or a florist. She is an artisan like any other, providing a sum of work for a sum of money. Her characteristic is above all not having any."[242] The most severe and often most lucid criticism came, predictably enough, from the abolitionist doctors.[243] Dr. Morhardt, after stressing the continuity between regulationism and the theory of the born prostitute, wrote in 1906: "Under Louis XII, the prostitutes were morally fallen creatures. Since Lombroso, they are physically fallen . . . Now, again, anything that is done to them is acceptable."[244]

It was G. Tarde, however, who, proposing an analysis innovative to an almost vertiginous degree, published the most profound critique of the Italian anthropology. He explained why the theories that it produced were unacceptable. The argument of this sociology professor at the Collège de France is simple enough: "Born enslaved to generation, love tends through civilization to free itself . . . From being simply a means of procreation, as it is in the lives of the animals, it tends to become an end in itself."[245] This "sterilization of love"[246] is, for Tarde, the major phenomenon of his time. In his opinion, the increase in pleasure that results from this sterilization should not be regarded as something "vile."

These new data lead one to reflect on "the utilitarian or aesthetic value of voluptuous pleasure, on its individual and social role";[247] from it a new ethics will spring. Indeed, "the morality of tomorrow will be what the convictions of tomorrow will be concerning the importance, the nature, and the meaning of sexual relations."[248] Depending on one's judgment of pleasure, "the entire view of marriage and of the family will follow, a whole system of sexual duties will be deduced."[249] If the primacy of the erotic is recognized, people's attitude toward prostitution will be radically transformed. Far from appearing, as Westermark claims, as a sequela of primitive promiscuity, it will develop with civilization. In fact it is an aesthetic profession, and it needed the arrival of Christian prudery for that profession to be associated with shame. Sterile, confined love, hemmed in by laws, becomes exalted. But prostitution fulfills a primordial function, making up for the inconveniences and defects of monogamous marriage, which is placed essentially at the service of generation. "Either prostitution, if it continues to be a dishonor in spite of its utility," the author concludes, "will fatally disappear and be replaced by some other institution that will remedy more efficiently the defects of monogamous marriage, or it will survive, but by becoming respectable, that is to say, by gaining respect whether people like it or not. This will happen gradually, when it is unionized, organized into a powerful corporation, which one will be able to join only by offering certain guarantees, in which certain professional virtues will be cultivated that will raise the moral level of the members."[250] Here the sociological analysis, diametrically opposed to the theories of Italian and Russian anthropology, confirms the claims of the libertarians.

One can only be struck at first sight by the coherence of the medical and anthropological discourse that, from Parent-Duchâtelet to the modest Dr. Simonot, tends to show the primacy of temperament over the influence of social structures. But the anthropology of the prostitute worked out at the turn of the century did not precisely continue the enterprise of the philanthropist of the July Monarchy, whose approach was in a sense presociological; it included the study of way of life and environment. The work of a Tarnowsky or a Lombroso accepts the primacy of the biological; the influence of environment gives in to hereditary inevitability. What had to be done was to convince people that prostitution was not a social category, whether or not it was marginalized, but a biological environment. At the same time there developed around the problem of prostitution a psychiatrizing temptation. To treat prostitution and "loose morals" in the upper reaches of society as a form of insanity, just as attempts were being made to treat crime, amounted to exorcising female sexual deviation by placing it outside normal behavior.

That prostitution should be regarded as an inherited predisposition and not as the result of a defective organization of society made it possible to avoid a lot of problems; by pretending to rest the theory of innateness on a scientific basis, medical discourse brought comfort to regulationism.

To believe that prostitution and sexual license were due to a morbid heredity was, finally, a way of mobilizing against prostitution and the sexual freedom of women the terror of degeneracy that was then taking root in public opinion. "Heredity is the modern term for Fatum,"[251] Dr. H. Colin wrote in 1890, and we have seen how this same concept was used by the propagandists of the venereal peril. In each case this naturalization of immorality brought about by the notion of hereditary morbidity helped to increase sexual anxiety, especially in women.

If one wishes to observe the synchrony of the three events in the history of public opinion on sexuality represented by the denunciation, both exaggerated and intentionally partial, of the white slave trade, the dramatization of the venereal peril, and the desire to link prostitution and degeneracy, one must recognize the existence in medical, police, and military circles and among the members of the morality societies of a common desire to exert surveillance over prostitutes and, through that, to effect a project of sexual moralization, or at least an attempt to stem, by stressing its many dangers, a liberation in morals. And this happened at precisely the moment when the radicals, who supported the abolitionists, came to power. It remains to be seen which of these two currents turned out to be the stronger and succeeded in imposing its policy on prostitution.

7. The De Facto Triumph of Neoregulationism

By 1898 prostitution and, as we have seen, the problems that it gave rise to were once again at the forefront of public attention. Various intellectual bodies were concerning themselves with the fate of the prostitute; investigations of unprecedented scope were being undertaken; a vast movement of questioning opinion reflected the curiosity that the general public had about venal sex. But even before it became exhausted, just prior to the war, this enormous discourse on prostitution, often of abolitionist inspiration, had proven sterile. It had led to no more than a few minor reforms, which expressed the grip of neoregulationism while doing nothing to address the marginalization of the prostitute. It did not really succeed in breaking the legislative silence. This decline, this discrepancy between the discursive and the political, characterized better then anything else this stage in the history of public opinion and of institutions connected with the subject of prostitution.

Inquiries into Public Opinion

The Abolitionist Attempt to Profit from the Political Situation

The links initially forged between the radicals and the adversaries of the vice squad explain the attention paid by Combes to the fate of the prostitute. Above all, the role of Clemenceau, first as minister of the interior, then as president of the council (prime minister) in 1906, seemed to pave the way for the victory of abolitionism. In 1903, as editor of *L'aurore,* he had demanded the abolition of the vice squad. When he became minister of the interior, he gave a speech at Draguignan on October 14, 1906, in which he suggested that profound reforms in favor of prostitutes were imminent; no sooner was he installed in the place Beauvau than he set out to investigate the treatment of the female prisoners in Saint-Lazare. In that same year the establishment of a Ministry of Labor and Social Welfare, headed by Viviani, further encouraged the hopes of the abolitionists and helped to explain the increased interest in official circles in anything to do with prostitution.

The abolitionists tried to benefit from the favorable circumstances. By the end of 1896, the movement was nearly dead. The members of the committees that had initially been formed at Paris, Lyons, and Marseilles in the early 1880s had finally decided to leave the British and Continental Federation and to found the Ligue française pour le relèvement de la moralité publique. Article 1 of the program of this association demanded the abolition of the vice squad and of the regulationism that dishonored the police, compromised the magistrature, and established inequality between men and women. In fact, as is apparent in the content of its organ, *Le relèvement social,* the league, whose proclaimed aim in 1887 had been "the reconstitution of the home," was as much, if not more, concerned with the struggle against alcoholism, the white slave trade, immoral literature, and license in the streets as with the regulation of prostitution; indeed, its efforts in this direction came up against strong criticism from certain of its members who defended the vice squad in the name of morality.

It was for this reason that Louis Comte, one of the leaders of the league, decided, with Auguste de Morsier, to bring out, on January 1, 1897, a *Supplément* to *Le relèvement social* that would be devoted entirely to the struggle against the regulation of prostitution. That same year, during a visit to France by Josephine Butler, a group of abolitionists, brought together by Auguste de Morsier, took steps to form a French branch of the International Abolitionist Federation. After a few months of preparation, a public appeal was launched in May 1898 with a view to obtaining members, and the new organization was officially represented at the international abolitionist conference held in London that year.[1]

In 1902, drawing up a balance sheet of the work that had been done,[2] Auguste de Morsier called for socialists and libertarians to adhere to the cause. He pointed out that the abolitionist precepts were being received with a great deal of sympathy by the workers' movement, in the labor exchanges, and in the people's universities. Nonetheless, he deplored the fact that only a small number of doctors had rallied to the campaign and that, on the whole, the Catholics and the clerical party, mainly concerned, as always, with preserving and improving morality, still showed hostility toward the movement.[3]

The nature of the recruitment explains the slight shift in the abolitionist discourse in the circles around the federation. Auguste de Morsier, who nevertheless declared himself to be a Christian and who refrained from attacking the family, asserted that the leaders of the French branch no longer had any moralizing intent. For him, the support of the socialists and libertarians necessitated this new attitude, so far removed from that of the league. The only aim of the campaign was now the abolition of the vice squad and the triumph of the principle of a single morality for both sexes. From this point of view, he even went so far as to declare that the leaders of the French branch had no difficulty accepting the principles of free union, and that they refused to identify legal marriage with the family.[4]

Between 1898 and 1907, under the leadership first of Auguste de Morsier, then of Mme. Avril de Sainte-Croix, the abolitionist organization took on a new dynamism. The conference that met at Lyons in 1901[5] represented the peak of the campaign. Lyons had been chosen because its mayor, Professor Augagneur, had accepted the chairmanship of the conference, and because the Protestant Center and the Midi had always been the heartland of abolitionism. During those years the action of the adversaries of the vice squad was moving forward on several fronts. In Paris, Mme. de Sainte-Croix (under the pseudonym of "Savioz"), de Morsier, Dr. Sicard, and Yves Guyot gave lectures; they also attended the section meetings on the League for the Rights of Man, the lay church groups, the Masonic lodges, the labor exchanges, the people's universities, church youth groups, and even the libertarian groups. These activities were backed up by lecture tours in the provinces. Mme. de Sainte-Croix founded L'oeuvre libératrice, whose aim was to provide a refuge for registered prostitutes. This propaganda was supported by a cross-section of the press. *Le siècle,* run by Yves Guyot, and *La fronde* openly supported the campaign; *L'aurore, Le rappel, La petite République, L'evénement,* and *L'eclair* provided less outspoken support. The *Revue de morale sociale,* founded in Geneva and Paris in 1899, was entirely devoted to abolitionism.

The propaganda also took other forms: Léon Frapié published *La proscrite* and dedicated this story of the life of a prostitute to the abolitionist federation. Jules Hoche published his novel *Saint-Lazare,* in which he denounces the abuses of the "plague-ridden house." In 1906 at Lille, Marius Véran produced *L'entôleuse,* an abolitionist propaganda play in which La Rouquine, condemned to prostitution out of poverty, after being seduced by her employer, commits suicide rather than present herself to the health service doctor, whom she has recognized as her younger brother.

The leaders of the French branch officially approached leading personalities with a view to obtaining their support; in this way they won that of Jaurès and Zola, while Frédéric Passy renewed his. On October 25, 1906, at a time when the presence of Clemenceau at the Ministry was a great source of hope, the abolitionists organized a protest meeting in Paris against regulation.[6] The meeting attracted over seven hundred people, a large number of them women, but it was broken up by anarchists, led by Libertad[7]; before being expelled from the hall, these anarchists attacked those taking part in the meeting as pharisees.

The rebirth of an organized abolitionism was only one aspect of the increased public interest in prostitution. As we have seen, the two world feminist conferences, which met in Paris in 1900 on the occasion of the Universal Exposition, had given a lot of time to the subject of venal sex. At the instigation of the French branch, in 1901 the League for the Rights of Man organized a great debate on regulation and the vice squad and concluded, for the time being, in favor of a moderate neoregulationism.[8] During the following years, many sections of the league rallied unambiguously to the abolitionist causes. In the end, thanks to the influence of its president, the socialist deputy for the Rhône, Francis de Pressensé, the league produced a firm condemnation of regulation at a conference meeting in Bordeaux in May 1907. The debate and decisions of the Paris municipal council in 1904 had an even greater impact. Faithful to tradition, and despite the reforming ideas expounded by the prefect Lépine, the councillors demanded abolition of both regulation and the vice squad.

The country's leaders were not going to be able to remain outside the movement. After the government had been questioned by the radical-socialist deputy for the Aube, Paul Meunier, Combes, who had already ordered a statistical investigation of the subject, proceeded on July 18, 1903, to appoint an extraparliamentary commission to investigate the vice squad. This body, made up of seventy-three members consisting of doctors, administrators, publicists, and lawyers, was to work from November 3, 1903, to December 7, 1906. The commission concluded its enormous labors[9] by adopting a parliamentary bill largely inspired by the abolitionist position. Despite his enthusiasm, Senator Bérenger had been unable to get his views accepted.

Dr. Fiaux perfectly defined the spirit of the commission's conclusions: the question, in his view, was one of substituting "for an arbitrary obligation partially imposed by the regulation of prostitution on a tiny category of individuals, a moral, legal obligation imposed on everybody without distinction of social rank and sex."[10] "What we wanted to create," he writes, "was a sexual conscience,"[11] especially in men. The members of the commission found little support. Apart from its provisions concerning the prostitution of minors, the bill was killed at the express request of the neoregulationists. In the end, the commission had more of an effect through the immense work of investigation that it had carried out than through the actual result of its proposals.

Recourse to Public Opinion

The debate on prostitution went beyond official circles; several investigations into the state of public opinion were also undertaken. The appeal for the creation of a male "sexual conscience" lay at the heart of this debate, which explains the importance then assumed by the suggestions for making intersexual contamination an offense, tirelessly propounded by Dr. Fiaux. These investigations into public opinion took various forms: *La revue de morale sociale,* for example, was content to organize a referendum on the problem of "injured parties" and asked various individuals for their opinion on the extent to which the state should intervene in the matter of sexual relations.[12]

In fact, it was the opinion of the medical profession that people were most anxious to discover. In 1903 *Le français*[13] organized an inquiry among doctors on the subject of the vice squad, and 337 replies were received. All condemned the system as it was then functioning; 175 (52 percent) declared themselves to be in favor of prostitution coming back under the common law, and 155 (46 percent) favored maintaining a reformed regulation. Among these neoregulationists, 48 (14 percent) wanted to see profound changes in the system. The success of these investigations proves the extent to which the medical profession was sensitive to the venereal threat at the time. The results, regarded as unexpected by the newspaper, were not to be confirmed. In 1904 the Société française de prophylaxie sanitaire et morale set up an enormous opinion survey of its members, who, as we know, largely belonged to the medical profession. Out of a total of 863 members, 410 (47.5 percent) declared themselves to be in favor of maintaining regulation, and only 51 (6 percent) considered it preferable to leave prostitution free.[14] Of course, the membership of this society already supported the neoregulationist position.

The investigation carried out by the extraparliamentary commission into the opinion of local mayors as to the advisability of maintaining or abolishing the *maisons de tolérance* had a more official character. Eighty-seven of them replied to the questionnaire; of this total, seventy-four expressed approval of the *maison de tolérance*, thirty-two regarded it as "indispensable," twenty-eight as "necessary," and fourteen as "useful." Thirteen were hostile to it, but often with reservations.

The arguments advanced by the seventy-four advocates of the officially tolerated *maison* were simple: its abolition would compromise public health (35 answers), increase unregistered prostitution (21), encourage an increase in the number of drinking places (15), harm public morality (11), lead to an increase in soliciting (9), and compromise the morality of minors (3). It might be noted, then, that although the mayors expressed greater concern for public health than for the preservation of public morality, the latter was nevertheless mentioned by many.

The commission also asked the mayors to express an opinion on the proposal to allow freedom of association for women to practice prostitution together in a house or apartment, without a keeper or any link with the local authorities or the police. Seventy-one declared this idea to be "disastrous," "inadmissable, or "very dangerous" on the grounds that it would compromise public health, morality, or security (42 answers), lead to a return of the *maisons de tolérance* without any guarantees (24), bring about an increase in the number of pimps (11), stimulate the white slave trade (9), and encourage robbery (7).[15]

The morality societies, for their part, investigated public opinion with a view to demanding that the authorities clean up the streets. In 1894, in order to support the bill that he was presenting in the Senate, Bérenger, president of the Ligue pour la lutte contre la licence des rues, had already initiated a petition in Paris demanding an energetic suppression of public soliciting. In a few months he collected twenty thousand signatures. The league consulted the general councils on the same subject and found that sixty-one of them, including that of the department of the Seine, favored the senator's action.[16]

Legislative Silence and the Policy of "Small Doses"

Despite the revival of interest in the problem of prostitution in the last years of the century, the deputies still refused to deal with the issue. Let us now look into the reason for this legislative silence, whose persistence might seem surprising. In the first place, a large number of parliamentarians were themselves clients of venal women and therefore found it difficult, if not disagreeable, to discuss prostitution in public. This argument, which was often put forward by contemporaries, partly explains the legislators' reticence. Nevertheless, it might be more to the point to suggest that the members of the two assemblies had remained faithful to the Augustinian view of prostitution, which they still claimed to regard as no more than a question of public order and of the administration of the thoroughfares. This is certainly what emerges from the declarations of ministers, especially from successive Gardes des Sceaux (senior law officers in the government); all reaffirmed before senators or deputies the trust that they placed in the administration and the police.

We should add that the hilarity that gripped the parliamentarians whenever the question of prostitution arose does indicate the deep unease that they felt in approaching sexual questions. Their conviction that such a subject should remain a private matter meant that, for them, it ought not to be openly discussed in parliament; there was a feeling that such a subject was obscene and would demean both parliament and the Republic. Tarde goes further and blames the psychology of the politicians: ambitious, desperate for power and wealth, they were led to pass "on the things relating to love, on all that side of the human soul that was opposed to theirs, the summary, contemptuous judgment of ignorance."[17] But, as the sociologist remarked in 1904,[18] it was becoming urgent for the legislators to deal with these problems, precisely because religion, which had once concerned itself with the matter of love, was declining in influence.

The refusal to legislate on the subject was deliberate; it was certainly noted and often denounced by contemporaries. Vallée, the Garde des Sceaux, made this clear in the Senate before the vote on April 3, 1903. On the change proposed to Article 334 of the penal code, he declared: "This is the first time that the legislator has thought fit to enter a domain that has hitherto been the preserve of the police."[19] Albert Gigot, a former prefect of police, in the report that he read to the Société générale des prisons on December 23, 1903, declared in turn: "What strikes us is the absolute silence, the determined silence of the legislator. Not only does the law not regulate these matters, but the legislator avoids mentioning them and even making any reference to them whatsoever. It is a subject that it has been agreed to pass over in silence."[20] At the same session Honnorat, chief of the first division of the prefecture of police, declared: "As long as current ideas on morals prevail, as long as it is regarded as shocking to speak of prostitutes and of venereal diseases, parliament will never deal with these questions, except in small doses."[21] Lucid and disillusioned, he was to add a little later on the subject of a proposed law: "By the time we get it, I'm afraid we'll all be dead and buried."[22]

It must be said, in any case, that the application of possible legislation would have come up against the reticence of the legal profession. The opinions expressed by magistrates during the debates of the Société générale des prisons in 1904 and 1908 are highly revealing.[23] The risk of seeing an increase in the number of cases going before the courts, fear of scandals coming to light during hearings, and the repulsion felt by judges for settling such questions led them to advocate the intervention of the administrative authorities in such matters. We must also take into account the inability of the magistrates of the time to judge laws of a social nature.[24]

Tirelessly, however, three parliamentarians—Georges Berry, the radical-socialist Paul Meunier, and above all Senator Bérenger—did their best to break this legislative silence. The history of these abortive attempts is significant.

The first assaults were mounted in 1894 and 1895. On November 23, 1894, Georges Berry presented a bill on the regulation of prostitution.[25] It was the first coherent attempt to overcome the reticence of the legislature. Not particularly original, of course, since it drew its inspiration largely from the sanitary neoregulationism advocated by the Richard Report, this bill was never debated. Its author advocated maintaining registration and the *maison de tolérance,* which, he advised, should include the *maison de rendez-vous.* Echoing ideas popularized by Bérenger, Georges Berry advocated the creation of an offense of soliciting, in order to clean up the streets, and called for showing greater severity toward pimps. Yet he also proposed the foundation of dispensaries, the opening of special departments for venereal patients in general hospitals, and an increase in open consultations.

In fact it was Bérenger who was to succeed in forcing parliament to debate this hitherto disreputable subject. Urged on by the anxiety about sexual matters so typical of the closing years of the century, the senator, as part of a wider struggle for safeguarding public morality, presented to the Senate on April 27, 1894, "a bill on prostitution and outrages against good morals." His essential aim was to "purge" the streets and public places, to struggle "against the teaching of immorality through the eyes."[26] He admitted the primacy of moral preoccupations: the precocious immorality born from the ease with which young people's curiosity and appetites could be satisfied brought with it a taste for pleasure and a disinclination to work, accustomed them to easy gains, and encouraged social tensions. Furthermore, the spectacle of public immorality, for the senator, undermined virility, affronted moral and physical health, destroyed the innocence of young girls and honest women. But for him the most serious effect was not so much the existence of venal sex as "the public soliciting of prostitution." "What great moral and intellectual strength we would believe we were giving out young people if we could impose chastity on them!" the senator exclaimed.[27]

From this sprang a series of propositions that placed Bérenger between the most exalted regulationists and the fiercest adversaries of the vice squad. His initial bill favored the enclosure of commercial sex and therefore the existence of the renovated *maison de tolérance*. Violently hostile to the arbitrary action of the vice squad, however, Bérenger proposed making an offense of "public soliciting of prostitution," which he identified as an outrage to public decency. The decision to register should belong, he believed, to the legal authorities. Furthermore, the senator called for stiffer penalties on pimps, procuresses, keepers of unregistered brothels, and traffickers in women. Finally, he demanded that the fate of minors should be determined by courts of summary jurisdiction.

Explaining his bill of May 27, 1895, to the assembled senators, Bérenger launched into a violent attack on the arbitrary powers of the vice squad. The next day, Trarieux, the Garde des Sceaux, refused to support the establishment of an offense of soliciting; it was easy for him to show that soliciting and the practice of prostitution were inseparable. Moreover, he declared himself hostile to any legislation concerning venal sex: for him, the passing of a bill was unthinkable, for it would prove to be unenforceable and would make the sanitary service quite ineffective.[28] In the name of "social interest," he cried: "I shall even go so far as to say that here *the right is, to a certain extent, in the arbitrary*," thus confirming officially the maintenance of a legislative silence on prostitution. He added: "From every point of view, we must resign ourselves to the inevitable. We must resign ourselves to living today as we have lived for twenty centuries." With these words he comforted the senators with the notion that prostitution is outside history and that its immutable character justifies its not benefiting from the progress of civilization.[29]

This time the vice squad was defended by the majority of moderate republicans (nonroyalist, moderate conservatives), who were then in power, and the Bérenger bill was rejected, despite the support of a heterogeneous group that included not only Chesnelong and the conservative aristocrats but also Jules Simon, Buffet, Waddington, Wallon, and Barthélemy-Saint-Hilaire. The bill to legislate on prostitution brought out the traditional divisions. It should be said, however, that Bérenger's bill, which tended at the same time to bring the prostitutes back under common law and to make soliciting an offense, was highly ambiguous. Among its opponents were the abolitionist Scheurer-Kestner and men of such different opinions as Constans, Floquet, Waldeck-Rousseau, Arago, Freycinet, and Teisserenc de Bort.

The failure of Article 1 of his bill led Bérenger to water it down, and it was a somewhat truncated bill that was finally passed by the senators on June 14 and June 27, 1895. The notion of bringing the prostitutes back under common law and regulating their situation had been abandoned; the bill confined itself to the pimps, procurers, and keepers of unregistered lodging houses, and to increasing the penalties on owners of drinking places and bringing minor prostitutes before the courts. This bill, we know, was never debated by the deputies.[30]

Between 1902 and 1910, when the mood of questioning had reached the most apparently refractory circles, the parliament, which was still hostile to any bill that treated prostitution as a whole, began to act in "small doses." Combes's decision to set up an extraparliamentary commission to investigate prostitutional structures in depth seems, indeed, to have sprung as much from a wish to reject any bold decision as from a concern to solve the problems later. For the first time in the history of investigations into prostitution, however, there was no fear this time of studying prostitution in the higher reaches of society[31] and of defending street prostitutes.

Even before the appointment of the extraparliamentary commission, Georges Berry, returning to the attack, tabled a neoregulationist bill in the Chamber of Deputies on June 4, 1903, that represented a vehement denunciation of the venereal threat; it was never debated. The passing of the law of April 3, 1903, which implemented the decisions of the Paris conference concerning the white slave trade, was certainly the most important legislative measure that had been taken in defense of the prostitute. Yet on February 1, 1904, the Chamber of Deputies rejected, after a lively debate, an amendment by Deputy Le Peletier by which acts of prostitution could be brought before justices of the peace.

The abolitionists awaited impatiently for Clemenceau and his successors in the government to bring the revolutionary project passed by the extraparliamentary commission in December 1906 before the parliament. They were to be bitterly disappointed. On June 7, 1907, Paul Meunier proposed a bill that followed quite closely, with some amendments,[32] the commission's conclusions. His motion was not debated. Of the enormous amount of work done by the commission all that emerged in the end was the law of April 11, 1908, on the prostitution of minors. This was largely because a counteroffensive on the part of the neoregulationists was under way; it was carried out simultaneously by the Société de prophylaxie, the Société de médecine militaire, which saw its influence increasing, and by the Académie de médecine. On December 7, 1908, a delegation from the Société de prophylaxie, led by Bérenger, met Clemenceau and, stressing the danger of the conclusions of the extraparliamentary commission, presented a counterproject drawn up by Dr. Butte. The delegation seemed convincing.

The prostitution of minors had long been a subject of serious concern, especially among conservatives and clericals anxious to protect them. The Comte d'Haussonville, haunted by the threat represented by the army of vagabond children, a breeding ground for crime and political violence, had set about, during the first decade of the Republic, producing, like Parent-Duchâtelet, a veritable anthropological study of vagabond children.[33] For him, prostitution was merely one form of vagabondage, all of a piece with the large number of illegitimate births, the promiscuity that reigned in working-class families, the bad example set by parents, and above all the pernicious influence of the dance hall. He blamed noisy popular music for the downfall of young women, echoing the fear felt by the ruling classes at the prospect of the people gathering together for a "good time."

The attention paid to the prostitution of minors is also explained by the widespread sense of the increasing precocity of debauchery and vice. Revealing in this regard is Marc Réville's *Prostitution des mineurs selon la loi pénale,* published in 1896. In a veritable utopia imbued with the sternest regulationism, the author takes the decline of modesty among girls as a reason to demand establishing the moral supervision of workshops and a system of coercion inspired by the conviction that a propensity to debauchery is a disease.

To this was later added, especially in the early years of the twentieth century, a fear of perversion and the development of a taste among men for young girls. In 1891 Catulle Mendès had described at length the tragic fate of Liliane, a young dancer, "a very small, pretty, monstrous prostitute, feeling neither desire nor pleasure,"[34] a victim "of vile passive precocities."[35] Then, too, there was the tirelessly denounced fashion for soliciting on behalf of false minors;[36] procuresses, disguising themselves as duennas, would dress prostitutes who were of age but looked younger as little girls, with pigtails, short skirts, and sometimes even a doll in their arms or a cake in their mouths, and would offer them to passersby.[37] The fact that the names of underage girls appeared on the registers of official prostitution had always been a subject of scandal. In 1882 Senator Roussel had carried out, on behalf of a senatorial commission, a vast investigation into child delinquency. The thirteenth question on his survey concerned the prostitution of minors. Fifty-seven prefectures replied to the questionnaire; they reported 1,338 minors registered as prostitutes in the towns of their departments at this time.[38]

Despite the growing reluctance of the authorities to register underage prostitutes, large numbers of them continued to work both in Paris and in the provinces, even though in the capital their numbers were in a steady decline.[39] Of the 400 municipal by-laws analyzed by Hennequin in 1904,[40] 337 contained no reservation concerning the registration of minors; only 26 by-laws stipulated that registration was reserved for women who had reached their majority; in some towns registration was still being carried out for girls of fourteen, thirteen, and even twelve.[41] In the course of 1904,[42] out of 3,809 underage girls arrested in the provinces for prostitution, 2,026 (53 percent) were registered; of this total, 45 (2.2 percent) were under sixteen, 385 (19 percent) were sixteen or seventeen, and 1,596 (78 percent) were eighteen, nineteen, or twenty. In Paris the prefecture of police was now showing more discernment; in 1902, 1,832 minors regarded as prostitutes had been arrested; 457 of them (25 percent) were registered, and all were eighteen or over.

On June 30, 1905, Bérenger proposed a bill in the Senate concerning the prostitution of minors. Haunted by the notion that debauchery was spreading, and realizing that the incidence of venereal disease was particularly high among young prostitutes, the senator proposed that prostitutes under eighteen should be sent to reformatories. The debate was adjourned, awaiting the recommendations of the extraparliamentary commission. When these were at last available, the government, in the spirit of its conclusions, passed the law of April 11, 1908, which made provision for the placing of prostitutes under the age of eighteen in such homes.[41]

This law, which, it is worth repeating, was the only positive result of the labors of the extraparliamentary commission, was to prove inapplicable for several years. The schools and homes proposed had not yet been set up, and not knowing what to do with the girls they arrested, the police ran the risk of having to give up surveillance of minors after April 16, 1909, the date on which the new legislation came into force. Clemenceau, alerted by Dr. Le Pileur's report, which noted a sharp increase in venereal disease, extended the delays envisaged for the application of the law of 1908.

The last attempts to legislate on prostitution were received with indifference and came to nothing. On July 11, 1912, Paul Meunier, supported by the socialists and certain of the radicals, again called on the government to consider the arbitrary action of the vice squad. He said that, despite the completion of the work of the extraparliamentary commission, nothing had yet been done, and he launched still another attack on the prison of Saint-Lazare. Steeg, the minister of the interior, pointed out that Clemenceau, once a staunch opponent of the arbitrary action of the vice squad, had reformed nothing during his long tenure in the government, and that the law of 1908 had itself remained a "dead letter."[44] Finally, by 320 votes to 241, the Chamber rejected the invitation to the government to present a bill on the vice squad. Next day, at Steeg's suggestion, Paul Meunier presented a proposal for a bill based on the conclusions of the extraparliamentary commission and proposed the abolition of registration and the health check. This bill, after due consideration, was never debated.

The break-up of the Bloc des Gauches (a coalition of radicals and socialists), the decline in influence of the radicals in the Chamber, the vigorous attempt to moralize youth, the consistent failure of various modest proposals adopted over previous years, the advance made by neoregulationism among public opinion and in particular inside the medical profession, and the relative success of the reforms inspired by this doctrine explain how legislative silence was maintained right up to the outbreak of the war.

The Reforms Are Carried Out

This legislative silence was accompanied, in the area of administration, by a great gap between intentions, promises, and solemn declarations on the one hand and the reforms that were actually enacted on the other.[45] The official recognition of the Parisian *maison de rendez-vous* and the humanization of the treatment of venereal patients are essentially all the reforms that were achieved.

Recognizing the Maison de Rendez-vous in Order to Improve Surveillance

Before the debates that took place in the Paris municipal council, and even before the extraparliamentary commission was set up, the prefect of police, Lépine, who had already declared to the Senate in 1895 that he had put an end to "the era of raids," officially recognized, in the by-law of February 14, 1900, what was taking place in the *maisons de rendez-vous;* by the same token, he was encouraging the development of new prostitutional structures.

The growth of the *maison de rendez-vous* merely reflected the triumph and the social diffusion of the model of the bourgeois home, that is to say, an end to overcrowding. But this meant that the institution involved, as L'épine understood very well, a certain opacity. Theodore Zeldin is only partly right when he writes of the prefect's reforms: "The pleasures of the middle class were thus liberated from state control."[46]

Of course, it cannot be denied that the new regulationism was simpler than that applied to the *maisons de tolérance,* but at the same time—and this, it seems to me, is the main point—Lépine wanted to supervise establishments that had hitherto eluded police observation. In the purest regulationist tradition this was to allow the spread of a new type of "clean" brothel[47] and to continue the fight against the spread of the "perversions" and "depravities" to be found in the *maisons de tolérance.*

The by-law of 1900 merely codified practices that had developed spontaneously; it confirmed the principle that prostitutes should live outside the brothels in which they worked, a process that had begun some decades before. The surveillance of the new establishments was handed over to the department responsible for lodging houses, since the Paris *maisons de rendez-vous* were now regarded as such. According to the by-law, all the women in these now-tolerated establishments had to have their names and photographs recorded by the *patronne* in a register; they had to undergo regular medical checks, the result of which had to be recorded in this register. The windows of the *maisons de rendez-vous* had to be kept closed, like those of the *maisons de tolérance,* and no external sign was allowed to indicate the nature of the establishment to the passer-by. All forms of advertising and soliciting at the doorway were forbidden. There were to be no drinks for sale in the building, and the *patronne* was not to tolerate the presence of women whose names were not in her register. As Honnorat, head of the first division,[48] explained, Prefect Lépine "has instructed that we shall be concerned at first with those houses where the entrance fee is 40 francs and less, which has been done." He also decided that "in exceptional circumstances, certain women, clients of the larger houses who may not wish to observe this system of registration, would be authorized to produce a card bearing their photograph, but not their name." As for the *maisons de tolérance,* in the strict sense, they too would have to become more discreet and avoid all advertising.

Between 1904 and 1908, a transitional period began for the Parisian brothels. Awaiting the results of the considerations under way, Lépine decided in 1904 to abolish the existing general regulation while advising the keepers to continue to abide by it. The keepers of the *maisons de tolérance* were no longer required to have prefectural permission; they were no longer obliged to keep a register; they could admit unregistered prostitutes; all that remained was the compulsory health check. The bars adjoining the establishments were now regarded quite simply as public drinking places. All regulation was abolished for the lower- and middle-level *maisons de rendez-vous,* but the keepers were still held responsible for the health of the women who frequented their establishments. This liberalization gave rise to sharp increase in the number of such houses; as for the *patronnes* of the first-class establishments, they were now content to inform the prefecture of their activities.

In short, awaiting parliament's decision, which was thought to be imminent, the authorities were attempting to put the policies advocated by the municipal council and the extraparliamentary commission into effect. As is proved by his remarks in the council and before the members of the commission, even Lépine was highly influenced by neoregulationism. He wanted to give a legal basis to regulation, which would bring about the abolition of prior inspection, the special commission, and punishments. According to him, it would be enough for the woman who wanted to prostitute herself, under penalty of being brought before the courts, to make a declaration to the prefecture of police and be given a health certificate by the physician of her choice. He proposed to abolish any confusion between treatment and punishment. These reforms would also make it possible, he hinted, to do away with the surveillance of the *maisons de rendez-vous,* and in particular the compulsory photograph.

The failure of the attempts to provide for the legislation of prostitution forced the police to resort to temporary devices. The order of August 4, 1908, abolished the special commission for the registration of prostitutes and provided for the setting up of a vice court under the local government. In fact, this body did not work, and in 1911 it was declared to be illegal by the Council of State. The by-law of February 15, 1910, forbade any lodging-house keeper or café owner in Paris to receive prostitutes on a regular basis. Above all, the by-law of April 4, 1912, once again codified the functioning of the *maisons de rendez-vous* in the capital. Its provisions were almost identical with those of the by-law of 1900; these included declaration to the prefecture of police that such an establishment was being opened, the prohibition of any external sign or advertisement, and any soliciting on the doorstep, in addition to the obligation to keep a register.

Just as people were coming to terms with the failure of the attempt to legislate on prostitution, the prefecture of police went back to the arrangements that had been in force prior to the period 1903-1907. This proves that, despite the reforming intentions advanced by Lépine, the police had certainly decided to exercise surveillance over the new establishments. Nevertheless, the regulation that went into effect between 1900 and 1910 confirmed the decline of the *maison de tolérance;* it both registered and permitted the proliferation of the discreet *maison de rendez-vous,* inside which the prostitute, who usually lived elsewhere, was no longer as directly under the keeper's control as she had previously been.

The Humanization of the Treatment of Venereal Patients

The application of the sanitary principles of neoregulationism profoundly affected the treatment of venereal patients at this time. The Hôpital Saint-Louis and its dermatological department acted as models in this respect.[49] Professor Landouzy pointed out to his colleagues on the extraparliamentary commission that over half the venereal patients in Paris were now being treated in the general hospitals. This development had occurred spontaneously; at the Hôpital Ricord, the former Hôpital du Midi, there were now only mixed departments of venereology and dermatology. In 1890 Professor Brocq had set about turning Lourcine, which was to become the Hôpital Broca, into a dermatological establishment and not a specifically venereological one. Since venereal and dermatological patients had been mixed, the soliciting of procuresses inside the hospital had ceased.

In 1904 the general council of the department of the Seine decided to set up a free venereological dispensary at Saint-Lazare. This dispensary, which bears the name of its first director, Toussaint-Barthélemy, was opened in 1906. Its success was considerable. In 1912 it carried out 12,531 medical examinations.[50] Women were not afraid to go there. In short, in the years just prior to the war a profound change had taken place in the attitude of venereal patients in Paris.[51]

The neoregulationists, however, were to be disappointed by the failure of innumerable attempts to reform the prison infirmary of Saint-Lazare. The scandal caused by the decrepitude of this establishment was an inexhaustible theme at this time. Almost every year following the debate in 1902 between Waldeck-Rousseau and the deputy Maillet the budget of Saint-Lazare was attacked in the Chamber. Even in 1902 the general council of the Seine had voted a sum of 5 million francs for the rebuilding of the prison; in 1906 it adopted the future site. But up to the outbreak of war, nothing had been done.

The humanization of treatment was apparent in the large provincial cities. At Bordeaux out-patient consultation for venereal patients had been established at the Hôpital Saint-Jean. Just prior to the war, the venereal patients of Nancy left the Maison de Secours.[52] A more ambitious reform was carried out at Lyons[53] where, ever since 1910, when the compulsory hospitalization of sick prostitutes had been abandoned, the prostitutes of the town had been flooding in for consultation and treatment.

An investigation begun in 1908 by the prison administration, which looked into the ways in which registered prostitutes suffering from venereal diseases were treated, made it possible to assess, for all the regions, the progress made since Bourneville's studies. Prostitutes were now admitted to hospitals almost everywhere; treatment in the local prisons had become exceptional.[54] This did not mean, however, that prostitutes were no longer kept in hospital establishments by force; on June 14, 1913, the subprefect of Briey, learning that a mining hospital was to be built, requested that "the new building should be arranged in such a way as to facilitate surveillance and prevent escapes."[55]

The Intensification of Surveillance in the Years before the War

Increased Pressure from the Morality Societies

During the years prior to the war, with campaigns concerning the dangers of venereal disease and the white slave trade, an attempt had been made to warn people, especially young people, off sex. Meanwhile, the activities of the morality societies and all those who were engaged in the struggle against pornography and licentiousness intensified. The campaigns of the regional press in favor of cleaning up the streets and forbidding unregistered prostitution became more frequent and more thoroughgoing. In 1907 *La croix du Nord*,[56] in an article entitled "Stinking Lille," declared war on the prostitutes operating in the center of the city. The newspaper published a petition signed by sixty well-known visitors to the city, who expressed their indignation at the licentiousness reigning there. Most of the other regional newspapers supported the Catholic organ and published the text of the petition. In 1912 *Soleil du Midi*[57] carried the headline "A Clean Sweep, Please" and demanded that the struggle against prostitution in Marseilles be intensified.

In Paris the campaign was organized at the district level. The struggle against prostitution that took place in the district of Goutte d'Or is a good example. Early in 1913 a "defense committee of the moral interests of the district" was formed, bringing together socialists, radical-socialists, and members of the morality societies; its organizer was Marcel Cachin, then a municipal councillor. On June 21, after an appeal was launched to "honest folk," a protest meeting against licentiousness in the streets attracted at least 1,500 people.[58] Cachin was pleased to see that this morality campaign involved all political tendencies, proof that this was *"a question of order, security, and cleanliness above all questions of party."*[59] Prostitution "was poisoning the district";[60] it was bad for business, discouraged employers, who were unwilling to hire women working at home, and led to a rise in delinquency. Cachin intervened with the prefect of police and the minister of the interior. He demanded that prison sentences be handed out to brothel-keepers. Speaking after him, Dr. Desormeaux, a radical-socialist and a losing candidate in the recent elections, accused capitalist society of being responsible for the increase in prostitution. Finally, Lefebvre-Ortozoul, vice president of the Ligue de protection sociale, offered the support of thirty thousand members of his organization "to clean up the mess in the rue de la Charbonnière and other streets,"[61] while suggesting that the inhabitants of the district should do the work themselves.

These were not isolated events. In that same month, June 1913, the residents of the place Cambronne sent a petition to the prefect of police asking him to put an end to public prostitution.[62] These isolated facts testify to the scope of the campaign being carried out in favor of public morality and of the decline in the movement to show sympathy for the prostitute, which, in the past, had been fed by abolitionism and redemptorist literature.

Extension of Sanitary and Police Supervision

Several facts suggest that police supervision of the prostitute in the years prior to the First World War was more severe than it had been fifteen years earlier. As we have seen, a large-scale offensive was then being waged at Marseilles against the unregistered *maisons de rendez-vous;* the authorities officially declared those establishments, then outside its supervision, as "places of debauchery" and also set out to close the public lavatories, traditionally devoted to low-class prostitution.

It was just before the war that the authorities hastily organized health checks among the rural population; this made it possible to turn young barmaids into registered prostitutes. An identical process had taken place in the area around the garrison of Toul at the expense of the women from the surrounding countryside who frequented the soldiers. More generally, an examination of archival documents shows that, by a sort of capillary action, regulation was beginning to reach the small towns, even the rural townships that had not yet experienced it, and it was under the pretext of supervising public health that the surveillance and police control of prostitution increased.

It was at about this time that repression of drugs, whose proliferation had been tied to that of unregistered prostitution, was first organized systematically. On June 14, 1913,[63] the procurator general of the court of appeals at Rennes wrote triumphantly that all the demimondaines who ran smoking dens had been expelled from Brest and that the vice admiral had removed from the port all the officers who had made up their clientele.

Despite the campaigns of the abolitionists and the neoregulationists, administrative punishment had far from disappeared; health checks sometimes concealed severe police repression.[64] The investigation carried out in 1908 by the prison administration allows us to discern the general persistence of punishment by imprisonment. At Nancy in 1907, 3,117 days of detention had been handed out to prostitutes,[65] and in 1914, the venereal patients of the city were transferred to the new hospital under police guard.[66]

It should be noted that the current of public opinion that tended to support the suppression of immorality did not concern only prostitutes and pornography. The answers given in 1912 by the procurators-general to the Garde des Sceaux, who had questioned them about the state of public morality in their areas, shows that almost everywhere people were in favor of increasing the penalties on pimps.[67] On September 30, 1910, the general council of the Vosges proposed sending vagabonds and "apaches" to the Foreign Legion. On May 27, 1911, the general council of Allier also demanded harsher punishments. The policy toward the drinking places was equally severe;[68] in 1907, at Clemenceau's request, the prefects advised mayors to restrict the number of such places opened. On July 30, 1913, an additional clause to the finance act provided that, henceforth, the prefect could, like the mayor, forbid the setting up of drinking places in certain areas. In the course of 1914 this permission was to be used in forty-three departments. A memorandum from the minister of the interior, dated February 20, 1914, urged a more severe policy toward alcoholism and prostitution in places of entertainment.

Imprisonment and the Revolt of the Young Prostitutes

It was the application of the law of April 12, 1906, that, under the pretext of protection, best expressed the wish for the moralization of youth and the suppression of prostitution. Indeed, the raising of the age of penal majority from sixteen to eighteen led to the arrest of large numbers of girls for vagabondage and prostitution. For the first year they were sent to the *maisons de correction* of Cadillac and Doullens and to private establishments in Montpellier, Bavilliers near Belfort, Limoges, and Rouen. From the first days of their confinement the young prostitutes showed the utmost exasperation.[69] They did not understand why they were to be kept in custody until they were eighteen, since prostitution was not a crime and many of them had been registered by the authorities. Considering that venal sex was their true profession, most of them refused any apprenticeship to other jobs. "Nous sommes des filles de noce" ("We are good time girls"), they repeated. They had no intention of working and spent their time chatting with their pimps and clients.

It was in this atmosphere of exasperation that the most violent revolts of prostitutes that had ever been seen took place. In all the institutions in which they were confined there were uprisings, and only the prostitutes took part in them. The authorities then decided to concentrate the mutineers in the reformatories at Doullens and Rouen. Scarcely had they arrived at the establishment at Rouen than a revolt broke out; informed before the outbreak of the disturbances, the authorities locked up two groups of these prostitutes in the city prison. *La dépêche de Rouen* reported tumultuous scenes as the girls were being transferred. The first contingent refused to get into the police van. "A policeman who accompanied the van and another policeman on a bicycle were hit in the face; police were bitten and kicked. In the midst of all this the detainees yelled out the filthiest abuse they were capable of."[70] During the journey the women tore their clothes to shreds; some offered themselves to the police. The transfer of the second group was, according to the press, even more dramatic: "Scenes of joy, anger, and despair followed one another in the space of half an hour. Some yelled out abominable songs; another collapsed, her legs folding under her, when she caught sight of the van . . . Drunk with fury, one of the prisoners jumped free, threw herself at a window, and smashed it, yelling abuse; she cut her wrist and refuse to have it bandaged. Another put up a terrific fight; it took four policemen to carry her off."[71]

After a short stay at the Rouen prison, the young rebels were sent to Saint-Lazare, where they immediately fomented another rebellion, which broke out on July 13, 1908. They smashed windows and furniture. A group of mutineers had to be transferred to Fresnes. Clemenceau, who came in person to supervise the precautions being taken to prevent a repetition of such scenes, was received with obscene gestures.[72]

Until the new penitentiary colony of Clermont d'Oise was finished, the authorities did not know what to do with the rebels; they were constantly moved from one institution to another in the hope that this would prevent them from organizing disturbances: "Traveling rebellion is being put on show."[73] In the autumn those who had been transferred to Clermont were the cause of new incidents. On October 7, after mutinying and trying to escape along the platforms of the Gare du Nord, the women got off the train, bodices open. Then, *L'eclair* reports,[74] they lifted up their skirts, exposed their bellies, and attracted passers-by with their shouts. On January 14, 1909, after a new mutiny a group of the detainees had to be transferred to the prison of Bonne-Nouvelle; throughout the journey they continually sang the "Internationale."

8. The Twentieth Century: The New Economy of Bodies

To write the history of venal sex under the Third Republic, from 1871 to 1914, is to retrace the slow, partial breakdown of the carceral procedures set up during the first part of the century. Gradually, prostitution ceased to be the seminal drain intended by the likes of St. Augustine and Parent-Duchâtelet. As a result of an evolution in socioeconomic structures, the male sexual sensibility was evolving; demand was being transformed; and the spread of the notion of the bourgeois home, the reduction of certain forms of sexual privation, and the social displacement of frustration meant that sexual relations now tended to become imbued with feelings. Turning to a prostitute was felt more and more to be a last resort, and during such encounters men would try to satisfy the deep need for fully relational sexuality that was developing in urban society; in relations with prostitutes, too, the erotic was gaining ground over the genital.

This was perceptible at every social level, as can be seen in the growth in procuring in drinking places frequented by workers and soldiers, the increase in unregistered mobile prostitution at the expense of the brothel, the enthusiasm felt by young men for *filles de brasserie* and *café-concert* singers, and the growth of venal adultery in the *maisons de rendez-vous;* the redemptive theme that was then appearing in literature was also an expression of this evolution.

It is understandable, then, that the stereotype of the prostitute should be breaking down and that the studies inspired by Parent-Duchâtelet seemed, by 1900, unrealizable, even pitiful projects. By the same token, the portrait of the bourgeois wife was also blurring as it became apparent that the models of the prostitute and the "honest woman" were defined in terms of one another and that the existence of a stereotyped prostitute had made it possible to exorcise pleasure within the legal couple. Women ceased to be angels or devils. The decline of medical discourse concerning the specificity of female nature is further evidence of this change; the destiny of Madame Bovary, a metamorphosis of the *petite bourgeoise* into a woman who tries to assume her sexual impulses, was exemplary and further spread anxiety.

The fear of confusion and the anxiety caused by the breakdown of such barriers were sharpened by the intense propaganda that tended to install the prostitute at the heart of the tragedy of this time. A synthesis of the scourges on which biological fear was focused, the venereal, alcoholic, consumptive, degenerate prostitute appeared to be the symbol of all the threats facing society.

A new calculus of transparency now seemed necessary; it was to find its place in an outlook inspired by eugenism. In it we may witness the development, followed by the triumph, of neoregulationism. The purpose of this system was to resolve the fundamental contradiction posed by the existence of prostitution. As a technology of sexual "drainage," and insofar as it fulfilled a socially orthopedic role, it helped to maintain the bourgeois home and to encourage the proletarian to exploit his capacity for labor. But at the same time, it represented a threat to health and, therefore, to the nation's ability to produce and to defend itself. It must, therefore, be maintained, but it must also be made clean.

The *maison de tolérance* corresponded to a stage in hygienist thinking dominated by the conviction that it was possible to avoid biological and moral contagion by separation. At the end of the nineteenth century it had become clear that this was not so and that it would be better to devise new techniques of surveillance. Neoregulationism may be regarded, then, as the supreme attempt to exert selection, normalization, and power over those involved in prostitution, in the name of hygiene.

The shift from enclosure to surveillance can also be found in the strategies adopted by employers. The regulated *maison de tolérance* could, from this point of view, be regarded as the manifestation both of a will to set people to work and of a shutting away of the prostitute that corresponds to that found in the organization of workshop-homes for girls. Yet the growth of neoregulationism also brought about a new strategy characterized by the search for the transparency of behavior achieved through hygienic supervision.

When the First World War broke out, little remained of the initial regulationist system and its innumerable confinements. The "disenclosure" of prostitutes was becoming a reality: most of them could now sell themselves and get treatment without being locked up. The dikes that had held back vice were partially breached; the proliferation of the *maison de rendez-vous* and the relative freedom allowed the women who frequented it are also evidence of the spread of prostitutional behavior throughout society as a whole. Neoregulationism triumphed in public opinion; the skillful exploitation of the fear aroused by venereal disease, the white slave trade, and all the threats to the vigor of the race allowed the medical profession to overcome the liberalizing intentions of abolitionism. The health check was both strengthened and extended; by this means the authorities were able to observe those prostitutes who had hitherto escaped their attention. The recognition of the *maisons de rendez-vous* now made it possible to exercise a discreet but effective supervision of those establishments. This victory of surveillance became part of the moralizing offensive that also found expression, in the years prior to the war, in the concern with organizing soldiers' leisure time and in a determination to combat licentiousness in the streets and halt the growth in drinking places and the spread of drugs and pornography.

This evolution, the implementation and ultimate victory of the new strategies, was carried out outside political decisions and without the legislative silence being broken. This is hardly surprising. Government uncertainty and inaction rested on a profound sense of disarray that sprang from the very contradictions at the heart of prostitution. Indispensable to the preservation of the virginity of young women and the fidelity of wives, a bastion against the threat represented by bachelors, in short, the means of diverting the drives created by sexual privation, venal sex, by facilitating late marriages, retarded plans to expand the population and flouted the rules of conduct acquired by young bourgeois males from the somatic culture of their class.

In any case, the anxiety aroused by the possible liberation of female sexuality had been exorcised; a concern for promoting social hygiene had made it possible to maintain the marginalization of the prostitute. Psychology and anthropology placed debauchery outside the field of normality; eroticism remained a specialty, a commercial object. The Salome of the salons may make Herod her slave and hold aloft the head of John the Baptist, but such women remained under the supervision of the prefect of police.

The work that I projected in my preface is now complete, but during the period of its writing a major development occurred that I could not ignore, namely, the prostitutes' movement, manifested in the occupation of churches. It is incumbent on a specialist in the past to try to discover the roots of this event. The discussion that follows makes no claim to rival sociological studies based on a thorough knowledge of the environment, still less the accounts of their lives that have been published by prostitutes. What I shall try to do in this brief final section is to put contemporary events in a historical context, to throw some light on their genesis, to distinguish between what is really new and what is rooted in the past, to point out the major facts affecting the more recent history of prostitution. Unfortunately there are no archives for studying this period, so I shall have to be content with published sources, firsthand testimony that is difficult to assess, often-sketchy studies, unestablished hypotheses, even stereotypes that later research will be led to correct and perhaps disprove. So it is with some anxiety that a historian of the nineteenth century leaves the firm ground of the past for the shifting sands of the present.[1]

The Age of Sanitarism: 1914–1960

The Good Times of the War

The First World War interrupted the evolution of prostitutional structures that had been in existence for close to fifty years. The conflict gave rise to an increase in sexual privation. The imminence of danger sharpened the wish to enjoy the moment; the daily presence of death led men to abandon all concern about disease and lifted the prohibitions that, in civilian life, surrounded inadmissible expenditure. The relative anonymity of the soldier in relation to his background and the constant change of scene imposed on him also encouraged a recourse to venal sex.[2] Moreover, observers agree that this period saw an increase in the number of part-time prostitutes; the hardship felt by many widows and wives left alone, who now had to meet the expense of supporting a family, is enough to explain a phenomenon that enforced abstinence must have helped exacerbate.

The aggravation of sexual privation and the authority conferred on the army for the duration of the war brought to a speedy, if temporary, end the process of enclosure and gave a new lease on life to the *maison de tolérance*. The example of Paris[3] will make it possible to discern the stages in this process, which ran counter to previous developments and which, we must recognize, did not emerge immediately. Mobilization created tremendous anxiety among the prostitutes, who feared that they might be expelled from Paris and sent, as in 1870, to work camps. This anxiety and a wish to be closer to their army clientele caused, in the summer of 1914, an exodus to the provinces; this movement principally involved the unregistered prostitutes, who almost disappeared from the streets of Paris. The German advance accelerated the flight to the south and southwest. Three-quarters of the brothels in the capital shut their doors, while the others continued to operate with reduced staff; the health dispensary saw a sharp decline in the number of visits.

The victory of the Marne brought many of the women back to the capital; by the end of autumn a large number of the brothels had reopened, despite competition from new brothels opened near the front. In 1915 the introduction of leave, the increase in time off for convalescence, and the arrival of the Allies introduced a period of prosperity for prostitution, especially for enclosed prostitution. A change had occurred in the geography of prostitution in Paris, as the statistics on arrests[4] show: the areas around the railway stations had become the centers of intensest activity, and the tenth arrondissement, which, before the war, had ranked fourth, now rose to the top, and by a wide margin.

Between 1916 and the signing of the armistice, new brothels were set up, while others were turned into deluxe establishments. Some opened branches; several keepers organized English lessons for their inmates. "Men write from the front to book a particular woman for their next leave."[5] The German advance of 1918 changed nothing; the *maisons de tolérance,* with all their lights out, continued to function long after the cafés and restaurants had closed; some even had air raid shelters.

It is understandable, then, that repression should also have increased, especially since the first years of the conflict were marked by a revival of venereal disease. The new policy was expressed at first by extra efforts to track down the unregistered prostitutes. From the beginning of the war, the military authorities had set about removing from the front all prostitutes who were not natives of the region in which the fighting was taking place. Surveillance of the areas around railway stations, hospitals, and barracks was increased.[6] A new commission was formed, on November 18, 1916, with a view to studying ways of countering venereal disease. On December 27 penalties for procuring were increased; the law of October 1, 1917, forbade the employment of prostitutes in drinking places.

Medical surveillance was also increased; the inmates of the Paris brothels now had health checks twice a week; soldiers were examined every two weeks, and in additional surprise inspections; furthermore, men on leave appeared before the medical officer on their departure and their return. Patients were placed in venereological centers near the front, so that their illness would not stop them from taking part in battle. Furthermore, attempts were made to provide the soldier with medical information and to promote his moralization. "Acceptance of continence doubles one's strength against the enemy"[7] was more than ever the rule of the day: it was necessary "during both the nervous hours preceding the sublime preparation for combat and the long, healthy repose that follows it."[8] Very revealing, in this respect, are the numerous directives from the undersecretary of state, Justin Godart. An abundant literature linked the war and morality.[9] Despite the expansion of enclosed prostitution, which they refused to accept, the abolitionists congratulated themselves[10] on a policy that vaunted the repression of sexual interests and organized the medical surveillance of the men. If we are to believe Professor Gaucher, whose analyses of the time display great perspicacity,[11] this policy proved ineffective with older soldiers but had considerable influence over the behavior of the young recruits.

The prosperity of the brothels, which continued during the year following the cessation of hostilities, was brought to a sudden end by the postwar economic crisis. This brought with it the disappearance of a large number of *maisons de tolérance,* which were turned into hotels and offices. Prefect of Police Morain decided that the authorities should give no further permission to open brothels; some landlords used the immorality clause to get rid of certain brothel-keepers as tenants. In short, the decline of enclosed prostitution, temporarily interrupted by the war, was confirmed; by 1920 no more than thirty real *maisons de tolérance* were left.

Taylorized Prostitution and the Prophylactic Brothel: 1919–1939

As in the years after the defeat of 1871, there were many witnesses who, after victory, denounced the spread of "semiprostitution";[12] it was a repetitive discourse that deplored the liberalization of morals and the rise of women's role in society. These new "liberated" women frequented cafés alone, drank cocktails, spent their evenings in the dance hall, drove their own cars, and flaunted themselves, as single women, on the fashionable beaches. The extension of pleasure and the practice of the English five-day week helped to propagate such behavior. In the world of love, the partner had replaced the "sister soul."[13] Beyond the moralizing campaign of the years prior to the war, the "crazy years" echoed the Belle Epoque. The daring of Victor Margueritte's novel *La garçonne (The bachelor girl)* terrified the public. Was not Juliette Romanet demanding the opening of establishments in which women could satisfy their desires and instincts?[14] For the heirs of Maxime du Camp a reign of confusion was beginning: "Prostitution is no longer confined to the bottom end of society and its oil stain is spreading upwards," Dr. Léon Bizard was to write. "Which is the marquise, the wife of the immensely rich industrialist, or simply the woman of easy virtue? What an embarrassing question and what a difficult problem to solve."[15]

The places and techniques of soliciting were changing, however. The war had destroyed the old structures of the "milieu"; the transformation of the city itself did the rest. In Paris, the disappearance of the old fortifications and the growth of the suburbs put an end to a whole prostitutional folklore; the *fille des remparts* and the *pierreuse* were disappearing; the *apache,* or Parisian tough, did not survive his time in the trenches. The decline of the music halls, whose promenades had been their stalking grounds, forced the prostitutes to change their tactics. The number of cinemas was expanding, but they did not lend themselves to soliciting. Other changes, however, did favor their activities: the larger cafés now accepted unaccompanied women; fashionable bars, tea shops, and hotel lounges took the place of the music hall promenades; the *entraîneuses* (dance hall hostesses) supplanted the *verseuses* (barmaids).

Women no longer hesitated to solicit openly in the streets; for Parisian prostitution the years around 1925 saw a promotion of the sidewalk and an increase in "ces dames de la Madeleine,"[16] those aristocrats of the street who operated only at certain times and were already accepting personal checks. At about the same time, the practice of soliciting from cars made its appearance.[17] On the eve of the Second World War, practices that were to be premonitory of the future began to appear: certain women offered themselves openly in advertisements, while a number of "middle" women were already fixing up appointments by telephone,[18] proof that the call girl was not just a borrowing from the American way of life.

The traditional *maison de tolérance,* with its closed shutters and large house number, which had found a new lease on life during the war, continued its decline. "The brothel is dying! Soon the brothel will be dead," deplored Bizard[19] in 1935, tolling the bell for an institution that, in fact, was moribund. At that time there were only twenty-seven *tolérances* left in Paris. The fashion for sport and the promotion of the virtues of fresh air could not fail to militate against the *maison close,* to the advantage of establishments that had a right to light and air. The statistics revealed a decline in the numbers of women working in the *maisons de tolérance* and an increase in those working in the *maisons de rendez-vous,* the number of which had reached sixty-five in 1935.[20]

In fact, a fusion was gradually taking place between the two kinds of establishments. The recognition and surveillance of the *maison de rendez-vous* and the partial enfranchisement of the inmates of the *tolérance* more or less implied identity in the long term; during the 1930s this had practically been achieved, at least in the capital. At this time the clientele of the *maisons de rendez-vous* had become "democratized."[21] In the city of Lyons, which has always been in the avant-garde of developments in prostitutional structures, the *maisons de tolérance* in the strict sense had already disappeared for lack of clients; they were replaced by forty *hôtels de passe*, which Dr. Carle had persuaded the authorities to supervise from a sanitary point of view, and thereby recognize.[22] Throughout the country the practice of holding back money to cover debts was disappearing and the weekly day off from work was spreading. Prostitutes enjoyed more freedom; at Lille in the 1920s they had only to pay "rent" to their employer and could keep all the money paid by their clients.[23]

There is nothing surprising in these developments; they merely continued the process that I have presented and confirm that, for the traditional brothel, the game was up by the end of the nineteenth century. It should be noted, however, that many brothels sprang up in small localities that had not previously had one, and this tended to prolong the agony. A careful analysis of the *Guide rose,* the successor to the *Annuaire reirum,* makes this development clear; by an ordinance of January, 8, 1926, the mayor of Pouzin, a small commune in the Ardèche, decided to establish a brothel in his commune.[24]

In Paris five or six of the most expensive brothels survived and, by that very fact, prevented the public from fully realizing what was taking place. Those establishments, which, according to Jean-José Frappa, "are so to speak theaters subsidized by prostitution,"[25] acted as brothel-museums, "in which everything is done," Francis Carco wrote, "to reawaken memories of childhood and of reading for any man who can boast a good education."[26] Where enclosed prostitution was concerned, there had been a long history of innovations intended to attract a rich clientele: thus the *maison-théâtre* of the immediate postwar years, which did not survive for long,[27] and the *maison-dancing* that succeeded it, which was regarded as out-of-date by 1934.

But the real direction of developments is not to be found there. Concentration, rationalization, and standardization characterize the establishments between the wars, and, from this point of view, the new-style *maison d'abattage* showed real evidence of modernity. In these establishments, which represented "modern times" in sex, Taylorized coitus was practiced. Of course the *maisons d'abattage* had existed in the nineteenth century, but, it must be stressed, the activity of the women who frequented them was far inferior to what was now being performed;[28] "conveyor-belt" sex is a creation of our own twentieth century.

The most striking change was an increase in the average number of women employed by these establishments; it rose from about twenty to over fifty. The prostitute who worked in a *maison d'abattage* usually lived elsewhere; she received on average between thirty and fifty clients a day, according to the most reasonable estimates.[29] The keepers, who had their own Amicale, or trade association, had come to consider forty clients a day as normal. In theory, therefore, a *maison d'abattage* could satisfy between 600 and 2,500 individuals a day.[30] The figures for the male visitors were to reach their height in establishments set up for the use of black troops at the outset of the Second World War.[31]

The descriptions of the brothels in the rue de la Charbonnière in the Monjol district, that of the Moulin Galant in the rue de Fourcy, or the *maison d'abattage* in Toulon are so many leitmotifs of prostitutional literature.[32] These establishments functioned between 10 A.M. and 11 P.M. The client entered directly into a bar; there were no seats so that he would not be tempted to hang around. Here order reigned: only non-intoxicating drinks were served; alcohol was prohibited. The gentleman would go to the counter, pay six, eight, or ten francs, and be given a towel and a small piece of soap, which would be taken by the girl, with whom he would stay for a few minutes before making room for the next man. Drunks and minors were refused entrance. The *maison d'abattage* symbolizes better than any previous such establishment the seminal drain imagined by the regulationists in the early nineteenth century.

Progress in hygiene was the other major development in the history of prostitution between the wars; the tendency was toward the prophylactic brothel that was to be set up by the German occupiers and which represented a link in the chain leading to the Eros Centers. This development resulted from the arrival of a new generation of keepers. Younger than their predecessors, they had neither the appearance nor the attitude of the traditional matron and were convinced that only good health and disease prevention could guarantee the survival of their establishments. Between the wars, brothels acquired central heating and hot water; a washroom per room became the rule. Regulationist literature was now nothing but an endless hymn to hygiene; the interest of such works lies more in the ideology that they convey than in the somewhat dubious evidence that they provide. Thus Jean-José Frappa[33] describes almost with pride the inmates who practice physical culture and sunbathe on the terrace, as if replacing infantile clothes with bathing costumes, doing exercises, and exposing oneself to the sun justified the survival of establishments that public opinion had once been determined to close. The new waiting rooms, painted with enamel, with medical cupboards and batteries of injectors on the walls, were reminiscent of clinics. Every establishment had showers, with cloakrooms; in the basement, the staff dining room led, in the very best establishments, to ultramodern kitchens and hairdressing and manicure salons; sometimes the cellar included an air raid shelter. In wartime, the keepers were keen to point out, the establishments could easily be turned into clinics.[34]

There remains the delicate problem of structures. The essential fact is, in this area, the creation of an unofficial Amicale des maîtres et maîtresses d'hôtels meublés de France et des colonies. This group brought together almost all the brothel owners and was to prove capable, on the publication of the Sellier bill, of producing a general assembly of 627 members from France and the colonies out of a total of 1,300. This led to the setting up of a support fund, amounting to 49,472,000 francs, intended to finance an intense propaganda campaign aimed at defeating the government bill.[35] This organization was defensive; in its own way it gave expression to the threats that weighed on prostitutional establishments. It also reflected concentration and standardization, themselves made possible by the systematic exploitation of sexual privation among the proletariat and, more particularly, of the dramatic situation of immigrant workers. All that the Amicale lacked was official recognition; the corporatism of Vichy was to bring it even this.[36]

The period between the two wars lay, as far as prostitutional policy was concerned, in the wake of the triumph of neoregulationism. In this area there was little new thinking. On April 20, 1920, at the instigation of the new minister of health, the commission for preventing venereal diseases was reformed. In 1925 it presented a neoregulationist bill, which, once again, was to lead nowhere.[37] In practice, sanitarism had triumphed, it should be said that the use of more effective medication and the dissemination of Wassermann's discoveries meant that syphilis was no longer regarded as an incurable disease. The number of venereological dispensaries increased considerably: in 1936 they numbered 1,821, not including the 387 departments especially reserved for prostitutes.[38] Medical checks on prostitutes were more thorough and more effective than ever: samples of blood and vaginal fluid were taken regularly; analysis now detected unerringly the presence of venereal disease. Indeed, the improvement in prostitutes' health was proclaimed almost unanimously by the specialists. It was a time of medical triumphalism.[39]

By the same token, the activity of the police seemed increasingly subordinate to that of the doctors, and the movement was toward that sanitary policing advocated by practitioners in the last years of the century. On the eve of the Second World War, Saint-Lazare lost its penitentiary vocation; the delinquent women were transferred to the Petite Roquette. After 1934 the prostitutes were no longer mixed with female criminals.[40] For the rest, police surveillance survived, in markedly similar forms, as is shown unambiguously by the content of an important memorandum from the minister of the interior dated June 1, 1919.[41] Most of the larger cities, however, deprived the police of the right to inflict administrative punishments; abusive soliciting and failure to attend health checks came more and more frequently under the court of summary jurisdiction.[42]

In a more discreet development, but one with a rich future, this period saw the emergence of the determination to exercise a "medico-psychical" surveillance of prostitution. Although Lombroso's theories had already been discredited, and although the thought of his adversary Morasso, who saw the practice of prostitution as a result of an irresistible sexual impulse, had led nowhere, the same cannot be said of the insidious theory of the "potential prostitute." This theory, which derived from the eclecticism of the modern anthropological school of Dr. Vervaerk, tried to combine, in its explanation of the genesis of prostitutional behavior, the influence of heredity with the role of environment, once theorized by Dr. Lacassagne. "A tainted woman from an immoral background is a potential prostitute."[43] This eclecticism received the implicit support of a number of doctors; it inspired the medico-psychical surveillance practiced by the Institut de médecine légale et sociale at Lille.[44] Shortly afterwards, concluding that the prostitute was above all a sadomasochistic neurotic, Dr. Allendy formulated a theory that in turn was to enjoy a long future.[45] Meanwhile, the appearance in France of Havelock Ellis's book on prostitution had scarcely any practical consequences. This book, which is a dense, highly documented synthesis of various works on venal sexuality, avoids the psychiatrizing temptation. It forms a link between Tarde's thinking and that of the avant-garde of the movement that is now activating in favor of a liberated prostitution, even a liberation of women through prostitution.[46]

In the face of triumphant neoregulationism and the survival of the brothel, the abolitionist struggle continued without any real change. Within the Union temporaire contre la prostitution réglementée et la traite des femmes, Professor Gemähling, its president, and Mme. Legrand-Falco, its indefatigable secretary, continued to wage an active propaganda war; the abolitionist literature is immense.[47] More significant in this area was the considerable reaction to certain events. With the support of the autonomists, the movement had found a favorable terrain in Alsace; the brothels were closed down at Haguenau in 1925, at Strasbourg in 1926, and at Mulhouse in 1927. Following a major scandal, the prefect of the Lower Rhine had ordered the closing of fifteen brothels in Strasbourg. On the occasion of a sports event that, from May 30 to June 1, 1925, had brought together in the city 12,000 gymnasts, aged between sixteen and twenty, accompanied by younger boys, the brothels had worked to full capacity; according to the abolitionists, some of the youths had spent three consecutive nights in them. In 1930 the municipalities of Roubaix, Hazebrouck, Sarreguemines, Oyonnax, and above all Grenoble decided in turn to close down their brothels. The experiment made at the central town of the Isère by the mayor, Paul Mistral, under the influence of Dr. Hermite and Charles Richard-Molard, was to serve as a test case;[48] his success was to be referred to at the Liberation by Marthe Richard and her supporters.[49]

The rise to power of the Popular Front raised as much hope among the abolitionists as the election of the Clemenceau government had once done. The new ministry could hardly avoid the problem: policies in favor of closing the brothels had been enacted in 1930 by the radicals and radical-socialists, in 1931 by the Republican Federation of France, and in 1932 at the congress of the Popular Democratic party, and were followed, some years later, by a declaration from the secretary of the Communist parliamentary group in 1937. On November 5, 1936, the government proposed a motion, in the name of the minister of public health, Henri Sellier, clearly inspired by a plan drawn up by the lawyer Le Poittevin. The text was based on work that had been produced several years before by the eminent venereologist Professor Jeanselme, intended to stress the dangers of venereal disease. It revealed the continuing grip of neoabolitionism, a doctrine that tried to combine abolitionist theory with the supposed need for health supervision, just as neoregulationism had tried, fifty years before, to adapt outdated regulationism to scientific discoveries. What this amounted to was that, when adherents of either point of view acceded to positions of responsibility, the supervision of venereal patients came to be regarded as inevitable.

The bill proposed abolishing arbitrary action by public authorities and the police, having recourse to the courts, and making an offense of soliciting. Apart from a few exemptions related to exceptional circumstances, Henri Sellier also proposed shutting down the brothels; nevertheless, the dominant notion behind the bill was that of public health. The bill gave doctors the task of identifying venereal patients, envisaged making an offense of contamination, and tried to make treatment compulsory; if the patient refused, he or she would be "taken to a public hospital establishment."

The bill, which was approved, with serious reservations, by the abolitionists, triggered a veritable panic in the world of prostitution; we know that the Amicale des tenanciers, the brothel-keepers' professional body, was able to prevent its adoption. In his memorandum of December 23, 1936, however, Henri Sellier declared that the opening of new brothels would henceforth be subject to the permission of the ministers of public health and of the interior.

Under cover of the war, the dying Third Republic was to make some attempt to translate into fact the principles that had inspired the bill; it was during the first months of the conflict that, for the first time in France, a legislative measure was to give official approval to the notion of a health authority in relation to the prevention of venereal disease. The decree and law of November 29, 1939,[50] represented, by that very fact, a significant stage in the rise of sanitarism. The law made it compulsory on venereal patients, under penalty of imprisonment, to allow a doctor to warn the health authorities[51] of the patient's condition and made it possible, in certain circumstances, to demand of any individual that he or she provide a medical certificate declaring him or her to be free from venereal disease. These measures tended to strengthen the effectiveness of the work being done by the army medical corps and to facilitate the increased repression being exerted on unregistered prostitution. Thus the first months of the war were marked, at Lyons, by an intensification of the struggle against soliciting and, at Marseilles, by the reorganization of the vice squad.

The Vichy Era: From Toleration to Official Recognition of the Brothel

The taking of almost 2 million prisoners, who enjoyed no leave, the cost of living, and unemployment once again led some women "to engage in prostitution for the duration of the war."[52] Furthermore, the absence of fathers diminished parental authority, permitting young people to give in more easily to the temptation of venal sex. So it is understandable that the matrimonial status of prostitutes was now somewhat altered: never had the proportion of married women and unmarried mothers been so high. Out of 1,900 unregistered prostitutes treated at Lille, 1,142 were married; 758 of them had one or more children; unmarried mothers accounted for 145 of them.[53] The war also brought about a relative decline in enclosed prostitution; the number of women practicing in an establishment was lower in 1945 than in 1939, although the total number of registered prostitutes had increased between those two dates.[54] It should be added that this was the case despite the policy of both the Vichy government and the German authorities to restore enclosed prostitution. It would seem that the influence exerted by the "milieu" on the prostitutes had altered somewhat; it should be said that the black market now represented a better source of profit.

The measures taken by Vichy represented a victory for a neoregulationism favorable to enclosure over the neoabolitionist tendencies previously expressed by the Sellier bill. The policy of the Vichy state combined in an original way a wish to defend the brothel and a determination to apply scientific disease prevention. One finds here the subtle mixture of traditionalism and technocratic modernity that characterized the regime. The policy implemented by Vichy manifested itself in three particular ways.

First, the legislation revealed an undeniable wish to fight the procurers, who were seen as symbols of the immorality that had led to defeat. The law of July 20, 1940—and one should note the speed with which it was passed—increased the penalties on convicted pimps; it was no longer necessary for their activities to be regular for them to face prosecution. Three years later the law of March 12, 1942, widened the definition of the procurer. It now regarded as such anybody who assisted prostitution, who protected the prostitution of others, or who benefited from it, including any individual living with a woman, even her husband, who knew that she engaged in prostitution. Furthermore, the law covered intermediaries and, again, increased penalties.

Second, the policy of the Vichy regime also found expression in a wish to encourage enclosed prostitution. The brothel, which had previously been no more than tolerated, was given official status for the first time; it now enjoyed a theoretical quasimonopoly[55] and was treated like any other kind of business. This amounted to a set of measures that might seem to go against the desire to stop procuring; but one has only to analyze Parent-Duchâtelet's book to understand how regulationist theory, from the beginning, overcame such a contradiction. The Vichy government first tried to establish a uniform set of regulations over the whole of the national territory. On December 24, 1940, a memorandum and a model decree emanating from the minister of the interior, Peyrouton, were sent to the prefects under the stamp of the Direction de la famille. The document asserted in particular that the *maison de tolérance* must occupy the whole of the building, and that it must contain no bar open to the public or bear any distinctive signs. Yet the keepers were given permission to form limited companies or partnerships. Venal sex, now treated as a business, could be an investment for available capital; by the same token, the profits derived from the business of selling women were officially recognized. Finally, it should be noted that the model decree remained completely silent about the minimum age at which women could prostitute themselves in such a brothel.

The law of December 31, 1941, was to perfect the government's work in regulating the fiscal aspect. The *maisons de tolérance* were now categorized as entertainment establishments of the third degree and taxable as such; the tax revenue was put at the disposal of the communes. The municipalities now had every interest in encouraging the opening of new brothels. As a logical consequence of these measures, the Amicale des tenanciers, after expressing their approval of this move at a meeting held at Lyons on February 18, 1942, was given membership, on April 11 of the same year, in the Comité d'organisation professionelle de l'industrie hôtelière, along with overnight shelters and subsidized homes for the elderly. Corporatism turned out to be the salvation of a once-threatened profession.

Third, and perhaps above all, the Vichy regime was to strengthen sanitary supervision and perfect the work begun during the last years of the Third Republic.[56] In practice, the vice squad doctors admitted that health checks had become more severe since July 1940. The health policy, whose direction was suggested by a memorandum from the minister of health, dated January 14, 1941, found more detailed expression in the law of December 31, 1942,[57] which established an obligation on doctors to report venereal patients to the authorities and to perform compulsory treatment on such patients.[58] Indeed, the law provided for the compulsory hospitalization of recalcitrant patients, a measure that represented the logical culmination of the neoregulationism formulated in the nineteenth century. Furthermore, under penalty of a fine, the doctor had to carry out an epidemiological investigation with a view to identifying the contaminator. Later regulations were to confer a key role on social workers, who would be assigned to patients to bring them back under hospital orders, before the intervention of the prefectural authorities. Under the law of 1942 the question was no longer simply one of setting up a sanitary police but of making doctors themselves, together with social workers, the primary agents of this policing.

The Brothel of Europe

The policy carried out by the Germans under Adolf Hitler, first in the occupied zone, then over the whole of France,[59] differed quite sharply from that in force within the Reich itself.[60] While allowing regulation to survive, the occupying authorities set up a parallel prostitutional system for the use of their own soldiers; the new organization expressed a very keen wish to avoid disease and made a systematic search for the carriers. The Germans were able to enact the most extravagant dreams of the hyperregulationist doctors of the Belle Epoque.

From the earliest days of the Occupation,[61] the Kommandantur, after carrying out meticulous health checks, decided to requisition certain brothels and to reserve them for the use of German troops. In Paris six establishments were assigned to officers (in particular, 12 rue Chabanais, 50 rue Saint-Georges, 39 rue Pasquier, and, for one year, Le Sphynx and 122 rue de Provence) and sixteen to enlisted men. In the Seine-et-Oise all thirty-four brothels were requisitioned; the same was true in the city of Rouen. La Féria in Rennes and in Toulon, after the occupation of the free zone, Le Luxuriant, Les Petits Carreaux, and Le Flamboyant were also reserved for the German troops. The occupying forces were even responsible for reopening establishments at Roubaix.

The brothels intended for the use of the Germans had to be equipped with sanitary equipment of high quality. A picket of nurses usually awaited the client at the door. Those civilians authorized to frequent the establishment had to present an *Ausweis* (identity card); inside, the authorized prices were posted. As he went upstairs, the client was given a visiting card on which were written the first name of his partner and the room number; if he later observed the appearance of venereal symptoms, he had only to hand the card to his medical officer. Since the woman's photograph was to be found in the keeper's album, and all inmates had to remain at least one month in the establishment, it would be difficult for an infected woman to escape detection. It should be added that the use of condoms was compulsory. Finally, the medical supervision of the prostitutes was strengthened; underzealous doctors could be brought before the courts for attempting to sabotage the Wehrmacht.

The German authorities were also keen on keeping a contingent of unregistered prostitutes for their soldiers' use. In Paris 1,200 of them, recruited during raids carried out mainly on part-time prostitutes, were given registration cards and brought under special regulations; any failure to comply could lead to detention in Nanterre prison for up to six months. In the provinces the women ran the risk of being sent to labor camps.[62] On December 16, 1942, when a rumor was current that certain women were intentionally infecting German soldiers, an ordinance issued by the Wehrmacht ruled that a prostitute found guilty of such a crime would be condemned to forced labor. It should be added that five or six hundred women, after signing such a contract, agreed to become prostitutes in foreign countries then under German domination. Some of them had opened bank accounts in Paris that regularly received payments from the occupying authorities.[63] The duality of the regulations seems to have given rise to jealousy; undeniably some prostitutes, thanks to their enemy clientele, managed to lead the good life throughout the Occupation. For their part, the keepers who benefited from the favors of the Kommandantur made considerable profits.[64]

Liberation and the Height of Sanitarism

Most witnesses agree that there was a rise in prostitutional activity after Liberation. The influx of Allied soldiers who ignored orders from their superiors not to frequent the brothels and the return of prisoners of war suddenly increased the clientele and gave rise to "patriotic prostitution."[65] The Liberation also accelerated the process of "disenclosure." The authority of the keepers had been weakened by the fall of the Vichy regime; some of them had been compromised by it, and many of the inmates left the brothels to find a new clientele elsewhere. Finally, the prostitutes seem to have shared the longing for freedom and the wish to escape any form of constraint that characterized this period.[66] Confronted by such a situation, the authorities had recourse to the age-old procedures: the police once again took up their hunt for unregistered prostitutes;[67] they issued blue-colored health booklets to the employees of massage parlors and buff-colored ones to dance-hall hostesses. The army hastened to open brothels inspired by the German model for the use of its troops.[68]

The history of prostitution in the twentieth century is remembered for only one legislative episode, one bound up with the attractive, mysterious figure of a heroine of the First World War. The event should take primacy in our own diachronic perspective. The legislation of 1946 marked a resumption of a logical process. It was the direct heir of Henri Sellier's bill; it marked the death throes of the old enclosed prostitution, as tolerated in the past, and, from this point of view, represented the triumph of neoabolitionism, a near-prohibitionism that had developed between the wars. But all this was merely the epilogue to a movement that had long been under way. The important point was rather that the new legislation confirmed, and in many ways strengthened, the sanitarism that had been developing since the end of the nineteenth century. Taken as a whole, the laws of 1946 must be regarded as a culmination; no sooner had they been passed than the sanitary measures were superseded, criticized, and condemned by the United Nations organization. The setting up of the sanitary and social file represented the last expression of a doctrine that France was to abandon in 1960; the high point of sanitarism brought one period to an end rather than opening up a new one. The real legislative turning point was to occur in 1960.

Several circumstances combined to favor the adoption of the measures of April 1946: the Vichy government's attempt to return to a system of control involving imprisonment sounded the death knell of traditional neoregulationism. The then-dominant view that a rise in the birth rate should be encouraged revived the repopulationist discourse of the early years of the century and quietly encouraged prohibitionism. Most of the medical profession abandoned neoregulationism in favor of a neoabolitionism underpinned by serious sanitary measures.[69] The electoral success of the MRP (Mouvement républicain populaire, a new party of Catholic inspiration, stretching from the center-left to the center-right) and of the parties that had supported the Popular Front governments in the years before the war was enough to make the abandonment of regulation predictable. The collusion of certain brothel-keepers with the enemy provided an excellent additional argument for those who wanted to shut the brothels down; indeed, it was to be the only argument made by Marcel Roclore, introducing the bill to the National Assembly on April 9, 1946. In many ways the new legislation was presented as an attempt at purification. It was preceded by a press campaign that pointed out the collaborationism practiced by many of the members of the Amicale; the scandals that had taken place at 50 rue Saint-Georges and at Marcel Jammet's One Two Two were then made much of. Professor Paul Gamälhing did not hesitate to write that the brothels represented a danger for national defense;[70] Daniel Parker denounced the keepers who had handed over young Frenchwomen to the "lust of the master race."[71] The success of Maxence Van der Meersch's book *Femmes à l'encan,* however, helped to rally public opinion to abolitionism.

The so-called Marthe Richard law was not the work of a single woman; it had been preceded by a number of partial measures. As early as September 7, 1944, Pasteur Vallery-Radot had addressed a letter of abolitionist inspiration to the prefects in which he called for the repeal of the Peyrouton decrees.[72] On February 8, 1945, the minister of reconstruction refused to consider the "reconstruction" of the brothels; nevertheless, the keepers were affected by the taxation of illicit profits made during the war. After December 1944 there was a sharp increase in the number of decrees closing down the brothels; in turn, the departments of Savoie, Ardèche, Moselle, Oise, and the towns of Saint-Brieuc, Lille, Saint-Etienne, and Trouville-Deauville decided to prohibit them. It was in this context that, on December 13, 1945, Marthe Richard demanded, at a meeting of the Paris municipal council, the closing of establishments practicing prostitution. After a very detailed report by Pierre Corval overcame people's final hesitations, the decision of Prefect Luizet to shut down within three months the brothels in the department of the Seine was approved, on December 17, by sixty-nine votes to one. The council refused to follow M. Amiot, who advocated the nationalization of the brothels.

The decision certainly made news, especially abroad; from then on it seemed that the passing of a law was inevitable. The general mobilization of the procurers turned out to be ineffective; the keepers tried to stress the principles of hygiene, to construct a theory by which their establishments could be considered special clinics, and to anticipate the protests of foreign clients, but to no avail.[73] The minister of the interior, the socialist Le Troquer, gave them false hopes by asking, on March 9, 1946, that all administrators suspend measures then being taken to close down the brothels; but this was merely an attempt to harmonize decisions so that the situation would not become chaotic.

When, on April 9, 1946, Marcel Roclore presented the report of the commission for the family, population, and public health, which had been entrusted with the task of examining the bill proposed by Pierre Dominjon, it was met this time not by amusement but by silence. Indeed, no debate took place; the president of the National Assembly declared that the commission had expressed the wish that there would be "no useless discussion."[74] The text of the report brought out the ambiguities of the future law that its authors claimed to be abolitionist, whereas it was quite clearly of prohibitionist inspiration and implicitly advocated maintaining the surveillance of prostitutes.[75]

According to Article 1, "all *maisons de tolérance* are forbidden throughout the national territory"; municipal authorizations would therefore be withdrawn. The time given for this measure to take effect depended on the size of the commune; the closing of such establishments would not give their owners any right to compensation, and the prefects would take over the abandoned premises. The text of Articles 334 and 335 of the penal code were changed; soliciting was now an offense liable to heavy fines and procuring was very severely dealt with. On this matter, the new text closely followed the 1943 act; it affected a man who protected a woman or helped her prostitute herself, as well as one who received income from such a prostitute, acted as an intermediary for her, or lived with her without being able to account for income of his own. The novelty lay in the text of Article 335, which concerned men who "run or manage an establishment of prostitution or who habitually tolerate the presence of one or several prostitutes." Among the sanctions envisaged were withdrawal of license, closing, and prohibition from entering the town or area. If taken literally, the bill adopted on April 9, 1946, was unquestionably prohibitionist. It even went so far as to bring landowners under its jurisdiction; they could be made to pay damages for disturbing the peace in a particular area.

Article 5 asserted, with what was probably unconscious humor, that "the existing registers and files shall be destroyed as a sanitary and social national file is established." Indeed, on April 11, the National Constituent Assembly adopted a motion inviting the government to submit a plan "to combat venereal diseases *and public immorality*" and passed a bill presented by Denis Cordonnier, which seems to me to be crucial. This bill envisaged the establishment of a sanitary and social file of prostitution for the whole of France; it amounted to centralizing information collected on prostitutes, assisting the hold exerted by the "milieu," and above all preventing women from "disappearing." The setting up of the file, which would be confidential only in theory, affecting what, for the prostitutes, had hitherto been the most effective mode of freedom—that is to say, the ability to move about or to merge into the population of a large city and thus move back into society—was the supreme refinement of panoptical procedures.[76]

The application of the first clauses of the laws of April 1946 did not present any serious problem; the closings, followed by sales of the contents, took place without any trouble. The premises of former brothels were turned into student accommodations or into offices for trade union organizations. But, very soon, opposition began to grow again inside parliament itself. The Marthe Richard law was strongly criticized soon after it had taken effect.[77] The reopening of the brothels was now demanded from time to time.[78] Moreover, misapplication of the new legislation gave rise to a number of protests. In 1954 Francine Lefebvre was to cause laughter in the Chamber once more when she declared that the law had been violated. In October 1956, in the name of the Poujardiste group, Deputy Nerzic posed a series of written questions on this subject to the government. In this area traditional political divisions were still inoperative. Indeed, it should be noted that enclosed prostitution still survived overseas in its traditional forms; this was because the deputies regarded it as necessary that governments of the Fourth Republic should refuse to sign the international convention of 1949.

The Golden Age of Surveillance, 1946–1960

Sudden "disenclosure" presented delicate problems of readaptation. Some inmates of brothels, incapable of turning themselves into streetwalkers, preferred to emigrate and went off to fill the brothels of North and sub-Saharan Africa; others went out into the streets and helped to create a new prostitutional folklore. The women who worked in the *maisons d'abattage* managed to impose, on the sidewalk, a ritual fairly close to that which had once reigned in their old establishments. It was also the transposition of the family-style behavior of the *filles de maison* that gave rise to the *chandelles* (candles), prostitutes who would solicit while standing motionless, often outside an *hôtel de passe*.

Of course, the keepers also had to adapt to the new ways, and this led to some bitter conflicts. At first the owners of *hôtels de passe* made substantial profits; indeed, enclosed prostitution, now forbidden, adapted quite naturally to the model of what had been practiced officially at Lyons, for example, between the wars. In other words, the *hôtels de passe* replaced the *maisons de tolérance*. The old keepers then tried to exert their control over this new market; it would seem that they succeeded, after bitter conflicts with the hotel owners, who often had to give up their establishments to newly formed networks. It was during this period that the "court," composed of representatives of the pimps and the hotel owners, supposedly functioned. The purpose of this body, which, it was said, met on the first Wednesday of each month at the back of a café in the rue de Vaugirard, was to regulate the prostitution market and to make sure that the "deontology of the sidewalk"[79] was respected.

There was another result, which the legislator had not foreseen: the closing of the *maisons de tolérance* increased the role of the pimp, who now became an indispensable element in the smooth running of the system controlled by the owners of the *hôtels de passe*. These owners now desperately needed not only touts and procurers but real pimps, who would teach the new code of practice of the "milieu" and who would guarantee that the women behaved as they should.

Otherwise,[80] the legislation of 1946 hardly altered the everyday life of the prostitutes, who were more closely supervised now than ever before.[81] The vocabulary expresses this permanence. Of course, the card had been abolished and replaced by a "medical certificate," a vague copy of the premarital certificate stamped on the day of the medical examination. This did not stop the women talking among themselves of the "card," just as they went on calling the central health file the *sommier* (register). The police always carried out a compulsory health registration of prostitutes charged with soliciting,[82] although some women managed to elude supervision. In 1960, at the time of its abolition, the health file held details of 30,000 prostitutes; at the same date, the police estimated the number of part-time or "unregistered" prostitutes to be in the region of 100,000.

Sanitarism, the culmination of that long movement whose gestation we have followed, was already anachronistic when it was established in its ultimate form in 1946. It could not be maintained for long, and, for the second time, the surveillance and marginalization of the prostitute would have to be based on other arguments. From this point of view, the legislation of 1960 introduced a new period: our own. From now on, it was the struggle against procuring and not the fight against venereal disease that, by a subtle reversal, was to make it possible to keep the prostitute outside common law. I shall now examine these new procedures and the rebellion to which they gave rise.

The Ambiguities of the War against Procuring

The Era of Certainties and Good Conscience

The advent of the Fifth Republic coincided with the official abandonment of the procedures of medical surveillance that had, from the end of the nineteenth century, taken over from traditional regulationism. While prostitution was officially denounced as a social scourge, much like homosexuality, police surveillance was now justified by the need to fight the procurers. Since 1946, soliciting had in fact proved difficult to repress; the courts hesitated to pass the heavy sentences laid down by the law on offenders. On December 23, 1958,[83] in order to assist in the maintenance of order, what had hitherto been an offense became a mere contravention, and the notion of passive soliciting was introduced. "Those whose attitude on the thoroughfare is of such a nature as to provoke debauchery" would be subject to fines of between 300 and 2,000 francs; "a penalty of imprisonment for five days at the most will be imposed for second contraventions." Furthermore, this ordinance extended the definition of the procurer still further;[84] this resulted in depriving the prostitutes of any private life whatsoever.

The convention on the trade in human beings, adopted on December 2, 1949, by the General Assembly of the United Nations, envisaged the abandonment of any discriminatory measure against prostitutes and the abolition of procedures that tended to maintain such prostitutes in their way of life. The existence of the medical and social file had prevented France from adhering to the convention. Since the beginning of decolonization, however, it was becoming easier to harmonize legislation with the United Nations text. Furthermore, the decline in venereal disease and, still more, the fact that prostitutes were no longer regarded as the main agents of contamination,[85] made the sanitarist procedures less and less defensible.

In July 1960[86] parliament authorized the Debré government to ratify the 1949 convention and to take steps against the social scourges; several ordinances were to make it possible to adapt legislation to this dual aim. The medical and social file was abolished and replaced by a medical and social department set up in the offices of the directors of health and population in each department. The new bodies were conceived as centers of reeducation and occupational training, in which social workers would confine themselves to urging prostitutes to take care of their health and rehabilitate themselves. Furthermore, funds were allocated to set up establishments for the moral protection of children.

To destroy the networks without preventing the prostitutes from earning their bread and butter was, in theory, the official policy; the legislation of 1960 was also very harsh on procurers. The measures of 1958 were confirmed: the notion of presumed procuring was introduced; the mere fact of preventing the rehabilitation of a prostitute was now regarded as an offense; the ordinance of November 25, 1960, envisaged at last a more determined struggle against procuring in hotels. As for so-called liberal prostitution, it could now be practiced freely. In fact, the idea of repression had not been abandoned; far from it. The notion of passive soliciting was retained. The police were empowered to prevent scandal and disorder in the public thoroughfare and even, according to the minister of health,[87] to supervise and compulsorily hospitalize prostitutes who infected their clients.

In this area the 1960s were a period of certainties and good conscience. A reading of the major works devoted to French prostitution reveals the consensus that had been achieved among those who, in their various domains, exercised supervision over prostitutes. There could be no better example than the harmony reigning between the convictions of the psychiatrist Dr. Durban,[88] the politician R. A. Vivien,[89] the policeman M. Sicot, the judge M. Sacotte,[90] and the educationist Dr. Le Moal.[91] An analysis of this quintet of male voices clearly shows that, although the ordinances of 1960 represented a major turning point in the area of legislation, those who exercised power over the prostitutes remained mired in backward-looking theories.

The discrepancy that I have detected between the legislation of 1960 and the way in which those responsible for its implementation exposed their ideas at that time on the surveillance of prostitution explains why police practice could so easily depart from the spirit and even the letter of the law and carry on much as it had in the past. From December 1960, the suppression of procuring in hotels intensified; the new legislation allowed an increase in police raids. During the years that followed, the police launched some major operations: in Paris the prostitution intended for North African workers was practically eliminated from the quadrilateral formed by the boulevard de la Chapelle, the boulevard Barbès, the rue Ordener, and the rue Marx-Dormoy;[92] raids were organized against the prostitutes working in the Bois de Boulogne.[93]

The procedure of questioning made it possible to carry out large-scale raids.[94] The repression of passive soliciting meant that more prostitutes were "taken away" than before; the "grande cage de l'Opéra," that is to say, the cells into which the local prostitutes were crowded, functioned more than ever.[95] The number of contraventions was such that the prostitutes often reached the point of wishing for a return to regulation. Each evening police vans would take two hundred prostitutes to the reception center at Saint-Lazare.[96] Since the official abolition of sanitarism, this daily raid was intended to put the women in contact with social workers.

The repressive action culminated in the formation of a new police file for prostitution, which was in fact quite illegal,[97] and the establishment of a veritable zoning system.[98] The persistence of the repressive mentality found expression in a particularly clear way at the level of vocabulary: in the police stations, and even in ministerial offices, the terms used were still those of the old regulationism, a language of exclusion, supposedly borrowed from the offenders,[99] which tended to make prostitution a domain reserved to a group of initiates.

The "milieu" had welcomed the new legislation with some anxiety. In the early days many hotel owners refused to receive prostitutes. That was why, on December 12, 1960, as the result of a call from Jo l'Auvergnat, several hundred prostitutes went to demonstrate before the Palais-Bourbon demanding free use of rooms in the *hôtels de passe*. The events that took place on that day in Algeria and the promptness with which repression was implemented[100] explain why the demonstration had little effect on public awareness. In any case, it was really no more than a false alarm; by the summer of 1961, after taking note of the relative clemency of the courts, the hoteliers resumed their activities. A new modus vivendi was established between the police and the "milieu": the syndicate that had functioned since 1946 was apparently replaced[101] by a more flexible organization whose role was to avoid any conflict with the authorities, to see that the oral instructions of inspectors were respected, and to prevent sick prostitutes from working.

The prostitution of the 1960s was characterized by the continuation of certain forms of behavior and by a balance between activities of a different type. The wealth of analytical vocabulary used by the authors of works of that time devoted to venal sex is reminiscent of the approach of the nineteenth-century regulationists. This vocabulary tends, by its very precision, to codify and solidify a wide range of behavior. In the wake of police and investigators, the general public now began to recognize *chandelles,* the *marcheuses* or *roulantes,* who walked the streets, the *bucoliques,* who operated in the woods and public parks, the *ama-*

zones, who solicited in cars, the *échassières,* who awaited their clients perched on a barstool, or the *caravelles,* who frequented the air terminals and hotels built close to motorways.

The society formed by the pimps preserved its old structures, however. North Africans ruled over "low" prostitution, and "metropolitans" (Corsicans, Marseillais, and Parisians) dominated the rest. Fines, sales, and "repurchases" of women remained current practice. In the evening the pimp still came to get his daily payment; on Sundays he would take his wife off to the country, to his child's nurse, followed by a visit to a restaurant and cinema. With age he would become a *père tranquille* or use his savings to buy a bar, which would allow him to remain in contact with his old acquaintances. The premonitory signs of a profound mutation were, it is true, already perceptible,[102] but observers evidently did not yet realize their significance.

The Rise of Long-Distance Procuring

After the late 1960s the world of prostitution swung into modernity. If we ignore the degree of change that then took place, we cannot understand the movement of 1975. Once again the process was driven by changes in demand.[103] The relative liberalization of morals taking place among youth deprived prostitution of its traditional function of initiation. Prostitutes' clients were now predominantly men between forty and sixty. The publication of the Simon Report dismissed the belief in the existence of a group of psychopathic clients;[104] it soon became clear that, in France,[105] it was occasional clients who provided the prostitutes with a living.

The highly eroticized atmosphere of everyday life and the awareness of a liberalization among youth stimulated the sexual desires of mature men. The growth in the sex industries, expressed first in the increase in the number of sex shops, then in the success of pornographic films and magazines for men, the eruption of eroticism on television, the fashion for works on sexology, and, even more, the permanent visual solicitation, reinforced between 1957 and 1969, by the fashion for miniskirts, leather boots, and bare breasts, all helped to stimulate fantasy. Receptionists, models, "sexy" secretaries, and beauticians for men, whose suggestive politeness often implied soliciting, strengthened the ambient eroticization. These newcomers provided a model of behavior in terms of which the new prostitution took shape; everyday contact with them brought about subtle transitions and facilitated recourse to a new type of *femme galante.*

Prostitution had to provide its mature clients not with a mere outlet for immediate sexual needs but with the promise of "sleeping with their dreams";[106] more than ever before, venal sex acted as a palliative for the frustrations of married men. The client, more difficult to please than formerly, once more demanded the illusion of seduction, especially when his partner belonged to the age group that he considered liberated. The ritual of the "short time," with its conveyor-belt sex, no longer filled new needs. The years 1967–1969 saw the success of the *coeurs compris*.[107] Given the age of the clientele, the activity of the prostitute soon tended to include that of the confidante, the *petite soeur du coeur*.[108] The client felt that need to confide that characterizes our times and expected sympathy and understanding from his partner. Indeed, it seems that a fairly large number of prostitutes appreciate this role, especially since the individual grip exerted over them by the pimp has now been relaxed. Richard-Molard believes that, for some of them, it has even become a real need.[109]

More than ever the future, in this area, lies with the women who distance themselves from the familiar, codified form of prostitution; it belongs to a kind of venality that denies being any such thing, for as soon as it appears as such, prostitution becomes off-putting. As in other sectors of marketing, the product now has to be presented in a constantly changing way.

At the same time, structures are also changing. The repression of hotel owners has given rise to a long-distance procuring[110] that no longer rests on the open relationship of one individual to another. The old-time pimp, who expected his everyday "cut" at the street corner, is disappearing, a reject of industrialization.[111] He has often been replaced by the "guard dog" of a racket organization, who simply waits for young women to appear on the sidewalk, without having to use the combination of seduction and violence that the pimp needed when prostitutional behavior was rarely spontaneous.[112]

Nevertheless, the essential factor is the expansionism of a form of procuring that no longer profits directly from the prostitutional activity itself but which tends to control the places and means indispensable to its exercise; this new kind of procuring is succeeding in inserting the prostitute into a system in which she pays more and more for the services that are indispensable to her. This new economy of bodies is probably the most profound revolution that prostitution has undergone for a century. Controlling the rooms where sex takes place, the studios, the bars, the saunas, even the shops in which the prostitute meets her client has become the key to success. These procedures define a form of procuring tied up with property that tends to become more and more diluted[113] and which no longer involves even opening Eros Centers, on the grounds that they might provoke public opinion and disturb the balance of the system. This mutation would not have happened so rapidly if not for the crisis that hit the "milieu." As we know, ideological upheavals and the advance of the protest movement have disorganized this underground society, with its hitherto very delicately codified rituals. Changes in the nature of the process of procuring are only one aspect of an overall reconstruction that cannot be analyzed here.

The double mutation in the nature of demand and in the structures of procuring has brought profound changes in the appearance and behavior of the women themselves. To begin with, for some years now prostitution brought about by poverty[114] is the only type to have declined, which makes analyses based on the primacy of poverty less and less adequate. Moreover, long-distance procuring allows the prostitute greater freedom in her everyday life and makes it easier for her to look after her children. Even the timetable has altered: the number of hours devoted to prostitutional activity has been reduced. Above all, the new conditions of practice have given rise to long-term ambitions; to become the owner of a studio apartment is now a widely shared aim, and indeed one cleverly used by the procurers. The government's tax policy has had a similar effect, in that it forces the prostitute to handle her own income. As early as 1975, the prostitutes of Lyons estimated that they needed five thousand francs a month to run their business. All this has resulted in a loss of spontaneity and a decline in specific attitudes. The evolution taking place is preparing the ground for the prostitute's social integration and for a real normalization of her activities.

If the complaints of the older members of the "milieu" are to be believed, the young express a wish to free themselves of all the forms of authority that weigh on them. The power of procurers of all kinds is becoming more and more difficult to exercise. Feminist propaganda has even reached prostitutes. The young no longer accept the old ways; it is quite often the woman who now decides how much of her income is to be handed over to her friend or protector;[115] she is motivated less and less by need, more and more by feeling. At Lyons for quite a long time now it has been the prostitutes themselves who have drawn up the regulations and controlled behavior on the sidewalk.[116] This spirit of independence finds expression in hostility toward the abusive client; more and more frequently, prostitutes exercise the luxury of rejecting men whose looks they don't like.[117] All these changes make the general rise in the intellectual level of prostitutes understandable.[118]

For several decades now[119] the call girl has been the very image of the emancipated prostitute. Seldom very young, she lasts longer than the streetwalker; her intellectual level, the nature of her clientele, consisting of a few serious, carefully chosen individuals, her relative autonomy in relation to the "milieu," the fact that she is practicing or claims to be practicing a profession that gives her a certain independence, allow her to work when she feels like it, and, when the time comes, to change her way of life. This explains how she has become the model in terms of which the new face of prostitution has been determined.

The lifting of sexual inhibition among the young, the contraction of future prospects as a result of economic crisis, the lowering of the age of majority, and the growing demand for this kind of woman help explain the recent increase in the number of young *michetonneuses*. To prostitute oneself has, for most, become a voluntary decision; the rejection of factory, office, or shop and the attraction of a life that takes place in a highly eroticized atmosphere[120] have given rise to a fluid, initially intermittent prostitution, but one that tends to become permanent once new needs have been created. It should be added that for some young women venality is seen as a way of expressing one's aggressiveness toward the established order. The practice of prostitution is thus prepared, among a gang of "pals," by a vague sense of venality based on subtle exchanges of services or, quite simply, on gratitude.[121]

These new forms of behavior are facilitated by the links that young prostitutes keep with their roots; they are less marginalized, less guilt-ridden than in the past. Jean Feschet notes that in Marseilles, half of them still live with their parents.[122] The same author reports that more and more teenage girls have become aware that it is possible to combine money with pleasure.[123] This poses the problem that has become crucial today to those concerned with the future of prostitution. It is obvious that true liberation would involve enjoyment without shame with a few clients chosen, if not actually desired, by the prostitute herself. In fact, among the prostitutes, a revolutionary vanguard is trying to integrate pleasure into their activities.

Such an attitude implies the destruction of the taboos imposed by the "milieu," which has always shown the greatest contempt for the woman who actually enjoys sex with her client. To dispossess the prostitute of her own body, to arouse in her a feeling of guilt about the pleasure experienced with clients, to lead her to regard her activity as a form of self-punishment were indispensable to preserving the pimp's profits. Quite naturally, the new face of prostitution acts as a challenge to such traditional attitudes;[124] sociofantastic aspirations are developing among the women as well as among their clients. The grip of the taboos is such, however, that no sudden change can be expected.[125]

The Occupation of the Churches and the Movement of 1975

It is obvious that the upheavals that I have described have created new hopes and ambitions, as well as new forms of hitherto unknown anxiety for the prostitutes. It is this that lies behind the prostitutes' movement in 1975 to occupy churches. This action had many roots. The revolt of the prostitutes was above all a protest against increased repression and against the threat of a return to earlier prison practices. It also expressed a rejection of the prostitutional structures that were emerging; in this sense, it was a backward-looking reaction that fed on the anxiety raised by the conviction that changes were taking place without the prostitutes themselves being consulted. Perhaps above all the movement manifested a wish on the part of the women to be heard. It did not express a truly revolutionary project, however, but this has already been made abundantly clear.[126] The militant women of 1975 formulated what were above all immediate claims; they wanted to arrange the practice of prostitution differently and, in the longer term, to be given status as prostitutes. The movement resulted from a wish for the institutionalization and integration of venal sex in the established social system. It cannot be denied, however, that the revolt also expressed a deep wish to establish new relations with the population and to change the way in which prostitutes are seen. As for the intervention of the pimps, which had been spoken of by the minister of the interior, this remained problematic; it was as if the "milieu" had allowed a movement to develop that had originated outside itself.

The prelude to the affair is well known. The wish of Jean Lecanuet, the Garde des Sceaux, to implement legislation that had so far never been implemented was soon to demonstrate that the struggle against procuring would culminate in preventing the free practice of prostitution. Events were soon to expose the ambiguities of this policy, since it could express equally well a wish to free the prostitute from controls in order to allow her to act freely, and a wish to fight the very existence of prostitution. Although prostitution may not be a legal offense, it is still regarded as a social scourge.

At Lyons, repression intensified from 1973 on.[127] The police, acting with all the more keenness in that they had been dragged through the mud, called systematically on the *hôtels de passe,* stepped up questioning for passive soliciting, and treated the women themselves with increased brutality. The fines levied by the police became exorbitant (according to the prostitutes, they amounted to between 320 and 1,280 francs every two weeks). This new attitude, which reached Paris and the other provincial cities the following year,[128] forced the prostitutes to work in their own premises, in studios. Despite the acquisition of dogs and the use of tear gas, they no longer enjoyed the same conditions of security as in the past, especially since they were forbidden to work together in the same apartment.

On May 15, 1974, the discovery, in the Lyons suburbs, of the corpse of Chantal Rivier, a twenty-five-year-old prostitute who had been tortured before being murdered, brought the scandal to light; it was the fourth crime committed against prostitutes in under a year in the region. At Lyons and in Paris the prostitutes organized, supported by a few lawyers, several journalists, and the militants of *Le nid*. A catalogue of claims was drawn up; in June an initial collective text demanded measures intended to provide real security. In September a group of prostitutes, tired of the victimization to which they had been subjected, broke the windows of the police van in which they were being taken to a reception center, smashed the crockery in the refectory, and overturned the furniture, shouting, "Saint-Lazare! Prison!" In this way their actions were reminiscent of the archaic gestures of the rebels in the early years of the century. In order to prepare their defense, the women formed themselves into an action committee and their lawyers into a collective; in fact, the affair fizzled out, since the judge dismissed the case sine die. In November two requests were addressed to the procurator of the Republic in order to stop the victimization; this action effectively brought to an end the use of Saint-Lazare as a reception center.

In early spring 1975 the agitation sprang up again. It was known that a law was being prepared that would sharpen the battle against procuring. Above all, the authorities were applying for the first time the article that established imprisonment as the penalty for prostitutes convicted a second time of soliciting. At Lyons the repression was so severe that the very exercise of prostitution seemed to be brought into question. At the same time, a new tax policy was adopted; prostitution, now regarded as a source of noncommercial income, came under Article 92 of the general code on taxation. By the same token, several prostitutes found that they were liable for tax arrears covering the four previous years.

On April 29, Ulla, the spokeswoman of the Lyonnais prostitutes, took part in the television program "Les dossiers de l'écran." Her fellow prostitutes demanded, she said, the right to think for themselves and to decide their own fate. The following month the prostitutes in Montpellier wrote to Simone Veil, and the militant prostitutes of Lyons, centered around *Le nid,* asked for an audience with the Garde des Sceaux, in order to explain to him the circumstances under which they had to work.

The announcement of the first imprisonments triggered off the movement that now, for these prostitutes, represented a turning point. On Monday, June 2, the Lyonnais prostitutes decided to occupy not Saint John's Cathedral but the parish church of Saint-Nizier, where the priest, Father Béal, turned out to be cooperative. For one week a community was established inside the building, while new relations were forged with the population; during long discussions that took place in the church square, the women tried, often successfully, to change the attitude of the people of Lyons. Journalists arrived from all over the world. Mayor Pradel agreed to a meeting; the archbishop, Monsignor Renard, received Ulla in secret. Meanwhile, the rebels of Saint-Nizier addressed a written message to the public and a letter to the president of the Republic.

The movement spread. Prostitutes from Montpellier, Saint-Etienne, and Grenoble, as well as a delegation from Paris, met at Saint-Nizier. Churches were occupied at Marseilles, Grenoble, and Montpellier. There were strikes at Toulouse, Caen, Nice, and Saint-Etienne. On Sunday, June 8, a group of Parisian prostitutes invaded the chapel of Saint-Bernard at Montparnasse; the minister of the interior, Michel Poniatowski, decided to have them removed. On Tuesday, June 10, at 5:30 A.M., the police burst into the churches. At Saint-Nizier force was used. Ulla and another prostitute, Barbara, were roughly treated. At Saint-Denis de Montpellier, by contrast, the expulsion was carried out peacefully.

The movement was not crushed. On June 30, at the Lyons Labor Exchange, the Estates General of Prostitution were held. The meeting brought together three hundred women who had come from Saint-Etienne, Grenoble, Marseilles, and Paris, and 1,500 sympathizers. A majority of the militants demanded that the movement take on a political character and be guided by revolutionary principles. At this point a misunderstanding was revealed between the women and those who supported them; it was to grow worse. The only concrete decision to arise out of the meeting was that a demonstration would be organized in the park of the Château de Chanonat, the property of the president of the Republic.

On August 23 at 3 A.M., in several towns throughout the country, prostitutes daubed slogans on the front of pornographic cinemas and sex shops. What Jean Bernard calls "the purifying action of the prostitutes of France"[129] merely linked up with the most traditional regulationism, which understood prostitution to be the only healthy, normal outlet for unsatisfied sexual needs.

The movement culminated[130] on November 18, with the holding of a national conference in Paris, in the Salle de la Mutualité. In fact, the meeting was a failure. Pasolini's film *Accatone,* which was shown, reflected an outdated situation. The status of stardom assumed by Ulla, who appeared in a low-cut dress, offended many of the prostitutes present.[131] Amid all the confusion the women were presented with a heteroclite series of speakers, many of whom seem to have come only to give vent to personal preoccupations. After such outpourings it soon became evident that the misunderstandings could not be overcome.

The avowed aims of the prostitutes were to be allowed to practice in dignity and safety an activity that hurt nobody, and at some later date to see it given official status. The notion of passive soliciting struck them as completely out of date at a time of sex shops and hard-core pornography. They demanded an end to the disdain, insults, and rough treatment handed out to them by the police. The women insisted on the right to practice in hotels of their choice, but categorically rejected the setting up of specific establishments in which they would be relegated to the status of workers specializing in sex. They denounced the legislation that, under the pretext of fighting procuring, prevented them from renting or buying apartments. They demanded the freedom to work together in the same premises, in order to guarantee their safety, and protested against tax demands. The rebellious prostitutes called for the right to a private life: "The situation in which we are put," one of them said, "prevents us from having our own bodies."[132] Thus they demanded the abolition of the article in the code that defined any individual living with a prostitute as, ipso facto, a pimp.

The militant women who lived through this movement known as "the churches" were struggling to emerge from the ghetto of contempt and pity in which they felt they had been enclosed by a society that regarded them as unclean while demanding that they be clean.[133] What they really wanted, it seems, was no longer to be regarded any differently from other women, not to have to put on two faces in the course of a day, not to have to be afraid when children looked at them. Only such a liberation, certain of the militants claimed, would allow the prostitute to be fully human, to show herself to be available to her clientele, and to be able to admit without shame, when the time came, the nature of her activities to her own children.

For the rest, the prostitutes questioned agreed that certain forms of procuring should continue. They had been asking since 1975 to benefit from Social Security, family allowances, and old-age pensions. They drew up a proposed statute that they would present to Councillor Guy Pinot. "I believe that prostitutes have the most peaceful, most harmless dreams imaginable: a home, children, peace, and comfort . . . My dream is that my daughter should have a white wedding, as a virgin," one of the Lyons prostitutes was to say.[134] Even if it is true that she was not speaking for all prostitutes, one can understand the hesitation of the revolutionaries who had supported the movement initially.

The movement ended in failure: it was unable to prevent the passing of the law of July 11, 1975, which, in particular, made it possible for prostitutes working in the same apartment to be found guilty of mutual procuring. After that date a few initiatives were carried out: on December 11 a regional conference on prostitution was held at Marseilles; on May 15, 1976, the prostitutes of Lyons addressed an open letter to the president of the Republic, asking him to present the Pinot Report to the Council of Ministers. Thereafter nothing more was done. Why? A number of arguments were brought to bear to convince public opinion that the affair was best forgotten. Between the theory of manipulation by pimps, presented by Michel Poniatowski, and declarations that the movement had chosen the wrong target or had been penetrated by Poujadism, a sort of consensus had grown up justifying an abandonment of the whole question. The most subtle of censorships, the complaint "We've heard enough about that!" seems to have come into play. The police cleverly aroused the hostility of law-abiding prostitutes for the "troublemakers" by maintaining that the latter were responsible for the new repressive policy. It is clear that the silence of Françoise Giroud, then minister for the condition of women, and to an even larger extent the results of an opinion poll carried out on June 7, 1975, showing that a majority of public opinion was in favor of regulation, put an end to all hope of change.[135]

All in all, the essential contribution of the movement seems to me to be the emergence of a new discourse. Anne Salva,[136] Michèle,[137] Marie-Thérèse, Xavière, and Jeanne Cordelier, Ulla, Chantal, Barbara, and the prostitutes interviewed by Claude Jaget and Judith Belladona[138] have told their stories over and over again; confessions, memoirs, and demands have nourished a proliferating discourse whose richness would make any attempt to analyze its content a distortion.[139] It is a discourse from the inside, the emergence of a mentality and behavior that had previously been concealed and which the admissions dragged out of the women by doctors and psychologists had not revealed. What had hitherto been private was now exposed in a continuing process of unburdening, just as the disorganization of the prostitutional "milieu" was lifting tacit forms of censorship. The prostitute began to tell her own story, explain her own point of view, and in doing so challenged the notion of sexual privation; the theme of the perspicacity of the prostitute, who had become the unmasker of our society, cropped up in most commentaries.

I shall merely point out two aspects of this new saga of prostitution: most of the old stereotypes (a sense of modesty, frigidity, the frequency of homosexuality, meanness with money, love of children, the "romantic" side) have, for the most part, been confirmed, and sex has been demythified. Several of the life stories suggest that a time of hope and ambition has arrived. Prostitution no longer appears to be simply a dead end, the way of death; it is even seen sometimes as a way of getting on in society.[140]

Professionalism, or Women Crazy about Their Bodies

Among those who are striving to work for the liberation of prostitution[141] there are two opposing groups, each supporting an antithetical strategy.

Among the leaders there has emerged a temptation to work out a status for prostitution that would give the women real freedom to practice; this policy is close to that demanded by the prostitutes themselves. It was this outlook that guided the writing of the Guy Pinot Report. Given a mission to look into the question of prostitution, this lawyer was regarded as a specialist in dangers to children when Simone Veil presented him to the press on July 23, 1975. A man interested in dialogue, he was to listen for over three hours, on September 30, 1975, to a national delegation of prostitutes that had come to present him with a draft statute. Some weeks later, he was to talk to Barbara and three other women about the lack of any policy concerning prevention and reintegration. After a period of intense work he submitted, at the end of the year, a text that supposedly would have to be studied by the Council of Ministers. We now know that this did not happen.

The Pinot Report is lucid and courageous on more than one account. On the theoretical plane it represents, in a sense, the antithesis of earlier work published by R. A. Vivien. This gives us some idea of how much progress was made, even within the ruling circles of the Fifth Republic, between 1960 and 1975. The investigator refuses absolutely to regard the prostitute and her client as particular human types. He claims that the legislation of 1960 had never really been applied,[142] that army brothels have survived. Furthermore, he shows that measures intended to strike at the pimps have in fact been used as ways of repressing prostitution. A veritable prostitute hunt has become established, and the idea that repression has a dissuasive effect is still widely held. The policy carried out, for example, in places where prostitution is current shows very well that the abolitionist legislation has been interpreted as a set of prohibitionist measures. In such a context the social reintegration of the prostitute, officially advocated, remains extremely problematic.

A series of propositions flows from this analysis: to begin with, Pinot advises abandoning all forms of police repression specifically directed at prostitutes. This involves the repeal of Article R 34-13 of the penal code on passive soliciting and a change in the direction of greater precision in Article R 40-11, concerning active soliciting. He rejects all procedures of incarceration and points out the illegality of zoning.

Furthermore, he advises that the prostitute should be allowed to have a private life and an emotional relationship with the man of her choice; indeed, any other policy has the effect of classifying her among antisocial individuals. In order to achieve this, Pinot proposed that loopholes should be inserted into the legislation concerning procuring. Furthermore, the law should be altered so that the prostitute is able to use premises in which she can carry out her work in dignity. The Pinot Report frankly rejects the opening of brothels and special centers, and indeed any measures that would have the effect of making the prostitute's reentry into normal life more difficult. He approved the women's claims concerning Social Security and advised that they should be granted through measures planned in 1978. (This has since been done.) To refuse to tax prostitutes would be equivalent, according to Pinot, to regarding them once again as creatures apart; he also tended to favor a moderate taxation. He did advise, at least in a transitional stage, against the procedure of summonses and arrests. If a prostitute gives up her work, the tax inspector should grant a generous postponement so that she is not forced to resume prostituting herself in order to pay her taxes. Here the Pinot Report moves firmly away from the opinion of the social services, which is that such a policy might lead to making prostitution an officially recognized occupation.[143] Indeed, it is undeniable that what the judge proposes does implicitly represent recognition of function, at least in a temporary capacity. So it is understandable that the women should have demanded that the report be studied by the Council of Ministers; it is also understandable, given the heterogeneous nature of the majority in parliament, that the president of the Republic should have so far refused this.

The Pinot Report also aroused strong criticism from certain advocates of liberalization.[144] For them the policy that he advocated would lead to integrating the practice of prostitution into the system of capitalist profit, which entails two major risks: (1) encouraging the true proletarianization of the prostitute, who would be reduced to the rank of an unskilled worker in the service of a procurer-employer or procurer-state; and (2) killing the revolutionary potential that the prostitute has within her. An instructor in pleasure, who also teaches a relaxed attitude toward money, she is presented as the model of the woman who rejects norms, who builds up her own means of liberation against the male order[145] or against the capitalist system. The "skilled worker" prostitute, by contrast, would run the risk of losing her desire for prostitution, just as the ordinary working woman loses the taste for work. The Pinot Report tends to turn sexual freedom to profit and not to encourage the permanent search for the pleasure principle;[146] it tends essentially to plan things in such a way as to absorb and control them, the ultimate in diffuse illegality. From this point of view, the urge to protest felt by the women at the level of their own bodies should not be prevented, and the exercise of a prostitution in the process of conquering and presenting itself, refusing to flow into the mold prefabricated by power, should be allowed to continue.

It is understandable that in such a discourse, which obviously belongs to the libertarian tradition, the central problem should be to reconcile the two halves of the prostitutional couple in order that each should be capable of receiving pleasure. A prostitution distanced from its rituals, which seeks to regain pleasure,[147] and which is capable of magnifying the pure violence and beauty of male desire, and not an institutionalized prostitution, integrated into that which has already invaded sight (pornographic cinema) and speech (sexology), leading to a decorporalization of the individual: this is what Judith Belladona, for one, preaches with such lyrical force. So the task now becomes not only to invite the prostitutes to accept their prostitution but also to invest them with an innovative mission, a profoundly revolutionary role in sexual education. Prostitution would no longer be a job but a way of living one's sexuality, a form of debauchery that would link up with a more or less fantastic past before the process of "somatic *dressage*" takes place. In the meantime, the important thing is to keep the prostitute outside the field of wage labor at the service of capital—that is to say, to spare her the most terrible forms of physical appropriation. The notion of redemption is thereby denied, since it is in fact equivalent to throwing the prostitute back into the "social melting-pot" of her "hysteria."[148]

The present debate is expressed, therefore, in simple terms. The problem now is to decide whether, after onanism, masturbation, premarital sexual relations, homosexuality, and the use of contraceptive methods that facilitate pleasure, the social body is ready to accept the free exercise of venal sex, that is, the right to prostitution for women and the freedom of a couple consisting of two human beings who, at a given moment, want a temporary sexual relationship in which money replaces any lasting commitment.

Such an attitude would imply both the strict application of the 1960 legislation and the abandonment of the notion of social scourge that it implies as the legal measures against homosexuality used to imply it. This would also presuppose the abolition of that policing, which, through successive arguments (respect for morality and order, the maintenance of physical and mental health, the struggle against procuring) and endlessly changing laws, represents only one aspect of a vast policing of bodies and pleasure that is giving ground on other fronts.[149] The return of prostitutes to common law would also imply the abolition of the contempt in which they are held and, by the same token, the attenuation and eventual disappearance of the guilt and the mechanisms of self-punishment that it engenders—that is to say, of the masochism that in our society prostitution conceals. The return to the common law would probably involve a straining of the relations that prostitutes have at present with their "milieu," especially as the role of the police would amount to protecting the prostitute against any pressure to continue working when she actually wanted to restructure her life.

If, however, those who exercise social control refuse to allow prostitutes to return to the common law, one can imagine a recourse to the whole gamut of procedures of surveillance, exclusion, and repression, of which history provides abundant examples: enclosure (the "sex clinic"), more or less impregnated with psychological sanitarism, tough surveillance, and loss of a private life under cover of a policy of "redeeming" the prostitutes and combating procuring, or, quite simply, prohibition accompanied by enforced work.

Given the hypothesis of a triumph of the liberal solution, it still remains uncertain whether prostitution would be regarded as a recognized profession, practiced by "hostesses," with the risk of proletarianization that this involves, or as a deliberately chosen form of sexual behavior. Would this be the ultimate form of sexual enslavement or a profound rejection of male domination? A symbol of capitalist alienation or a revolt against the monotony of factory, office, and shop? A temptation to self-destruction or the expression of a wish for an intense life in a highly eroticized atmosphere? The existence of the prostituted person still poses its questions; it has vertiginous implications. Otherwise how can we explain the refusal to discuss it or even to think about it, and the cries of "We've heard enough about it," subsidized perhaps by the procurers, but which come as a secret relief to almost all our political leaders? The issue will probably find a solution only as part of a more general solution to all those acute problems confronting us in the politics of bodies.

Notes

Bibliography

Index

Notes

Source citations in this volume follow the form used in the original French edition.

1. The Regulationist Argument

1. Dr. Parent-Duchâtelet, *De la prostitution dans la ville de Paris considérée sous le rapport de l'hygiène publique, de la morale et de l'administration.*

2. Parent-Duchâtelet's book had an immediate influence. It was in reference to this work and with the avowed aim of completing it with the account of a policeman's experience that A. Béraud published, in 1839, *Les filles publiques de Paris, et la police qui les régit.* It was in the work of Parent-Duchâtelet that Buret, Frégier, and Ducpétiaux found their quantitative data on prostitution. When, between 1839 and 1842, Dr. Potton wrote *De la prostitution et de la syphilis dans les grandes villes, dans la ville de Lyon en particulier,* it was because he was driven by a desire to see Parisian regulationism, so well described by Parent-Duchâtelet, applied in Lyons. Only Alphone Esquiros (*Les vierges folles,* 1844) tried to react against the thinking of the regulationist doctor, by whom, nonetheless, he himself had been inspired.

3. See Louis Chevalier, *Classes laborieuses et classes dangereuses,* pp. 29–31.

4. Béraud, it is true, differs in this respect. He also refuses to deal with *"femmes galantes,* kept women, and courtesans of high degree" (op. cit., I, 18–19). Unlike Dr. Potton, who regards them as identical (op. cit., p. xiv), he recognizes that being a rich man's mistress is different from being an ordinary prostitute (op. cit., I, 47). Such is his obsession with unregistered prostitution and his desire to extend police surveillance, however, that through the proposed by-laws that he draws up at the end of his book, he attempts to define courtesans and kept women of all kinds as prostitutes (op. cit., II, 296–298). He sees this as the only way to guarantee medical surveillance of prostitution, of protecting the fortunes of prodigal sons, and above all of repressing and keeping confined "the immorality that, in public, is an insult to impoverished virtue." Béraud, who adopts a more impassioned and more resolutely moralizing tone than Parent-Duchâtelet, advocates extreme regulationism.

5. This notion of timelessness characterizes even more the histories of prostitution that appeared under Louis-Philippe and during the Second Republic; see

Sabatier, *Histoire de la législation sur les femmes publiques et les lieux de débauche* (1818) and Dufour, *De la prostitution chez tous les peuples* (1852). It is to be found in Béraud (op. cit., I, 9–58), and in Potton (op. cit., pp. 7ff.).

6. Esquiros (op. cit., p. 19) writes, quite wrongly, that Parent-Duchâtelet considered prostitution "a stagnant, perpetual fact, always the same."

7. Almost all the authors agree in recognizing this, including, in 1835, Dr. Guépin (*Nantes au XIXᶜ siècle,* p. 636), though, it is true, with some reservations. Béraud (op. cit., I, 15) also sees prostitution as an indispensable "safeguard of the major part of sex worthy of our respect and homage" (p. 16). For Esquiros (op. cit., pp. 182, 205), prostitution is a necessary if temporary evil; it will disappear when civilization has mastered this sequela of primitive promiscuity. Meanwhile, prostitutes should be brought into "the general order of society" by subjecting them to a temporary regulationism.

8. Op. cit., II, 513.

9. Ibid., p. 512.

10. See, on this matter, the arguments of Louis Chevalier, op. cit., p. 30.

11. The regulationists refer tirelessly to the thought of Saint Augustine: "Abolish the prostitutes and the passions will overthrow the world; give them the rank of honest women and infamy and dishonor will blacken the universe" (*De ordine* 2.4.12).

12. Op. cit., II, 41.

13. Unlike the socialists (see Chapter 5), he never questioned the bourgeois marital model in the course of his reflections on the genesis of prostitutional behavior.

14. As the publishers emphasize (op. cit., I, 3), "M. Béraud's principal aim is the abolition of unregistered prostitution." Potton (op. cit., p. 38), for his part, regards the unregistered prostitute as a hundred times more dangerous than the registered one. Frégier (*Des classes dangereuses de la population dans les grandes villes et des moyens de les rendre meileures,* 1840, I, 153–154) shares Béraud's regulationist optimism and holds that unregistered prostitution should be eliminated.

15. Op. cit., II, 14.

16. Indeed, the success of Louis Chevalier's fine work runs the risk of making us lose sight of this notion. For Frégier it is the combination of poverty and vice within the same individual that makes him dangerous (op. cit., I, 7). Although he does not regard as belonging to the "dangerous classes" individuals "who foment popular sedition" (I, 13), he places the prostitutes, their lovers, and their pimps and keepers among "the dangerous elements of the vicious class" (I, 44). Finally, Frégier deplores the fact that the "idle, erring, and vicious class" (p. 7)—one is reminded here of the *lumpenproletariat*—"with all its unleashed passions" (p. 11) cannot remain the object of statistical analysis and that vice, more than crime, eludes such an analysis (p. ix). The idea of annual statistics for vice (and Frégier seems to be thinking above all of drunkenness) goes beyond the regulationist project but stems from the same obsessions.

17. Op. cit., II, 33.

18. Potton, it is true, places much more emphasis on the venereal danger in his work on prostitution. Nevertheless, at this time public opinion held that syphilis, if as widespread as before, constituted a less serious threat. See Dr. Guépin, op. cit.,

p. 644, and Cullerier, s.v. "syphilis," *Dictionnaire des sciences médicales.* Potton (op. cit., p. 3) criticizes this belief.

19. Op. cit., I, 4.

20. Ibid. As Balzac has Carlos Herrera say to Esther, "since you are, in the police files, a figure outside the world of social beings" (*Splendeurs et misères des courtisanes,* p. 684).

21. These ideas were taken up again by Béraud (op. cit., II, 34). For Esquiros, however (op. cit., p. 69), prostitutes were not excluded from society; they had not yet entered it.

22. Still guided by the reigning organicism, Esquiros writes: "It always becomes dangerous, in the long term, for a society to allow its members to separate from the center: it is these forces, outside, separated off, that in time lead to certain violent, sterile disorders. *There are two natural sisters in the world: prostitution and riot*" (op. cit., p. 201).

23. In 1839, in a somewhat academic way, Béraud tried to complete, for his own purposes, Parent-Duchâtelet's categorization (op. cit., I, 54–91).

24. Op. cit., I, 153.

25. Op. cit., I, 180.

26. Although Béraud remarks that he was wrong to confuse *filles d'amour,* apprentices admitted without any payment by the keepers, with *filles en numéro,* who received part of the payment made by the client (op. cit., I, 57–60).

27. Op. cit., I, 188.

28. "Debauchery," Béraud writes, "is a fever of the senses carried to the point of delirium; it leads to prostitution (or to early death) without being as debasing or as incurable as it" (op. cit., I, 42).

29. A subject that Béraud refrains from mentioning because he was writing for the general public.

30. Op. cit., I, 90.

31. Ibid., I, 95.

32. Ibid., I, 94.

33. We know that the philanthropists and empirical sociologists of this time accorded much importance to the influence of the environment. On the subject of prostitution Guépin wrote in 1835: "We call upon those who draw up statistics to provide information on the background and social position of these women, on the circumstances of their upbringing, on the morality of their parents, in a word, on their *environment*" (op. cit., p. 637). According to him, such work ought to be carried out by a "benevolent police force."

34. As an example, poverty is recognized as a cause of prostitution by E. Buret (*De la misère des classes laborieuses en Angleterre et en France,* 1840, II, 251–256), Frégier (op. cit., passim), Potton (op. cit., pp. 7ff.), Ducpétiaux (*De la condition physique et morale des jeunes ouvriers et des moyens de l'améliorer,* 1843, I, 325, 330), and Esquiros (op. cit., p. 30). But this does not stop these same authors from mentioning, in the wake of Parent-Duchâtelet, all the causes stemming from individual temperament. During the second half of the century the discourse on the causes of prostitution would split; one does not again find so exhaustive an analysis of the various processes leading a young woman to prostitute herself.

35. See Béraud (op. cit., II, 36). It was Esquiros, however, who elaborated this

theme at greatest length. His wide knowledge of phrenology and the talks he had
with Broussais led him to a belief that prostitutes remained "in a childhood state"
(op. cit., p. 68). According to him, there was "a class of women who perpetuate
among us the childhood of the human race . . . who have remained . . . in the primitive state of nondevelopment" (op. cit., p. 69). The criminal anthropology of the
latter part of the century (see Chapter 6) was to take up this notion. By the same
token, Esquiros justifies administrative surveillance: "the social age" (op. cit.,
p. 229) of the women means that they are kept not in a state of slavery but in one
of *guardianship* in order to give them the sense of selfhood that, according to Broussais, they lack.

36. See also Esquiros, op. cit., p. 37.

37. The prostitution of young women appeared to many as the equivalent of
vagabondage among young men. "Prostitutes are essentially mobile creatures, who
pass for no good reason from the most sullen mistrust to absolute trust. They are,
in this, below the animal," writes Balzac (*Splendeurs et misères des courtisanes,*
p. 682).

38. A. Daumard, *La bourgeoisie parisienne de 1815 à 1848,* p. 211.

39. Frégier (op. cit., II, 259) calls on the police superintendents to try to persuade the prostitutes to invest their savings in a bank.

40. Op. cit., I, 223.

41. If only through the existence of the *mangeuse,* that is, the friend with whom
the imprisoned prostitute shared her food.

42. "Prostitutes are particularly fond of three things in the world," writes
Esquiros, "the sun, flowers, and their hair" (op. cit., p. 161). This theme was to
enjoy great literary currency.

43. Only Esquiros, an enthusiastic phrenologist, draws a fairly precise stereotype of the prostitute (op. cit., pp. 52ff.). In particular, it contains the following
features: "large, well-shaped breasts; fleshy shoulders, a thick, powerful, Herculean
neck; the whole face lively rather than beautiful; low forehead, flared nostrils; a
large, toothy mouth . . . short, thick, soft hands." According to him, there is a link
between race and a penchant for prostitution; thus "the black woman is naturally a
prostitute" (op. cit., p. 54).

44. Op. cit., I, 279. Similar observations are to be found in Villermé's work.

45. This feature was to be stressed by Balzac (*Splendeurs et misères des courtisanes,*
p. 671), by Victor Hugo (*Les misérables,* p. 265), and by Maupassant (*Le port*).

46. Registration, Frégier writes, prevents the woman who knows that she is
registered and therefore under surveillance to abandon herself to excess (op. cit., I,
155). What haunts him about unregistered prostitution is just "its horrible excess"
(p. 185).

47. This is a fundamental principle of regulationism, as Béraud remarks.
Béraud's recommendation (op. cit., I, 10) is "to confine prostitution" within such
bounds that it can no longer be an affront to decency; in order to achieve this he
wishes to remove all provocation from the public thoroughfare (p. 17) by compulsory confinement of prostitutes to a *maison de tolérance* (p. 178). "The concentration
of organized debauchery is an improvement" for "public decency" and for "the general safety and prosperity of the brothel-keepers. Béraud had been the right-hand
man of Mangin, the prefect of police who, in 1830, had tried, with some success,

to ban prostitutes from public places. "Concentrating vice is the safest guarantee that morality may be given," wrote Potton (op. cit., p. 247). Esquiros thought that concentrating prostitutes in *maisons de tolérance* would encourage their moral progress and allow them to move more easily toward eventual salvation—that is, to marriage.

It is worth noting that Balzac too was an advocate of concentrating vice (see *Splendeurs et misères des courtisanes*, p. 672).

48. See Béraud, op. cit., I, 4. Richard Cobb (*La protestation populaire en France, 1789–1820*, p. 221) remarks that prostitution was the profession about which the police of the period were best informed.

49. "Le panoptisme," in *Surveiller et punir* (Paris, 1975).

50. Whose importance was pointed out by Michel Foucault.

51. Parent-Duchâtelet, op. cit., II, 250.

52. Op. cit., I, 308.

53. Op. cit., I, 292.

54. In his plan for regulation Béraud wrote: "When the windows are open, for the time that is strictly necessary to air the place, the venetian blinds and curtains will be constantly closed. These curtains will be of a thick, dark material" (op. cit., II, 161).

55. Op. cit., I, 429–430.

56. Ibid., I, 292. The increase in the number of *maisons de tolérance* was demanded by all the regulationists. See Béraud, op. cit., I, 184–185, and Potton, op. cit., p. 251.

57. Op. cit., II, 49.

58. Guépin (op. cit., p. 642) thought that "only moral regeneration" would put an end to syphilis. Frégier (op. cit., II, 256) believed that only doctors and police officers could reclaim prostitutes; he proposed that the authorities should urge doctors to dispense moral advice.

59. Op. cit., II, 86.

60. It should be noted, because they have often been criticized, quite wrongly, for it, that the regulationists of the July Monarchy did not regard venereal disease as a just punishment; on the contrary, using as their argument the large number of innocent victims, they welcomed the abandonment of corporal punishment and demanded a humanization of treatment (see Béraud, op. cit., II, 59).

61. Op. cit., II, 495. Béraud sets out at length to show that "arbitrariness is indispensable" (op. cit., II, 24ff.).

62. Op. cit., II, 261.

63. Esquiros comes out strongly against this form of reformation (op. cit., p. 193). According to him, the prostitutes should be brought under common law (p. 205); they should no longer be treated with contempt but should be treated as women and grouped together in reformed *maisons de tolérance*. These establishments would be for them simply temporary places of residence; "in the end marriage would invade prostitution as the light of day invades the empire of night" (p. 233).

64. Op. cit., I, 115.

65. See C. Tilly, "The Changing Place of Collective Violence," in *Essays in Social and Political History*, and E. Shorter and C. Tilly, "Le déclin de la grève violente en France de 1890 a 1935," *Le mouvement social* (July-September 1971), 95–118.

66. See Chapter 3.

67. Op. cit., II, 268.

68. Ibid.

69. Frégier denounces more strongly these "advance posts of unregistered prostitution" (op. cit., I, 181).

70. Op. cit., I, 109.

71. Ibid., I, 22.

72. Ibid., I, 23.

73. Ibid., I, p. 255, 23. With Quételet, the Comte d'Angeville, and Ducpétiaux, Parent-Duchâtelet belongs to the group of sociologists who advanced the cause of social statistics. On the subject of the growth of statistical investigation in France, see B. Gille, *Les sources statistiques de l'histoire de France* (1964).

74. Op. cit., I, 372ff.

75. See the remark by M. Perrot, *Enquêtes sur la condition ouvrière en France au XIXe siecle*, p. 33.

76. It should be noted that in the study of the geographical origin of the Paris prostitutes, he too discerns the celebrated Saint-Malo–Geneva line.

77. Dr. O. Commenge, *La prostitution clandestine à Paris*.

78. Indeed, the third edition of Parent-Duchâtelet's book dates from 1857; in particular, it contains in appendixes studies by A. Trébuchet and Poirat-Duval.

79. Among the main ones I would mention are C. J. Lecour, *La prostitution à Paris et à Londres, 1789–1871* (1872), and *De l'état actuel de la prostitution parisienne* (1874); Maxime du Camp, "La prostitution," in *Paris, ses organes, ses fonctions et sa vie*, vol. 3 (1872); Dr. Jeannel, *De la prostitution dans les grandes villes au XIXe siècle et de l'extinction des maladies vénériennes* (1868); Dr. Homo, *Etude sur la prostitution dans la ville de Château-Gontier, suivie de considerations sur la prostitution en général* (1872); Flévy d'Urville, *Les ordures de Paris* (1874); Charles Desmaze, *Le crime et la débauche à Paris* (1881); Dr. J. Garin, *Le service sanitaire de Lyon, son organisation médicale et ses résultats pratiques* (1878). Certain works from a later period have the same inspiration: Dr. Mireur, *La prostitution à Marseille* (1882), and Dr. L. Reuss, *La prostitution au point de vue de l'hygiène et de l'administration en France et à l'étranger* (1889).

80. Yves Guyot, *La prostitution* (1882).

81. "Neither was man created for woman, but woman for man," 1 Corinthians 11:9.

82. See C.-J. Lecour, *La prostitution à Paris*, chap. 15, pp. 241ff.; Maxime du Camp, op. cit., pp. 428ff.; and Jeannel, op. cit., p. 174: "Laziness, greed, disorder, hereditary debauchery, unregistered prostitution, utter abandonment, and a distaste for work, these are the true sources of public prostitution." Homo, op. cit., pp. 125ff.; Mireur, *La prostitution à Marseille*, pp. 333–335; Reuss, op. cit., pp. 24–49. It is in this work that the catalogue of the causes cited by the regulationists is most specific; the author lists in turn "genetic instinct, precocious, natural perversion," "indolence, laziness," "indecency and promiscuity in poor families," "illegitimate birth," "the remarriage of the father or mother," "bad upbringing," "the lack of careers open to women," "advances in education," "the desertion of the countryside," "low wages," the mixing of the sexes in shops and factories, an excessive number of servants, "the lure of pleasure and a taste for luxury," "obscene books

and engravings," and "an initial seduction." Above all, he stresses that "there is a close link between the causes of prostitution and the social question" (p. 49), and that "political revolutions," "financial setbacks," and the disappearance of "the religious principles that have for so long kept the working class steadfast and honest" play an essential role.

83. Dr. Homo's nostalgia for the modest brothel of earlier times, now in competition with the luxurious establishment, is revealing in this respect (op. cit., pp. 6–7, 70).

84. Heroine of "Le lit 29."

85. Léon Bloy, "Repaire d'amour," *Sueurs de sang*.

86. "L'enfance à Paris," *Revue des deux-mondes* (October-December 1876, March 1877).

87. Homo, op. cit., p. 70.

88. Garin, op. cit., p. 39.

89. Lecour, *La prostitution à Paris*, p. 137.

90. Mireur, *La prostitution à Marseille*, p. 228.

91. Mireur, *La syphilis et la prostitution dans leurs rapports avec l'hygiène, la morale et la loi*, p. 368.

92. Reuss, op. cit., p. 97.

93. Garin, op. cit., p. 12.

94. Op. cit., pp. 424ff.

95. Bloy, *Sueurs de sang*, p. 60. *Pétroleuses* was the name given to women who started fires during the Commune.

96. C.-J. Lecour, *La prostitution à Paris*, p. 338. Paul Cère, for his part, notes that the police had been more severe toward the prostitutes since the two sieges (*Les populations dangereuses et les misères sociales*, 1872, p. 235).

97. Prof. Mauriac, *Leçons sur les maladies vénériennes professées à l'hôpital du Midi*, lesson 4 (1875) p. 145.

98. Op. cit., pp. 454ff.

99. Flévy d'Urville (op. cit., pp. 155ff.) says that "leprosy is at its height."

100. F. Carlier, *Les deux prostitutions*, published quite late, in 1887, in fact concerns the Second Empire.

101. According to Charles Desmaze (op. cit., p. v), one can no longer "enumerate" debauchery. "In the past, prostitution was limited to certain women: they were known, registered, wore gilt belts, and were confined to certain districts. Nowadays, in Paris, they are everywhere, filling the streets, wearing whatever they like. *In the past debauchery could be enumerated by a certain fixed figure;* now, its name is legion and its ranks are swollen each day, by the shops, factories, and theaters, in this pellmell of ages, sexes, ingenuities, vices, *any virtue may be bought.*"

102. According to Cère (op. cit., p. 229), *femmes galantes* and prostitutes can no longer be told apart. Furthermore, the *grisette*, who reserved her favors for a single lover, has disappeared (p. 3). "I suppose there is still some difference between the words *gallantry, bad behavior, concubinage,* and *prostitution!*" Mireur wrote rather increduously in 1883 (*La prostitution à Marseille*, p. 210). He too is describing unregistered prostitution, that "army of depravity and ruin that has us so firmly in its grip at this time that it seems to obstruct every avenue of our lives" (ibid.). Even more categorically Reuss was to write: "In general, all debauched women are unreg-

istered prostitutes: a grand lady who has lovers is, from this point of view, at the same level as the unregistered prostitute soliciting on the boulevard" (op. cit., p. 164).

103. Op. cit., p. 465.

104. Prof. H. Diday, "Assainissement méthodique de la prostitution," *Bull. de l'acad. de méd.* (1888), 492.

105. Op. cit., p. 65.

106. Ibid., p. 69.

107. This betrays the progress in the influence of hygienism and reflects the preoccupations of the medical profession. As early as 1867 the international medical congress in Paris placed the struggle against venereal disease high on its agenda.

108. See Mireur, *La syphilis et la prostitution,* passim. It should be noted, however, that, in 1867, Mireur devoted his thesis to heredity and syphilis (*Essai sur l'hérédité de la syphilis*).

109. Dr. Mougeot, cited by Lecour, *La prostitution,* pp. 13–14.

110. Homo, op. cit., p. 75.

111. Ibid., p. 75.

112. Op. cit., p. 490.

113. Ibid., p. 458.

114. Ibid., p. 460.

115. Flévy d'Urville, op. cit., p. 26.

116. Maxime du Camp, op. cit., p. 460.

117. Cère, op. cit., p. 231.

118. Flévy d'Urville, op. cit., p. 40.

119. Op. cit., p. 44.

120. Op. cit., sec. 2, introduction.

121. *La prostitution à Marseille,* p. viii.

122. Drs. Crocq and Rollet, *Prophylaxie internationale des maladies vénériennes* (1869), p. 28.

123. It should be noted that at the international medical congresses at Philadelphia (1876) and Geneva (1877), this matter no longer appeared on the agenda.

124. Garin, op. cit., p. 13.

125. *La prostitution à Marseille,* p. 327.

126. Ibid., p. 330.

127. Arch. dept. Seine-Inférieure.

128. Op. cit., p. 397.

129. *La prostitution à Marseille,* p. 233.

130. "Suppression de la syphilis" (Paris, 1846), quoted by Desprès, op. cit., p. 174.

131. Prof. Diday, *La gazette médicale* (1850), 198.

132. According to Mireur (*La syphilis,* p. 82) by Ratier, Petermann, Acton, de Sandouville, Bertherand, and Davila.

133. Dr. Rey, *Congrès médical international de Paris* (1867), p. 312.

134. After examining each of these suggestions, Mireur rejected them (*La syphilis,* pp. 82–97).

135. Jeannel, op. cit., p. 377.

136. Op. cit., p. 121.

137. Ibid.

138. Op. cit., p. 89.

139. Ibid.

140. Potton, op. cit., II, 442, quoted by Homo.

141. *La prostitution à Marseille,* p. 336.

142. Ibid., p. 336.

143. Ibid., p. 337.

144. Ibid., p. 338.

145. Ibid., p. 339.

146. Dr. Bertillon, memorandum, "L'influence du mariage sur la vie humaine," Acad. de méd., November 24, 1874, published in *Gazette hebdomadaire,* 43 (1871), 686ff.

147. Diday, "Assainissement méthodique de la prostitution," p. 492.

148. Ibid.

149. We know the extent to which Zola made himself the echo of this set of fantasies; according to him, Nana "dissolves everything she touches, she is the yeast, the nakedness, the anus, that brings the decomposition of our society . . . She is the central flesh" (Zola Papers, Bibliothèque nationale, French manuscripts, new acquisitions, sec. 211–212). He rebelled against this process, however: Nana seems more an agent of decomposition than a threat.

2. The Enclosed World of Regulationism

1. The term *les filles ordonnées au vice* was used by a registered prostitute of the Seine-Inférieure in a letter to the authorities requesting her removal from the register (arch. dept. Seine-Inférieure).

2. Règlement Gigot, October 15, 1878, 1, 2.

3. See O. Commenge, op. cit., pp. 142–175. The author cites examples of this correspondence.

4. See Chapter 3.

5. Dr. H. Mireur, *La prostitution à Marseille,* pp. 130–151, and various documents of the departmental archives of Bouches-du-Rhône.

6. At Toulon, as late as 1902, the cards were sold for 1 franc and the proceeds distributed to police personnel (report of the police commissioner, March 24, 1902, arch. dept. Var).

7. The results appear in an appendix, Gigot, op. cit., pp. 485–555.

8. Extraparliamentary Commission on the Regulation of Vice, *Annexes au rapport général présenté par M. F. Hennequin,* pp. 41–133.

9. See Henri Hayem, "Enquête sur la police des moeurs en province," *Revue pénitentiaire* (1904), 251ff.

10. Hennequin, op. cit., appendixes, p. 91.

11. Hayem, op. cit., p. 258.

12. Dr. Jeannel, op. cit., p. 236.

13. Mireur, *La prostitution à Marseille,* p. 150.

14. Table drawn up with the help of memoranda from the 1902 enquiry, arch. dept. Finistère, Seine-et-Oise, Charente-Inférieure, Hérault, and Meurthe-et-Moselle.

15. In this case the change I have noticed runs the risk of being amplified by the makeup of the sample, which tends to minimize the importance of southern France.

16. Dr. Louis Fiaux, *La police des moeurs,* I, 199.

17. Balzac is exaggerating when he has Esther, who is not yet nineteen, subjected to a two-year probationary apprenticeship on leaving Mme. Meynardie's *maison* (*Splendeurs et misères des courtisanes,* p. 677).

18. Mireur, *La prostitution à Marseille,* p. 201.

19. Hennequin, op. cit., p. 97.

20. Dr. Reuss, op. cit., p. 261.

21. See appendixes to Hennequin's report and Paul Meunier's report, p. 392.

22. C.-J. Lecour, *La prostitution à Paris,* p. 126.

23. Garin, op. cit., table.

24. E. Richard, *La prostitution à Paris* (1890), p. 50.

25. Dr. A. Desprès, *La prostitution en France* (1883).

26. Detailed memoranda of this inquiry into the "statistics of morals" ordered by the circular of February 1, 1879, are to be found in most of the departmental archives. For example, arch. dept. Bouches-du-Rhône, Charente-Inférieure, Gironde, Var, Finistère, Seine-Inférieure, and Seine-et-Oise. This makes it possible to check the accuracy of the printed tables.

27. I shall make extensive use of this inquiry later. Important fragments of it are to be found, for example, in the following archives: arch. dept. Charente-Inférieure, Hérault, Meurthe-et-Moselle, Var, Seine-et-Oise, Finistère, and Bouches-du-Rhône.

28. Report by Senator Théodore Roussel, *Documents parlementaires: Sénat,* appendix to the meeting of July 25, 1882. Documents in appendixes, answers to question 13, pp. 291–296.

29. See Hayem, op. cit.

30. Notice should be taken of the acquisition of Nice and Savoy, where official prostitution was not extensive, and of the loss of Alsace-Lorraine, where it was.

31. Hayem, op. cit., p. 251.

32. Drawn up with the help of the documents cited in note 27.

33. The situation in Toulon is explained by the policy of "enclosure" carried out after 1900 by the police commissioner (see his report, 1902, arch. dept. Var); there were 250 "independent" prostitutes in 1899, 89 in 1901, and 16 in 1902.

34. Desprès, op. cit., passim.

35. Information taken from Desprès's work.

36. J. Rossiaud carried out a detailed study of the structures of prostitution in the Rhône Valley during the Middle Ages. See "Prostitution, jeunesse et société dans les villes du Sud-Est au XV^c siècle," *Annales E.S.C.* (March–April 1976), 289–326.

37. It should be noted, however, that official prostitution satisfied a sexual demand that existed in a sense outside urban society (among soldiers, students, commercial travelers, tourists, recent immigrant workers, and other "marginals"), whereas unregistered prostitution was better suited to the demands of individuals who were well integrated into that society. This is one of the reasons why it appeared to be more threatening.

38. Reuss, op. cit., p. 19.

39. Mireur, *La prostitution à Marseille,* p. 158. It should be noted that, according to the author, many applicants would claim to be older in order to be registered more easily.

40. Prof. Barthélemy, "La prophylaxie des maladies vénériennes chez la femme," *Revue de médecine légale* (1900), 124.

41. These conclusions confirm those of Dr. Martineau concerning unregistered prostitutes (see Chapter 3). Fifty-two prostitutes from Château-Gontier had admitted to Dr. Homo the age at which they had lost their virginity: two of them had lost it before the age of ten, seventeen between ten and fifteen, twenty-five between fifteen and eighteen, and nine between eighteen and twenty-one. The average age for loss of virginity was fifteen years, four months. Forty-three of fifty-two had had a child before being registered as a prostitute. Many of them had been kept before joining a *maison de tolérance* (Homo, op. cit., p. 45). These figures make interesting comparisons with those provided for the same period by Dr. Le Moal in his *Etude sur la prostitution des mineures* (Paris, 1969).

42. It was to be taken up again at the abolitionists' congress at Lyons in 1901.

43. Dr. L. Le Pileur, cited by Regnault, *L'évolution de la prostitution,* pp. 87–88.

44. Dr. Martineau, *La prostitution clandestine,* pp. 42–66.

45. Arch. dept. Var and Seine-et-Oise.

46. This prejudice underpinned the whole passage devoted to prostitution by E. Ducpétiaux in his work *De la condition physique et morale des jeunes ouvriers et des moyens de l'améliorer.* Fantine in *Les misérables* was, of course, illegitimate.

47. Mireur, *La prostitution à Marseille,* p. 169.

48. Homo, op. cit., p. 40.

49. Prefect Delasalle, February 18, 1882, in T. Roussel, op. cit., p. 294.

50. It should be noted, however, that among the young girls caught prostituting themselves, and whom the authorities refused to register in view of their age, the influence of family background appears clearer. It should not be forgotten, in this respect, that official prostitution, which I am describing here, was not representative of prostitution as a whole.

51. Homo, op. cit., p. 36.

52. Mireur, *La prostitution à Marseille,* p. 170.

53. Reuss, op. cit., p. 17.

54. Arch. dept. Bouches-du-Rhône.

55. Arch. dept. Seine-et-Oise, Finistère.

56. Reuss, op. cit., p. 13.

57. Mireur, *La prostitution à Marseille,* pp. 166–168.

58. Not counting the fifty-eight women born in Algeria.

59. Arch. dept. Bouches-du-Rhône. The situation in Toulon followed the Marseilles model (see arch. dept. Var).

60. Homo, op. cit., p. 31.

61. Discussed later in this chapter.

62. Mireur, *La prostitution à Marseille,* pp. 171–173.

63. Although it is likely that a large proportion of those listed as servants in Table 5 were agricultural laborers.

64. See Chapter 3.

65. Mireur, *La prostitution à Marseille,* p. 176.

66. See Chapter 4.

67. See Chapter 3.

68. Reuss, op. cit., p. 15.

69. Mireur, *La prostitution à Marseille*, p. 174.

70. Arch. dept. Bouches-du-Rhône.

71. Arch. dept. Seine-et-Oise.

72. Arch. dept. Var.

73. Arch. dept. Charente-Inférieure.

74. Arch. dept. Bouches-du-Rhône.

75. Arch. dept. Seine-et-Oise.

76. See, on this subject, Friedlander, *Histoire et psychanalyse*.

77. Fiaux, *La police des moeurs*, I, 212.

78. The main works of this type are those that I have cited by the following authors: Homo, Lecour, Garin, Mireur, Macé, Reuss, Fiaux, Goron, and the documents of the commission set up by the Paris municipal council in 1878, or the Extraparliamentary Commission on Vice.

79. For example, the work cited by Coffignon and Virmaître.

80. On this subject, see the critique of Fiaux's works by Virmaître, *Trottoirs et lupanars*, p. 28.

81. To this type belong, by way of example, the works of Yves Guyot.

82. Arch. dept. Rhône. Register (September 7, 1885, to July 27, 1914) of the house run since September 19, 1896, by Espérance Salvador, 1 bis, rue de la Monnaie; the establishment had twenty-two rooms. Register of the maison Beillot (August 2, 1907, to August 3, 1914). Register (October 22, 1898, to July 18, 1914) of the *maison* kept by Joséphine Chevillat, widow Blanc, since July 25, 1879, 2 rue Smith; the establishment had ten rooms.

83. Arch. dept. Bouches-du-Rhône.

84. Arch. dept. Bouches-du-Rhône.

85. While sometimes referring to slightly later documents.

86. Mireur, *La prostitution à Marseille*, p. 156, and the report of the police commissioner of December 15, 1876, which mentions eighty-six *maisons de tolérance* as having been "closed" (arch. dept. Bouches-du-Rhône).

87. Guyot, *La prostitution*, appendix, p. 488.

88. Report of the mayor, March 25, 1902 (arch. dept. Var).

89. Arch. dept. Var.

90. Arch. dept. Hérault.

91. Arch. dept. Bouches-du-Rhône.

92. Reuss, op. cit., p. 407.

93. Arch. dept. Finistère.

94. Hennequin, op. cit., p. 106.

95. Servais and Laurend, *Histoire et dossier de la prostitution*, p. 203.

96. See R. Ricatte, *La genèse de la fille Elisa*, p. 120.

97. See Chapter 3.

98. See, on this subject, Fiaux's description in *Les maisons de tolérance, leur fermeture*, p. 251.

99. In the *maison de tolérance* described by Maupassant in *Ami Patience*, the salon is decorated with a fresco representing Leda stretched out beneath the swan.

The use of mythology, which we find again in the decoration of the *brasseries à femmes,* is reminiscent of the subterfuges used by bourgeois academic painters, who, wishing to evoke prostitutional settings without shocking their clientele, would use representations of Oriental harems, slave girls won in war by barbarian chieftains, slave markets, the temptations of Saint Anthony, or portraits of Mary Magdalen. On this subject, see Alexa Celebonovic, *Peinture kitsch ou réalisme bourgeois: L'art pompier dans le monde.*

100. Maupassant, *L'ami Patience.*

101. See Coffignon, *Paris vivant: La corruption à Paris,* p. 43.

102. Coffignon, op. cit., p. 39.

103. Jeannel, op. cit., p. 194.

104. It should be noted, however, that in most provincial towns the keepers of *maisons de tolérance* were forbidden at this time to serve drinks or to operate a *café-brasserie* on the ground floor; this applied at Amiens, Rouen, Rennes, Brest, Nantes, and Toulouse. At Lyons it was allowed. L. Fiaux, *La police des moeurs en France et dans les principaux pays d'Europe* (1888), p. 184.

105. E. de Goncourt, *La fille Elisa.* G. de Maupassant, *La maison Tellier* and *Le port.*

106. At least according to witnesses; but experience shows (see Chapter 3 on the subject of *filles à soldats*) that we must mistrust such stereotypes when not supported by a quantitative analysis.

107. G. Macé, *La police parisienne: Gibier de Saint-Lazare,* p. 206.

108. Champon, the mayor of Salins, states that this was practiced at Nevers. A. de Morsier, *La police des moeurs en France et la campagne abolitionniste,* appendix, "Report of M. Champon," p. 155.

109. Toulon, report of the police commissioner, March 24, 1902, arch. dept. Var.

110. Report of the mayor of Brest to the subprefect, arch. dept. Finistère.

111. Lardier, op. cit., p. 13.

112. G. de Maupassant, *La maison Tellier.*

113. See Chapter 3.

114. See Chapter 3.

115. Most of the descriptions concern liaisons with *femmes galantes,* kept women, or other unregistered prostitutes.

116. This type of clientele was revealed only when some scandal erupted. Late in 1883 just such a scandal occurred at Arles; it soon appeared that a large number of well-known men in the town, "civil servants, solicitors, barristers, municipal councillors, property owners, and merchants," were frequenting the *maison de tolérance* run by a Mme. Rougier, who was accused of prostituting underage girls (Report of the special commissioner for railways, November 30, 1883, arch. dept. Bouches-du-Rhône).

117. Hennequin, op. cit., p. 108.

118. Otherwise they resorted to the independent or unregistered prostitute.

119. Paul Bourget, *Physiologie de l'amour moderne,* p. 78.

120. Ibid., p. 79.

121. Ibid., p. 82.

122. In particular in tourist regions. According to the police commissioner for Hyères, "During the winter season most of the hotel waiters in the town—and there

are a great many of them—frequent the brothels" (Report of March 16, 1902, arch. dept. Var).

123. See Homo, op. cit., p. 179, and Lardier, op. cit., p. 6.

124. Fiaux, *Les maisons de tolérance,* p. 126.

125. Lardier, op. cit., p. 13.

126. Fiaux, *Les maisons de tolérance,* p. 125.

127. Coffignon, op. cit., p. 41.

128. A. Corbin, *Archaïsme et modernité en Limousin,* I, 218.

129. The mayor of Toulon observed in 1902 that "out of a population of 100,000 inhabitants, there are sometimes, either in the harbor or in the barracks, 15,000 bachelors in the town." He believed that if prostitution were abolished, homosexuality would spread (arch. dept. Var).

130. See Chapter 4.

131. In his *Physiologie de l'amour moderne,* Paul Bourget makes an interesting study of sexual exclusion: to the categories I have listed, he adds the shy.

132. See, in Chapter 3, the testimony of a Paris brothel-keeper (arch. préfect. de police, B A 1689).

133. Bergeret (d'Arbois), "La prostitution et les maladies vénériennes dans les petites localités," *Annales d'hygiène publique et de médecine légale* (1866), 348.

134. Homo, op. cit., p. 179.

135. In many cases the license could be given to a man, but in most large towns only women were allowed to keep a *maison de tolérance* (that is, live there); this was also true in Rennes, Le Mans, Amiens, and Marseilles.

136. Arch. dept. Bouches-du-Rhône.

137. See Chapter 3.

138. C.-J. Lecour, *De l'état actuel de la prostitution parisienne,* p. 138.

139. Carlier, *Les deux prostitutions,* p. 177.

140. Arch. nat. BB 18 2314.

141. Which, as we know, the by-laws often required them to do. These practices are described by Lecour, Macé, and Fiaux.

142. Carlier, op. cit., p. 153.

143. Macé, op. cit., p. 283.

144. Op. cit., p. 152.

145. Champon, op. cit., p. 156.

146. Report of the police commissioner of Versailles, arch. dept. Seine-et-Oise.

147. Report of the police commissioner for Toulon, March 24, 1902, arch. dept. Var.

148. Report of March 14, 1902, arch. dept. Finistère.

149. Arch. dept. Var.

150. Report of the police commissioner for La Seyne-sur-Mer, March 28, 1902, arch. dept. Var.

151. Report of the mayor, arch. dept. Finistère.

152. Four or five in Paris, according to Carlier, op. cit., p. 175.

153. In the *maisons ouvertes* of Toulon in 1902, the entrance fee varied between one franc and two francs and that of a *coucher* between five and ten francs (arch. dept. Var). At Brest in 1902 the entrance fee was two francs and that of the *coucher* five francs (Report of the mayor, arch. dept. Finistère). The same applied at

Versailles; here, however, soldiers paid only one franc for admission (Report of the police commissioner, March 14, 1902, arch. dept. Seine-et-Oise).

154. At Toulon in 1902 at a *maison fermée* admission cost five francs and at a *coucher* between ten and twenty francs, depending on the *fille* and the class of the client (Police commissioner's report, op. cit.).

155. Report of the mayor, arch. dept. Finistère.

156. See, on this subject, Mme. Legrain's communication to the abolitionist congress at Lyons in 1901 (A. de Morsier, *La police des moeurs en France*, pp. 184ff.

157. Ibid., p. 187.

158. Champon, op. cit., p. 156.

159. Ibid.

160. Op. cit., p. 154.

161. Fiaux, *Les maisons de tolérance*, p. 301.

162. Hennequin, op. cit., pp. 106–110.

163. Macé, op. cit., p. 265.

164. Fiaux, *Les maisons de tolérance*, p. 296.

165. *Les maisons de tolérance*, p. 113.

166. Reuss, op. cit., p. 135.

167. See Chapter 5.

168. Sometimes, however, novices decided to join the *maison de tolérance* directly; thus, among the inmates of the Brest brothels in 1902, "two had come from the convent, in which they had been placed against their will" (mayor of Brest, March 13, 1902, arch. dept. Finistère).

169. Macé, op. cit., p. 258.

170. Fiaux, *Les maisons de tolérance*, p. 49.

171. Ibid.

172. Ibid.

173. The atmosphere of the waiting rooms of these agencies is magnificently described by Octave Mirbeau in *Journal d'une femme de chambre*, pp. 262–263 (Paris, 1968).

174. Guyot, op. cit., p. 165.

175. Arch. nat. BB 18 2314.

176. Fiaux, *Les maisons de tolérance*, pp. 41–42.

177. Inquiry of 1902, arch. dept. Seine-et-Oise.

178. When pimps recruited underage girls they were forced, in order to hoodwink the authorities, and often the keeper herself, to fabricate false papers. In order to do this, writes the police commissioner for Toulon, they would go into cemeteries, note down from the gravestones the names and biographical details of dead girls, and then write to the mayors of the native communes for a birth certificate, giving some plausible reason (arch. dept. Var).

179. Arch. nat. BB 18 2386 II.

180. Police commissioners for La Seyne and Toulon, op. cit., arch. dept. Var.

181. Fiaux, *Les maisons de tolérance*, p. 41.

182. Inquiry of 1902, arch. dept. Finistère.

183. See L. Fiaux, *Rapport . . . au conseil municipal de Paris* (1883).

184. Cited by Fiaux in this report, appendixes to Léo Taxil, *La prostitution contemporaine*, p. 370, n. 1.

185. Reuss, op. cit., p. 411. In March 1902 the mayor of Brest confirmed the description of this network (arch. dept. Finistère).

186. Report of the police commissioner, 1902, arch. dept. Var.

187. Arch. dept. Rhône.

188. One must understand that the residence of the prostitutes at the time of their registration in a Lyons *maison* is different from that of their place of birth (discussed earlier in this chapter).

189. Each keeper had her own methods; thus Espérance Salvador recruited mainly in Paris, while Beillot and Chevillat found their personnel in Lyons.

190. Thirty declared that they did not know where they were going; only three "disappeared in secret"; eleven claimed to be going home, without making clear where that was; nine were dismissed because they were suffering from venereal disease and four because their papers were not in order; two had been jailed; only one had been removed from the register; and the last one died during her stay in the *maison*.

191. Charts in Figure 8 are produced from documents in the departmental archives of Seine-et-Oise, the Var, and Bouches-du Rhône.

192. Arch. dept. Finistère.

193. Arch. dept. Rhône.

194. I have eliminated the other stays because their duration did not seem significant; this method has the effect of minimizing the duration of the real stay of certain inmates (see Figure 8).

195. Diagrams produced from answers to the 1902 inquiry, departmental archives of the Seine-et-Oise, the Var, and the Bouches-du-Rhône (see Figure 9).

196. Report by the mayor, arch. dept. Finistère.

197. Report cited by the police commissioner for Toulon, arch. dept. Var.

198. This "namelessness" of the prostitute has been pointed out, in the context of the eighteenth century, by Simone Delesalle, in "Lecture d'un chef-d'oeuvre: *Manon Lescaut.*" Victor Hugo presents Fantine, who was to keep her anonymity even to the grave: "She emerged from the unfathomable depths of society's darkest corners and bore on her brow the sign of anonymity" (*Les misérables,* p. 129).

199. Except when this pseudonym was already borne by an inmate of the new *maison.*

200. Arch. dept. Rhône.

201. The relative popularity of this pseudonym may be explained in part by Alphonse Daudet's heroine.

202. Fiaux, *Les maisons de tolérance,* p. 90.

203. Report cited by the police commissioner for Toulon, arch. dept. Var.

204. By contrast, at Versailles in the same period a prostitute managed to earn only one franc or one franc fifty centimes a day. This shows the wide diversity in practices from region to region (arch. dept. Seine-et-Oise).

205. Arch. nat. BB 18 2359.

206. See discussion later in this chapter.

207. Guyot, op. cit., p. 305.

208. Hennequin, op. cit., pp. 106–107.

209. Certain by-laws were astonishingly precise. The by-laws of Clermont-de-l'Hérault, not passed until 1911, established in particular that "the rooms [of the

maisons de tolérance] will each have a number, placed on the door, in figures measuring at least seven centimeters high" (Article 5) and that "the steps of the staircase must not be more than 17 cm high or less than 30 cm deep" (Article 20) (arch. dept. Hérault).

210. Fiaux, *Les maisons de tolérance*, p. 238.

211. Fiaux, *Rapport . . . au conseil municipal de Paris*.

212. E. de Goncourt has left a fascinating description of this in *La fille Elisa*, which Zola made much use of later.

213. See Chapter 3.

214. Dr. Patoir, "La prostitution à Lille," *Echo médical du Nord*, September 7, 1902, 425, speaks of the skill of the Lille keepers in handling the speculum and nitrate pencil. They knew how to drain a Bartholin gland of its drop of pus and to remove any "stubborn, too adherent mucosity" around the neck of the vagina.

215. Cited by Fiaux, *Les maisons de tolérance*, p. 130.

216. Police commissioner for La Seyne, arch. dept. Var.

217. This refers to the number of clients and not to the number of acts of intercourse (Fiaux, *Les maisons de tolérance*, p. 131).

218. Ibid., p. 131.

219. Op. cit., p. 207.

220. Fiaux, *Les maisons de tolérance*, p. 132. Testimony confirmed in 1901 by Champon, op. cit., p. 156.

221. See Chapter 3.

222. Hennequin, op. cit., p. 107.

223. Ibid., p. 106.

224. Macé, op. cit., p. 267. It goes without saying that the situation was noticeably different in the provinces. Readers of Goncourt will remember the description of the inmates' bedroom in a brothel at Bourlemont in *La fille Elisa*.

225. Fiaux, *Les maisons de tolérance*, p. 50.

226. Ibid., p. 263.

227. See Goncourt, *La fille Elisa*, and Maupassant, *L'ami Patience*.

228. Macé, op. cit., p. 266. Reuss, op. cit., pp. 122ff.

229. Reuss, op. cit., p. 124.

230. Fiaux, *La police des moeurs* (1888), p. 184.

231. Hennequin (op. cit., p. 112) shows, on this matter, that several by-laws forbade brothel-keepers "to put out flags and illuminations" on July 14.

232. It should be remembered, however, that this was extremely rare in the three Lyons *maisons* whose archives have been preserved (see n. 190).

233. Arch. nat. BB 385. Cited by Pierre Arches, *Une ville et son maire: Parthenay en 1872* (1975), pp. 34–35.

234. See discussion later in this chapter.

235. See Chapter 7.

236. G. de Molinari, *La viriculture*, p. 156.

237. Lion Murard and Patrick Zylberman, *Le petit travailleur infatigable*, passim.

238. Op. cit., p. 152.

239. Arch. dept. Var.

240. See discussion later in this chapter.

241. Fiaux, *Rapport . . . au conseil municipal*, p. 372.

242. According to statements made by Coué before the municipal commission.

243. Jeannel, op. cit., p. 203.

244. Arch. dept. Bouches-du-Rhône.

245. Arch. dept. Bouches-du-Rhône.

246. This district comprised in particular rues Récollettes, Thubaneau, Lemaître, du Musée, Mazagran, du Théâtre-Français, and Sénac.

247. Arch. dept. Bouches-du-Rhône.

248. Arch. dept. Charente-Inférieure.

249. Arch. dept. Meurthe-et-Moselle.

250. See n. 190, concerning the three Lyons *maisons de tolérance*.

251. Reuss, op. cit., p. 72.

252. This is what emerges from the results of the hospital inquiry of 1865 (Arch. nat. F 20 282).

253. In 1882 (Guyot, op. cit., appendixes, pp. 486–555) exclusion was practiced, for example, by the mutual aid societies of Montpellier, Reims, Brest, Chalon, Nantes, Niort, Saint-Quentin, Pau, and Troyes; very often this clause in the by-laws was also aimed at alcoholics and victims of brawls.

254. "The government's penis" was a name given by the prostitutes of North Africa to the speculum, which was used in health checks (M. Moty, "Prophylaxie des maladies vénériennes," *Echo médical du Nord*, August 17, 1902, 391).

255. Reuss, op. cit., p. 291.

256. Jeannel, op. cit., p. 178.

257. See Guyot, op. cit., pp. 302–303, and works by Fiaux, passim. "The chair in which she sat for the medical examination filled her with fear and shame," Zola writes of Nana (p. 1315). Rops has described in a striking way this conception of the use of the speculum.

258. Mireur, *La prostitution à Marseille*, p. 244.

259. Guyot, op. cit., p. 489.

260. Fiaux, *La police des moeurs* (1888), pp. 184ff. Guyot's inquiry of 1882 showed that this was the most common frequency of health checks.

261. Hennequin, op. cit., p. 114.

262. Mireur, *La prostitution à Marseille*, p. 243.

263. Report by the health department, arch. dept. Finistère.

264. Mireur, *La prostitution à Marseille*, p. 246.

265. Ibid.

266. Hennequin, op. cit., pp. 116ff. In some towns—at Grenoble for example—hospital fees were also partly covered by a tax imposed on the keepers of the *maisons de tolérance*. At Orléans it was the prostitutes themselves who had to pay two francs for each day of treatment (Hayem, op. cit., p. 260).

267. Arch. dept. Seine-Inférieure.

268. See Chapter 1.

269. Mireur, *La prostitution à Marseille*, pp. 100ff.

270. Guyot, op. cit., appendixes, p. 523.

271. See Fiaux, report to the Paris municipal council, op. cit., p. 417, and E. Richard, op. cit., p. 124.

272. Fiaux, op. cit.

273. Guyot, op. cit., p. 294.

274. Cited by Guyot, op. cit., p. 293.

275. Guyot, op. cit., p. 295, and Fournier, passim.

276. The prostitutes were particularly attached to their hats, especially since the by-laws usually forbade them to wear hats while soliciting.

277. Patoir, op. cit., p. 425.

278. Garin, op. cit.

279. There is a very revealing passage on this subject in the book by Dr. Corlieu, *La prostitution à Paris*, pp. 100ff.

280. By *syphilization* I mean here the appearance of syphilis and not the voluntary contamination practiced, for example, by Professor Auzias-Turenne.

281. Arch. dept. Bouches-du-Rhône.

282. Dr. Maireau, *Syphilis et prostituées*, p. 78.

283. "Les vénériennes de Saint-Lazare," *Revue de médecine légale* (1900), 81ff.

284. Barthélemy, op. cit., *Revue de médecine légale* (1900). The results obtained are to be accepted only with caution; if Barthélemy is to be believed, the syphilization of prostitutes would appear to have occurred at a later age than the average age for all venereal patients! (See, on this subject, Fournier, op. cit., p. 389.)

285. *Bulletin de la Société française de prophylaxie sanitaire et morale* (1909), 127.

286. Title of the article by Dr. Langlet, *Union médicale et scientifique du Nord-Est*, July 30, 1905.

287. Op. cit., pp. 310ff. In the timetable that he supplies, Guyot seems to confuse prisoners and patients.

288. See the details provided by Reuss, op. cit., pp. 336ff.

289. Corlieu, op. cit., p. 63. Treatments varied, of course, from hospital to hospital; see the results of the Guyot inquiry, especially the details concerning Dunkirk, Valenciennes, and Saint-Quentin.

290. Op. cit., p. 312.

291. Op. cit., p. 338.

292. Op. cit., p. 312.

293. Op. cit., p. 69.

294. Corlieu, op. cit., p. 70.

295. Garin, op. cit., p. 40. In 1888 (that is, after the reform) Fiaux mentions 244 beds for venereal patients and 92 beds for men (*La police des moeurs*, 1888, p. 760).

296. Garin, op. cit., p. 31.

297. Mireur, *La prostitution à Marseille*, p. 313.

298. Fiaux, *La police des moeurs*, p. 760.

299. Mireur, *La prostitution à Marseille*, p. 319.

300. Cited by Fiaux, *La police des moeurs*, I, 434.

301. It should be noted that at the Hôpital de Lourcine in Paris, the isolation cell was maintained until Fournier had it abolished (Fiaux, *La police des moeurs*, p. 776). The Guyot inquiry suggests, however, that in 1882 the venereal patients of Rouen and Valence were well treated. The average duration of treatment for the former was then forty-two days (Guyot, op. cit., appendixes, pp. 492–493, 544).

302. Louis Spillmann and J. Benech, *Du refuge à la Maison de secours* (1914).

303. According to Dr. Etienne (*Etudes sur la prostitution*, Nancy, 1901, p. 14), the average number of syphilitics confined to the Maison between 1882 and 1885 rose to 122.

304. Spillmann, *L'évolution de la lutte contre la syphilis*, pp. 2–3.

305. Ibid., p. 5.

306. Ibid.

307. Prof. Bourneville, "Quelques notes sur l'hospitalisation des vénériens de province," *Le progrès médical* (1887). This testimony is very enlightening, although one must admit that the campaign he launched in the review belonged to a wider, anticlerical polemic. See, on this subject, the accusations in *La province médicale* (March 1887).

308. *Loire médicale,* 4 (1887), 103.

309. Ibid.

310. *La province médicale,* 13 (March 26, 1887), 208.

311. M. Perrot, "1848, révolution et prisons," *Annales historiques de la Révolution française* (July-September 1977), 321.

312. Bourneville, op. cit. (1887), pt. 1, p. 431.

313. Ibid.

314. Op. cit. (1887), pt. 2, p. 53.

315. Report by the director of the childbirth course, arch. dept. Finistère.

316. Homo, op. cit., p. 27.

317. Letter from Viator to Bourneville, *Progrès médical* (1887), pt. 2, p. 52.

318. *Progrès médical* (1887), pt.2, p. 69.

319. Patoir, op. cit., p. 424.

320. Reuss, op. cit., p. 414.

321. Guyot, op. cit., appendixes, p. 488.

322. Langlet, op. cit., p. 154.

323. *Progrès médical* (1887), pt. 1, p. 232.

324. Hennequin, op. cit., p. 115.

325. Public acts of indecency. The definition of these terms was to evolve during the nineteenth century.

326. See Vivien, *Etudes administratives,* II, 216ff; Batbie, *Traité de droit public et administratif;* Faustin-Hélie, *Théorie du code pénal,* III, 104.

327. *Le moniteur,* 192 (12 Germinal, Year V).

328. See Chapter 7.

329. See the remarks by Léon Renault on March 28, 1872, before a meeting of the Paris municipal council; by Voisin on November 30, 1876; and by Naudin before the vice squad commission on April 28, 1879. This is also the argument developed in the work cited by Dr. Reuss.

330. See, before the law of 1884, the memorandums of Beugnot (1814), Argout (1833), and Delangle (1859).

331. See Reuss, op. cit., p. 353.

332. An argument taken up by Léon Renault on March 28, 1872, and by C. J. Lecour (*La prostitution à Paris,* p. 40).

333. Exhaustively cited in Léo Taxil, *La prostitution contemporaine,* p. 397.

334. Ibid.

335. Ibid.

336. For example, Georges Martin, *Bulletin municipal de la ville de Paris,* February 8, 1883, contains a report of the session of January 25.

337. A long list can be found in Fiaux, *La police des moeurs,* I, 59ff.

338. See Chapter 5.

339. By an order dated March 9, 1881.

340. As well as Article 10 of the order of October 25, 1883, on the policing of the lodging houses.

341. Guyot, op. cit., p. 131.

342. See Chapter 5.

343. Reuss, op. cit., p. 418.

344. Ibid., p. 407.

345. Mireur, *La prostitution à Marseille,* chap. 3.

346. Translator's note: "country," in the sense of "going to the country" for a break. Reuss, op. cit., p. 377.

347. Op. cit., p. 145.

348. See M. Perrot, *Les ouvriers en grève,* I, 182.

349. See Chapter 3. A movement that coincided chronologically with the conservative Catholic counteroffensive in the country as a whole.

350. This decline is also to be found in the repressive policies directed at workers; see Perrot, op. cit., I, 182.

351. Op. cit., p. 295.

352. Guyot, op. cit., appendixes, p. 491.

353. Report by the police commissioner, 1884, arch. dept. Nord.

354. Arch. dept. Bouches-du-Rhône.

355. To speak of 21,943 prostitutes is inaccurate, however, since many of them were detained several times.

356. Arch. dept. Var.

357. Only a systematic analysis of the prison registers preserved in the departmental archives would enable us to determine this.

358. Fiaux, *La police des moeurs,* II, 217. (remark by M. Auffret to the extraparliamentary commission).

359. Arch. dept. Bouches-du-Rhône.

360. Arch. dept. Bouches-du-Rhône.

361. See Chapter 1. The progress made in confining prostitutes to their haunts was noted in 1877 by the police commissioner (arch. dept. Bouches-du-Rhône).

362. Detailed descriptions of the prison are to be found in Reuss, op. cit., p. 374; Guyot, op. cit., pp. 136ff; d'Haussonville, op. cit., pp. 900ff.

363. See Guyot's report to the municipal council, October 19, 1880.

364. Coffignon, op. cit., p. 246.

365. Count d'Haussonville, "Le combat contre le vice," p. 809.

366. If Police Commissioner Dietze is to be believed (arch. dept. Bouches-du-Rhône).

367. Coffignon, op. cit., p. 248.

368. Mireur, *La prostitution à Marseille,* pp. 204ff.

369. Report by the police commissioner, March 24, 1902.

370. Maxime du Camp (op. cit., pp. 439ff.) has left an astonishing description of the way the prostitutes were interrogated.

371. Reuss, op. cit., p. 373.

372. Cited by Fiaux.

373. Richard, op. cit., p. 135, and Fiaux, op. cit., pp. 389ff.

374. Reuss, op. cit., p. 376.

375. It is true that with half their earnings they could, twice a day, treat themselves to a *gobette* (coffee, milk, or a glass of wine at the canteen)(Reuss, ibid.).

376. On this matter, Guyot and Richard, op. cit., are of the same opinion.

377. Richard, op. cit., p. 136.

378. Maxime du Camp, op. cit., p. 444.

379. By-laws of 1875.

380. E. Richard, op. cit., p. 137, inspired by Caroline de Barrau's report to the abolitionist congress in London, 1886.

381. On the problem of Saint-Lazare in the twentieth century, see Chapter 7.

382. Prefect's report, February 18, 1887, arch. dept. Seine-Inférieure.

383. Reuss, op. cit., p. 419.

384. Hennequin, op. cit., p. 123.

3. The Failure of Regulationism

1. Information for this figure is taken from Fiaux, *Les maisons de tolérance,* pp. 343ff., and above all *La police des moeurs,* II, 907–908. I have used documents assembled by F. Hennequin in writing this analysis.

2. This change is noted by Dr. Patoir (op. cit., 1902, p. 379), who remarks, however, that the decline in the number of *maisons de tolérance* was accompanied by increasing rotation of the personnel among the remaining establishments; those at Lille now saw an annual turnover of between 200 and 220 women.

3. Report to the prefect, arch. dept. Finistère.

4. It affected, for example, the cities of Belgium and those of the Russian empire.

5. That is to say Lyons, Bordeaux, Rouen, Toulouse, Rennes, Amiens, Limoges, Dijon, and Bourges.

6. This table uses information provided by the 1902 inquiry. It should be noted, however, that the information concerning Brest and Montpellier do not concur either with that of the 1879 inquiry or with that provided by Dr. Fiaux. The vagueness of the definition of the *maison de tolérance* no doubt explains the discrepancies.

7. See Carlier, op. cit., pp. 146ff.

8. H. Hayem, op. cit., pp. 260–261.

9. See Chapter 4.

10. See discussion later in this chapter.

11. Cited by Fiaux, *La police des moeurs,* II, 213.

12. On this matter, see the reflections of Fiaux, *La prostitution cloîtrée,* p. 86.

13. See arch. préfect. de police, BA 1689, and arch. dept. Bouches-du-Rhône.

14. Op. cit., p. 147. On this matter, interesting documents are to be found in bundles F 7 9304–5 in the Arch. nat.

15. See discussion later in this chapter.

16. Arch. préfect. de police, BA 1689.

17. Ibid.

18. Ibid.

19. Arch. dept. Bouches-du-Rhône.

20. Arch. dept. Meurthe-et-Moselle.

21. This, it should be remembered, was illegal.

22. Ibid.

23. Arch. dept. Meurthe-et-Moselle.

24. Arch. dept. Var.

25. Ibid.

26. Several works kept this utopia alive; see, in particular, Charles Richard, *La prostitution devant le philosophe* (1881).

27. Regnault, "De l'évolution de la prostitution," *La France médicale* (1892), 565.

28. Evidence given by Paul Dubois to the commission set up by the Paris municipal council.

29. A. Champon, op. cit.

30. Arch. dept. Meurthe-et-Moselle.

31. Fiaux, *Les maisons de tolérance,* p. 256.

32. Ibid., p. 230.

33. Regnault, op. cit., p. 547.

34. See the evocation of the animated streets of the *quartier réservé* in Maupassant, *Le port.*

35. Report by the subprefect to the prefect, July 4, 1907, arch. dept. Hérault.

36. Ibid.

37. Ibid.

38. Meunier, *Annexes au rapport de M. Hennequin,* pp. 421ff.

39. Ibid., p. 424.

40. Ibid.

41. Fiaux, *La police des moeurs,* I, 214.

42. Fiaux, *Les maisons de tolérance,* p. 179.

43. Ibid, p. 180.

44. This was already in use in the early years of the century: see Canler's memoirs, cited by Léo Taxil, *La prostitution contemporaine,* pp. 168ff. There were also shows in certain small-town *tolérances,* but they soon caused a scandal. In September 1911 several officers from the garrison of Saint-Mihiel, accompanied by their friends, went to a *maison de tolérance* and persuaded two of the inmates "to undress and, lying on a mattress, to indulge in obscene practices with one another." The small group of friends spent the evening in the establishment and did not leave until the early hours of the morning, after consuming quantities of champagne (Report of the procurator general of the Court of Nancy, September 16, 1911, Arch. nat. BB 18 2466). What the magistrates seem to have been most concerned about during the investigation was whether the officers' women friends had averted their gaze or not. The manuscript of *La fille Elisa* contains a scene of flagellation of naked prostitutes by a subkeeper; this passage does not appear in the published text (see R. Ricatte, op. cit., pp. 213–215).

45. Fiaux, *Les maisons de tolérance,* pp. 182–183.

46. The police reports confirm the existence of dogs specially trained to do this (see arch. préfect. de police, BA 1689, report of October 11, 1893, concerning 6 rue de Provence). Dr. Bouglé describes at length the practice of bestiality in his work *Les vices du peuple* (Paris, 1888). The work is of hyperregulationist inspiration.

47. Fiaux, *Les maisons de tolérance,* p. 165.

48. Léo Taxil, op. cit., p. 165. This work contains a very detailed description of

all the practices indulged in by the inmates; the instruments of flagellation are described precisely in Meunier, op. cit., p. 157.

49. Fiaux, *Les maisons de tolérance,* p. 165. The same goes for those cited by Carlier (op. cit., p. 102): long needles, thongs studded with pinheads, knotted cords; everything covered with dried blood.

50. Fiaux, *Les maisons de tolérance,* p. 166.

51. Taxil, op cit., p. 167.

52. Fiaux, *Les maisons de tolérance,* p. 166.

53. Taxil, op. cit., p. 166.

54. Cited by Fiaux, *Les maisons de tolérance,* p. 162.

55. Taxil, op. cit., p. 165.

56. Dubois, op. cit.

57. Taxil, op. cit., p. 171.

58. See the works on the history of biological behavior cited in the bibliography.

59. See, for example, the testimony of Canler and Carlier.

60. See M. Callu's master's thesis, "Approche critique du phénomène prostitutionnel parisien dans la seconde moitié du XIXᵉ siècle par le biais d'un ensemble d'images: Oeuvres de Constantin Guys, Félicien Rops, Gustave Moreau," University of Tours, 1977.

61. On this matter, see G. Deleuze, *Présentation de Sacher-Masoch: Le froid et le cruel* (1973).

62. Krafft-Ebing, *Psychopathia sexualis.*

63. Michel Foucault, *La volonté de savoir,* pp. 69–99.

64. Homo, op. cit., p. 70.

65. Ibid., p. 69.

66. H. Turot, *Le prolétariat de l'amour,* p. 181.

67. Published by H. Turot.

68. J. K. Huysmans, *A rebours,* Collection 10–18 (1975), pp. 136–140.

69. Carlier, op. cit., pp. 20ff.

70. Op. cit., p. 164.

71. See A. Dumas *fils, Théâtre complet,* vol. 1, unpublished prefaces.

72. See Coffignon, op. cit., p. 142.

73. Ibid., p. 143.

74. Dumas *fils,* unpublished prefaces.

75. Dr. Homo, for example (op. cit., p. 52).

76. He regards as prostitutes women who "make an occupation and profession of their sexual relations," that is, "any woman who . . . gives herself to the first comer, in exchange for financial remuneration, . . . and has no other means of subsistence than the temporary relations she has with a more or less large number of individuals" (op. cit., pp. 43–44).

77. Dr. L. Butte, "Syphilis et prostitution" (1890).

78. Homo (op. cit., p. 52), after demanding their registration, also excludes from his study of prostitution kept women, whom he regards as pseudowives.

79. See Chapter 1.

80. A calculation carried out by E. Richard, op. cit., p. 60, according to the method advocated by F. Carlier, "Etude statistique sur la prostitution clandestine," *Annales d'hygiène publique,* 36 (1871), 302.

81. See Chapter 1.

82. C. J. Lecour, *La prostitution à Paris et à Londres*, p. 120. It should be noted that the author includes *filles soumises* in this total.

83. Fiaux, *Rapport au nom de la commission spéciale*, p. 378.

84. Statement to the commission set up by the municipal council, second hearing, p. 25.

85. Op. cit., p. 9.

86. Quoted by Richard, op. cit., p. 58.

87. Lassar, *Die Prostitution zu Paris: Ein Bericht* (1892).

88. Op. cit., p. 60. The same year Miron calculated that 24,000 prostitutes were working in Paris, and Strohmberg calculated 20,000 (cited by Dr. P. E. Morhardt, *Les maladies vénériennes et la réglementation de la prostitution*, pp. 113–114).

89. Dr. Lutaud, "La prostitution patentee," *Journal de médecine de Paris* (June 1903), 229.

90. *Bull. de la soc. fr. de prophylaxie sanit. et morale* (1905), 189.

91. *Bull. de la soc. fr. de prophylaxie sanit. et morale* (1908), 9.

92. See Chapter 2.

93. Op. cit., p. 9. On the conditions of this inquiry, see Chapter 2.

94. Mireur, *La prostitution à Marseille*, p. 217. Even more unsoundly based and practically devoid of any interest are the estimates emanating from the authorities in sixteen municipalities, who, when polled by Yves Guyot in 1881, replied to the question concerning the number of unregistered prostitutes. It should be noted on this matter that half the municipal administrations considered that it was impossible to calculate the extent of unregistered prostitution.

At the conclusion of his inquiry, Henri Hayem calculated, in 1903, that there were 2,000 unregistered prostitutes at Marseilles, 1,500 at Nancy, and between 150 and 200 at Grenoble (op. cit., pp. 254, 256). In 1907 Dr. E. Hermite (*Prostitution et réglementation sanitaire de la police des moeurs à Grenoble*, p. 9) estimated that between 1,000 and 1,200 prostitutes were working in that city.

95. This is the opinion of Richard, op. cit., p. 64.

96. Martineau, *La prostitution clandestine*, p. 4.

97. Such picturesque details may be found in the following works: for the Second Empire, Carlier, op. cit., pt. 1, chap. 2, and Delvau's work as a whole; for the later period, Macé, op. cit., passim; Coffignon, op. cit., pp. 122ff; Andrieux, *Souvenirs d'un préfet de police*, passim; Goron, *Les industries de l'amour*; and Virmaître, *Trottoirs et lupanars*, pp. 143ff. Among the works of fiction, one might also point out Pierre de Lano, *Courtisane*, preceded by an interesting preface, and *L'affaire Clemenceau*, by Dumas *fils*. Iza, the heroine of this novel, is a demimondaine who indulges in venal sex without her husband's knowledge.

98. Numerous examples cited by C. J. Lecour (*La prostitution à Paris*), Dr. Jeannel, and Léo Taxil (op. cit., p. 211).

99. In the novel by Pierre de Lano, the lover of Berthe de la Pierre-Taillade is Adrien Darbois, prime minister and minister of the interior.

100. In the sense given the term by Adeline Daumard (op. cit., p. 272).

101. Taxil, op. cit., pp. 210ff.

102. Reuss, op. cit., p. 422.

103. See Chapter 3. The activities of Sidonie Rougon as described by Zola in *La curée* illustrate the transition very well.

104. To use the rather felicitous title of Goron's book.

105. P. Alexis, *La fin de Lucie Pellegrin.*

106. P. de Lano, op. cit., preface, p. vii. This hieratic aspect of the courtesan is the source of her literary success. A sphinx, an unsolved riddle, at once a dispenser of pleasure and yet marmoreal, the courtesan symbolizes the contradictions of woman. Furthermore, as Paul de Saint-Victor (cited by H. Mitterand, *Nana,* p. 1689) points out, the society of the courtesans was, for the bourgeois male, the world of the unexpected, of the "happening," as we might say nowadays.

107. After 1884, of course.

108. Dr. Reuss provides statistics on this matter (op. cit., p. 371). The departmental archives of the Bouches-du-Rhône include an interesting collection of files on expulsions on moral grounds.

109. This is also the opinion of Reuss (op. cit., pp. 169ff.).

110. Again in the sense understood by Adeline Daumard (op. cit., p. 250).

111. As she is described by E. and J. de Goncourt, in *La lorette.*

112. A fine collection of photographs is to be found in Joanna Richardson, *The Courtesans: The Demimonde in 19th Century France* (London, 1967).

113. Gavarni, Daumier, and Granville for the earlier period, then Mars, Stop, and Grévin.

114. *Nana,* pp. 165–195.

115. Macé, op. cit., pp. 103ff.

116. Coffignon, op. cit., p. 133. Sylvia, Maxime's young mistress (*La curée*), is the representative in Zola's world of the *femme galante.*

117. Coffignon, op. cit., p. 127.

118. See Taxil, op. cit., p. 211.

119. Macé, op. cit., p. 67.

120. A. Armengaud, *Les Populations du Sud-Est aquitain à l'époque contemporaine,* p. 284.

121. Unfortunately, we do not have for the nineteenth century studies of this phenomenon as detailed as the one made by J. Depauw on the end of the ancien régime, "Amour illégitime et société à Nantes au XVIIIᵉ siècle," *Annales, économies, sociétés, civilisations* (July-October 1972), 1155–82.

122. See Chapter 4.

123. Magnificently described by Huysmans in *Marthe* and in *Les soeurs Vatard.*

124. For some months this is what happens to Marthe; by contrast, Cyprien *(Les soeurs Vatard)* proves to be kinder toward Céline.

125. L. Puibaraud, *Les malfaiteurs de profession,* p. 112.

126. J. Vidalenc, *Le département de l'Eure sous la Restauration,* p. 494.

127. Reuss, op. cit., p. 423.

128. Ibid., p. 416.

129. Report of the special commissioner, November 12, 1885, arch. dept. du Nord. In 1885 *Le matin* devoted an article to this matter.

130. See Chapter 5.

131. Guyot, op. cit., appendixes, p. 552.

132. A. Corbin, *Archaïsme et modernité en Limousin,* I, 113.

133. G. Désiré-Vuillemin, "Une grève révolutionnaire: Les porcelainiers de Limoges en avril 1905," *Annales du Midi* (January-March) 1971, 54ff.

134. Maurice Barrès, *Les déracinés* (1965), p. 110. Balzac pointed out that, in

Paris, "vice perpetually welds rich and poor together" (*Splendeurs et misères*, p. 826).

135. The attitude of Huysmans' heroes is revealing in this respect.

136. The divided loyalties of the working-class woman are a theme commonly treated by Huysmans and Charles-Louis Philippe.

137. Homo, op. cit., p. 179.

138. Reuss, op. cit., p. 413.

139. See the discussion later in this chapter of the *maisons de rendez-vous*.

140. Mireur, *La prostitution à Marseille*, p. 216.

141. Op. cit., p. 21.

142. Coffignon, op. cit., pp. 109ff.

143. Richard, op. cit., p. 63.

144. *Nana*, p. 1312.

145. *Bubu de Montparnasse*, pp. 107–109.

146. *L'assommoir*, p. 771.

147. Coffignon, op. cit., pp. 110ff.

148. Macé, op. cit., p. 58.

149. Coffignon, op. cit., p. 111.

150. Ibid., p. 112.

151. Ibid., p. 115.

152. Martineau, op. cit., p. 81.

153. Virmaître, *Trottoirs et lupanars*, p. 139.

154. According to Commenge, op. cit., p. 123.

155. Virmaître, *Trottoirs*, p. 151. Also described by Maupassant in *Bel ami*.

156. Carlier, op. cit., p. 23, and above all d'Haussonville, "L'enfance à Paris," *Revue des deux-mondes*, June 15, 1878, 898.

157. Taking into account what I have just said and the location of the *maisons de tolérance*.

158. These nuclei of popular space amount to what J. Rougerie regards as "police space" or "abandoned space" ("Recherche sur le Paris populaire: Espace populaire et espace révolutionnaire, Paris, 1870–1871," *Recherches et travaux: Institut d'histoire économique et sociale de l'université de Paris*, 1, no. 5 (January 1977).

159. Rougerie, op. cit., p. 82.

160. Unless one regards debauchery as the elementary form of popular protest.

161. J. P. Aron, *Le mangeur au XIXᵉ siècle*.

162. J. Gaillard, *Paris: La ville*, passim.

163. As is shown now by the survival of popular and sadomasochistic prostitution in the district of Les Halles and the Beaubourg.

164. Virmaître, op. cit., p. 140.

165. Patoir, op. cit., p. 421.

166. Léon Bloy, "Barbey d'Aurevilly: Espion prussien," *Sueurs de sang*. See also the catalogue of oaths used by prostitutes in Virmaître's book, p. 139.

167. Coffignon, op. cit., p. 119, cites soliciting in omnibuses.

168. Developing a remark by Flaubert to the effect that "in the provinces, the window is replacing theaters and walking out" (*Madame Bovary*, Garnier edition, p. 130), Edgard Pich writes, "The theme of prostitution is closely bound up with that of the window . . . it is in a way a substitute for the *maison close* and the side-

walk" ("Littératures et cadres sociaux: L'antiféminisme sous le Second Empire," *Mythes et représentations de la femme,* p. 182, n. 7).

169. Macé, op. cit., p. 78.

170. Ibid.

171. Op. cit., p. 502.

172. Coffignon, op. cit., p. 79.

173. Reuss, op. cit., p. 203.

174. In *Nana* (p. 1320), Zola describes one such police raid in a lodging house.

175. Hence the hero's surprise in Barbey d'Aurevilly's novella "La vengeance d'une femme" when he realizes how sexually accomplished the duchesse de Sierra Leone is.

176. Reuss, op. cit., p. 422.

177. Arch. dept. Bouches-du-Rhône.

178. On this matter, see Carlier, op. cit., p. 36; Martineau, op. cit., p. 82; and Coffignon, op. cit., pp. 80ff.

179. Op. cit., p. 114.

180. Reuss, op. cit., p. 184.

181. See Regnault, *L'évolution de la prostitution,* p. 114.

182. As far as Marseilles is concerned, see the discussion later in this chapter.

183. Reuss, op. cit., pp. 424, 404.

184. Martineau, op. cit., p. 97, and Coffignon, op. cit., p. 312.

185. Arch. dept. Haute-Garonne.

186. Op. cit., p. 83.

187. Virmaître, op. cit., p. 115.

188. Commenge, op. cit., p. 62. It should be noted, however, that the author tends to exaggerate all the threats to the private life of the bourgeois household.

189. Virmaître, op. cit., p. 67.

190. Arch. dept. Bouches-du-Rhône. The prostitution practiced in the *chalets de nécessité* had already been pointed out by Regnault in *L'évolution de la prostitution,* p. 113.

191. Arch. dept. Bouches-du-Rhône.

192. Arch. dept. Bouches-du-Rhône.

193. J. Le Yaouanq observes a similar process in the fourth arrondissement.

194. As far as Nancy is concerned, Dr. Vigneron provides a detailed description of these back rooms, which were sometimes separated from the public room by no more than a curtain. "We have seen such dark rooms, giving on to the first, public room," he writes. "It is easy enough to know what is going on there; one can hear and see all too easily" (*La prostitution clandestine à Nancy,* p. 25). One senses here the fear of seeing sexuality spill over from the marital bedroom and become perceptible.

195. According to Février, three-fifths of the barmaids suffering from syphilis at Nancy were under twenty-one (cited by Vigneron, op. cit., p. 62).

196. Arch. dept. Var.

197. Arch. nat BB[18] 2198.

198. Cf. Pierre Pierrard, *La vie ouvrière à Lille sous le Second Empire,* pp. 281–289.

199. Prof. H. Leloir, "La syphilis et les cabarets dans la région du Nord: Les brasseurs," *Journal des connaissances médicales* (November 1887), 371–372.

200. Hayem, op. cit., p. 252.

201. Guyot, op. cit., appendixes, p. 551.

202. Ibid.

203. Arch. dept. Nord.

204. Hayem, op. cit., p. 253.

205. Reuss, op. cit., p. 424.

206. Prof. G. Etienne, *Etudes sur la prostitution,* p. 13.

207. Arch. nat. BB 18 2498.

208. Bergeret, op. cit., passim.

209. Report of the police commissioner to the prefect, arch. dept. Hérault.

210. Ibid.

211. A particularly revealing example of these complaints is provided by the inhabitants of Bastide-Bordeaux (arch. dept. Gironde), who complained about five café owners in the avenue Thiers. After questioning them at length, the police commissioner wrote to the prefect on July 10, 1881: "Sometimes a client has been seen kissing one of the barmaids; on another occasion, a barmaid kissed a young man. In other circumstances, it has been observed that a customer pulled one of these barmaids on to his knees, another took her by the waist. Sometimes, barmaids go off in *open carriages* with young men and smoking cigarettes. Familiar, sometimes obscene language has been heard." A twenty-six-year-old merchant declared that his sister-in-law, aged thirteen, was not allowed by her father to visit her friends because she would have had to pass in front of these cafés. Ladies stopped visiting the library because it was situated close to these establishments.

212. Report of the police commissioner, July 1, 1903, arch. dept. Charente-Inférieure.

213. See the description by Reuss, op. cit., p. 277.

214. According to the physician in chief Debrie and Major Rudler, certain women prostituted themselves to the soldiers of the garrison at Belfort for five and sometimes even for two or four sous; *Bull. soc. fr. de médecine militaire,* 7,8 (1909).

215. Bloy, "La boue," in *Sueurs de sang,* p. 128.

216. Ibid. See also the striking description of the *pierreuse* murdered by Moosbrugger in Robert Musil's novel *Man without Qualities.*

217. A similar process was observed, it is true, around other garrisons, but the documentation is not nearly as rich. Thus, from 1889 an intercommunal system of health surveillance was organized in the area around Brest (arch. dept. Finistère).

218. Arch. dept. Meurthe-et-Moselle.

219. Like G——, the licensee who forced his nineteen-year-old barmaid to prostitute herself and, in order to attract customers, to stand, in the evening, on a table, lift her skirts, and allow the soldiers to touch her obscenely. By way of a change, G—— frequently sent his barmaid to church to take communion.

220. In all, 153 prostitutes gave rise to 177 arrests.

221. Report of the commissioner, arch. dept. Meurthe-et-Moselle.

222. Until August 1904 caravans were parked in a field close to the 156th and 160th regiments. Under pressure from the authorities the landowner refused, after that date, to give permission to park on his land.

223. Lucienne C——, aged nineteen, arrested in 1908, declared that she slept "in the stables of a boat-hauling firm." She prostituted herself on the banks of the canal.

When arrested in March 1906, Louise B——, aged twenty, was exploring the terrain where the thirty-ninth artillery regiment of La Justice was practicing maneuvers, as well as the canal banks. She took her clients "into a wooden hut in a garden at the place known as Moulin-le-Bas."

224. Arch. dept. Charente-Inférieure.

225. Vigneron, op. cit., p. 56.

226. Arch. dept. Hérault.

227. Arch. dept. Gironde.

228. Report of the subprefect of Brest to the prefect, October 4, 1876, arch. dept. Finistère.

229. Bergeret, op. cit., p. 343.

230. Report of the subprefect of Marennes, April 11, 1902, arch. dept. Charente-Inférieure.

231. Arch. dept. Hérault. See table of answers to the 1902 inquiry.

232. Arch. dept. Var.

233. Results of the inquiry, arch. dépt. Var.

234. Ibid.

235. Ibid.

236. For example, two prostitutes, aged eighteen and twenty-one, one of whom was a day worker and a widow, living in the hamlet of Mathéou, a commune of Cantenac in the Gironde, sold themselves to young men who arrived at their living quarters in gangs (Report of the gendarmerie of Cantenac, arch. dept. Gironde).

237. Op. cit., p. 15. The same opinion is expressed by Regnault, *L'évolution de la prostitution*, p. 89.

238. Ibid., p. 17.

239. Ibid., p. 15.

240. On the occasion of a charge of robbery, brought on November 23, 1907, we thus learn that Charles F——, a married agricultural laborer living at Bouvron, came regularly to Toul "to have carnal relations on the edge of the bed" with Céline M——, a twenty-eight-year-old prostitute (arch. dept. Meurthe-et-Moselle).

241. See Lion Murard and Patrick Zylberman, op. cit.

242. According to the police commissioner of Briey, July 7, 1908, arch. dept. Meurthe-et-Moselle.

243. Ibid.

244. The diatribes against the popular dance hall were, for the police too, an inexhaustible theme.

245. Report of the mining engineer, July 5, 1912, arch. dept. Meurthe-et-Moselle.

246. Ibid.

247. Spillmann, "A propos de la prophylaxie des maladies vénériennes: L'état sanitaire dans le bassin de Briey," *Revue médicale de l'Est* (1908), 77.

248. Ibid., p. 91.

249. Op. cit.

250. Arch. dept. Meurthe-et-Moselle. At this date about 127 prostitutes had been registered: 35 at Joeuf, 23 at Homécourt, 18 at Jarny, 1 at Valleroy, 8 at Tucquenieux, 4 at Mancieulles, 2 at Trieux, 20 at Piennes, 3 at Mont-Bonvillers, 9 at Villerupt, 4 at Thil, 3 at Crusnes, 2 at Longlaville, 1 at Longwy, and 3 at Réhon.

251. See Chapter 7.

252. Arch. nat. BB 18 2363.

253. It is because he approaches her too suddenly and too brutally that Goncourt's *fille* Elisa murders the soldier who is her *amant de coeur.*

254. This is the case of Céline in *Soeurs Vatard.*

255. Op. cit., p. 78.

256. This is the case in the novella by P. Alexis, *La fin de Lucie Pellegrin.*

257. Op. cit., pp. 75–76.

258. L. Puibaraud, *Les malfaiteurs de profession,* p. 97.

259. On this matter, see Charles-Louis Philippe, *Bubu de Montparnasse,* p. 28.

260. Meunier, op. cit., p. 173 ("Prices Charged by the Bar Whores"). This paper appears to have been found in a pimp's rooms in the place Maubert.

261. See the use made by R. Ricatte (*La gènese de la fille Elisa,* pp. 172ff.) of the letters found in a brothel on the Ile de la Cité when the quarter was being demolished.

262. Albert Leblond and Arthur Lucas, *Du tatouage chez les prostituées* (1899). I have borrowed from this book most of the information concerning tattoos.

263. C. J. Lecour, *La prostitution à Paris,* p. 207.

264. Reuss, op. cit., p. 77.

265. All the authors who have attempted to describe prostitution have tried to sketch a portrait of the *souteneur,* notably Carlier, op. cit., pp. 218–230; Reuss, op. cit., pp. 75–95; Martineau, op. cit., pp. 118ff.; Coffignon, op. cit., p. 212ff.; Commenge, op. cit., pp. 91ff.; Maxime du Camp, op. cit., pp. 470ff.; L. Puibaraud, op. cit., pp. 90–106; Macé, op. cit., p. 111; and Meunier, op. cit., p. 171.

266. Coffignon, op. cit., p. 214.

267. Arch. dept. Seine-et-Oise.

268. Carlier, op. cit., p. 218.

269. Arch. dept. Bouches-du-Rhône.

270. Arch. dept. du Nord.

271. Coffignon, op. cit., p. 215.

272. Commenge, op. cit., p. 93.

273. Puibaraud, op. cit., p. 115.

274. Op. cit., p. 94.

275. *Le droit des femmes* claims, in its edition of March 15, 1884, that a union of *souteneurs* had been formed in Paris.

276. This is also the opinion of Martineau, op. cit., p. 121.

277. Like those of Bubu and Le Grand Jules in *Bubu de Montparnasse,* pp. 64ff.

278. On this matter, one may remember the role played by Fernand in L. F. Céline's *Mort à credit.*

279. Report by Police Commissioner Dietze, arch. dept. Bouches-du-Rhône.

280. Ibid.

281. Op. cit., pp. 226–227.

282. Op. cit., p. 94.

283. Report by the prefect to the procurator general, arch. dept. Seine-Inférieure.

284. Report of December 9, 1902, arch. préfect. de police, BA 1689.

285. Ibid.

286. See "Exploits de souteneurs," *L'humanité,* October 25, 1906.

287. Arch. préfect. de police, BA 1689.

288. Commenge, op. cit., p. 100.

289. Homo, op. cit., p. 51.

290. For this we have at our disposal Dr. Martineau's work on the venereal patients of Lourcine, that of Dr. Commenge, who analyzed ten thousand files on unregistered prostitutes suffering from venereal disease, originally kept by the physician of the dispensary of the prefecture of police, and Dr. Mireur's inquiry into the unregistered prostitutes of Marseilles. We also have the work of Dr. Etienne, and above all that of Dr. Vigneron, on the unregistered prostitutes at Nancy; and we should not forget the oldest work, to which I have frequently referred, that by Dr. Homo on the prostitutes of Château-Gontier. Unfortunately, the first three authors, who are those who did the most work on the subject, used different samples. The most scientific of them is certainly that of Dr. Martineau; since no registered prostitute was treated at Lourcine, this hospital was the headquarters of unregistered prostitution. His work concerns only those prostitutes suffering from venereal disease, however, and is not, therefore, entirely representative of the whole. Dr. Mireur's work enables us to compare, among the prostitutes who appeared before the Marseilles vice squad, those who were registered (see pp. 72ff.) with those who were released; but this last category is not representative, it goes without saying, of unregistered prostitution as a whole. Dr. Commenge's study of unregistered prostitutes arrested and recognized as suffering from venereal disease comprises both a majority of prostitutes who were to be registered immediately and a minority of prostitutes allowed to return to unregistered prostitution.

291. Mireur, *La prostitution à Marseille*, p. 221; this is also the source of details provided in the following paragraph.

292. Op. cit., p. 42, and, for what follows, pp. 302–379.

293. Results generally confirmed by the reports of Police Commissioner Dietze (arch. dept. Bouches-du-Rhône), concerning underage prostitutes arrested in 1875 and 1876.

294. Report of the head of the vice squad, arch. dept. Seine-Inférieure.

295. Etienne, op. cit., p. 13.

296. Vigneron, op. cit., p. 20.

297. Op. cit., pp. 42–66.

298. It should also be noted that among the eleven unregistered prostitutes at Château-Gontier who, at the end of the Second Empire, replied to Dr. Homo's questions (op. cit., p. 57), one claimed to have lost her virginity in her twelfth year, another in her thirteenth year, four around the age of fourteen, two around fifteen, one around sixteen, and one at seventeen; the last one was married as a virgin at the age of nineteen.

299. With the exception of certain inmates of *maisons de rendez-vous*, but when the police investigated them, they did so with tact and discretion.

300. For example, Barthélemy and Devillez, "Syphilis et alcool: Les inviteuses," *France médicale*, (1882), 302ff.

301. In fact, these establishments were the successors of the *caboulots* (low dives), which became widespread in the capital in 1860, but which, after an ordinance issued by Prefect of Police Boitelle on September 19, 1861, began to decline (Lecour, *La prostitution à Paris*, p. 226).

302. Data in Table 10 are from Macé (op. cit., p. 127) and Virmaître (*Trottoirs et lupanars*, p. 273).

303. Reuss, op. cit., p. 196.

304. Macé, op. cit., p. 136.

305. The fashion for the grotto during the last third of the century would be worth a systematic study. It played an important part in both stage design and symbolist architecture, as well as in the decoration of "erotic" temples. One also finds it in a religious context, for example, in the growing number of edifices based on the model of the grotto at Lourdes.

306. Macé, op. cit., p. 141.

307. Op. cit., p. 81.

308. Macé, op. cit., p. 142.

309. Coffignon, op. cit., p. 101.

310. Macé, op. cit., p. 199.

311. J. L. Huysmans, *A rebours*, Collection 10–18, pp. 271–274. For des Esseintes, these establishments "corresponded to the state of mind of a whole generation and he *derived from them the synthesis of the period*," a mixture of "foolish sentimentality" and "practical ferocity." "Young Parisians who, when the blood was up . . . could not bring themselves to go in, to drink, to pay, and to leave . . . had not yet realized that the barmaids in the dives were, from the point of view of physical beauty, from the point of view of artful poses and necessary attire, far inferior to the inmates of the better-class brothels!"

312. Barrès, *Les déracinés* (1965), p. 113.

313. Ibid., p. 112.

314. Ibid., p. 108.

315. Ibid., p. 105.

316. Ibid., pp. 73–74.

317. Ibid., p. 107.

318. Hayem, op. cit., p. 252.

319. Commenge, op. cit., p. 57.

320. Arch. dept. Haute-Garonne.

321. Arch. dept. Bouches-du-Rhône.

322. Inquiry of 1902, arch. dept. Var.

323. Arch. nat. BB 18 2488.

324. Ibid.

325. See the map in André Ibels, *La traite des chanteuses*, pp. 128ff.

326. Arch. dept. Meurthe-et-Moselle.

327. Indeed, it should be remembered that, in certain regions at least, choral or other singing held a considerable attraction for workers. See P. Pierrard, op. cit., pp. 296–299, for the Nord, and A. Corbin, op. cit., I, 412–417, for the Limousin.

328. Obviously this depends on individual cases and regional habits. In the north and northeast, the *patrons* of the *bouisbouis* often took a direct cut from the professional earnings of the women. J. B. D—— owned two *cafés-concerts* at Longwy; according to a report dated 1895, he charged the client and "took one-tenth of what the artists earned from their contacts with men" (arch. dept. Meurthe-et-Moselle).

329. Op. cit., p. 78.

330. Abel Hermant, in *Le cavalier Miserey* (1886), 379–383, gives a description of the raffle collection and of the atmosphere of a Rouen *beuglant*.

331. Report by Louis Comte, *La répression de la traite des blanches: Compte rendu du 3ᶜ congrès international tenu à Paris* (1906), pp. 226ff.

332. *La répression de la traite des blanches, congrès de Madrid* (1912), p. 145.

333. Martineau, op. cit., p. 86.

334. Reuss, op. cit., p. 192. On the scandal in one of the *maisons* in the rue Duphot in which he was compromised, see Andrieux, op. cit., vol. 2, chap. 59, "L'affaire de la rue Duphot."

335. Indeed, a certain time lag may be observed in the spread of the *maisons de rendez-vous* in Paris and in the provinces.

336. Fiaux, *La police des moeurs,* I, 219.

337. Fiaux, *La femme, le mariage et le divorce* (1880).

338. See Chapter 7.

339. Virmaître, *Trottoirs et lupanars,* p. 101; on pp. 89ff. the author provides a list, with addresses, of the Parisian *maisons de rendez-vous.*

340. Fiaux, *La police des moeurs,* I, 218.

341. *Le prolétariat de l'amour,* p. 175.

342. See Chapter 7.

343. Fiaux, *La police des moeurs,* I, 219.

344. Meunier, op. cit., p. 436.

345. Ibid., p. 445. It would seem that it was this type of establishment that Courtial des Péreires frequented in *Mort à crédit.*

346. Meunier, op. cit., p. 437.

347. Fiaux, *La police des moeurs,* I, 219.

348. Meunier, op. cit., p. 448.

349. Fiaux, *La police des moeurs,* I, 221.

350. Ibid.

351. See Chapter 7.

352. Op. cit., p. 32.

353. Coffignon, op. cit., p. 154.

354. Marie-Jeanne Dury, *Flaubert et ses projets inédits.* On this matter, see Jean-Paul Sartre, *L'idiot de la famille,* III, 627ff.

355. Turot, op. cit., p. 185.

356. Op. cit., p. 81.

357. Coffignon, op. cit., p. 159.

358. Zola, *La curée*; G. de Maupassant, *Le signe.*

359. See, by way of example, André Couvreur, *Les mancenilles.*

360. An inexhaustible theme that cannot be adequately dealt with here.

361. Fiaux, *La police des moeurs,* I, 219, and Meunier, op. cit.

362. Goron, *Les industries de l'amour,* p. 18.

363. Op. cit., pp. 229–244.

364. Ibid., p. 236.

365. Ibid., p. 237.

366. Op. cit., p. 439, and Fiaux, *La police des moeurs,* I, 220.

367. These files are to be found in the departmental archives of the Bouches-du-Rhône. All the quotations in this discussion are taken from these documents. Following a press campaign orchestrated by *Le petit Provençal* and *Le tout-Marseille,* the

prefect decided to apply an ordinance of July 8, 1907, of which Article 9 forbade "the keeping of *maisons de passe*" and Article 20 forbade prostitutes to frequent "unregistered houses of debauchery." This policy was part of the increased repression evident in the years prior to the First World War.

368. For the rest, a file concerns an unregistered *maison de tolérance* that functioned in every way like an authorized establishment; another concerns a café-restaurant in the suburbs of Marseilles, another a public lavatory, and nine *maisons de passe* (lodging houses for unregistered prostitutes). These last establishments usually occupied almost the whole of the buildings in which they were set up.

369. Four of these women had opened two such establishments during the period under consideration.

370. But four were found in the rue Pavillon, three in the rue de Musée, and two each in the rue Sénac, rue Saint-Ferréol, and rue de la République.

371. One of them was not even a subtenant.

372. We have details of thirteen of the thirty-six apartments: six of them comprised five rooms, three had four rooms, and the others had three, six, seven, and eight rooms, respectively.

373. It is true that my study of the keepers of *maisons de tolérance* (see Chapter 2) concerns women who had been authorized to open a brothel, whereas here, on the contrary, I am dealing with establishments that the authorities closed down.

374. The Nord, the Landes, the Ariège, the Basses-Pyrénées, the Hautes-Alpes, and Corsica.

375. It should be added that two of the keepers declared that they had private incomes.

376. This was the case with four of those whose files I have analyzed.

377. The presence of these women is specified in five *maisons de rendez-vous*.

378. This practice was noted in only one of the *maisons* studied.

379. They were usually posted in the street, near the building, sometimes actually on its staircase. Some policemen carried the conscientious performance of their duties to the point of moving into the building opposite and trying to observe the couples *in flagrante delicto*. Policeman X saw at first a couple kissing at Madame S——'s. With his colleague he watched the couples undressing, but, he complained in his report, "we were not witnesses to their sexual relations, since, from the place where we were, we could not see the bed." Could we have a better example of the persistence of police supervision of unlicensed sexual activities?

380. Some keepers sent men out to advertise their services when boats disembarked.

381. Twenty-five minutes or half an hour in three establishments, three-quarters of an hour in three other establishments, one hour in two, and an hour and a half in the last.

382. One of the establishments received four clients per afternoon, two others seven, and two others between fifteen and twenty.

4. Sexual Privation and the Demand for Prostitution

1. Louis Chevalier, *La formation de la population parisienne au XIXe siècle*.

2. Jeanne Gaillard, *Paris: La ville (1852–1870)*, pp. 217ff.

3. See Louis Chevalier, *Classes laborieuses,* pp. 380–392. See also, on the subject of Lille, Pierre Pierrard, op. cit., pp. 118–124.

4. On the development of these familial structures, see the whole of J. L. Flandrin and F. Lebrun, *La vie conjugale sous l'ancien régime.*

5. A. Corbin, "Migrations temporaires et société rurale au XIXᵉ siècle; Le cas du Limousin," *Revue historique,* 500 (September-December 1971), and *Archaïsme et modernité en Limousin,* I, 218. On the "immorality" of the temporary migrants, see Abel Châtelain, *Les migrants temporaires en France de 1800 à 1911,* pp. 1068–73, and Martin Nadaud, *Mémoires,* republished almost simultaneously by Maspéro and Hachette, with introductions by J. P. Rioux and Maurice Agulhon.

6. Gaillard, op. cit., p. 525.

7. In *Splendeurs et misères des courtisanes* (p. 671), Balzac describes the rue de Langlade and the adjacent streets "criss-crossed by strange creatures that belonged to no world; white, half-naked shapes stand against the walls; the shadows move backward and forward. Between the wall and the passer-by there flows a procession of walking, talking dresses." See also the description of the rue de la Mortellerie in *Les mystères de Paris,* and, at a later date, that of the rue Basse-du-Rempart by Barbey d'Aurevilly ("La vengeance d'une femme," in *Les diaboliques*).

8. As the whole of the book by Jeanne Gaillard, op. cit., shows.

9. Gaillard, op. cit., p. 220.

10. Châtelain, op. cit., p. 1069, notes the progress of conjugal fidelity among the temporary migrants in the second half of the century.

11. Op. cit., p. 221.

12. Pierrard, op. cit., pp. 119ff.

13. M. Perrot, "L'éloge de la ménagère dans le discours ouvrier français au XIXᵉ siècle," in *Mythes et représentations de la femme au XIXᵉ siècle,* p. 110.

14. Op. cit., p. 228.

15. A. Daumard, *Les fortunes françaises au XIXᵉ siècle,* p. 152.

16. P. Léon, *Géographie de la fortune et structures sociales à Lyon au XIXᵉ siècle,* pp. 120–135. The silk worker, in particular, saw his condition improve, especially after 1870; he "manifests an ever-marked tendency to become like a bourgeois" (p. 127).

17. Yves Lequin, *Les ouvriers de la région lyonnaise (1848–1914),* vol. 2, "Les intérêts de classe et la République," p. 92.

18. F. Codaccioni, *De l'inégalité sociale dans une grande ville industrielle: Le drame de Lille de 1850 a 1914,* p. 430.

19. Chevalier, *Classes laborieuses,* pp. 461–462.

20. A. Corbin, "Pour une étude sociologique de la croissance de l'alphabétisation au XIXᵉ siècle," *Revue d'hist. econ. et soc.,* 1 (1975), and, with a wider scope, F. Furet and J. Ozouf, *Lire et écrire.*

21. *The Rebellious Century, 1830–1930,* pp. 78ff.

22. Michelle Perrot, *Les ouvriers en grève,* II, 586.

23. Ibid.

24. Michelle Perrot, "Délinquance et système pénitentiaire en France au XIXᵉ siècle," *Annales eco. soc. civ.* (January-February, 1975).

25. M. Foucault, *Surveiller et punir,* passim.

26. Perrot, *Les ouvriers en grève,* II, 624.

27. I have written about the persistence of this image, nourished by innumerable fantasies, among the workers of Limoges.

28. On the subject of the miners, see R. Trempé's thesis "Les mineurs de Carmaux."

29. *Le petit travailleur infatigable,* p. 153.

30. Ibid., p. 198.

31. Ibid., p. 259.

32. Ibid.

33. Ibid., p. 202.

34. Ibid.

35. Ibid.

36. Ibid.

37. Jean Borie, *Le célibataire française,* passim.

38. Lion Murard and Patrick Zylberman, op. cit., p. 202.

39. Ibid., p. 20.

40. This is what emerged from the session of the *Société de démographie historique,* February 5, 1977, following remarks by, in particular, M. Gilet, M. Frey, and G. Jacquemet, to whom I refer later.

41. Familialization and moralization go together; this subject has been dealt with at great length by Jacques Donzelot, *La police des familles* and *Recherches,* 28, *Disciplines à domicile.*

42. Michelle Perrot, speech before the Jean Jaurès colloquium, November 1976.

43. Gaillard, op. cit., p. 207.

44. Daumard, *Les fortunes,* pp. 149ff.

45. A critical analysis of this concept is to be found in C. Baudelot, R. Establet, and J. Malemort, *La petite bourgeoisie en France,* pp. 29ff.

46. Léon, op. cit., pp. 105ff.

47. Cited by Gaillard, op. cit., p. 384.

48. Ibid.

49. Maurice Lévy-Leboyer, "Le patronat française a-t-il été malthusien?" *Le mouvement social* (July-September 1974), 22–28.

50. On traveling conditions for British tourists in France, see Sylvaine Marandon, *L'image de la France dans l'Angleterre victorienne,* pp. 145ff.

51. It was during a train journey that Léon Mirat caught the syphilis that drove him to suicide (Michel Corday, *Vénus ou les deux risques.*)

52. See Proust's description of the building of a deluxe brothel on the Normandy coast, near Balbec, in *Sodome et Gomorrhe (Cities of the plain).*

53. A visit by a provincial notable to the local prostitute is described by Huysmans in *Un dilemme.*

54. Marguerite Perrot, *Le mode de vie des familles bourgeoise, 1873–1953.*

55. See, concerning the socialist discourse on prostitution, the discussion in Chapter 5.

56. T. Zeldin, *Ambition, Love, and Politics,* p. 291.

57. See *Contributions à la psychologie de l'amour,* and passages by Jean Borie on this subject in *Le célibataire français,* p. 47.

58. See Yvonne Knibiehler, "Le discours médical sur la femme, constances et ruptures," in *Mythes et représentations,* p. 45.

59. Op. cit., p. 291.

60. Noami Schor, "Le sourire du sphinx," in *Mythes et représentations,* p. 193.

61. Op. cit., pp. 65ff.

62. T. Zeldin, op. cit., pp. 299ff.

63. See Knibiehler, op. cit., and "La nature féminine au temps de code civil," *Annales eco. soc. civ.* (July-August 1976).

64. Dr. L. Fiaux, *La femme, le mariage et le divorce: Etude de physiologie et de sociologie,* pp. 122, 94.

65. See *Revue de gynécologie.* These articles are full of advice on the positions to adopt during intercourse.

66. See A. Forel, *La question sexuelle exposée aux adultes cultivés,* passim. For Dassy de Lignières (op. cit., p. 33), the average duration of sexual intercourse during this period in his circle was close to that of soft-boiling an egg, that is, three or four minutes. By contrast, Charles-Louis Philippe, describing the sexual activities of Berthe and her pimp, regards them "as a good, hygienic thing between a man and his wife, which amuses one for a quarter of an hour or so before you go to sleep" (*Bubu de Montparnasse,* p. 28). According to the Simon report, the average duration was eleven minutes during this period.

67. Fiaux, *La femme, le mariage et le divorce,* p. 198.

68. Ibid., pp. 197–198.

69. Ibid., p. 116.

70. Op. cit., p. 303.

71. A fictional example of a husband condemned to continence for this reason occurs in Octave Mirbeau's *Journal d'une femme de chambre.*

72. See T. Zeldin, op. cit., pp. 292ff. One will find in this book references to the works of those few authors (G. Droz, J. P. Dartigues, A. Debay) who were then demanding a woman's right to orgasm.

73. *Nana,* p. 1223.

74. On this subject, see L. Boltanski, *Prime éducation et morale de classe,* passim.

75. See J. Le Yaouanq, "La boutique du IVe arrondissement," speech before the Institut française d'histoire sociale, 1976.

76. P. Léon (op. cit., pp. 117–118) writes in particular about this "proliferating" category: "Ever-more numerous, the clerks appear . . . as victims of an overall evolution, from which they profit only very little; at the fundamental level of wealth, they represent a declining group." Lequin (op. cit., I, 187ff.). also discusses the rapid growth of this group; the number of clerks in Lyons increased by 934 percent between 1866 and 1891.

77. See Comte d'Haussonville, "Les non classées et l'émigration des femmes aux colonies," *Revue des deux-mondes* (June 1898), 787, and the fictional descriptions by Charles de Rouvre (*L'employée, A deux*).

78. Gaillard, op. cit., p. 221.

79. P. Guillaume, *Bordeaux au XIXe siècle.*

80. See Borie, op. cit., p. 49.

81. P. Gerbod, *La condition universitaire en France au XIXe siècle.*

82. Stendhal, *La vie d'Henri Brulard* ("La Pléiade" edition), pp. 317, 320, and 322.

83. See, by way of example, Huysmans, *Un dilemme.*

84. J. L. Flandrin (*Amours paysannes,* p. 158) speaks of the "sexual ghetto" created by adolescence.

85. See Chapter 2. There is a fine description of the first relations between a schoolboy and a prostitute in Huysmans, *En ménage,* Collection 10–18, pp. 168–169.

86. Later, young bourgeoises were more understanding. See M. Prévost, *Les demi-vierges;* M. Proust, *A la recherche du temps perdu,* passim; and on the subject of the Austrian bourgeoisie, Walter's confidences about his engagement to Clarisse in Musil's novel *The Man without Qualities.* But it should be said that, outside France, long bourgeois engagements frequently gave rise to what Freud, who had experienced one himself with Martha Bernays, calls the fiancé's neurosis. But, as Zeldin notes, this practice was to remain very infrequent in France; this helps to explain the sexual behavior of young Frenchmen.

87. See discussion later in this chapter.

88. Op. cit., p. 24.

89. See Chapter 3 on the garrison at Toul, and Fiaux, *La police des moeurs,* II, 174 (the remarks by Prof. Landouzy).

90. See M. Perrot, Jean Jaurès, colloquium, op. cit., and Y. Lequin, *Les ouvriers de la région lyonnaise,* passim.

91. On this subject, Michel Lobrot draws a distinction between the genital and the erotic in *La libération sexuelle.*

92. The theme of the client's hasty departure is treated by Huysmans in *Un dilemme* and *A vau-l'eau.* Most contemporaries regarded the proposition "Animal triste est post coïtu" as a dogma.

93. This insistence on a semblance of seduction does not contradict the collapse of the Don Juan myth observed by Jean Borie (op. cit., p. 52). Insofar as the practices of seduction were intended for prostitutes, they were devalued. Don Juan in the salon of a *maison de rendez-vous* was certainly one of the elements of the psychopathology of the myth. The real contradiction lies at another level: it is at the point where the scientific literature speaks of the satisfaction of the genetic instinct—that is to say, of animality in the individual—that the prostitute's triumph demands more feeling. Is there a time lapse here between discourse and actual behavior? A simpler explanation might be that, frustrated at both poles of his sexuality by marriage, man pursues with the prostitute the satisfaction of a self-contradictory need for unbridled sex with a pure, angelic partner.

94. J. P. Aron, *Le mangeur au XIXe siècle.*

95. Op. cit., p. 543.

96. Chalmin, *L'officier française de 1815 à 1870,* p. 145.

97. See W. Serman, *Les officiers français, 1848–1870,* pp. 1071–79.

98. Along with the theater, for the officers in provincial garrisons.

99. Dr. L. Fiaux, *L'armée et la police des moeurs: Biologie sexuelle du soldat,* p. 116.

100. A. Corbin, "Le péril vénérien: Prophylaxie sanitaire et prophylaxie morale," *L'haleine des faubourgs: Recherches,* 29, (1977).

101. Gaillard, op. cit., p. 528.

102. *Histoire de Lyon et du Lyonnais,* (Privat, 1975).

103. On the subject of Lille.

104. That is to say, prostitutes were asked not to stand in groups, to keep moving, and to allow free circulation.

105. Pierrard, op. cit., p. 216.

106. Gaillard, op. cit., p. 246.

107. The Comte Muffat is all the more fascinated by the spectacle of Nana's body in that, in his circle, women do not exhibit their nakedness. After over twenty years of life together, he "had never seen the Comtesse Muffat put on her garters" (*Nana*, p. 1213).

108. See, on this subject, the envious reflections of M. Hennebeau, the elderly *patron* in *Germinal*, when confronted by the display of proletarian sexuality. The same envious view of the sexual behavior of the workers is to be found in the character of Cyprien in *En ménage* (see the monologue to the cat).

109. See Chapter 2.

110. Richard Cobb, *La protestation populaire*, pp. 220–226.

111. In *Le pornographe*.

112. Louis-Sébastien Mercier, "Matrones," in *Tableau de Paris*. The author describes the activity of "the "matrons" who attracted into their establishments young bourgeois women and shopgirls who wanted to be able to buy dresses. In eighteenth-century Paris, dancers, actresses, governesses, and linen workers already nourished the world of venal sex.

113. Simon, *L'ouvrière*, pp. 228–229.

114. Commenge, op. cit., pp. 337–339.

115. Savioz, "La question du sixième," *Relèvement social: Supplément*, March 15, 1906.

116. Dr. Morin, "Le sixième étage et les jeunes domestiques," *Bull. de la soc. fr. de prophylaxie san. et morale* (1912), 139.

117. See Vellini's servant girl in *Une vieille maîtresse*.

118. Could there be a better example of this proximity than the relations described throughout Marcel Proust's work between the hero and his domestic staff?

119. See Raoul Dumès' escapades in Rose's room in Victor Margueritte's *Prostituée*.

120. E. and J. de Goncourt, *Germinie Lacerteux* (1877), p. 53. The erotic function of the chambermaid is clearly brought out by Marcel Proust in the case of Mme. Putbus' maid (see *Sodome et Gomorrhe*).

121. De Ryckère, *La servante criminelle*, p. 293, an essential work on this subject.

122. *Psychopathia sexualis*, p. 223.

123. Described in detail in *Au Bonheur des Dames*.

124. F. Parent-Lardeur, *Les demoiselles de magasin*, p. 36–37.

125. Which makes the couple formed by the student and the shop assistant a logical one. See Parent-Lardeur, op. cit., p. 37.

126. H. Mercillon, *La rémunération des employés*, p. 48, n. 3.

127. It should be recognized, however, that, very often, concubinage with a shop assistant approximated a true marriage. Indeed, a new mode was being established in these circles in which loss of respectability attached only to a multiplicity of lovers; this was the case of Clara in *Au bonheur des dames*.

128. See the statement by M. Beauchamp, a departmental head, to Zola (author's notes made before writing the novel).

129. Statement made by Mme. Dulit, a saleswoman, to Zola, ibid.

130. Gaillard, op. cit., p. 440.

131. Ibid., p. 439.

132. Ibid., p. 216.

133. Op. cit., p. 296.

134. Charles Benoist, *Les ouvrières de l'aiguille à Paris*, pp. 115ff.

135. L. Bonnevay, *Les ouvrières lyonnaises travaillant à domicile: Misères et remèdes*, p. 90.

136. This is shown in detail by Zola through the character of Denise Baudu in *Au bonheur des dames.*

137. *Réforme sociale*, 2 (1901), 57ff., according to Gonnard, op. cit., p. 134.

138. Admirably described, albeit in the case of the male work force, by L. F. Céline in *Mort à crédit.*

139. See the role of the dressmakers in Marcel Proust's work. Morel's fiancée, the niece of the waistcoat-maker Jupien, is received into a good bourgeois milieu (*La prisonnière*).

140. Simon, op. cit., p. 90.

141. J. K. Huysmans, *Marthe, Les soeurs Vatard.*

142. Bonnevay, op. cit., p. 90.

143. Simon, op. cit., p. 145.

144. *Au bonheur des dames,* p. 681.

145. Zola, *Au bonheur des dames,* p. 500.

146. Michelle Perrot, "Delinquance et système pénitentiaire," p. 75; one is reminded of the character of Mme. de Boves in *Au bonheur des dames.*

147. Count d'Haussonville, "Les non classées," p. 779.

148. The history of urban society after 1870 is, as we know, an area in which much research is being done (see J. Le Yaouanq and G. Jacquemet, among others, and the colloquium of economic historians devoted on this subject). Unfortunately, apart from P. Guillaume's work on Bordeaux, this investigation has not yet borne fruit.

149. See Servais and Laurend, op. cit., pp. 209ff.

150. The effects of economic circumstances on prostitutional activity are indeed complex; they are a good deal more so than Engels suggests when, on the subject of Berlin, he notes the increase of prostitutional supply in a period of economic crisis. Indeed, it should not be forgotten that, unlike recession, economic prosperity tends to increase demand and also, by this very fact, plays a stimulating role.

151. This is what emerges from the work of all the historians working on this period, which was regarded by Simiand as phase A of a new Kondratieff. On the acceleration in the growth rate at this time, see, in particular, the work of T.J. Markovitch, M. Lévy-Leboyer, and F. Crouzet.

152. Léon, op. cit., p. 380.

153. See C. Macilhacy, *Le diocèse d'Orléans sous l'épiscopat de Mgr. Dupanloup.*

154. See J. Van Ussel, *La répression sexuelle,* and J. Solé, *L'amour en Occident.*

155. The rise of the theme of prostitution also reflects, it is true, the fascination with characters' falls and self-destruction, which affected many novelists from Barbey d'Aurevilly to Huysmans and Léon Bloy. Finally, one might celebrate "that spiritual form of lechery that is satanism" (Huysmans, *Certains,* on the work of Rops).

156. On this subject, see F. Ronsin's thesis, "Mouvements et courants néo-

malthusiens en France," University of Paris, 1974, and A. Armengaud, *Les Français et Malthus.*

157. For example, the work of Madeleine Pelletier and, in particular, *L'émancipation sexuelle de la femme.*

158. Which finds expression in the success of the popularized works of sexologists, such as the book by Forel.

159. See Knibiehler, "Le discours médical," p. 46.

160. Ibid., p. 41.

5. The System Challenged

1. See the text of fundamental importance published by Maurice Allem in "Notes et variantes" and the Pléiade edition of *Les Misérables,* pp. 1624–41. Victor Hugo abandons his description of Fantine's prostitutional activities; he presents his heroine not as a prostitute by temperament but as a woman led astray. Apart from her weakness for brandy, her raucous voice, her volubility and sudden bursts of anger, he avoids stereotypes. He does not evoke the threat that prostitution represented to society as a whole and to the bourgeoisie in particular; there is no mention in his book of the venereal danger. What he does do is retrace the itinerary of decline; he launches into a severe attack on society: prostitution is merely the last stage of a process; it carries Fantine from the condition of a social shadow to that of a ghost. The novel violently denounces arbitrary police action and the selfishness of bourgeois males. The romantic theme of the purity of the prostitute-martyr, already treated in *Les mystères de Paris,* carries within itself, in an inherent state, the redemptorism of the end of the century. The earthly hell that engulfs this woman, sold so that her daughter might live, prepares the way for her entry into paradise. "The cesspit is a sanctuary in spite of itself," and "putrefaction can become idealized if one glimpses the soul through it . . . Beside Parent-Duchâtelet, who records, Jérémie is capable of sobbing" (pp. 1631, 1637). Comparing the destinies of Jean Valjean and Fantine, Victor Hugo builds up, in describing the Montreuil-sur-Mer dreamed of by M. Madeleine, a countersociety from which poverty, prostitution, and crime have been banished. It is the policeman Javert who puts an end to this utopian vision: "A blackguard from a place where the galley slaves are magistrates and the prostitutes are treated like countesses! But all that is going to change! And not before time!" (p. 307).

2. See Yves Guyot, op. cit., chap. 2. The account of this campaign is based mainly on Guyot's work, on Josephine Butler's *Souvenirs personnels d'une grande croisade,* on the *Bulletin continental* series, and on police reports in the archives of the prefecture of police (BA 1689).

3. Jules Favre was to return to the subject before his death; in the preface to Albert Decourteix's book *La liberté individuelle et le droit d'arrestation,* he calls for a profound reform of the vice squad.

4. This campaign was chronicled at some length by the press; the many reports from policemen ordered by the prefecture to observe the activities of the English militants also provide us with a clear picture of the campaign.

5. J. Butler, *Souvenirs,* p. 64.

6. Ibid., p. 63.

7. Ibid., p. 63.

8. Ibid., p. 67.

9. Ibid., p. 65.

10. Ibid., p. 190.

11. *Bulletin continental: Revue mensuelle des intérêts de la moralité publique: Fédération britannique et continentale pour l'abolition de la prostitution spécialement envisagée comme institution légale ou tolérée,* December 15, 1882.

12. *Bulletin continental,* no. 15, June 1882, text of the appeal of the Comité parisien pour le relèvement de la moralité publique.

13. Butler, op. cit., p. 138.

14. "Why waste much time on the idea that the needs of the flesh must be satisfied?" asks Tacussel, author of the first work devoted to the white slave trade (*La traite des blanches,* p. 28).

15. A. Corbin, "Le péril vénérien au début du siècle: Prophylaxie sanitaire et prophylaxie morale," in *L'haleine des faubourgs.*

16. Report by Brissaud, officer of the peace, on the meeting held on January 28, 1877, at the Union chrétienne de la jeunesse (arch. préfect. de police, BA 1689).

17. Butler, op. cit., pp. 186–187.

18. See Caroline de Barrau, *Bulletin continental,* 12, (November 15, 1876), 92.

19. On Codet, see A. Corbin, *Archaïsme et modernité,* vol. 2, passim.

20. The *Bulletin continental* of 1877 gives an account of the congress (arch. préfect. de police, DB 410).

21. Ibid. Also features in the arch préfect. de police, BA 1689.

22. First Pastor Adrien Gory then Pastor Borel had made abolitionist lecture tours in the provinces. See *Bulletin continental* (1878), 76.

23. Butler, op. cit., p. 322.

24. *Bulletin continental* (1879).

25. In *Bulletin continental* (1878), 9, one reads: "France is now the country that gives most hope of a prompt, radical suppression of the vice squad. This institution is incompatible with the Republic; the democratic press proclaims it; the working classes will soon be unanimous in recognizing it."

26. Guyot, op. cit., p. 425ff.

27. On Maria Deraismes and the principal leaders of feminism, see Marie-Hélène Zylberberg-Hocquard, "Féminisme et syndicalisme en France avant 1914," thesis, University of Tours, 1973, pp. 17ff.

28. See *Bulletin continental,* April 15, 1879, 29ff.

29. Arch. préfect. de police, BA 1689.

30. Ibid.

31. See my discussion later in this chapter.

32. *Bulletin continental,* June 15, 1883, 70. On the fate and activities of this society, see F. Ronsin, op. cit., passim.

33. The dwindling of the *Bulletin continental* reflects the decline.

34. See Chapter 6.

35. I need only mention the severity of the judgments made about it by Louis Reybaud in 1841 in *Revue des deux-mondes.* Somewhat later, *Le temps,* on November 30, 1867, strongly criticized its functioning (see Guyot, op. cit., pt. 3, chap. 1). During the Second Empire, Bouchard waged an obscure struggle against the exis-

tence of enclosed prostitution in his commune of Beaune; having become mayor in 1871, he suppressed, by order, the brothel that functioned in the city. This measure allowed him to be regarded by the abolitionists as their leader (*Bulletin continental,* 1878).

36. Arch. préfect. de police, DB 407.

37. This campaign was related at length by C. J. Lecour and Yves Guyot (op. cit.) and in the newspapers cited.

38. Among the newspapers supporting the campaign were *L'événement, Le bien public, La France, Le Gaulois, L'homme libre, Le national, Le ralliement, Le rappel, Le siècle, La tribune,* and, for the time being, *La République française.* Mention might also be made of *L'estafette, La gazette des tribunaux, La liberté, Le républicain,* and *La Révolution,* not to mention the feminist press, and in particular *L'avenir des femmes. Le petit Lyonnais* and *La tribune des travailleurs* also took part in the campaign, as did *Le républicain* at Saint-Etienne and *La Gironde* at Bordeaux. On Bel-Ami's duel, Maupassant echoes these campaigns, which so activated the press at the time.

39. Quickly replaced, it is true, by *Le radical,* which disappeared in turn in June 1877.

40. To this account should be added the initiative of Martin Nadaud, who, on March 22, 1878, demanded the abolition of the vice squad in the Chamber.

41. Founded by Sigismond Lacroix after the disappearance of *Le radical.*

42. C. J. Lecour, *La campagne contre le préfecture de police* (1881).

43. On September 25, even before Yves Guyot and Fernand Xau had opened fire in *La Marseillaise,* followed by Charles Laurent in Emile de Girardin's *La France;* there then followed *L'estafette, La rappel,* and *Le Voltaire* (in articles by Aurélien Scholl), which criticized the prefecture of police and succeeded in getting Superintendent Luciani, who had been responsible for the arrest of Augustine B——, suspended. *Le temps, Le petit Parisien,* and *Le XIXᵉ siècle,* however, continued to support the prefecture.

44. The chronology of this commission is complex. According to Dr. L. Fiaux's report, it was elected on December 11, 1876, and renewed on December 14, 1878. It began its work on January 27, 1879, suspended it on February 23, 1880, resumed it on January 6, 1883, and completed it on April 5 of the same year.

45. *Bulletin continental,* June 15, 1881.

46. Andrieux explains this in his *Souvenirs d'un préfet de police,* op. cit., vol. 2, chap. 59.

47. *Bulletin continental,* June 15, 1883.

48. P. Sorlin, *Waldeck-Rousseau,* p. 321.

49. Thus *Le Figaro,* October 6, 1881, and Juliette Adam's *Nouvelle revue,* September 1, 1881, took up this position.

50. E. Richard, *La prostitution à Paris* (1890).

51. One exception, however, was Dr. Fiaux, who was one of the apostles of this abolitionism.

52. Op. cit., p. 452.

53. Although certain references to Herbert Spencer prove that Fiaux drew a distinction between freedom of sexual behavior and immorality.

54. Fiaux, *Les maisons de tolérance,* p. 320.

55. See Guyot, op. cit., pp. 420–421, 459.

56. Ibid., p. 473.

57. Fiaux, op. cit., p. 326, and *La police des moeurs,* II, 865.

58. Guyot, op. cit., p. 438.

59. See Pillon's articles in *La critique philosophique, politique, scientifique et littér-aire,* November 23, 1876, and March 14, 1878, and above all the article by Ren-ouvier himself, May 6, 1882.

60. A burning subject and a measure much feared among the bourgeoisie of the time; see Huysmans, *Un dilemme.*

61. Guyot, op. cit., pp. 41, 455. "Bring order into establishments, clean the latrines . . . but I forbid you to lay your hands on me, on my person, or to subject me to your experiments," Guyot declared to the hygienist he was attacking.

62. Ibid., pp. 302–303.

63. Thus Fiaux denounces the practice by which the police put well-known actresses under surveillance (*Rapport à la commission,* p. 384).

64. Guyot, op. cit., p. 107; Fiaux, *Rapport,* pp. 373ff.

65. Guyot, op. cit., pp. 123ff.; Fiaux, *Rapport,* p. 380.

66. References given in Chapter 2. These opinions are often invoked; see Fiaux, *Rapport,* p. 391, and Guyot, op. cit., p. 231.

67. Guyot, op. cit., pp. 267–268.

68. *Les maisons de tolérance,* p. 321.

69. Guyot, op. cit., p. 215.

70. Ibid., p. 215.

71. Ibid., p. 222.

72. Inspired by a quite different ideology, Barbey d'Aurevilly rallied against the moralists who "right, like overturned flowerpots, fallen women" ("La vengeance d'une femme," in *Les diaboliques,* p. 256). For him, only the priests could right such falls. The conviction of the irremediable fall of a woman provides a moral justifica-tion for enclosure.

73. Fiaux, *Les maisons de tolérance,* p. 282.

74. Guyot, op. cit., pp. 294ff., and Fiaux, *Rapport,* pp. 417ff.

75. See Guyot, op. cit., pp. 334ff.

76. Fiaux, *Les maisons de tolérance,* p. 325.

77. Fiaux, *Rapport,* p. 436.

78. C. J. Lecour, *La campagne contre la préfecture de police,* p. 435.

79. M. H. Zylberberg-Hocquard, op. cit., p. 6.

80. Cf. Savioz, *La serve: Une iniquité sociale,* and "Le mouvement féministe fran-çais et la réglementation de la prostitution," report by Mme. J. Hudry-Menos, Lon-don Conference, 1898, in *Le relévement social: Supplément,* September 1, 1898.

81. See the action by Mme. Potonié-Pierre at Maria Pognon's Solidarité des Femmes (Ligue française pour le droit des femmes), Mme. Griess-Traut (Société pour l'amélioration du sort de la femme), Mme. Schmahl (*L'avant-courrière*), and Mme. Vincent (*L'égalité*).

82. Savioz, *La serve,* p. 10.

83. Arch préfect. de police, DB 1689.

84. We know that the question of women later occupied a lesser place in trade-union conferences; after 1888 the only remaining problem was that of women's work, which was almost always treated together with that of children (see M. Perrot, "L'éloge de la ménagère," p. 107).

85. Speech quoted in the *Bulletin continental,* (1878).

86. Christine Dufrancastel, "Hubertine Auclert et la question des femmes à l'immortel congrès," in *Mythes et représentations*, p. 135.

87. Who, however, was to reject the establishment of new brothels in his town.

88. In England, between 1870 and 1879, 9,667 petitions containing 2,150,941 signatures had demanded the repeal of the Contagious Diseases Acts (Guyot, op. cit., p. 437).

89. See Corbin, "Le péril vénérien au début du siècle."

90. C. Andler, *Le manifeste communiste de Karl Marx et F. Engels* ("harem of the capitalist," p. 151).

91. Charles-Albert, "La prostitution," *Les temps nouveaux*, November 26–December 2, 1898 ("disgorger of the virility of the poor").

92. Louis Devance, "Femme, famille, travail et morale sexuelle dans l'idéologie de 1848," in *Mythes et représentations*, describes in detail the attempt at subversion that shook sexual morality in the early 1830s, following the spread of Fourier's ideas and thanks to the influence of Enfantin; he shows how feminism then proved to be radical. The year 1848, however, was obviously a period of "reduction of the dissonances in the ethics of socialism" (p. 86). Proudhon, Cabet, Eugénie Niboyet, Jeanne Deroin, and even the Société des vénusiennes allowed themselves to be influenced by the then-triumphant discourse on female nature. Pauline Roland was converted to the dominant familialism. Victor Hennequin and above all Jules Gray were about the only exceptions, along with, from the working class, the Lyonnais Greppo.

Moreover, we know of the profound divergences that separated the two theoreticians whose influence largely determined the later position of French socialism on matters of sexuality, that is, Fourier and Proudhon. A double mania led the first to advocate complete freedom in love and the second to restore paternal, marital authority (see Louis Devance, "La question de la famille dans la pensée socialiste," thesis, University of Dijon, 1972). Proudhon expounded his views on prostitution at length; for him, any woman who had sexual relations outside marriage was a prostitute; the wife who sought pleasure with her husband, without being guided by absolute devotion for him, also deserved the same description. Indeed, there is no gratuitous love, outside the reciprocal devotion of spouses. Furthermore, everyday dealings with men lead a woman, even a chaste one, to "become de-natured," like a prostitute, and to become "hideous to view" (Oeuvres complètes, *La pornocratie*, pp. 372–374).

Pierre Leroux, Pecqueur, Vidal, and Louis Blanc accepted monogamous union while demanding more equality for women and a free choice of spouse. Finally, Marx and Engels, without defining the nature of the future conjugal bond in detail, analyzed the vices of the bourgeois union that the new organization of society would remedy.

93. Benoît Malon, *Le socialisme intégral*, vol. 1, chap. 7, "L'évolution familiale et le socialisme."

94. Charles Bonnier, *La question de la femme*, 1897, extract from *Devenir social*.

95. Andler, *Le manifeste communiste de Karl Marx*.

96. Edouard Dolléans, La police des moeurs, and his account of the Brussels conference, Le mouvement socialiste (1902), pp. 1784–91. Paul Lafargue does not approach the problem in his book *La question de la femme* (1904).

97. *La police des moeurs*, p. 90.

98. Op. cit., p. 129.

99. Ibid., p. 120.

100. Andler, op. cit., p. 152.

101. Malon, op. cit., p. 362.

102. Ibid., p. 363.

103. Op. cit., p. 77.

104. The model of which, indeed, is not described.

105. Bebel, op. cit., p. 79.

106. Dolléans, op. cit., p. 90.

107. See Andler, op. cit., pp. 150–151.

108. See Chapter 1 on the philanthropists of the Louis-Philippe period.

109. Guilbert, op. cit., pp. 189ff.

110. Bonnier, op. cit., p. 42.

111. Op. cit., p. 364.

112. Bebel, op. cit., p. 88.

113. Ibid., pp. 120ff.

114. Ibid., p. 122. This theory was expounded in the Academy of Medicine in 1866 (see Perrot, "L'éloge de la ménagère," p. 109).

115. Guilbert, op. cit., p. 188.

116. Dolléans, *La police des moeurs,* p. 166.

117. This reluctance was noted by the socialist deputy F. de Pressensé, who, in 1903, at a public meeting, deplored that his friends should have remained outside the battle (arch. préfect. de police, BA 1689).

118. This is what emerges from an article published by Benoît Malon, "Un congrès socialiste," *L'intransigeant,* July 19, 1883.

119. The divergences are obvious. Thus Malon envisaged a free, human, natural, working-class family, based on love and intellectual and moral affinities, the duration of which would be limited by the free will of each partner. Dolléans, by contrast, subjected the family of the future to the duty of procreation; he became the apostle of continence and sexual control on the part of youth because, for him, the obligation to reproduce took precedence over the right to enjoy pleasure.

120. See Charles Sowerwine, "Le groupe féministe socialiste, 1899–1902," *Le mouvement social* (January-March 1975), 87–120.

121. See Chapter 7.

122. See Chapter 7.

123. This is what emerges from an examination of the *Supplément* to *Relèvement social.*

124. See Chapter 7.

125. Speech by F. de Pressensé to the meeting cited in arch. préfec. de police, BA 1689.

126. Charles-Albert, "La prostitution," *Les temps nouveaux,* December 10–16, 1898. Charles-Albert was to reproduce these articles in *L'amour libre* (1900).

127. In particular in *Le libertaire, Le père Peinard,* and *Les temps nouveaux.*

128. "La prostitution," *Les temps nouveaux,* November 26–December 2, 1898.

129. For example, "Le droit du cuissage," *Le père Peinard* (February 1889); Louis Grandidier, "Le droit de cuissage," *Le libertaire,* April 22–28, 1897; and "Le droit de jambage à Limoges," *Le libertaire,* April 23, 1905.

130. It should be noted that Dolléans also asked himself, "Cannot the prostitu-

tional contract be compared to the work contract?" *Le mouvement socialiste* (1902), p. 1790. One finds this idea again in Bonnier, op. cit., p. 42. This tends to show that the distinction that I am drawing here in order to differentiate the two currents is somewhat crude.

131. Title of an article by Léon Wolke, *Le libertaire,* November 13, 1896.

132. R. C., "Salariat et prostitution," *Les temps nouveaux,* April 29, 1899.

133. Arch. préfect. de police, BA 1689.

134. Henri Duchmann, "Etudes feministes, la prostitution," *Le libertaire,* August 20–27, 1904.

135. Charles-Albert, *Les temps nouveaux,* December 10–16, 1898.

136. The work by Lion Murard and Patrick Zylberman, *Le petit travailleur infatigable,* shares this viewpoint.

137. Charles-Albert, *Les temps nouveaux,* December 10–16, 1898.

138. *Les temps nouveaux,* November 26–December 2, 1898.

139. Ibid.

140. Grandidier, op. cit., *Le libertaire,* April 22–28, 1897.

141. *Les temps nouveaux,* December 10–16, 1898.

142. On this matter one should draw attention to the effort undertaken by *Guerre sociale* after February 2, 1910.

143. One has only to think of the work of the *chansonnier* Aristide Bruant as a whole and of the success of Nini Peau-de-chien.

144. D. Snop, "Margot," *Le libertaire,* July 11–17, 1896, and in Gaston Kleyman, "La serve d'amour," *Le libertaire,* June 27–July 3, 1896, who keeps in her heart the unsatisfied image of the ideal lover.

145. Sonia, in *Crime and Punishment,* appears redeemed and redeeming.

146. See the character Katusha in *Resurrection.*

147. See his novel *Femme-enfant.*

148. Léon Bloy is the most typical of this tendency. The hero of *Le désespéré,* Marchenoir, after losing one mistress, a former prostitute, begins a relationship with Véronique, a converted prostitute, a tumultuous union during which the woman finds herself torn between divine love and her lover. In her thirst for mysticism, she mutilates herself and has herself shut up in an enclosed house, which Léon Bloy describes on the model of a bedroom in a *maison de tolérance* consecrated to divine love. This theme of God's prostitute, inspired by the character of Mary Magdalen, is sometimes magnified into a heavenly vision. Huysmans, now converted, put an invocation to the Virgin in the mouth of Durtal, ("Tenancière des glorieuses Joies," in *La cathédrale*).

149. Jacques Damour, "Les yeux des putains," *Le libertaire,* November 12, 1899:
And the humble eyes of whores
With veiled lashes, expert at deceit . . .
And the humble eyes of whores
Console us more than the saints.

150. Apollinaire, "Marizibil" and "La chambre du mal-aimé," in *Alcools* ("Regrets of the Whore's Eyes").

151. Alla, "Un syndicat de prostituæs," *Le libertaire,* November 12, 1899.

152. Ibid.

153. Léopold Lacour, *Humanisme intégral: Le duel des sexes: La cité future,* p. 128,

then inspired by Edward Carpenter, *Woman, and Her Place in a Free Society* (Manchester: Labour Press Society, 1894).

154. Henri Duchmann, "La prostitution," *Le libertaire,* August 20–27, 1904.

155. Henri Duchmann, "Etudes féministes: Le droit des vierges," *Le libertaire,* June 17, 1904.

156. Henri Duchmann, "Etudes féministes: La liberté sexuelle," *Le libertaire,* September 17, 1904, criticizes the moderation of the feminists on this matter. Curiously enough, Madeleine Pelletier, in her book devoted to *L'emancipation sexuelle de la femme,* remains silent on the problem of prostitution. .

157. Duchmann, "La prostitution."

158. Charles-Albert, "La prostitution," *Les temps nouveaux,* December 24–30, 1898.

159. Paul Robin, *Propos d'une fille.* On Robin himself, see the thesis by F. Ronsin, who has, however, ignored Robin's attitude toward prostitution.

160. Michel Corday, *Vénus ou les deux risques.*

161. On this matter, see Ronsin, op. cit.

162. Robin, op. cit., p. 9.

163. Ibid.

164. Ibid.

165. Ibid., p. 10.

166. Ibid., p. 15.

167. Paul Robin was the founder of a famous school at Cempuis.

168. It was at this time that requests were sent to parliament for the setting up of a body to take charge of public health. See Dr. Corlieu, *La prostitution à Paris,* pp. 170ff.

169. The fact that the term *peril* has been confined to this form of illness is revealing.

170. C. Mauriac, *Leçons sur les maladies vénériennes professées à l'Hôpital du Midi,* p. 198.

171. The way he regards the risks of prostitutional activity is different, therefore, from that of the Marxists and is based on changes in demand.

172. Mauriac, op. cit., p. 126.

173. Ibid., p. 186–187.

174. Richard, op. cit., p. 23. A critical examination of the statistical methods used shows that these estimates should be viewed with caution.

175. Prof. Barthélemy, "Exposé des mesures en vigueur en France, et d'un projet de réorganisation de la surveillance de la prostitution," address to the congress of dermatology and syphilography held in Paris, August 18, 1889 (arch. préfect. de police, DB 407). Here the venereological discourse comes close to that of the regulationists of "moral order" (see Chapter 1).

176. Being unable to show that the Republic of September 4 and the Commune had led to an overall revival in venereal diseases, since the statistics that he compiled proved the opposite, Mauriac chose, nevertheless, to remark that those periods saw the greatest spread of "the filthiest" of those diseases, the soft canker so common in the depths of society (op. cit., p. 177).

177. Mauriac's results differ quite notably from those obtained by Dr. Léon Le Fort at the Hôpital du Midi in 1866 and 1867. Out of 4,070 cases of contamination

whose origin was known, 2,302 (58 percent) had come from "prostitutes met in the street or in public dance halls," and 780 (19 percent) from prostitutes at *maisons de tolérance,* but 988 cases of disease (22 percent) had been contracted with lawful wives or mistresses in the course of sexual relations that were not paid for (*Bull. acad. de médecine,* 1888, pp. 262ff.). Mauriac tended, no doubt, to exaggerate the influence of venal sex in the process of contamination.

178. H. Mireur, *La syphilis et la prostitution,* pp. 120ff. This work, which appeared in 1875, contains a progress report on the matter.

179. Exploratory probe, tongue depressor, speculum; see, on this subject, *Bulletin médical,* May 15 and 18, 1895.

180. Commenge, op. cit., p. 505.

181. Prof. A. Fournier, "Documents statistiques sur les sources de la syphilis chez la femme," *Bulletin de l'académie de médecine,* 18 (1887), 538.

182. Ibid., conclusion.

183. Prof. H. Diday, *Le péril vénérien dans les familles* (1881), p. 54.

184. Op. cit., pp. 17ff.

185. See Tardieu, *Etude médico-légale sur les attentats aux moeurs* (1859), p. 72. It is this prejudice that, in Victor Margueritte's novel *Prostituée,* drives Raoul Dumès to deflower Annette, the young seamstress.

186. Sixty-two percent of the venereal patients treated at the Hospice générale at Rouen by Dr. A. Hébert had had recourse initially to "charlatans" (20 percent to pharmacists, 17 percent to herbalists, 16 percent to "friends," 4 percent to cobbler-quacks, and 1 percent to an "unqualified doctor"). G. Hébert, *Où se prennent les maladies vénériennes?,* p. 39.

187. Mireur poses the problem in *La syphilis et la prostitution,* p. 67.

188. It is described by Dr. Martineau, op. cit., p. 10.

189. To the crusade begun by Josephine Butler to spread abolitionism, the neo-regulationists were content to oppose a "sanitary crusade."

190. "It's even better to sleep with one's wife" are the words that Folantin discovers, angrily traced, in a brothel under advertisements for "depuritives" advocated for venereal sufferers. J. K. Huysmans, *A vau-l'eau,* Collection 10–18, p. 389.

191. See his jokes about the cankers that afflicted him and the attitude of Dr. Vaucorbeil toward the infected Pécuchet. (On this see Borie, op. cit., pp. 82–83.)

192. J. K. Huysmans, *En ménage,* p. 168.

193. Huysmans, *A vau-l'eau,* p. 388.

194. Huysmans, *En ménage,* p. 303.

195. Huysmans, *A rebours,* pp. 163, 170ff.

196. Cf. Jacques Marles's nightmare in *En rade,* pp. 208ff.

197. J. K. Huysmans, *Certains* (1908), pp. 77–118.

198. Huysmans, *En ménage,* pp. 298–299.

199. Barbey d'Aurevilly, "La vengeance d'une femme," *Les diaboliques.*

200. See G. de Maupassant, *Le lit 29.*

201. See Chapter 6.

202. It should be noted, however, that Molé-Tocqueville's lecture had already proposed a set of almost similar measures. See Conférence Molé-Tocqueville, "Rapport extrait de l'annuaire 1879-1880" Paris, 1886 (arch. préfect. de police, DB 410).

203. It included, notably, Larrey, Ricord, Legouest, Dujardin-Beaumetz, Clerc, Fournier, Passant, Boureau, Martineau, and Le Pileur.

204. Dr. Le Pileur, *Prophylaxie de la syphilis, réglementation de la prostitution à Paris: Rapport adressé à M. le préfet de police* (1887).

205. See *Bulletin de l'académie de médecine* (1888), sessions of January 31, February 7, 21, and 28, March 6, 13, 20, and 27, 1888.

206. Op. cit., p. 162.

207. Op. cit., p. 34.

208. Op. cit., p. 558.

209. There is one reference to Laborde.

210. Mauriac, op. cit., p. 103. This does not mean, however, that moral preoccupations did not underpin this new medical discource. See Chapter 6.

211. Speech by Léon Le Fort, *Bulletin de l'acad. de méd.* (1888), 261.

212. See Martineau, op. cit., p. 196.

213. Le Pileur, op. cit., p. 25.

214. Ibid., p. 18.

215. Molé-Tocqueville, op. cit. One is thinking here of an "asylum" for immorality, like those already set up for insanity.

216. Le Pileur, op. cit., p. 21.

217. Proposed by Le Pileur, ibid., p. 24, and by Gustave Lagneau, *Bulletin de l'acad. de méd.*, February 7, 1888, 188.

218. Ibid., session of February 28, 1888, p. 292.

219. Ibid., p. 276.

220. Docteur A. Malécot, *Les vénériens et le droit commun* (1888).

221. Op. cit., pp. 161ff.

222. Op. cit., pp. 107ff.

223. Docteur Verchère, "De la réorganisation de Saint-Lazare au point de vue de la prophylaxie des maladies vénériennes," *Bulletin médical*, March 19, 1890, 267ff.

224. Op. cit.

225. Richard, *La prostitution à Paris.*

226. At most one could cite the ordinance of Prefect Léon Bourgeois, who, on March 1, 1888, set up the recruitment of doctors for the vice squad by competition, as well as a few alterations in the regulations of Saint-Lazare.

6. The Need for Surveillance

1. This is an issue that I have discussed at length elsewhere. See "Le péril vénérien au début du siècle: Prophylaxie sanitaire et prophylaxie moral," *Recherches*, 29 (1977), *L'haleine des faubourgs.*

2. Prof. A. Fournier, *Ligue contre la syphilis*, lecture given at the Hôpital Saint-Louis in April 1901 (published in 1904), p. 12. For his part, Dr. F. Raoult (op. cit., p. 33), writes: "From the day that syphilis became duplicated by parasyphilis, its prognosis has increased in seriousness to a considerable degree."

3. Prof. Burlureaux, "Rapport concernant la prophylaxie individuelle," Second International Conference at Brussels, 1902, p. 5.

4. Dr. L. Le Pileur, "De la mortalité infantile causée par la syphilis," *Journal des maladies vénériennes, cutanées et syphilitiques*, (June 1889), 78ff. See also on this subject J. H. Doléris, "Statistiques sur l'avortement," *Bulletin de la soc. fr. de proph. san. et mor.* (1906), 136–150.

5. *Bulletin de la soc. fr. de proph. san. et mor.* (1901), 37.

6. Ibid., p. 80.

7. Raoult, op. cit., pp. 39ff., and Mignot, op. cit., p. 28, and the observations by Drs. Porak and Ribemont-Dessaignes.

8. And, in particular, that of secondary heredity, which affects the grandchildren, sometimes in a more virulent form than primary heredity.

9. Dr. Edmond Fournier, *Les stigmates dystrophiques de l'hérédosyphilis* (Paris, 1898), with color plates. All his later work was to be devoted to inherited syphilis.

10. A. Fournier, *Danger social de la syphilis* (1905), p. 56.

11. "I am convinced that it is increasing," declared A. Fournier, *Ligue contre la syphilis*, p. 7. This was also the opinion of Dr. Paul Berthod, "Le péril vénérien," *Revue de médicine légale* (1899), 86ff.

12. Dr. Léon Issaly, *Contribution à l'étude de la syphilis dans les campagnes* (Paris, 1895).

13. Dr. Le Noir, Report to the Brussels conference, 1899, cited by A. Fournier, op. cit.

14. Cited by Dr. Morhardt, op. cit., p. 60. These estimates are close to those proposed by Blaschko for the city of Copenhagen.

15. Emile Duclaux, *L'hygiène sociale* (1902), p. 237.

16. Prof. Février, Dr. Vigneron, and even more so Prof. Spillmann in 1913 considered that the recrudescence of venereal morbidity was unquestionable in the city of Nancy. Dr. V. Vigneron, *La prostitution clandestine à Nancy: Esquisse d'hygiène sociale* (Nancy, 1901), p. 8. Prof. Février, "Du rôle du médecin dans la prophylaxie de la syphilis," *Revue médicale de l'Est* (1903), 385. L. Spillmann and Zuber, "Syphilis et prostitution à Nancy," *Société de médicine de Nancy* (1913), p. 299. Intervening in the discussion, Dr. G. Etienne observed that venereal morbidity was increasing among the workers of the Compagnie de l'Est.

17. Morhardt, op. cit., p. 88.

18. See, in particular, the report cited by Alfred Fournier to the Commission extra-parlementaire du régime des moeurs.

19. Dr. Edmond Fournier, "A quel âge se prend la syphilis," *Presse médicale* (1900), 164–167. Furthermore, the age of contamination varied according to social category. "One catches syphilis at an earlier age in the working classes than in the bourgeoisie," E. Fournier concludes (p. 165), after comparing the patients in his father's private practice with those of the Hôpital du Midi and Hôpital Saint-Louis.

20. A. Fournier, report to the extraparliamentary vice squad commission, p. 152.

21. Dr. Patoir, "La prostitution à Lille," *Echo médical du Nord*, August 10, 1902, 373.

22. On this matter, we should remember that the conviction that the disease would inevitably spread had already given rise to the plan for a voluntary and systematic univeral syphilization in the form of vaccination.

23. And yet at this time there was no shortage of eminent doctors to create a scandal and to call on the exalted syphilographers to show greater lucidity. In this they did no more than take up the ideas of Herbert Spencer, who, as early as 1873, in his *Studies of Sociology,* had noted the discrepancy between the true importance of venereal diseases and the image that, in his opinion, people tended to have of them. Among these thoughtful individuals, we might cite the few doctors who supported

the abolitionist proposals on the matter of regulating prostitution, in particular Dr. Louis Fiaux and the mayor of Lyons, Professor Augagneur.

24. We should mention the failure of an ephemeral Société de prophylaxie contre les maladies vénériennes, founded in 1896 at the instigation of Dr. Boureau, which came up against a great deal of prejudice; see *Bull. soc. fr. de proph. san. et mor.* (1902), 280.

25. It should be noted that this was a turning point in the history of antivenereal prophylaxis. Hitherto this had almost been confused with the steps taken to supervise prostitution. This attempt to promote a moral, individual prophylaxis, through the work of the neoregulationists, was connected with the abolitionist ideas defended by Yves Guyot and Dr. Louis Fiaux.

26. A. Fournier, *Ligue contre la syphilis,* p. 25.

27. Ibid.

28. Burlureaux, op. cit., p. 13.

29. Dr. Debove, "Rhumatisme blennorragique: Prophylaxie des maladies vénériennes," *Revue de thérapeutique médico-chirurgicale* (June 1904), 400.

30. Dr. L. E. Monnet, *Conseils aux avariés,* pp. 55–56. It should be remembered that genital herpes was then regarded as a venereal disease.

31. Prof. Moty (op. cit., p. 390) wrote, "If every man knew only one woman and vice versa, the venereal diseases would soon die out."

32. Burlureaux, op. cit., p. 23.

33. Dr. Queyrat, *La démoralisation de l'idée sexuelle,* (1902). The idea that early marriage was the best way of preventing venereal disease was a veritable leitmotif. It is to be found again in Georges Hébert, *Où se prennent les maladies vénériennes? Comment elles sont soignées, comment elles devraient l'être* (Paris, 1906), p. 49.

34. Queyrat, op. cit., p. 5.

35. Ibid., p. 6.

36. Ibid., p. 7.

37. Prof. Burlureaux, *Pour nos jeunes filles quand elles auront seize ans.*

38. Prof. A. Fournier, *Pour nos fils quand ils auront dix-sept ans.*

39. Dr. Manquat, "Prophylaxie de la syphilis et des maladies vénériennes," p. 25.

40. Prof. Delorme, "La syphilis dans l'armée," *Bull. de l'acad. de médecine,* April 23, 1907.

41. Burlureaux, op. cit., p. 20.

42. The results obtained by this commission were later to be used by the extra-parliamentary vice squad commission.

43. Edouard Rod, preface to the first French edition of Ibsen's *Ghosts (Les revenants)* (1889).

44. Ibid.

45. According to Lombroso (cited by T. de Wyzewa, *Le temps,* March 9, 1899: "Le crime et la folie dans la littérature"), the reference was to general paralysis.

46. Dr. H. Mireur, *L'avarié, étude d'hygiène sociale,* p. 7.

47. Ibid., p. 1.

48. André Couvreur, preface to *Les mancenilles* (Paris: Plon, 1900).

49. Ibid., p. 217.

50. Maxime, the hero, sleeps with Frida, "whose bed became the emunctory of

all the colored individuals in the district, bringing their vices and perhaps their diseases from all four corners of the earth!" (ibid., p. 121). In the end it is an Armenian who contaminates Simone, another of Maxime's mistresses.

51. Ibid., p. 363.

52. Ibid., p. 188.

53. Ibid., p. 195.

54. The public was then convinced that the discovery of an antisyphilis serum was imminent.

55. M. Corday, *Vénus* (1901), p. 78.

56. Op. cit., p. 166.

57. Ibid., p. 247.

58. Ibid., p. 252.

59. Dr. L. E. Monnet, *Conseils aux avariés,* p. 86.

60. See the report by Prof. Delorme.

61. Those of Médecin-major Ramally and Dr. Mathieu.

62. On this matter, see Granjux, "Prophylaxie de la syphilis dans l'armée, 101–11," *Bull. soc. fr. de proph. san. et mor.* (1911), 60ff.

63. Abraham Flexner, *La prostitution en Europe,* p. 309.

64. Ibid., p. 308.

65. Charles-Louis Philippe, *Bubu de Montparnasse,* p. 57.

66. Ibid., p. 65.

67. This is, of course, propagandist literature, but on a quite different plane.

68. This allowed the libertarian press to play on the words *civilization* and *syphilization,* and to joke about the civilizing or syphilizing work of the French troops in Madagascar. See "La syphilisation à Madagascar," *Le père Peinard,* November 28–December 5, 1897.

69. Victor Margueritte, *Prostituée,* p. 82. Prof. Moty (op. cit., p. 390) considered as a cause favoring the spread of venereal morbidity (whose decline he notes elsewhere) "civilization, which, through vapor, multiplies the cases of syphilis," and advances the idea that the venereal threat is proportional to the prosperity of trade.

70. Emile Duclaux, "La syphilis," in *L'hygiène sociale,* pp. 224–266.

71. Ibid., p. 263.

72. Dr. Fischer, "Essai de prophylaxie des maladies vénériennes," *La presse médicale,* April 2, 1902, 317–318.

73. Dassy de Lignières, Prostitution et contagion vénérienne (Paris: Barthe, 1900), pp. 36, 38.

74. Ibid., p. 11.

75. Ibid.

76. Manquat, op. cit.

77. Report of the Lyons conference in *Annales d'hygiène,* 6 (1906), 358–360. This throws some light on the ironic remarks made by Dr. Lutaud, who expresses disagreement with most of his colleagues. The safety that they are in search of, he tells them, "will exist (and will even then be relative) only when you have turned the 85,000 prostitutes in Paris into civil servants, locked away, like soldiers in barracks, in an incalculable number of *maisons;* when coitus is permitted only in those establishments, when every candidate with an erection is examined by an inspecting physician." According to him, they were trying to realize the old dream of Restif de

la Bretonne. (Dr. Lutaud, "La prostitution patentée," *Journal de médecine de Paris* (June 1903).

78. *Prophylaxie des maladies vénériennes et police des moeurs* (Lyons, 1905), p. 87.

79. And by which Michel Foucault, quite logically, seems to have been essentially inspired in *La volonté de savoir*.

80. Could it be otherwise when the venereological discourse, which by definition associates sex with pain, constitutes the antithesis of a discourse on pleasure?

81. A. B., "La traite des blanches," *La République*, July 27, 1902, called it "one of the worst scourges of our time."

82. Jules Lenoble, *La traite des blanches et le congrès de Londres* (1900).

83. *Revue pénitentiaire*, March 19, 1902.

84. F. Tacussel, *La traite des blanches* (1877).

85. *Ministère des affaires étrangères: Documents diplomatiques, conférence internationale pour la répression de la traite des blanches* (Paris, 1902), p. 183.

86. What I am trying to do here is to trace the rise of the theme of the white slave trade in public opinion. It goes without saying that the expression had long been in use. Thus Lucien de Rubempré uses it in a conversation with Corentin (*Splendeurs et misères des courtisanes*, p. 862).

87. Lord Monroe, *Le clarisse du XIXᵉ siècle, ou la traite des blanches* (Brussels, 1881).

88. Such episodes had long been cropping up in novels. See the fate of Lydie in *Splendeurs et misères des courtisanes*.

89. Dr. Minime, *La prostitution et la traite des blanches à Londres et à Paris*, p. 92.

90. Paul Appleton, *La traite des blanches*, p. 103.

91. See Chapter 7.

92. Paul Robiquet, "La traite des blanches," in *Histoire et droit*, pp. 179–192.

93. Savioz (Mme. Avril de Sainte-Croix), "La traite des blanches," *La grande revue* (1902), 282.

94. Moncharville, *La traite des blanches et le congrès de Londres: Rapport présenté au comité français de participation au congrès*, p. 14.

95. Ferdinand Dreyfus, *Misères sociales et études historiques*, p. 60.

96. The *rapporteurs* of the French committee were Moncharville and H. Joly.

97. This contradiction, which had been noted in 1895 by Robiquet during the penitentiary conference, was later to be repeated many times in those bodies that, in France, had set out to study this problem. Thus, in 1902, in the Société générale des prisons, it was to oppose Gigot, the former prefect of police, and Bérenger, who both refused to regard as an offense any commerce in human flesh, to Feuilloley and Puibaraud, who demanded that such commerce be defined as an offense.

98. It should be noted, however, that the French delegates had been forced to concede to their opponents that the decisions being taken were no more than minimal.

99. J. Lenoble, op. cit., p. 69–78.

100. Vittorio Levi, *La prostitution chez la femme et la traite des blanches*, p. 6. On April 5, 6, and 7, 1910, an international Jewish conference on the white slave trade was held in London.

101. On this subject, apart from Joly's report, see Lenoble, op. cit., and Savioz, op. cit.

102. One session was devoted to it in September 1899, during the conference of the Union internationale de droit pénal held in Budapest; see Louis Layrac, *De l'excitation à la débauche.*

103. Indeed, the organization of this white slave trade had its roots back in the distant tradition of transporting lost girls, immortalized by the Abbé Prévost.

104. In his report to the London conference.

105. An inexhaustible theme, as we know, in the Western.

106. In *Le matin* of April 21, 1902, one reads, on the subject of the organization that had its center at Andrésy: "The gang includes touts, pimps, inspectors, travelers; there are even bookkeepers and a treasurer, to whom one must add agents who have come 'to replenish their stock' from the four corners of the earth."

107. *Chambre des Députés: Débats parlementaires: Séance du 26 mars 1912,* report by Pierre Goujon, pp. 328–329.

108. All the files in series BB 18 in the Arch. nat. dealing with the white slave trade have been studied, as has bundle DB 411 in the archives of the prefecture of police and the documents preserved in the departmental archives.

109. Meeting of March 19, 1902, in *Revue pénitentiare,* p. 509.

110. *Revue pénitentiaire* (1902), 517.

111. Feuilloley, *Revue pénitentiaire* (1902), 509–510.

112. Arch. préfect. de police, DB 411.

113. Ferdinand Dreyfus, *La répression de la traite des blanches: Compte rendu du 3ᵉ congrès international, Paris,* p. 362.

114. Op. cit., p. 286.

115. Ibid.

116. Concerning Andrésy, see the reports in *Le matin* beginning April 21, 1902.

117. It must be recognized, however, that the activities that gave rise to judicial inquiries, some trace of which has been preserved in the archives, rarely seem to have been so perfectly organized.

118. See Feuilloley and Savioz, op. cit. This assertion, it is true, is not based on an accurate quantitative study, since I found it impossible to consult the four hundred files on victims drawn up by the Ministry of the Interior in the early years of the century.

119. *Le matin,* May 25, 1902, devotes an article to this problem.

120. *Revue pénitentiaire* (1902), 508.

121. Op. cit., pp. 42–43. This is also what emerges from consulting files in series BB 18 in the Arch. nat.

122. The judicial and police archives indeed show that they usually traveled alone.

123. *Revue pénitentiaire* (1902), 535.

124. Savioz, op. cit., p. 284.

125. See Moncharville, Lenoble, and Appleton, op. cit.

126. Savioz, op. cit., p. 290.

127. Report by Prince Sergei Wolkowski.

128. Cited by Appleton, op. cit., p. 33.

129. See the Paulucci de Calboli report cited by Appleton, op. cit., p. 37.

130. Arch. dept. Gironde, Bouches-du-Rhône.

131. Savioz, op. cit., p. 287.

132. The importation of women survived, however; according to one inquiry carried out in the United States in 1908–09 by the Immigration Commission on the Importation and Lodging of Women for Immoral Purposes, most of them were consenting. They had usually been bought by correspondence for sums varying between $200 and $2,000 (Arch. nat. BB 18 2167 2). A law was passed by Congress in 1910 in an attempt to eliminate this commerce.

133. English and Irish girls continued to supply the markets on the coast and in New Orleans, where the Storyville district, the cradle of jazz and the center of prostitution, was then experiencing its hour of glory.

134. It should be noted that in Brazil, prostitution was mainly in the hands of *caftes,* traffickers who had originated in Hungary, Galicia, Poland, or southern Russia. The few prostitutes of French origin who settled in that country usually eluded their grip. *Rapport Wagener: Compte rendu du congrès de Paris* (1906), p. 402.

135. Op. cit., p. 328.

136. *Le relèvement social: Supplément,* June 1, 1897.

137. Levi, op. cit., p. 54.

138. Bérenger, "La traite des blanches et le commerce de l'obscénité," *Revue des deux-mondes* (July 1910), 85.

139. Op. cit., p. 34.

140. *La répression de la traite des blanches* (1906), p. 337.

141. Op. cit., p. 53.

142. Report by Dr. Ismail Kemal Bey to the London conference, cited by Appleton, op. cit., p. 35.

143. *La répression de la traite des blanches* (1906), p. 337.

144. Appleton, op. cit., p. 37, and *Revue pénitentiaire* (1902), 768–769.

145. Bérenger, "La traite des blanches," p. 87.

146. An analysis of the four hundred files on the white slave trade drawn up by the Ministry of the Interior between 1902 and 1906 allowed Ferdinand Dreyfus to emphasize the importance of this emigration of French prostitutes to South Africa.

147. Wagener, op. cit., p. 404.

148. A decline that was also beginning to be observed in Egypt (see Levi, op. cit., p. 53). At the end of this overview of the white slave trade, it should be noted how difficult it is to make a quantitative study of the phenomenon. The immigration statistics are no help, because a prostitute or future prostitute was seldom declared or regarded as such. Only registers of official prostitution could provide series of statistical data that would be in any sense valid. Unfortunately, this type of source is lacking for the countries of the East; this fact may have led me to overestimate the relative size of the trade with the regulationist states of Latin America. As for the legal archives, they concern only cases involving legal offenses; as we shall see, these were extremely rare and probably unrepresentative. Reading certain files does, however, provide a vivid picture of the dealers. For the trade with Lisbon (the Chat Noir establishment) see the departmental archives of Charente-Inférieure and the Gironde; for Barcelona, see Arch. nat. BB 18 2184; for Buenos Aires, see arch. dépt. Gironde and Bouches-du-Rhône, Arch. nat. BB 18 2231 and 2514; for Port Said, see arch. dept. Bouches-du-Rhône; for Poland and the Russian empire, see Arch. nat. BB 18 2250; for South Africa, see Arch. nat. BB 18 2249 and 2250; for Senegal, see arch. dept. Gironde.

149. Robiquet, *Histoire et droit,* II, 181.

150. Op. cit., p. 281.

151. Robiquet, op. cit., p. 179.

152. Op. cit.

153. See n. 81.

154. See Jacques Teutsch, *L'association pour la répression de la traite des blanches: Revue pénitentiaire,* report delivered to congress in Frankfurt, 1902, p. 1134.

155. G. Baal has shown the extent of the movement in public opinion aroused by the coming to power of Emile Combes and the hopes of his supporters. See "Combes et la République des comités," *Revue d'hist. mod. et contemp.* (April-June 1977), 260–285.

156. C. Brunot, "La traite des blanches," *Revue philanthropique,* May 10, 1902, 13.

157. For May 8, 1902, one read in *L'aurore* that it was the press that imposed the theme on public opinion.

158. *La petit Parisien,* August 17, 1906.

159. *La lanterne,* of course (April 24, May 19, June 4, August 9 and 25, September 2); *L'aurore* (May 8 and 12, August 8); *La libre parole* (May 5); *Le père Duchêne* (May 17); *La journée* (May 20, August 30); *Le rappel* (May 31, September 1, December 30); *La presse* (June 8, November 18); *Le radical* (June 14, November 10 and 28); *Le libertaire* (June 13); *Le Français* (June 22); *Le journal des débats* (July 22); *La République* (July 27); *La petite République* (August 8); *La patrie* (August 6); *Le temps* (August 26); *L'eclair* (October 10); *La tribune française* (November 28); *L'echo de Paris* (December 4); and *La fronde* (December 6, 17, and 28); not forgetting the series of articles that appeared in *Le matin, Le journal,* and *Le petit Parisien.*

160. Jean Marestan, "La traite des blanches," *L'aurore,* May 8, 1902.

161. In the edition for May 5, 1902.

162. *La tribune française,* November 28, 1902.

163. *Le journal,* August 27, 1902.

164. *La répression de la traite des blanches* (1906), p. 99, gives an account of the proceedings.

165. It should be noted, however, that the left-wing press, and in particular the anarchist press, sometimes acknowledged the contradiction. See G. Amyot in *Le libertaire,* June 13, 1902. As far as the socialists are concerned, see the article by Louis Maurice in *La petite République* for August 8, 1902. On August 30, in *La journée,* under the signature of Alexandre Boutique, the confessions of a former "meat merchant" brought out the correlation existing between trafficking in women and tolerated prostitution. Finally, it goes without saying that the same went for the proabolitionist press (see *La lanterne,* September 2, 1902).

166. Ferdinand Dreyfus, *Revue pénitentiaire* (1902), 1135.

167. The others were Austria, Belgium, Brazil, Denmark, Germany, Great Britain, Hungary, Italy, the Netherlands, Norway, Portugal, Russia, Spain, Sweden, and Switzerland. France was represented by Bérenger, Ferdinand Dreyfus, the lawyer Louis Renault, the prefect of police Lépine, and Hennoquin, head of the first division of the prefecture of police.

168. Thus, as far as France is concerned, only Articles 334 (habitual incitement of minors to debauchery), 354–357 (seizure or corruption of minors), and 341–

344 (illegal arrests and sequestration of persons) of the penal code concerned the white slave trade, and even then very indirectly.

169. See Chapter 6.

170. Austria-Hungary, the United States, and Brazil were later to adhere to it.

171. And in particular the newspaper *Le temps*.

172. It is true that the final protocol established that the recommended measures should be regarded as minimal.

173. Arch. préfect. de police, DB 411.

174. It should be noted, however, that the text of the convention, like the final protocol, remained silent on "the holding of a girl against her will in a house of debauchery"; the problem of trafficking with the colonies, however, was confronted.

175.. The fourth international conference of the federation was held in Madrid; the problem of regulation was still not officially faced, but a collective comment on the sources and roots of the white slave trade made it possible to confront it indirectly. See *La répression de la traite des blanches: Compte rendu du IVᵉ congrès international tenu à Madrid les 24–28 octobre 1910,* question 6, pp. 146ff.

176. Report cited by Ferdinand Dreyfus at the Paris conference, p. 359.

177. Ibid., p. 360. It should be noted that in Paris a special brigade, known as the mobile brigade, whose task it was to enforce the law of 1903, had been set up in the criminal investigation department.

178. See Chapter 7.

179. Dreyfus, op. cit., p. 363.

180. Pierre Goujon, in his report to the Chamber of Deputies, March 26, 1912. This member of parliament took up the figures cited in the account of the Madrid conference (1910), question 3, p. 85. It should be added that the preservation societies were no less active in trying to outwit the maneuvers of the traffickers; it was with this purpose in mind that *Oeuvre des gares* was founded in October 1905.

181. In a speech to the general assembly of the Association pour la répression de la traite des blanches et la préservation de la jeune fille, published in the *Journal des débats,* July 21, 1902, Georges Picot appealed to the isolated girl "to form a group with other girls with a view to sharing their means of defense, until such time as she has crossed *the perilous defile of her youth* and isolation has been corrected by the only moral solution: marriage." He launched urgent appeals to "private charity" to set up protective ramparts around the young female; he demanded an increase in havens of all kinds. Now this has hardly anything to do with international trafficking, but it reveals, on the part of the members of the association, deep anxiety at the idea that a sexual liberation of youth might take place. It was the same individuals who refused to attack the regulation and institution of the brothel, aware as they were of the close correlation between maintaining the virginity of young bourgeois girls and the existence of prostitution.

182. Esquirol, *Maladies mentales,* p. 47.

183. *Dictionnaire des sciences médicales,* XXXII, 483.

184. Parent-Duchâtelet, op. cit., I, 262–266.

185. Dr. Rossignol, *Aperçu médical sur la maison de Saint-Lazare* (1856).

186. Griesinger, *Traité des maladies mentales,* p. 175.

187. Guislain, *Leçons orales sur les phrénopathies,* p. 73.

188. Renaudin, *Etudes médico-psychologiques sur l'aliénation mentale,* pp. 312–316.

189. Chatelain, *Causeries sur les troubles de l'esprit*, pp. 32, 123ff.

190. Dr. Reuss, *Annales d'hygiène* (January–June 1888), 301.

191. Krafft-Ebing, *On Insanity, Based on Clinical Observation*, p. 130.

192. Except for Dr. Reuss.

193. Dr. F. Gras, *L'aliénation mentale chez les prostituées.*

194. On this subject, see the more recent histories of hysteria, and in particular the one by Dr. Ilza Veith.

195. Dr. P. Briquet, *Traité clinique et thérapeutique de l'hystérie*, p. 123.

196. Op. cit., I, 259.

197. See Gérard Wajeman, "Psyché de la femme, note sur l'hystérique au XIXᵉ siècle," in *Mythes et preésentations*, pp. 56–66.

198. His aim was to draw up a comparison with a sample of venereal patients at the Hôpital Lourcine. The enterprise turned out to be lacking in interest because the patients treated in that establishment were largely unregistered prostitutes, a fact that Briquet, curiously enough, seems to have forgotten.

199. Of whom 32 were subject to hysterical attack and 74 presented "continuous or almost continuous symptoms of hysteria, without the attacks" (op. cit., pp. 124–125).

200. Ibid., p. 125.

201. See H. Colin, *Essai sur l'état mental des hystériques*, pp. 38ff. It should be noted that it was with the aim of describing the progress of "misogynous" hysteria in a prostitute that Edmond de Goncourt wrote *La fille Elisa* (Ricatte, op. cit., p. 64).

202. Op. cit., p. 125.

203. Cited by F. Gras, op. cit., p. 13.

204. H. Colin, "L'hystérie dans les prisons et parmi les prostituées," op. cit., pp. 37–43. This work also contains very interesting biographies of prostitutes.

205. Ibid., p. 41.

206. Cf. Octave Simonot, "Psycho-physiologie de la prostituée," *Annales d'hygiène* (1911), 498–567.

207. Ball, *Leçons sur les maladies mentales*, p. 383. Balzac echoes this belief of the phrenologists in the innateness of prostitution. "'You're a whore, you'll always be a whore, you'll die a whore,' Carlos Herrera declares to Esther, 'for, despite the attractive theories of animal breeders, one cannot become on this earth what one is not. The bumps man was right. You've got the love bump.'" (*Splendeurs et misères des courtisanes*, p. 710). The indelible character of crime and prostitution is reaffirmed several times in the novel (see pp. 1046–50). "Prostitution and theft are two living protests, male and female, of the natural state against the social state" (p. 1046).

208. Dr. Moreau (de Tours), *La psychologie morbide*, pp. 379–381.

209. Pauline Tarnowsky, *Etude anthropométrique sur les prostituées et les voleuses* (1889). Lombroso and G. Ferrero, *La femme criminelle et la prostituée (1896).*

210. According to Lombroso (op. cit., p. 265), "In the higher capacities, honest women surpass them by five or six times."

211. Ibid., p. 269.

212. Ibid., p. 338. In his *Pornocratie*, Proudhon had already written, "Parent-Duchâtelet might have added that the faces of these women alter in the same way as their morals: they become deformed, take on the appearance, voice, and manner

of men, and preserve of their sex, in the physical as well as the moral sense, only the gross matter, what is strictly necessary" (pp. 372–373).

213. Op. cit., p. 345.

214. Cited by S. Icard, *La femme pendant la période menstruelle* (1890), p. 197.

215. Here Lombroso runs counter to the traditional anthropological discourse by which the female nature was characterized by its sex and great sensitivity (Y. Knibiehler, "Le discours médical sur la femme," pp. 49–50.)

216. Lombroso, op. cit., p. 409.

217. On "moral insanity," see the work of Schüle. In the *Annales médico-psychologiques* (1899), 482ff., there is a summary of the criticisms concerning this notion.

218. Op. cit., p. 556.

219. Ibid., p. 542.

220. Lombroso, op. cit., p. 585.

221. C. Féré, *Dégénérescence et criminalité*, p. 103.

222. Ibid., p. 103.

223. Ibid., p. 107.

224. Ibid., p. 104.

225. Dr. Corre, *Crime et suicide*, pp. 273–276, with details on pp. 277–291.

226. Dr. Emile Laurent, "Prostitution et dégénérescence," *Annales médico-psychologiques (1899), 353ff.*

227. The conviction that the prostitute was usually a degenerate also imbues the writings of certain of the abolitionists. See, for example, the portraits sketched by Jules Hoche during his visits to Saint-Lazare, in "Une visite à la prison de Saint-Lazare," *La grande Revue* (March 1901), 697–721.

228. Op. cit., p. 562.

229. Ibid., p. 516.

230. Ibid., p. 499.

231. Ibid., p. 543.

232. Ibid., p. 510.

233. Ibid., p. 511.

234. Ibid., p. 514.

235. Ibid., p. 518.

236. Ibid., p. 520.

237. Ibid., p. 530.

238. Ibid., p. 548.

239. Ibid., p. 567.

240. For example, E. Dolléans, *La police des moeurs*, pp. 95ff.

241. In Germany and Austria, Binswanger, Mendel, Baer, Meynert, and Naecke refused to consider "moral insanity" a morbid entity. In France, Dr. Lacassagne gave preeminence to the role of environment in the genesis of prostitutional behavior.

242. Dr. G. Daniel, "Etudes de psychologie et de criminologie: Contribution à l'étude de la prostitution," *Revue de psychiatrie*, (1897), 80.

243. Dr. Poppritz, *La prostituée-née existe-t-elle?* The work is a systematic refutation of this theory.

244. Op. cit., p. 151.

245. G. Tarde, "La morale sexuelle," *Archives d'anthropologie criminelle* (1907), 29.

246. Ibid., p. 29
247. Ibid., p. 23.
248. Ibid., p. 23.
249. Ibid., p. 23.
250. Ibid., p. 39.
251. Colin, op. cit., p. 48.

7. The De Facto Triumph of Neoregulationism

1. The *Supplément* to *Le relèvement social* became, from June 1 on, "the organ of the Ligue française de la moralité publique and of the French branch of the International Abolitionist Federation against Regulated Prostitution." In fact, until July 1902, it was the subeditor, Auguste de Morsier, who with the help of a few friends wrote the contents of the *Supplément*.

2. Auguste de Morsier, "La campagne abolitioniste française, 1897–1902," *Le relèvement social: Supplément,* May 1, 1902.

3. It is true that two months later, four French archbishops and four bishops were to declare themselves hostile to the regulation of prostitution (*Le relèvement social: Supplément,* July 1, 1902).

4. A. de Morsier, "Explications nécessaires," *Le relèvement social: Supplément,* December 1, 1899, and "Seconde explication," January 1, 1900.

5. See A. de Morsier, *La police des moeurs en France et la campagne abolitionniste* (1901); this work is an account of the congress.

6. Arch. préfect. de police, BA 1689.

7. See Chapter 5.

8. *Bulletin officiel de la ligue des droits de l'homme,* sessions of the central committee of December 23 and 27, 1901, and January 6, 13, 20, and 27, 1902.

9. The progress of this work can be followed in the printed accounts of the commission's fifty-three sessions, preserved, for example, in the Bibliothèque Sainte-Geneviève and in Hennequin's report. Louis Fiaux, *La police des moeurs,* also provides a useful summary of the commission's debates.

10. Fiaux, *La police des moeurs* II, 865.

11. Ibid.

12. *La revue de morale sociale* (1902–1903), 90ff.

13. The results appeared in *Le français,* August 2, 1903.

14. *Bulletin de la société fr. de proph. san. et morale* (1904), 543.

15. Fiaux, *La police des moeurs* II, 162ff.

16. *Journal officiel: Débats parlementaires: Sénat.* See session of May 30, 1895, remarks by Senator Bérenger.

17. Tarde op. cit., p. 29.

18. Ibid., p. 35.

19. Session of April 3, 1903.

20. *Revue pénitentiaire,* on session of December 23, 1903, 43.

21. Ibid., p. 69.

22. Ibid., on session of March 16, 1904, 548.

23. See remarks by Paul Jolly, *Revue pénitentiaire* (1904), 525.

24. See declaration by M. A. Rivière, *Revue pénitentiaire* (1904), 385.

25. *Journal officiel: Débats parlementaires: Chambre des Députés,* appendixes to the session of November 23, 1894.

26. *Sénat: Documents parlementaires: Annexes,* 81 April 27, 1894. "Proposition de loi sur la prostitution et les outrages aux bonnes moeurs," by M. Bérenger.

27. Cited by Trarieux in the Senate, session of May 28, 1895.

28. Senate, session of May 28, 1895. It should be noted that for the Garde des Sceaux himself, it was the health check that justified the maintenance of arbitrary action.

29. A reading of the *Journal Officiel* shows that the sessions of May 28 and 30, 1895, in the course of which the senators debated the bill, were treated extremely lightheartedly. The fun reached its height when Bérenger declared that he had "taken on the fairly painful duty of examining these things at close hand" and added, "I, I repeat, and I think I know what takes place, and, in the streets . . ." The frequent use of Latin also reveals the deep embarrassment felt at dealing with this question in the Senate.

30. And yet, according to Senate practice, it was sent to the president of the Chamber in 1895, 1898, 1902, 1914, 1919, and yet again in June 1924 by Gaston Doumergue.

31. See the report cited by Paul Meunier.

32. Since, contrary to the wishes of the commission, Meunier proposed that the *maisons galantes* should be allowed to continue.

33. D'Haussonville, "L'enfance à Paris: Les vagabonds et les mendiants," *Revue des deux-mondes,* (June 1878), 598–627.

34. Catulle Mendès, *Femme-enfant,* p. 435.

35. Ibid., p. 599.

36. I have already cited examples from Marseilles, *maisons de rendez-vous.* In addition, in 1898 a scandal broke out at Elbeuf. The regional press declared that Mme. M—— was prostituting underage girls in her lodging house. The police superintendent confirmed the fact; among the clients, he mentions merchants, industrialists, landowners, *rentiers,* the mayor of a nearby commune, and several other notables of the town "whom respect for the rule of anonymity prevents me from naming too explicitly" (arch. dept. Seine-Inférieure).

37. Fiaux, *La police des moeurs* I, ccxlii, and II, 17. One may remember the description of these child prostitutes in *Mort à crédit.*

38. A total that in fact has little significance, since the majority of underage prostitutes operated unofficially.

39. See the statistics in H. Turot, p. 153.

40. Op. cit., pp. 93–94.

41. According to Turot, op. cit., p. 213.

42. Fiaux, *La police des moeurs* I, ccxxi.

43. By extending the penal majority from age sixteen to eighteen, the law of April 12, 1906, had already posed the problem of the fate of prostitutes under the age of eighteen (see discussion later in this chapter).

44. Chamber of Deputies, session of July 11, 1912.

45. Noted by E. Skandha, "La prostitution et la police des moeurs," *La revue blanche,* September 1, 1902, 49.

46. Op. cit., p. 308.

47. Ibid.

48. Letter to the head of the lodging houses department, March 31, 1900, arch. préfect. de police, DB 408.

49. The success of this establishment derives from the fact that it contained both special departments and general departments and that in this respect it resembled a general hospital.

50. Arch. préfact. de police, DB 408.

51. After the war, the dispensaries of venereology were to function at full capacity; in *Mort à crédit* Céline describes the clientele of one of these institutions.

52. L. Spillmann and J. Benech, *Du refuge à la maison de secours.*

53. See Carle, *Paris médical,* March 1, 1913.

54. In Charente-Inférieure, Seine-et-Oise, Hérault, and Meurthe-et-Moselle (see departmental archives), all the women were, at this date, treated in hospitals.

55. Arch. dept. Meurthe-et-Moselle.

56. *La croix du Nord,* December 27, 1907.

57. *Le soleil du Midi,* July 4, 1912. The years before the war saw an increase in such petitions (see arch. dept. Bouches-du-Rhône).

58. Arch. préfect. de police, BA 1689.

59. Ibid. The participation of the socialists and radical-socialists in this campaign, side by side with members of the morality societies, is significant. It proves that the extreme-lift militants were now regarded as "moralizers," as honorable people. The ancient confusion between holding democratic ideas, drunkenness, and debauchery had come to an end. This contraction of the area of evil is a fundamental donnée in understanding the history of French politics under the Third Republic (see, on this subject, the ideas expressed by Maurice Agulhon during his seminars at the Ecole normale supérieure).

60. Marcel Cachin, account of the meeting (arch. préfect. de police, BA 1689).

61. Ibid.

62. Arch. préfect. de police, BA 1689.

63. Arch. nat., BB 18 2488.

64. The discrepancy between the declared wish for liberalization and the progress of regulation emerges quite clearly from a reading of the memoranda of the investigation of 1902; the situation in the department of the Hérault (arch. dept.) is very clear in this respect.

65. Arch. dept. Meurthe-et-Moselle.

66. See the photograph of this transfer in the work cited by L. Spillmann and J. Benech.

67. Arch. nat., BB 18 2363.

68. See J. Lalouette, who notes the growth, in the years prior to the war, of public anxiety about the danger to public hygiene of the large number of cafés and drinking places.

69. On this matter, see Eugène Prévost, *De la prostitution des enfants: Etude juridique et sociale (loi du 11 avril 1908),* and, in particular, the appendixes: "Resultats de l'envoi en correction des prostituées mineures de 16 à 18 ans," pp. 295ff.

But is it really possible to speak of a growth in complaints by prostitutes in the decades prior to the war? The complaints of the prostitutes were a tradition, as is proved by the petitions submitted by the prostitutes of the Palais-Royal during the

Restoration, and it is difficult to say with any degree of certainty that they had become more numerous. It would seem, however, that, thanks to the encouragement given by the abolitionists, and sometimes even by the judiciary, the prostitutes were more often challenging the authority of the police. What is revealing in this regard is the attitude of the prostitutes of Bordeaux and Marseilles when the abolitionist lawyer Goguillot encouraged them to resist and when the procurator had the imprisoned prostitutes freed by the mayor; this occurred at Marseilles in 1905 and at Bordeaux in 1910 (arch. dept. Bouches-du-Rhône and Gironde). In 1907 the police, who had brutally interrogated a registered prostitute at Marseilles, were reprimanded and punished; following that event, wrote the procurator-general to the prefect, the prostitutes, "demand to be simply questioned, and no more" (arch. dept. Bouches-du-Rhône). Among the individual requests one might cite that of a prostitute from La Seyne in 1901 (Arch. nat. BB 18 2199) and that of another prostitute from Chambéry in 1905 (Arch. nat. BB 18 2318), as well as a supposed petition from the prostitutes of Lyons in 1906 (Arch. nat. BB 18 2342).

70. *La dépêche de Rouen,* June 13, 1908.

71. *La journal de Rouen,* June 27, 1908.

72. Prévost, op. cit., p. 299.

73. Ibid., p. 301.

74. *L'eclair,* October 7, 1908.

8. The Twentieth Century

1. The references appearing in the notes to this chapter complement the bibliography.

2. On this subject see Prof. Gaucher's analyses cited in the preface to L. Fiaux, *L'armée et la police des moeurs.*

3. See particularly Dr. Léon Bizard, *Les maisons de prostitution de Paris pendant la guerre* (Poitiers, 1922), and Dr. Le Pileur, *Indications sur la prostitution vulgivague à Paris depuis le début de la guerre.*

4. Le Pileur, op. cit., pp. 16ff., inquiry concerning 1,074 prostitutes.

5. Bizard, op. cit., p. 5.

6. On this policy, see Fiaux, *L'armée et la police des moeurs,* pp. 264ff. (in particular the analysis of Gallieni's investigations), and M. Carle, *La prophylaxie des maladies vénériennes,* pp. 48ff.

7. Justin Godard, cited by Fiaux, op. cit., p. xii.

8. Ibid., p. xi.

9. See Albert Nast, *La vie morale et la guerre.*

10. By way of example, Mme. Avril de Sainte-Croix and Louis Comte, *Vous êtes braves, restez forts: Les vrais héros.*

11. Contributions by Prof. E. Gaucher, *Bull. acad. de méd.,* March 28, 1916, 357, and December 26, 1916, 576.

12. Dr. Bizard, *La vie des filles,* p. 93. The passage that follows borrows considerably from this author's analyses.

13. F. Carco, *L'amour vénal* (Paris: Albin Michel, 1927), p. 69.

14. Juliette Romanet, *Le n° 17* (Paris, 1929).

15. *La vie des filles,* pp. 95ff. and 46.

16. Ibid., p. 110.

17. Paul-Jean Cogniart, "La prostitution: Etude de science criminelle," law thesis, University of Nancy, 1938, p. 119, stigmatizes the motor car as "a moving house of debauchery." See also Bizard, *La vie des filles,* p. 108, and Jean-José Frappa, *Enquête sur la prostitution,* p. 47.

18. Frappa, *Enquête,* pp. 80 and 83.

19. *La vie des filles,* p. 203.

20. Cogniart, op. cit., p. 135.

21. On this subject, see Emile Massart's plan, presented to the Paris municipal council on June 20, 1922, cited by Maurice Hamel and Charles Tournier in their public opinion poll in *La prostitution* (Nice, 1927), pp. 269–279.

22. Dr. M. Carle, *La prophylaxie des maladies vénériennes,* passim; and Frappa, op. cit., p. 174.

23. Cogniart, op. cit., p. 136.

24. Jacques Roberti, *Maisons de société: Choses vues* (Paris: Fayard, 1927), pp. 8ff. and 217.

25. Op. cit., pp. 137–138.

26. Op. cit., p. 71.

27. Bizard, *La vie des filles,* p. 158.

28. From this point of view, no discordant note is to be found in the testimony collected.

29. Such, for example, is the estimate of Paul-Jean Cogniart (op. cit., p. 139). The most moderate witnesses report between ten and fifteen clients a day.

30. Insofar as not all the prostitutes were permanently occupied.

31. On this subject, see Emmanuel Davin, *La prostitution à Toulon* (Toulon, 1940), pp. 78–79. In racist language that I find shocking, the author describes a brothel in the rue de la Chapelleria in which eight women were reserved exclusively for the use of black troops. "The 'short time,' charged at five francs, took place in line on the stairs, at the rate of one good, proud Senegalese per step. The patient Black awaited his turn, as if he were under orders."

32. By way of example, see Roberti, op. cit., pp. 273ff., and A. Scheiber, *Un fléau social: Le problème médico-policier de la prostitution* (Paris: Lib. de Mécicis, 1946), p. 66, on the subject of the Moulin Galant.

33. His work, which appeared in 1937, is the prototype of the books whose aim is to exalt the prophylactic *maison de tolérance.*

34. According to Jean-José Frappa (although this is not the opinion of A. Scheiber), hygiene also reigned in the *maisons d'abattage:* "In the drawer of the nightstand was a tube of calomel ointment and, on the washbasin, a small bottle of Botot water for the teeth . . . Furthermore, well displayed was a notice, published by the Public Health services, listing the precautions to be taken to avoid all contamination" (op. cit., p. 117).

35. M. Van Der Meersch (*Femmes à l'encan,* pp. 99ff.) claims that he himself had seen the official account of the meeting. A. Scheiber provides the same information, but it is now impossible to verify it.

36. At this time there also developed the practice of the *condé,* a pact established between the vice squad officers and the prostitutes, to tolerate soliciting in exchange for certain favors.

37. In 1921 the government had proposed a bill of similar inspiration; later, Dr. Sicard de Plauzolles (*Principes d'hygiène sociale*) was to formulate similar proposals. On the subject of these attempts, see N. M. Boiron, *La prostitution devant l'histoire,* pp. 243ff.

38. Salim Haïdar, *La prostitution et la traite des femmes et des enfants* (Paris: Domat-Montchrestien, 1937), p. 392.

39. Testimony of Dr. Bizard concerning Paris, and of Dr. Cavaillon on Lyons and Nancy; on this subject, see Cogniart, op. cit., p. 168.

40. The neoregulationist literature began to praise "the admirable work of the social workers," in terms almost identical with those used by Parent-Duchâtelet of the *dames patronnesses,* or charity ladies (Bizard, op. cit., p. 266).

41. The text of this memorandum is found in M. Sicot, *La prostitution dans le monde* (Paris: Hachette, 1964), pp. 46–47.

42. At Nancy, for example; see Boiron, op. cit., p. 238.

43. Cogniart, op. cit., p. 77.

44. On the "medico-psychical" surveillance of prostitutes at the Institut de médicine légale et sociale de Lille, see Cognairt, op. cit., pp. 75ff.

45. *Crapouillot* (September 1937), 49ff.

46. Havelock Ellis stresses the normality of the two partners in the venal couple; he gives a determining place to the repression of orgiastic impulses and links the growth of new forms of prostitution with the constraints of capitalist society. This leads him to exalt what, for him, was the "cultural value" of prostitution, "an element of gaiety and variety in the ordered complexity of our modern life and of rest from the monotony of its mechanical routine, of distraction from its deadly, respectable grayness (Havelock Ellis, *Prostitution: Its Causes, Its Remedies,* p. 147). "There can be no doubt," he writes, "that the principal motive in women to adopt temporarily or definitively the life of a prostitute is to obtain the means of self-development that are restricted in the system of our civilization, based on mechanical labor" (p. 149).

From this point of view, early marriage would not, in his opinion, remove the desire for prostitution. His highly exculpating book exalts the mission of the prostitute, who "thus takes her clients for a time out of the desecrating atmosphere of artificial thought and unreal feelings in which most civilized beings are forced to waste most of their lives" (p. 174). At the end of a book that, before its time, implicitly advocates a politics of bodies, Havelock Ellis demands, on the part of moralists, a more generous, more dynamic attitude toward prostitution and a reexamination of the sexual rights and duties of all women.

47. It features in the work by S. Haïdar, pp. 409–424.

48. Among the innumerable contradictory accounts of this experience, see P. Marcovici, "L'expérience de Grenoble," medical thesis, University of Paris, 1937. Dr. Bütterlin, *L'exemple de Grenoble: La situation vénérienne et l'état de la prositution à Grenoble, de 1931 à 1941 inclus,* and D. Dallayrac, *Dossier prostitution,* pp. 99–103. I should point out the role of the Abri Dauphinois, founded at Grenoble in 1934. This asylum for prostitutes wanting to leave their profession served as a model for readaptational organizations set up after the war.

49. Abolitionist doctrines did make progress on an international level. Article 23 of the foundation agreement gave the League of Nations the mission to concern itself with the problem. As early as September 30, 1921, the General Assembly

decided to turn the wishes expressed on July 5 by an international conference into a convention; from now on, reference was to be made to the trading in women and children rather than the white slave trade. In 1926 a wide-ranging investigation carried out in the West by the League concluded by condemning the *maison de tolérance*. The obvious link between the white slave trade and enclosed prostitution, which the London conference had refused to make in 1899, was clearly exposed. This amounted to an official condemnation of regulationism. Finally, a conference that met in Geneva in 1933 led to an international convention, which France signed on October 11. All forms of trading in women were now condemned, including those involving consenting adults. All that remained was to adapt French legislation to the text of the new convention, since the law of 1903 had become inadequate. (On international policy, see Haïdar, op. cit.)

50. The decree of application was signed, it is true, on March 19, 1940.

51. That is to say, the Inspection départementale d'hygiène.

52. Scheiber, op. cit., p. 127.

53. Ibid., p. 128.

54. Ibid., pp. 59–61, 222, 297. Officially the number of *filles de maison* was 8,784 and of "registered prostitutes operating on the highway" 9,192 in 1939, that is, a total of 17,976 prostitutes; in 1945 the numbers were, respectively, 6,649, 12,355, and 19,004 prostitutes. It should be noted, however, that the real figures were probably somewhat in excess of these government ones; unfortunately we have at our disposal no others that can in any way be trusted.

55. Theoretical because, at the same time, a list of the places where soliciting was authorized was drawn up.

56. In doing so it drew inspiration from German and Scandinavian models.

57. The decree of application dated from July 27, 1943.

58. Each doctor was to fill out a stub book, from which he would have to extract an opinion of contagiousness to be given to the patient and a report to be sent to the health authority. In the case of a prostitute or a person whose way of life or profession made him or her particularly contagious, or of a patient who refused treatment, the declaration would necessarily be nominal.

59. In order to understand the attitude of the occupying forces and even the policy carried out by the Vichy government, we have to remember a few facts about Germany. The law of February 18, 1927, which in many respects foreshadowed the French legislation of 1946, had set up a neoabolitionism that was prohibitionist in tendency. It had forbidden enclosed brothels and similar establishments, abolished the segregationist legislation then in force, and, in theory, authorized so-called liberal prostitution. At the same time, medical surveillance was strengthened and treatment made compulsory. Furthermore, provision was made for assistance and education under the health authority. This law, which in fact was poorly applied, since, by way of example, one reserved street was rebuilt at Bremen in 1933, was later made more specific and somewhat modified, as can be seen in the prohibition of prostitution in towns with fewer than 20,000 inhabitants.

It should also be remembered that Hitler, given his eugenic attitudes, regarded a policy toward prostitution as being of the greatest importance. Fiercely prohibitionist, he denounces in *Mein Kampf* the poisoning of young people's sexual lives. The Führer considered that the struggle against syphilis was a national duty on which the very future of the Reich depended. These various attitudes suggest the links to be found between fascism, sanitarism, and eugenics by anyone concerned with the distant roots of these phenomena, which give a particular definition to our century.

In line with the Führer's convictions, the laws of October 18, 1935 had made the premarital medical examination compulsory, forbidden those suffering from venereal diseases (and others) to marry, and envisaged for them, as well as those found guilty of offenses concerning sexual morals, sterilization by castration. By this measure sanitarism came very close to eugenism.

60. Indeed, it should be noted that, on this matter, the attitude adopted was very different in the various countries that came under German occupation.

61. On the subject of German policy in this field, see Scheiber, op. cit., pp. 130–138.

62. Like the one set up at Ponchaillou, near Rennes.

63. It must be recognized, however, that it has not been satisfactorily established that such a practice actually existed.

64. According to the evidence left by the women, it seems that the correct behavior, the kindness, even the sensitivity of the German soldiers made them highly appreciated by the prostitutes. By contrast, the women were often to reproach the Allied soldiers for their drunkenness, their crudity, and above all the contempt that they were to show for them. On this matter, see Marie-Thérèse, *Histoire d'une prostituée* (Paris: Gonthier, 1964), p. 86.

65. Scheiber, op. cit., p. 178.

66. Phenomena that, of course, nourished once again the complaints of those who repeated that the demarcation line had become unclear between the prostitute and most other women, that venal sex now affected every milieu, and that it even involved women who did not need to earn money in this way.

67. Memorandum from the minister of the interior, March 5, 1945. Over 12,000 women were apprehended in Paris in 1945. Scheiber, op. cit., p. 178, and BMO, Ville de Paris, December 1945, p. 427.

68. Memorandum from the Direction du service de santé, July 31, 1945. The text is included in Scheiber, op. cit., pp. 187–188. That year regulations were laid down by the ministries of the Interior and Public Health.

69. Dr. Cavaillon, who had already inspired Sellier's bill, was to exert a profound influence in this area.

70. Paul Gemaehling and Daniel Parker, *Les maisons publiques, danger public* (Paris: L.F.R.M.P.), p. 39.

71. *Témoignage chrétien,* March 23, 1945.

72. But on April 15, 1945, the minister for public health was led to confirm the measures taken to combat the venereal peril.

73. The brothel-keepers were also accused, but without any evidence being offered, of advocating the organization of scandals if the *maisons* were closed. They would, it seems, have called upon the prostitutes to rob their clients on a massive scale and to solicit actively on the sidewalk; they would even have incited them to refuse to cooperate in any official investigations.

74. All the quotations that follow are taken from *Le journal officiel.*

75. Taking up once more a wish formulated by the Société française de dermatologie, the commission demanded sanitary measures "suitable to intensify the

struggle against the dangers of prostitution in all its forms and, in particular, *unregistered prostitution.*" The speaker had obviously forgotten that the bill that he was suggesting the Assembly should pass involved the abolition of regulation and therefore implied the disappearance of such notions as toleration and registration!

76. The file envisaged by the law was indeed the most complete of all those that I have analyzed; it was to be drawn up in duplicate, the first copy intended for the ministry, the second for local authorities; it was intended to follow the prostitute on her travels.

77. See, on December 27, 1947, the remarks by Mme. Rastier-Caillé, RPF (Gaullist), in the Paris municipal council. See Pierre Dominique and Jean-Gabriel Mancini, *Pour, contre: La réouverture des maisons closes* (Paris, Berger-Levrault, 1967), and BMO, Ville de Paris, December 27, 1947, pp. 741–744.

78. On November 6, 1951, by Jean Durand, RGR (a small centrist party), senator for the Gironde; on January 3, 1952, by the socialist deputy Pierre Mazuel. The bill was to be rejected in committee on February 20. See Romi (Robert Miquel), *Maisons closes,* p. 503.

79. Dallayrac, *Dossier prostitution,* p. 311. In the absence of archive documents, the existence of this court remains problematic.

80. For the period prior to the turning point of 1960, the most detailed description is still that of Dr. P. Filhol, *Le monde des particulières* (Paris, 1959).

81. Thus, in 1953, the prefect of the Rhône introduced zoning (Sicot, op. cit., p. 37).

82. It should be noted, however, (see Filhol, op. cit., p. 185), that it required about three years for the new system to be fully installed and for the file to cover the 10,000 prostitutes then in practice.

83. That same day a circular was published and a decree and ordinance issued.

84. It regards as such anyone who knowingly lives with a woman who practices prostitution habitually, whether or not he can account for the income on which he lives.

85. In 1960 only 1,500 cases of syphilis were reported in France; in 1946 the number has been as high as 4,400. In 1960 prostitutes were responsible for 30 percent of contaminations.

86. For the 1960 legislation, see "Dispositions récentes contre la prostitution et l'alcoolisme," *Notes et études documentaires,* 2777 (May 8, 1961).

87. Bernard Chenot, minister of public health and population, press conference, November 16, 1960.

88. Dr. P. Durban, *La psychologie des prostituées* (1969).

89. R. A. Vivien, vice president of the Counseil général de la Seine, *Solution de la prostitution* (1960).

90. Marcel Sacotte, *La prostitution* (1965).

91. Dr. Le Moal, *Etude sur la prostitution des mineurs* (1965).

92. Sacotte, op. cit., p. 95.

93. See the account of the "Amazone B" operation in Dallayrac, *Dossier prostitution,* pp. 473–476.

94. R. Delpêche, *L'hydre aux mille têtes* (Paris: Karolus, 1961), p. 85, "La razzia de ce soir."

95. On this police repression, see Jeanne Cordelier, *La Dérobade.*

96. Since the first and for a long time the only readaptation body envisaged by

the law was the former sanitary establishment, itself the successor of the ancient penitentiary. Later, centers were to be set up in the Nord, Rhône, Bouches-du-Rhône, Hérault, and Gironde. Moreover, rehabilitation has given rise to a number of organizations; among the more effective, mention should be made of Le Nid and the work of Abbé Talvas, the Bienvenue, founded by Hélène Tzaut, and the Equipes d'action.

97. On this matter, see the revelations of Commissaire Ottavioli in Dallayrac, *Dossier,* p. 314.

98. It should be added that, during 1961, the military campaign brothels continued to function in Algeria; it is thought that between 12 and 15 percent of soldiers in the contingent frequented them regularly.

99. Very revealing on this matter is the work by R. Delpêche, which was endorsed by Marthe Richard, and recounts a descent into a forbidden world in the company of the police.

100. *Le monde,* December 14, 1960.

101. Dallayrac, *Dossier,* p. 312.

102. See M. Sacotte, op. cit., pp. 84, 87, 109.

103. It is actually very difficult now to decide what, in the evolution of demand, is systematically aroused by the new sex industrialists.

104. Dr. Pierre Simon, *Rapport sur le comportement sexuel des Français* (Paris: Julliard, 1972), pp. 230ff. In particular, we learn that 33 percent of men aged twenty and over admit that they have had sexual relations with a prostitute, while 45 percent reply that they have never had such relations with a prostitute, and 14 percent do not respond. "The number of prostitutes with whom the interested parties declared that they have had sexual relations is 7.8 on average; the median number is 3" (p. 230). This average number rises with age, reaching 10.1 for men over fifty. Among the inhabitants of the larger cities belonging to this age group, the median number rises to 9.

105. The Kinsey Report had noted this earlier for the United States. It should be added that prostitutes did not regard "regulars" as ordinary clients.

106. Claude Jaget, *Une vie de putain* (Paris: Presses d'aujord'hui, 1975), p. 150.

107. This term—literally, "understood hearts"—is Dallayrac's.

108. G. Richard-Molard, *Avec les prostituées* (Lyons: Chalet, 1976), p. 60.

109. Ibid., p. 64.

110. See D. Dallayrac, *Le nouveau visage de la prostitution* (Paris: Laffont, 1976), pp. 98ff.

111. Jaget, op. cit., p. 182.

112. Some pimps, it is true, seem to have adapted; they operate intermittent control, either by stop checks, or through contacts, or they subject their women to a fixed taxation, a practice that is very close to simple racketeering.

113. By way of example, the hotels in which call girls work are owned by corporations for which the profit derived from prostitution is only one element in the balance sheet.

114. See in particular, Dallayrac, *La nouveau visage,* p. 25.

115. Jaget, op. cit., pp. 153ff.

116. Barbara and Christine de Coninck, *La partagée* (Paris: Editions de Minuit, 1978), pp. 18ff.

117. Jaget, op. cit., p. 149.

118. On this matter the authors that I have consulted are unanimous. To practice venal sex becomes "a difficult activity, which does not tolerate too low an intellectual quotient," Dr. Durban noted in 1961 (op. cit., p. 66).

119. Sacotte, op. cit., pp. 147ff.

120. See the long passages devoted to these upheavels in Dallayrac, *Le nouveau visage,* pp. 27ff.

121. The new behavior of the young prostitute is clearly expressed in the life stories of and interviews with such women; contrary to what we found in relation to the nineteenth century, it is no longer the account of defloration, formerly accompanied by violence, that is seen as the decisive turning point and which arouses the curiosity of the investigator and reader, but the account of the first experience of prostitution. Claude Maillard, *Les prostituées: Ce qu'elles disent quand elles parlent à une femme* (Paris: Laffont, 1975), pp. 41ff.

122. Op. cit., p. 121.

123. Ibid., p. 127.

124. Dallayrac notes that there is also unique pleasure in prostituting oneself and being chosen (*Le nouveau visage,* p. 150).

125. The insistence with which prostitutes exalt the significance of the kiss, to which they transfer the prohibition that in the rest of society surrounds coitus, thus illustrates the rigidity of the ritual.

126. By way of example, see Annie Mignard, "Propos élémentaires sur la prostitution," *Les temps modernes* (March 1976). This article contains a strong criticism of the movement and, more than that, represents a cry of indignation against the acceptance, by the prostitutes themselves, of the schizoid experience that they undergo. Mignard stresses with some vehemence that women do not *have* but *are* their own bodies; she considers that rape, abortion, and prostitution belong to the same problematic.

127. Following the repercussions of the affair involving Tonnot, a police superintendent compromised in procurement.

128. On Montpellier, see Chantal and Jean Bernard, *Nous ne sommes pas nées prostituées* (Paris: Editions Ouvrières, 1978), passim. I have depended heavily on this book for information concerning the central town of the Hérault. On Lyons, see Barbara, Christine Coninck, and Claude Jaget, op. cit.

129. Op. cit., p. 76.

130. After a demonstration took place in Marseilles on the Canebière, on October 23, for the freeing of Michèle D——, on whom the taxation office had levied a fine amounting to 42,000 francs.

131. Such were the reactions of Chantal (op. cit., pp. 79ff.) and, according to her, of Sonia and Carole la Marseillaise; as for Barbara, she preferred not to attend the meeting (op. cit., p. 113).

132. Jaget, op. cit., p. 120.

133. Ibid., p. 88.

134. Ibid., pp. 98–99.

135. "L'opinion d'août 1974 à juillet 1975," *Sondages: Revue française de l'opinion publique,* 3 and 4 (1975), pp. 81–85, "La prostitution," the result of an investigation carried out for *Le progrès* of Lyons into the distribution area of this newspaper, based on a sample of persons over eighteen. Forty-two percent of the people questioned

(51 percent of the men, 34 percent of the women) 42 percent disapproved of the demonstrations of prostitutes in the Lyons region. Seven percent of those questioned (3 percent of the men, 9 percent of the women) preferred "the total prohibition of any form of prostitution," 10 percent "the maintenance of the present situation of toleration" (a curious question in view of the fact that toleration had been abolished in 1946 and that any form of regulation had disappeared since 1960!), and 78 percent "permission for prostitution to be practiced in the context of an adapted regulationism." Five percent of those questioned expressed no view on the matter. To the question "Most prostitutes wait for their clients in the street; is this, in your opinion, normal, acceptable, abnormal, or unacceptable?" the answers were as follows: normal 9 percent, acceptable 14 percent, abnormal 37 percent, unacceptable 36 percent, no view 4 percent.

In June 1970 a Gallup Poll revealed that 17 percent of Frenchmen and 9 percent of Frenchwomen regarded prostitution as necessary, that 59 percent of men and 55 percent of women regarded it as inevitable but thought that it ought to be contained, while 20 percent of men and 31 percent of women thought that it was intolerable and ought to disappear at all costs (*The Gallup International Public Opinion Polls: France 1939, 1944–1975,* p. 808). According to another poll carried out at Lyons in June 1974 by the same organization, 59 percent of those questioned favored an official recognition of the status of prostitutes (ibid., p. 1058). Everything seems to suggest that the public distinguishes very little between the notion of regulation and that of the prostitute's status.

136. Anne Salva, *Je n'en rougis pas.*

137. *Histoire de Michèle* (Paris: Fayard, 1971).

138. Apart from the works already cited, see *Ulla,* ed. Charles Denu; Judith Belladona, "Femmes folles de leur corps," *Recherches,* 26, (1977); "Se prostituer," *Sorcières,* 3; Sonia, *Respectueusement vôtre* (Presses de la Cité); and Griséldis Réal, *Le noir est une couleur* (Balland).

139. The novelty lies essentially in the accumulation of individual evidence, because there were a great many texts emanating from prostitutes collectively addressed to the authorities during the Revolution and Restoration.

140. One of the prostitutes queried by Claude Jaget declared: "For me to be a prostitute is to have an ideal, an ideal for later" (op. cit., p. 165).

141. I shall do no more than mention the positions of those who belong to one of the tendencies analyzed in the book, without really introducing anything new. I am referring to advocates of regrouping in sexual clinics inherited from the healthy, corrective brothel of Parent-Duchâtelet, such as Dr. Peyret, deputy for the Vienne (*Touma,* October 5–19, 1970) or of all those who, more or less in the long term, predict or desire the disappearance of prostitution through the setting up of an overt or implicit prohibitionism. (On this matter, see the responses of several political parties, "Politique, société et prostitution," *Femmes et monde,* 39).

142. After, it is true, Michel Poniatowski himself. A detailed commentary of the penal report is to be found in the work of Richard-Molard.

143. On this matter, the councillor remarked that all income, even occasional income, is taxable.

144. It has also aroused criticism, quite obviously, from opponents of liberalization and from all those fighting prostitution. There can be no question here of going

over the arguments, which have already been developed at length. It might be worth noting, however, as far as Marxists are concerned, the more subtle position expressed in *Rouge,* June 17, 1978: "A status for prostitution, no. Rights for prostitutes, yes."

145. The position of the feminists is ambiguous. For some, prostitution remains the symbol of male order and the extreme form of the oppression of women. Following Kate Millett's *Prostitution Papers: A Candid Dialogue,* Benoîte Groult wrote in the preface to *La dérobade:* "What clients go to a prostitute's room for . . . is not so much sex as sexual power." She sees prostitution as "virilism carried to the point of horror." As a result, prostitutes are perceived as women's "political prisoners" (Millett, op. cit., p. 83). See also "Dossier prostitution," *Cahiers du féminisme,* 5 (June-August, 1978), 21. For others, while being a proof of the sexism to which women are subjected, the state of prostitution is less alienating for them than marriage: "Sale limits physical use to sexual use. Marriage, on the other hand, extends physical use to every possible form of this use"; Colette Guillaumin, "Pratique du pouvoir et idée de Nature: L'appropriation des femmes," *Questions féministes* (February 1978), 13. Considered as a lesser evil, prostitution seems able to open up the way of liberation, especially as it allows women "to swing into a total presence of one's own body" ("Se prostituer," *Sorcières,* no. 3, 9). See also, on the revolutionary implications of prostitution, the evidence of Grisélidis, March 9, 1979, during the meeting organized by the review *Marge: Le monde,* March 14, 1978.

146. On this precise point, see Dallayrac, *Le nouveau visage,* passim.

147. To decode prostitutional relations appears, again, difficult, if one bears in mind that for a very long time, both in medical discourse and in public opinion, the prostitute has been the antithesis of the nymphomaniac, of the woman who seems possessed, and is regarded above all as the woman who is able to resist pleasure. It is probably at this level that the true success of the project of those who have established regulationism is situated. To create a debauchery that is experienced by women (and often by men) as the negation of pleasure was the best way of exorcising the threat that female sexuality and debauchery itself represented to the social order.

148. Belladona, op. cit., p. 68.

149. While trying, it is true, to work through sex education and sexology.

Bibliography

This is not an exhaustive bibliography. I have systematically excluded works dealing with prostitution outside France and, with only a few exceptions, those dealing with venal sex in periods prior or subsequent to the one under examination. The comprehensive bibliography prepared by Vern L. Bullough and Barrett W. Elcano—*Annotated Bibliography of Prostitution,* Reference Library in Social Science, no. 25, New York, Garland, 1976, 430 pp.—will readily fill any gaps left here.

I have not included works in fields such as music and the visual arts that deal incidentally with venal sex; the few books I do cite concerning the history of sexuality are those that provided the information used directly in the preparation of this work. In short, this is not a bibliography of the sexological history of the second half of the nineteenth century.

The theme of prostitution traverses almost all the fiction of the period: I have therefore listed only a few particularly representative selections.

Many of the works to which I refer in the book do not appear in this bibliography, specifically those that deal with the growth of economic and social structures, which have been indispensable to me in understanding the development of prostitution as a phenomenon (see in particular the works cited in Chapter 4).

Finally, newspaper articles devoted to venal sex, even those cited in the text, do not appear here; to list them would have made this bibliography excessively unwieldy.

Manuscript Sources

National Archives

Series F 7 9304–9305: *femmes publiques* (investigations of the Restoration period)
Series BB 18. Files concerning affairs involving prostitution: 1884, 2156, 2167, 2184, 2189, 2198, 2199, 2223, 2231, 2249, 2250, 2252, 2260, 2261 A, 2278, 2314, 2318, 2342 I, 2359, 2363 2, 2386 2, 2390 2, 2415, 2436 2, 2466, 2482, 2488 2, 2490 2, 2498, 2514 2, 2518 1

Archives of the Prefecture of Police

Particularly valuable files: BA 1689, DB 407, DB 408, DB 410, DB 412

Departmental Archives

Bouches-du-Rhône: M 6 1747, 1889, 2329, 2458, 2729, 3336, 4816, 4817 A and
    B, 4820, 6356, 6569, 6570, 6573, 6574
Charente-Inférieure (Maritime): 6 M 415
Finistère: Series M, unclassified, numbered in pencil, 397 1, 2
Gironde: 4 M 337, 4 M 340
Haute-Garonne: M 284, 446, 447
Hérault: 62 M 6, 7, 8
Meurthe-et-Moselle: 4 M 134, 4 M 135
Nord: M 201/13, M 201/15, M 201/18
Rhône: unclassified, registers of three *maisons de tolérance* in the city
Seine-Inférieure (Maritime): 4 M P 4564, 4 M P 4565
Seine-et-Oise: 6 M 7, 8, 9, 10. A fine collection of registers
Var: 8 M 52
My research in the archives of the Indre-et-Loire and the Orne was not productive.

I consulted some of the prison registers of the departmental archives of Indre-et-
Loire, but I abandoned using hospital archives (on this subject, see G. Désert, op.
cit.). The information they provide draws on only a small sample, much less representative of prostitutes as a whole than the lists, registers, and inquiries produced
by the vice squad. These last documents comprise an enormous quantity of still
unsorted documentation; I do not believe, therefore, that for the time being hospital
archives should be treated as a privileged source—except, of course, concerning the
treatment of venereal patients.

Published Inquiries and Official Documents

Results of the censuses of 1851, 1856, 1872
Journal officiel: Débats parlementaires et annexes. Set of projects for bills mentioned
    in Chapter 7, reports and debates to which they gave rise. Parliamentary reports
    concerning the prison of Saint-Lazare by Boucher (1893), Codet (1904),
    Girard and Morlot (1904).
*Ministère des affaires étrangères: Documents diplomatiques: conférence internationale
    pour la répression de la traite des blanches.* Paris, Imp. nat., 1902, 211 pp.
*Ministère de l'intérieur et des cultes: Commission d'étude des questions relatives à la pro-
    phylaxie de la syphilis et des maladies vénériennes.* Melun, Imp. adm., 1902.
*Annexes au rapport général présenté par M. F. Hennequin . . . sur les travaux de la
    commission extra-parlementaire du régime des moeurs.* Melun, Imp. adm., 1908,
    534 pp.
Conférence internationale de Bruxelles sur la prophylaxie des maladies vénériennes. Min-
    utes of sessions, Brussels, Lamertin, 1899.
Commission extra-parlementaire du régime des moeurs. Reports of sessions, 1909. Pre-
    served in the archives of Bouches-du-Rhône and in the Bibliothèque Sainte-
    Geneviève.

A number of reports appear below under the names of their authors or of the bodies to which they were addressed.

Periodicals

The Bibliothèque Marguerite Durand contains a series of files on prostitution (most of them collections of press clippings), under the following reference numbers: 050 P Bul., DOS 351 FED, DOS 351 OEU, DOS 351 PRO.

Le bulletin continental: Revue mensuelle des intérêts de la moralité publique: Fédération britannique et continentale pour l'abolition de la prostitution spécialement envisagée comme institution légale et tolérée. Neuchâtel, December 15, 1875–1884.

Le relèvement social: Supplément, 1897–1914.

Bulletin de la Société française de prophylaxie sanitaire et morale, 1901–1914.

These three periodicals, which are essential sources, have been examined completely for the dates cited.

Bulletin de l'Académie de médecine. Sessions of January 31, February 21 and 28, March 6, 13, 20 and 27, 1888. Discussion of Prof. A. Fournier's project concerning the reform of the vice squad.

Bulletin de la Société française de philosophie. "L'éducation sexuelle." Vol. II (1911): 30–52.

Bulletin officiel de la Ligue des droits de l'homme, 1902. Debate on the vice squad. Sessions of the central committee, December 23 and 27, 1901.

Le français. May 31–August 2, 1903. "Référendum: La police des moeurs."

Revue de morale sociale. Geneva, 1899–.

Revue pénitentiaire. Bulletin de la Société générale des prisons. 1896, 1902, 1903, 1904. Reports and debates concerning prostitution and the white slave trade.

Samplings carried out:

1. 1902: all press reports concerning the white slave trade.
2. Anarchist press: articles dealing with prostitution during the period, in particular: *Les temps nouveaux, Le père peinard, Le libertaire, La guerre sociale, Le révolté.*
3. Samplings in the feminist press.
4. *Bulletin de l'oeuvre des libérées de Saint-Lazare.* Mme. Caroline de Barrau and Isabelle Bogelot.

Books

Acton, Dr. William. *Fonctions et désordres des organes de la génération chez l'enfant, le jeune homme, l'adulte et le vieillard, sous le rapport physiologique, social et moral.* Paris, V. Masson, 1863. Trans. of *The Functions and Disorders of the Reproductive Organs in Youth, in Adult Age, and in Advanced Life.* London, J. Churchill, 1857.

———— *Prostitution Considered in Its Moral, Social, and Sanitary Aspects in London and Other Large Cities and Garrison Towns.* 2d ed. London, J. Churchill, 1870.

Agrippa, Dr. J. *La première flétrissure.* Paris, L. Hurta, 1877.

Alexis, Paul. *Les femmes du père Lefèvre.* 1877.

———— *La fin de Lucie Pellegrin.* Paris, G. Charpentier, 1880.

Alhoy, Maurice. *La lorette.* Paris, Imp. de Raçon, 1856.

———— *Physiologie de la lorette.* Paris, Aubert, 1841.

Allem, Maurice. *La vie quotidienne sous le Second Empire.* Paris, Hachette, 1948, 288 pp.

Andler, C. *Le manifeste communiste de Karl Marx et F. Engels.* "Introduction historique et commentaire." Paris, Rieder, 209 pp.

Andrieux, L. *Souvenirs d'un préfet de police.* Paris, Rouff, 1885, 2 vols.

Annuaire-Reirum: Indicateur des adresses des Maisons de Société de France, Algérie, Tunisie et des principales villes de Suisse, Belgique, Hollande, Italie et Espagne. Paris, Th. Murier, 39 rue Lamartine.

Appleton, Paul. *La traite des blanches.* Lyons, Paris, Arthur Rousseau, 1903, 300 pp.

Arches, Pierre. *Une ville et son maire, Parthenay en 1872.* 1975, on the prostitutes' revolt.

Aron, J.-P. *Le mangeur au XIXe siècle.* Paris, Laffont, 1973, 371 pp.

Augagneur, V. *Contre la police des moeurs: Critiques et rapports.* Paris, Cornély, 1904, xvii + 147 pp.

———— *De l'influence de la réglementation de la prostitution sur la morbidité vénérienne.* Melun, Imp. adm., 1904, 50 pp.

Augier, Emile, and Edouard Foussier. *Les lionnes pauvres,* 1858.

Avon, Dr. Philippe. *Contribution à l'histoire des maladies vénériennes dans l'armée française.* Lyons, Dugas et Cie, 1968, 71 pp.

Avril de Sainte-Croix, Mme. *L'esclave blanche.* Alençon, Coueslant, 1913, 46 pp.

Balzac, H. de. *Splendeurs et misères des courtisanes,* "La Pléiade" edition.

Barberet, Joseph. *La bohème du travail.* Paris, Hetzel, 1889.

Barbey d'Aurevilly, J. *Les diaboliques.* "La vengeance d'une femme," "La Pléiade" edition.

Barlay, Stephen. *L'esclavage sexuel.* Paris, A. Michel, 1969, 315 pp.

Barrès, Maurice. *Les déracinés.*

Barthélemy, Dr. Toussaint. *Etude d'hygiène sociale. Syphilis et santé publique.* Paris, J. B. Baillière, 1890. xiv + 352 pp.

———— *Exposé des mesures en vigueur en France, et d'un projet de réorganisation de la surveillance de la prostitution.* Paris, Gaston Née, 1889, 20 pp.

———— "La prophylaxie des maladies vénériennes chez la femme." Brussels Conference, 1899. *Revue de médecine légale.* 1900, pp. 115ff.

Barthélemy and Devillez. "Les inviteuses des brasseries." *La France médicale,* 25 (February 28, 1882): 289ff.

Barthes, Roland. *La mangeuse d'hommes. Guilde du Livre, Bulletin mensuel,* 20 (June 1955).

Bataille, Georges. *L'érotisme.* Paris, Ed. de Minuit, 1957.

Beaufils, Marcel. *Parsifal.* Paris, Aubier, 1964, on Kundry.

Bebel, Auguste. *La femme dans le passé, le présent et l'avenir.* Trans. Henri Ravé. Preface by Paul Lafargue. Paris, Ed. Carré, 1891, viii + 375 pp.

Becquerel, Dr. A. *Traité élémentaire d'hygiène privée et publique.* Paris, 5th ed. Completed by Beaugrand, 1873.

Benoist, Charles. *Les ouvrières de l'aiguille à Paris.* Paris, Léon Chailley, 1895, 296 pp.

Béraud, F. F. A. *Les filles publiques de Paris et la police qui les régit.* Paris, Desforges, 1839, 2 vols. in one.

Bérault, Gustave. *La maison de tolérance considérée au point de vue hygiénique et social.* Paris, J. B. Baillière, 1904.

Berck, Armand. *Quelques aperçus sur la prostitution au point de vue social, économique et moral.* Paris, G. Carré, 1885.

Bérenger, Senator. "La traite des blanches et le commerce de l'obscénité." *Revue des deux mondes,* July 1, 1910.

Bergeret d'Arbois, Dr. L. F. E. "La prostitution et les maladies vénériennes dans les petites localités." *Annales d'hygiène publique et de médecine légale,* 25, ser. 2, 1866.

Bergeret, Dr. *Les passions, dangers et inconvénients pour les individus, la famille et la société. Hygiène morale et sociale.* Paris, J. B. Baillière, 1878, IV, 336 pp.

Berry, Georges. *Les petits martyrs. Mendiants et prostituées.* Preface by J. Simon. Paris, G. Charpentier et E. Fasquelle, 1892, 36 pp.

Berthod, Dr. Paul. "Le péril vénérien: La réglementation actuelle de la prostitution: Ruine du système." *Revue de médecine légale et de jurisprudence médicale* (March 1899): 86ff.

———— "Le traitement des maladies vénériennes: Le mode d'assistance qui leur convient." *Journal de médecine de Paris,* June 19, 1904.

Biographie des nymphes du Palais-Royal. Paris, 1823.

Bizard, Dr. Léon. *Histoire de la prison de Saint-Lazare du Moyen Age à nos jours.* Paris, Ed. de Boccard, 1925, xv + 279 pp.

———— *La vie des filles.* Paris, Grasset, 1934, 286 pp.

Bloy, Léon. *Sueurs de sang.* "La boue" and "Repaire d'amour." 1892–1894.

———— *Le désespéré.* Paris, Mercure de France, 1964, 339 pp.

Bluzet, Jules. *La prostitution officielle et la police des moeurs.* Lyons, A. Rey, 1903, 84 pp.

Bogelot, Isabelle. *Fédération britannique, continentale et générale: Rapport présenté à la conférence de Lausanne à propos de l'oeuvre des libérées de Saint-Lazare à Paris.* September 6, 1887. Paris, C. Noblet, 1887, 14 pp.

Boiron, N. M. *La prostitution dans l'histoire, devant le droit, devant l'opinion.* Nancy, Paris, Berger-Levrault, 1926, 291 pp. An excellent summary of the legal history relating to prostitution.

Boltanski, L. "Les usages sociaux du corps." *Annales E.S.C.,* January–February 1971, pp. 205ff., on the idea of "culture somatique."

———— *Prime éducation et morale de classe.* Paris, La Haye, Cahiers du centre de sociologie européenne, Mouton, 2d ed., 1977, 152 pp.

Bonneff, L., and M. *La vie tragique des travailleurs: Enquêtes sur la condition économique et morale des ouvriers et ouvrières d'industrie.* Paris, J. Rouff, 1908, 339 pp.

Bonnevay, L. *Les ouvrières lyonnaises travaillant à domicile—Misères et remèdes.* Paris, Guillaumin, 1896, 148 pp.

Bonnier, C. *La question de la femme.* Paris, Giard et Brière, 1897, 59 pp.

Borie, J. *Le tyran timide: Le naturalisme de la femme au XIXᵉ siècle.* Paris, Klincksieck, 1973, 161 pp.

Borie, Jean. *Le célibataire français.* Paris, Sagittaire, 1976, 191 pp.

Bouglé, Dr. *Les vices du peuple.* Paris, G. Carré, 1888, 220 pp.

Bourdieu, P. "Célibat et condition paysanne." *Etudes rurales,* 1962, nos. 5, 6.

Bourgeois, Dr. L. X. *Les passions dans leurs rapports avec la santé et les maladies: L'amour—le libertinage.* Paris, J. B. Baillière, 1860–1861.

Bourget, P. *Physiologie de l'amour moderne.* Paris, Lemerre, 1891, 431 pp.

Bourneville, Professor. Enquête entreprise par le docteur Bourneville dans l'Est de la France sur le traitement des vénériens parue dans le *Progrès médical,* 1887.

Braun. *The "Courtisane" in the French Theater from Hugo to Becque (1831–1885).* Baltimore, 1947.

Bricon, P. "Révolte des vénériennes à Lyon." *La province médicale,* no. 13 (March 20, 1887): 208.

Bridel, Louis. *Mélanges féministes: Études de droit et de sociologie.* Paris, Giard et Brière, 1897, 251 pp.

Brieux, E. *Les avariés.* Paris, Stock, 1902, 228 pp.

Briquet, Dr. P. *Traité clinique et thérapeutique de l'hystérie.* Paris, J. B. Baillière, 1859, pp. 123ff.

Brouardel, Dr. G. *Traité d'hygiène.* Paris, Baillière, 1911.

Bru, Paul. *Histoire de Bicêtre (hospice, prison, asile).* Paris, *Progrès médical,* 1890, xviii + 480 pp.

Brunot, Ch. "La traite des blanches." *Revue philanthropique,* May 10, 1902.

Bullough, Vern L., and Bonnie L. *The history of prostitution.* New York, University Books, 1964, 304 pp.

Bunting, Percy von. "La traite des femmes." *Revue de morale sociale,* no. 3 (July–September 1899): 273–283.

Buret, E. *De la misère des classes laborieuses en Angleterre et en France.* Paris, Paulin, 1840, 2 vols., vi + 432 pp. and vii + 492 pp.

Buret, Dr. F. *La syphilis à travers les âges: La syphilis aujourd'hui et chez les anciens.* Paris, Soc. d'éditions scient., 1890, 257 pp.

———— *Les mesures répressives à l'égard des vénériens, autrefois, aujourd'hui.* Clermont (Oise), Imp. de Daix frères, 1890, 12 pp.

———— *Le gros mal du Moyen Age et la syphilis actuelle.* Paris, Soc. d'édit. scient., 1894, 319 pp.

Burguière. "Histoire et sexualité." *Annales E.S.C.* (July–August 1974). Présentation, pp. 973ff. Proposes a "historical theory of desire."

Burlureaux, Dr. Charles. *Société française de prophylaxie sanitaire et morale: Le péril vénérien, conseils aux jeunes filles.* Paris, C. Delagrave, 1904, 41 pp.

————. *Deuxième conférence internationale pour la prophylaxie de la syphilis et des maladies vénériennes.* (Bruxelles, 1902.) "Rapport de . . . prophylaxie individuelle. (Quels sont les moyens de vulgarisation auxquels il convient d'avoir recours pour éclairer la jeunesse et le public . . .)," Brussels, Imp. de Hayez, 1902, 33 pp.

Butler, J. *Souvenirs personnels d'une grande croisade.* Paris, Fischbacher, 1900, xxii + 366 pp. Trans. of *Personal Reminiscences of a Great Crusade.* London, Marshall, 1896.

Butte, Dr. L. *Prostitution et syphilis, action du dispensaire de salubrité de la ville de Paris pendant les trente dernières années.* Paris, G. Masson, 1890, 30 pp.

———— *Etat sanitaire au point de vue de la syphilis des filles soumises dans les maisons de tolérance de la ville de Paris, depuis 1872 jusqu'en 1903 inclus.* Paris, F. R. de Rudeval, 1903, 5 pp.

———— *Rapport sur un projet de réglementation de la prostitution présenté au nom de la société de prophylaxie sanitaire et morale par le docteur Lucien Butte.* Paris, P. Renouard, 1908, 27 pp.

Callu, Martine. *Approche critique du phénomène prostitutionnel parisien de la seconde moitié du XIXᵉ siècle par le biais d'un ensemble d'images: Oeuvres de Constantin Guys, Félicien Rops, Gustave Moreau.* Mémoire de maîtrise, Tours, 1977, 215 pp.

Canler, M. *Mémoires de Canler, ancien chef du service de sûreté.* Paris, J. Hetzel, 1862, 446 pp.

Carco, Francis. *Visite à Saint-Lazare.* Paris, Lesage, 1925, 57 pp.

Carle, Dr. M., *La prophylaxie des maladies vénériennes.* Paris, Doin, 1921, 320 pp.

Carlier, Félix. *Etude de pathologie sociale: Les deux prostitutions (1860 à 1870).* Paris, Dentu, 1887, 514 pp.

——— "Etude statistique sur la prostitution clandestine à Paris de 1855 à 1870." *Annales d'hygiène publique et de médecine légale.* 1871, vol. 36.

Cazalis, Dr. Henry. *La science et le mariage: Etude médicale.* Paris, O. Doin, 1900, 184 pp.

Celebonovic, Aleksa. *Peinture kitsch ou réalisme bourgeois: L'art pompier dans le monde.* Paris, Seghers, 1974, 198 pp.

Céline, L. F. *Mort à crédit.* 1936.

Cère, Paul. *Les populations dangereuses et les misères sociales.* Paris, Dentu, 1872, 378 pp.

Chabrol de Volvic, Count Gilbert-J. Gaspard. *Recherches statistiques sur la ville de Paris et la département de la Seine.* Paris, Imp. Royale, 1821–1829, 4 vols.

Chatelain, Abel. *Les migrants temporaires en France de 1800 à 1914.* Lille, P.U.L., 1976, vol. 1, pp. 512 ff., on immigration connected with prostitution.

Chéry, Dr. C. "Syphilis: Maladies vénériennes et prostitution." Medical thesis. Toulouse, 1911–1912, Dirion, 576 pp.

Chevalier, Louis. *Classes laborieuses et classes dangereuses à Paris pendant la première moitié du XIXᵉ siècle.* Paris, Plon, 1958.

Cinquante années de visites à Saint-Lazare par Mme. d'A (sister of Caroline de Barrau). Paris, Fischbacher, 1889.

Clavel, Dr. A. *La morale positive.* Paris, G. Baillière, 1873, 381 pp.

Cobb, Richard. *La protestation populaire en France, 1789–1820.* Paris, Calmann-Lévy, 1975, 322 pp. Trans. as *The Police and the People: French Popular Protest, 1789–1820.* Oxford, Clarendon Press, 1970.

Coffignon, A. *Paris vivant: La corruption à Paris.* Paris, Librairie illustrée, 1888, 401 pp.

Colin, Dr. H. *Essai sur l'état mental des hystériques.* Paris, Rueff, 1890, chap. 4, "L'hystérie dans les prisons et parmi les prostituées," pp. 37–43.

Colin, Dr. Léon. *Paris: Sa topographie, son hygiène, ses maladies.* Paris, G. Masson, 1885.

Commenge, Dr. O. *Recherches sur les maladies vénériennes à Paris dans leurs rapports avec la prostitution clandestine . . . de 1878 à 1887.* Paris, G. Masson, 1890, 52 pp.

——— *Les maladies vénériennes dans les armées anglaise, française et russe.* Paris, G. Masson, 1895, 47 pp.

——— "La question de la prostitution devant le Sénat." *Bulletin médical,* July 14, 1895.

——— *Hygiène sociale: La prostitution clandestine à Paris.* Paris, Schleicher frères, 1897, xi + 567 pp.

Conférence internationale pour la répression de la traite des blanches. Brussels, October 21–24, 1912. Brussels, Imp. Nat., 1912, 137 pp.

Conférence Molé-Tocqueville. *Rapport présenté au nom de la commission . . . sur la police des moeurs.* Paris, 1886, 54 pp.

Corbin, Alain. *Archaïsme et modernité en Limousin au XIXe siècle (1845–1880).* Paris, Rivière, 1975, vol. 1, 112–115, on prostitution.

——— "Le péril vénérien au début du siècle, prophylaxie sanitaire et prophylaxie morale." *Recherches,* no. 29 (1977).

Corday, Michel. *Vénus.* Paris, Charpentier, 1901, 277 pp.

Cordelier, Jeanne, and Martine Laroche. *La dérobade.* Paris, Hachette, 1976, 407 pp.

Corlieu, Dr. A. *La prostitution à Paris.* Paris, J. B. Baillière, 1887, 127 pp.

Courcelle, L. *Répertoire de police administrative et judiciare.* Edited by M. Lépine. Paris, Berger-Levrault, 1896–1899, 2 vols.

Couvreur, André. *Les dangers sociaux: Les mancenilles.* Paris, Plon, Nourrit et Cie, 1900, 421 pp.

Crocq, Dr. J., and Dr. Rollet. *Prophylaxie internationale des maladies vénériennes.* Lyons, L. Perrin, 1869, 84 pp.

Cuisin, P. *Les nymphes du Palais-Royal.* Paris, Roux, 1815, 104 pp.

Cullerier, Michel. *Notes historiques sur les hôpitaux établis à Paris, pour traiter la maladie vénérienne.* Paris, Year XI, 72 pp.

Dallayrac, Dominique. *Dossier prostitution.* Paris, Ed. J'ai Lu, 1973, 563 pp.

Daniel, Dr. G. "Etudes de psychologie et de criminologie: Contribution à l'étude de la prostitution." *Revue de Psychiatrie* (1897), 75ff.

Dassy de Lignières. *Prostitution et contagion vénérienne.* Paris, Barthe, 1900, 47 pp.

Daubié, Mlle. J. V. *La femme pauvre au XIXe siècle.* Paris, Guillaumin, 1866, 450 pp.

Daudet, A. *Sapho: Moeurs parisiennes.* Paris, G. Charpentier, 1884.

Daumard, Adeline. *La bourgeoisie parisienne de 1815 à 1848.* Paris, S.E.V.P.E.N., 1963, 670 pp.

——— *Les fortunes françaises au XIXe siècle.* Paris, La Haye, Mouton, 1973, 605 pp.

Debove, Dr. "Rhumatisme blennorragique: Prophylaxie des maladies vénériennes." *Revue de thérapeutique médico-chirurgicale* (June 1904): 397–400.

Debray, Dr. T. F. *Histoire de la prostitution et de la débauche chez tous les peuples du globe depuis l'antiquité la plus reculée jusqu'à nos jours.* Paris, S. Lambert, 1879, 810 pp., anecdotal.

Decante, R. *La lutte contre la prostitution.* Paris, V. Giard et E. Brière, 1909, 334 pp.

Decaux, Alain. *Histoire des françaises.* Paris, Perrin, 1972. Vol. 3, *La révolte: Les contradictions de la liberté,* 606 pp. Vol. 4, *La révolte: De l'obéissance à la contestation.*

Defrance, Eugène. *La maison de Mme. Gourdan.* Paris, Mercure de France, 1908, 239 pp.

Delaitre, J. *Rapport sommaire sur . . . les jeunes mineurs se livrant habituellement à la prostitution.* Imp. adm. Melun, 1906, 12 pp.

Delannoy, J. C. *Pécheresses et repenties: Notes pour servir à l'histoire de la prostitution à Amiens du XIVe au XIXe siècle.* Amiens, 1943, 24 pp.

Delesalle, Simone. "Lecture d'un chef-d'oeuvre: Manon Lescaut." *Annales E.S.C.* (May–August 1971): 723–740.

Deleuze, Gilles. *Présentation de Sacher-Masoch: Le froid et le cruel.* Paris, U.G.E., 1973, 317 pp.

Delorme, Dr. E. "Mémoire sur la syphilis dans l'armée avec quelques considérations sur sa prophylaxie." Read at the Academy of Medicine, April 23, 1907. In L. Fiaux, *La police des moeurs devant la commission.* Vol. 3, pp. 548–562.

Delvau, Alfred. *Grandeur et décadence des grisettes.* Paris, A. Desloges, 1848, 104 pp.

—— *Les Dessous de Paris.* Paris, Poulet-Malassis et De Broix, 1860, 288 pp.

—— *Les Cythères parisiennes: Histoire anecdotique des bals de Paris.* Paris, E. Dentu, 1864, 281 pp.

—— *Dictionnaire érotique moderne par un professeur de langue verte.* Freetown, Imp. de la Bibliomaniac society, 1864, x + 319 pp.

—— *Histoire anecdotique des barrières de Paris.* Paris, E. Dentu, 1865, 301 pp.

—— *Le grand et le petit trottoir.* Paris, A. Faure, 1866, 343 pp.

—— *Les plaisirs de Paris.* Paris, A. Faure, 1867, 299 pp.

Dennie, Dr. Charles Clayton. *A History of Syphilis.* Springfield, 1962, 137 pp.

Depauw, J. "Amour illégitime et société à Nantes au XVIIIᵉ siècle." *Annales E.S.C.* (July–October 1972): 1155–82.

Descaves, Lucien. *Sous-offs, roman militaire.* Paris, Stock, 1889, 443 pp.

Désert, Gabriel. "Prostitution et prostituées à Caen pendant la seconde moitié du XIXᵉ siècle (1863–1914)." *Les archives hospitalières. Cahier des Annales de Normandie,* no. 10 (1977): 187–208.

Desmaze, Charles. *Le crime et la débauche à Paris: Le divorce.* Paris, G. Charpentier, 1881, 364 pp.

Desprès, Dr. A. *La police des moeurs et la morale: Discours prononcés à Paris, en janvier et février 1877 par Mme. Joséphine Butler, et MM. A. Humbert, Butler, Donat, Sautter et le docteur Desprès, avec un appendice contenant le compte rendu . . . des études du Conseil municipal de Paris sur le service des moeurs.* Paris, Sandoz et Fischbacher, 1877, 108 pp.

—— *La prostitution en France: Etudes morales et démographiques avec une statistique générale de la prostitution en France.* Paris, J. B. Baillière et fils, 1883, viii + 203 pp.

Devance, Louis. "Femme, famille, travail et morale sexuelle dans l'idéologie de 1848." *Mythes et représentations de la femme au XIXᵉ siècle.* Paris, Champion, 1976.

Diday, Dr. Paul. *Exposition critique et pratique des nouvelles doctrines sur la syphilis suivie d'une étude sur les nouveaux moyens préservatifs des maladies vénériennes.* Paris, J. B. Baillière, 1858, 560 pp.

Diday, Professor P. "Nouveau système d'assainissement de la prostitution." In *Annales de dermatologie et syphiligraphie* (1873–1874). Paris, Masson, 1874, 23 pp.

—— *Le péril vénérien dans les familles.* Paris, Asselin, 1881, xix + 448 pp.

—— "Assainissement méthodique de la prostitution." *Bullet. de l'acad. de méd.* (1888): 491ff.

Didiot, Dr. P. A. *Etude statistique de la syphilis dans la garnison de Marseille.* Marseilles, Arnaud et Cayer, 1886, 43 pp.

Dolléans, E. "L'hygiène sociale." *Le mouvement socialiste,* 1902, pp. 1784–91.

—— *La police des moeurs.* Paris, L. Larose, 1903, 262 pp.

Donzelot, Jacques. *La police des familles.* Paris, Ed. de Minuit, 1977, 224 pp.

Dreyfus, Ferdinand. "Des réformes proposées et des moyens déjà mis en pratique par le tribunal de la Seine pour réprimer la prostitution des filles mineures de seize ans." *Comité de défense des enfants traduits en justice.* Report presented at the meeting of February 5, 1896. Paris, Kugelmann, pp. 57–78.

——— *Misères sociales et études historiques.* Paris, Ollendorff, 1901, 285 pp. "Le congrès de Londres et la traite des blanches," pp. 57–78.

Drouineau, Dr. G. (de La Rochelle). "Discussion du rapport de M. le docteur Vibert sur la réglementation de la prostitution." *Revue d'hygiène et de police sanitaire* (1884): 62–68.

——— "La réglementation de la prostitution." *Revue d'hygiène et de police sanitaire* (1898): 508.

du Camp, Maxime. *Paris: Ses organes, ses fonctions et sa vie dans la seconde moitié du XIXᵉ siècle.* Paris, Hachette, 1869–1875. 6 vols. Vol. 3, 1872.

Duclaux, Emile. *L'hygiène sociale.* Paris, F. Alcan, 1902, iv + 271 pp.

Ducpétiaux, Edouard. *De la condition physique et morale des jeunes ouvriers et des moyens de l'améliorer.* Brussels, 1843, 2 vols.

Dufour, Pierre. (Pseud. of Paul Lacroix, who nonetheless disclaimed authorship of this work.) *Histoire de la prostitution chez tous les peuples du monde depuis l'antiquité la plus reculée jusqu'à nos jours.* Paris, Seré, 1851–1853, 6 vols.

Dumas, Alexandre, père. *Filles, lorettes et courtisanes.* Paris, Dolin, 1843, 338 pp.

Dumas, Alexandre, fils. *L'affaire Clemenceau.*

——— *Théâtre complet.* Paris, 1868. Preface.

Durban, Dr. Pierre. *La psychologie des prostituées.* Paris, Maloine, 1969, 239 pp.

Dutasta, Emile. *Compte rendu des travaux de la police présenté à M. le maire de Bordeaux par M. E. Dutasta. Année 1854.* Bordeaux, Imp. de G. Gounouilhou, 1855, 35 pp., maps.

Ellis, Havelock. *Etudes de psychologie sexuelle.* Paris, 1908. Published in English as *Studies in the Psychology of Sex.* Philadelphia, Davis, 1903.

——— *La prostitution: Ses causes, ses remèdes.* Vol. 9 of *Studies.* Philadelphia, Davis, 1904.

Elouin, M., A. Trébuchet, and E. Labat. *Nouveau dictionnaire de police.* Paris, Béchet jeune, 1835, 2 vols.

Engels, Friedrich. *L'origine de la famille, de la propriété privée et de l'Etat.* Paris, G. Carré, 1893, 291 pp. Published in English as *The Origins of the Family, Private Property, and the State.* Chicago, Kerr, 1902.

Esquiros, Adèle. *Les marchandes d'amour.* Paris, F. Pick, 1865, 224 pp.

Esquiros, Alphonse. *Les vierges folles.* Paris, A. Le Gallois, 1840, 128 pp.

Etienne, Professor G. *Etudes sur la prostitution.* Nancy, 1901, 74 pp.

Fallot, T. *La femme esclave.* Paris, Fischbacher, 1884, 81 pp.

Femme, La, dans la nature, dans les moeurs, dans la légende, dans la société. Vol. 4. "Le féminisme." Paris, 1910.

Féré, Dr. C. *Dégénérescence et criminalité.* Paris, Alcan, 1888, 179 pp.

——— *La pathologie des émotions: Etudes physiologiques et cliniques.* Paris, F. Alcan, 1892, xii + 605 pp.

Feschet, J. *A seize ans au trottoir, piégées par le système.* Paris, Ed. ouvrières, 1975, 240 pp.

Fiaux, Dr. L. *La femme, le mariage et le divorce. Etude de physiologie et de sociologie.* Paris, G. Baillière, 1880, iii + 236 pp.

———— *Rapport présenté au Conseil municipal de Paris sur les résultats de l'enquête concernant la police des moeurs.* Paris, Imp. municipale, 1883.

———— "La question de la prostitution devant l'Académie de médecine." *Revue socialiste,* no. 41, (May 15, 1888).

———— *La police des moeurs en France et dans les principaux pays de l'Europe.* Paris, E. Dentu, 1888, vii + 1010 pp.

———— "Note sur la rareté des maladies vénériennes dans la population ouvrière de Paris." *Gazette des hôpitaux,* September 18, 1890; February 10, September 10, 1891.

———— *Les maisons de tolérance: Leur fermeture.* Paris, G. Carré, 1892, v + 394 pp.

———— *L'organisation actuelle de la surveillance médicale de la prostitution est-elle susceptible d'amélioration?* Brussels, Lamertin, 1899, 121 pp.

———— *La prostitution réglementée et les pouvoirs publics dans les principaux états des deux mondes.* Vol. 1. Belgium, Russia, France, and Switzerland. *Progrès médical* (1902).

———— *La prostitution cloîtrée: Etude de biologie sociale.* Paris, F. Alcan, 1902.

———— *Le délit pénal de contamination intersexuelle.* Paris, Alcan, 1907, 261 pp.

———— *La police des moeurs devant la commission extra-parlementaire du régime des moeurs. Introduction. Rapports. Débats. Abolition de la police des moeurs. Le régime de la loi. Documents inédits.* Paris, Alcan, 1907–1910, 3 vols.

———— *L'armée et la police des moeurs. Biologie sexuelle du soldat. Essai moral et statistique.* Paris, Alcan, 1917, 325 pp.

Filhol, *Le monde des particulières.* Paris, Gallimard, 1959, 262 pp.

Fischer, Dr. G. "Essai de prophylaxie des maladies vénériennes." *La presse médicale,* April 2, 1902, 217–318.

Flandrin, J. L. "Contraception, mariage et relations amoureuses dans l'Occident chrétien." *Annales E.S.C.* (November–December 1969): 1370–90, an essential source.

———— "Mariage tardif et vie sexuelle: Discussion et hypothèses de recherche." *Annales E.S.C.* (November–December 1972): 1351ff.

———— *Les amours paysannes (XVIᵉ–XIXᵉ siècle).* Paris, Julliard, 1975, 256 pp.

Flaubert, G. *Bouvard et Pécuchet.*

Fleury, Dr. Maurice de. *Les mères de demain: L'éducation de la jeune fille d'après sa physiologie.* Paris, 1902.

———— *Nos enfants au collège: Le corps et l'âme de l'enfant,* Paris, A. Colin, 1899–1905, 2 vols.

Flévy d'Urville. *Les ordures de Paris.* Paris, Sartorius, 1874, 302 pp.

Flexner, Abraham. *La prostitution en Europe.* Preface by H. Minod. Paris, 1919. (Published in New York in 1913.)

Fodéré, F. E. *Traité de médecine légale et d'hygiène publique ou de police de santé.* Paris, Mame, 1813, 6 vols.

Folles femmes de leur corps. Recherches, no. 26 (March 1977), 246 pp.

Forel, Professor A. of Zurich. *La question sexuelle exposée aux adultes cultivés.* Paris, Steinheil, 1906. viii + 604 pp.

Foucault, Michel. *Surveiller et punir. Naissance de la prison.* Paris, Gallimard, 1976, 323 pp. Trans. as *Discipline and Punish* by Alan Sheridan. New York, Pantheon, 1977.

———— *Histoire de la sexualité.* Vol. 1. *La volonté de savoir.* Paris, Gallimard, 1976,

211 pp. Trans. as *The History of Sexuality* by Robert Hurley. New York, Pantheon, 1978.

Fournier, Professor Alfred-Jean. *Clinique de l'hôpital de Lourcine: Leçons sur la syphilis, étudiée plus particulièrement chez la femme.* Paris, A. Delahaye, 1873, 1108 pp.

———— "Documents statistiques sur les sources de la syphilis chez la femme," and "La syphilis des honnêtes femmes." *Bulletin de l'Académie de Médecine,* October 25, 1887, 339–549; October 2 and 9, 1906, 190–206, 232–246.

———— *Traitement de la syphilis.* Paris, J. Rueff, 1894, 600 pp.

———— *Prophylaxie de la syphilis.* Paris, J. Rueff, 1903, 558 pp.

———— *Ligue contre la syphilis.* Paris, Delagrave, 1904, 57 pp.

———— *Commission extra-parlementaire du régime des moeurs.* Report. Melun, 1904, 68 pp.

———— *Danger social de la syphilis.* Paris, Delagrave, 1905, 84 pp.

Fournier, Christiane. *Ces filles perdues.* Paris, Centurion, 1963, 174 pp.

Fournier, Professor E. "A quel âge se prend la syphilis?" *Presse médicale,* April 4, 1900, 164–167.

Fournier, Dr. H. *L'onanisme: Causes, dangers et inconvénients pour les individus, la famille et la société.* Paris, J. B. Baillière, 1876, 178 pp.

France, Hector. *Marie-Queue-de-Vache.* Paris, Lib. du progrès, 1883, 481 pp.

Francillon-Lobre, Dr. Marthe. *Essai sur la puberté chez la femme: Etude de psycho-physiologie féminine.* Paris, Félix Alcan, 1906, v + 300 pp.

———— *Hygiène de la femme et de la jeune fille.* Paris, C. Delagrave, 1909, vii + 200 pp.

Frapié, Léon. *La proscrite.* Paris, C. Lévy, 1907, 314 pp.

Frappa, Jean-José. *Enquête sur la prostitution: Ce qu'elle est aujourd'hui—les trottoirs de Paris—les agences—prostituées clandestines—maisons de tolérance—maisons de rendez-vous—maisons d'abattage—Faut-il réglementer la prostitution ou l'émanciper?* Paris, Flammarion, 1937, 212 pp.

Frégier, H. A. *Des classes dangereuses de la population dans les grandes villes, et des moyens de les rendre meilleures.* Paris, J. B. Baillière, 1840, 2 vols., xii + 435 pp.

Freud, S. *Sur la sexualité féminine.* Paris, P.U.F., 1969.

Froment, M. *La police dévoilée depuis la Restauration et notamment sous MM. Franchet et Delavau.* Edited by M. Guyon. Paris. Lemonnier, 1829, 3 vols.

Gaillard, Jeanne. *Paris: La ville, 1852–1870.* Paris, Champion, 1977, 686 pp.

Garin, Dr. Joseph. *De la police sanitaire et de l'assistance publique dans leurs rapports avec l'extinction des maladies vénériennes.* Paris, V. Masson et fils, 1866, viii + 191 pp.

———— *Le service sanitaire de Lyon: Son organisation médicale et ses résultats pratiques.* Paris, G. Masson, 1878, 62 pp.

Garnier, Dr. P. *Célibat et célibataires: Caractères, dangers et hygiène chez les deux sexes.* Paris, Garnier frères, 1887, 542 pp.

Gaucher, Professor. "Des moyens propres à prévenir la prostitution." *Bulletin de la Société internationale de prophylaxie sanitaire et morale.* Brussels. no. 4 (1901): 313–318.

Geffroy, Gustave. *L'apprentie.* Paris, E. Fasquelle, 1904, 319 pp.

Geremek, Bronislaw. *Les marginaux parisiens aux XIV^c et XV^c siècles.* Paris, Flammarion, 1976, 355 pp.

Gide, Professor Charles. "L'influence de l'immoralité sur le mouvement de la population." *Revue de morale sociale*. Paris, Alcan, December 1903, pp. 411–433.

——— *Rapport sur la moralité publique*. Melun, Impr. Administr. 1903, 22 pp.

Goncourt, E. de. *La fille Elisa*. Paris, Charpentier, 1877.

Goncourt, E., and J. Huot de. *La lorette*. Paris, Dentu, 1853.

——— *Germinie Lacerteux*. Paris, Charpentier, 1864, viii + 279 pp.

——— *Journal: Mémoires de la vie littéraire*. Monaco. Imp. nat., 1956–1958.

Gonnard, R. *La femme dans l'industrie*. Paris, A. Colin, 1906, 283 pp.

Goron, M. F. *L'amour à Paris*. Paris, Flammarion, 1899. Vol. 2, *Les industries de l'amour*. Vol. 4, *Le marché aux femmes*.

Grandpré, Mlle. Pauline Chevalier de. *Les condamnées de Saint-Lazare: Mémoires par Mme* . . . Paris, F. Curot, 1869, 336 pp.

——— *La prison de Saint-Lazare depuis vingt ans*. Paris, Dentu, 1889, 434 pp.

Gras, Dr. François. "L'aliénation mentale chez les prostituées." Thesis. Lyons, 1901, 106 pp.

Grauveau, A. *La prostitution dans Paris*. Paris, 1867, 153 pp.

Graux, Dr. Lucien. *Les arrêtés municipaux et les lois sanitaires des 15 et 19 février 1902 et 7 avril 1903*. Paris, Rousset, 1905; 19 pp.

Grimal, P., ed. *Histoire mondiale de la femme*. Vol. 4, *Sociétés contemporaines*, Book 2, *La femme au XIXᵉ siècle*, chap. 1, "La femme en France au XIXᵉ siècle," by Nicole Bothorel and Marie-Françoise Laurent, pp. 101–161. Paris, Nlle Librairie de France, 1966.

Guépin, A. and E. Bonamy. *Nantes au XIXᵉ siècle: Statistique topographique, industrielle et morale*. Nantes, Prosper Sebire, 1835, 650 pp.

Guiard, Dr. F. P. "Le danger vénérien pour la santé publique: Urgence d'une réglementation nouvelle de la prostitution pour le combattre." *Revue de médecine légale* (1899): 18.

Guilbert, Madeleine. *Les femmes et l'organisation syndicale avant 1914*. Paris, Ed. du C.N.R.S., 1966, 509 pp.

Guillaume, P. *La population de Bordeaux au XIXᵉ siècle: Essai d'histoire sociale*. Paris, A. Colin, 1972, 304 pp.

Guyot, Yves. *La prostitution*. Paris, G. Charpentier (E. Fasquelle), 1882, iv + 580 pp.

——— *Un drôle*. Paris, Flammarion, 1885, 384 pp.

——— *La traite des vierges à Londres*. Paris, G. Charpentier (E. Fasquelle), 1885, xxxvi + 285 pp.

Haussonville, Count d'. "L'enfance à Paris." *Revue des deux-mondes*, October 1– December 1, 1876; March 1, 1877; June 1878.

——— "Le combat contre le vice: L'inconduite." *Revue des deux-mondes* (December 1887).

——— "Les non-classées et l'émigration des femmes aux colonies." *Revue des deux-mondes*, June 15, 1898.

——— *Salaires et misères des femmes*. Paris, Calmann-Lévy, 1900, 314 pp.

Hayem, Henri. "La police des moeurs en province." In *Bulletin de la Société des prisons: Revue pénitentiaire*. (February 1904): 251–262.

Hébert, Dr. G. "Où se prennent les maladies vénériennes? Comment elles sont soignées comment elles devraient l'être." Thesis. Paris, 1906, 53 pp.

Hennequin, F. *Rapport de M. Hennequin, Chef de bureau au ministère de l'Intérieur, sur la réglementation de la prostitution en France (Seine, Algérie et colonie exceptées)*. Melun, Imprimerie administrative, 1903, 100 pp.

Hennique, Léon. "L'affaire du grand 7." *Les soirées de Médan*.

Hermant, A. *Le Cavalier Miserey*, Paris, G. Charpentier, 1887.

Hermite, Dr. E. *Prostitution et réglementation sanitaire de la police des moeurs à Grenoble*. Grenoble, 1907, 17 pp.

Hesnard, Dr. *Traité de sexologie normale et pathologique*. Paris, Payot, 1939, 718 pp.

Hoche, Jules. *Saint-Lazare: Roman social*. Paris, Lib. Contemp., 1901, xiv + 399 pp.

———— "Une visite à Saint-Lazare." *Grande revue*, March 1, 1901.

Homo, Dr. Hippolyte. *Etude sur la prostitution dans la ville de Château-Gontier suivie de considérations sur la prostitution en général*. Paris, J. B. Baillière, 1872, vi + 183 pp.

Hugo, Victor. *Les Misérables*, with notes and variants by M. Allem. Paris, Gallimard, "La Pléiade" edition.

Huysmans, J. K. *Marthe, histoire d'une fille, Les soeurs Vatard, En ménage, A vau-l'eau, A rebours, En rade, Un dilemme, Certains*.

Ibels, André. *La traite des chanteuses (moeurs de province), beuglants et bouis bouis, le prolétariat de l'art ou de . . . l'amour?* Paris, F. Juven, 1906, 320 pp.

Ibsen, *Les revenants*. Paris, 1894. Published in English as *Ghosts*.

Icard, Dr. S. *La femme pendant la période menstruelle*. Paris, F. Alcan, 1890, 283 pp.

Influence des expositions universelles sur l'état sanitaire des prostituées à Paris. Paris, 1901, 8 pp.

Issaly, Dr. Léon. "Contribution à l'étude de la syphilis dans les campagnes." Thesis. Paris, 1895.

Jeannel, Dr. Julien F. *Mémoire sur la prostitution publique et parallèle complet de la prostitution romaine et de la prostitution contemporaine, suivis d'une étude sur le dispensaire de salubrité de Bordeaux . . . et d'un essai statistique de l'infection vénérienne dans les garnisons de l'Empire*. Paris, G. Baillière, 1862, 241 pp.

———— *De la prostitution dans les grandes villes au XIXᵉ siècle et de l'extinction des maladies vénériennes*. Paris, J. B. Baillière et fils, 1868, x + 416 pp.

Joly, Adolphe. *La prostitution au XIXᵉ siècle: Exposé des causes régénératrices de cette plaie sociale et indication de réformes humaines seules capables de la cautériser*. Paris, A. Pierre, n.d.

Joly, Henri. *Les maisons du Bon-Pasteur*. Paris, secrétariat de la Société d'économie sociale. 1901. 24 pp.

———— *L'enfance coupable*. Paris, Lecoffre. 1904. 222 pp.

Jullien, Dr. "Les vénériennes de Saint-Lazare." In *Journal des maladies cutanées et syphilitiques*, Clermont (Oise), Daix, 1900, 16 pp.

Knibiehler, Y. "Les médecins et la nature féminine au temps du code civil." *Annales E.S.C.* (July–August 1976): 824–845.

———— "Le discours sur la femme: Constantes et ruptures." *Mythes et représentations de la femme au XIXᵉ siècle*. Paris, Champion, 1976.

Krafft-Ebing, *Psychopathia sexualis*. Paris, G. Carré, 1895, 595 pp.

Lacassagne, Dr. A. *Les tatouages: Etude anthropologique et médico-légale*. Paris, J. B. Baillière et fils, 1881.

Lafargue, P. *La question de la femme*. Paris, Ed. de l'Oeuvre nouvelle, 1904, 24 pp.

Lagneau, Dr. G. *Mémoire sur les mesures hygiéniques propres à prévenir la propagation des maladies vénériennes.* Paris, J. B. Baillière, 1856, 107 pp.

Lambert-Thiboust, P. A. *Les filles de marbre.* Paris, Michel Lévy, 1853, 76 pp.

Langlet, Professor. "La cure de prison." *Union médicale et scientifique du Nord-Est,* no. 30 (July 1905).

Lano, Pierre de. *Courtisane.* Paris, Rouveyre, 1883, 220 pp.

Lardier, Dr. P. *Les vénériens des champs et la prostitution à la campagne.* Paris, Doin, 1882, 40 pp.

Lassar, *Die Prostitution zu Paris: Ein Bericht.* Berlin, Klin. Wochenschr., 1892.

Laurent, Dr. Emile. *Les habitués des prisons de Paris: Etude d'anthropologie et de psychologie criminelles.* Lyons, A. Storck, 1890, 616 pp.

——— *L'amour morbide: Etude de psychologie pathologique.* Paris, Soc. d'Ed. Scientifiques, 1891, x + 287 pp.

——— *L'anthropologie criminelle et les nouvelles théories du crime.* Paris, Soc. d'éd. scientifiques, 1893, 242 pp.

——— "Prostitution et dégénérescence." *Annales médico-psychologiques* (1899): 353ff.

——— *Fétichistes et érotomanes.* Paris, Vigot frères, 1905, 270 pp.

——— *La criminalité infantile.* Paris, Maloine, 1906, 168 pp.

Layrac, Louis. "De l'excitation à la débauche." (Law of April 3, 1903). Thesis. Bordeaux, 1904, 242 pp.

Le Blond, Maurice, ed. *Nana.* Notes and commentary, with extracts from Zola's notebook. Paris, Ed. Bernouard, 1928.

Leblond, Dr. Albert, and Dr. Arthur Lucas. *Du tatouage chez les prostituées.* Paris, 1899, 96 pp.

Le Clec'h, Jules. *La prostitution des mineures, commentaire des lois du 11 avril 1908 et 19 juillet 1909 et des décrets des 5 mars et 13 juin 1910.* Paris, n.d., 144 pp.

Leclerc, Adhémar. *Etudes sociales. Les cancers. La femme déchue. L'exploiteur. L'homme déchu.* Paris, Librairie universelle de Godet, 1876, 35 pp.

Lecour, Charles-Jérôme. *Police médicale: De la prostitution et des mesures de police dont elle est l'objet à Paris au point de vue de l'infection syphilitique.* Paris, P. Asselin, 1868, 32 pp.

——— *La prostitution à Paris et à Londres, 1789–1870.* Paris, P. Asselin, 1870, vi + 372 pp.

——— 2d ed. contains additional chapters on prostitution in Paris during the Siege and under the Commune, and new statistical information. Paris, P. Asselin, 1872, vi + 416 pp.

——— *De l'état actuel de la prostitution parisienne.* Paris, Asselin, 1874, 59 pp.

——— *La campagne contre la préfecture de police, envisagée surtout au point de vue du service des moeurs.* Paris, Asselin, 1881, viii + 503 pp.

Le Foyer, Lucien. *Des conséquences juridiques de la contamination syphilitique.* Paris, Giard et Brière, 1902, 34 pp.

Legouvé, E. *Histoire morale des femmes.* Paris, G. Sandré, 1849, vii + 450 pp.

Lejeune, P. "Le dangereux supplément: Lecture d'un aveu de Rousseau." *Annales E.S.C.* (July–August 1974): 1009–22.

Leloir, H. "La syphilis et les cabarets dans la région du Nord: Les brasseurs." *Journal des connaissances médicales,* November 24, 1887, 371.

Le Moal, Dr. Paul. *Etudes sur la prostitution des mineures.* Paris, Editions sociales françaises, 1965, 220 pp.

Lenoble, Jules. *La traite des blanches et le congrès de Londres de 1899: Etude sur la protection de la jeune fille en France et à l'étranger.* Paris, L. Larose, 1900, 102 pp.

Le Pileur, Dr. Louis. *Prophylaxie de la syphilis: Réglementation de la prostitution à Paris, rapport adressé à M. le Préfet de Police au nom de la sous-commission.* Clermont (Oise), Imp. de Daix frères, 1887, 48 pp.

———— "De la mortalité infantile causée par la syphilis: Documents recueillis à la prison de Saint-Lazare." *Journal des maladies cutanées et syphilitiques* (June 1889): 78.

———— *De l'hospitalisation des prostituées vénériennes.* Paris, J. B. Baillière et fils, 1889, 24 pp.

———— *A propos du projet de loi de M. Bérenger, sénateur, visant le racolage sur la voie publique.* Paris, Maloine, 1895, 40 pp.

———— *Rapport sur la conférence internationale tenue à Bruxelles en septembre 1899 pour la prophylaxie de la syphilis et des maladies vénériennes présenté à M. le ministre de l'Intérieur.* Clermont (Oise), 1901, 141 pp.

———— *Indications sur la prostitution vulgivague à Paris depuis le début de la guerre.* Paris, Imp. de Tancrède, 1918, 20 pp.

Lépine, Prefect L. *Rapport de M. Lépine, préfet de police, sur la réglementation de la prostitution à Paris et dans le département de la Seine.* Imp. administrative de Melun, 1904, 28 pp.

Leroy-Allais, Mme. Jeanne. *Le rôle des mères dans l'éducation de leurs fils au point de vue de la morale.* Paris, Maloine, 1905, 16 pp.

———— *Comment j'ai instruit mes filles des choses de la maternité.* Paris, Maloine, 1907, 134 pp.

Leroy-Beaulieu, Paul. *De l'état moral et intellectual des populations ouvrières et de son influence sur le taux des salaires,* Paris, Guillaumin, 1868, xxviii + 303 pp.

———— *Le travail des femmes au XIX* siècle.* Paris, Charpentier, 1873, 468 pp.

Lévéque, P. "Prophylaxie des maladies vénériennes et police des moeurs." Thesis. Lyons, A. Rey, 1905, 271 pp.

Lévi, Vittorio. *La prostitution chez la femme et la traite des blanches.* Naples, Imp. Castiglione, 1912, 128 pp.

Lewinsohn. *Histoire de la vie sexuelle.* Paris, Payot, 1957, 409 pp.

Lobrot, Michel. *La libération sexuelle.* Paris, Payot, 1975, 217 pp.

Lohse, Félix. *La prostitution des mineures en France avant et après la loi du 11 avril 1908.* Paris, A. Rousseau, 1913, 696 pp.

Lombroso, C., and G. Ferrero. *La femme criminelle et la prostituée.* Paris, F. Alcan, 1896, xvi + 679 pp.

Londres, Albert. *Le chemin de Buenos-Aires.* Paris, A. Michel, 1927, 258 pp.

Lutaud, Dr. A. "Considérations sur la réglementation de la prostitution à Paris." *Bulletin et mémoires de la Société de médecine pratique de Paris,* February 15, 1888.

———— "La prostitution patentée." *Journal de médecine de Paris.* June 7, 1903.

Macé, G. *La police parisienne.* Vol. 4. *Gibier de Saint-Lazare.* Paris, Charpentier, 1888, 320 pp.

Maillard, Dr. Claude. *Les prostituées: Ce qu'elles disent quand elles parlent à une femme.* Paris, R. Laffont, 1975, 232 pp.

Maireau, Dr. *Syphilis et prostituées et principalement contribution à l'étude de la syphilide pigmentaire.* Paris, J. Le Clère, 1884, 95 pp.

Malécot, Dr. A. *Les vénériens et le droit commun.* Paris, Carré, 1888, 24 pp.

Malon, Benoît. *Le socialisme intégral.* Paris, F. Alcan, 1890–1891. Vol. 1. chap. 7, "L'évolution familiale et le socialisme."

Mancini, Jean-Gabriel. *Prostitution et proxénétisme.* Paris, P.U.F., "Que sais-je?", 1972, 126 pp.

Margueritte, Victor. *Prostituée.* Paris, E. Fasquelle, 1907, 500 pp.

Martineau, Dr. L. *La prostitution clandestine.* Paris, Delahaye, 1885, iv + 216 pp.

Matter, Paul. *Le trafic de la débauche et les délits internationaux: Commentaire théorique et pratique de la loi du 3 avril 1903.* Paris, Bureau des Lois Nouvelles, 1903, 90 pp.

Maupassant, Guy de. "Le Horla," "L'odyssée d'une fille," "Le port," "Le signe," "L'ami Patience," "Le lit 29," "La maison Tellier," "Les tombales."

Mauriac, Dr. C. *Leçons sur les maladies vénériennes, professées à l'hôpital du Midi.* Paris, J. B. Baillière et fils, 1883, pp. 108ff. "Du régime de la prostitution dans la ville de Paris."

Mendès, Catulle. *La femme-enfant.* Paris, Charpentier, 1891, 631 pp.

Mercier, Louis-Sébastien. *Tableau de Paris.* 1781, 2 vols.

Mignot, Dr. F. *Le péril vénérien et la prophylaxie des maladies vénériennes.* Paris et Nantes, Doin et Dugas, 1905, 238 pp.

Millett, Kate. *La prostitution: Quatuor pour voix féminines.* Paris, Denoël, 1972, 128 pp. Published in English as *Prostitution Papers: A Candid Dialogue.*

Minime, Dr. A. Lutaud. *La prostitution et la traite des blanches à Londres et à Paris.* Paris, Marpon et Flammarion, 1886, 1 vol., 274 pp.

Ministère de la Guerre. Statistique médicale de l'armée. Annual since 1851.

Minod, H. *Ve Congrès international des Patronages. IVe session—IIIe section—*"Patronage des mendiants et vagabonds." 2d question (La prostitution). Liège, August 1905, 120 pp.

———. *Simple exposé du but et des principes de la Fédération abolitionniste internationale.* 5th ed., Geneva, 1912.

Mirbeau, Octave. *Le journal d'une femme de chambre.* Paris, Fasquelle, 1900, 519 pp.

Mireur, Dr. Hippolyte. *La syphilis et la prostitution dans leurs rapports avec l'hygiène, la morale et la loi.* Paris, G. Masson, 1875, ii + 475 pp.

———. *La prostitution à Marseille: Histoire, administration et police, hygiène.* Paris, E. Dentu, 1882, xiii + 404 pp.

——— *L'avarie, origine, symptômes, contagion, traitement, prophylaxie.* Paris, Stock, 1906, iv + 161 pp.

Mithouard, A. *Conseil municipal de Paris, 17 novembre 1908.* "Rapport au nom de la commission sur l'application de la loi du 15 avril 1908 concernant la prostitution des mineures présenté par A. Mithouard et Ranvier."

Molinari, G. de *La viriculture.* Paris, Guillaumin, 1897, 253 pp.

Moll, Dr. Albert. *Les perversions de l'instinct génital: Etude sur l'inversion sexuelle.* Paris, G. Carré, 1893, 327 pp.

Moncharville, M. *La traite des blanches et le congrès de Londres: Rapport présenté au comité français de participation au congrès par M. Moncharville.* Paris, P. Mouillot, 1900, 26 pp.

Monnet, Dr. L. E. *Conseils aux avariés.* Paris, Vigot, 1902, 148 pp.

Monod, Henri. "Prostitution." In *Encyclopédie d'hygiène et de médecine publiques.* Edited by Jules Rochard. Paris, Vigot, 1897, Vol. 8, fol. 41, pp. 512ff.

Monroe, Lord. *La clarisse au XIXe siècle ou la traite des blanches.* London, Paris, Brussels, 1881, 367 pp.

Monselet, C. *Le musée secret de Paris.* Paris, Michel Lévy, n.d., 200 pp.

Morali-Daninos Dr. André. *Histoire des relations sexuelles.* Paris, P.U.F., 1970, 128 pp.

——— *Evolution des moeurs sexuelles.* Paris, Casterman, 1972, 171 pp.

Morel, Dr. Benedict A. *Traité des dégénérescences physiques, intellectuelles et morales de l'espèce humaine.* Paris, J. B. Baillière, 1857, 700 pp.

Morel de Rubempré, Dr. M. J. *La pornologie, ou histoire nouvelle, universelle et complète de la débauche.* Paris, 2 vols., 1848, 302 pp.; 1850, 306 pp.

Morhardt, Dr. Paul-Emile. *Les maladies vénériennes et la réglementation au point de vue de l'hygiène sociale.* Paris, Doin, 1906, 216 pp.

Morsier, Auguste de. *Fédération abolitionniste internationale, branche française: Rapport au Congrès de Londres (12–15 juillet 1898) sur la lutte contre la prostitution réglementée en France.* Alençon, de Guy, 1898, 32 pp.

——— *La police des moeurs en France et la campagne abolitionniste.* Paris, Stock, 1901, 217 pp.

——— *Le droit des femmes et la morale intersexuelle: Une question d'éducation sociale.* Geneva, H. Kundig, 1903, 88 pp.

Moty, Dr. M. "Prophylaxie des maladies vénériennes." *Echo médical du Nord,* August 17, 1902.

Mullem, Louis. *Chez Madame Antonin.* Paris, Stock, 1887, v + 304 pp.

Murard, Lion, and Patrick Zylberman. *Le petit travailleur infatigable. Recherches,* no. 25 (1976), 292 pp.

Noonan, John T. *Contraception et mariage.* Paris, Ed. du Cerf. 1969, 722 pp.

Osmont, Alain. *La prostitution et le monde des prostituées à Caen dans la seconde moitié du XIXe siècle.* Mémoire de maîtrise, Caen, 1977.

Pachot, ed. "Le régime actuel des moeurs en France: Sa réforme." *Archives d'anthropologie criminelle et de médecine légale.* (October–November 1908): 687–721.

Palais-Royal, Le, ou les filles à bonne fortune. Paris, 1815.

Parent-Duchatelet, Dr. Alex. J. B. *De la prostitution dans la ville de Paris.* Paris, J. B. Baillière, 1836, 2 vols. 3d. ed. completed with new documents by MM. A. Trébuchet, Poirat-Duval. Paris, J. B. Baillière et frères, 1857, 2 vols.

Parent-Lardeur, *Les demoiselles de magasin.* Paris, Ed. Ouvrières, 1969, 159 pp.

Patoir, Dr. "La prostitution à Lille." *Echo médical du Nord,* August 10, 1902.

Payenneville, Dr. J. *Le péril vénérien.* Paris, P.U.F., 1965.

Pelacy, Dr. "Rapport fait au Conseil de salubrité de la ville de Marseille." *Annales d'hygiène,* 25, ser. 1, pp. 297ff.

Pelletier, Madeleine. *L'émancipation sexuelle de la femme.* Paris, Giard et Brière, 1911, 87 pp.

Perrot, Jean-Claude. *Genèse d'une ville moderne: Caen au XVIIIᵉ siècle.* Paris, La Haye, Mouton, 1975, pp. 839ff., on prostitution.

Perrot, Michelle. *Les ouvriers en grève: France, 1871–1890.* Paris, La Haye, Mouton, 1973, 2 vols., 901 pp.

———— "L'éloge de la ménagère dans le discours des ouvriers français au XIXᵉ siècle." In *Mythes et représentations de la femme au XIXᵉ siècle.* Paris, Champion, 1976.

Philippe, Charles-Louis. *Bubu de Montparnasse.* 1901. Livre de poche.

Philippon, Odette, *L'esclavage de la femme dans le monde contemporain: Le trafic des femmes: L'esclavage du siècle.* Ed. Téqui, 1954, 1956, 1969.

Pierrard, Pierre. *La vie ouvrière à Lille sous le Second Empire.* Paris, Bloud et Gay, 1965, 532 pp.

Pignot, Dr. Albert. "L'Hôpital du Midi et ses origines. Recherches sur l'histoire . . . de la syphilis à Paris." Ph.D. diss., Paris, 1885, 147 pp.

Plaintes et révélations nouvellement adressées par les filles de joie de Paris à la Congrégation. Paris, Garnier, 1830, 38 pp.

Police des moeurs, La. Réunion de la salle Lévis du 10 avril 1880. Paris, 1880, 95 pp.

Pottet, Eugène. *Histoire de Saint-Lazare, 1122–1912.* Paris, 1912, 340 pp.

Potton, Dr. Ariste. *De la prostitution et de la syphilis dans les grandes villes, dans la ville de Lyon en particulier.* Paris, J. B. Baillière, 1842, xvi + 291 pp.

Potton, Dr. F. F. A. *De l'hospice de l'Antiquaille.* Lyons, Imp. de L. Perrin, 1845, 77 pp.

Pradier, Dr. F. H. *Histoire statistique et médicale et administrative de la prostitution dans la ville de Clermont-Ferrand.* Clermont-Ferrand, P. Hubler, 1859, 157 pp.

Prévost, Eugène. *De la prostitution des enfants: Etude juridique et sociale.* Paris, Plon, 1909, 336 pp.

Prévost, M. E. *Les demi-vierges.* Paris, A. Lemerre, 1894, 361 pp.

Proudhon, P. J. *Oeuvres complètes.* Vol. II. *La pornocratie.* Paris, M. Rivière, 1939.

Puibaraud, Louis. *Les malfaiteurs de profession.* Paris, E. Flammarion, 1893, vii + 416 pp. Chap. 5 "Les souteneurs," pp. 90–106.

Queyrat, Dr. Louis. *Contribution à la défense sociale contre le péril vénérien: La démoralisation de l'idée sexuelle.* Paris, Rueff, 1902, 31 pp.

Raisson, H. *Histoire de la police de Paris.* Paris, Levasseur, 1844, 404 pp.

Ranc. Municipal Council of Paris, ordinary budget session, 1871–1872. *Rapport complémentaire présenté au nom de la 8ᵉ commission par M. Ranc sur l'administration centrale de la préfecture de police,* on the vice squad.

Raoult, Dr. Ferdinand. *Etude sur la prophylaxie de la syphilis.* Paris, G. Steinheil, 1902, 238 pp.

Raux, *Nos jeunes détenus: Etude sur l'enfance coupable avant, pendant et après son séjour . . . correctionnel.* Paris, Lyons, Storck, and Maloine, 2d ed., 1890 and 1902, 372 pp.

Raynaud, Ernest. "Les écrivains de filles." *Mercure de France,* July 1, 1890.

———— *Souvenirs de police, au temps de Félix Faure.* Paris, Payot 1925, 251 pp.

———— *Souvenirs de police: La vie intime des commissariats.* Paris, Payot, 1926, 267 pp.

———— *La police des moeurs.* Paris, Soc. franç. d'éd. litt. et tech., 1934, 191 pp.

Regnault, Dr. Félix. "De l'évolution de la prostitution et plus spécialement de la maison." *La France médicale* (August–September 1892).

——— "Hygiène sociale, réglementation, abolition." *Revue moderne de médecine et de chirurgie,* no. 8 (August 1905): 270–279.

——— *L'évolution de la prostitution.* Paris, Flammarion, 1906, vii + 354 pp.

Reich, W. *La révolution sexuelle.* Paris, Plon, 1968, Published in English as *The Sexual Revolution.* London, Vision, 1961.

Renon, Dr. L. *Etude médico-sociale: Les maladies populaires: Maladies vénériennes, alcoolisme, tuberculose.* Paris, Masson, 2d ed., 1905, 477 pp.

Répression de la traite des blanches, La. Compte rendu du IIIe congrès international tenu à Paris les 22–25 octobre 1906. Paris, Soc. ann. de publ., 1907, 455 pp.

Répression de la traite des blanches, La. Compte rendu du IVe congrès international tenu à Madrid les 24–28 oct. 1910. Madrid, 1912.

Restif de la Bretonne. *Le pornographe ou idées d'un honnête homme sur un projet de réglement pour les prostituées.* London, La Haye, 1769, 368 pp.

Reuss, Dr. Louis. "Influence de la prostitution habituelle sur la santé des prostituées: Fréquence des maladies communes et générales chez les prostituées." *Annales d'hygiène* (January–June 1888).

——— *La prostitution au point de vue de l'hygiène et de l'administration en France et à l'étranger.* Paris, J. B. Baillière, 1889, viii + 636 pp.

Réville, Marc. *La prostitution des mineures selon la loi pénale.* Paris, Fischbacher, 1896, 36 pp.

"Révolte des vénériennes de Lyon." *La province médicale,* no. 13 (March 20, 1887): 208.

Rey, J. L. *"Des prostituées et de la prostitution en général," par J. L. Rey, commissaire de police au Mans.* Le Mans, Julien, Lanier et Cie, 1847, 185 pp.

Ricatte, Robert. *La genèse de "la Fille Elisa."* Paris, P.U.F., 1960, 220 pp.

Richard, Charles, mayor of Toulon. *La prostitution devant le philosophe.* Paris, Ghio, 1881, 176 pp.

Richard, Emile. *La prostitution à Paris,* Paris, J. B. Baillière, 1890, 295 pp.

Richard, Marthe. *Appel des sexes.* Paris, les éd. du Scorpion, 1951, 298 pp.

Richardson, Joanna. *Les courtisanes. La demi-monde au XIXe siècle.* Paris, Stock, 1968, 272 pp. Published in English as *The Courtesans: The Demimonde in 19th Century France.* London, 1967.

Ricord, Dr. Philippe. *Clinique de l'hôpital du Midi: Leçons sur le chancre . . . rédigées et publiées par Alfred Fournier . . . suivies de notes et pièces justificatives.* Paris, A. Delahaye, 1860, viii + 541 pp.

——— *Traité complet des maladies vénériennes.* Paris, J. Rouvier, 1862, 201 pp.

Robin, Paul. *Propos d'une fille recueillis par . . .* Paris, Librairie de Régénération, 1905, 16 pp.

Robiquet, Paul. *Histoire et droit,* Paris, Hachette, 1907.

Rogeat, Marcel. *Moeurs et prostitution: Les grandes enquêtes sociales.* Paris, Nouvelles éditions latines, 1935, 354 pp.

Rollet, Henri. *Les enfants en prison, études anecdotiques sur l'enfance criminelle par Guy Tomel.* Paris, Plon, 1891, 303 pp. Pt. 1, chap. 4, "Les petites prostituées."

Romi, *Maisons closes dans l'histoire, l'art, la littérature et les moeurs.* Paris, Serg, 2 vols., 1965, 309 pp. and 240 pp.

Ronsin, Francis. "Mouvements et courants néo-malthusiens en France." Thesis. Paris VII, June 1974.

Rossiaud, J. "Prostitution, jeunesse et société dans les villes du Sud-Est au XVe siè-cle." *Annales E.S.C.* (March–April 1976): 289–325.

Rougerie, J. "Recherche sur le Paris du XIXe siècle." *Recherches et travaux.* Institut d'histoire économique et sociale, University of Paris I, no. 5 (January 1977).

Roussel, Théophile, Senator. *Journal officiel: Sénat: Documents annexes no. 451. Séance du 25 juillet 1882.* Report on legal proposals concerning the protection of abandoned children. Responses to question 13 on the prostitution of minors, pp. 272 and 291–296.

Rouvre, C. de. *L'employée.* Paris, 1894, xv + 215 pp.

Ryan, Michael. *Prostitution in London with a Comparative View of That of Paris and New York.* London, H. Baillière, 1839, xx + 447 pp.

Ryckère, Raymond de. *La servante criminelle: Etude de criminologie professionnelle.* Paris, Maloine, 1908. 461 pp.

Sabatier, *Histoire de la législation sur les femmes publiques et les lieux de débauche.* Paris, J. P. Roret, 1828, 267 pp.

Sacotte, Marcel. *La prostitution.* Paris, Buchet-Chastel, 1965, 183 pp.

Sartre, J. P. *L'idiot de la famille: Gustave Flaubert de 1821 à 1857.* Vol. 3. Paris, 1971.

Savioz, Avril de Sainte-Croix, Mme. "Les femmes à Saint-Lazare." *La Fronde,* December 15, 16, 17, 1897.

———— *La serve: Une iniquité sociale.* 1901.

———— "La traite des blanches." *La grande revue,* 2 (1902): 281–294.

Schelsky, H. *Sociologie de la sexualité.* Paris, Gallimard, Collect. Idées, 1966, 255 pp.

Schor, Noami. "'Le sourire du sphinx': Zola et l'énigme de la féminité." In *Mythes et représentations de la femme au XIXe siècle.* Paris, Champion, 1976.

Schreiber, Hermann. *Le plus vieux métier du monde.* Paris, A. Michel, 1968, 251 pp.

Serman, W. "Les officiers français, 1848–1870." Thesis. Paris, 1977, typewritten copy, pp. 1078ff., concerns relations with prostitutes.

Servais, Jean-Jacques, and Jean-Pierre Laurend. *Histoire et dossier de la prostitution.* Paris, Ed. Planète, 1967, 458 pp.

"Sexualité et capitalisme," *Crapouillot,* 1961, 74 pp.

Simonot, Dr. Octave. "Psychologie physiologique de la prostituée." *Annales d'hygiène* (1911): 498–567.

Skandha, E. "La prostitution et la police des moeurs." *La revue blanche,* September 1, 1902, 49–62.

Société médicale de l'Elysée. *Discussion sur la réglementation de la prostitution.* Meetings of April 4, June 6, and July 4, 1898. Clermont d'Oise, Daix, 1898, 24 pp.

Solé, Jacques. "Passion charnelle et société urbaine d'Ancien Régime: Amour vénal, amour libre et amour fou à Grenoble au milieu du règne de Louis XIV." *Annales de la Faculté des lettres et sciences humaines de Nice,* nos. 9, 10 (1969): 211–232.

Sorr, Angelo de. *Les filles de Paris.* Paris, Comptoir des imprimeurs-unis, 1848, 3 vols.

Spencer, Herbert. *Introduction à la science sociale.* Paris, Baillière, 1874, 438 pp.

Spillmann, Professor L. *Du Refuge à la Maison de Secours (1614–1914): Histoire de la clinique de dermato-vénéréologie de Nancy.* With M. J. Benech. Imprimeries réunies de Nancy, July 1914.

———— *L'évolution de la lutte contre la syphilis: Un bilan de 25 ans (Nancy 1907–1932).* Paris, Masson, 1933, 291 pp.

Spillmann, L., and Zuber. "Syphilis et prostitution à Nancy." *Société de médecine de Nancy* (1913): 298ff.

Sue, Eugène. *Les mystères de Paris.* Paris, C. Gosselin, 1842–1843.

Surbled, Dr. G. *La vie de jeune homme.* Paris, Maloine, 1900, v + 160 pp.

———— *La vie de jeune fille.* Paris, Maloine, 1903, 256 pp.

Tacussel, F. *La traite des blanches.* Paris, J. Bonhoure, 1877.

Talmeyr, Maurice. *La fin d'une société: Les maisons d'illusion.* Paris, F. Juven, 1906, viii + 285 pp.

Tarde, G. "La morale sexuelle." *Archives d'anthropologie criminelle* (1907), 23ff.

Tarnowsky, Dr. Pauline. *Etude anthropométrique sur les prostituées et les voleuses.* Paris, Lecrosnier et Babé, 1889, vi + 226 pp.

Taxil, Léo. *La prostitution contemporaine: Etude d'une question sociale.* Paris, Lib. populaire n.d., 508 pp.

Teutsch, Dr. Robert. *Morale de l'instinct sexuel: Prophylaxie par les maisons de tolérance réformées.* Paris, Coccoz, 1902, 54 pp.

Thibierge, Dr. Georges, of Broca. *Syphilis et déontologie.* Paris, Masson, 1903, xi + 296 pp.

———— *L'avènement des doctrines syphiligraphiques modernes: L'oeuvre de Joseph Rollet, chirurgien major de l'hospice de l'Antiquaille à Lyon, de 1855 à 1864: Sa vie 1824–1894.* Paris, Masson, 1924, 75 pp.

Thulié, Dr. H. *Les enfants assistés de la Seine.* Paris, Delahaye et Lecrosnier, 1887, 700 pp.

Timon-David, Chanoine. *Traité de la confession des enfants et des jeunes gens.* Paris, V. Sarlit, 1865.

Tolstoy, Leo. *Résurrection.* Paris, Perrin, 1900, 2 vols. Published in English as *Resurrection,* trans. Vera Trevill. London, Hamish Hamilton, 1947.

Turot, Henri. *Le prolétariat de l'amour.* Paris, Librairie universelle, 1904, with a historical introduction by M. Paul-Louis Garnier, 344 pp.

Turot, Henri, Adrien Mithouard, and Maurice Quentin. *Conseil municipal de Paris: Rapport au nom de la deuxième commission sur la prostitution et la police des moeurs.* Paris, 1904.

Van der Gun, W. H. *La courtisane romantique et son rôle dans la Comédie humaine de Balzac.* Assen van Gorcum et Cie, n.d.

Van Ussel, J. *Histoire de la répression sexuelle.* Laffont, 1972, 351 pp.

Vast-Ricouard, R. and G. *Vices parisiens.* Paris, Derveaux, 1879, 276 pp.

Veith, Dr. Ilza. *Histoire de l'hystérie.* Paris, Seghers, 1972, 285 pp.

Venot, Dr. J. B. *Aperçu de statistique médicale et administrative sur l'hospice des vénériens de Bordeaux.* Paris, Baillet, 1837, 86 pp.

———— *Comment s'opposer aux ravages de la syphilis? Les mesures d'hygiène auxquelles on soumet les prostituées sont-elles suffisantes?* Bordeaux, Imp. de A. Péchade, 1846, 16 pp.

———— *Hygiène: Rapprochements statistiques entre les deux prostitutions, inscrite et clandestine, au point de vue de la syphilis.* Bordeaux, Imp. de G. Gounouilhou, 1857, 16 pp.

———— *De la pseudo-syphilis chez les prostituées, envisagée au point de vue de l'hygiène publique.* Bordeaux, Imp. de G. Gounouilhou, 1859, 32 pp.

Verchère, Dr. "De la réorganisation de Saint-Lazare." *Bulletin médical*, March 19, 1890.

Vernet, Madeleine (Mme. Louis Tribier). *L'amour libre*. Paris, 1907.

Véron, L. *Mémoires d'un bourgeois de Paris*. Paris, G. de Gonet, 1853–1855, 6 vols.

Véron, Pierre. *Paris amoureux*. Paris, C. Lévy, 1891, 308 pp.

Vibert, Dr. "Rapport sur la prostitution dans ses rapports avec la police médicale." *Revue d'hygiène*. 1883, pp. 912ff.

Vigneron, Victor. "La prostitution clandestine à Nancy: Esquisse d'hygiène sociale." Thesis. Nancy, 1901, 103 pp.

Villermé, Dr. Louis-René. *Tableau de l'état physique et moral des ouvriers employés dans les manufactures de coton, de laine et de soie*. Paris, J. Renouard, 1840, 2 vols.

Villette, Armand. *Du trottoir à Saint-Lazare: Etude sociale de la fille à Paris*. Paris, Lib. Universelle, 1907, ii + 284 pp.

Vintras, Dr. *On the Repressive Measures Adopted in Paris, Compared with the Uncontrolled Prostitution in London and New York*. London, 1867.

Virmaître, Charles. *Paris impur*. Paris, C. Dalou, 1889, 302 pp.

——— *Paris galant*. Paris, L. Genonceaux, 1890, 300 pp.

——— *Trottoirs et lupanars*. Paris, H. Perrot, 1893, 285 pp.

——— *Les flagellants et les flagellés de Paris*. Paris, C. Carrington, 1902, xcii + 303 pp.

Wajeman, Gérard. "Psyché de la femme: Note sur l'hystérique au XIXe siècle." In *Mythes et représentations de la femme au XIXe siècle*. Paris, Champion, 1976.

Winaver, Dr. *Vie sexuelle et risques vénériens*, Paris, Casterman, 1972, 161 pp.

Weidmann, Peter. *Die Venerologie in Paris von 1800–1850*. Zurich, Juris-Verlag, 1965, 67 pp.

Wylm, Dr. *La morale sexuelle*. Paris, F. Alcan, 1907.

Yvaren, Dr. *Les métamorphoses de la syphilis*. Paris, J. B. Baillière, 1854.

Zeldin, Theodore. *France 1848–1950*. Vol. 1. *Ambition. Love. Politics.*

Zola, Emile. *Les Rougon-Macquart. (La curée, L'assommoir, Nana, Pot-Bouille, Au Bonheur des Dames, Germinal.)* Paris, Gallimard, "La Pléiade" edition, introduction by H. Mitterand.

Zylberberg-Hocquard. "Feminisme et syndicalisme en France avant 1914." Thesis. Tours, 1973.

Index

Abolitionism, 37, 53, 54, 71, 88, 94, 99,
100, 101, 106, 111, 128, 261, 309,
310–313, 336, 365; and Josephine
Butler, 214–220; and Yves Guyot, 221–
229, 233; health issues in, 218, 225,
227, 229, 230, 246–258, 265, 273,
315; police issues in, 216, 218, 220–
234, 238, 243, 262, 273, 310–315;
public opinion on, 310–315; and
socialism, 231–240; twentieth-century
developments, 341–343; and white slave
trade, 275–280, 290–291, 297. *See also*
Neoabolitionism
Adultery, 175, 212
Advertising, 79–80, 178, 323, 337
Age distribution, of prostitutes, 34, 42–
44, 148, 149, 160, 163–165, 344; in
maisons de rendez-vous, 181–182, 184;
and Parisian white slave trade, 284–285;
of pimps, 160; and venereal disease, 92–
93
Alcohol, 7, 9, 19, 57–59, 66, 78, 118–
119, 154, 172, 298, 299, 302, 304,
328, 333, 339; and *brasseries à femmes*,
169; wine-shop procuring, 145–148,
150, 151
Alexis, Paul, 199
Anal sex, 125
Anarchism, 241–246, 313
Andler, Charles, 235
Andrieux, Prefect of Police, 106, 219,
223, 224, 233
Anthropology, criminal, 298, 300–308,
341

Appleton, Paul, 285, 288
Apprenticeship, 69, 209, 285
Aron, J. P., 142, 201
Art, 58, 60, 126, 205, 212
Artiste-prostitutes, 171–174
Atheism, 19
Augagneur, Professor, 265, 312
Austria, 277–278, 286, 287, 296

Bachelors, 137–138, 247, 333; bourgeois,
190–191, 197–206
Background of prostitutes: registered, 44–
53; unregistered, 162–163
Barbey d'Aurevilly, Jules, 142, 212, 252
Barrès, Auguste Maurice, 170–171
Barthélemy, Professor, 42, 92, 247, 248,
254, 257, 264, 265
Bebel, Ferdinand August, 235, 237, 278
Beer halls, 146–147
Belgium, 153, 262, 276; white slave trade,
276–277, 286, 287
Béraud, A., 4, 16, 17
Berenger, Senator, 173, 258, 278, 279,
297, 313, 315, 317–319, 321
Bergeret, Dr., 63, 147, 151
Berry, Georges, 257, 268, 317, 319
Bestiality, 124, 125
Béziers, 42, 122, 147
Birth control, 237, 245
Birthplace of prostitutes, 44–46
Birth rate, 8, 23–24, 52, 264, 347–348
Bizard, Léon, 336, 337
Blanc, Louis, 215
Bloc des Gauches, 261, 322

Bloy, Léon, 20, 142, 148, 244
Bonnier, Charles, 235
Bon-Pasteur houses, 15, 44
Bordeaux, 25, 33, 39, 70, 84, 88, 89, 96,
  105, 115, 131, 144, 189, 198, 204, 325
Borie, Jean, 194, 195, 198
Born prostitute, theory of, 300–308
Bourgeoisie, 24–25, 235; changing
  demands for prostitution by, 186–213,
  236–237; male sexual frustration, 194–
  206, 236, 242; marriage and home,
  189, 194–198, 235–244, 261, 322,
  331, 332
Bourneville, Professor, 95, 97, 98, 255,
  326
Brasseries à femmes, 168–171
Brest, 37, 39, 44, 55, 59, 66, 71, 72, 75,
  88, 89, 98, 105, 115, 132, 147, 163,
  171, 328
Brieux, Eugène, 269–270
Briey, 153–154, 192, 326
Briquet, Pierre, 299, 300
British abolitionists, 214–220, 227
British and Continental Federation for the
  Abolition of Prostitution, 218–220,
  222, 225, 239, 278, 311
Brothel-keepers, 11–12, 31, 53, 54, 61,
  63–84, 89, 103, 107, 117–121, 226,
  228, 291, 323; twentieth-century
  developments, 339–340, 348–349, 351;
  and white slave trade, 275, 282, 285
Brothels, 20, 26, 31, 44, 47, 53–84, 227–
  229, 331; clientele, 57–63, 70, 79–82,
  120–123; decline of *maisons de tolérance,*
  115–128, 139, 174, 201, 203, 254,
  274, 281, 324, 334, 337–338;
  functioning of, 63–84; and
  neoregulationism, 322–325, 333;
  Parent-Duchâtelet on, 10–12; pimps of,
  158; and police surveillance, 53, 54, 56,
  65, 68, 70, 78, 103–107, 117–121;
  profits, 66–69, 77–78, 117, 123, 175;
  topography and typology of, 54–60;
  twentieth-century changes in, 332–351,
  365
Brussels, 276–277; conferences on veneral
  diseases, 262–268
Burlureaux, Professor, 266–268
Butler, Josephine, 110, 214–220, 221,
  222, 231, 234, 277, 311
Butte, Dr. L., 129, 254, 320

By-laws, municipal, 32–35, 81–85, 88,
  89, 101–104, 107, 110–111, 122, 176,
  228, 254, 321, 323, 324

Cachin, Marcel, 239, 326–327
Cafés-concerts, 171–174
Call girls, 357–358
Capitalism, 192, 193, 235–237, 240–243,
  365–366
Carco, Francis, 338
Carle, Dr., 274, 338
Carlier, F., 22, 64, 65, 67, 90, 111, 118,
  130, 138, 159, 160, 176
Causes of prostitution, 7, 19, 28
Château-Gontier, 22, 23, 44, 46, 98, 126,
  138
Cherbourg, 33, 39, 147
Chevalier, Louis, 186–187
Cholera, 23, 248
Church occupation (1975), 333, 361–362
Circus prostitution, 151
Clandestine prostitution. *See* Unregistered
  prostitution
Clemenceau government, 173, 223, 233,
  290, 310, 313, 319, 320, 321, 328,
  329, 342
Clientele, 5–6, 42, 43, 66–67, 116, 186;
  of artiste-prostitutes, 172; bourgeois,
  changing needs of, 186–213, 236–237;
  competition for, 86, 121, 123; of
  femmes de brasserie, 169–171; lesbian,
  125; of *maisons de rendez-vous,* 174–185;
  of *maisons de tolérance,* 57–63, 70, 79–
  83, 120–123; partnerships, 86; student,
  61–62, 170–171, 198–199; twentieth-
  century developments in, 337–339,
  345–347, 356, 358; of unregistered
  prostitutes, 133–154. *See also* Military
  prostitution and clientele
Clothes shops, 143–145
Clothing, 19, 20, 59, 78, 82, 109, 170,
  175, 183, 207, 355
Combes, Emil, 290, 313, 319
Commenge, Dr., 17, 130, 143, 159, 162,
  167, 206, 253, 254
Commune, 17, 18, 21, 24, 106, 107, 111,
  130
Compulsory registration, 31–34
Condoms, 245
Contagious Diseases Act, 215, 216, 229,
  265

Contraception, 237, 245
Corlieu, Dr., 95, 253, 254, 257
Council of the Five Hundred, 101
Countryside prostitution, 148–154
Cour de Cassation, 102, 103
Crime, 189, 304. *See also* Police and police surveillance; Prisons
Criminal anthropology, 298, 300–308, 341

Dames de maisons. See Brothel-keepers
Darwinism, 247
Daumard, A., 189, 193, 197
Debré government, 352
Debts, prostitutes', 78–79, 134, 228, 338
Definitions of prostitution, 3, 128–129
Degas, Edgar, 58, 60
Degeneracy, 298–309
Demand for prostitution, changes in, 186–213
Demimondaines, 134–135, 158
Democratic League for the Improvement of the Lot of Women, 231
Demographic weakening, 23–24
Desprès, Dr., 36, 130, 131, 132, 215, 218
Diday, Dr., 22, 26, 28, 250, 257
Divorce, 135, 174, 212, 249, 250, 261
Domestic servants, 47, 49–51, 68–69, 163–167, 206–207
Dressmakers, 208–210
Dreyfus, Ferdinand, 282–283, 295
Dreyfus affair, 261, 290
Drugs, 124, 171, 327–328, 333
Du Camp, Maxime, 20, 21–22, 24, 94, 130, 336
Duchmann, Henri, 244–245
Duclaux, Emile, 264, 273
Dupanloup, Monsignor, 211, 219

Education, 17, 27–28, 52, 168, 189, 198–199, 210, 212; sex, 262, 266–271
Empire, 3, 18, 106, 115, 118, 129, 138
Enclosed prostitution, 9–111; decline and failure of, 115–185, 201, 203, 204, 254, 334, 337–338, 343; Parent-Duchâtelet on, 9–16; twentieth-century developments, 334–338, 344–345, 350. *See also* Abolitionism; *Maisons de tolérance;* Registered prostitution; Regulationism
Engels, Friedrich, 236, 238
Erotic equipment and practices, 123–128

Esquirol, 298
European economic expansion, 280–281
Evangelical abolitionism, 219–220, 234
Expenses, prostitutes', 66–69, 77–79, 81, 117, 120, 143

Factory workers, 137–138, 163, 167, 190, 237, 238
Family, 19, 23–24; background, of prostitutes, 44–53, 162–163; bourgeois, 189, 194–198, 235–244, 261, 322, 331, 332; twentieth-century changes in, 331–332; working-class, 188–193, 199–200, 235–238
Fees, clients', 66–69, 77–78, 81, 117, 123, 143, 176, 184. *See also* Profits
Feminism, 212–213, 214–215, 219, 261, 313, 357; and abolitionism, 231–234, 239, 243
Femmes d'attente, 136–139
Femmes de brasserie, 168–171
Femmes de café, 136
Femmes galantes, 132–136, 155
Fertility. *See* Birth rate
Fiaux, Louis, 53, 67, 69, 81, 82, 121, 123, 124, 125, 127, 130, 176, 195, 196, 225, 226, 227, 229, 233, 256, 257, 265, 313–314
Fifth Republic, 352, 364
Filles de beuglants, 171–174
Filles de maison, 37–44. *See also* Brothels
Filles en carte, 30–42, 84–86, 88, 89, 91, 104, 105, 139, 143, 200–201
Filles insoumises. See Unregistered prostitution
Filles soumises. See Registered prostitution
Flagellation, 124, 176
Flaubert, Gustave, 135, 176, 198, 212, 251
Food, 82, 94, 108, 109, 110
Foucault, Michel, 9, 189, 195, 275
Fournier, Alfred, 196, 247–258, 263, 264, 265, 266, 268
Fournier, Edmond, 263, 264
Fourth Republic, 350
Frappa, Jean-José, 338, 339
French League for the Rights of Women, 231
French Revolution, 206
"French system," 9, 111, 214, 216, 246, 297

Freud, Sigmund, 194
Fronde, La, 232, 239, 312

Gaillard, J., 142, 188, 189, 201, 204, 208
Gambling, 7, 19
Garin, Dr., 20, 25, 26, 35, 254
Geneva congress (1877), 216, 218, 219,
    232
Genevan abolitionists, 215, 216, 218, 219,
    279
Genoa congress (1880), 218–219
Geographical distribution: of *maisons de
    tolérance*, 54–60; of registered
    prostitution, 36–42, 70–74, 115–116;
    of unregistered prostitution, 131–132,
    141, 162–163; of white slave trade,
    283–289
Germany, 153, 278, 286, 287, 295, 296,
    297, 345–346
Gigot, Albert, 106, 219, 222, 223, 233,
    316; Gigot regulations, 31, 32, 55, 80,
    108
Goncourt, Edmond de, 57, 59, 162, 207,
    212
Gonorrhea, 80, 92, 154, 196, 229, 264.
    See also Venereal diseases
Goujon, Pierre, 281, 289, 297
Gras, François, 299, 304, 306
Great Britain, 214–215; and white slave
    trade, 276–280, 286, 287, 293, 295
Guyot, Yves, 18, 36, 79, 81, 94, 95, 105,
    130, 216, 217, 219, 221–229, 233,
    234, 269, 275, 277, 312

Haussmannization, 204, 208
Haussonville, Comte d', 20, 108, 210,
    212, 320
Hayem, Henri, 37, 147, 171
Health and hygiene, 8–9, 12, 15, 19, 21,
    23, 31, 71, 86–100, 154, 246–258,
    317; abolitionists on, 218, 225, 227,
    229, 230, 246–258, 265, 273, 315;
    Contagious Diseases Act, 215, 216,
    229, 265; neoregulationists on, 246–
    258, 265, 273–275, 323, 325–328; and
    police surveillance, 87, 90, 91, 92, 100,
    103–104, 106, 107, 229, 247–248,
    254, 255, 273–275; prison treatment,
    93–100, 229, 230, 254, 255; ratios of
    illness, 92–93; and registered
    prostitution, 86–100, 254–256;
    regulationists on, 20–21, 26–27, 86–

100, 265, 273–275; twentieth-century
    developments, 332, 333, 335, 339–343,
    345, 351–353; and unregistered
    prostitution, 148, 254, 255, 256. *See
    also* Health checks; Hospitals; Hysteria;
    Mental illness; Venereal diseases
Health checks, 12, 27, 31, 32, 68, 79, 84,
    86–93, 100, 103–104, 106, 107, 122,
    147, 162, 227, 229, 256, 274, 323,
    328, 333, 335, 340, 341, 345
Hennequin, F., 32, 34, 85, 293, 321
Heredity, 19, 299, 300–308, 341
Hermaphrodism, 124, 303
Hoche, Jules, 312
Holland, 172, 280, 283, 286
Homo, Dr., 20, 22, 23, 26, 27, 44, 126
Homosexuality, 69, 81, 84, 108, 124, 125,
    126, 159, 303, 352, 367; Parent-
    Duchâtelet on, 5, 6, 7–8, 12, 19
Hospitals, 10, 12–13, 18, 20–21, 26–27,
    86–100, 162, 248–249, 345; and
    neoregulationism, 254–258, 325–326,
    328; prison, 93–100, 229, 230, 254,
    255; revolts, 97, 98; venereal disease
    treatment, 87–100. *See also* Health and
    hygiene
Hugo, Victor, 215, 231
Hungary, 277, 286, 287, 288
Husbands of prostitutes, 32, 33, 64, 67,
    68–69, 140, 158
Huysmans, Joris Karl, 162, 170, 198, 212,
    251, 252, 272
Hygiene. *See* Health and hygiene
Hyperregulationism, 21, 24, 27, 205, 243,
    273, 274
Hysteria, 8, 126, 298–300, 305–306, 308

Ibels, André, 172, 173, 275
Ibsen, Henrik, 207, 251, 269
Illegitimacy, 44, 52, 162, 187, 191, 320
Illiteracy, 17, 52, 168, 189
Immaturity of prostitutes, 7, 9, 19
Immigration, 40, 61–62, 118; and
    changes in prostitution, 186, 187, 188,
    192
Independent prostitutes. *See Filles en carte*
Industrialization, 19, 40, 42, 46, 56–57,
    124, 137–138, 236, 237, 356; and
    changing demands for prostitution,
    186–213
Infant mortality, 263
"Inherited insanity," 305–306

International Abolitionist Federation, 240, 311–312
International Society for Sanitary and Moral Prophylaxis, 265
International tourism, 193–194
International white slave trade, 283–298
Italian criminal anthropology, 301–308
Italy, 153, 286
Itinerant prostitution, 139–143, 148

Jaurès, Jean Léon, 240, 313
Jeannel, Dr., 25, 27, 90, 254
Jewish Association for the Protection of Girls and Women, 280
Jews, 192, 281, 286, 292
Journal des femmes, 231, 232
July Monarchy, 3, 18, 86, 94, 100, 115, 308
Juvenile prostitution. *See* Minors

Kept women, 131, 136–139, 201
Krafft-Ebing, Richard von, 126, 207, 299

Landouzy, Dr., 265, 299, 325
Languedoc, 40, 132
Lanterne, La, 222, 223, 275
Lardier, Dr., 152, 250
Late marriages, 198, 235–236, 237, 333
Launching of prostitutes, 133–134, 158–159
Leases, brothel, 65–66
Lecour, Léopold, 20, 21, 23, 35, 64, 101, 106, 130, 215, 221, 222, 244, 254
Le Fort, Léon, 253, 254, 256
Legislation, 25, 101–103, 155, 212, 230, 239, 255–256, 268, 278, 280, 295–296, 313–314, 315; "small doses" policy, 315–322, 324, 333; twentieth-century developments, 340, 342–345, 347–354, 362, 364–367. *See also* By-laws, municipal
Le Havre, 39, 115, 147, 160, 163, 233
Léon, P., 189, 193, 197
Le Pileur, Dr., 43, 93, 131, 252, 253, 254, 263, 321
Lépine, Prefect, 131, 176, 296, 313, 322–324
Lesbianism, 69, 81, 84, 108, 124, 125, 126, 303, 352, 367; Parent-Duchâtelet on, 5, 6, 7–8, 12, 19
Limoges, 33, 137

Literature, 7, 57, 59, 60, 126, 130, 135, 136, 148, 176, 177, 188, 198, 199, 202, 206–207, 212, 243–244, 251–252, 262, 269–273, 303–304, 312, 336; regulationist, 20–29
Lombroso, Cesare, 301–308, 341
London conference on white slave trade (1899), 278–280, 286, 289
Long-distance procuring, 355–358
Louis-Philippe period, 28, 170, 186, 193, 209, 249, 298
Lyons and Lyonnais prostitution, 25–26, 101, 115, 171, 189, 204, 215, 232, 247, 312, 337, 343, 357; health issues in, 87, 88, 89, 91, 95, 97–98, 264, 325; *maisons de tolérance*, 71–74, 77, 79; police surveillance in, 104–105, 110; prostitutes' movement in, 359–363; unregistered prostitution, 131, 132, 133, 137, 142, 143, 144, 147

Macé, Jean, 106, 136, 142, 170, 178
Maisons closes, 120–123
Maisons d'abattage, 338–339, 350
Maisons de débauche, 123–128
Maisons de rendez-vous, 174–185, 201, 317, 331, 337; recognition of, 322–325, 327, 333, 337
Maisons de tolérance, 10–12, 16, 20, 26, 30, 34, 46, 53–84, 183, 202, 225, 227–229, 233–234, 283, 314–315, 317, 318, 323, 332, 349, 351; building owners, 64–66; clientele, 57–63, 70, 79–83, 120–123; decline of, 115–128, 139, 174, 201, 203, 254, 274, 281, 324, 334, 337–338; duration of prostitute's stay in, 70–76; functioning of, 63–84; pimps of, 158; and police surveillance, 53, 54, 56, 65, 68, 70, 78, 103–107, 117–121, 175; profits, 66–69, 77–78, 117, 123; topography and typology of, 54–60; twentieth-century developments, 334–338, 344–345
Maisons ouvertes, 122
Makeup, 80, 82, 91, 302
Manquat, Dr., 264, 268, 274
Marcère (Minister of the Interior), 106, 219, 222, 223
Marginalization, 9, 111, 187–193, 225, 227, 258, 261, 306, 310, 333
Marginal clients, 61–62
Marguerite, Victor, 272–273, 336

Marriage, 23, 28, 32, 33, 34, 35, 44, 61, 62, 137, 138, 174, 175, 176, 178, 182, 183, 247, 307, 343; bourgeois, 189, 194–198, 235–244, 261, 322, 331, 332; late, 198, 235–236, 237, 333; twentieth-century changes in, 331–332; and venereal diseases, 249, 250, 266–267, 270, 271; working-class, 188–193, 199–200, 235–238; working girl's chances of, 206–211

Marseilles and Marseillais prostitution, 25, 26, 27, 42, 44, 47–49, 52, 111, 115, 171, 204, 215, 232, 326, 327, 343, 358, 361, 363; area of recruitment, 45–46; *filles en carte*, 84–85; health issues, 88, 89, 90, 92, 95–96; *maisons de rendez-vous*, 174, 179–185; *maisons de tolérance*, 54–55, 63, 64, 72, 75–76, 80, 119, 121, 122; pimps, 158, 159, 160; police surveillance, 105–111; registered prostitution, 32, 33, 34, 37, 38, 39; unregistered prostitution, 131, 132, 138, 142, 143, 145, 147, 158, 159, 160, 162–164, 168

Marthe Richard law, 342, 348, 350

Martineau, Dr., 43, 130, 132, 144, 163, 165, 170, 254, 257

Marxism, 235, 236, 238, 240

Masturbation, 61, 148

Maupassant, Guy de, 20, 59, 126, 136, 197, 198, 207, 212, 252

Mauriac, Dr., 21, 247–249, 253, 254

Memoirs of prostitutes, 54

Menstrual periods, 80, 196

Mental illness, 298–300, 305–306, 308; and venereal diseases, 270, 274, 275, 299, 300

Meunier, Paul, 156, 179, 240, 313, 317, 319, 321–322

Middles Ages, 18

Midi, 33, 54, 120, 132, 312

Military prostitution and clientele, 27, 54, 57, 59, 62, 66, 148–150, 167, 199, 201–203, 271–272, 274, 327, 334–336, 345–347

Mining areas, 152–154, 190, 192, 326

Ministry of the Interior, 36, 110, 130, 173, 224, 282, 294, 296

Minors, 37, 77, 92, 103, 109, 181–182, 228, 230, 254, 258, 297–298, 319–321; imprisonment and revolt, 328–330; male, 61, 228; and white slave trade, 276, 285, 295, 297

Mireur, Dr., 20, 25, 26, 46, 84, 88, 96, 108, 131, 163, 229, 254, 269

Mistresses of *maisons de rendez-vous*, 176–184

Mobility of prostitutes, 35, 70–76, 130, 142, 152, 331

Monnet, Dr. L. E., 267, 269, 271

Monod, Dr. Gustave, 215, 218, 220

Montpellier, 42, 55, 88, 361

Morality societies, 326–327

Moralization, 186–213, 217, 234, 258, 262, 328, 333, 335

Morhardt, Dr., 264, 307

Morsier, Auguste de, 219, 240, 311, 312

Morsier, Emilie de, 215, 219, 231

Mortality rate, 263, 264

Motherhood and sexuality, 195–197

Names of prostitutes, 77

Nancy, 40, 96–97, 120, 147, 163, 164, 325, 328

Nantes, 39, 88, 115

National Council of French Women, 232

Nationalism, 262

National Vigilance Association, 278–279

Neisser, Albert, 196, 247, 273

Neoabolitionism, 342, 343–344, 347–349

Neoregulationism, 23, 88, 99, 100, 101, 106, 110, 111, 129, 225, 234, 246, 301, 310–333, 340, 341, 343–344, 347–348; and police surveillance, 252–258, 273–275, 322–324, 327–330; public opinion and, 310–315, 328, 333, 363; recognition of *maisons de rendez-vous*, 322–325, 327; and venereal diseases, 246–258, 265, 273–275, 323, 325–328; and white slave trade, 276, 297

Newspapers, 262; on white slave trade, 283, 290–292

Number of prostitutes: registered, 36–42; unregistered, 130–132, 163

Occupations, 179, 183, 197; and disease, 248–249; as factor in seduction, 166–168; of fathers of prostitutes, 46–49, 52; previous, of prostitutes, 47–52, 150, 163, 164, 166–167, 206–211

Opium, 171, 328

Oral sex, 9, 125, 126, 196

Orphans, 44, 162

Parent-Duchâtelet, Alex, 46, 54, 62, 94, 100, 127, 128, 130, 188, 206, 225, 233, 298, 299, 305, 320, 331, 344; views on regulationism, 3–18, 22, 24, 28

Paris and Parisian prostitution, 25, 26, 42, 44, 46, 52, 81, 111, 121, 128, 172, 232, 247, 248, 321, 326; abolitionist campaign, 215–222, 227, 232, 312, 313; *brasseries à femmes*, 168–171; changing bourgeois demands for, 186– 187, 189, 192, 193–194, 198, 204, 205, 208; *filles en carte*, 84–86; health issues in, 87–95, 98, 100, 248, 252, 257, 264, 325; *maisons de rendez-vous*, 174–179, 180, 185, 322–325; *maisons de tolérance*, 55–60, 62, 65, 67, 69–72, 75, 79, 80, 81, 82, 83, 115, 116–119, 123, 126, 127, 174, 334–336, 337; pimps, 158, 159, 161; police surveillance in, 101–111; registration in, 30–39; twentieth-century changes in, 337–338, 345–346, 353–354, 360, 361, 362; unregistered prostitution, 131, 132, 133, 136, 137, 138, 139– 146, 158, 161, 162–164, 166; white slave trade, 278–297

Patoir, Dr., 99, 264

Patriotic prostitute, 19–20

Peasants, 151–152, 187

Perrot, Michelle, 189, 190, 192

Philippe, Charles-Louis, 139, 156, 198, 272

Photography, 124, 126, 175, 324

Physical characteristics of prostitutes, 8–9, 70, 82, 301–302

Pierrard, Pierre, 188, 204

Pimps, 64, 86, 146, 155–161, 174, 228, 283, 296, 328; prostitutes' feelings for, 156–157; twentieth-century developments, 344, 351, 355, 356, 359, 362, 363, 364

Pinot Report, 362, 363, 364–365

Police and police surveillance, 9–16, 18, 19, 21, 25–26, 85, 86, 101–111, 169, 205, 308, 316, 318, 321–322; and abolitionist campaign, 216, 218, 220– 234, 238, 243, 262, 273, 310–315; and health issues, 87, 90, 91, 92, 100, 103– 104, 106, 107, 229, 247–248, 254, 255, 273–275; of *maisons de rendez-vous*, 175, 179–184; of *maisons de tolérance* and registered prostitution, 31–37, 47, 53, 54, 56, 65, 68, 70, 78, 103–107, 117–121; and neoregulationism, 252– 258, 273–275, 322–324, 327–330; Parent-Duchâtelet on, 9–16; and pimps, 158–161; raids, 104, 221, 228, 353; twentieth-century developments, 340– 343, 345, 347, 352–354, 359–363, 365, 367; of unregistered prostitution, 133, 147, 149–151, 154, 156, 158, 159, 161–162; and white slave trade, 282, 283, 295, 296

Political issues, 105–107, 213, 310–322, 342, 350

Popular Front, 342, 348

Population distribution and growth, 36– 42, 115–116

Pornography, 124, 125, 258, 326, 333, 355

Poverty, 6, 19, 53, 189, 237, 299, 357

Pregnancy, 80, 196

Pressensé, Edouard de, 217, 218, 220, 240, 258

Press laws, 212

Pretext shops, 143–146, 181

Prison, 26, 35, 55, 100–111, 321; health treatment in, 93–100, 229, 230, 254, 255; minors in, 328–330; and neoregulationism, 325–326, 328–330; Parent-Duchâtelet on, 7–15; procedures, 107–111; twentieth-century developments, 340–341, 347, 354, 360–361; and white slave trade, 295, 296. *See also* Saint-Lazare prison

Procuring and procuresses, 133–134, 139, 144, 176; twentieth-century developments in, 352–358, 362, 364– 367; wine-shop, 145–148, 150, 151. *See also* Brothel-keepers; Pimps; Recruitment

Profits: of artiste-prostitutes, 172, 173; of *filles à brasserie*, 170; of *maisons de rendez-vous*, 175, 176, 177, 179, 184; of *maisons de tolérance*, 66–69, 77–78, 117, 123; twentieth-century changes in, 338, 344, 346, 351, 356, 365–366; of unregistered prostitutes, 134, 143, 156

Prostitutes' movement (1975), 333, 359– 363

Proudhon, Pierre Joseph, 236, 241, 242

Psychological factors of prostitution, 7, 9, 19, 70, 298–309, 341; and heredity, 300–308; and mental illness, 298–300, 305–306, 308

Public lavatory prostitutes, 145
Public opinion, 118, 168, 219, 234, 250, 261, 267, 274, 281–282, 308; and international white slave trade, 289–298; and neoregulationism, 310–315, 328, 333, 363

Quartiers réservés, 54, 55

Raids, police, 104, 221, 228, 353
Rape, 43, 277
Recruitment, 139, 168, 226, 344, 351; of artiste-prostitutes, 172–174; and changing demands of bourgeoisie, 203–211; of *femmes de brasserie*, 168–171; *maisons de rendez-vous*, 176–185; and pimps, 155–161; of registered prostitutes, 43–47, 69–76, 117, 122, 283; of unregistered prostitutes, 133–135, 139, 143–161, 162; white slave trade, 275, 282–286, 292. *See also* Procuring and procuresses
Registered prostitution, 30–129, 162, 182, 200–201, 225, 228, 299; *filles en carte*, 30–42, 84–86, 104; geographical distribution, 36–42, 70–74; health issues, 86–100, 254–256; methods of, 30–36; numbers of, 36–42; Parent-Duchâtelet on, 9–16; removal from register, 33–35; sociological factors, 42–53; twentieth-century developments, 334–336, 344–345. *See also* Abolitionism; Enclosed prostitution; *Maisons de tolérance;* Regulationism
Regulationism, 3–111, 187–188, 225, 300, 332, 344; epistemological implications, 16–17; failure of, 22–23, 53, 92, 111, 115–185, 213; Parent-Duchâtelet on, 3–18, 22, 24, 28; sociological factors, 42–53. *See also* Enclosed prostitution; Hyperregulationism; *Maisons de tolérance;* Neoregulationism; Registered prostitution
Religion, 18, 19, 20, 54, 83, 196, 267; and abolitionism, 217, 219–220; declining influence of, 211–212, 316
Renault, Louis, 276, 294
Restoration, 3, 18, 25, 28, 56, 118, 137, 204
Retail trade, 143–145, 197, 207–211
Reuss, Dr., 18, 20, 22, 25, 26, 69, 95, 128, 155, 156, 299

Revolts, 83, 329–330; hospital, 97, 98; prostitutes' movement (1975), 333, 359–363
Richard, E., 35, 129, 130, 225, 257–258
Richard, Marthe, 342, 348, 350
Ricord, Professor, 125, 126, 247
Robiquet, Paul, 278, 289
Rossignol, Dr., 298, 302
Rouen, 110, 159, 160, 329
Russia, 172, 281, 285, 286, 287, 288, 296
Russian criminal anthropology, 301–308

Sadomasochism, 81, 125, 156
Saint Augustine, 18, 331
Saint-Lazare prison, 12, 20, 21, 31, 42, 43, 89, 91–95, 98, 100, 105, 109, 110, 165, 215, 221, 254, 300, 305, 311, 321, 325, 329, 340, 354, 360
Salesgirls, 207–208
Sanitarism, age of, 334–352
Schoelcher, Victor, 215, 219, 223
Seamstresses, 208–210
Second Empire, 18, 21–26, 98, 111, 116, 117, 128, 130, 132, 135, 136, 159, 169, 188, 189, 198, 205, 211, 218, 246, 247
Sellier, Henri, 340, 342, 344, 347
Senate, 101, 316, 317–321
Seniority, 73, 76
Sex education, 262, 266–271
Sexual ghettos, increase in, 197–200
Sexual privation: among bourgeois men, 194–206, 236, 242; and World War I, 334–336
Simon, Jules, 188, 195, 206, 210, 215, 318
Simon Report, 355
Socialism, 231–240, 241
Société de prophylaxie, 265–269, 271, 314, 319
Society for Sanitary and Moral Prophylaxis, 131
Society for the Revival of Public Morality, 258
Society of Saint-François-Régis, 188
Sociological factors of prostitution, 308; and changing demands for sex, 186–213; Parent-Duchâtelet on, 5–16; in registered prostitution, 42–53; in unregistered prostitution, 130–132, 141, 160–168
Souteneurs. See Pimps
South Africa, 288, 289, 292–293, 296

South America, 287, 289, 292

Stereotypes, prostitution, 7, 8, 19, 28, 43, 44, 54, 130, 138, 148, 229, 298–299; twentieth-century changes in, 331–332, 363–364

Sterility, 24

Stillbirths, 263

Student clientele, 61–62, 170–171, 198–199

Submistresses, 69

Supplier-agents, 282, 283, 284

Supply and exchange of prostitutes, 69–76

Surveillance, 20–29, 103–111; turn-of-the-century, 261–309; twentieth-century developments in, 326–330, 334–336, 340–343, 345, 347, 350–354, 359–363, 365, 367. *See also* Enclosed prostitution; Health checks; Police and police surveillance; Prison; Registered prostitution; Regulationism

Switzerland, 214–215, 278, 286, 287

Syphilis, 21, 23–27, 31, 80, 92, 95, 100, 111, 154, 229, 230, 246–258, 261–275, 299, 340; development of, 246–247; inherited, 263–264, 269, 270, 273. *See also* Venereal diseases

Syphilography, 100, 247, 253, 263–264

Syphilophobia, 5, 271

Tarde, G., 307, 316, 341

Tarnowsky, Pauline, 301–308

Tattoos, 19, 156–158, 249, 302

Taxes, 89–90, 357, 360, 362, 365

Television, 355, 360

Theatrical artists, 135, 136, 171–174

Third Republic, 3, 4, 6, 12, 56, 80, 89, 91, 94, 96, 125, 126, 135, 139, 185, 211, 220, 234, 235, 331, 343

Tolerance. *See* Registered prostitution

Tolstoy, Leo, 207, 244

Tortures, sexual, 124

Toul, 40, 148–150, 160, 327

Toulon, 37, 38, 39, 52, 55, 59, 66, 71, 72, 74–76, 107, 108, 132, 146, 171, 339

Toulouse, 42, 88, 144, 171, 189, 204, 361

Toulouse-Lautrec, Henri de, 58, 60, 205

Tourism, 193–194

Trade union, prostitutes', 244

Turot, Henri, 127, 131, 175, 238, 240

Twentieth-century prostitution, 331–368

United Nations, 347, 352

United States, 287

Universal Exposition of 1867, 169

Unregistered prostitution, 4, 16, 24, 32, 36, 40, 47, 56–57, 64, 69, 83, 84, 86, 92, 104, 107–108, 119, 121, 128–168, 182, 200–201, 203, 299; clientele of, 133–154; in the countryside, 148–154; forms of, 128–168; and health issues, 148, 254, 255, 256; police surveillance of, 133, 147, 149–151, 154, 156, 158, 159, 161–162; profits, 134, 143, 156; sociological factors, 130–132, 141, 160–168; World Wars I and II, 334–335, 346, 347

Upholsterers, 134, 136, 208

Urban development, 23, 39–42, 46–47, 56–57, 115–116; and changing demands for prostitution, 186–213

Vagina, 8, 91

Venereal diseases, 12, 21, 23–27, 31, 62, 80, 111, 148, 169, 196, 198, 246–258, 299, 321; abolitionists on, 229, 230, 246–258, 265, 273, 315; fear of, 5, 23–25, 87, 249–252, 269–275, 333; health checks and treatment, 86–100; neoregulationists on, 246–258, 265, 273–275, 323, 325–328; and occupations, 248–249; Parent-Duchâtelet on, 12–13; public concern, 261–275; ratios of illness, 93–94; regulationists on, 12–13, 20–21, 26–27, 86–100, 265, 273–275; and sex education, 262, 266–271; twentieth-century developments, 332, 333, 335, 339–343, 345, 351–352; and unregistered prostitution, 150–151, 154. *See also* Gonorrhea; Health and hygiene; Syphilis

Versailles, 40, 44, 52, 70, 72, 74–76, 131, 158

Vice squads. *See* Police and police surveillance

Vichy government, 343–345, 347

Vienna congress (1873), 25, 26

Vignernon, Dr., 151, 199

Violence, 25, 83, 97, 98, 189, 192, 221, 329–330

Virginity, loss of, 42–43, 163, 165, 302

Voisin, Félix, 221, 222

Voluntary registration, 30–34

Voyeurism, 124

Waddington, William Henry, 222, 223, 318
Wages, 6, 236, 237
Waldeck-Rousseau, Pierre, 224, 268, 290, 318, 325
Wealth, shifts in, 193, 197, 211
White slave trade, 47, 71, 117, 154, 239, 258, 261, 262, 275–298, 319, 326, 333; development of, 280–281; geographical distribution, 283–289; public opinion on, 289–298; recruitment, 275, 282–286, 292
Widows, 44, 135, 174, 177, 181
Wine shops, 56–57, 58, 118; procuring in, 145–148, 150, 151
Wives' sexual behavior, bourgeois attitudes on, 195–197

Working class, 249, 311; and abolitionism, 233–246; family, 188–193, 199–200, 235–238; and socialism, 234–240
World War I, 88, 98, 154, 159, 203, 205, 230, 239, 258, 332; and prostitution, 334–336; surveillance prior to, 326–330
World War II, 337, 339, 343, 345–347

Zeldin, Theodore, 194, 196, 322
Zola, Émile, 29, 104, 130, 133, 135, 136, 139, 141, 176, 197, 204, 207, 208, 210, 212, 251, 303, 313